ALGEBRA 1
An Integrated Approach

ALGEBRA 1

An Integrated Approach

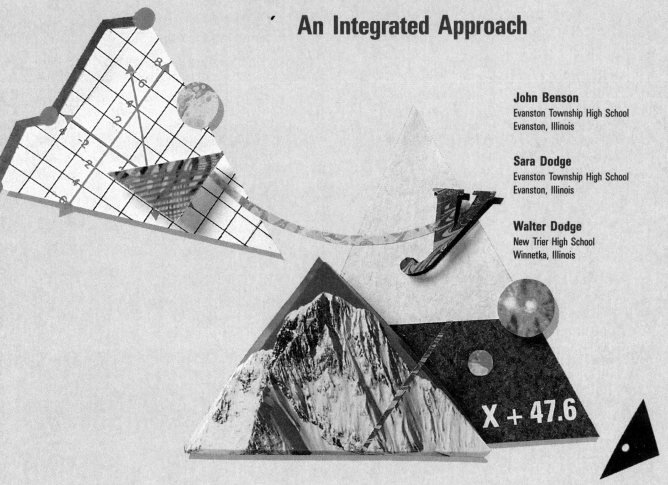

John Benson
Evanston Township High School
Evanston, Illinois

Sara Dodge
Evanston Township High School
Evanston, Illinois

Walter Dodge
New Trier High School
Winnetka, Illinois

Charles Hamberg
Illinois Mathematics and
Science Academy
Aurora, Illinois

George Milauskas
Illinois Mathematics and
Science Academy
Aurora, Illinois

Richard Rukin
Evanston Township High School
Evanston, Illinois

ML McDougal, Littell & Company

Evanston, Illinois
New York   Dallas   Sacramento   Columbia, SC

Reviewers

Sheldon Berman
Kensington High School
Philadelphia, Pennsylvania

Chris Comins
Pueblo County High School
Pueblo, Colorado

Richard Dube
Taunton High School
Taunton, Massachussets

Robert Jones
Greenwood Lakes Middle School
Lake Mary, Florida

Nancy King
Tascosa High School
Amarillo, Texas

Elizabeth Lashley
Picken County School District
Easley, South Carolina

Sue McLeod
Galena Park High School
Galena Park, Texas

Fred Symonds
Sehome High School
Bellingham, Washington

ISBN 0-8123-5860-0

Copyright © 1991 by McDougal, Littell & Company
Box 1667, Evanston, Illinois 60204

92 93 94 / 15 14 13 12 11 10 9 8 7 6 5

A Special Thank You

A special thank you to the teachers, students, and administrators who helped field test *Algebra 1, An Integrated Approach*, for the full school year 1986-1987. Their suggestions, comments, and criticisms were invaluable.

Mr. Jack Adams
Glenbrook High School South
Glenview, IL

Mr. Dennis Caughy
North Campus, White Bear
Lake Area High School
White Bear Lake, MN

Ms. Susan Ebdon
Saxe Middle School
New Canaan, CT

Mr. Don Esty
Falmouth High School
Falmouth, ME

Ms. Jennifer Foutch
Shelby County High School
Shelbyville, KY

Ms. Jeanne Hayman
Willowbrook High School
Villa Park, IL

Mr. Spike Herrick
Falmouth High School
Falmouth, ME

Ms. Carol Johnson
Richardson North Junior High
School
Richardson, Texas

Mr. Richard Kaplan
Lakeview High School
Chicago, IL

Mr. James Keenan
Lane Tech High School
Chicago, IL

Mr. Donald Kuusinen
Grand Rapids Middle School
Grand Rapids, MN

Ms. Lisa Love
Richardson North Junior High
School
Richardson, Texas

Mr. Mike McLaughlan
Hillcrest High School
Country Club Hills, IL

Mr. David Neuberger
Beaver Dam Junior High School
Beaver Dam, WI

Mr. Keith Peak
Oak Forest High School
Oak Forest, IL

Ms. Sharon Rainwater
Hurst Junior High School
Hurst, Texas

Ms. Sandy Spalt
Red Bud High School
Red Bud, IL

Mr. Marcy B. Streight
South Lyons High School
South Lyons, MI

Ms. Mary Thacker
Mulberry Grove High School
Mulberry Grove, IL

Mr. James Treadway
Kaukauna High School
Kaukauna, WI

Mr. Ron Vandenberg
Kaukauna High School
Kaukauna, WI

In addition, thank you to the approximately 7,500 students, their teachers and administrators throughout the country who used versions of this book in pre-publication form for a full school year during 1987-1988 and/or 1988-1989. Their feedback helped shape this final published book.

More information on the field-testing and piloting is available on request.

CONTENTS

LETTER TO STUDENTS

Welcome to algebra! As high school teachers, we have each spent many years teaching students very much like you. We have written this book to help make algebra a more interesting, useful, and challenging course.

Expect to learn something new each day. Some days you may feel confused and that is appropriate. Sometimes it is necessary to work on an idea over a period of several days before you understand. The most important fact is that you will understand.

We have written this book for you. We want you to be able to read it and to use it as a reference. Let us tell you about some parts of the book.

The opening page of a chapter tells you about the ways algebra shapes our lives today. In each section the list of objectives tells you what you will learn in that lesson. The information in

Part One: Introduction

explains concepts and skills. Examples show these ideas in practice.

Part Two: Sample Problems

apply the information from Part One. These problems, along with the Examples, are models you can refer to when you solve the Exercises and Problems.

Part Three: Exercises and Problems

are where you practice and really learn the concepts and skills of algebra. This is where you learn to be a problem solver, one of the most important tasks you have this year. We have tried to make these exercises and problems worthwhile. In each section you will find problems that

▲ practice the ideas in today's lesson

▲ review the ideas from yesterday's lesson, last week's lesson, and last month's lesson to apply today's ideas

▲ introduce ideas you will learn tomorrow or next week or even later.

Thus, you will learn the concepts of algebra over days, weeks, and months so that by the end of the year, all these different concepts that seemed puzzling when you first saw them will be firmly integrated in your understanding. To give you an idea of how practice, review, and introducing all work in a practice set, we have labeled the problems in Sections 1.4 and 2.2.

At the end of each chapter, you will find a

CHAPTER SUMMARY   *of ideas, vocabulary, and skills;*
REVIEW PROBLEMS
CHAPTER TEST
PUZZLES AND CHALLENGES   *some problems that are fun to think about.*

Good luck. We wish you well and hope that by the end of this year you share some of our excitement about mathematics.

John Benson   Charles L. Hamberg

Sara H. Dodge   George Milauskas

Walter Dodge   Richard Rukin

1 | A PREVIEW OF ALGEBRA

To send a spacecraft into a designated orbit, scientists must solve a complex array of problems. For example, when the planetary probe *Magellan* left the cargo bay of the shuttle *Atlantis*, *Magellan*'s speed was too great to enable it to intersect the designated orbit. By firing its rockets, *Magellan* was able to slow its speed and fall the necessary distance in order to enter an orbit around the planet Venus.

Scientists faced a very different problem when planning to launch the planetary probe *Galileo*. In this case, the launch rocket lacked the power to send the spacecraft all the way to Jupiter. So *Galileo* was sent toward Venus intead, in such a way that the planet's gravity would give it an energy boost. *Galileo* was scheduled to receive two more "gravity assists" from the Earth before it would finally have enough speed to reach Jupiter.

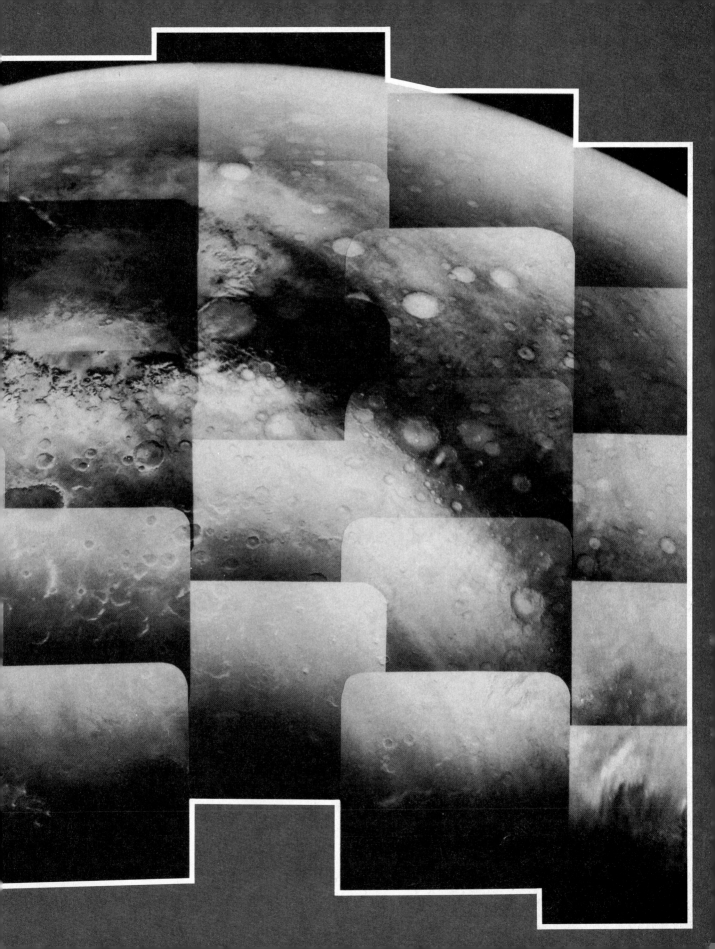

GETTING STARTED

Objectives
After studying this section, you should be familiar with
- What algebra is and why we study it
- What you will learn in this year's study of algebra

What Algebra Is and Why We Study It
Algebra is generalized or abstract arithmetic. It uses symbols such as
x and n to represent numbers. Using symbols in this way makes it
easier to study number patterns and to solve problems.

There are several reasons for studying algebra. The logical
thinking and problem-solving skills of mathematics are important in
our lives. Algebra builds on the skills you already have, helps you
develop new skills, and helps you become a better problem solver.
Mathematics is also necessary in most careers. In fact, it is becoming
difficult to find a career where math is not important.

This Year's Study of Algebra
Three key elements of algebra that you will study throughout this
year are
- Equations and inequalities
- Graphing
- Translating words into symbols and symbols into words

Each of these elements is built on many skills. In this chapter, you
will be introduced to these skills, but **you will not be given many
rules nor will you be expected to master all the ideas.** Mastery will
come as you use these ideas throughout this book.

This book is written in a style that you can read and understand. You will be more successful if you **read** each section, **study**
the diagrams, examples, and sample problems, and **do each homework assignment** carefully.

If you are able to use a scientific calculator, many problems will be easier to solve. Some sections also include suggested computer programs. If you have access to a computer, you will be able to enter and run these programs. By using a calculator and a computer, you will learn how each can be useful in algebra. You will also see that each has its limitations.

Solving algebra problems can be interesting and enjoyable. Here is one kind of problem you will often see.

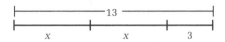

Can you guess what number x represents?

Warm-up Exercises

1 Find the length of segment AB.

2 Find which of the numbers 15, 7, 12, or 2 should be put in the box if the subtraction problem has the least possible result.

$$24 - \boxed{} = ?$$

In problems 3–5, use the information in rectangle ABCD. You may refer to the formulas on page 666.

3 Find 30% of the area of rectangle ABCD.
4 Find the area of triangle BCD.
5 Find the ratio of the area of triangle BCD to the area of the rectangle ABCD.

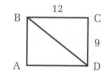

6 Name the longer segment.

7 True or False   The figure is a square. Explain your answer.

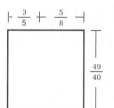

8 Find the value of x for which the figure is a square.

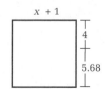

Problem Set

In problems 9–14, simplify.

9 $\frac{7}{8} - \frac{5}{6}$

10 $12.3 - 7.54$

11 5^3

12 10% of 24

13 6% of 35.3

14 $(8.4)^2$

---

15 Find the area and perimeter of the rectangle.

7.23 cm

18.7 cm

16 The sales tax is 7%. Quincy bought a jacket that cost $58.95 before tax.

  a How much tax did Quincy pay?

  b What was the total cost of the jacket?

  c The jacket went on sale a week later at 15% off. Including tax, how much money would Quincy have saved if he had waited until the sale?

17 Four pieces of lumber are nailed together as shown to form a post. Each piece is $1\frac{5}{8}$ inches wide by $3\frac{1}{2}$ inches long.

  a Find the perimeter of the inner square region enclosed by the wood.

  b Find the perimeter of the outer square formed by the post.

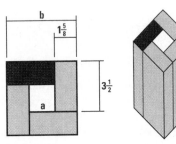

 In problems 18–23, compute the answer. The symbol to the left means that a calculator or a computer makes the problem easier to solve.

18 $156.7 \div 0.087$

19 $\sqrt{1369}$

20 $12.3 - (3.2 + 5.9)$

21 $\frac{1}{5.5}$

22 Change $\frac{5}{8}$ to a decimal.

23 $90 \div (39 - 19)$

24 If the wooden block shown at the right is sanded and $\frac{1}{8}$ of an inch is removed from the top and from the bottom, how much is the volume of the block decreased?

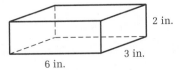

2 in.

3 in.

6 in.

 In problems 25–28, explain what happens when you try to do each of the following on your calculator.

25 7 $\boxed{\div}$ 0

26 6 $\boxed{+/-}$

27 6 $\boxed{\div}$ 2 $\boxed{X \leftrightarrow Y}$ $\boxed{X \leftrightarrow Y}$ $\boxed{X \leftrightarrow Y}$ ...

28 3 $\boxed{\times}$ $\boxed{\times}$ $\boxed{=}$ $\boxed{=}$ $\boxed{=}$

29 The yearly profits of a company are shown in the graph.

a Find the average profit for the five years shown.

b Copy the graph and draw a horizontal line across the graph to show the average profit.

c How many years had profits that were above average?

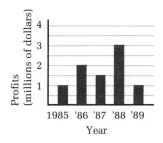

30 Phil Maker is buying a camera for $100, including 6% sales tax.

a Find the cost of the camera before sales tax.

b What is the amount of the sales tax?

MATHEMATICAL EXCURSION

PERFECT NUMBERS
A fascinating mathematical challenge

1, 2, 11,   1, 2, 4, 7, 14

Nothing is perfect it is said. Not so! A few whole numbers satisfy the definition of what mathematicians call a *perfect number,* a whole number that is equal to the sum of all its divisors except the number itself. The smallest perfect number is 6. Its divisors, except for 6, are 1, 2, and 3, which add up to 6.

We know very few perfect numbers. Ancient mathematicians knew of only four. The two largest of these are 496 and 8128. Not until the twelfth century was the fifth perfect number discovered. It is 33,550,336.

High-speed computers have greatly simplified the job of finding perfect numbers. Exactly thirty are now known. The largest has 130,100 digits. Written out, it would fill more than forty pages of this book. All of the known perfect numbers are even, although no one has ever proven that they must be. However, an important step in the proof was taken in 1985 when a crucial theorem about odd perfect numbers was proven for the first time—by Michael Friedman, a high school senior from Brooklyn.

One of these numbers is the second smallest perfect number: 22, 28, 32. Which one is it?

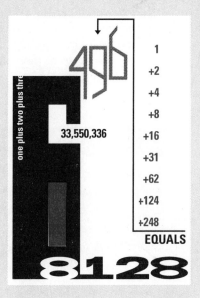

1.2 EXPRESSING NUMBERS

Objectives

After studying this section, you should be familiar with
- Representing approximate answers
- Representing multiplication and division in algebra
- Evaluating a number in exponent and square root forms

Part One: Introduction

Approximating Answers

There are many problems in mathematics that do not have exact answers. The interest on a bank account or bank loan, for example, may have many decimal places. Since we are using money, however, only two decimal places have any meaning. In baseball, a player's batting average (the number of hits divided by the number of times at bat) can be calculated to any number of decimal places. However, a batting average statistic is rounded to three decimal places.

The key to approximating answers is to do what makes sense in the situation. Here are some guidelines to help.

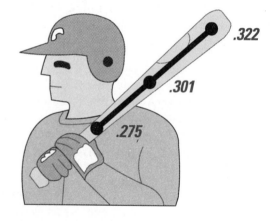

Approximating Answers

1. If a problem involves money, use two decimal places.

2. If a problem involves measurement (time or length), round to the nearest appropriate value.

3. If all the decimal numbers in a problem are given to the same number of places, approximated answers should be rounded to the same number of places.

4. In all other problems in this book, round to the nearest hundredth.

To show approximate answers, we use the symbol ≈, meaning "is approximately equal to."

Example   *Use approximation to answer the following. (The solution is given below.)*

    a *What is 45% of $165.89?*
        45% of 165.89 is 74.6505. The problem indicates money, so we represent the answer rounded to two decimal places, $74.65.

    b *The time is now 10:56:23 A.M. Lunch is about an hour from now. What time is lunch?*
        The time is almost 11 A.M., and lunch is about one hour from now. So lunch is, approximately, at noon.

Multiplication and Division in Algebra

In algebra, each of the following indicates the multiplication of 4 times 5.

$$4 \cdot 5 \qquad (4)(5) \qquad 4(5) \qquad (4)5 \qquad 4*5$$

We do not use the × symbol because it is too easily confused with the variable x. We will learn about variables in the next section.

You may remember that when two numbers are multiplied, each number is called a *factor* of the product. To find the factors of a number, we find all *whole numbers* that are exact divisors of that number. For example,

Product	Factors
12	1 and 12 or
	2 and 6 or
	3 and 4

A whole number greater than or equal to 2 is called a *prime number* if its only factors are 1 and itself. For example, 13 is a prime number. Its only factors are 1 and 13. A whole number with more than one prime factor is called a *composite number*. The number 27 is a composite number.

Some prime numbers	Some composite numbers
2, 11, 13, 29, 37	8, 9, 27, 51

Division is also indicated in several ways. Each of the following indicates that 24 is divided by 6.

$$24 \div 6 \qquad \frac{24}{6} \qquad 24/6$$

Exponents

In the expression 3^5, which is read "three to the fifth power," 3 is called the *base* and 5 is called the *exponent*. The exponent indicates how many times the base is used as a factor.

For example,

6^4 means $(6)(6)(6)(6)$ and is read "six to the fourth."
4^3 means $(4)(4)(4)$ and is read "four cubed."
5^2 means $(5)(5)$ and is read "five squared."

Computer languages use ↑ or ∧ to denote exponents, and 3^4 would be written 3 ↑ 4 or 3 ∧ 4.

Example *Use an exponent to write "two to the sixth power."*

Two to the sixth power is written 2^6. For a computer, we would write 2 ↑ 6 or 2 ∧ 6.

Example *If the area of the square is 32 square inches, find the numerical value of side s.*

The area of a square is $A = s^2$.
If the area is 32, then $32 = s^2$.
To find s, we take the square root of 32.

$$\sqrt{32} = s$$
$$5.6568542 \approx s$$

Since s is the side of a geometric figure, we can round to 5.7 inches.

Example *Evaluate 7^8.*

Using a calculator, we press 7 $\boxed{x^y}$ 8 $\boxed{=}$ to obtain 5,764,801. Some calculators use a $\boxed{y^x}$ key.

Square Roots

The term $\sqrt{25}$ is read "the square root of 25." It means "find a positive number that is 25 when squared." Since 5^2 is 25, we write $\sqrt{25} = 5$.

Example *Find each square root. (The solutions are given below.)*

a $\sqrt{9}$ b $\sqrt{121}$ c $\sqrt{\frac{4}{9}}$

$\sqrt{9} = 3$ $\sqrt{121} = 11$ $\sqrt{\frac{4}{9}} = \frac{2}{3}$

because $3^2 = 9$ because $11^2 = 121$ because $\left(\frac{2}{3}\right)^2 = \frac{4}{9}$

Example *Find $\sqrt{5}$.*

If you do not have access to a calculator, use the Table of Square Roots on page 663. If you use a calculator, press 5 $\boxed{\sqrt{}}$. Your calculator will show $\boxed{2.23606797749}$, an approximate answer, not an exact answer, so we write $\sqrt{5} \approx 2.23606797749$. Square the answer that your calculator displayed. Is the answer close to 5? The chart reviews how to round the approximate value of $\sqrt{5}$ to a specific number of decimal places.

Decimal Place	Number of Decimal Places	Approximate Value
ten thousandth	4	2.2361
thousandth	3	2.236
hundredth	2	2.24
tenth	1	2.2
integer (units)	0	2

Part Two: Sample Problems

Problem 1   Find 12.5% *of* $251.45.

Solution
$$12.5\% \text{ of } \$251.45 = 0.125 \ (251.45)$$
$$= 31.43125$$

Since we are dealing with money, we round to the nearest cent. Therefore, 12.5% of $251.45 is $31.43.

Problem 2   *If 4.64705 days = 4 days 15 hours 31 minutes and 45.12 seconds, give a reasonable approximation for each of the following.*

a *A visit to Disney World lasting 4.64705 days*
b *A space mission lasting 4.64705 days before reentry*

Solution   We approximate with respect to what makes sense in the problem.

a An appropriate approximation would be $4\frac{1}{2}$ or $4\frac{2}{3}$ days.

b Only the exact time, 4 days 15 hours 31 minutes and 45.12 seconds, is appropriate.

Problem 3   *Express 56 in prime factored form.*

Solution

$56 = 2(28)$	$56 = 4(14)$	$56 = 7(8)$
$= 2(4)\ (7)$	$= (2)\ (2)\ (2)\ (7)$	$= 7(2)\ (4)$
$= 2(2)\ (2)\ (7)$	$= 2^3(7)$	$= 7(2)\ (2)\ (2)$
$= 2^3(7)$		$= 2^3(7)$

Although 56 has many factors, its **prime factored form**, $2^3(7)$, is unique. The factors can be listed in different order, but the prime factors are unique.

Problem 4   *The side of a square is 6.32 centimeters. What is the numerical value of the area?*

Solution   The area of a square is

$$A = s^2$$
$$A = (6.32)^2$$
$$A = 39.9424 \text{ cm}^2$$

6.32 cm

Since the length of a side is given to two decimal places, we round our answer to 39.94 cm².

Problem 5   *Evaluate and round answers to two decimal places. (The solutions are given below.)*

a $(1.05)^5$ **b** $\sqrt{7}$ **c** $(1.05)^5 + \sqrt{7}$

$(1.05)^5$	$\sqrt{7}$	$(1.05)^5 + \sqrt{7}$
≈ 1.28	≈ 2.65	≈ 3.92

Be careful! In part **c,** rounding and then adding does not give the same approximation as adding and then rounding. It is more accurate to evaluate using your calculator and round as a last step.

Part Three: Exercises and Problems

Warm-up Exercises

In problems 1–3, rewrite using a base and an exponent.

1 (6) (6) (6) (6) (6)   **2** $x \cdot x \cdot x \cdot x \cdot x$ **3** $6^2 \cdot 6^7$

4 Approximate the area of the triangle to the nearest tenth.

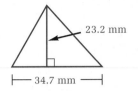

23.2 mm

34.7 mm

5 Find the area of each figure. Round your answer.

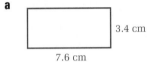

a 3.4 cm / 7.6 cm

b 5.12 mm

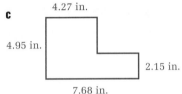

c 4.27 in. / 4.95 in. / 7.68 in. / 2.15 in.

6 The cost of an item is $11.93. The sales tax on this purchase is 6.5%. Determine the tax and the total bill for the item.

7 Give an approximation for 57.8945 seconds in each instance.
   a When it is the time left in a basketball game
   b When it is the time in which a swimmer completes an event

8 The chart shows top speeds.

Animal	Speed (miles per hour)
Cheetah	70
Quarter horse	47.5
Greyhound	39.35
Giraffe	32
Grizzly bear	30
Domestic cat	30
Man	27.89
Elephant	25
Pig	11
Garden snail	0.03

   a Explain why the times of the quarter horse, greyhound, and man are computed to decimals, whereas those of most of the others are not.
   b Explain why the snail's time is computed to hundredths.
   c How do you suppose the information was collected?
   d Can a zebra run faster than a greyhound?
   e Do you suppose someone watched a snail crawl a mile and timed it with a stopwatch?
   f The speeds above were reported in an article written in 1974. For which animals will these numbers be out of date?

Problem Set

9 Use exponents to write the prime factorization of each number.

    a 13   **b** 32   **c** 198

10 Evaluate each expression if x is replaced by 5.

    a $x + x + x$ **b** x^3 **c** $3x$

 In problems 11 and 12, use a calculator to evaluate each expression.

11 $\sqrt{64009}$ **12** $(x_2)^2$ if $x_2 = 1.24$

13 Find the value of x.

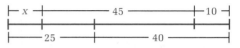

In problems 14–16, list all the factors of each number.

14 28   **15** 17
16 24

17 If $z^2 = 6^2 + 8^2$, what is the value of z?

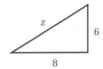

18 The chart shows the average weekly income of the residents of Littletown. Estimate the increase in average weekly income between 1980 and 1988.

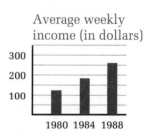

Average weekly income (in dollars)

19 Evaluate.

    a $(x^2)(x^3)$ if $x = 2$ **b** x^5 if $x = 2$

20 Evaluate the expression $3x + 2$ for $x = 1, 2, 3, 4,$ and 5. Copy and complete the table.

x	1	2	3	4	5
$3x + 2$	5			14	

21 Find the average of the numbers 3.57, 10.8, and 7.2.

22 Find the value of d if $d = \sqrt{(x_2 - x_1)^2 + (y_2 - y_1)^2}$ and $x_1 = 4$, $x_2 = 7$, $y_1 = 8$, and $y_2 = 12$.

23 Evaluate $x_1 + x_2 + x_3$ if $x_1 = 7$, $x_2 = x_1 + 3$, and $x_3 = 2x_1$.

24 The area of the triangle is what percent of the area of the rectangle?

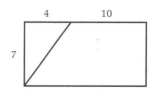

BEGINNING TO WORK WITH ALGEBRAIC EXPRESSIONS

Objectives

After studying this section, you should be familiar with
- Showing multiplication and division using numbers and variables
- Evaluating an expression
- Using the correct order of operations to evaluate expressions

Part One: Introduction

Using Variables to Represent Numbers

A *variable* is a symbol used to represent a number. The most common variable is the letter x, but any symbol can be used.

Example   *Use any variable to represent the length of segment DF.*

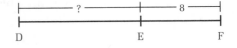

Here are some possible answers:

$x + 8$ $x_1 + 8$ $y_2 + 8$ $\triangle + 8$ $NUM + 8$

Note: The variable x_1 is read "x sub one"; y_2 is read "y sub two." The $_1$ and $_2$ are called *subscripts.*

In algebra, if a number and a variable are written side by side, or if two or more variables are written side by side, the operation of multiplication is understood. For example,

4x means "4 times x."
abc means "a times b times c."
37rs means "37 times r times s."

Example   *Write an expression for the perimeter of the hexagon.*

The perimeter is the sum of the lengths of the sides.

$P = 8 + 9 + 4 + 8 + x + y$
$P = 29 + x + y$

Evaluating an Algebraic Expression

An *expression* contains operations with numbers, variables, or numbers and variables. To *evaluate* an expression means to find a numerical value for the expression. To evaluate an expression that contains a variable, we must replace the variable with a number.

Example   *Evaluate each expression below if* x = 7.

    a $4x$ **b** $4 + x$ **c** $\dfrac{x}{4}$ **d** $\dfrac{x + 5}{4}$

In each, replace x with 7. Then perform the indicated operation.

a	$4x$	**b**	$4 + x$
Multiply	$= 4(7)$	Add	$= 4 + 7$
	$= 28$		$= 11$

c $\dfrac{x}{4}$

Divide $= \dfrac{7}{4}$

$= 1.75$ or $1\frac{3}{4}$

d $\dfrac{x + 5}{4}$

Add, then divide $= \dfrac{7 + 5}{4}$

$= \dfrac{12}{4}$

$= 3$

Order of Operations

You might evaluate $1 + 2 \cdot 3$ in either of two ways.

Procedure 1 $1 + 2 \cdot 3$
Add first, then multiply $= 3 \cdot 3$
                        $= 9$

Procedure 2 $1 + 2 \cdot 3$
Multiply first, then add $= 1 + 6$
                        $= 7$

Only the second way is correct. In algebra, we follow an agreed-upon *order of operations.* **It is important that you learn the order of operations before you complete this chapter so that you can evaluate expressions correctly.**

Order of Operations

1. **Simplify expressions within grouping symbols, such as parentheses, brackets, and fraction lines.**

2. **Simplify exponents and roots.**

3. **Do multiplication and division in order from left to right.**

4. **Do addition and subtraction in order from left to right.**

Example   *Evaluate* $6 + 12 \div 2 \cdot 3$.

Divide 12 by 2	$6 + 12 \div 2 \cdot 3$
Multiply 6 by 3	$= 6 + 6 \cdot 3$
Add	$= 6 + 18$
	$= 24$

Example

The area of a trapezoid is given by the formula $A = h\left(\dfrac{b_1 + b_2}{2}\right)$.

Evaluate the formula if $h = 3$, $b_1 = 6$, and $b_2 = 12$.

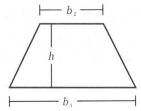

$$A = h\left(\frac{b_1 + b_2}{2}\right)$$

Substitute the given values for b_1, b_2, and h. The fraction line groups the 6 + 12.

$$= 3\left(\frac{6 + 12}{2}\right)$$

Divide

$$= 3\left(\frac{18}{2}\right)$$

Multiply

$$= 3\,(9)$$

The area of the trapezoid is 27.

$$= 27$$

Example

Evaluate $(2 + x) \uparrow 4 / 8 + y$ when $x = 1$ and $y = 7$.

Remember $(2 + x) \uparrow 4$ is $(2 + x)^4$ and / means divide in computer language.

$(2 + x) \uparrow 4 / 8 + y$	or	$(2 + x)^4 \div 8 + y$
$= (2 + 1) \uparrow 4 / 8 + 7$		$= (2 + 1)^4 \div 8 + 7$
$= 3 \uparrow 4 / 8 + 7$		$= 3^4 \div 8 + 7$
$= 81/8 + 7$		$= 81 \div 8 + 7$
$= 10.125 + 7$		$= 10.125 + 7$
$= 17.125$		$= 17.125$

Part Two: Sample Problems

Problem 1

Evaluate.

a $\sqrt{x + 3}$ if $x = 13$ **b** $2\sqrt{x} + 3$ if $x = 8$

Solution

a Substitute for x $\sqrt{x + 3}$

Add 13 + 3 $= \sqrt{13 + 3}$

Find the square root $= \sqrt{16}$

          $= 4$

b The square root symbol does not include the 3.

Substitute for x $2\sqrt{x} + 3$

Take the square root $= 2\sqrt{8} + 3$

Multiply by 2 $\approx 2(2.828427125) + 3$

Add 3 $\approx 5.65684249 + 3$

          ≈ 8.65684249

          ≈ 8.66

The following symbols are used to write inequalities.

Symbol	Meaning
$\neq$	**is not equal to**
$<$	**is less than**
$\not<$	**is not less than**
$>$	**is greater than**
$\not>$	**is not greater than**
$\leq$	**is less than or equal to**
$\geq$	**is greater than or equal to**

An inequality sign separates an inequality into two parts, the *left side* of the inequality and the *right side*.

Part Two: Sample Problems

Problem 1   *Solve for x if x is 30% of 70.*

Solution   We know that 30% of 70 means 0.30 times 70.

$x = 0.30(70)$
$x = 21$

Problem 2   *If $y = mx + b$, solve for y if $m = \frac{1}{2}$, $x = 6$, and $b = 18$.*

Solution   We solve for y by substituting $\frac{1}{2}$ for m, 6 for x, and 18 for b.

$y = mx + b$
$y = \frac{1}{2}(6) + 18$
$y = 3 + 18$
$y = 21$

Problem 3   *Solve $x^2 + 3 - 4x = 0$, using values for x from $\{1, 3, 5, 7\}$.*

Solution   We test each possibility by substituting for x.

Try $x = 1$	**Try $x = 3$**	**Try $x = 5$**	**Try $x = 7$**
$1^2 + 3 - 4(1)$	$3^2 + 3 - 4(3)$	$5^2 + 3 - 4(5)$	$7^2 + 3 - 4(7)$
$= 1 + 3 - 4$	$= 9 + 3 - 12$	$= 25 + 3 - 20$	$= 49 + 3 - 28$
$= 4 - 4$	$= 12 - 12$	$= 28 - 20$	$= 52 - 28$
$= 0$	$= 0$	$= 8$	$= 24$

So, $x^2 + 3 - 4x = 0$ for $x = 1$ or $x = 3$.

Problem 4   If $x_1 = 5$, determine whether $x_1 - 2 \leq 7x_1 - 2(3)$.

Solution   We substitute 5 for x_1 and compare the left side and the right side.

Left Side	Right Side
$x_1 - 2$	$7x_1 - 2(3)$
$= 5 - 2$	$= 7(5) - 2(3)$
$= 3$	$= 35 - 6$
	$= 29$

Since $3 \leq 29$, the answer checks. If $x_1 = 5$, then $x_1 - 2 \leq 7x_1 - 2(3)$.

Part Three: Exercises and Problems

Warm-up Exercises

As explained in the "Letter to Students," this is one of the problem sets that has been labeled for you.

Practice

In problems 1–4, replace x with 5. Evaluate the expressions and indicate which symbol ($=$, $<$, or $>$) replaces the question mark.

1 $30 \div x + 2$? $7 + 2 - 1$

2 $2x + 4 \div 2$? $(2 + 16) \div 2$

3 $5^2 - \sqrt{25}$? $3(x + 2)$

4 $3x - 10 \div 2$? $3^2 + 1$

Practice

5 Solve for k if k is 25% of 76.

Practice, Review

In problems 6–9, solve for x.

6 $2x = 7^2 + 1$

7 $(21 + 3) \div \sqrt{8 \cdot 3 - 15} = 4x$

8 $24 \div 3 - \sqrt{3^2 - (2 + 3)} = 3x$

9 $8x = 2(6^2 - 4)$

Practice, Introduce

10 If PQ = RS, find x.

Problem Set

Practice

11 If $y = 2$, determine whether $2y + 3y = 10$.

Practice

In problems 12 and 13, say whether each sentence is True or False.

12 If $x = 0$, then $2x + 7x + 5 \leq 4^2 - 5 \cdot 3$.

13 If $y = 19$, then $2(y + 3) = 4(3^2 + 2)$.

Practice, Introduce

14 If $x_1 = 7$, determine whether $x_1 + 5 \geq 2x_1 - 1$.

Practice

15 If $A = \pi * 6.5 \uparrow 2$, find the value of A.

Practice, Review

16 Write an equation that states

    a the perimeter of ABCD is 60

    b the area of ABCD is 100

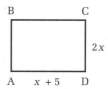

Practice

Practice,
Review

Practice,
Review

Practice

Practice

Practice,
Review

Practice,
Introduce

Practice,
Introduce

Practice,
Review

Practice,
Introduce

In problems 17–20, find the value of x that makes each sentence true if x is chosen from {1, 3, 5, 7}.

17 $2x + 5 \geq 11$

18 $x^2 + 15 = 8x$

19 The perimeter is greater than 18.

20 Area of ABCD ≠ area of EFGH

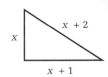

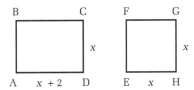

21 Use the variable n to write an expression for "6 added to 4 times a number."

22 Solve for a if $a = 1.14(2.36 + 4.73)$.

23 If $x = \sqrt{7.64 + 2.64}$, solve for x.

24 Find the value of y if $y = 3x + 5$ and $x = 6$.

25 What must the temperature be on Friday to have a 5-day average of 48°?

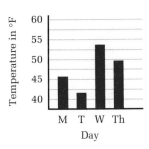

26 Find the value of y if $y = x^2 - 6$ and $x = 7$.

27 Find S_n if $S_n = (n - 2)180$ and $n = 10$.

28 For each exact value in the left column, give an approximation rounded to the indicated accuracy.

Exact Answer	Nearest Thousandth	Nearest Hundredth	Nearest Tenth
.70473			
.73			
$\frac{7}{16}$			
$\frac{5}{7}$			
$\sqrt{7}$			

29 One half cup of milk has the following.

60 calories	4 g protein	2 g fat	50 mg sodium

The chart shows nutrition information for one-half cup of each cereal without milk. Rewrite it showing totals for each cereal with one-half cup of milk.

Cereal	Calories	Grams Protein	Grams Fat	Milligrams Sodium
Oat Way	100	4	2	160
Wheat Ho	90	3	1	120
Rice Crunchies	110	2	0	290

Problem Set, *continued*

Practice

30 Determine which values of x in {1, 2, 3, 4, 5, 6, 7} will make $x^2 - 7x + 10 = 0$ a true statement.

Practice,
Review

31 Find the area of the circle to the nearest tenth. (Hint: The formula for the area of a circle is $A = \pi r^2$.)

7 ft

Practice,
Review

32 The radius of a circle is 12.6 centimeters. Find its area to the nearest tenth.

Practice,
Review

33 If each of the numbers 1, 2, 3, 4, and 5 is substituted for x, how many of the substitutions will make $x + 8 \geq 11$ a true statement?

Practice

In problems 34 and 35, solve for x.

34 $x = 3.24 - 5.36(2.18)$

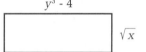 **35** $x = 2.15(4.37)(10.1) - 4.16^3$

Practice,
Introduce

36 Solve for x_1 if $x_1 + x_1 = 13$.

Practice

37 If $x = 13 + 5(4)$, is 9 a factor of x?

Practice,
Introduce

38 Find the area of the rectangle if (x, y) = (50, 3).

$y^3 - 4$

$\sqrt{x}$

Practice,
Introduce

39 If $x_1 = 3$ and $x_2 = 1$, is $2x_1 - 4 > x_2 + 1$ a true statement?

Practice

40 Use x to write an equation that represents the diagram. Then solve the equation for x.

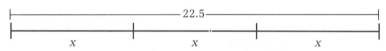

22.5

x x x

Practice,
Introduce

41 If $m = \dfrac{y_2 - y_1}{x_2 - x_1}$, find m for the following values.

a $y_2 = 8$, $y_1 = 4$, $x_2 = 7$, and $x_1 = 5$
b $x_1 = 10$, $x_2 = 7$, $y_1 = 56$, and $y_2 = 68$

Practice

42 Find a value for x such that $\dfrac{12}{x - 3} > 15$.

Practice

In problems 43 and 44, determine whether each statement is true Always, Sometimes, or Never.

43 If x represents some number between $\frac{1}{2}$ and 2.3, then $3x > 3$.

44 If x represents some number between 0.1 and 0.9, then $\frac{2}{x} > 2$.

WAYS TO REPRESENT DATA

Objectives

After studying this section, you should be familiar with
- Using sets of numbers to solve equations and inequalities
- Using ordered pairs to solve equations and inequalities
- Organizing data in a matrix

Part One: Introduction

Sets of Numbers

A *set* is a collection of objects. Each object in a set is called a *member* or *element* of the set. Braces, { }, enclose the elements of a set. If A is the set consisting of the numbers 1, 2, 3, 4, and 5, then we write A = {1, 2, 3, 4, 5}.

Equal sets contain exactly the same elements. For example,

$$\{1, 2, 3, 4, 5\} = \{4, 2, 1, 3, 5\}.$$

These two sets are equal even though the elements are in different order.

The *solution set* of an equation is the set that contains all the numbers that are the solutions for that equation. For example, {0, 1} is the solution set for the equation $x^2 = x$ since $0^2 = 0$ and $1^2 = 1$, and $x^2 \neq x$ for any other number.

Ordered Pairs

An *ordered pair* contains two elements in a designated order. Parentheses, ( ), enclose the elements of an ordered pair. For instance, (5, 2) and (3, 8) are ordered pairs. The ordered pair (5, 2) is different from the ordered pair (2, 5).

Matrices

A *matrix* organizes numbers into rows and columns. Brackets, [ ], are used to enclose the rows and columns of a matrix. The plural of *matrix* is *matrices*. Here are several matrices.

$$\begin{bmatrix} 4 & 6 \end{bmatrix}, \begin{bmatrix} 4 & 5 \\ 8 & 7 \\ 1 & 3 \\ 5 & 0 \end{bmatrix}, \begin{bmatrix} 4 \\ 1 \\ 6 \end{bmatrix}, \begin{bmatrix} 6, 3, 7 \end{bmatrix}$$

Two matrices are equal if each element of one matrix is equal to the corresponding element of the other matrix. For example,

$$\begin{bmatrix} 6+7 & 9 \\ 8-3 & 4\cdot 5 \end{bmatrix} = \begin{bmatrix} 13 & 9 \\ 5 & 20 \end{bmatrix} \text{ but } \begin{bmatrix} 13 & 5 \\ 9 & 20 \end{bmatrix} \neq \begin{bmatrix} 13 & 9 \\ 5 & 20 \end{bmatrix}$$

Part Two: Sample Problems

Problem 1 Choosing from the set {0, 12, 24}, solve for x if $\frac{x}{6} + 3 = 7$.

Solution We need to check each number by substituting it in the equation and seeing if the left side then equals 7.

Try x = 0	**Try x = 12**	**Try x = 24**
$\frac{0}{6} + 3 = 3$	$\frac{12}{6} + 3 = 5$	$\frac{24}{6} + 3 = 7$

The solution set is {24}.

Problem 2 If $(x_1, y_1) = (6, 8)$ and $(x_2, y_2) = (14, 32)$, solve $m = \dfrac{y_2 - y_1}{x_2 - x_1}$ for m.

Solution By substitution, $m = \dfrac{y_2 - y_1}{x_2 - x_1}$

$$= \frac{32 - 8}{14 - 6}$$

$$= \frac{24}{8}$$

$$= 3$$

Problem 3 The matrix gives data about the caps and scarves that are in stock at a store.

$$\begin{array}{r} \\ \textbf{Caps} \\ \textbf{Scarves} \end{array} \begin{array}{ccc} \textbf{Red} & \textbf{Blue} & \textbf{Yellow} \\ \begin{bmatrix} 5 & 8 & 3 \\ 6 & 4 & 9 \end{bmatrix} \end{array}$$

Determine what each of the following represents.
a The number in row 2, column 3
b The sum of the elements of the second column
c The sum of the elements of the first row
d The sum of all the elements in the matrix

Solution We interpret each number using the row and column labels. Rows go across; columns go down.

a The 9 represents 9 yellow scarves.
b 8 + 4 = 12 represents a total of 12 blue items.
c 5 + 8 + 3 = 16 represents a total of 16 caps.
d 5 + 8 + 3 + 6 + 4 + 9 = 35 represents the store's total stock of caps and scarves.

Part Three: Exercises and Problems

Warm-up Exercises

For problems 1–4, find the solution set if z is chosen from $\{2, 4, 6, 8\}$.

1 $3z - 4 = 14$

2 $(z - 2)(z - 4) = 0$

3 $RT = 13$ cm

4 Area = 24 cm^2

R ⊢— $2z - 1$ —⊦— $z + 2$ —⊣ T, with S between

$z + 2$, height z

5 If the two matrices are equal, find the values of w, x, y, and z.

$$\begin{bmatrix} 2x & w - 4 \\ y + 7 & \frac{z}{3} \end{bmatrix} = \begin{bmatrix} 16 & 12 \\ 13 & 14 \end{bmatrix}$$

6 If $(x, y) = (4, 6)$, evaluate $3xy - y^2 + x$.

7 Do $x + 5 = 7$ and $3x = 6$ have equal solution sets? If so, what is the value of x?

8 Are $\{1, 2, 4\}$ and $\{4, 2, 1\}$ equal sets?

9 Five ordered pairs, (day, temperature), can be read from the chart. If the first pair is (Monday, 50°), write the other four.

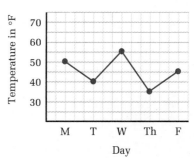

Problem Set

In problems 10–12, identify each as a set, an ordered pair, or a matrix.

10 (x, y)

11 $\begin{bmatrix} x \\ y \end{bmatrix}$

12 $\left\{ \frac{1}{2}, \frac{3}{4}, 1\frac{1}{4} \right\}$

In problems 13–16, solve for x.

13 $2x = 1 + 15^2 - 8 \div 2$

14 $3x = (2^3)(3^2)$

15 $5x = 2 \cdot 6 + \dfrac{8 - 1 \cdot 2}{1^2 + 1^3}$

16 $2x = 15\sqrt{3^4(12 - 2 \cdot 4)} - 34 \cdot 2$

In problems 17–19, determine whether the sentence is True or False. If the answer is False, explain.

17 If $y = 12$, then $3y + 2 \geq 38$.

18 If $x_1 = 7.2$, then $3.2 + 4.8x_1 = 57.6$.

19 If the sum of a number x and 18 is 32, then $18x = 32$.

20 If $y = 3x + b$, solve for b when $(x, y) = (2, 15)$.

Problem Set, *continued*

In problems 21–23, choose from {3, 5, 6, 10, 20} and find the solution set.

21 $14 = x - 6$

22 $3(y + 4) = 27$

23 $3z < 20$

24 Al, Bob, and Carl went fishing. Al brought 6 worms, 12 minnows, and 5 crayfish. Bob brought 15 worms, no minnows, and 10 crayfish. Carl brought 9 of each. The matrix shows this data.

$$\begin{bmatrix} 6 & 12 & 5 \\ 15 & 0 & 10 \\ 9 & 9 & 9 \end{bmatrix}$$

    a What does the second column represent?
    b What does the 15 in the second row, first column, represent?
    c Find how many minnows they had all together.

25 When sales of computer discs began to drop, the store owner made a graph of daily sales, s, and price, p. To fit the data, he developed the equation $s = 90 - 5p$.

    a If discs cost $0.17, what would the equation predict for daily sales?
    b How many would be sold at 2 for $0.17?
    c If discs were free, what would the equation predict?
    d According to the equation, what price would produce no sales of discs?

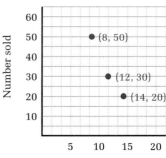

In problems 26–31, look for patterns as you solve the equations.

26 $x + x = 6$

27 $2x = 6$

28 $3x_2 + 2x_2 = 20$

29 $5x_2 = 20$

30 $2y - 8 = 20$

31 $2y = 28$

32 If Henry paints an entire wall in 20 minutes, how much of the wall can he paint in 1 minute?

33 If $x_1 - 4 = 11$ and $x_2 + 5 = 17$, determine whether $x_1 > x_2$.

34 Determine whether the ordered triplet $(x, y, z) = (9, 2, 6)$ is a solution to the equation $\sqrt{x} + 7z - y^3 = z^2$.

35 Solve for x, y, and z.

$$\begin{bmatrix} 2 & y & 3 \\ x + 1 & 5 & 3z \end{bmatrix} = \begin{bmatrix} 2 & 1 & 3 \\ 4 & 5 & 6 \end{bmatrix}$$

In problems 36 and 37, solve for x.

36 $\left(\frac{2}{3}\right)x = 5$

37 $x^2 - 4x = 0$

GRAPHING

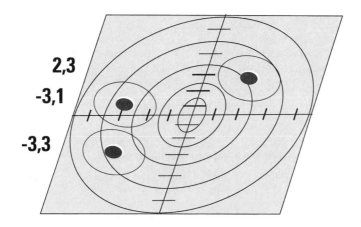

2,3

-3,1

-3,3

Objectives
After studying this section, you should be familiar with
- Constructing a rectangular coordinate system
- Graphing points on a rectangular coordinate system
- Making a table of values for an equation and drawing its graph

Part One: Introduction

The Rectangular Coordinate System

A *rectangular coordinate system* is constructed by drawing two lines that intersect to form right angles at point O, called the *origin.*

The horizontal line through the origin is the *x-axis,* and the vertical line through the origin is the *y-axis.* The two *axes* divide the flat surface, or *plane,* into four regions, called *quadrants* (I, II, III, IV). Each point in the plane can be represented by a unique ordered pair of numbers, called *coordinates.* The first number of the ordered pair is called the *x-coordinate,* or *abscissa.* The second number is called the *y-coordinate,* or *ordinate.* A rectangular coordinate system is also called a *Cartesian coordinate system,* after the French mathematician René Descartes (1596–1650).

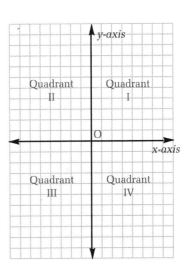

Graphing Points

In an ordered pair (x, y), the x-coordinate tells how far a point is to the right or left of the origin, and the y-coordinate tells how far a point is up or down from the origin.

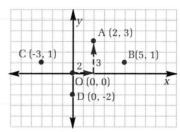

The coordinates of the origin are $(0, 0)$. Point A, in Quadrant I, is represented by $(2, 3)$ because, starting at point O, you get to point A by moving 2 units to the right and then 3 units up. Similarly, point B, in Quadrant I, has an abscissa of 5 and an ordinate of 1 and is represented by $(5, 1)$.

The negative sign $(-)$ indicates a point to the left of or down from the origin. Point C, in Quadrant II, has coordinates $(-3, 1)$ because it is 3 units to the left of point O and 1 unit up. Point D is not in a quadrant, but on the y-axis. It is represented by $(0, -2)$ because no move to the left or right of point O is needed, only a move 2 units down.

Graphing an Equation

To graph an equation in two variables, x and y, we first construct a *table of values.*

Example *Graph the equation $y = 2x - 1$.*

We choose a value for x from some set, say $\{1, 2, 3, 4, 5\}$, substitute that value for x, and solve for y. We have then found an ordered pair (x, y).

Choose $x = 1$
$y = 2x - 1$
$\quad = 2(1) - 1$
$\quad = 2 - 1$
$\quad = 1$
So, $(x, y) = (1, 1)$

Choose $x = 2$
$y = 2x - 1$
$\quad = 2(2) - 1$
$\quad = 4 - 1$
$\quad = 3$
So, $(x, y) = (2, 3)$

By choosing more values for x and solving for y, we can make a table of values for $y = 2x - 1$.

x	1	2	3	4	5
y	1	3	5	7	9

Now we graph, or **plot,** these ordered pairs on a coordinate system. The line through the points is the graph of $y = 2x - 1$.

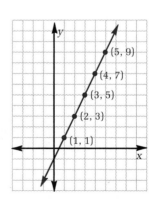

Part Two: Sample Problems

Problem 1   *For the graph of points A–E, determine the quadrant in which each point lies.*

Solution   We remember that the quadrants are numbered counterclockwise, beginning in the upper right quadrant.

A is in Quadrant I.
B is in Quadrant I.
C is in Quadrant II.
D is in Quadrant III.
E is not in any quadrant. (E is on the x-axis.)

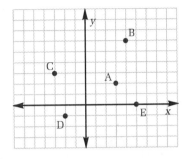

Problem 2   *Make a table of values and graph the equation y = 3x + 2.*

Solution   We substitute values for x and solve for y.

x	0	1	2	3
y	2	5	8	11

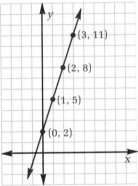

Problem 3   *Find the point of intersection of lines y = 2x and y = 3x − 1.*

Solution   We make a table of values for each equation, then graph each line.

y = 2x

x	0	1	2
y	0	2	4

y = 3x − 1

x	1	2	3
y	2	5	8

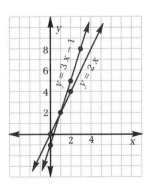

We can see from the graph and verify from the table of values that the point of intersection is (1, 2).

Part Three: Exercises and Problems

Warm-Up Exercises

1 Use the graph to determine the coordinates and quadrant of each point.

a point A　　　　　　**b** point B
c point C　　　　　　**d** point D
e point E　　　　　　**f** point F
g point G　　　　　　**h** point H

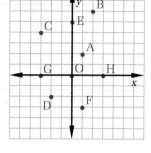

2 Refer to the graph and name the points.

  a Which point lies on the y-axis?
  b What is the name given to point O?
  c Name all labeled points that lie in Quadrant IV.

3 Name the following for point C.

  a The abscissa　　　　**b** The ordinate

4 If Aimee puts her pencil on point A and moves it 2 to the right and 1 up, what are the coordinates of the point where she ends?

Problem Set

5 Complete the table of values for $y = 3x - 2$.

x	1	2	3	4
y				

6 If P represents the perimeter of the figure, find P.

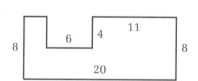

7 The matrix shows the earnings (in dollars) of three part-time employees of Pentomino's Pizza Place during the past four weeks.

	Pat	Juan	Rosa
First Week	50	85	75
Second Week	60	60	80
Third Week	55	90	60
Fourth Week	75	75	80

  a Who earned the most in the first week?
  b How much did Juan earn during the four weeks?
  c What was the total paid by Pentomino's Pizza Place to all three employees during the third week?
  d Who earned the most during the four-week period?

8 If $x = 2$ and $y - 3 = \dfrac{2x^2 - 3}{3}$, find the value of y.

9 Make a table of values and graph the equation $y = x + 2$.

10 If Henry can paint a wall in 30 minutes, how much of the wall can he paint in 1 minute?

11 If x represents a number, write an algebraic sentence that indicates that the sum of this number and 10 is 16.

12 Refer to the diagram to answer the following questions.

   a Point M is in the middle of segment AB. What are the coordinates of M?

   b What is the distance from M to B?

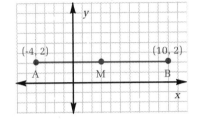

13 If Superman can fly 720 miles per hour, how many miles can he fly in 4 hours?

14 Choosing from $\{11, 14, 15\}$, solve for x if $3(x - 4) = x + 16$.

15 Evaluate $3x^2 - 12 + 3\sqrt{y^2 - x^2} \div y$ for $(x, y) = (2, 3)$.

16 The lines appear to intersect at the point $(3, 2)$. Test these coordinates in the equations of the lines to prove whether $\left(3\frac{1}{4}, 2\frac{3}{4}\right)$ is the actual point of intersection.

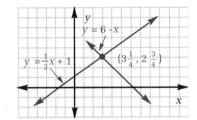

In problems 17 and 18, make a table of values and graph the equation.

17 $y = \frac{1}{2}x + 3$ **18** $x + y = 12$

19 In the diagram of a rectangle, find the coordinates of the unlabeled vertices.

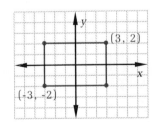

20 Solve for x, y, and z.

$$\begin{bmatrix} 5 & 0 & y \\ 4 & 7 & 11 \\ z & 3 & 9 \end{bmatrix} = \begin{bmatrix} x & 0 & 3x \\ 4 & 7 & 11 \\ x + y & 3 & 9 \end{bmatrix}$$

21 Use the given table to draw the graph of $y = 3x + 1$. Explain what is wrong.

x	0	1	2	3	4	5
y	1	4	9	10	13	16

22 Graph the equations $y = 3x - 4$ and $y = x + 2$ and find their point of intersection.

23 For the equation $y = \sqrt{x - 4}$, complete the table of values and graph the equation.

x	4	6	8	10	12
y					

TRANSLATING BETWEEN WORDS AND SYMBOLS

Objective

After studying this section, you should be familiar with
- Translating words into algebraic symbols and translating algebraic symbols into words

Part One: Introduction

Words and Algebraic Symbols

Here are several suggestions for translating words into algebraic symbols and algebraic symbols into words.

Four Suggestions for Translations

1. **Ask yourself if you have seen a similar problem.**

2. **Translate words and phrases step-by-step.**

3. **Try convenient numbers and look for a pattern.**

4. **Organize information to show a pattern, draw a diagram if it seems reasonable, and then make generalizations.**

Part Two: Sample Problems

Problem 1   Translate each phrase by using a variable.

a The sum of a number and 8   b Twice a number
c 2 dollars less than Judy had   d 25 percent of a number
   yesterday

Solution   The following are possible translations.

a $x + 8$ b $2y$ c $d - 2$ d $0.25z$

Problem 2   Give a possible word translation for each algebraic expression.

a $y + 9$ b $x - 17$ c $2x_1 + 3x_1$ d $\dfrac{x}{x + 5}$

Solution   The following are possible translations. You will be able to think of other correct translations.

a The sum of a number and 9

b 17 less than a number

c The sum of twice a number and 3 times the same number

d A number divided by 5 more than itself

Problem 3   *If Chris can do x sit-ups per minute, how many can he do in 3 minutes?*

Solution   We can try a number example in order to see the pattern. If x were 15 sit-ups per minute, Chris would do 3 · 15 = 45 sit-ups in 3 minutes. In general, he can do 3 · x sit-ups in 3 minutes.

Problem 4   *If Debbie can stock a shelf in y minutes, how much of the shelf can she stock in 1 minute?*

Solution   Again, let's try a number example. If y were 30 minutes, Debbie would stock $\frac{1}{30}$ of the shelf per minute. Generalizing this relationship, we say that she can stock $\frac{1}{y}$ of the shelf per minute.

Problem 5   *The length of $\overline{GH}$ (segment GH) is 12. Write an equation to describe the length of $\overline{GH}$.*

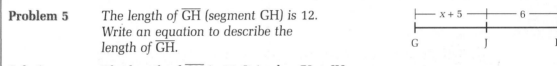

Solution   The length of $\overline{GH}$ is 12. It is also GJ + JH.

We can write an equation

$$GH = GJ + JH$$
$$12 = (x + 5) + 6$$

Problem 6   *Write an equation to represent $\frac{1}{3}$ the area of MNOP.*

Solution   First, we write an equation for the area of MNOP.

$\frac{1}{3}$ of the area is

$$A = lw$$
$$A = (2x)(4)$$
$$\tfrac{1}{3}A = \tfrac{1}{3}(2x)(4)$$

Part Three: Exercises and Problems

Warm-up Exercises

In problems 1–5, translate each phrase or sentence using a variable.

1 Five times a number
2 Four more than a number
3 Six less than a number
4 Divide the sum of a number and six by four.
5 Square the quotient of a number and three.

In problems 6–8, give a possible word translation for each algebraic expression.

6 $\dfrac{x_1 + x_2}{2}$ **7** $y - 15$ **8** $3w + 6$

Problem Set

9 Translate each phrase by using a variable.
  a Seven decreased by a number
  b The square of four more than a number

10 Let $(x_1, y_1) = (2, 4)$ and $(x_2, y_2) = (5, 6)$. Find the value of m if $m = \dfrac{y_2 - y_1}{x_2 - x_1}$.

11 Write an expression using x to describe the length of $\overline{AB}$.

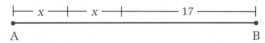

In problems 12 and 13, solve for x.

12 $3x + 4x = 28$ **13** $7x = 28$

14 If Patrick can walk x kilometers per hour, how far can he walk in 2 hours?

15 If Tricia has q quarters, how many cents does Tricia have?

16 If Roger needs y minutes to wax the floor, how much of the floor does he wax in 1 minute?

In problems 17 and 18, evaluate each expression.

17 $\dfrac{7 + xy}{10}$ if $x = 5$ and $y = 6$ **18** $\dfrac{4 + 3(x^2 - 6)}{7}$ if $x = 5$

19 Graph the line $y = x - 1$.

20 Choosing from $\{0, 1, 2, 3, 4\}$, solve for x.
  a $x^2 + 3 = 7$ **b** $x^2 + 3 \le 7$

21 Translate each phrase by using a variable.
  a A number multiplied by 8 less than itself
  b One-half a number increased by the square root of 17

22 If b bananas cost p cents and each banana costs the same amount, find the cost of one banana.

23 A triangle has one side 8 centimeters long and one side 14 centimeters long. The perimeter is 38 centimeters.

    a Write an equation to represent the information.

    b Find the length of the third side.

24 Give the coordinates of the point that is five units to the left of and seven units down from $(3, -1)$.

25 Find the value of $b^2 - 4ac$ if $(a, b, c) = (1, 7, 4)$.

26 Chart A lists the August shipment of television sets to Littell's Appliances. Chart B is the September shipment. Chart C shows how many sets Littell's sold in August and September. Fill in Chart D to show how many of the sets from these two shipments the store has at the end of September.

	Brand X	Brand Y	Brand Z
A	12	8	14
B	5	10	2
C	10	7	5
D			

27 Find the value of x and y.

$$\begin{bmatrix} x - 4 \\ 2y + 3 \end{bmatrix} = \begin{bmatrix} 0 \\ 4 \end{bmatrix}$$

28 Refer to the coordinate system.

    a Find the coordinates of points A, B, C, and D.

    b Find the distance from point A to point B and the distance from point B to point C.

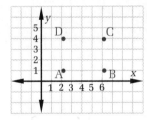

29 If Henry can paint a wall in 20 minutes and Peter can paint the same wall in 30 minutes, how much of the wall can Henry and Peter paint if they work together for 1 minute?

30 At a recent dance, the ratio of girls to boys was $5:3$. If there were 90 more girls than boys, which of the following equations represents a translation of the conditions?

    a $3x + 5x = 90$ **b** $3 + x + 90 = 5 + x$

    c $3x + 90 = 5x$ **d** $\frac{g}{b} = \frac{5}{3} + 90$

31 Graph the two equations $y = 5x - 17$ and $y = x - 1$ and find their point of intersection.

Problem Set, *continued*

32 Find the perimeter of rectangle ABCD.

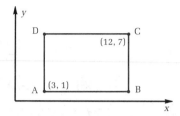

SAFE SKIES, HAPPY LANDINGS

The goal of Margaret Sanchez, air traffic control specialist

Near misses. Crowded skies. Nearly 2 million people flying every day. No wonder the job of air traffic controller has been characterized as one of today's most challenging occupations. The controller's challenge is to keep track of dozens of blips on a radar screen, mentally translating them into three-dimensional pictures of planes in complex patterns of altitudes, speeds, and directions. For Margaret Sanchez, an air traffic control specialist in Fort Worth, Texas, the challenge also involves helping lost pilots get their bearings.

"I process flight plans and provide weather briefings to pilots prior to their departure, advising them on the best routings around bad weather," says Ms. Sanchez. "And when pilots get lost, I try to get them back on track." If the plane has the right equipment, the process can be simple. If not, the lost pilot can turn to geometry and the convenient principle that two nonparallel lines must cross at a single point.

Under Ms. Sanchez's guidance, the pilot tunes in to an airport navigational aid, allowing the controller to obtain a first bearing. The pilot flies along that line of position until the controller gets a second bearing—a *cross fix*—thereby pinpointing the plane's exact location.

Ms. Sanchez has been an air traffic controller for five years. To anyone thinking about a career as a controller, she emphasizes the importance of being able to visualize complex relationships in space. This problem, taken from a recent test for air traffic control specialists, measures that ability. There is a relationship among the symbols in the first box, and a similar relationship among those in the second box. See if you can figure out which symbol in the third box can best be substituted for the question mark.

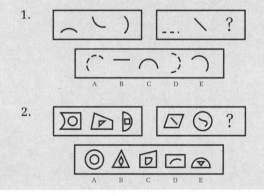

1.8 PROBABILITY

Objectives

After studying this section, you should be familiar with
- Defining probability
- Calculating probabilities of events

Part One: Introduction

Probability

The ***probability*** of an event is the ratio of favorable outcomes, called winners, to all outcomes of the event, called possibilities.

$$\text{probability of an event} = \frac{\text{number of winners}}{\text{number of possibilities}}$$

All probabilities range from 0, when none of the possible events are winners, to 1, when all of the possible events are winners.

Example   *If you choose one number at random from* {1, 2, 3, 4, 5, 6, 7, 8}, *what is the probability that it is a solution for $x \geq 3$?*

We count all possibilities. There are eight.
We then count the favorable outcomes, or winners.

Favorable	**Not Favorable**
$3 \geq 3$ is true	$1 \geq 3$ is false
$4 \geq 3$ is true	$2 \geq 3$ is false
$5 \geq 3$ is true	
$6 \geq 3$ is true	
$7 \geq 3$ is true	
$8 \geq 3$ is true	

$$\text{Probability} = \frac{6 \text{ winners}}{8 \text{ possibilities}} = \frac{3}{4} \text{ or } .75$$

Part Two: Sample Problems

Problem 1   *If x is selected at random from {0, 1, 2, 3, 4, 5}, find the probability that the line segments AB and CD will be equal in length.*

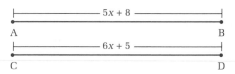

Solution   Let's make a table to find the winners.

x	AB = 5x + 8	CD = 6x + 5	Winner?
0	5(0) + 8 = 8	6(0) + 5 = 5	No
1	5(1) + 8 = 13	6(1) + 5 = 11	No
2	5(2) + 8 = 18	6(2) + 5 = 17	No
3	5(3) + 8 = 23	6(3) + 5 = 23	Yes
4	5(4) + 8 = 28	6(4) + 5 = 29	No
5	5(5) + 8 = 33	6(5) + 5 = 35	No

$$\text{Probability} = \frac{1 \text{ winner}}{6 \text{ possibilities}} = \frac{1}{6} \approx 0.17$$

Problem 2   *If 3 of the 4 figures are selected at random, find the probability that all three will have perimeters greater than 28. Assume that figures A–C are equilateral (have all sides equal).*

A	**B**	**C**	**D**
square	pentagon	hexagon	trapezoid

Solution   Let's calculate the perimeters.

Figure	Perimeter
A	8 · 4 = 32
B	5 · 5 = 25
C	6 · 6 = 36
D	sum of all sides = 30

A winner occurs when all three of the figures chosen at random have a perimeter greater than 28.

Threesomes	Perimeter	Winner?
ABC	32, 25, 36	No
ABD	32, 25, 30	No
ACD	32, 36, 30	Yes
BCD	25, 36, 30	No

$$\text{Probability} = \frac{1 \text{ winner}}{4 \text{ possibilities}} = \frac{1}{4} \text{ or } .25$$

Problem 3   *If we solve each equation and then pick 2 of the solutions at random, what is the probability that both solutions are greater than 6?*

$$x + 7 = 15 \qquad 4y - 1 = 27 \qquad z - 8 = 12 \qquad 0.5x_1 = 3$$

Solution   We solve each of the equations to find $x = 8$, $y = 7$, $z = 20$, and $x_1 = 6$.

A winner occurs when both numbers are greater than 6.

Twosomes	Winner?
8 and 7	Yes
8 and 20	Yes
8 and 6	No
7 and 20	Yes
7 and 6	No
20 and 6	No

$$\text{Probability} = \frac{3 \text{ winners}}{6 \text{ possibilities}} = \frac{1}{2} = 0.5$$

Part Three: Exercises and Problems

Warm-up Exercises

1 If a number is chosen at random from {1, 2, 3, 4, 5}, what is the probability that it is a solution of $x < 4$?

2 If two numbers are selected at random from {1, 2, 3, 4, 5}, what is the probability that the sum of the numbers is greater than 6? (A number can only be used once in a sum.)

3 If a number is chosen at random from {1, 2, 3, 4, 5}, what is the probability that it is a solution to the equation $y^2 = 36$?

4 If a point is chosen at random from {A, B, C, D, E, F, G, H}, what is the probability that it is more than one unit from E?

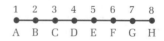

5 The first digit of a two-digit number is randomly selected from {1, 2}. The second digit is randomly selected from {1, 2, 3}. What is the probability that the two-digit number is a prime number? (Hint: List all possible outcomes.)

6 If z is chosen at random from {1, 2, 3, 4, 5}, what is the probability that in the rectangle,

a the area is more than 65 sq in.?
b the perimeter is less than 25 in.?

Problem Set

In problems 7–10, if one of the members of {1, 2, 3, 4, 5, 6} is chosen at random, find the probability that the number

7 is a factor of 24

8 is prime

9 is a solution of $2x + 1 \leq 9$

10 is a solution of $5x - 2x = 0$

Problem Set, *continued*

In problems 11 and 12, if two of the members of {1, 2, 3, 4, 5} are chosen at random, find the probability that

11 at least one of the two is an even number

12 they both are solutions of x ≥ 3

13 If the value of x is randomly selected from {1, 2, 3, 4, 5}, find the probability that $\overline{XY}$ and $\overline{PR}$ will be equal in length.

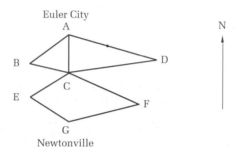

14 Which choice from **a–c** correctly translates the expression 4x?

    a 4 more than a number   **b** 4 times a number   **c** fourth power of a number

15 Matthew travels from Euler City to visit his girlfriend in Newtonville. How many different routes can he travel if he always travels in a southerly direction and stays on the roads shown in the figure?

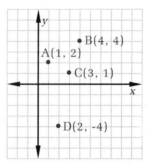

16 Refer to the graph of points A, B, C, and D.

    a Determine whether the coordinates of point C make the equation 4x + 2y = 14 a true statement.

    b Give the coordinates of the point that is 4 units to the right of and 3 units below point A.

    c If two of the points A, B, C, and D are selected at random, find the probability that they both lie in Quadrant I.

17 There were 14 people at Perry's party. Perry ordered 7 pizzas and cut each into 8 slices. There were 7 slices left over. On the average, how many slices did each person eat?

18 Solve $y = \dfrac{6 + 8 - 3(2 + 1)^2}{1 + 2(2)}$.

19 Two of the points A, B, C, D, and E are selected at random; what is the probability that the distance between them is 2?

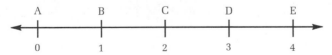

20 Refer to the circle with a radius of 1.7 centimeters.

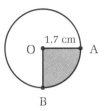

  a If lines OA and OB intersect at a 90 degree angle and if O is the center of the circle, find the area of the shaded region, correct to the nearest tenth.

  b If a point is selected at random from inside the circle, find the probability that the point is in the shaded region.

21 A number is selected at random from {2, 3, 4}, and a second number is selected at random from {2, 4, 6}. Find the probability

  a that the two numbers are equal.

  b that both are even

22 Determine whether $x^2 > x$ is true Always, Sometimes, or Never. Explain.

A PROFESSIONAL MATHEMATICIAN

Ronald L. Graham shows what math can do

Meet Ronald L. Graham, director of Bell Laboratories Mathematical Studies Center. Mr. Graham is one of the world's leading authorities on the Ramsey theory, a difficult field of theoretical mathematics. In working on this theory, he used the largest number ever used in a mathematical proof, a feat that landed his name in the *Guinness Book of World Records*.

Mr. Graham runs a huge department that is responsible for finding the most efficient way to route millions of telephone calls a day. The techniques he has developed have important applications in economics and computer science as well as a host of other fields. Mr. Graham has used them, for example, to help NASA develop schedules for astronauts to follow on space flights.

Currently Mr. Graham is looking for ways to get specific information from huge banks of data. For example, census figures tell us the average age of farmers in the United States.

Are the ages of individual farmers hidden in that figure? If so, can they be found? A relatively easy example of the problem follows.

The average age of Althea and Bartles is thirty-five. The average age of Althea and Cuthbert is twenty-six. The average age of Bartles and Cuthbert is thirty-seven. How old is each?

1 CHAPTER SUMMARY

PROCEDURES AND CONCEPTS

After studying this chapter, you should be familiar with
- Evaluating an expression (1.2)
- Finding the prime factorization of a number (1.2)
- Working with exponents and square roots (1.2)
- Following the order of operations when evaluating an expression (1.3)
- Using sets of numbers to solve equations and inequalities (1.4)
- Organizing information in solution sets, ordered pairs, and matrices (1.5)
- Drawing the graph of an equation by making a table of values and using ordered pairs to plot the points (1.6)
- Translating words into algebraic symbols and algebraic symbols into words (1.7)
- Finding the probabilities of events (1.8)

VOCABULARY

abscissa, x-coordinate (1.6)
axis (1.6)
base (1.2)
composite number (1.2)
coordinates (1.6)
element (1.5)
equal sets (1.5)
equation (1.4)
evaluate (1.3)
exponent (1.2)
expression (1.3)
factor (1.2)

inequality (1.4)
matrix (1.5)
member (1.5)
order of operations (1.3)
ordinate, y-coordinate (1.6)
ordered pair (1.5)
origin (1.6)
plane (1.6)
plot (1.6)
prime factored form (1.2)
prime number (1.2)

probability (1.8)
quadrant (1.6)
rectangular, or Cartesian, coordinate system (1.6)
set (1.5)
solution set (1.5)
subscript (1.3)
table of values (1.6)
variable (1.3)
x-axis (1.6)
y-axis (1.6)

SYMBOLS

$=$	is equal to
$\neq$	is not equal to
$<$	is less than
$\not<$	is not less than
$>$	is greater than

$\not>$	is not greater than
$\leq$	is less than or equal to
$\geq$	is greater than or equal to
$\approx$	is approximately equal to
$\sqrt{}$	square root symbol

REVIEW PROBLEMS

1 Simplify $\dfrac{6 + 4^2}{2}$.

2 Choosing from {1, 3, 5, 7}, find all replacements for x such that $2(x + 3) \geq 14$.

In problems 3 and 4, solve for y.

3 $3y + y = 8$ **4** $4y = 8$

5 Solve the equation $x_1 = 6 \div 1 \cdot 2$ for x_1.

6 If $x_1 = 5$ and $x_2 = 6$, evaluate $\dfrac{2x_1 + 3x_2}{2}$.

7 Lee's quiz scores are shown on the graph.

   a What is Lee's average score?

   b What must Lee's grade be on quiz 7 for Lee's new average to be 80?

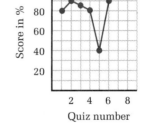

8 Evaluate $\sqrt{x + y}$ if $(x, y) = (7, 4)$.

9 Determine in which quadrant the point $(-3, 4)$ is located.

10 If $x = 14$, solve for y in $y = 2x + 11$.

11 For what value of w will the area of the rectangle be 54?

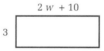

12 If $(x, y) = (7, 8)$, determine whether the point $(7, 8)$ is on the line $y = 4x - 20$.

13 Find the area of the circle to the nearest tenth.

14 Write the prime factorization of 40.

15 Make a table of values for $y = x + 3$ and graph the equation.

16 Write an algebraic expression that represents a translation of "four more than twice a number."

Review Problems, *continued*

17 Using a variable, write a translation of the phrase "four less than a number."

18 Find the point that is 2 units to the left of and 3 units up from the point (7, 6).

19 Solve for q, r, s, and t.
$$\begin{bmatrix} \sqrt{q} & 2.5 \\ r - 3 & \frac{1}{4} \end{bmatrix} = \begin{bmatrix} 4 & 2.5s \\ 5.5 & \frac{3}{t} \end{bmatrix}$$

In problems 20 and 21, solve for r.

20 $r = 180 - 5 \cdot 2^2 + 10$

21 $2r = 64 \div 16 \cdot 2$

22 If $QR = ST$ and $PQ = RS$, find the length of PT.

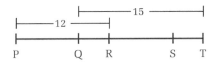

23 If Melissa has d dimes, how many cents does she have?

24 A jet flies 615 miles per hour. To the nearest tenth of a mile, how many miles does it fly in 5 hours and 20 minutes?

25 Using algebraic symbols, translate the statement "three more than twice a number is 39."

26 Evaluate the perimeter of the quadrilateral (4-sided figure) if $(x, y) = (3, 10)$.

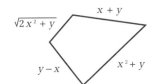

In problems 27 and 28, if one of $\{1, 2, 3, 4, 5\}$ is chosen at random, find each probability.

27 The number is even.
28 The number is the solution of $3x + 4 < 19$.

29 Choosing from $\{1, 2, 3, 4, 5\}$, solve $x^2 = 5x - 6$ for x.

30 If the perimeter of the triangle is 60 yards, find the length of the longest side.

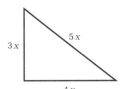

31 Solve for d if $d = \sqrt{(x_2 - x_1)^2 + (y_2 - y_1)^2}$, $(x_1, y_1) = (3, 4)$, and $(x_2, y_2) = (12, 37)$.

32 If $(x_1, y_1) = (5.17, 4.38)$, $(x_2, y_2) = (4.6, 8.12)$, and $m = \dfrac{y_2 - y_1}{x_2 - x_1}$, find m to the nearest hundredth.

In problems 33 and 34, solve for y.

33 $y + 3 = 4^5 + 2\sqrt{36} - 49.982 \div 3$

34 $2y = 6(14 - \sqrt{16 - 7}) + \dfrac{3^2 - 3}{2}$

35 Evaluate the BASIC expression $4 + 2^\wedge 4/2$.

36 Let $A = \{(2, 3), (4, 5), (6, 8), (12, 7)\}$. If an ordered pair is chosen at random from the set A, what is the probability that $x^2 + y^2 < 100$?

37 To build a doghouse you need boards, shingles, and nails. There are three types of doghouses: the old-fashioned design, the contemporary design, and the split-level design.

	Old-fashioned	Contemporary	Split-level
Boards	10	15	25
Shingles	20	35	38
Nails	40	75	120

a What does the 35 represent?
b What does the third column represent?
c How many nails are needed to build two old-fashioned doghouses and one split-level doghouse?

In problems 38–40, evaluate each expression for $x = 2$ and $y = 3$.

38 $(y^x + xy)(y + x)$ **39** $(y^x + xy)y + x$ **40** $y^x + xy \cdot y + x$

41 If the sides of a triangle are represented by $2x$, $3x$, and $4x$ and the perimeter of the triangle is 27 feet, find the length of the longest side of the triangle.

42 If 8 loaves of bread cost $11.20, find the cost of 12 loaves.

43 Find the point of intersection for the two lines $y = x - 3$ and $y = 2x - 8$.

44 If a point is chosen at random from inside the diagram, what is the probability that it lies in the shaded region? What is the probability that it lies outside the shaded region?

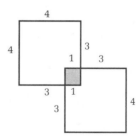

45 If two of the following equations are selected at random, what is the probability that 4 is a solution of both equations?

a $x_1 + 6 = 10$ **b** $x_1^2 + 5x_1 - 36 = 0$

c $4.63x + \frac{x}{2.4} = 20.18$ **d** $x_3 + x_3^2 = 64$

CHAPTER TEST

1 Find all values of r in {3, 4, 5, 6} so that the area of a circle with radius r is greater than 25 and less than 55.

2 A, B, C, D, E, and F are points on the line. If one of these points is selected at random, what is the probability that the point is between B and E?

3 Use the formula y = 2x + 3.

   a Complete the table.
   b Plot the points from the table on a coordinate system.

x	0	1	2	3	4
y					19

In problems 4–9, evaluate each expression if x is replaced by 5.

4 $x + x + x$ **5** x^3 **6** $3x$

7 $x + 7 \cdot 9$ **8** $3(x)^6$ **9** $3 + 4x_1 - 3x_1$

10 If Meg has 20 dimes, how many cents does she have?

11 If (x, y) = (12, 10), find the area of a rectangle with sides x and y.

12 Solve the equation $x + \sqrt{9} = \sqrt{16}$ for x.

13 The radius of a circle is 12.6 centimeters. Find its area to the nearest tenth.

14 If 3x = 18 and y + 12 = 23, determine whether x > y.

15 Assume that Peter is now x years old and that his father is 3 times as old.

   a Write an algebraic expression to indicate how old Peter will be 5 years from now.
   b Write an algebraic expression to indicate how old Peter's father will be 5 years from now.
   c Write an inequality comparing the ages of Peter and his father 5 years from now.

16 Using {4, 7, 9, 11, 13}, find all values of x that make the length of $\overline{MN}$ greater than 30 and less than 40.

PUZZLES AND CHALLENGES

Throughout history, people have enjoyed challenging problems. Using imagination helps us become better problem solvers in general. If nothing else, we hope you enjoy these puzzles.

1 At Anston High School, Benz, Ruke, and Doj are the head math coach, the first assistant, and the second assistant—although not necessarily in that order. The following facts are known.
  a The head coach eats pizza as though it were going out of style.
  b Ruke is allergic to number bases and Italian food.
  c Benz and the first assistant are constantly in need of direction.
  Place each of the three in the proper position.

2 Choosing from {16, 17, 23, 24, 39}, show how you can make a sum of exactly 100.

$$\text{SEND}$$
$$+\ \text{MORE}$$
$$\overline{\text{MONEY}}$$

3 An alphametic is a puzzle in which each letter of a word stands for a digit. The same letter must be used to represent the same digit throughout the problem. Different digits must be represented by different letters. See if you can solve this famous addition alphametic.

4 If a farmer has $2\frac{13}{27}$ and $4\frac{10}{11}$ haystacks, find how many haystacks he will have if he puts them together.

5 How many squares of any size are showing in the figure?

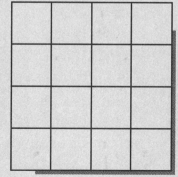

2 | THE RULES OF ALGEBRA

How can we estimate a galaxy's distance from the Earth? Today, astronomers measure the speed of the galaxy and use two mathematical relationships. Thanks to these relationships, this roundabout method works.

When a galaxy is speeding through space, the emitted light is shifted in color because of the galaxy's motion. The amount of shift in color is related to the galaxy's speed and this spectral shift, called the Doppler effect, can be measured by the astronomers.

According to another mathematical relationship called Hubble's law, a galaxy's speed is directly proportional to its distance from the Earth. Therefore, if the speed of a galaxy, in relation to the earth, is found to be twice as fast as the speed of a second galaxy, the first galaxy must be twice as far away.

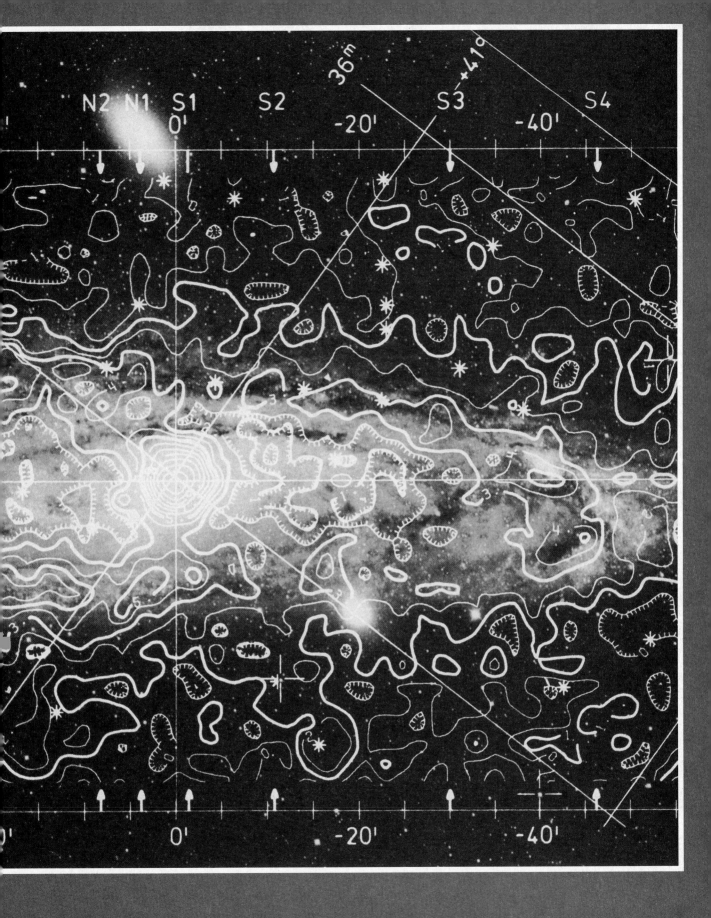

ALGEBRAIC BASICS

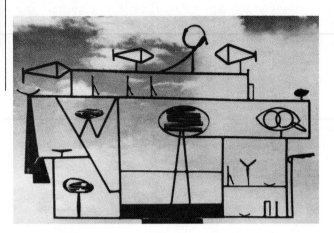

Objectives

After studying this section, you will be able to
- Recognize equalities, inequalities, and expressions
- Find solutions to equations
- Simplify expressions

Part One: Introduction

Recognizing Equations, Inequalities, and Expressions

Algebra is used as a tool to solve problems—from finding the most efficient way to route millions of phone calls to designing more efficient cars. First, you need to learn the language of algebra.

In algebra, information is presented symbolically in three standard forms: equations, inequalities, and expressions. These were defined in Chapter 1.

An *equation* has an equal (=) sign.
An *inequality* has a $<$, $>$, $\leq$, $\geq$, or $\neq$ sign.
An *expression* has neither an equality nor an
    inequality sign.

Note how the symbols indicate each form.

$3 + x = 2x + 4$ is an equation.
$91 - 75 \geq x + 45$ is an inequality.
$xy + 3z - 7^3$ is an expression.

A ***statement*** in mathematics is an equation or inequality that is either true or false.

$3 + 8 = 14 - 3$ is an example of a true statement.
$14 - 2 \geq 10 + 9$ is an example of a false statement.

In an equation or inequality, when you replace the variable with a number, you form a statement that is either true or false.

Equation	$x + 5 = 8$	
Replace x with 7	$7 + 5 = 8$	False statement
Replace x with 3	$3 + 5 = 8$	True statement
Inequality	$y - 5 < 10$	
Replace y with 12	$12 - 5 < 10$	True statement
Replace y with 19	$19 - 5 < 10$	False statement

Solving Equations

To *solve* an equation means to find all the values for a variable or variables that will make the equation true. These values are called *solutions* of the equation. To solve the equation $x + 14 = 21$, we find all values of x that make the equation true. If we replace x with 7, the equation becomes $7 + 14 = 21$, so 7 is a solution.

Example   *Choosing from $\{0, 2, 4, 6\}$, solve $a^2 - 4a = 0$ for a.*

Value of a	Value of $a^2 - 4a$	A solution?
0	$0^2 - 4(0) = 0$	Yes
2	$2^2 - 4(2) = -4$	No
4	$4^2 - 4(4) = 0$	Yes
6	$6^2 - 4(6) = 12$	No

Both 0 and 4 are solutions of the equation.

Simplifying Expressions

Expressions are made up of *terms*, the products of numbers and variables.

$3x + 2x$ has two terms, $3x$ and $2x$.
$6 - 4y^2 + 3zw$ has three terms, 6, $-4y^2$, and $3zw$.

Like terms have exactly the same variables raised to the same exponent. For example, $5x$ and $7x$ are like terms, but $6y$ and $4y^2$ are *not*. Now, let's evaluate $2x + 3x$ and $5x$ for various values of x.

Value of x	Value of $2x + 3x$	Value of $5x$
4	$2(4) + 3(4)$ or 20	$5(4)$ or 20
7	$2(7) + 3(7)$ or 35	$5(7)$ or 35

If you evaluated both expressions for other values of x, the results would always be the same. Such expressions are called *equivalent expressions*. Like terms can be combined by addition or subtraction.

Expression	Simplified form	Notice
$3x_1 + 9x_1 - 2x_1$	$10x_1$	There are 3 like terms.
$4y + 8y_2 + 3y + 2y_2$	$7y + 10y_2$	y and y_2 are not like terms.
$6x^2 + 5x^2 - 4x$	$11x^2 - 4x$	x^2 and x do not have the same exponent.

Each expression above appears in a *simplified form* that combines like terms. An expression and its simplified form are equivalent expressions.

Part Two: Sample Problems

Problem 1 Simplify each expression.

a $7x^2 + x^2 - 3x^4$ **b** $7\sqrt{q} - 3\sqrt{q} + 2\sqrt{r}$

Solution
a $\quad 7x^2 + x^2 - 3x^4$
$\quad = 7x^2 + 1x^2 - 3x^4$
$\quad = 8x^2 - 3x^4$

b $\quad 7\sqrt{q} - 3\sqrt{q} + 2\sqrt{r}$
$\quad = 4\sqrt{q} + 2\sqrt{r}$

Problem 2 Write an equation to represent the diagram and then solve that equation.

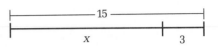

Solution We can represent the combined length of the two segments as x + 3. The length of the entire segment is given as 15. The equation is x + 3 = 15, and the solution is x = 12. The length of the longer segment is 12.

Problem 3 Is $(x, y) = (3, 5)$ a solution for $2x - y = y - x - 1$?

Solution We replace x with 3 and y with 5 to check the solution.

Left Side	**Right Side**
$2x - y$	$y - x - 1$
$= 2(3) - 5$	$= 5 - 3 - 1$
$= 6 - 5$	$= 2 - 1$
$= 1$	$= 1$

Since substituting x = 3 and y = 5 makes the left side of the equation equal to the right side, (3, 5) is a solution.

Problem 4 Find two numbers whose sum is 7 and whose product is 12.

Solution We pick some numbers whose sum is 7 and check their product.

Sum is 7	**Product is**	**Correct choice?**
$0 + 7 = 7$	$0 \cdot 7 = 0$	No
$1 + 6 = 7$	$1 \cdot 6 = 6$	No
$2 + 5 = 7$	$2 \cdot 5 = 10$	No
$3 + 4 = 7$	$3 \cdot 4 = 12$	Yes

The numbers are 3 and 4.

Part Three: Exercises and Problems

Warm-up Exercises

In problems 1–9, determine whether each is an equation, an inequality, or an expression.

1 $15 - 5 = 10$ **2** $8 + 2 > 9$ **3** $x - 1$
4 $2(2) + 1 \le 7$ **5** $2b + 1$ **6** $2x + 1 = 7$
7 $7(2 + 3)$ **8** $2(10 + 12) \le 44$ **9** $2 \cdot 4 = 2^3$

In problems 10–13, simplify each expression.

10 $6x_3 + 7x_3 + 2x_3$

11 $3x^2 + 5x^2 - 7x$

12 $4 + 7(8) - 23$

13 $4y^2 + y - 36$

In problems 14–16, determine whether $x = 9$ solves the inequality.

14 $\sqrt{x} \geq 3$

15 $\sqrt{x} \leq 4$

16 $3x + 5 < 32$

Problem Set

In problems 17 and 18, simplify each expression.

17 $5x^3 - 3x^3 + 3x$

18 $3\sqrt{x} - 2\sqrt{x} + x^2$

19 Does $(x, y) = (6, 3)$ solve the inequality $2x - y < 9$?

20 Write an equation to represent the sentence "If 7 is subtracted from a number, the result is 12."

21 Write an equation to represent each diagram.

22 Does $(x, y) = (4, 1)$ solve the equation $x + y = 6$?

23 Choosing from $\{0, 1, 2, 3\}$, solve the equation $y^2 - 3y = 0$.

24 Find two numbers whose product is 30 and whose sum is 13.

25 Simplify the expression $2.56x + 4.1y + 18.345x - 0.3y$.

26 Choosing from $\{0, 5, 10, 15\}$, solve the equation $2x + 4 = 12$.

In problems 27 and 28, evaluate each expression if $x = 6$ and $y = 2$.

27 $x(3y - 4)^2 + 3^4 - \frac{2}{6x}$

28 $3x^2 - 4\left[2y - \frac{4}{12}\right] + 8$

In problems 29–31, translate each phrase and then simplify each expression.

29 The value in cents of n nickels

30 The value in cents of three dimes and q quarters

31 The value in cents of two pennies, seven dimes, two quarters, and n nickels

32 Determine whether $x = 17$ will make the equation $x - 4 = 13$ a true statement.

33 Evaluate the expression $\sqrt{b^2 - 4ac}$ if $a = 1$, $b = 5$, and $c = 4$.

Problem Set, *continued*

In problems 34 and 35, simplify each expression.

34 $7y^2 + 2y - 2y$ **35** $4x + 8x^3 + 6y^3 - 2x^2 + 4y^3$

In problems 36–38, solve each equation.

36 $6x = 0$ **37** $0x = 0$ **38** $0x = 8$

39 Write an equation to represent this diagram.

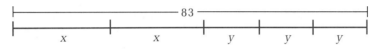

40 Write an equation to represent the sentence "If 3 is added to the square of a number, the sum is 28."

41 If a letter is selected randomly from {a, b, c, d, e, f, g, h}, what is the probability that the letter is a vowel?

42 Is $x = 3.1$ a solution of $4.2x + 6.5 \leq 2x^2$?

43 Find the ordered pair or pairs (x, y) in {(8, 2), (2, 8), (0, 2), (1, 5), (4, 13)} that solve the equation $y - 3x = 2$.

44 Write an equation to represent the sentence "The sum of twice a number and three times another number is 83."

45 Refer to the triangle.
   a Express the perimeter in algebraic terms.
   b Find the perimeter if $x = 3.4$.

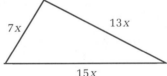

46 Make a table of values and graph the line $y = \frac{1}{2}x + 3$.

47 Is $x = 5$ a solution of the equation $2x = 25$?

In problems 48 and 49, compute.

48 $5 \cdot 2^3 - 3 \cdot 2^3 + 3 \cdot 2$ **49** $3\sqrt{4} - 2\sqrt{4} + 4^2$

50 Choosing from {1, 2, 3, 4, 5}, solve $5 + 2(x + 1)^2 \leq 40$.

51 The sum of two numbers is 19, and their product is 78. Find the numbers.

In problems 52 and 53, solve each equation.

52 $3x + 2x = 20$ **53** $8x - 2x = 12$

54 Find $\frac{1}{x}$ if $3 + 2x = 31$.

55 Evaluate the matrix if $x = 10$ and $y = 6$.
$$\begin{bmatrix} x - y & x^2 - y^2 \\ (x - y)^2 & \sqrt{x + y} \end{bmatrix}$$

56 If $3x = 4y$, what is the ratio of x to y?

57 The sum of the digits of a three-digit number is 25. The number is divisible by 4. Find the number.

58 Find all ordered pairs (x, y) that will solve the equation $xy = 0$.

59 Find the two solutions to the equation $x^2 - 5x + 6 = 0$. (Hint: Try some numbers.)

HISTORICAL SNAPSHOT

CHILD PRODIGIES
When does genius first show itself?

Two of history's great mathematicians, Blaise Pascal of France and Carl Friedrich Gauss of Germany, displayed their talents early.

Pascal was born in 1623, a time when it was thought unwise for a child to study mathematics before the age of twelve. Anxious to learn but denied a teacher, Pascal invented mathematics on his own. By the time he was twelve, he had developed many of the theorems of geometry completely by himself.

Gauss, who was born in 1777, was even more precocious. One Saturday when he was three, he watched as his father worked out the weekly payroll of his employees. As the older Gauss completed his long computations, his young son spoke up: "Father, the calculation is wrong. It should be . . . ."

In the third grade, Gauss had the misfortune to have as his teacher a Mr. Büttner, who was feared by all his students. Büttner started the first day of school by telling his students to find the sum of the whole numbers from 1 to 100. He planned to spend the next hour daydreaming while his students struggled with the addition. But before Büttner reached his desk, Gauss gave him the correct answer.

Blaise Pascal

Carl Friedrich Gauss

The illustration shows the pattern that Gauss used to find the sum. Study the illustration and see if you can find a different shortcut.

$$1 + 2 + 3 + \ldots + 98 + 99 + 100$$

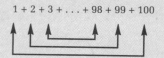

SOLVING EQUATIONS

Objectives

After studying this section, you will be able to
- Recognize equivalent equations
- Use inverse operations to solve equations

Part One: Introduction

Equivalent Equations

Equations with exactly the same solutions are called *equivalent equations.* For example, $x + 5 = 12$, $x + 9 = 16$, and $x = 7$ are equivalent equations because they have the same solution, 7.

 Given any equation, an equivalent equation will result if the same mathematical operation is applied to both the left side and the right side.

This can be shown as follows.

Subtract 21 from each side of the equation

$$x + 21 = 36$$
$$x + 21 - 21 = 36 - 21$$
$$x + 0 = 15$$
$$x = 15$$

The equations are equivalent because 15 is the solution of both.

Inverse Operations

Two operations are called *inverse operations* if one reverses the effect of the other. Addition and subtraction are inverse operations. Multiplication and division are inverse operations.

Example   *Use inverse operations to solve $x + 47.6 = 132.32$.*

Notice that in the original equation 47.6 is to be added to x. To solve for x, 47.6 is subtracted from each side.

$$x + 47.6 = 132.32$$
$$x + 47.6 - 47.6 = 132.32 - 47.6$$
$$x + 0 = 84.72$$
$$x = 84.72$$

Every time you solve an equation, it is helpful to check your answer. Substitute 84.72 for x in the original equation, and see if the left side equals the right side.

Check

Left Side   **Right Side**
  x + 47.6   = 132.32
= 84.72 + 47.6
= 132.32

If x = 84.72, the sides are equal, so the answer checks.

A Strategy for Solving Equations

How do you know what steps to take to solve an equation? Use inverse operations to write an equivalent equation in the form

variable = number

Example   *Solve the equation 9x + 13 = 76.*

Here, x is multiplied by 9, and 13 is added to the result. To solve the equation, we apply the inverse operations *in reverse order.*

$$9x + 13 = 76$$

Subtract 13 from each side

$$\underline{\quad -13 \quad -13}$$

$$9x + 0 = 63$$

$$9x = 63$$

Divide each side by 9

$$\frac{9x}{9} = \frac{63}{9}$$

$$1x = 7$$

$$x = 7$$

Check to be sure that x = 7 is the correct solution.

Part Two: Sample Problems

Problem 1   *Solve the equation $\frac{7}{3}y - 83 = 78$.*

Solution   In this equation, y is multiplied by $\frac{7}{3}$, and 83 is subtracted from the result. To solve it, we apply the inverse operations in reverse order.

$$\frac{7}{3}y - 83 = 78$$

Add 83 to each side

$$\underline{\quad +83 \quad +83}$$

$$\frac{7}{3}y + 0 = 161$$

$$\frac{7}{3}y = 161$$

Divide each side by $\frac{7}{3}$

$$\frac{\frac{7}{3}}{\frac{7}{3}}y = \frac{161}{\frac{7}{3}}$$

Remember $161 \div \frac{7}{3} = 161 \cdot \frac{3}{7} = 69$

$$1y = 69$$

$$y = 69$$

Check

Left Side	Right Side
$\frac{7}{3}y - 83$	$= 78$

$$= \frac{7}{3} \cdot 69 - 83$$
$$= 7 \cdot 23 - 83$$
$$= 161 - 83$$
$$= 78$$

If $y = 69$, the sides are equal, so the answer checks.

Problem 2 Solve the equation $15.3 + 22.5 = 0.5y_1 + 0.2y_1 - 15.8$.

Solution

$$15.3 + 22.5 = 0.5y_1 + 0.2y_1 - 15.8$$

Combine like terms

$$37.8 = 0.7y_1 - 15.8$$

Add 15.8 to each side

$$\underline{+\ 15.8 \qquad\qquad +\ 15.8}$$
$$53.6 = 0.7y_1 + 0$$
$$53.6 = 0.7y_1$$

Divide each side by 0.7

$$\frac{53.6}{0.7} = \frac{0.7y_1}{0.7}$$
$$76.6 \approx 1y_1$$

Since each number in the original equation is rounded to the nearest tenth, we also round our answer to the nearest tenth. We save the unrounded number in the calculator's memory to use in the check.

Check

Left Side	Right Side
$15.3 + 22.5$	$0.5y_1 + 0.2y_1 - 15.8$
$= 37.8$	$\approx 0.5(76.571429) + 0.2(76.571429) - 15.8$
	$\approx 38.285714 + 15.314286 - 15.8$
	$\approx 53.6 - 15.8$
	≈ 37.8

If $y_1 \approx 76.6$, the sides are equal, so the answer checks.

Note: A calculator also rounds off. Because of round-off error, sometimes problem checks are only approximately equal.

Problem 3 George has the same number of pennies, nickels, and dimes for a total of $20.32. How many of each coin does George have?

Solution Let x = number of pennies that George has. Then
x = number of nickels that George has, and
x = number of dimes that George has.

We can use x for all three since he has the same number of each.

$1x$ = value of pennies in cents
$5x$ = value of nickels in cents
$10x$ = value of dimes in cents
2032 = value of all the money in cents

We can now write an equation and solve it.

Combine like terms

$$1x + 5x + 10x = 2032$$
$$16x = 2032$$

Divide each side by 16

$$\frac{16x}{16} = \frac{2032}{16}$$
$$x = 127$$

George has 127 pennies, 127 nickels, and 127 dimes. We then check this to see if the total value is $20.32.

Problem 4   *The sum of the digits of a two-digit number is 6. If we reverse the digits of this number, the value increases by 18. Find the original number.*

Solution   Let's try to solve this problem using logic.

Sum of digits is 6	Reversed number	How much larger?
15 (1 + 5 = 6)	51	36
24 (2 + 4 = 6)	42	18

The original number is 24.

Part Three: Exercises and Problems

Warm-up Exercises

As explained in the "Letter to Students," this is one of the problem sets that has been labeled for you.

Practice

In problems 1–4, state the inverse operation.

1 adding 47.1

2 subtracting 76

3 multiplying by $\frac{2}{5}$

4 dividing by $\frac{3}{2}$

Practice

In problems 5–10, solve each equation.

5 $\frac{m}{13} = 8$

6 $y - 32 = 15$

7 $z + 32 = 54$

8 $\frac{3}{4}m = 33$

9 $\frac{2}{3}s + 182 = 584$

10 $8x = 128$

Practice

11 If the lengths of $\overline{AB}$ and $\overline{CD}$ are equal, what is the value of t?

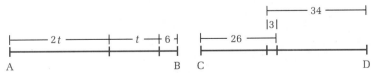

Practice

12 Aldo has the same number of dimes, quarters, and half-dollars. He has a total of $9.35. How many of each kind of coin does he have?

Practice

13 Solve for x. $2x + 39 + 31 = 217 - 43$

Problem Set

Practice

In problems 14–19, simplify the expressions or solve the equations.

14 $6x = 762$

15 $5x^2 + 3x - x^2 + 7x$

16 $157 = x - 987$

17 $2x_1 + 5x_1 + 3y + 8y - 3x_1$

18 $x + 47 = 183$

19 $3y + 1.5 + 4.7 - 3y + 2x$

Practice

20 An equilateral (all sides equal) triangle has a perimeter of 91 centimeters. What is the length of each side?

Practice, Introduce

21 Each person at Jim's party had 3 slices of pizza. There were 50 pieces to start with and 5 pieces left over. How many people were at Jim's party?

Practice, Introduce

22 Refer to the line AD.

a Write and simplify an expression that describes the length of $\overline{AD}$.

b Find the length of $\overline{AD}$ if $x = 4$ and $y = 6$.

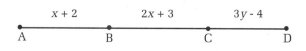

Practice

In problems 23–28, solve each equation.

23 $3x + 7 = 7$

24 $563 = a - 334$

25 $\frac{y}{17} = 0.14$

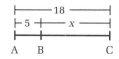 **26** $2x - 15 = \sqrt{63}$

27 $9y + 135 = 684$

28 $\frac{3x}{5} = 2.763$

Practice

29 Mr. Conners has singles, fives, and twenties in his wallet. He has the same number of each kind of bill. If he has a total of $364, how many bills of each kind does he have?

Practice, Introduce

30 Find x, the length from B to C.

Practice

In problems 31–40, solve the equation.

31 $24x - 56 = 2.8$

32 $2t - 0.16 = 0$

33 $\sqrt{x} = 4$

34 $5x - 18.7 = 0$

35 $\frac{2}{3}y + \frac{3}{4}y = 34$

36 $45 - 15 = 0.5w - 0.2w - 3$

37 $37x = 0$

38 $7y + 5y = 0$

 39 $m + 14 + 12m - 8 + 7m = 3 + 4(5^6)$

40 $5x + 4x + 3x = 5^3 + (13)(14) + 5$

Practice, Review

41 Solve $5*x - 3\wedge2 = 144/4$ written in BASIC.

Practice, Review

42 If a number is chosen randomly from {10, 11, 12, 13, 14, 15}, what is the probability that the number is prime?

Practice

43 The length of a rectangle is twice its width. If the perimeter is 174 inches, find the dimensions.

Practice, Introduce	**44** Van is moving from Orlando to Dallas. On the way, he stops for the night in Shreveport, Louisiana. Soon after he leaves Shreveport, he sees a sign that says Dallas is 134 miles ahead. He has been driving at a steady rate of 55 miles per hour for a total of 16 hours. How far is it from Orlando to Dallas?
Practice, Introduce	**45** Vera Wright is a bus driver. For the first 48 miles of her route, she travels at an average speed of 12 miles per hour. Then she realizes that she is allowed only 6 hours for her entire 144-mile route. How fast must she go for the rest of the route?
Practice, Introduce	**46** Jack and Jill went up the hill to fetch a pail of water. After having fetched the first pail together, they went back many times and each time brought back one pail apiece. Eventually they ended up with 5317 pails of water. How many trips did Jack and Jill each make up the hill?
Practice, Introduce	**47** Solve for x in terms of a and b if $a + x = b$.
Practice, Introduce	**48** Solve for x in terms of a, b, and c if $ax + b = c$ (where $a \neq 0$).
Practice	**49** Find the value of x if the average length of the three line segments is 80.

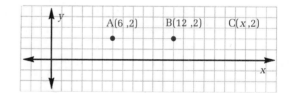

Practice, Introduce	**50** The length of $\overline{AC}$ is 12. **a** Find the length of $\overline{BC}$. **b** Find the value of x.

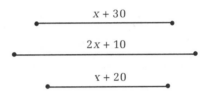

Practice, Introduce	**51** The longer sides of the rectangle increase by 20%, and the shorter sides decrease by 20%. Find the ratio of the new rectangle's perimeter to the old rectangle's perimeter.

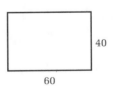

Practice	**52** Find the greatest area of the rectangle if x is selected from {5, 7, 9}.

Practice, Introduce	**In problems 53 and 54, solve for x.** **53** $x(x - 3) = 0$ **54** $\sqrt{x - 10} = 4$

2.3 PROPERTIES OF EQUALITY

Objective

After studying this section, you will be able to
- Use the properties of equality in solving equations

Part One: Introduction

Properties of Equality

The rules that allow you to perform the same operations on both sides of an equation are called *properties.*

Name of Property	Statement	Example
Addition Property of Equality	If $a = b$, then $a + c = b + c$	If $x = 4$, then $x + 3 = 7$
Subtraction Property of Equality	If $a = b$, then $a - c = b - c$	If $x + 4 = 37$, then $x = 33$
Multiplication Property of Equality	If $a = b$, then $ac = bc$	If $x = 5$, then $3x = 15$
Division Property of Equality	If $a = b$, where c is not 0, then $\frac{a}{c} = \frac{b}{c}$	If $3x = 45$, then $x = 15$

These properties state that you may add, subtract, multiply, or divide each side of the equation by the same number. Notice that the Division Property of Equality restricts the divisor so that $c \neq 0$. You cannot divide by 0. Try dividing 5 by 0 on your calculator. What happens?

Another important property is the Zero Product Property. This property states that if the product of two numbers is zero, then one or both of the numbers must be equal to zero.

Name of property	Statement	Example
Zero Product Property	If $ab = 0$, then $a = 0$ or $b = 0$ or $a = 0$ and $b = 0$	If $(x)(x - 3) = 0$, then $x = 0$ or $x - 3 = 0$

For example, if $x(x - 3) = 0$, then by the Zero Product Property, $x = 0$ or $x - 3 = 0$. You should check these solutions in the original equation.

Part Two: Sample Problems

Problem 1

Solve $6x - 13 = 101$, using a property of equality to justify each step.

Solution

To solve the equation, we use inverse operations in reverse order. First we add 13, and then we divide by 6.

$$6x - 13 = 101$$

Addition Property of Equality
$$\underline{+ 13 \qquad + 13}$$
$$6x + 0 = 114$$
$$6x = 114$$

Division Property of Equality
$$\frac{6x}{6} = \frac{114}{6}$$
$$1x = 19$$
$$x = 19$$

Check

Left Side	Right Side
$6x - 13$	$= 101$

$= 6 \cdot 19 - 13$
$= 114 - 13$
$= 101$

If $x = 19$, the sides are equal so it checks.

Problem 2

Solve $x(5 - x) = 0$, using properties of equality.

Solution

$$x(5 - x) = 0$$

Zero Product Property
$$x = 0 \quad \text{or} \quad 5 - x = 0$$

Addition Property of Equality
$$\underline{\qquad \qquad + x \qquad + x}$$
$$x = 0 \quad \text{or} \quad 5 = x$$

There seem to be two solutions. Let's check them both.

If $x = 0$

Left Side	Right Side
$x(5 - x)$	$= 0$

$= 0(5 - 0)$
$= 0(5)$
$= 0$

If $x = 5$

Left Side	Right Side
$x(5 - x)$	$= 0$

$= 5(5 - 5)$
$= 5(0)$
$= 0$

Both solutions check. The solution set is $\{0, 5\}$.

Part Three: Exercises and Problems

Warm-up Exercises

In problems 1–6, name the property that is illustrated.

1 If $x + 3 = 7$, then $x = 4$.

2 If $\frac{x}{7} = 11$, then $x = 77$.

3 If $x(2 - x) = 0$, then $x = 0$ or $2 - x = 0$.

4 If $x - 7 = 28$, then $x = 35$.

5 If $1.4x = 1.4$, then $x = 1$.

6 If $\frac{2}{3}x = 4$, then $x = 6$.

In problems 7–10, solve for x.

7 $4x = 0$

8 $x(x - 2) = 0$

9 $(x - 4)(x - 2) = 0$

10 $xy = 0$

Problem Set

In problems 11–19, solve each equation. Justify each step.

11 $x + 137 = 425$

12 $1254 = 6y$

13 $35.6 = x - 17.5$

14 $\frac{x}{15} = 13$

15 $\frac{2y}{3} = 18$

16 $2x + 15 = 47$

17 $3x - 9 = 72$

18 $15 = 2x - 39$

19 $2x + 3x = 505$

20 If a number is randomly selected from {0, 1, 2, 3, 4, 5} and substituted for x in $x(5 - x)$, what is the probability that the value will be greater than 1?

21 Find the value of x.

In problems 22–29, simplify each expression and solve each equation.

22 $3x + 45 = 99$

23 $12x + 15 + 9x - 3$

24 $4x - 50 = 9 - (3)(3)$

25 $\frac{1}{2}x + \frac{1}{4}x$

26 $\frac{1}{2}x + \frac{1}{4}x = \frac{3}{4}$

27 $6x = 0$

28 $9y_2 + 4y + 9y^2 + 5y - 6y_2$

29 $3(4^2) - 6(5)$

30 Find the value of w if the perimeter of the pentagon is 84 centimeters.

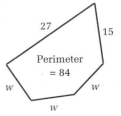

31 One ream of paper contains 500 sheets. A box contains x reams.

a Write an expression for the number of sheets of paper in one box.

b How many sheets of paper are there in 13 reams of paper?

c How many reams of paper should be purchased to make 1685 copies of a 25-page handbook?

In problems 32–37, solve each equation.

32 $x(6 - x) = 0$

33 $y(y - 13.2) = 0$

34 $0 \cdot z = 0$

35 $0 \cdot x = x$

36 $(x - 2)x = 0$

37 $(x - 4)(x - 7) = 0$

38 Evaluate $\sqrt{b^2 - 4ac}$ for $a = 2$, $b = 7$, and $c = 6$.

39 If $x + y = z$, $y = 134$, and $z = 2176$, solve for x.

In problems 40–47, solve each equation. Indicate which property of equality is used.

40 $56 = 23 + 6x$

41 $8z - 15.4 = 32.6$

42 $11.35 + 10x = 64.42$

43 $685 = \frac{5}{2}x$

44 $\frac{2}{3}x = 64$

45 $2x(x - 7) = 0$

46 $(5x - 72)(6x - 96) = 0$

47 $10.5m + 5.5m = 17.6$

48 Adrian picked a number and added 30% of 400 to the number. The resulting sum was 700. Write an equation to represent this problem. Then solve the equation to find the original number.

49 A thrown dart lands at random on any point within the circle. What is the probability that the dart will not land inside the square?

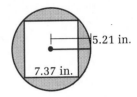

5.21 in.

7.37 in.

50 Find each probability.

a A number randomly selected from {0, 1, 2, . . . , 9} contains the digit 8.

b A number randomly selected from {0, 1, 2, . . . , 97, 98, 99} contains the digit 8.

c A number randomly selected from {0, 1, 2, . . . , 998, 999} contains the digit 8.

51 Andy is going from his house at A to Fred's at F. Andy will always take the shortest path, three blocks. If all possible routes are equally likely, what is the probability that he goes past Ethan's at E?

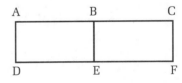

A B C

D E F

52 The ratio of AB to BC is 3 to 4. The ratio of BC to CD is 4 to 5. Find AB if AD = 60.

A B C D

53 Darts thrown at the board are equally likely to hit any point on the board. It is found that 38% of the darts hit inside the small square. What is the approximate value of x?

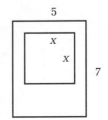

5

x

x

7

THE SUBSTITUTION AND DISTRIBUTIVE PROPERTIES

Objectives

After studying this section, you will be able to
- Use the Substitution Property to solve equations
- Use the Distributive Property of Multiplication over Addition or Subtraction

Part One: Introduction

The Substitution Property

As you solve equations, you will need to simplify expressions. You can simplify expressions with the Distributive Property of Multiplication over Addition or Subtraction. The Substitution Property will also help you solve equations.

When you replace a variable with a number or with an expression, the process is called *substitution.*

Example   Solve for x if $x + 6y = 432$ and $y = 48$.

Since we are given that $y = 48$, we *substitute* 48 for y in $x + 6y = 432$.
Then we solve the resulting equation.

$$
\begin{aligned}
x + 6y &= 432 \\
x + 6(48) &= 432 \\
x + 288 &= 432 \\
-288 &= -288 \\
x &= 144
\end{aligned}
$$

Check

Left Side	Right Side
$x + 6y$	$= 432$

$$
\begin{aligned}
&= 144 + 6(48) \\
&= 144 + 288 \\
&= 432
\end{aligned}
$$

If $x = 144$, the sides are equal so it checks.

Example   Solve for y if $x + 3y = 29$ and $x = y - 3$.

Since $x = y - 3$, we substitute $y - 3$ for x in $x + 3y = 29$. Then we solve the resulting equation.

	$x + 3y = 29$
Substitute $y - 3$ for x	$(y - 3) + 3y = 29$
Combine like terms	$4y - 3 = 29$
Add 3 to each side	$\underline{+3 \quad +3}$
	$4y \quad = 32$
Divide each side by 4	$\dfrac{4y}{4} = \dfrac{32}{4}$
	$y = 8$

The solution is $y = 8$.

Distributive Property of Multiplication over Addition or Subtraction

When we evaluate the expressions $5(3 + 7)$ and $5(3) + 5(7)$, we get the same value.

$5(3 + 7)$	$5(3) + 5(7)$
$= 5(10)$	$= 15 + 35$
$= 50$	$= 50$

This example illustrates the Distributive Property of Multiplication over Addition or Subtraction. It is one of the properties you will use frequently.

Name of Property	Statement	Example
Distributive Property of Multiplication over Addition or Subtraction	$a(b + c) = ab + ac$ or $(b + c)a = ba + ca$ $a(b - c) = ab - ac$ or $(b - c)a = ba - ca$	$3(x + 5) = 3x + 15$ $(x + y)z = xz + yz$ $3(x - y) = 3x - 3y$ $(3 - 5)x = 3x - 5x$

Example   *Multiply.*

a $3(4x + 8y)$ **b** $(x - 2y)6$

$\quad 3(4x + 8y)$ $\quad (x - 2y)6$
$= 3(4x) + 3(8y)$ $= (x)6 - (2y)6$
$= 12x + 24y$ $= 6x - 12y$

Example   *Use the Distributive Property of Multiplication over Addition or Subtraction to change the form of each expression.*

a $5x + 3x$ **b** $y^2 - 12y$

We will use the Distributive Property of Multiplication over Addition or Subtraction in reverse.

$\quad 5x + 3x$ $\quad y^2 - 12y$
$= (5 + 3)x$ $= y \cdot y - 12y$
$= 8x$ $= (y - 12)y$

In part **a** of the previous example, we have combined like terms. The Distributive Property of Multiplication over Addition or Subtraction is the reason that terms having the same variable, like $5x + 3x$, can be combined.

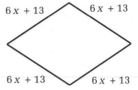

Problem 1
Find the value of x if the perimeter of the figure is 940 centimeters.

Solution

An equation for the perimeter is
$$4(6x + 13) = 940$$

Use the Distributive Property of Multiplication over Addition or Subtraction
$$4(6x) + 4(13) = 940$$
$$24x + 52 = 940$$

Subtraction Property of Equality
$$\frac{-52 \quad -52}{24x \qquad = 888}$$

Division Property of Equality
$$\frac{24x}{24} = \frac{888}{24}$$
$$x = 37$$

Then, x = 37 centimeters.

Check

Left Side	Right Side
4(6x + 13)	= 940

$= 4(6 \cdot 37 + 13)$
$= 4(222 + 13)$
$= 4(235)$
$= 940$

If x = 37, the sides are equal so it checks.

Problem 2
Solve for x if $x(2x - 3) = 0$.

Solution
This equation looks like one we should solve using the Distributive Property of Multiplication over Subtraction. Let's try that.

$$x(2x - 3) = 0$$
$$x(2x) - x(3) = 0$$
$$2x^2 - 3x = 0$$

We are no closer to solving this problem. Let's try another approach. Since the product is zero, we can use the Zero Product Property.

$$x(2x - 3) = \quad 0$$

Zero Product Property
$$x = 0 \text{ or } 2x - 3 = \quad 0$$

Addition Property of Equality
$$\frac{+3 \quad +3}{2x \qquad = \quad 3}$$

Division Property of Equality
$$\frac{2x}{2} = \frac{3}{2}$$
$$x = 1.5$$

The solution set is {0, 1.5}. Be sure to check each solution.

As you work through the book, you will learn when it is appropriate to use the Distributive Property of Multiplication over Addition or Subtraction or use the Zero Product Property.

Problem 3   *Solve $y^2 - 9y = 0$.*

Solution   The right side of the equation is 0. Can we change the form of the left side of the equation so that the Zero Product Property can be used? Let's first use the Distributive Property of Multiplication over Subtraction.

$$y^2 - 9y = 0$$
$$y \cdot y - 9y = 0$$

Distributive Property of
Multiplication over Subtraction $$(y - 9)y = 0$$
Zero Product Property $$y = 0 \text{ or } y - 9 = \quad 0$$
Addition Property of Equality $$\underline{\quad +9 \quad +9}$$
$$y = \quad 9$$

The solution set is {0, 9}. Check the solutions.

Part Three: Exercises and Problems

Warm-up Exercises

In problems 1–4, what equation will result if you substitute the given value for x into the first equation?

1 $x + y = 15$ and $x = 5$ **2** $2x + 3y = 11$ and $x = 4$

3 $x + y = 9$ and $x = y + 3$ **4** $2x + 3y = 6$ and $x = y - 2$

In problems 5–12, use the Distributive Property of Multiplication over Addition or Subtraction to change the form of each expression.

5 $2(x - y)$ **6** $12y - 10y$ **7** $(y - 2)y$ **8** $2y^2 + 5y$

9 $3x + 7x$ **10** $(x + 3)4$ **11** $x^2 + 9x$ **12** $y(3y + 4)$

In problems 13 and 14, solve for y.

13 $3(4y - 1) = 96$ **14** $\frac{1}{2}(8y + 18) = 42$

Problem Set

In problems 15–18, solve each equation for x.

15 $2(x + 5) = 20$ **16** $x(x + 5) = 0$

17 $4(y - 6) = 5$ **18** $x^2 - 5x = 0$

19 Which of the given expressions represent the area of the rectangle pictured?

    a $4x + 8$ **b** $4x + 2$ **c** $4(x + 2)$

    d $12 + 2x$ **e** $4 \cdot 2x$ **f** $8x$

    g $12x$ **h** $(x + 2)4$

20 If Julie carries 12 more books than Fred, how many books must Julie give Fred so each will carry the same number of books?

Problem Set, *continued*

In problems 21–24, apply the Distributive Property of Multiplication over Addition or Subtraction to each expression.

21 $(y + 4) \cdot 6$ **22** $3(2x - 5)$

23 $8n + 6n$ **24** $(5 + 2)k$

25 On fast forward, it takes Richard's VCR 40 seconds to advance the tape through a half-hour show. How long will it take to advance the tape through a show that is $2\frac{3}{4}$ hours long?

26 Find the value for x in the figure shown.

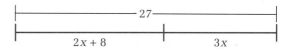

In problems 27–30, solve each equation.

27 $2(x - 7) = 12$ **28** $4(y + 2) = 29$

29 $16 = 5(x - 7) - 2x$ **30** $t^2 - 12t = 0$

In problems 31 and 32, evaluate each expression.

31 $(a + b)^2$ if $a = 4$ and $b = 8$ **32** $16a^2 + b^2$ if $a = 4$ and $b = 8$

In problems 33–36, find the probability that a number selected randomly from {1, 3, 5, 7} is a solution for the given equation.

33 $4(x + 2) = 4x + 8$ **34** $3x + 2x = 5x$

35 $5 + 4x = 9x$ **36** $x + 2x = 2x$

In problems 37 and 38, solve for x.

37 $8x + 11y = 24$ and $y = 0$ **38** $2x + y = 40$ and $y = 3x$

In problems 39 and 40, solve for p.

39 $3(p + 6) = 18$ **40** $p(p - 6) = 0$ $p = 0$ or

In problems 41–46, simplify the expression or solve the equation.

41 $3(x + 5) = 77$ **42** $4(3y + 2) + 5(2y + 3)$

43 $5x + 7x + 31 = 70$ **44** $21 = (3 + 4n) \cdot 2$

45 $(2x + 8) \cdot 4$ **46** $2(x + 3) + 3(x + 4) = 73$

47 Find x if the perimeter of the rectangle shown is 68 and y is 10.

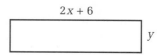

In problems 48 and 49, solve for w.

48 $3w + 2x = 22$ and $x = 4w$ **49** $3w + 2x = 6$ and $x = 2w + 3$

In problems 50 and 51, solve for x.

50 $5x + 8y = 81$ and $y = x + 2$
51 $2x + y = 38$, $y + z = 10$, and $z = 8$

In problems 52–55, apply the Distributive Property of Multiplication over Addition or Subtraction and simplify.

52 $12 + 5(2 + 3x)$ **53** $5y + 3(2y + 5)$
54 $5(x + 2y + 7)$ **55** $3(x - 4) + 3(4 - x)$

56 Write the equation $y = x(3x + 7)$ in BASIC.

57 Solve for x if $x + 2y + 3z = 100$, $y = x + 2$, and $z = 2x + 5$.

In problems 58 and 59, simplify.

58 $5[2 + 3(5 + x)]$ **59** $3(2x + 5 + 3x - 2)$

60 Use the diagrams to solve for x.

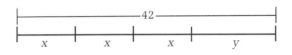

In problems 61–64, solve for x.

61 $(3x - 4)(2x + 5) = 0$
62 $4xy = 0$ and $y = 2x - 3$
63 $2x^2 - 6x = 0$
64 $y(x - 3) = 0$ and $y = 4x - 7$

65 Does the point $(5, 3)$ lie on the graph of $y = 2x - 7$?

66 Toni had $10. She rented three videos and bought a large bottle of soda and a large bag of popcorn. The popcorn cost $1.35, and the soda cost $1.50. She had $1.90 left. How much did she pay to rent each video?

67 A computer disc can store information on any of 40 tracks. Each track is subdivided into 16 sectors, and each sector can hold 256 bytes of information. Disc communication software requires 3 of the tracks on all discs. The remaining tracks are space for programming.

  a What percentage of the programming space on a disc remains after using 48,520 bytes to store a program?
  b How many 32,000-byte programs can be stored on a disc?
  c If a disc has 10 tracks unused, can a 56K program be stored on this disc? (Hint: 1K = 1024 bytes.)

APPLICATIONS OF EQUATION SOLVING

Objective

After studying this section, you will be able to
- Solve many types of problems by using algebra

Part One: Introduction

To solve a word problem, it is important to understand what the problem says.

Example *A plumber charges a base rate of $30 per visit plus $34 for each hour he is at your house. If the total bill comes to $166, how long did the plumber stay?*

Read the problem. You may need to read word problems several times. What do you know? What do you need to find? One way to get a feel for the problem is to try some numbers.

If he stays 1 hour, the bill is $30 + $\overset{\$34}{\underset{\text{1 hour}}{\rule{2cm}{0.4pt}}}$
$30 + 34 = 64$.

If he stays 2 hours, the bill is $30 + $\overset{\$34}{\underset{\text{1 hour}}{\rule{2cm}{0.4pt}}}\overset{\$34}{\underset{\text{1 hour}}{\rule{2cm}{0.4pt}}}$
$30 + 2(34) = 98$.

Now we see a pattern.

If he stays h hours, the bill is $30 + h(34)$.

You may be able to guess a solution. If not, try to write an equation. Then use algebra skills to solve the equation.

$$
\begin{aligned}
\text{total bill} &= 166 \\
30 + h(34) &= 166 \\
-30 \qquad\qquad &\quad -30 \\
\hline
h(34) &= 136 \\
\frac{h34}{34} &= \frac{136}{34} \\
h &= 4
\end{aligned}
$$

Read the problem again, and check your answer. What does the number mean? Does it make sense?

Part Two: Sample Problems

Problem 1

Ruth is jogging at a steady pace of 6.2 miles per hour. She jogs for a total of t hours.

a Write an expression for the distance traveled in t hours.
b If Ruth jogs for 2.3 hours, how far will she go?
c Write an equation to indicate that she jogged 20 miles in t hours at 6.2 miles per hour.
d Solve the equation in part **c** to find how long it took Ruth to jog 20 miles.

Solution

a The distance traveled is equal to the rate times the time ($d = r \cdot t$). Ruth's rate is 6.2 miles per hour, and her time is t.

The expression for the distance traveled is 6.2t, which represents the distance in miles.

b
$$d = 6.2t$$
Substitute 2.3 for t
$$d = 6.2(2.3)$$
$$= 14.26$$

Ruth will go approximately 14.3 miles if she jogs for 2.3 hours.

c If she jogged 20 miles, the equation is $20 = 6.2t$.

d
$$20 = 6.2t$$
Divide each side by 6.2
$$\frac{20}{6.2} = \frac{6.2t}{6.2}$$
$$3.2 \approx t$$

It took Ruth approximately 3.2 hours to jog 20 miles.

Problem 2   *Mr. T. F. Grader requires that a test be at least 92% correct in order for a student to earn an A. Let x be the number of questions on the test.*

a *Write an expression for the number of questions a student must answer correctly in order to get an A.*

b *If a student must answer at least 69 questions correctly in order to get an A, how many questions are on the test?*

Solution   **a** Since a student must correctly answer 92% of the x questions, the expression is $\left(\frac{92}{100}\right)$ x or 0.92x.

b 69 equals 92% of the x questions on the test.

Write the equation   0.92x = 69
Divide each side by 0.92   x = 75

The test had 75 questions. Check this answer on your calculator.

Part Three: Exercises and Problems

Warm-up Exercises

1 The Clemens family is driving from their house outside of Durango, Colorado, to Denver, a distance of 385 miles. They travel at an average speed (rate) of 50 miles per hour. Let *t* be the number of hours they have been traveling.

   a Give an expression for their distance from Durango after traveling for *t* hours.
   b Give an expression for their distance from Denver after *t* hours.
   c Write an equation to show that after *t* hours their distance from Denver is 35 miles.
   d If they are 35 miles from Denver, how long have they been traveling?

2 The Reliable Moving Company charges $55 per hour and $3.50 per mile of travel. How much would it cost for a move that takes *h* hours and is a distance of *m* miles?

Problem Set

3 Sandy wants to make a sand-and-brick patio. He discovers that sand is ordered in yards. A yard is one cubic yard of sand. The Burlington Sand & Gravel Company charges $23 per yard and an additional $45 for delivery.

   a What will be the total charge if 1 yard of sand is delivered? If 3 yards are delivered? If 6 yards are delivered?
   b Write an expression to represent the total charge if *y* yards are delivered.
   c Use the expression in part **b** to write an equation that indicates the total charge for *y* yards is $160.
   d Solve the equation in part **c.** How many yards would be delivered for $160?

4 To repair a TV set, Tooner's TV Repair Shop charges $24 plus $16.50 per hour for labor.

   a To repair Jerry's TV set requires 2 hours of work. How much will it cost Jerry?

   b To repair Juanita's TV set requires *h* hours of work. Write an expression that represents Juanita's total bill.

   c Juanita's bill was $65.25. Use the expression in part **b** to write an equation to represent Juanita's bill.

   d Solve the equation in part **c** to find out how many hours it took to repair Juanita's TV set.

5 Bricks for Sandy's patio are ordered in cubes of 500 bricks. There is a delivery charge of $50. The type of bricks that Sandy plans to use costs $635 per cube.

   a What would be the total cost if Sandy needs 500 bricks? If he needs 1000 bricks? If he needs 2495 bricks?

   b Write an expression to represent what Sandy would pay for *x* cubes of bricks.

   c Use the expression in part **b** to write an equation for the total cost *c* of *x* cubes.

   d What would be the total cost if 7 cubes of bricks are delivered?

   e Sandy estimates that he needs 3 yards of sand (see problem **3**) and 1500 bricks for his patio. What would be the cost?

6 Molly can ride her bike at a steady speed of 12 miles per hour.

   a How far can Molly travel in 3 hours? In 5 hours?

   b Write an expression representing the number of miles Molly can ride in *h* hours.

   c Molly rode 90 miles nonstop. Use the expression in part **b** to write an equation representing this.

   d Solve the equation in part **c** to find how long Molly rode.

7 A box of 10 computer discs costs $42.50 from Floppy's Computer Outlet, plus $2.25 per order for postage and handling.

   a Mac needs 40 discs. How much will his bill be?

   b Discs must be ordered in multiples of 10, and Chip needs 57 discs. How much will his bill be?

   c Write an expression that represents the total bill if Paige orders *b* boxes of discs.

   d Use the expression from part **c** to write an equation to represent the total bill of $1149.75 that Paige received after she ordered *b* boxes of discs.

   e Solve the equation in part **d** to determine how many boxes Paige ordered.

8 Marshall High School is building a new basketball court. The court will be 50 feet wide with 10 feet on each of two sides for the out-of-bounds area, the team benches, and the scorer's table. Each row of bleachers will be $3\frac{1}{2}$ feet wide.

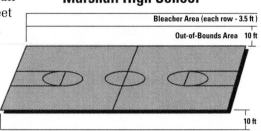

Marshall High School

Bleacher Area (each row - 3.5 ft)

Out-of-Bounds Area   10 ft

10 ft

a How wide must the gym be if there are 10 rows of bleachers on each side? If there are 14 rows of bleachers on each side? If there are 17 rows of bleachers on each side?

b Write an expression to represent the width of the gym if there are r rows of bleachers on each side.

c Use the expression in part **b** to write an equation that indicates the gym must be 280 feet wide.

d Solve the equation in part **c** to determine how many rows of bleachers there will be in the new gym.

e If each row of bleachers will hold 60 spectators, what is the seating capacity of the new gym?

9 The catalog price of a package of 12 pads of note paper is $7.68, plus a charge of $6.35 for delivery and handling. Barb ordered 225 packages. Through a mistake in the unit price, the bill came out $40.50 over the correct amount. The handling and delivery charges were correct. What mistake was made?

10 A plane starts at 10,000 feet and climbs at a rate of 123 feet per second. Let x be the number of seconds the plane climbs.

a If the plane climbs for 93 seconds, what is its altitude?

b Write an expression for the altitude of the plane after x seconds.

c How many seconds will it take the plane to climb to 35,000 feet?

11 On July 30, a zucchini is 4 inches long, and it grows 0.1 inch in length each time it rains. Let f be the number of times it rains in August. If by September 1 the zucchini has grown to 7 inches long, how many times did it rain in August?

12 According to state law, a speeder is fined $12 for every mile per hour over the speed limit. The speed limit on Elm Road is 45 miles per hour. Let s be the speed of the car.

a If Marlon is stopped by the police after their radar records that he is traveling 62 miles per hour, what is the amount of Marlon's fine?

b Write an expression for the amount of the fine in terms of the speed, s.

c The records show that Marilyn was stopped for speeding and fined $228. How fast was she traveling?

13 The Pizza Emporium charges $3.50 for a plain cheese pizza. Each additional topping costs $0.75. Let x be the number of additional toppings.

   a Write an expression for the cost of a cheese pizza with x toppings.

   b If a customer wants 8 different toppings, what is the cost of the pizza?

   c If Julio is charged $14.75 for a pizza, how many toppings were on his pizza?

14 A recent Indianapolis 500 race lasted for 2.9 hours.

   a The winner of the race traveled the full 500 miles. What was the winner's average speed for the race?

   b The tenth-place auto had finished only 187 laps by the end of the race. If each lap covers 2.5 miles, what was the tenth-place finisher's average speed for the race?

   c If the winner spent 0.4 hours stopped in the pits, what was his average speed for the race while he was actually driving out on the track?

15 Ms. Martinez requires that a student score at least 65% to earn a passing grade on an algebra test.

   a Suppose that there are 35 questions on the test. How many questions must a student answer correctly in order to pass the algebra test?

   b If the test has y questions, write an expression for the number of questions a student must answer correctly in order to pass the test.

   c Determine how many questions are on the test if a student needs to answer at least 39 questions correctly in order to pass the test.

16 Charlie can usually guess correctly on 35% of the questions on a multiple-choice test.

   a On Monday, Charlie did not know the answer to any of the questions on his history test, so he guessed at all 50. Assuming that he had his usual success at guessing, how many questions did Charlie answer correctly?

   b On Tuesday, Charlie knew the answers to half of the 80 questions on his English test. He guessed at the other half. How many questions did Charlie answer correctly?

   c On Thursday's algebra test, there were 5x questions. He did not know the answer to x of the questions. Write an expression to represent the number of questions Charlie answered correctly.

Problem Set, *continued*

17 Fran can run at an average speed of 1 mile every 6 minutes. Walking, she averages 1 mile every 15 minutes.

a After running for 45 minutes, Fran decided to walk the next 15 minutes. How far was she from her starting point?

b After running for half an hour, Fran decided to walk the next half hour. How far was she from her starting point?

c Fran ran for *r* minutes, then walked for *w* minutes, and arrived at a lake 10 miles from her starting point. Write an equation using *r* and *w* to express this situation.

2.6 FORMAL PROPERTIES

Objectives

After studying this section, you will be able to
- Use the properties of equality in solving equations
- Use the properties of operations and identity in writing equivalent expressions and in solving equations

Part One: Introduction

Properties of Equality

The formal properties you study in this section are the rules for the steps in solving an algebra problem. You can use these properties to justify some of the steps in your solution of an equation.

The following properties of equality are grouped together because they affect both sides of an equation. Each property is true for all numbers a, b, and c, unless otherwise noted.

Name of property	Statement	Example
Reflexive Property of Equality	$a = a$	$3.57 = 3.57$
Symmetric Property of Equality	If $a = b$, then $b = a$	If $3 = x$, then $x = 3$
Transitive Property of Equality	If $a = b$ and $b = c$, then $a = c$	If $x = 3$ and $3 = y$, then $x = y$
Addition Property of Equality	If $a = b$ and $c = d$, then $a + c = b + d$	If $x = 4$ and $y = 7$, then $x + y = 11$
Subtraction Property of Equality	If $a = b$ and $c = d$, then $a - c = b - d$	If $x + 4 = 37$ and $4 = 4$, then $x = 33$
Multiplication Property of Equality	If $a = b$ and $c = d$, then $ac = bd$	If $x = 5$ and $y = 3$, then $xy = 15$

Name of property	Statement	Example
Division Property of Equality	If $a = b$ and $c = d$, where c and d are not 0, then $\frac{a}{c} = \frac{b}{d}$	If $3x = 45$ and $3 = 3$, then $x = 15$
Zero Product Property	If $ab = 0$, then $a = 0$ or $b = 0$	If $(x)(x - 5) = 0$, then $x = 0$ or $x - 5 = 0$
Substitution Property	If $a = b$, then either one can be substituted for the other.	If $x + y = 20$ and $y = 11$, then $x + 11 = 20$

Properties of Operations and Identities

Properties of operations and identities are grouped together because these properties are used to transform or rename parts of equations. Usually, these properties affect only one side of an equation. Each property is true for all numbers a, b, and c.

Name of property	Statement	Example
Commutative Property of Addition	$a + b = b + a$	$3 + 6 = 6 + 3$
Commutative Property of Multiplication	$ab = ba$	$3 \cdot 7 = 7 \cdot 3$
Associative Property of Addition	$(a + b) + c = a + (b + c)$	$(3 + 4) + 7 = 3 + (4 + 7)$
Associative Property of Multiplication	$(ab) \cdot c = a \cdot (bc)$	$(3 \cdot 5)x = 3(5x)$
Additive Identity Property	There is a number 0, called the additive identity, such that $a + 0 = 0 + a = a$	$5 + 0 = 0 + 5 = 5$
Multiplicative Identity Property	There is a number 1, called the multiplicative identity, such that $1 \cdot a = a \cdot 1 = a$	$1 \cdot 7 = 7 \cdot 1 = 7$
Multiplicative Inverse Property	For every a, $a \neq 0$, there is a number $\frac{1}{a}$, called the multiplicative inverse (or reciprocal) of a, such that $a \cdot \frac{1}{a} = 1$	$6 \cdot \frac{1}{6} = \frac{6}{6} = 1$
Mutiplication Property of Zero	$0(a) = a(0) = 0$	$3(0) = 0(3) = 0$ $0x = 0$

Name of property	Statement	Example
Quotient Property	$a \cdot \frac{1}{b} = \frac{a}{b}$	$3 \cdot \frac{1}{4} = \frac{3}{4}$
Distributive Property of Mutiplication over Addition or Subtraction	$a(b + c) = ab + ac$ or $(b + c)a = ba + ca$ $a(b - c) = ab - ac$ or $(b - c)a = ba - ca$	$3(x + 5) = 3x + 15$ $(x + y)z = xz + yz$ $3(x - y) = 3x - 3y$ $(3 - 5)x = 3x - 5x$

These properties are the rules of algebra. Notice how they are used to explain the steps in the Sample Problems.

Part Two: Sample Problems

Problem 1   Solve $148 = 4x$ and give a reason for each lettered step.

Solution

a $148 = 4x$ Given

b $\frac{148}{4} = \frac{4x}{4}$ Division Property of Equality

c $37 = 1x$ Division

d $37 = x$ Multiplicative Identity Property

e $x = 37$ Symmetric Property

Check the answer.

Problem 2   If $xy = 56$ and $x = \frac{2}{3}$, find y. Give a reason for each lettered step.

Solution

a $xy = 56$ and $x = \frac{2}{3}$ Given

b $\frac{2}{3}y = 56$ Substitution Property

c $\frac{3}{2}\left(\frac{2}{3}y\right) = \frac{3}{2} \cdot 56$ Multiplication Property of Equality (We chose $\frac{3}{2}$ because it is the multiplicative inverse of $\frac{2}{3}$.)

d $\left(\frac{3}{2} \cdot \frac{2}{3}\right)y = \frac{3}{2} \cdot 56$ Associative Property of Multiplication

e $1y = 84$ Multiplication

f $y = 84$ Multiplicative Identity Property

Check the answer.

Part Three: Exercises and Problems

Warm-up Exercises

In problems 1–8, name the property that is illustrated.

1 $a + 7 = 7 + a$

2 $b \cdot \frac{1}{b} = 1$

3 $5(c \cdot 7) = 5(7 \cdot c)$

4 $4(15 + x) = 4(x + 15)$

5 $3 + (8 + K) = (3 + 8) + K$

6 If $\frac{1}{2}x + 5 = 12$, then $x + 10 = 24$.

7 If $3x - 4 = 16$, then $3x = 20$.

8 If $4x + 8y = 20$ and $y = 2$, then $4x + 16 = 20$.

Problem Set

In problems 9 and 10, use the Associative Property of Addition to write an expression equivalent to each of the given expressions.

9 $(x + p) + q$

10 $35 + (17 + y)$

In problems 11 and 12, name the property illustrated.

11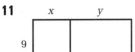

12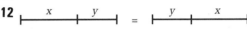

In problems 13–15, use the Commutative Property of Multiplication to write an expression equivalent to each of the given expressions.

13 $x \cdot 8$

14 $(x + 3) \cdot 5$

15 $3(4y)$

In problems 16–19, name the property illustrated.

16 $5(7 + p) = (7 + p)5$

17 $7 \cdot 12 + 7 \cdot 8 = 7(12 + 8)$

18 $5(x + 2) + 3(x + 2) = 8(x + 2)$

19 If $r(r - 2) = 0$, then $r = 0$ or $r - 2 = 0$.

20 Name the algebraic property that justifies each of the lettered steps used in simplifying the expression $0.38(19 + x) + 0.62(x + 19)$.

$$0.38(19 + x) + 0.62(x + 19) \quad \text{Given}$$
a $= 0.38(x + 19) + 0.62(x + 19)$
b $= (0.38 + 0.62)(x + 19)$
c $= 1(x + 19)$
$$= x + 19$$

In problems 21–28, which property is illustrated?

21 $5 + 7 = 7 + 5$

22 $x \cdot \frac{1}{x} = 1$

23 $x(yz) = (yz)x$

24 $x(yz) = (xy)z$

25 If $x_1 = y^2$ and $y^2 = \sqrt{z}$, then $x_1 = \sqrt{z}$.

26 If $x_1 = y$ and $a = b^2$, then $x_1 + a = y + b^2$.

27 $x + (y + 7) = (x + y) + 7$

28 $3x + 5x = 8x$

29 Name the properties applied in the solution of $5x + 3x = 96$.

$$5x + 3x = 96$$
a $(5 + 3)x = 96$
b $8x = 96$
c $\frac{1}{8}(8x) = \frac{1}{8}(96)$
d $\left(\frac{1}{8} \cdot 8\right)x = \frac{1}{8}(96)$
$$1x = 12$$
e $x = 12$

In problems 30 and 31, solve each equation.

30 $4(x - 2) + 3(x + 5) = 27$

31 $2x^2 - 9x = 0$

32 If $2y = z$ and $z = 156$, solve for y. State a property to justify each step.

33 Solve for x if $3x + 2y = 26$ and $y = x + 3$.

34 Scratch and Dents Car Rental charges $19.95 per day and $0.12 cents a mile to rent one of its cars. Let d be the number of days the car is rented and m the number of miles the car is driven.

 a Write an expression for the total bill, using d and m.
 b If the car is rented for 5 days and driven 357 miles, what is the total bill?
 c Jonathan rented a car for 4 days. The total bill was $166.80. How far did Jonathan drive the car?

In problems 35–37, give an example to illustrate each statement.

35 Subtraction is not commutative.
36 Subtraction is not associative.
37 Division is not commutative.

38 Explain why the expression $6(4x + 2)$ and $24x + 12$ are equivalent descriptions of the area of the rectangle shown.

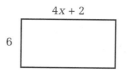

39 Determine the area of the larger rectangle from the answer choices below.

 a $6x + 12$ **b** $12 + x$
 c $6x$ **d** $6x + 2$
 e $(x + 2)6$ **f** $12x$

40 Define the operation $*$ by $a * b = a^2 + b^2$. For example, if $a = 4$ and $b = 2$, then

$$a * b = 4 * 2$$
$$= 4^2 + 2^2$$
$$= 16 + 4$$
$$= 20$$

 a Find $3 * 9$, $2.4 * 7.6$, and $4 * (7 * 9)$.
 b Is $*$ commutative? Is $*$ associative?
 c Is there a number x such that $x * a = a^2$ for all numbers a?
 d For what numbers x is $x * x = x$?
 e Does $4 \cdot (a * x) = (4 \cdot a) * (4 \cdot x)$? Why or why not?

CHAPTER SUMMARY

CONCEPTS AND PROCEDURES

After studying this chapter, you should be able to
- Recognize equalities, inequalities, and expressions (2.1)
- Simplify expressions (2.1)
- Find solutions to equations (2.1)
- Recognize equivalent equations (2.2)
- Use inverse operations to solve equations (2.2)
- Use the properties of equality (2.3)
- Use substitution (2.4)
- Use the Distributive Property of Multiplication over Addition or Subtraction (2.4)
- Solve application problems (2.5)
- Use properties of equality, operations and identities (2.6)

VOCABULARY

additive identity (2.6)
equivalent equations (2.2)
equivalent expressions (2.1)
inverse operations (2.2)
like terms (2.1)
multiplicative identity (2.6)
multiplicative inverse of a (2.6)

property (2.3)
simplified form (2.1)
solution (2.1)
solve (2.1)
statement (2.1)
substitution (2.4)
term (2.1)

PROPERTIES

Reflexive Property of Equality
Symmetric Property of Equality
Transitive Property of Equality
Addition Property of Equality
Subtraction Property of Equality
Multiplication Property of Equality
Division Property of Equality
Zero Product Property
Substitution Property
Commutative Property of Addition

Commutative Property of Multiplication
Associative Property of Addition
Associative Property of Multiplication
Additive Identity Property
Multiplicative Identity Property
Multiplicative Inverse Property
Multiplication Property of Zero
Quotient Property
Distributive Property of Multiplication over
    Addition or Subtraction

REVIEW PROBLEMS

In problems 1 and 2, choose from {4, 5, 6, 7, 8} to solve each equation.

1 $3x + 2 = 23$ **2** $x^2 - x > 30$

3 Refer to the diagram.

    a Write an equation to represent the diagram.

    b Solve the equation you wrote in part **a**.

    c Use your answer from part **b** to find the percentage of the total segment that is represented by the shorter segment.

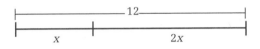

In problems 4–11, simplify each expression and solve each equation.

4 $6p + 9p - 3 = 14 + 37$ **5** $4.7q - 22.8 = (12.4)^2$

6 $6.51 + 3.24y = 19.7$ **7** $8.4 + \frac{2}{3}c + 1.2c + \frac{3}{5}$

8 $3x_1 + 9x_1 + 4x_1$ **9** $8w + 15 - 5w$

10 $14 = \frac{2}{3}m$ **11** $\frac{x}{16} = 7.5$

12 Refer to the diagram.

    a Write an equation to represent the diagram.

    b Solve the equation you wrote in part **a**.

    c Use your answer from part **b** to find the length of the longest side of the rectangle.

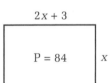

In problems 13–16, solve each equation.

13 $y(y - 15) = 0$ **14** $2y^2 - 16y = 0$

15 $4(y - 7) + 2y = 8$ **16** $3(y - 7) + \frac{1}{2}(y + 4) = 16$

In problems 17–20, simplify each expression if possible.

17 $4.3n + 19.8 - 2.1n - 3.7$ **18** $8.3x + 5.2y$

19 $9u^2 - 6u_2 + 7^2$ **20** $x^2 + x + 2x$

21 A car travels at the rate of $x + 7$ miles per hour for $4\frac{1}{2}$ hours. Find x if the car travels 180 miles.

Review Problems, *continued*

In problems 22 and 23, evaluate each expression.

22 $3x^2 + 8x$ if $x = 7$ **23** $\sqrt{x^2 + y^2}$ if $x = 36$ and $y = 27$

24 Christopher, a plumber, charges $45 for a service call plus $35 for each hour he works.

   a If Chris works for $3\frac{1}{2}$ hours, what is the total bill?

   b If h represents the number of hours Chris works on a job, write an expression to represent the total bill.

   c Write an equation to represent a total bill of $141.25.

   d Solve the equation from part **c** to determine how many hours Chris worked.

In problems 25–28, solve the equation.

25 $3(2s + 6) = 24$ **26** $7(2t - 3) = 3(4 + 3)$

27 $7(y + 8) = 7(5 + 8)$ **28** $(s - 7)3 = 30$

29 If $v = 4 + 2f$, solve $3v + 2f = 28$ for f and v.

30 If the perimeter of the rectangle is 52 centimeters and $y = 3$, find the other dimension of the rectangle.

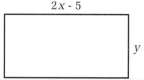

In problems 31–36, name the property illustrated.

31 $3(c + 2) = 3c + 6$ **32** $3m + (2w + 3e) = (3m + 2w) + 3e$

33 $r + (u + h) = r + (h + u)$ **34** If $\frac{2}{3}f + 4 = 10$, then $\frac{2}{3}f = 6$.

35 If $8g + 6 = 12$, then $4g + 3 = 6$.   **36** If $x = 2$, then $\frac{1}{3}(3x + 6) = \frac{1}{3}(12)$.

37 If a point is chosen at random from inside the diagram, what is the probability that it will lie in the shaded region?

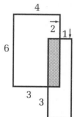

38 Refer to the diagram.

   a Write an expression to represent the diagram.

   b If $y = x + 1$, solve for x.

In problems 39–43, simplify each expression.

39 $5(m + n) + 6m + 4n$ **40** $4x^2 + 4.4x_2 + 44x^2$

41 $2(r + 3q) + 5(q + 3r)$ **42** $3.4j + \frac{2}{5}j + \frac{3}{4}j$

43 $\sqrt{9}\,x + 3^2x^2 + \sqrt{9 + 16}\,x^2 + (1 + 2)^3x$

44 Kirk had as many quarters as Gloria had dimes, as many dimes as Gloria had quarters, and as many nickels as Gloria had, and neither had any other money. Gloria had 5 more dimes than nickels and 10 more quarters than dimes. Kirk had $5.95.

   a If n is the number of nickels Gloria had, write an expression for the number of dimes she had.

   b If n is the number of nickels Gloria had, write an expression for the number of quarters she had.

   c If n is the number of nickels Gloria had, write an expression for the number of dimes Kirk had.

   d If n is the number of nickels Gloria had, write an expression for the number of quarters Kirk had.

   e If n is the number of nickels Gloria had, write an expression for the amount of money Kirk had, in terms of n.

   f Write an equation for the total amount of money Kirk had.

45 If $(x, y) = (7, 5)$ and $3x + 2y = z$, find the area of the rectangle pictured.

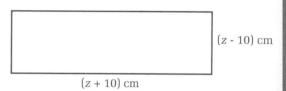

$(z - 10)$ cm

$(z + 10)$ cm

46 Two motorcycles start from Winnetka. Harley rides his bike at 30 miles per hour to Northbrook, then to Evanston, then on to Chicago. Beemer rides his bike directly to Evanston and on to Chicago at 10 miles per hour.

   a Which motorcycle arrives in Evanston first? How much sooner?

   b How far from Winnetka is Beemer when Harley arrives at Evanston?

   c How long after they left Winnetka will both riders be the same distance from Chicago?

47 The sale price of a radio is 30% below the original price of the radio, but a 7% sales tax is added to the sale price. Rob's total bill for his radio came to $97.54. What was the original price of the radio Rob bought on sale? (Hint: Let x be the original price of the radio. Write an equation to represent the problem and then solve it.)

48 The operation ▲ is defined by $a ▲ b = \frac{1}{a} + \frac{1}{b}$, $a > 0$, $b > 0$.

   a Find $2 ▲ 3$.

   b Is ▲ commutative? Why or why not?

   c Is there a number x such that $a ▲ x = \frac{1}{x}$? Why or why not?

   d For what values of a does $a ▲ a = 4$?

   e For what values of a does $a ▲ a = a$?

CHAPTER TEST

In problems 1–3, solve each equation.

1 $4m - 7 = 21$ **2** $3x(x - 5) = 0$ **3** $\frac{2}{5}x = 25$

4 If $x = 2.4$ and $5x + 3y = 19$, solve for y.

In problems 5–10, simplify each expression and solve each equation.

5 $5x - 3 = 8$ **6** $5(x + 3) + 3(x - 2)$

7 $3(x - 9) = 24$ **8** $24 = 2(x + 6) + 2(3x + 7)$

9 $(2x - 3)(x - 7) = 0$ **10** $\frac{1}{3} + \frac{5}{6}x = \frac{1}{2}$

11 Determine whether $x = 5$ is a solution of the equation
$4x - 5 = 25$.

In problems 12 and 13, simplify each expression.

12 $5y + 14x - 6x - 2y$ **13** $5x^2 + 4x_2 + 6x - 3x^2 + x_2 - 2x$

14 A model racing car travels along its track at 4 feet per second.
How long does it take the car to travel 22 feet?

15 Does $(x, y) = (2, 1)$ solve $2(y + 4) > 3(x + 3)$?

16 If a number is randomly selected from {2, 4, 6, 8}, what
is the probability that it is a solution of the equation
$2(x - 5) = 2x - 10$?

17 Write an equation to represent the diagram. Then solve the equation for w if
$x = 15$.

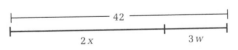

18 The Great American Pizza Emporium charges a fixed rate of
$8.35 for a cheese pizza. There is a charge of $1.35 for each
additional topping. Stephanie and her friends ordered 3 pizzas,
each with the same number of additional toppings. If their bill
was $37.20, how many additional toppings did they order on
each pizza?

19 Solve for w if $2x + 3 = w$ and $2x + 3 + 5w = 18$.

PUZZLES AND CHALLENGES

1 What phrase does each of the following suggest?

Mind   **LU CKY**
Matter

i i i
● ● ●

Now try these:

a DEATH LIFE   **b STAND**   **c DKI**   **d toMANwn**
                          DO YOU

e Make up some of your own.

2 A kind of puzzle you may not have seen is the cryptic crossword clue. In this kind of clue, a word is both defined and given a wordplay clue. The number in parentheses is the number of letters in the word.

a 54 Romans are subconsciously angry (5)

b Leave wasteland (6)

c The girl arranged loss of weight (7)

d Sounds like their location (5)

a LIVID (LIV is the Roman numeral for 54, ID means *subconscious*, and *livid* means "angry.")

b DESERT (DESERT has several meanings; one is *leave* and another is *wasteland*.)

c LIGHTER (*Arranged* implies an anagram. *The girl* is anagrammed to LIGHTER. *Loss of weight* implies LIGHTER, also.)

d THERE (*Sounds like* implies a homonym of *their*. THERE implies a *location*.)

Now try these:

3 Fashionable start in Chicago (4)

4 I doubt eccentric wins at auction (6)

5 Give someone the end of your arm (4)

6 Mixed-up kids lose control of car (4)

7 Make up some of your own clues.

3 | SIGNED NUMBERS

W hy is it that we can land someone on the moon but often cannot accurately predict the weather?

Edward Lorenz, a meteorologist at the Massachusetts Institute of Technology, has found a reason. Using a computer simulation, he found that the equations describing the weather yield an unpredictably different weather pattern whenever the initial conditions, such as air temperature and pressure, change by as little as one ten-thousandth of a percent. That's about the size of the change caused by the fluttering of a butterfly's wings. This is one reason why Lorenz's discovery is often referred to as the butterfly effect.

Meteorologists have begun to study the weather with a new mathematical tool called chaos theory. This new theory has been used as a technique for finding order in the type of chaotic changes Lorenz described.

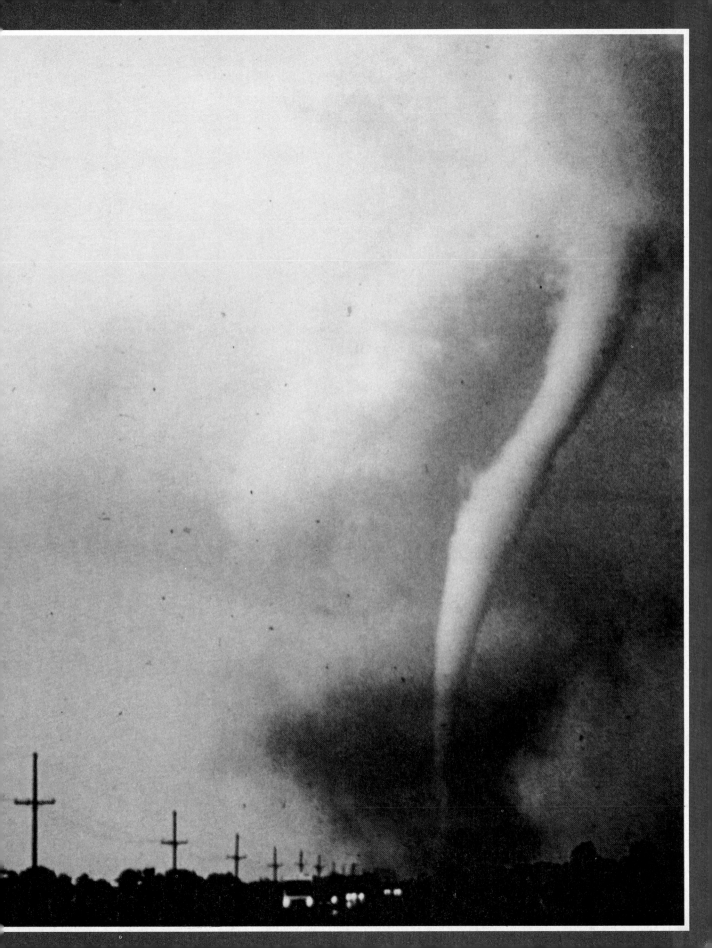

THE NUMBER LINE

Objectives

After studying this section, you will be able to
- Represent numbers on a number line
- Identify integers and rational numbers
- Identify irrational numbers
- Explain how the set of real numbers is formed

Part One: Introduction

Numbers on a Line

When you first learned to count, you used the set of **natural** or **counting numbers,** {1, 2, 3, 4, . . .}. Later, when you encountered the number zero, you used {0, 1, 2, 3, . . .}, the set of **whole numbers.** Later still, you needed to describe half an apple or $15.35 and included fractions and decimals in your work with numbers.

All the numbers you have learned about can be assigned to points on a line. Usually, zero is assigned to one of the points. We can then assign the natural numbers to evenly spaced points to the right of zero. Next, we assign fractions and decimals to points between the whole numbers.

$$0 \quad \frac{1}{2} \quad 1 \quad 1.75\,2 \quad\quad 3 \quad\quad 4 \quad\quad 5$$

The Integers and the Rational Numbers

Now we can expand the set of numbers we use by assigning **negative numbers,** such as -2, to all the points to the left of zero on the number line. The negative sign, $(-)$, indicates that a number is to the left of zero. Numbers to the right of zero are **positive numbers.** They may be written with the positive sign, $(+)$, such as $+5$, or without any sign, such as 5. The set { . . . , -3, -2, -1, 0, 1, 2, 3, . . . } is called the set of **integers.**

On a horizontal number line, the smaller numbers are to the left. Notice that -6 is less than -2, and -4 is greater than -8.

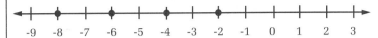

If all the fractions, both negative and positive, are then assigned to points on the number line, the combined set of integers and fractions is called the set of *rational numbers.* All of the following are rational numbers.

$$\frac{3}{5} \qquad -\frac{2}{3} \qquad 5 = \frac{5}{1} \qquad -7.62 = -7\frac{62}{100} = -\frac{762}{100}$$

There are two ways to describe a rational number.

- Each rational number can be written as $\dfrac{\text{an integer}}{\text{a natural number}}$.

- Each rational number, $\dfrac{a}{b}$, $b \neq 0$, can also be written as either a terminating decimal or a repeating decimal.

Example   *Express each rational number in decimal form. (The solutions are given below.)*

a $\dfrac{19}{8}$ **b** $\dfrac{1}{3}$ **c** 5

a $\dfrac{19}{8} = 2.375$ **b** $\dfrac{1}{3} = 0.333\ldots$ **c** $5 = 5.0$

In a repeating decimal, a bar is usually written over the repeating digit or digits. For example, $0.333\ldots = 0.\overline{3}$.

The Irrational Numbers

After all the rational numbers have been placed on a number line, there remain points that have not been assigned a number. These points correspond to irrational numbers. An *irrational number* is a number whose decimal form is nonterminating and nonrepeating. The following are irrational numbers.

$$\sqrt{5} \qquad \pi \quad \sqrt{3} \qquad \frac{\pi}{2}$$

For the value of π or any other irrational number, a calculator will give a decimal approximation to the precision of the calculator.

The Density Property states an interesting fact about the set of rational and the set of irrational numbers.

The Density Property

Between any two rational numbers you can always find another rational number, and between any two irrational numbers you can find another irrational number.

For example, between $\dfrac{5}{8} = 0.625$ and $\dfrac{2}{3} = 0.66\ldots$ is $0.63 = \dfrac{63}{100}$.

The Real Numbers

The set of rationals and the set of irrationals form the set of *real numbers.* This set and the points on the number line match up exactly.

Real Numbers			
Irrational Numbers	**Rational Numbers**		$7\frac{3}{8}$
$\sqrt{2}$ $\sqrt{19}$	**Integers**	17	$\frac{3}{4}$
$3\sqrt{5}$ $5+\sqrt{7}$	**Whole Numbers** 0 6		6.75
π 3π	**Natural Numbers** 1 8 -3		$-\frac{1}{3}$
	3 24 -81		-0.001

Part Two: Sample Problems

Problem 1 Classify each number as natural, whole, integer, rational, irrational, or real. Some numbers fit in more than one category.

$$-67 \qquad \frac{21}{7} \qquad \sqrt{7} \qquad 0 \qquad -\sqrt{9} \qquad -5\frac{3}{5} \qquad -5.\overline{2}$$

Solution We can organize the classifications in a table.

Naturals	Wholes	Integers	Rationals	Irrationals	Reals
$\frac{21}{7}=3$	$\frac{21}{7}$	$\frac{21}{7}$	$\frac{21}{7}$		$\frac{21}{7}$
	0	0	0		0
		-67	-67		-67
		$-\sqrt{9}=-3$	$-\sqrt{9}$		$-\sqrt{9}$
			$-5\frac{3}{5}=-\frac{28}{5}$		$-5\frac{3}{5}$
				$\sqrt{7}$	$\sqrt{7}$
			$-5.\overline{2}$		$-5.\overline{2}$

Problem 2 Find the distance on the number line between -4 and $+9$.

Solution We draw a number line, locate -4 and $+9$, and then count the spaces between them.

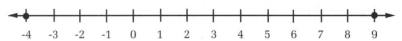

There are 13 spaces, so the distance is 13.

Problem 3   *Show that each number is rational by representing it as*
$$\frac{an\ integer}{a\ natural\ number}.$$

   a -4.1 **b** $4\frac{1}{3}$ **c** $\sqrt{6.76}$

Solution   **a** $-4.1 = \frac{-41}{10}$ **b** $4\frac{1}{3} = \frac{13}{3}$ **c** $\sqrt{6.76} = 2.6 = \frac{26}{10}$

Part Three: Exercises and Problems

Warm-up Exercises

In problems 1–6, determine which letter is closest to the location of each number below.

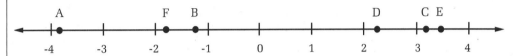

1 $3.\overline{47}$ **2** $2\frac{3}{10}$ **3** $-1\frac{3}{10}$

4 -3.93246 **5** $-\sqrt{3} \approx -1.7$ **6** $\pi \approx 3.1$

In problems 7–12, determine whether each statement is True or False.

7 $-\pi < 2$ **8** $-5 > -3$
9 All integers are rational.   **10** $-2.\overline{6}$ is rational.
11 A number can be both rational and   **12** Zero is neither positive nor negative.
       irrational.

Problem Set

In problems 13–24, classify each number as natural, whole, integer, rational, irrational, or real. Some numbers fit in more than one category.

13 -4 **14** $\frac{12}{3}$ **15** $\frac{-2}{3}$ **16** $\frac{11}{2}$
17 -891 **18** $\sqrt{81}$ **19** 3.3 **20** $\sqrt{15}$
21 $\frac{\pi}{2}$ **22** 0 **23** $7\frac{1}{4}$ **24** 2750

25 The temperature rises 10°, falls 16°, and then rises 2°. How many degrees higher or lower is the new temperature than the original?

In problems 26–29, draw a number line and plot the points with the given coordinates.

26 -5 **27** $\sqrt{21}$ **28** $-2\frac{3}{4}$ **29** 3.9

30 How far is -14 from 0 on a number line?

Problem Set, *continued*

31 On October 15, 1783, Jean-François Pilâtre de Rozier rode a hot-air balloon to a world-record height of 84 feet. Four days later, he broke his own record by floating 330 feet above ground. Determine how much higher Jean-François rode the second time.

32 Phineas Frog and Tiny Toad are at zero on a number line. Phineas can jump three times as far as Tiny.

  a Phineas jumps six times in the same direction and lands on -54. How many times must Tiny jump to catch his friend?

  b If Phineas started at zero and jumped four times to the left, on what number would he land?

  c If Tiny started at zero and jumped eight times to the right, on what number would he land?

  d If Phineas started at zero and jumped once to the left, twice to the right, and then three times to the left, on what number would he land?

In problems 33–35, which is the larger number?

33 -7 or 0   **34** -37 or -21 **35** $3\frac{1}{3}$ or 3.3

In problems 36 and 37, find a rational number between each pair of rationals.

36 $\frac{15}{4}$ and $3\frac{37}{43}$ **37** $2.\overline{6}$ and $2\frac{5}{8}$

38 The graph contains 12 points.

  a List the set of y-coordinates of the points on the graph.

  b Find the probability that the y-coordinate of a point chosen at random is negative.

  c Find the probability that 2 points chosen at random have the same y-coordinate.

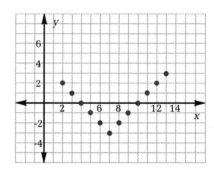

In problems 39–46, simplify each expression.

39 $8(d + 2) - 3(d + 2)$ **40** $4(x + 7) - 2(x + 30)$

41 $9(f + 4) + 7f$ **42** $x[2x + 5(3x + 9)]$

43 $4d^2 + 8d^3 + 12d^2 + 16d^3$ **44** $4a(a - 3) - a^2 + 4$

45 $4.2h + 7.23k + 5h + 9.3k + k$ **46** $x[2x + 3(x + 6)]$

47 Alice paid \$14 to get into Wonderland Amusement Park. She paid \$0.75 for each game she played and \$1.50 for a cup of tea. She went to the park with \$50 and left with \$7.50. How much money did Alice spend at the park? If r represents the number of games Alice played, write an equation in terms of r to represent the total amount of money she spent. Then solve the equation.

In problems 48 and 49, solve each equation.

48 $2y - 7 = 25$ **49** $4x(x + 5) = 0$

In problems 50 and 51, name the property illustrated.

50 $(5 + 3) + 9 = 5 + (3 + 9)$ **51** $3 + (4 + x) = (4 + x) + 3$

In problems 52–55, draw a rectangular coordinate system. Graph and label each point.

52 $(6, -1)$ **53** $(-3, -5)$ **54** $\left(\frac{1}{3}, 4\frac{2}{3}\right)$ **55** $(1.2, -3.5)$

In problems 56–59, find a number that is the same distance from zero on a number line as the given number but in the opposite direction.

56 15 **57** -2.6 **58** $-4\frac{2}{3}$ **59** π

In problems 60–63, write each rational number in the form $\dfrac{\text{an integer}}{\text{a natural number}}$.

60 $5\frac{7}{8}$ **61** -0.005 **62** $\sqrt{\frac{18}{32}}$ **63** $\frac{\sqrt{16}}{16}$

64 Ottavio's bank account was overdrawn by $14. He added $25 to the account. Determine his net balance.

65 Joan's outdoor thermometer read $-8°F$.

   a The temperature rose by 15 degrees. Determine the new temperature.
   b If the temperature fell 2 degrees from $-8°F$, what would the new temperature be?

In problems 66–71, solve each equation.

66 $x + 7.6 = 2.9$ **67** $0.07x - 2.3 = 9.6$ **68** $4x - 8 = 40$

69 $\frac{x}{5} + 3 = 18$ **70** $2.4x + 8.3 = 47.8$ **71** $\frac{2}{3}x - 13 = 45$

72 Refer to the number line to determine which real numbers correspond to the labeled points.

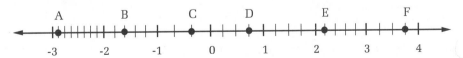

In problems 73 and 74, find the number on the number line halfway between the given numbers.

73 -12 and -4 **74** -15 and $+3$

Problem Set, *continued*

In problems 75–77, find the distance on the number line between the numbers in each pair.

75 12 and 21   **76** -3 and -10 **77** -7 and 19

78 Two clubs, the Woods and the Irons, are having a tug of war. There are 3 Woods pulling to the left and 9 Irons pulling to the right. Each Wood can pull with a force of 161 pounds. Each Iron can pull only 54 pounds. Determine who will win, and with what force and direction.

79 Refer to the diagram.

a Point Q is seven units to the right of the point P. Find the coordinates of the point Q.

b Point S is six units below point P. Find the coordinates of point S.

c Find the coordinates of point R, the fourth vertex of the rectangle.

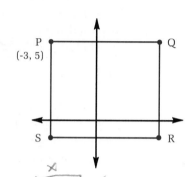

80 The longer sides of a rectangle are 5 millimeters longer than the shorter sides. The perimeter is 40 millimeters.

a Draw and label all four sides of the rectangle in terms of x, the length of the shorter side.

b Write and solve an equation to find x.

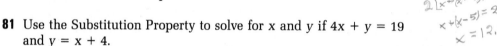

81 Use the Substitution Property to solve for x and y if $4x + y = 19$ and $y = x + 4$.

82 Judy noticed numbered signs at regular intervals on the highway. The first number she saw was 256, the next 255, and the next after that 254. Judy set her stopwatch and found that it took one minute to go from 254 to 253.

a If the speed Judy is traveling at remains constant, how long will it take her to go from 253 to 227?

b Explain what the numbered signs are.

c Determine how fast Judy's car is going.

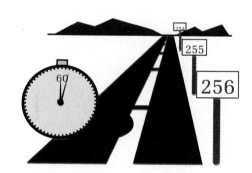

83 Find an irrational number between π and $\sqrt{11}$.

84 Peter randomly picked an x-coordinate for point P from the set $\{0, 1, -2, 3\}$ and a y-coordinate for point P from $\{-4, 5, -6\}$. He then correctly plotted the point. Determine the probability that Peter put point P in Quadrant II.

COMPARING NUMBERS ON THE NUMBER LINE

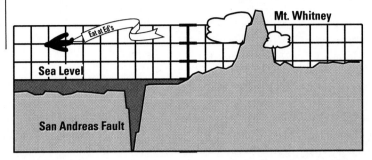

Objectives

After studying this section, you will be able to
- Find the absolute value of a real number
- Find the opposite of a real number
- Use inequality symbols with real numbers
- Graph inequalities on the number line

Part One: Introduction

Absolute Value

The *absolute value* of a real number is the number's distance from zero on the number line. The symbol for the absolute value of a number n is $|n|$.

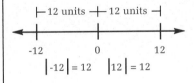

Both -12 and 12 are the same distance from 0.

Opposites

Numbers that have the same absolute value but are on opposite sides of zero on the number line are called *opposites.*

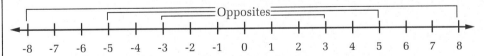

For example, -3 and 3 are opposites, 2.5 and -2.5 are opposites, and $\frac{1}{3}$ and $-\frac{1}{3}$ are opposites. Every real number has an opposite. Zero is its own opposite.

The symbol for the opposite of a number n is $-(n)$ or $-n$. For example, the opposite of 7 is written $-(7)$ or -7, and the opposite of -2 is written $-(-2)$ or 2. Another name for the opposite of a number is the ***additive inverse*** of the number. Consider the following example.

On their first down, the Saints gained 5 yards. On their second down, they lost 5 yards. The total yardage gained or lost for the two plays is 0 yards, which can be expressed as $5 + (-5) = 0$. This example illustrates the following rule.

 The sum of a number and its opposite is zero.

For example, $-7 + 7 = 0$, and $-(-5.12) + (-5.12) = 0$.

Inequalities

On a number line, the greater of any two numbers is to the right. The lesser number is located to the left.

On the number line, -1 is located to the right of -3, so -1 is greater than -3. In other words, $-1 > -3$. Since -2 is located to the left of 4, -2 is less than 4. In other words, $-2 < 4$.

> ***In general, if a is greater than (to the right of) b, we write $a > b$. If a is less than (to the left of) b, we write $a < b$.***

The inequality $7 > 3$ is equivalent to $3 < 7$, since saying 7 is greater than 3 is equivalent to saying 3 is less than 7.

Example   *Determine which numbers from {2, 4, 6} are solutions of $x + 3 \le 7$.*

We recall that $\le$ is read "is less than or equal to."
Since $2 + 3$ is less than 7, 2 is a solution.
Since $4 + 3$ is equal to 7, 4 is a solution.
Since $6 + 3$ is neither less than nor equal to 7, 6 is not a solution.

Graphing Inequalities

You can graph inequalities by using a number line to show all numbers that meet the given conditions.

Example   *Graph each inequality. (The solutions are given below.)*

a $x > 3$

b $x \le -1.5$

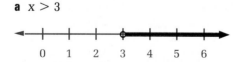
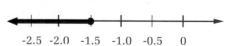

Use an open dot at 3 to show that 3 is not a solution.

Use a solid dot at -1.5 to show that -1.5 is a solution.

Part Two: Sample Problems

Problem 1   *Evaluate each expression.*

   a $|-3| + |25 - 12|$ **b** $|4| + |-10| - |-3|$ **c** $|3 + (-3)|$

Solution   The absolute value symbols are grouping symbols. We evaluate
expressions inside grouping symbols first.

   a $|-3| + |25 - 12|$ **b** $|4| + |-10| - |-3|$ **c** $|3 + (-3)|$
       $= |-3| + |13|$ $= 4 + 10 - 3$ $= |0|$
       $= 3 + 13$ $= 11$ $= 0$
       $= 16$

Problem 2   *Determine whether each statement is True or False.*

   a $|x|$ *is always positive.*   **b** $-x$ *is always negative.*

Solution   **a** False.   **b** False.
       Since $|0| = 0$ and 0 is not   If $x = -2$, then
       positive, $|x|$ is not always $-x = -(-2) = 2$, and
       positive.   2 is not negative.
       Note   Zero is the only exception.

Problem 3   *Points P, Q, and R are placed on a number line at -17, 4, and 10, in
that order.*

   a *Find the distance between P and Q.*
   b *Find the distance between P and R.*

Solution   We draw a number line and label points P, Q, and R.

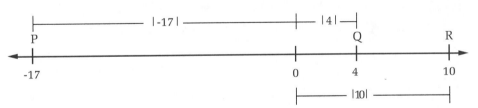

Since the points in each pair are on opposite sides of zero, the
distance between them can be found by adding the absolute values.

   a $|-17| + |4| = 21$, so the distance between P and Q is 21.
   b $|-17| + |10| = 27$, so the distance between P and R is 27.

Problem 4   *Solve the equations.*

   a $|x| = 17$ **b** $|x| = -17$ **c** $-x = 3$

Solution   **a** Since $|17| = 17$ and $|-17| = 17$, both 17 and -17 are solutions.
   b Since the absolute value of a number cannot be negative, there are
       no solutions.
   c Since $-(-3) = 3$, the solution is -3.

Problem 5   *Use the matrix below to answer each question.*

$$\begin{bmatrix} -4 & \sqrt{16} & -\frac{63}{9} \\ 7 & 0 & \sqrt{25} \end{bmatrix}$$

a *List opposites that are in the same row.*
b *List opposites that are in different rows.*
c *List opposites that are in the same row and the same column.*
d *Name a number with an opposite that is not in the matrix.*
e *In which column is the sum of the absolute values of the elements greatest?*

Solution   We see that some expressions are not in simplest form.

a In row 1, -4 and $\sqrt{16}$ are opposites.

b Opposites in different rows are $-\frac{63}{9}$ and 7.

c Zero is its own opposite in row 2 and column 2.

d The opposite of $\sqrt{25}$, -5, is not in the matrix.

e Column 1: $|-4| + |7| = 4 + 7 = 11$

Column 2: $|\sqrt{16}| + |0| = 4 + 0 = 4$

Column 3: $|-\frac{63}{9}| + |\sqrt{25}| = 7 + 5 = 12$

The sum of the absolute values of the elements in the third column is the greatest.

Part Three: Exercises and Problems

Warm-up Exercises

In problems 1–10, determine whether each statement is True or False.

1 $|-7.7| = 7.7$

2 $|365| = -365$

3 $|10 - 14| = |10| - |14|$

4 $-(8.8) = -8.8$

5 $-(-9) = 9$

6 $-2 > -3$

7 $-10 < -15$

8 $8 \geq 8$

9 If $3 < x$, then $x > 3$.

10 A number and its opposite have the same absolute value.

11 Match each inequality with its graph.

a $x \geq 3$

b $x < 3$

c $x + 2 > 5$

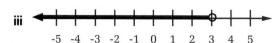

d $2x \leq 6$

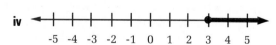

Problem Set

In problems 12–15, give the opposite of each number.

12 -9 **13** $\sqrt{7}$ **14** $5\frac{3}{4}$ **15** -8.8

16 Find the distance between points A and B.

In problems 17–25, simplify each expression.

17 $3x + (-3x)$ **18** $3x - 3x$ **19** $5x + 8 + (-8)$

20 $5x + 8y + (-8y)$ **21** $5(6 + 8) + 3(6 + 8)$ **22** $9[6 + (-6)]$

23 $-(-x)$ **24** $x + (-x)$ **25** $-x + x$

26 Find the distance between points S and T.

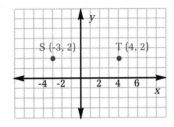

In problems 27–29, evaluate each expression.

27 $|-7| + |31 - 11|$ **28** $|-18| - |-7| + |5|$ **29** $|9 + (-9)|$

In problems 30–37, graph each inequality on a number line.

30 $x \leq 3.2$ **31** $x - 3 \geq 7$

32 $x < -2$ **33** $3x \leq 21$

34 $x \geq -1.5$ **35** $x > 5$

36 $0 > x$ **37** $4 \leq x < 8$

In problems 38 and 39, write an inequality to describe each graph.

38

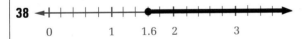

39

In problems 40–42, rewrite each inequality so that x is on the left side of an inequality sign and the inequality still has the same meaning.

40 $-16 < x$ **41** $\sqrt{5} \geq x$ **42** $7\frac{5}{8} > x$

In problems 43 and 44, evaluate the expression for the given value.

43 $|x| + (-x) + 7$ for $x = -10$ **44** $x^2 - x + \sqrt{x}$ for $x = 9$

45 Find the distance between each pair of points on a rectangular coordinate system.

   a (2, 9) and (11, 9)   **b** (5, 13) and (5, 7)   **c** $(-4, -2)$ and $(-4, 5)$
   d Explain how to find these distances without graphing.

46 Find the distance between points X and Y.

47 The hourly salaries of employees at Martinson's grocery store are represented by the matrix.

	Cashier	**Bagger**	**Stockperson**
1 Year's Experience	7.50	6.25	5.45
2 Years' Experience	8.25	6.75	5.95
3 Years' Experience	8.90	7.20	6.15

   a Determine the hourly wage for a stockperson with 1 year's experience.
   b Determine the hourly wage for a cashier with 2 years' experience.
   c Joshua is a bagger with 3 years' experience. Determine his wages for a 35-hour work week.

48 Find the area of the rectangle.

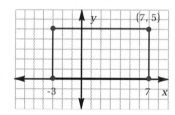

In problems 49 and 50, simplify each expression.

49 $-(3.4^2 - |15^2 + 12 \div 3|)$ **50** $-\left[-(53.2 - |5^2 - 25 \div 4|)\right]$

In problems 51–54, solve each equation.

51 $-x = 12$ **52** $x(x + 5) = 0$
53 $3(x - 4) = 24$ **54** $|x| = 2.6$

55 Make a table of values for $y = |x|$ and sketch the graph. (Be sure to use both positive and negative values for x.)

In problems 56 and 57, solve for *y*. Be sure to check your answers.

56 $|y| + 6 = 10$ **57** $|y|6 = 15$

In problems 58–60, find the distance between the points in each pair.

58 3.5 and 15.3   **59** -15 and 7   **60** -3.5 and -15.3

61 Two matrices can be added by adding their corresponding elements. Complete the addition.

$$\begin{bmatrix} 2.7 & 15 \\ 1\frac{1}{6} & 0 \end{bmatrix} + \begin{bmatrix} 0.6 & 14 \\ \frac{5}{6} & 3 \end{bmatrix} = \begin{bmatrix} 3.3 & ? \\ ? & ? \end{bmatrix}$$

62 Sandy checked over her savings account. Here is what she found.

8/9/90	Deposit	$1200
9/15/90	Deposit	$ 350
9/20/90	Withdrawal	$1000
10/3/90	Withdrawal	$ 480
10/30/90	Deposit	$ 760
11/15/90	Withdrawal	$ 820

a Determine her total deposits.
b Determine the total amount of her withdrawals.
c On 12/1/90 Sandy wants to withdraw $45. Can she do it?

63 Describe the graph in words.

64 Pete and Paul were asked to supply soft drinks for a party. Each carton contains 12 cans. If they need 144 cans for the party and Pete brings 5 cartons, how many cartons must Paul bring?

65 If $(x, y) = (6, 3)$, determine which perimeter is greater.

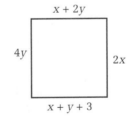

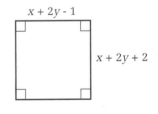

In problems 66–69, determine whether each is true Always, Sometimes, or Never.

66 $-x < 5$ **67** $-x \le x$
68 $-(-x) = x$ **69** $-x \le 0$

70 The price of a $100 suit was increased by 20%. A month later, the same suit went on sale at 20% off. What was the new cost of the suit? Explain. (Hint: The answer is not $100.)

ADDITION OF REAL NUMBERS

Objectives

After studying this section, you will be able to
- Add numbers with the same sign
- Add numbers with opposite signs
- Add like terms with signed coefficients
- Use a scientific calculator to add signed numbers

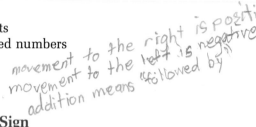

Part One: Introduction

Adding Numbers with the Same Sign

Positive numbers indicate a motion to the right on the number line. The diagram that follows shows the steps in the addition problem $2 + 9 = 11$. Starting at 2, you move 9 units, or spaces, to the right, arriving at 11.

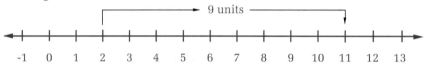

Negative numbers indicate a motion to the left on the number line. In the diagram that follows, the numbers -5 and -8 are added by moving 8 units to the left of -5.
You can see that $(-5) + (-8) = -13$.

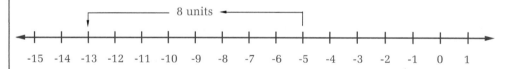

> **To add two numbers with the same sign, add their absolute values. The sign of the sum is the sign of the original numbers.**

Example   Add. (The solutions are given below.)

a $7 + 8\frac{1}{3}$

$$7 + 8\frac{1}{3} = \boxed{+ (|7| + |8\tfrac{1}{3}|)}$$

$$= (7 + 8\tfrac{1}{3})$$

$$= + 15\tfrac{1}{3}$$

Since both numbers are positive, the sum is positive.

b $-2.5 + (-4.7)$

$$-2.5 + (-4.7) = \boxed{-(|-2.5| + |-4.7|)}$$

$$= -(2.5 + 4.7)$$

$$= -7.2$$

Since both numbers are negative, the sum is negative.

Adding Numbers with Opposite Signs

To help you add -4 and 12, think of the number line.

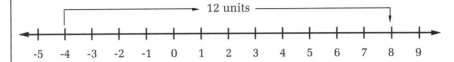

Notice that you start at -4 and move 12 units to the right to get to 8. This can be stated as $-4 + 12 = 8$.

To add $4 + (-6)$, you start at 4 and move 6 units to the left. The result is $4 + (-6) = -2$.

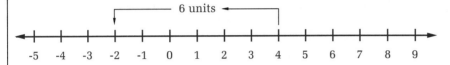

> *To add two numbers with opposite signs, subtract the smaller absolute value from the larger absolute value. The sign of the sum is the sign of the number with the larger absolute value.*

Example   *Add. (The solutions are given below.)*

a $-10 + 40$

$$-10 + 40 = \boxed{|40| - |-10|}$$

$$= 40 - 10$$

$$= 30$$

Since the number with the larger absolute value is positive, the sum is positive.

b $10 + (-40)$

$$10 + (-40) = \boxed{-(|-40| - |10|)}$$

$$= -(40 - 10)$$

$$= -30$$

Since the number with the larger absolute value is negative, the sum is negative.

Adding Like Terms

The terms $-17x$ and $-5x$ are like terms. The numbers multiplying the variables, -17 and -5, are called **coefficients** of the variables. To add like terms, we add their coefficients.

$$-17x + (-5x) = -22x$$
$$-6x^3 + 2x^3 = -4x^3$$
$$5\sqrt{x} + (-7\sqrt{x}) = -2\sqrt{x}$$

Using A Scientific Calculator

When you want to enter a negative number on a scientific calculator, you first enter the positive number, then push the change-sign key, $\boxed{+/-}$ or $\boxed{\text{CHS}}$. You should not use the subtraction key to enter negative numbers. For example, to enter -17 you press 17 $\boxed{+/-}$. Notice that the change-sign key is used *after* you enter the number.

Example   *Use a calculator to compute $33.7 + (-45.9)$.*

Press the change-sign key after 45.9   **33.7** $\boxed{+}$ **45.9** $\boxed{+/-}$ $\boxed{=}$

The display shows $\boxed{-12.2}$

Example   *Use a calculator to compute -11^2.*

Remember that -11^2 means "the opposite of the square of 11." We square 11 and then find the opposite of the result.   **11** $\boxed{x^2}$ $\boxed{+/-}$

The display shows $\boxed{-121}$
How would you find $(-11)^2$?

Part Two: Sample Problems

Problem 1   *Add the matrices.*

$$\begin{bmatrix} -1.0 & 4 & 3.7 \\ -2.1 & -8 & -15.0 \end{bmatrix} + \begin{bmatrix} -6 & -7 & -5.9 \\ 7 & 2 & -4.0 \end{bmatrix}$$

Solution   To add matrices, we add corresponding elements.

$-1 + (-6) = -7$	$4 + (-7) = -3$	$3.7 + (-5.9) = -2.2$
$-2.1 + 7 = 4.9$	$-8 + 2 = -6$	$-15 + (-4) = -19$

The sum of the two matrices is

$$\begin{bmatrix} -7.0 & -3 & -2.2 \\ 4.9 & -6 & -19.0 \end{bmatrix}$$

Problem 2   *Solve.*

a $y + (-10) = -17$ **b** $-2.6 + 4.1 = 6.5 + x$

Solution   We use additive inverses to solve each equation.

a $y + (-10) = -17$
$ \quad\quad + 10 \quad + 10$
$\overline{y = -7}$

b $-2.6 + 4.1 = 6.5 + x$
$ 1.5 = 6.5 + x$
$ - 6.5 \quad - 6.5$
$\overline{ -5.0 = x}$

Problem 3   *In a rectangular coordinate system, the coordinates of point A are* $(-5, -6)$*. Point B is 9 units to the right of and 4 units up from point A. Find the coordinates of point B.*

Solution   We can graph point A, then move 9 units to the right and 4 units up. We can also find the coordinates by adding. Moving right increases the x-coordinate, so $-5 + 9 = 4$. Moving up increases the y-coordinate, so $-6 + 4 = -2$. The coordinates of point B are $(4, -2)$.

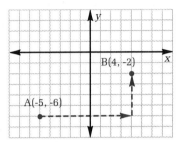

Problem 4   *Approximate* $-12\sqrt{5} + 9\sqrt{5} + (-3\sqrt{5})$ *to the nearest thousandth.*

Solution   Since these are like terms, we simplify first by adding the coefficients to obtain $-6\sqrt{5}$. Then we use the calculator.

6 $\boxed{+/-}$ $\boxed{\times}$ 5 $\boxed{\sqrt{}}$ $\boxed{=}$. The display shows $\boxed{-13.416407}$, so the approximate value is -13.416.

Part Three: Exercises and Problems

Warm-up Exercises

In problems 1–4, add.

1 $-6 + 12$ **2** $10 + (-8)$ **3** $-6 + (-9)$ **4** $-23 + 6$

In problems 5–7, combine like terms.

5 $4y + 10y - 15y$ **6** $-12x^2 + (-7x^2)$ **7** $\sqrt{7} + (-8\sqrt{7}) + (-2\sqrt{5}) + (-\sqrt{5})$

Problem Set

In problems 8–15, add the numbers.

8 $0.9 + (-4.9)$ **9** $-0.25 + 0.025$

10 $15 + |-15|$ **11** $9 + (-23) + 5 + (-4)$

12 $-45 + (-12) + (-19) + (-37)$ **13** $-125 + (-278) + 301$

14 $32 + (-63) + 51 + (-16)$ **15** $-0.35 + 2.17 + (-1.81)$

16 Approximate $-\left(-\sqrt{2}\right)$ to the nearest thousandth.

17 Given the point $(-12, -2)$, find the coordinates of the point that lies 7 units to the right and 10 units up.

Problem Set, *continued*

In problems 18–23, solve the equation or simplify the expression.

18 $x - 29 = -15$

19 $-5 = 2 + y$

20 $25x - 15x + 9x + 2x$

21 $2x + 17 + (-13) = -22 + (-5) + 40$

22 $-18y + (-19y) + 10x$

23 $-7a + 37b + 13a + (-45b)$

24 Complete the table of values for $y = x + (-2)$, and graph the equation on a coordinate plane.

x	-3	-2	-1	0	1	2	3
y							

25 A warehouse has 10 floors above ground, 9 floors below ground, and 1 floor at ground level. Christopher gets on an elevator at the lowest level and travels up 7 floors. He then goes up another 7 floors. He wants to get out at ground level. How many more floors must Christopher ride the elevator, and in which direction?

In problems 26–28, evaluate each expression for $x = -15$, $y = 9$, and $z = -6$.

26 $x + 2y$

27 $x + y + |z|$

28 $|x + z|$

In problems 29 and 30, add the matrices.

29 $\begin{bmatrix} -2.5 & -\dfrac{3}{4} \\ \dfrac{2}{3} & 0.75 \end{bmatrix} + \begin{bmatrix} -1.4 & -\dfrac{3}{10} \\ -\dfrac{5}{6} & -2.9 \end{bmatrix}$

30 $\begin{bmatrix} -3 & 7 & 11 \\ -13 & -9 & -5 \\ 4 & 0 & -1 \end{bmatrix} + \begin{bmatrix} -7 & -16 & -5 \\ 7 & -1 & 0 \\ -17 & -6 & -13 \end{bmatrix}$

In problems 31–34, graph each inequality on a number line.

31 $x < -10$

32 $x \geq -6$

33 $4 \geq x + 1$

34 $(7 + 9) < x$

35 Find the area of the circle if $(x, y) = (14, 3)$.

$x - 3y$

In problems 36–38, graph each set on a number line.

36 All real numbers that are 5 or less units from 0

37 All integers that are 5 or less units from 0

38 All whole numbers that are 5 or less units from 0

In problems 39 and 40, use a calculator to evaluate each expression.

39 Evaluate $(-35.4) + (-16.7) + (12.3) + (-1.8)$.

40 Approximate $6\sqrt{11} + 7\sqrt{11} + \left(-3\sqrt{11}\right) + 10\sqrt{11} + \sqrt{11}$ to the nearest hundredth.

In problems 41–44, evaluate each expression for $x = 3.5$ and $y = -2.1$.

41 $-x^2 + y$ **42** $-x + (-y)$ **43** $-y + 3x$ **44** $2(-y + 3x)$

In problems 45 and 46, name the property illustrated by each statement.

45 $4[5 + (-10)] = 4(5) + 4(-10)$

46 If $x(-5 + y) = 0$, then either $x = 0$ or $-5 + y = 0$.

47 Complete the table for $x + y = -2$, and graph.

x	-5	-4	-3	-2	-1	0	1	2	3
y									

48 Evaluate $19^2 + \left(-\sqrt{237}\right)$.

49 Find the average of -6, -3, and -23.

50 Find the area of the rectangle whose vertices are at $(-3, 1)$, $(11, 1)$, $(11, -6)$, and $(-3, -6)$.

51 Use the points $P(-8, 3)$ and $Q(-2, 19)$.

  a Plot the points in a coordinate plane.
  b How far to the right and how far up is Q from P?
  c Find the coordinates of the other two points that are corners of a rectangle with sides parallel to the x- and y-axes and opposite corners at P and Q.

In problems 52–57, simplify the expression or solve the equation.

52 $16(x - 4) + (-12x) = -10 + (-13)$ **53** $6x^2 + (-8x) + (-9x^2) + x$

54 $-[-37 + (-45)] - 5^2(2)$ **55** $-x(x + 4) = 0$

56 $4(x - 7) + (-5x) = -10$ **57** $2x^2 + 10x = 0$

58 The student body of Cramer High School decreases by 8% each year. In 1987 there were 1200 students in the school. Assuming half of the students are boys and 10% of the boys play football, in what year will the football coach not be able to field a team? (Hint: It takes 11 players to make up a football team.)

The Football Program at Cramer High School

600 Eligible to Play   10% Play Football

59 Write an expression whose product will be 5x + 10y + 35 when you apply the Distributive Property of Multiplication over Addition.

60 From a point on a graph, you move 23 units to the right and then 14 units up. If your resulting position is (9, − 2), what was your original position?

61 If *ax* = *b*, solve for x in terms of *a* and *b*, *a* ≠ 0.

TORNADO WATCH
Raymond Theiler tracks a tornado's path

On a peaceful spring day somewhere in the Midwest, a mass of cold air forces itself underneath a bank of warm, moist air along a cold front. The warm air begins to revolve faster and faster as it rises. Moisture condenses in the spinning air, forming a funnel-shaped cloud. Suddenly a tornado, the most violent of all windstorms, is moving across the countryside.

People living in the path of a tornado once had little hope of avoiding its destructive power. Today, however, weather scientists are able to predict when and where tornadoes are likely to occur and to issue warnings. It is work like this that occupies Raymond "Skip" Theiler, a weather service specialist with the National Weather Service in Albuquerque, New Mexico. Using a variety of techniques, Mr. Theiler can identify the atmospheric conditions that are likely to lead to tornadoes.

Mr. Theiler showed an early talent in science and math. "Both are very important in my field," he says. After attending college, he studied meteorology at the Air Force Weather School. To satisfy the requirements for becoming a forecaster with the weather service, a college degree—preferably in science or engineering—is needed. You also need to study math through differential and integral calculus.

One of a forecaster's major tools is radar. When a radar pulse is sent out toward a weather system, the pulse bounces off and returns, bringing important information about the speed and distance of the system. Here's a simple example of how it works.

The radar pulse travels at the speed of light. Forecasters see how long it takes a pulse to make a round trip to the system and back. Then they use the familiar formula "distance equals rate times time" to determine how far away the weather system is.

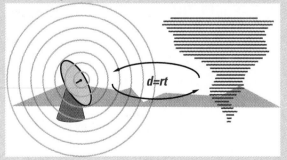

SUBTRACTION OF REAL NUMBERS

Objectives

After studying this section, you will be able to

- Subtract signed numbers
- Find opposites of quantities
- Use a scientific calculator to subtract signed numbers

Part One: Introduction

Subtraction

Subtraction is the inverse operation of addition. In order to understand subtraction of real numbers, let's study the following patterns and draw a conclusion.

Subtraction	Adding the Opposite	Subtraction	Adding the Opposite
$5 - 3 = 2$	$5 + (-3) = 2$	$-3 - 3 = -6$	$-3 + (-3) = -6$
$5 - 2 = 3$	$5 + (-2) = 3$	$-3 - 2 = -5$	$-3 + (-2) = -5$
$5 - 1 = 4$	$5 + (-1) = 4$	$-3 - 1 = -4$	$-3 + (-1) = -4$
$5 - 0 = 5$	$5 + 0 = 5$	$-3 - 0 = -3$	$-3 + 0 = -3$
$5 - (-1) = 6$	$5 + 1 = 6$	$-3 - (-1) = -2$	$-3 + 1 = -2$
$5 - (-2) = 7$	$5 + 2 = 7$	$-3 - (-2) = -1$	$-3 + 2 = -1$
$5 - (-3) = 8$	$5 + 3 = 8$	$-3 - (-3) = 0$	$-3 + 3 = 0$
$5 - (-4) = 9$	$5 + 4 = 9$	$-3 - (-4) = 1$	$-3 + 4 = 1$

The patterns in the equations above show that subtracting a number gives the same result as adding its opposite.

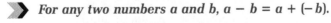 **For any two numbers a and b, $a - b = a + (-b)$.**

Example Subtract. (The solutions are given below.)

a	**b**	**c**
$14 - 19$	$-7 - 8$	$-3 - (-6)$
$14 - 19$	$-7 - 8$	$-3 - (-6)$
$= 14 + (-19)$	$= -7 + (-8)$	$= -3 + [-(-6)]$
$= -5$	$= -15$	$= -3 + 6$
		$= 3$

Opposites of Quantities

To find out how to determine the opposite of a quantity, compare the corresponding equations on the left and the right.

$$-(8 + 2) = -10 \qquad -8 + (-2) = -10$$
$$-(9 - 5) = -4 \qquad -9 - (-5) = -9 + 5 = -4$$

The equations above show that the opposite of a quantity can be expressed as the opposite of each of its terms.

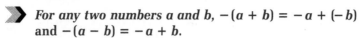 **For any two numbers a and b, $-(a + b) = -a + (-b)$ and $-(a - b) = -a + b$.**

Example   *Simplify each expression. (The solutions are given below.)*

a $-(x - 1) + x$ **b** $6x - 3 - (5x + 7)$

$-(x - 1) + x$ $6x - 3 - (5x + 7)$
$= -x - (-1) + x$ $= 6x + (-3) + [-(5x + 7)]$
$= -x + 1 + x$ $= 6x + (-3) + (-5x) + (-7)$
$= 1$ $= x + (-10)$
 $= x - 10$

Using A Scientific Calculator

To enter a negative number on a calculator, you use the change-sign key.

Example   *Use a calculator to evaluate $-31.45 - 43.04$.*

Enter numbers in the order shown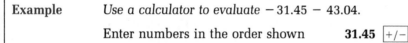
The display shows

Example   *Use a calculator to evaluate $45 - (-30)$.*

Simplify $45 - (-30)$ to $45 + 30$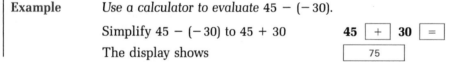
The display shows

Part Two: Sample Problems

Problem 1   *Are $3y - 7$ and $7 - 3y$ equivalent expressions?*

Solution   Let's substitute 4 for y and then evaluate each expression.

$3y - 7 = 3(4) - 7 \qquad 7 - 3y = 7 - 3(4)$
$ = 12 - 7 \qquad = 7 - 12$
$ = 5 \qquad = -5$

Since each expression yielded a different answer, the expressions are not equivalent. This problem shows that subtraction is not commutative.

Problem 2   *Subtract the matrices.*

$$\begin{bmatrix} 5 & 19 & -23 \\ -4 & -21 & 33 \end{bmatrix} - \begin{bmatrix} 14 & -8 & 5 \\ -6 & 25 & -44 \end{bmatrix}$$

Solution

To subtract the matrices, we subtract corresponding numbers.

$$5 - 14 = -9 \qquad 19 - (-8) = 27 \qquad -23 - 5 = -28$$
$$-4 - (-6) = 2 \qquad -21 - 25 = -46 \qquad 33 - (-44) = 77$$

The matrix solution follows.

$$\begin{bmatrix} -9 & 27 & -28 \\ 2 & -46 & 77 \end{bmatrix}$$

Problem 3   *Solve each statement, and graph each solution on a number line.*

        a $-(x + 24) = -42 - (-12)$ **b** $y + 2.3 \le -4.7$

Solutions

a
$$-(x + 24) = -42 - (-12)$$
$$-x + (-24) = -42 + 12$$
$$-x + (-24) = -30$$
$$ \quad +24 \quad +24$$
$$\overline{-x \qquad = \quad -6}$$
$$-x(-1) \quad = \quad -6(-1)$$
$$x \qquad = \quad 6$$

b
$$y + 2.3 \le -4.7$$
$$ \;\; -2.3 \quad -2.3$$
$$\overline{y \qquad \le -7}$$

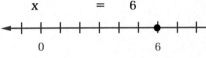
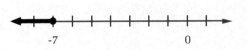

Problem 4   *Evaluate* $3(14x - 8) - (10x - 7)$ *if* $x = 3.9$.

Solution   Simplify the expression first. Then substitute 3.9 for x.

$$3(14x - 8) - (10x - 7)$$
$$= 42x - 24 - 10x + 7$$
$$= 32x - 17$$
$$= 32(3.9) - 17$$
$$= 124.8 - 17$$
$$= 107.8$$

Part Three: Exercises and Problems

Warm-up Exercises

1 Subtract the matrices.

$$\begin{bmatrix} -3 & 7 \\ 4 & -8 \\ -5 & -5 \\ 5 & -3 \end{bmatrix} - \begin{bmatrix} 6 & 3 \\ 10 & -2 \\ 3 & -3 \\ -3 & 5 \end{bmatrix}$$

In problems 2–4, simplify.

2 $2x - 7x$ **3** $-2x + 7x$ **4** $-2x - (-7x)$

In problems 5–7, describe the key sequence you would use on a calculator to compute each problem.

5 $78 - (-105)$ **6** $-6.92 - 2.37$ **7** $-\sqrt{2} - (-3)$

Problem Set

In problems 8–25, add or subtract.

8 $16 - 26$

9 $-5 - (-5)$

10 $-18 - 13 + 19$

11 $-5 - (3 - 11)$

12 $-22 - 11$

13 $-14 + (-33)$

14 $-23 + 3$

15 $-(5 - 3) - 7$

16 $233 - 300$

17 $95 - (-45)$

18 $8 - (3 + 4)$

19 $-(-9 - 2) - (-6)$

20 $32 - (-5)$

21 $33 - 44 + 55$

22 $-9 - (-7 + 2)$

23 $-4 - (6 + 18)$

24 $12 + (-13)$

25 $-7 - (-6)$

In problems 26–29, evaluate each expression for $a = 5$, $b = -3$, and $c = -8$.

26 $|a + b|$

27 $2a - c$

28 $c - 2a$

29 $a + c - b$

In problems 30–37, simplify each expression and solve each equation.

30 $x + 48 = -36$

31 $3 - (6y + 19)$

32 $-(x - 7) = -48 - 24$

33 $12 = 3x + 96$

34 $8 - x = -15$

35 $-(-7x - 3x) + 9x$

36 $-(4 - x) = 12$

37 $2x^2 - 8x = 0$

38 Subtract the matrices.

$$\begin{bmatrix} 19 & -7 & -44 \\ -25 & -6 & 5.7 \\ \dfrac{3}{10} & -\dfrac{5}{2} & -254 \end{bmatrix} - \begin{bmatrix} 10 & 14 & -4 \\ 5 & -15 & 8.8 \\ \dfrac{1}{2} & -\dfrac{1}{2} & -254 \end{bmatrix}$$

In problems 39–41, solve each inequality and graph the solution.

39 $x + 25 \geq 15$

40 $y + 2.5 > -5.7$

41 $5 + x < 5$

In problems 42–44, use a calculator to evaluate.

42 $16 - 34.006$

43 $-34.2 + (-15.3)$

44 $-34.2 - (-15.3)$

In problems 45–47, find the perimeters if $(x, y) = (9, 7)$.

45

$2x + 3y$

$x + y + 9$

$2x + y$

$3x - y$

46

$2x$

$2x + 1$

$x + y$

$x + y + 1$

$3x - 2y + 2$

$4x - 3y$

47

$4x - 3y$

In problems 48–53, add or subtract.

48 $1.6 + (-2.6)$

49 $-2.2 - 1.18$

50 $0.233 - 3$

51 $3.5 - (-1.7)$

52 $13.1 - 17.5 - 8.24$

53 $98.6 - 200.1 - (-19.84)$

54 A plumber charges \$48.50 for a house call plus \$35 for each hour she works. Al called the plumber to fix a broken faucet. If the plumber takes 90 minutes to repair the faucet, how much will she charge Al? If the plumber leaves Al a bill of \$127.25, how long did it take to fix the faucet?

In problems 55 and 56, approximate to the nearest ten-thousandth.

55 $3\sqrt{23} - 15\sqrt{23} + 4\sqrt{23}$ **56** $25\pi - 9\pi - 30\pi$

57 Evaluate $3(14x - 8) - (10x - 7)$ if $x = 2.6$.

58 Simplify.

$$\begin{bmatrix} -4 & -3 \\ 5 & 2 \end{bmatrix} - \begin{bmatrix} -8 & 2 \\ -1 & 9 \end{bmatrix} + \begin{bmatrix} -2 & 5 \\ -4 & 1 \end{bmatrix}$$

59 Starting at $(-6, 10)$, move 11 units to the left and 19 units down. What are the coordinates of the new location?

60 If $(x_1, y_1) = (14, 20)$ and $(x_2, y_2) = (22, 7)$, find m if $m = \dfrac{y_2 - y_1}{x_2 - x_1}$. (Write your answer as a fraction.)

61 Find the average of -12, 14, -22.9, -94, and 57.6 to the nearest hundredth.

In problems 62–64, evaluate for $z = -19$, $a = -7$, and $p = 9$.

62 $z - a - p$ **63** $|p - 23| + z$ **64** $z - (a - p)$

In problems 65–68, determine which property is illustrated.

65 $-(x - 4) = -x + 4$ **66** $-4(-5.9x) = [(-4)(-5.9)]x$
67 If $0.4x = 7$, then $2.5(0.4x) = 2.5(7)$.   **68** $5x - 3 = -3 + 5x$

In problems 69 and 70, solve for x. Be sure to check your answers.

69 $8 - x = -15$ **70** $3x + 6y = -15$ and $y = 7$

71 Find the area of the rectangle with vertices at $(-7, 5)$, $(3, -1)$, and $(-7, -1)$. Find the coordinates of the fourth vertex.

In problems 72 and 73, solve.

72 $|x| = 9$ **73** $|x| < 9$ where x is a real number

74 The vertices of a rectangle are $(5, 2)$, $(-3, 2)$, $(-3, -6)$, $(5, -6)$. A point is randomly selected in the interior of the rectangle.

  a In what quadrant is the point most likely to be?
  b Find the probability that the point is in Quadrant I.

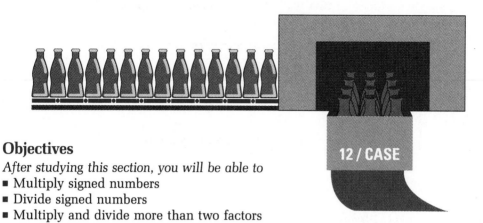

3.5 MULTIPLICATION AND DIVISION OF REAL NUMBERS

Objectives

After studying this section, you will be able to
- Multiply signed numbers
- Divide signed numbers
- Multiply and divide more than two factors

Part One: Introduction

Multiplication of Signed Numbers

In order to understand multiplication of signed numbers, let's look at the pattern for multiplication of whole numbers.

$5(3) = 15$	Notice that the prod-
$5(2) = 10$	ucts decrease by 5.
$5(1) = 5$	
$5(0) = 0$	

As the pattern continues, watch what happens as the second factor decreases by 1.

$5(-1) = -5$	The pattern shows that
$5(-2) = -10$	multiplying a positive
$5(-3) = -15$	number by a negative
$5(-4) = -20$	number results in a
	negative number.

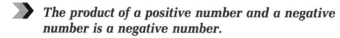 **The product of a positive number and a negative number is a negative number.**

Here are some examples of this rule.

$$4(-6) = -24 \qquad (-3.25)(6.78) = -22.035 \qquad \left(-\tfrac{1}{2}\right) \cdot \tfrac{3}{4} = -\tfrac{3}{8}$$

Now look at this pattern.

$(-3)3 = -9$	The pattern shows that
$(-3)2 = -6$	the products increase
$(-3)1 = -3$	by 3 as the second fac-
$(-3)0 = 0$	tor decreases by 1.

Watch what happens as the second factor continues to decrease by 1 and you multiply two negative numbers.

$$(-3)(-1) = 3$$
$$(-3)(-2) = 6$$
$$(-3)(-3) = 9$$

This pattern shows that when two negative numbers are multiplied, the product is a positive number.

> **The product of two negative numbers is a positive number.**

Here are some examples of this rule.

$$(-10)(-4) = 40 \qquad (-3.6)(-2.5) = 9 \qquad \left(-\tfrac{1}{3}\right) \cdot \left(-\tfrac{4}{5}\right) = \tfrac{4}{15}$$

Finally, from earlier arithmetic, you know the following rule.

> **The product of two positive numbers is a positive number.**

Division of Signed Numbers

In Chapter 2, you learned the Quotient Property, $\dfrac{a}{b} = a \cdot \dfrac{1}{b}$, which states that to divide two numbers, we multiply by the reciprocal of the denominator. The rules for division are therefore the same as the rules for multiplication.

> **The quotient of a positive number and a negative number is negative.**

For example, $-18 \div 6 = -3$, $\dfrac{21}{-6} = -3.5$, and $\dfrac{-21}{6} = -3.5$.
Also, $\dfrac{-1}{2} = -0.5$, $\dfrac{1}{-2} = -0.5$, and $-\dfrac{1}{2} = -0.5$.
The general statement is $\dfrac{-a}{b} = \dfrac{a}{-b} = -\dfrac{a}{b}$.

> **The quotient of two positive numbers or two negative numbers is positive.**

For example, $-15 \div (-3) = 5$, $\dfrac{-14}{-2} = 7$, and $-4.6 \div (-2.2) \approx 2.09$.

Repeated Multiplication or Division of Signed Numbers
Now consider these problems.

$$(-3)(-4)(0.5)(-0.2)(6)(-2)$$

$$= (12)(-0.1)(-12)$$
$$= (-1.2)(-12)$$
$$= 14.4$$

Here 4 factors are negative, and the product is positive.

$$\frac{(-3)(0.4)(-6)}{(0.2)(-5)}$$

$$= \frac{7.2}{-1}$$
$$= -7.2$$

Here 3 factors are negative, and the quotient is negative.

The rule for repeated multiplication or division of signed numbers follows.

 If there is an even number of negative values, then the product or quotient will be a positive number.

If there is an odd number of negative values, then the product or quotient will be a negative number.

Example   *Determine whether the product will be positive or negative.*

a $(-3)(-2)(-5)(2)$
There are 3 negative factors, so the product will be negative.

b $(-2)^4$
Since $(-2)^4$ means $(-2)(-2)(-2)(-2)$, there are 4 negative factors, and the product will be positive.

c -2^4
Be careful! The expression -2^4 means $-(2)(2)(2)(2)$. This is the opposite of a positive product, and the result will be negative.

Part Two: Sample Problems

Problem 1   *Evaluate $x^2 - 5x - y$ for $x = -7$ and $y = -4$.*

Solution   When we substitute the values for x and y, we enclose them in parentheses to make the operations more clear.

$$x^2 - 5x - y$$
$$= (-7)^2 - 5(-7) - (-4)$$
$$= (-7)(-7) + (-5)(-7) + (4)$$
$$= 49 + 35 + 4 = 88$$

Problem 2   *Solve each equation.*

a　$8 - 3x = 56$ 　　　　**b**　$x - (5 - 4x) = -10$

Solution

a
$$\begin{aligned} 8 - 3x &= 56 \\ -8 \qquad\quad &\ -8 \\ \hline -3x &= 48 \\ \frac{-3x}{-3} &= \frac{48}{-3} \\ x &= -16 \end{aligned}$$

b
$$\begin{aligned} x - (5 - 4x) &= -10 \\ x - 5 + 4x &= -10 \\ 5x - 5 &= -10 \\ +5 \quad\ &\ +5 \\ \hline 5x &= -5 \\ \frac{5x}{5} &= \frac{-5}{5} \\ x &= -1 \end{aligned}$$

Problem 3   *Multiply.* $\quad -5 \begin{bmatrix} 2 & -4 \\ -7 & -11 \end{bmatrix}$

Solution   To multiply a matrix by a number, we multiply each element of the matrix by the number. This is called *scalar multiplication.* The number -5 is called a **scalar.**

$$-5 \begin{bmatrix} 2 & -4 \\ -7 & -11 \end{bmatrix} = \begin{bmatrix} (-5)(2) & (-5)(-4) \\ (-5)(-7) & (-5)(-11) \end{bmatrix} = \begin{bmatrix} -10 & 20 \\ 35 & 55 \end{bmatrix}$$

Problem 4   *Multiply.*

$$-5\left(3x_2 + 4y^3 - 6\sqrt{7}\right)$$

Solution   We multiply each term by -5.

$$(-5)(3x_2) + (-5)(4y^3) + (-5)\left(-6\sqrt{7}\right)$$
$$-15x_2 - 20y^3 + 30\sqrt{7}$$

Part Three: Exercises and Problems

Warm-up Exercises

In problems 1–8, simplify.

1 $(-2)(-3)(-1)$ **2** $-6 \div 3$ **3** $\dfrac{(-2)(-3)}{-3}$ **4** $(-2)^3$

5 $\dfrac{(-2)^2}{-4}$ **6** -2^2 **7** -2^3 **8** $(-1)^{43}$

In problems 9 and 10, evaluate for $x = -2$ and $y = -3$.

9 $2x - y^2$ **10** $x^2 + 3y - x$

Problem Set

In problems 11–18, simplify.

11 $-15(-3)$ **12** $-15 + (-3)$ **13** $-15 - (-3)$ **14** $-15 \div (-3)$

15 $(6)(-8)$ **16** $(6) - (-8)$ **17** $\dfrac{6}{-8}$ **18** $(6) + (-8)$

19 Let x be a number such that 65% of the number is 95. Write this information as an equation involving x and solve it.

In problems 20 and 21, multiply.

20 $-6 \begin{bmatrix} -6 & \frac{1}{2} & -10 \\ 7 & -20 & -\frac{2}{3} \\ 123 & 2\sqrt{5} & 3.7 \end{bmatrix}$

21 $-\frac{2}{3} \begin{bmatrix} 6 & 12 & -3 \\ -15 & -9 & -12 \end{bmatrix}$

22 What property does $-3^2(-5)(-7) = (-5)(-3^2)(-7)$ illustrate?

In problems 23–26, evaluate each for $x = -6$ and $y = -4$.

23 $-x^2 - y$ **24** $-3x^3 - y^2$ **25** $\dfrac{-x - 4y}{x^3 y^3}$ **26** $\dfrac{x - 2y}{y^2}$

In problems 27–32, multiply or divide as indicated.

27 $\dfrac{-28}{4}$ **28** $\left(\dfrac{1}{7}\right) \cdot (7)$ **29** $\dfrac{-18}{-36}$

30 $\dfrac{30}{-12}$ **31** $\left(-\dfrac{2}{9}\right)\left(-\dfrac{15}{4}\right)$ **32** $(-1)^{35}$

Problem Set, *continued*

33 Find 20% of (-135).

34 Express (-18) as a percentage of -50.

35 A TV repairman charges $21 for a visit and $42 per hour of repair time. Let n represent the number of hours he works.
   a Write an expression for his total bill.
   b Determine how much he charges if he works 2.5 hours.
   c Write an equation to represent his total bill of $168.
   d Solve the equation from part **c** to find how long he worked.

In problems 36–41, simplify each expression.
36 $4x + (-12x) - (-16x)$ **37** $20k(-5k) + 100k^2$ **38** $4x - (3x - 2)$
39 $4x - (2 - 3x)$ **40** $(-1)^{46} - 1^{45}$ **41** $(-1)^{46} + (-1^{45})$

42 Complete the table of values for $y = 3x - 5$ and graph.

x	-4	-3	-2	-1	0	1	2	3
y		-14				-2		

In problems 43–45, solve each equation or inequality.
43 $-3 - 2y = -32$ **44** $y - (6 - 3y) = -12$ **45** $4x + 68 \geq 0$

46 Solve for x if $6x + 4y = 0$ and $y = -48$.

In problems 47–52, simplify.
47 $-10 + (20)$ **48** $-10 - (20)$ **49** $\dfrac{-10}{20}$

50 $(-6)^2$ **51** -6^2 **52** $(-3)^2 - \dfrac{(-2)(-24)}{-16}$

53 If one of the values a, b, c, or d is selected at random, what is the probability that the number will be positive?

$a = (-2)(-3)(\pi)(-1)$ $b = (-3) \div (-9)(-5)(-2)$
$c = (-2)^7 (-3)^4 (-4)$ $d = (0 - 7)(0 + 7)(-7)(7)$

In problems 54–56, simplify.
54 $\left(-\frac{5}{6}\right)\left(-\frac{3}{10}\right)$ **55** $\dfrac{-2.46}{-0.3}$ **56** $\dfrac{6 + 10}{6 - 10}$

In problems 57–59, multiply, using the Distributive Property of Multiplication over Addition and Subtraction.
57 $-7(3x^2 + 5x - 9)$ **58** $-5(-4p + 8q - 5r)$ **59** $3x(x - 4)$

In problems 60–62, use a calculator to evaluate each expression. You may find it easier to determine the sign of the answer first.

60 $(-5)^3(-4.2)^4$

61 $7.8(-2.4)^3(3)^7$

62 $\dfrac{18.27(-4.2)^2}{(-3.25)^3}$

In problems 63–65, solve for x and graph each solution on a number line.

63 $|x| = 6$

64 $|x| = 0$

65 $|x| = -4$

66 Evaluate.

$$(-2)\begin{bmatrix} 12 & -4 & 6 \\ 11 & 16 & -9 \end{bmatrix} + \begin{bmatrix} 8 & -6 & 13 \\ -4 & -3 & 0 \end{bmatrix}$$

In problems 67–69, find the value if $a = 1$, $b = 3$, and $c = -10$.

67 $\sqrt{b^2 - 4ac}$

68 $\dfrac{-b + \sqrt{b^2 - 4ac}}{2a}$

69 $\dfrac{-b - \sqrt{b^2 - 4ac}}{2a}$

70 Solve for x if $3x + y = 190$ and $y = 5x - 10$.

71 Solve $|x - 5| = 12$ for all values of x that make the equation a true statement.

MATHEMATICAL EXCURSION

THE GOLDEN RATIO
From ancient temples to modern art

Mathematics can be applied to art and architecture in fascinating ways. Let's look at a rectangle in which the lengths of the sides are related according to the equation $\dfrac{x + y}{x} = \dfrac{x}{y}$.

Artists and architects from the ancient Greeks to Le Corbusier and Mondrian in our own century have felt that this rectangle was unusually pleasing visually. They have called it the Golden Rectangle and have incorporated it into many of their designs.

In this rectangle, the ratio of length to width is an irrational number, approximately 1.61803, that has a habit of popping up in unexpected places. For example, consider the sequence of numbers called the Fibonacci sequence, in which each number is found by adding the two previous numbers.

1, 1, 2, 3, 5, 8, 13, 21, 34, 55, 89, . . .

Find the next three numbers in the sequence. Then use a calculator to divide each number by the preceding number. What can you say about each quotient?

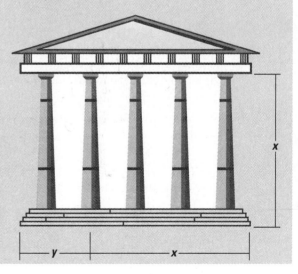

SPECIAL RELATIONSHIPS

Objectives

After studying this section, you will be able to
- Multiply by -1 to find the opposite of a quantity
- Find the reciprocal of a number
- Multiply two matrices

Part One: Introduction

Multiplying by -1

The relationships below show that the opposite of a number can be found by multiplying by -1.

The opposite of 12 is -12, and $-1(12) = -12$.
The opposite of -4 is 4, and $-1(-4) = 4$.

Now we can find the opposite of a quantity by multiplying the quantity by -1.

The opposite of $(x - 2)$ is $-x + 2$, and
$-1(x - 2) = -1(x) - (-1)(2) = -x + 2$.
The opposite of $(x + 5)$ is $-x - 5$,
and $-1(x + 5) = -1(x) + (-1)(5) = -x + (-5) = -x - 5$.

➤➤ *The opposite of x, written $-x$, is $-1(x)$.*
The opposite of a quantity $(x + y)$, written
$-(x + y)$, is $-1(x + y)$.

Reciprocals

The *reciprocal* of a nonzero number $\frac{p}{q}$ is the number $\frac{q}{p}$. The following pairs of numbers are reciprocals.

$$\frac{3}{4} \text{ and } \frac{4}{3} \qquad \frac{-22}{7} \text{ and } \frac{7}{-22} \qquad \frac{1}{-13} \text{ and } -13$$

Notice that reciprocals always have the same sign and their product is always 1.

On a calculator, a reciprocal can be found by using the $\boxed{1/x}$ key.

To find the reciprocal of 2.3, enter 2.3 $\boxed{1/x}$. The result is approximately 0.434782608.

Multiplying Matrices

To multiply matrices, we perform row-by-column calculations, matching each row in one matrix with each column in the other.

Example *Multiply the matrices M and N.*

$$M = \begin{bmatrix} 4 & 5 \\ -3 & 2 \end{bmatrix} \quad N = \begin{bmatrix} -6 & 7 \\ 1 & -8 \end{bmatrix}$$

To multiply matrices M and N, we do row-by-column calculations as shown below.

Column 1

Row 1 $\begin{bmatrix} 4 & 5 \end{bmatrix}\begin{bmatrix} -6 \\ 1 \end{bmatrix}$

$= (4)(-6) + (5)(1)$
$= -24 + 5$
$= -19$

The element -19 will be in Row 1, Column 1, of the new matrix.

Column 2

Row 1 $\begin{bmatrix} 4 & 5 \end{bmatrix}\begin{bmatrix} 7 \\ -8 \end{bmatrix}$

$= (4)(7) + (5)(-8)$
$= 28 + (-40)$
$= -12$

The element -12 will be in Row 1, Column 2, of the new matrix.

Column 1

Row 2 $\begin{bmatrix} -3 & 2 \end{bmatrix}\begin{bmatrix} -6 \\ 1 \end{bmatrix}$

$= (-3)(-6) + (2)(1)$
$= 18 + 2$
$= 20$

The element 20 will be in Row 2, Column 1, of the new matrix.

Column 2

Row 2 $\begin{bmatrix} -3 & 2 \end{bmatrix}\begin{bmatrix} 7 \\ -8 \end{bmatrix}$

$= (-3)(7) + (2)(-8)$
$= -21 + (-16)$
$= -37$

The element -37 will be in Row 2, Column 2, of the new matrix.

The answer is the matrix $MN = \begin{bmatrix} -19 & -12 \\ 20 & -37 \end{bmatrix}$ Row 1, Row 2 (Column 1, Column 2)

Part Two: Sample Problems

Problem 1 *Solve $\frac{-3}{5}x = -24$.*

Solution We multiply both sides of the equation by the reciprocal of the coefficient of x.

$$\frac{-3}{5}x = -24$$

$$\left(\frac{5}{-3}\right)\left(\frac{-3}{5}x\right) = \left(\frac{5}{-3}\right)(-24)$$

$$x = 40$$

Problem 2 *Simplify $3x - (4 - 2x)$.*

Solution First, we find the opposite of the quantity $(4 - 2x)$.

$3x - (4 - 2x)$
$= 3x + (-1)(4 - 2x)$
$= 3x + (-1)(4) + (-1)(-2x)$
$= 3x + (-4) + 2x$
$= 5x - 4$

Problem 3 *Multiply.*

$$\begin{bmatrix} 3 & -2 \\ -4 & 7 \end{bmatrix}\begin{bmatrix} 5 \\ -6 \end{bmatrix}$$

Solution

Column 1

$$\textbf{Row 1}\begin{bmatrix} 3 & -2 \end{bmatrix}\begin{bmatrix} 5 \\ -6 \end{bmatrix}$$

$$= (3)(5) + (-2)(-6)$$
$$= 27$$

Column 1

$$\textbf{Row 2}\begin{bmatrix} -4 & 7 \end{bmatrix}\begin{bmatrix} 5 \\ -6 \end{bmatrix}$$

$$= (-4)(5) + (7)(-6)$$
$$= -62$$

The product is

$$\begin{bmatrix} 27 \\ -62 \end{bmatrix}$$

Problem 4 *Evaluate* $(-5)^2$ *and* -5^2.

Solution Be careful! The expression $(-5)^2 \neq -5^2$. The expression -5^2 means the opposite of 5^2.

$$(-5)^2 = (-5)(-5) \qquad\qquad -5^2 = (-1)5^2$$
$$= 25 \qquad\qquad\qquad = (-1)(5)(5)$$
$$= -25$$

Part Three: Exercises and Problems

Warm-up Exercises

In problems 1–4, multiply.

1 $-1(x - 3)$ **2** $-1\left(-\frac{3}{5}\right)$ **3** $(-3)\left(-\frac{1}{3}\right)$ **4** $\left(5\frac{2}{3}\right)\left(-\frac{1}{17}\right)$

In problems 5–8, find the reciprocal.

5 1.5 **6** $2\frac{1}{4}$ **7** -2.3 **8** $-3\frac{2}{5}$

In problems 9 and 10, multiply the matrices.

9 $\begin{bmatrix} -3 & 2 \\ 4 & -1 \end{bmatrix}\begin{bmatrix} 0 & 4 \\ -2 & 3 \end{bmatrix}$ **10** $\begin{bmatrix} -5 & 1 \\ 2 & 3 \end{bmatrix}\begin{bmatrix} -2 \\ 0 \end{bmatrix}$

In problems 11 and 12, find the opposite of the quantity.

11 $(3x - 4)$ **12** $(-5b + 3c - 8)$

Problem Set

In problems 13–22, find the reciprocal of each number.

13 $\frac{15}{4}$ **14** -22 **15** $\frac{5}{-7}$ ▦ **16** $\sqrt{2}\frac{1}{\sqrt{2}}$ or

17 $3\frac{1}{2}$ ▦ **18** 3.5 **19** $\frac{2}{3}$ ▦ **20** $\sqrt{10}$

21 -0.8 ▦ **22** $\pi \frac{1}{\pi}$ or

In problems 23–25, solve each equation.

23 $-\frac{2}{3}x = 14$ **24** $-(x - 4) = -17$ **25** $\frac{-1}{2}x = -9.2$

26 If $(x, y) = (-2, 14)$, find the perimeter of the rectangle.

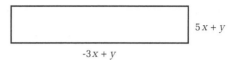

$5x + y$

$-3x + y$

In problems 27–32, solve each equation.

27 $\frac{2}{3}x = 1$ **28** $\frac{1}{x} = \frac{2}{3}$ **29** $-y = 32$

30 $(-1)y = -3.5$ **31** $-7.5y = 7.5$ **32** $\frac{3}{5}y = -\frac{3}{5}$

33 If $(x_1, y_1) = (4, 1)$, $(x_2, y_2) = (9, -11)$, and $d = \sqrt{(x_2 - x_1)^2 + (y_2 - y_1)^2}$, find the value of d.

In problems 34 and 35, simplify each expression.

34 $-3a + 7a + 9a$ **35** $(7y_1 - 19y_1)(-3)$

In problems 36–38, solve each equation.

36 $\frac{2}{3}y = 0$ **37** $-16 + \frac{4}{7}k = 4$ **38** $-13 = -6.5x$

39 Find the area of the rectangle for each value of x.

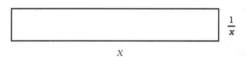

$\frac{1}{x}$

x

 a $x = 7$ **b** $x = 1.39$

 c $x = \frac{1}{3}$ **d** $x = \sqrt{7}$

In problems 40 and 41, graph the numbers on a number line. Then graph the reciprocals of these numbers on the same number line.

40 $1, 2, 3, 4, 5, 6$ **41** $-6, -5, -4, -3, -2, -1$

42 Multiply the matrices.

$$\begin{bmatrix} 5 & 9 \\ -4 & -8 \end{bmatrix} \begin{bmatrix} 5 & -3 \\ -2 & 11 \end{bmatrix}$$

In problems 43 and 44, evaluate each expression if $(x, y) = (-3, 5)$.

43 $x^2 + y^2$ **44** $(x + y)^2$

45 Is the equation $(-x)^2 = -x^2$ true Always, Sometimes, or Never? Explain.

In problems 46–49, simplify each expression.

46 $\frac{1}{2}(8x - 12) + 4(2x + 11)$ **47** $-(x - y) - (x + y)$

48 $-4(6y - 6x) - 2(6y - 3x)$ **49** $-(3x + 2y - 5z) - (5z - 2y)$

50 If a number is picked at random from $\left\{-2.7, -\frac{3}{5}, 0, 4, \frac{19}{2}\right\}$, determine the probability that the number does not have a reciprocal.

In problems 51–54, solve each equation.

51 $8k + 36 = 0$ **52** $-100 = 25(2x - 90)$

53 $4x - (2x - 4) = 26$ **54** $-(x - 2)x = 0$

In problems 55–58, find the opposite of the reciprocal of each number.

55 2 **56** $-\frac{2}{3}$ **57** $\frac{4}{5}$ **58** 0.125

In problems 59 and 60, multiply the matrices.

59 $-2\begin{bmatrix} 4 & -6 \\ 2 & 8 \end{bmatrix}\begin{bmatrix} 3 \\ 5 \end{bmatrix}$ **60** $\begin{bmatrix} 1 & 0 \\ 0 & 1 \end{bmatrix}\begin{bmatrix} 3.7 & -4.8 \\ -16 & 13.7 \end{bmatrix}$

61 Refer to the figure.

a Write an expression for the area of the shaded region.

b Find the area of the shaded region if $a = b = 4$ ft and $c = d = 9$ ft.

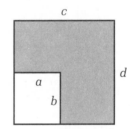

62 Solve for y if $3x + 2y = .49$ and $x = y + 2$.

63 A chemical reaction in one reaction chamber manufactures a chemical at the rate of 4 grams per hour. In another reaction chamber, the temperature is 50° lower, and the chemical is manufactured at a rate equal to the reciprocal of the rate in the hotter chamber. The cooler chamber starts to produce chemical 10 hours before the hotter one. Let $t =$ the number of hours the hotter chamber has been manufacturing chemical.

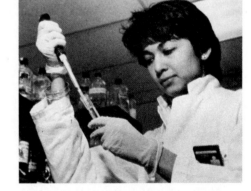

a Write an expression for the amount of chemical manufactured by the hotter chamber.

b Write an expression for the amount of chemical manufactured in the cooler chamber after t hours.

c Write an equation that can be used to calculate how many hours it will take before the hotter chamber has manufactured as much of the chemical as the cooler one.

In problems 64–68, determine whether each statement is true Always, Sometimes, or Never.

64 If two numbers are reciprocals, their product is 1.

65 The sum of a number and its reciprocal is greater than the number.

66 The reciprocal of a positive integer is less than 1.

67 The reciprocal of the reciprocal of x is x (if x ≠ 0).

68 The opposite of the reciprocal of a positive integer is less than or equal to −1.

69 If a number is chosen at random from along $\overline{AB}$, what is the probability that its reciprocal will be a point on $\overline{CD}$?

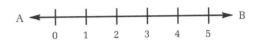

In problems 70 and 71, consider the following matrices.

$$L = \begin{bmatrix} -1 & -2 \\ 4 & -2 \end{bmatrix} \qquad M = \begin{bmatrix} 3 & -4 \\ -2 & 6 \end{bmatrix} \qquad N = \begin{bmatrix} 5 & 7 \\ -3 & 10 \end{bmatrix}$$

If you have access to a computer, use the following BASIC program, which will multiply two 2 × 2 matrices and give a 2 × 2 matrix as the product.

```
10 REM     Multiply two 2 X 2 matrices
20 PRINT   "What is the top row of the first matrix"
30 INPUT   "(Separate the elements by a comma)"; a, b
40 INPUT   "What is the bottom row of the first
           matrix"; c, d
50 INPUT   "What is the top row of the second matrix";
           e, f
60 INPUT   "What is the bottom row of the second
           matrix"; g, h
70 REM     Compute product
80         I = A*E + B*G
90         J = A*F + B*H
100        K = C*E + D*G
110        L = C*F + D*H
120 PRINT: Print "the product is"
130 PRINT: Print i, j
140 PRINT: Print k, l
150 END
```

70 a Evaluate LM and ML.
 b Evaluate MN and NM.
 c Draw a conclusion from your results.

71 a Evaluate (LM) · N and L · (MN).
 b Evaluate (NL) · M and N · (LM).
 c Draw a conclusion from your results.

MORE PROPERTIES OF EQUALITY AND OPERATIONS

Objectives

After studying this section, you will be able to
- Determine whether a set is closed under a given operation
- Identify more properties of algebra used in simplifying expressions and solving equations and inequalities

Part One: Introduction

Closure Properties

If set A is $\{-1, 0, 1\}$, what happens if you pick any pair of numbers from the set (you may pick the same number twice) and multiply? Is the product always in set A?

$$
\begin{array}{lll}
(-1)(-1) = 1 & (-1)(0) = 0 & (-1)(1) = -1 \\
(0)(0) = 0 & (0)(1) = 0 & (1)(1) = 1
\end{array}
$$

Yes, the product of any two numbers in set A is also a member of set A. Set A is closed under multiplication.

What happens if you add all possible pairs of elements in set A? Is the sum always in set A? The answer is no. Add $1 + 1$. The sum, 2, is not in set A. Set A is not closed under addition.

The Closure Property

A set *S* is closed under the operation ☆ if whenever *a* and *b* are in *S*, *a* ☆ *b* is in *S*.

Example Is $\{0, 1, 2, 3, \ldots\}$ *closed under addition? Under subtraction?*

The set of whole numbers is closed under addition because the sum of any two whole numbers is another whole number.

The set of whole numbers is not closed under subtraction since $2 - 4 = -2$, which is not a whole number.

To show a set is *not closed* under an operation, it is necessary to find only one example that has a result not in the set. To show a set is *closed* under an operation, you need to show that every possible case has a result that is in the set. Since you will not always be able to try every case, try enough cases to convince yourself.

More Properties of Algebra

The following list of properties includes some properties listed in Section 2.6. The properties are true for all real numbers a, b, and c.

Name of Property	Statement	Examples
Addition Identity Property	There is a number 0, called the additive identity, such that $a + 0 = a$ and $0 + a = a$.	$7 + 0 = 7$ $0 + 7 = 7$ $0 + (-2.7) = -2.7$ $-2.7 + 0 = -2.7$
Additive Inverse Property	For every a, there is a number $-a$, called the additive inverse, or opposite, of a, such that $a + (-a) = 0$ and $-a + a = 0$.	Given the number -7, there is a number 7, such that $-7 + 7 = 0$ and $7 + (-7) = 0$. 7 and -7 are additive inverses of each other.
Difference Property	$a - b = a + (-b)$	$3 - 7 = 3 + (-7)$ $9 + (-11) = 9 - 11$
Multiplicative Identity Property	There is a number 1, called the multiplicative identity, such that $a \cdot 1 = a$ and $1 \cdot a = a$.	$(9 \cdot 7)(1) = 9 \cdot 7$ $(1)(9 \cdot 7) = 9 \cdot 7$
Multiplicative Inverse Property	For every number a, $a \neq 0$, there is a number $\frac{1}{a}$, called the multiplicative inverse, or reciprocal of a, such that $a \cdot \frac{1}{a} = 1$ and $\frac{1}{a} \cdot a = 1$.	Given the number 5 there is a number $\frac{1}{5}$, such that $5 \cdot \frac{1}{5} = 1$ and $\frac{1}{5} \cdot 5 = 1$
Multiplication Property of -1	$a(-1) = -a$ and $-1(a) = -a$	$(-3)(-1) = 3$ $(-1)(7) = -7$
Property of the Opposite of a Quantity	$-(a + b) = -1(a + b)$ $\quad = (-a) + (-b)$ $-(a - b) = -1(a - b)$ $\quad = -a + b$	$-(x + 3) = -1(x + 3)$ $\quad = -x - 3$ $-(x - 3) = -1(x - 3)$ $\quad = -x + 3$ $\quad = 3 - x$
Trichotomy Property	Given any two numbers a and b, one of the following must be true. $a > b$ or $a < b$ or $a = b$	If x is not less than y and x is not greater than y, then $x = y$.
Transitive Properties of Inequality	If $a < b$ and $b < c$, then $a < c$. If $a > b$ and $b > c$, then $a > c$.	If $-3 < -1$ and -1 is < 2, then $-3 < 2$. If $20 > 11$ and $11 > 10\frac{1}{2}$, then $20 > 10\frac{1}{2}$.

Example   Determine which is larger, $\frac{2}{3}$ or 0.68.

It is easier to compare numbers that are in the same form. So, let's change $\frac{2}{3}$ to decimal form by dividing 2 by 3.

$$\frac{2}{3} \approx 0.6667$$

Since 0.68 is larger than 0.6667, 0.68 is larger than $\frac{2}{3}$.

Part Two: Sample Problems

Problem 1   Determine whether each statement is True or False.

a The set of positive real numbers is closed under division.
b The set of irrational numbers is closed under addition.
c {0, 1} is closed under subtraction.
d $-a$ is always negative.
e $|a|$ is never negative.
f The set of negative numbers is closed under division.

Solution   **a** True. The quotient of any two positive real numbers is a positive real number.
b False. $\pi + (-\pi) = 0$, which is not irrational.
c False. $0 - 1 = -1$, which is not in {0, 1}.
d False. If $a = -7$, then $-a = -(-7) = 7$.
e True. Distance is not negative.
f False. Negative ÷ negative = positive.

Problem 2   Solve the equation $3x + 59 = 4682$. Give a reason for each step.

Solution   The steps and reasons follow.

a $3x + 59 = 4682$ — Given
b $(3x + 59) + (-59) = 4682 + (-59)$ — Addition Property of Equality
c $3x + [59 + (-59)] = 4682 + (-59)$ — Associative Property of Addition
d $3x + (59 - 59) = 4682 - 59$ — Difference Property
e $3x + 0 = 4623$ — Subtraction
f $3x = 4623$ — Additive Identity Property
g $\frac{3x}{3} = \frac{4623}{3}$ — Division Property of Equality
h $1x = 1541$ — Division
i $x = 1541$ — Multiplicative Identity Property

Problem 3   Determine whether the statement is True or False.
If $a < b$ and $c < d$, then $ac < bd$.

Solution   We can try combinations of positive and negative numbers.

$2 < 3$	$3 < 7$	$-5 < -2$	$-9 < 10$
$4 < 9$	$-4 < 2$	$-6 < -4$	$-5 < -1$
Is $8 < 27$?	Is $-12 < 14$?	Is $30 < 8$?	Is $45 < -10$?
True	True	False	False

We can find at least one contradictory case. The statement is false.

Part Three: Exercises and Problems

Warm-up Exercises

In problems 1–5, determine whether each statement is True or False.

1 The set $\{-1, 1\}$ is closed under division.
2 The set $\{-1, 1\}$ is closed under addition.
3 The set $\{-1, 0, 1\}$ is closed under division.
4 The opposite of a is $-a$.
5 If $a = b$, then $-a = -b$.

In problems 6–9, name the property that justifies each statement.

6 If $a \neq 0$ and a is not positive, then $a < 0$.
7 $-1(3x - 4y) = -3x + 4y$
8 $(7)\left(\frac{1}{7}\right) = 1$
9 $-12a + 0 = -12a$

10 Give a reason for each step.

$$3(5y + 2x)$$
a $= 3(5y) + 3(2x)$
b $= (3 \cdot 5)y + (3 \cdot 2)x$
$$= 15y + 6x$$

Problem Set

11 Determine whether $\{-1, 0, 1\}$ is closed under multiplication. Explain.

12 Determine whether the set of negative integers is closed under subtraction. Explain.

13 Find the area of the rectangle.

14 Supply the missing reasons.

	$43 = 91 - 6x$	Given
a	$-91 + 43 = -91 + 91 - 6x$	
	$-48 = 0 - 6x$	Add. Inv. Prop.
b	$-48 = 0 + (-6x)$	
c	$-48 = -6x$	
d	$\dfrac{-48}{-6} = \dfrac{-6x}{-6}$	
	$8 = 1x$	Division
e	$8 = x$	
f	$x = 8$	

Problem Set, *continued*

In problems 15–18, simplify each expression and solve each equation.

15 $3(2x - 11) - (3x - 23)$

16 $5y + 4(2x_1 + 6y) - x_1$

17 $-3(2k + 12) = 390$

18 $4.6 = 3y + 1.82$

19 A number is added to the reciprocal of 4 to get 7. Find the number.

20 Write an inequality that describes the relationship between each pair of distances.

  a x and y   **b** y and z   **c** x and z

21 Solve for x if $x(x + 3) = 0$.

22 Complete the table of values for the equation $y = -3x + 7$.

x	-5	-4	-3	-2	-1	0	1	2	3	4
y										

23 $4 > 2$ and $2 > -3$. Use the transitive property to determine the relationship between 4 and -3.

24 Supply a reason for each step used to solve $\frac{1}{3}x = 24$.

  a $\frac{1}{3}x = 24$

  b $3\left(\frac{1}{3}x\right) = 3(24)$

  c $\left(3 \cdot \frac{1}{3}\right) x = 3(24)$

  d $1x = 72$

  e $x = 72$

In problems 25–30, name the property illustrated in each statement.

25 $4 + (-4) = 0$

26 $16 \cdot \frac{1}{16} = 1$

27 $17 + 0 = 17$

28 $3 - 4 = 3 + (-4)$

29 $a \div b = a \cdot \frac{1}{b}$

30 $-(3x - y) = -3x + y$

In problems 31–33, evaluate each expression.

$$M = \begin{bmatrix} 2 & -4 \\ -1 & 6 \end{bmatrix} \quad N = \begin{bmatrix} -3 & 7 \\ 9 & -2 \end{bmatrix}$$

31 $M + N$

32 $4N$

33 MN

34 Find all possible pairs of consecutive integers with a product of 30.

35 Simplify $-3(2x + 7) + 4$. Give a reason for each step.

36 Solve for x if $-x(2x + 13) = 0$.

In problems 37 and 38, determine whether each statement is True or False.

37 If $a > b$ and $c < d$, then $a + c > b + d$.

38 If $a < b$ and $c < 0$, then $\frac{a}{c} < \frac{b}{c}$.

39 Find the values of x and y.

$$\begin{bmatrix} 3 & 2x \\ \frac{1}{3}y & 5 \end{bmatrix} = \begin{bmatrix} 3 & -6 \\ 1 & 5 \end{bmatrix}$$

In problems 40–42, solve each equation.

40 $|2x| = 12$ **41** $-3(2x - 5) = 27$ **42** $-4.5x - 12.4 = 6.5$

43 Two numbers have a sum of 12. The reciprocal of their product is $\frac{1}{32}$. Find the two numbers.

44 $M = \begin{bmatrix} a & b \\ c & d \end{bmatrix}$ and X is another matrix.

  a Solve for X if $M + X = M$.
  b Give an appropriate name to Matrix X.
  c Determine the matrix that must be added to M to get X.
  d Give a name to the matrix in part **c**.

45 The Trichotomy Property states that if $x + y \neq 0$, exactly one of the following is true. If $x > 1$ and $y > 1$, determine which statement is true. Explain.

  a $\dfrac{xy}{x + y} > \dfrac{1}{x + y}$ **b** $\dfrac{xy}{x + y} = \dfrac{1}{x + y}$ **c** $\dfrac{xy}{x + y} < \dfrac{1}{x + y}$

In problems 46 and 47, use matrices M and R to evaluate each expression.

$$M = \begin{bmatrix} 2 & 5 \\ 1 & 3 \end{bmatrix} \quad R = \begin{bmatrix} 3 & -5 \\ -1 & 2 \end{bmatrix}$$

46 MR **47** RM

48 The intensity I of light shining on a wall is 60 times the reciprocal of the square of the distance d, in feet, of the light from the wall. The formula is $I = 60 \cdot \dfrac{1}{d^2}$. Find I for each given distance of the light from the wall.

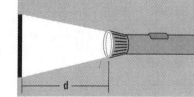

  a 2 feet **b** 4 feet **c** 8 feet

49 If $A = \{\text{all multiples of 3}\} = \{\ldots, -12, -9, -6, -3, 0, 3, 6, 9, \ldots\}$, determine whether A is closed under each operation.

  a addition **b** multiplication **c** subtraction **d** division

LINE GRAPHS, BAR GRAPHS, AND FREQUENCY POLYGONS

Objectives

After studying this section, you will be able to
- Analyze line graphs
- Analyze bar graphs
- Analyze frequency polygons

Line Graphs

The numbers below represent the numbers of games won by the Apollo High School football team in the 22 seasons from 1966 through 1987. The team never played more than 12 games per season.

1, 2, 4, 5, 6, 5, 7, 5, 8, 8, 9, 4, 7, 5, 6, 10, 8, 7, 6, 8, 9, 8

One way to show the frequency of each number of wins is to use a ***line graph.*** To do this, we draw a horizontal line and mark it to represent the number of possible wins per season. Above each number on the line, we place an x to represent each season the team won that number of games.

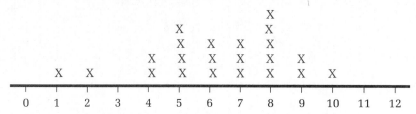

Number of Wins per Season for the Apollo H. S. Football Team
1966–1987

Problem 1   *Use the graph to determine each of the following.*

    a *The greatest number of wins per season*
    b *The total number of wins Apollo's team had in 22 years*
    c *The number of times Apollo won 4 games in a season*
    d *The number of wins per season that had the greatest frequency*
    e *The greatest number of losses per season*

Solution   **a** The greatest number of wins was 10.
    b The sum of all 22 numbers is 138.
    c Apollo won 4 games in a season two times.
    d The number of wins per season with the greatest frequency is 8, which occurs 5 times.
    e The answer cannot be determined from the given data. Why not?

Bar Graphs

You can show the same data on the frequency of Apollo's wins per season by using a *vertical* or *horizontal bar graph.*

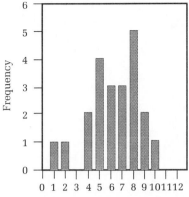

Number of Wins per Season for the
Apollo H.S. Football Team 1966-1987

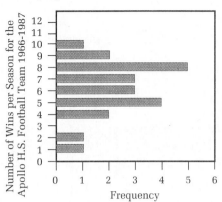

Let's suppose that you now have a record of the number of losses as well as the number of wins in each season. Both types of information can be represented on a double bar graph.

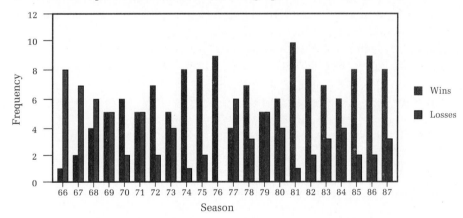

Problem 2   Use the graph to determine each of the following.

    a The year Apollo won the most games and the number of games it won
    b The percentage of the 22 years Apollo won more games than it lost
    c The average number of losses per season from 1966 to 1987
    d The years Apollo won 50% of its games.

Solution   **a** Apollo won the most games, 10, in 1981.

    b Apollo had a winning season $\frac{15}{22} \approx 0.68$, or 68% of the time.

    c Apollo lost an average of $\frac{77}{22}$, or 3.5 games per season.

    d The answer cannot be determined. There may have been ties.

Frequency Polygons

Data represented by a bar graph can also be represented by a *frequency polygon*, or broken line graph. A frequency polygon is formed by connecting consecutive points representing the data. The graph shows two frequency polygons for the wins and losses of the Apollo football team.

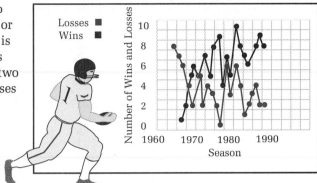

Problem 3   *Use the frequency polygon to determine the following.*

a *In how many years the number of wins exceeded the number of losses*

b *In how many years the number of wins equaled the number of losses*

c *In what years the number of losses exceeded the number of wins*

d *In what years the number of losses exceeded 50% of the games played during the season*

e *In what year the team attained its 100th victory during the 22-season time period*

Solution   **a** Wins exceeded losses in 15 years.

b Wins equaled losses in 3 years.

c Losses exceeded wins in 1966, 1967, 1968, and 1977.

d The answer cannot be determined because there may have been tie games.

e The team had its 100th victory in 1982.

Problem Set

1 The chart records the number of days in each year from 1975 through 1985 that snow fell in the town of Fairmont, Wyoming.

Year	1975	1976	1977	1978	1979	1980	1981	1982	1983	1984	1985
Number of Snow Days	23	18	16	20	22	11	10	13	25	17	26

a Draw a line graph and a bar graph for the data.

b In what year did the greatest increase in number of snow days from the previous year occur?

c Determine the year in which the greatest amount of snow fell.

d Determine which 3-year period had the fewest days of snow.

2 Refer to the bar graph.

a What percentage of the freshmen made the honor roll in 1985?

b Could more sophomores have made the honor roll in 1985 than in 1986? Explain.

c Find the class and year that had the smallest percentage of students making the honor roll.

d If there were 420 juniors in 1986, determine how many juniors did not make the honor roll.

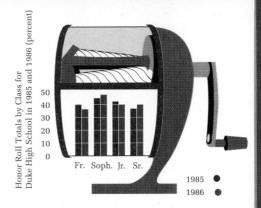

Honor Roll Totals by Class for Duke High School in 1985 and 1986 (percent)

1985 ●
1986 ●

3 The table represents the average high and average low temperatures for July in nine U.S. cities.

a Draw a frequency polygon for the average high and average low temperatures.

b Which city has the least difference between the average high and average low temperature? The greatest difference?

City	Average High	Average Low
Denver	87°F	59°F
Honolulu	83°	74°
Las Vegas	102°	68°
Los Angeles	75°	60°
Miami	88°	76°
New York	85°	70°
Phoenix	104°	77°
San Francisco	69°	51°
Washington	88°	70°

4 The graph shows the results of a survey in Littleton, New York. It shows the percentages of households having certain products.

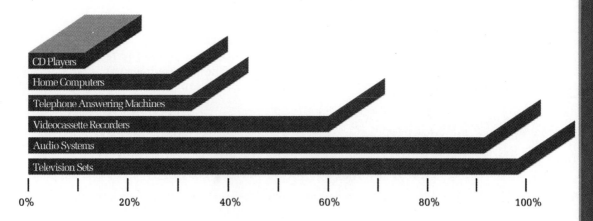

CD Players
Home Computers
Telephone Answering Machines
Videocassette Recorders
Audio Systems
Television Sets

0%   20%   40%   60%   80%   100%

a Find the approximate number of households having each product if there are 3920 households in Littleton.

b Express the number of households having compact disc players as a percentage of those having home computers.

c Determine the approximate number of households that do not have telephone answering machines.

CHAPTER SUMMARY

CONCEPTS AND PROCEDURES

After studying this chapter, you should be able to

- Represent real numbers on the number line and classify real numbers as natural, whole, integer, rational, or irrational (3.1)
- Find the absolute value, the opposite, and the reciprocal of a real number (3.2) (3.6)
- Use inequality symbols with real numbers (3.2)
- Graph inequalities (3.2)
- Add like terms with signed coefficients (3.3)
- Add, subtract, multiply, and divide signed numbers, with and without a calculator (3.3) (3.4) (3.5)
- Find the opposites of quantities (3.4) (3.6)
- Multiply matrices (3.6)
- Determine whether a set is closed under a given operation (3.7)
- Use the properties discussed in this chapter and in Chapter 2 to solve equations and inequalities (3.7)
- Analyze line graphs, bar graphs, and frequency polygons (3.8)

VOCABULARY

absolute value (3.2)
additive inverse (3.2)
coefficient (3.3)
counting number (3.1)
frequency polygon (3.8)
horizontal bar graph (3.8)
integer (3.1)
irrational number (3.1)
line graph (3.8)
natural number (3.1)

negative number (3.1)
opposites (3.2)
positive number (3.1)
rational number (3.1)
real number (3.1)
reciprocal (3.6)
scalar (3.5)
scalar multiplication (3.5)
vertical bar graph (3.8)
whole number (3.1)

PROPERTIES (3.7)

Additive Identity Property
Additive Inverse Property
Closure Property
Density Property
Difference Property
Multiplicative Identity Property

Multiplicative Inverse Property
Multiplication Property of -1
Property of the Opposite of a Quantity
Trichotomy Property
Transitive Properties of Inequality

REVIEW PROBLEMS

In problems 1–6, evaluate each expression.

1 $-8(-12) + 16(-3)$

2 $8 - (-6)(4)$

3 $\dfrac{(-3)(4) - 12}{-8}$

4 $(-3)^2 + (-2)^2$

5 $(-3 + -2)^2$

6 $|-3|^2 + |-2|^2$

In problems 7–10, evaluate each expression for $x = -3$ and $y = 2$.

7 $x^2 + y^2$

8 $(x + y)^2$

9 $y^2 - x^2$

10 $(y - x)(y + x)$

11 Solve for x if $3x + 4y = 18$ and $y = 6$.

In problems 12–17, simplify each expression.

12 $3x - (2x + 4)$

13 $(-8x)(4 - 4)$

14 $-(3x + 5y) - (6x - 3y)$

15 $3(2x + 5) + 4x - 1$

16 $4(2a - 3b) - (2a - b)$

17 $\frac{1}{2}(6x - 12y) - (3x - 6y)$

18 Let $a = (-1)^3(-5)(6)$, $b = (-3)^2(5)^3(-4)$, $c = 5 + (-8) + (-2)$, and $d = (-1)^3 + (-5) + 6$. One of the numbers a, b, c, or d is chosen at random.

a Find the probability that the number is positive.
b Find the probability that the number is negative.
c Find the probability that the number is neither positive nor negative.

In problems 19–24, solve each equation.

19 $13x + 147 = -73$

20 $-(2x - 4) = -23$

21 $\frac{4}{5}x - 7 = -39$

22 $2(3x - 4) = -25$

23 $12 - 18 = -4(2x - 7) - 3x$

24 $-2x(3x - 12) = 0$

In problems 25–28, simplify.

25 $-3 \begin{bmatrix} -18 & 7 \\ -5 & -4 \end{bmatrix}$

26 $\begin{bmatrix} -5.1 & 14.6 \\ 11.8 & -5.17 \end{bmatrix} - \begin{bmatrix} 16.4 & 12.9 \\ -5.5 & -2.7 \end{bmatrix}$

27 $\begin{bmatrix} 4 & -5 \\ -2 & 10 \end{bmatrix}\begin{bmatrix} 6 \\ 15 \end{bmatrix}$

28 $\frac{3}{4}\begin{bmatrix} -16 & -20 \\ 24 & 22 \end{bmatrix}$

29 Express the rational number $\frac{23}{11}$ in decimal form.

In problems 30 and 31, graph each inequality on a number line.

30 $x < -4$

31 $y \geq -2$

Review Problems, *continued*

In problems 32–35, solve each equation.

32 $9x + 158 = 23$ **33** $6k - 42 = 0$

34 $15 = 8y - 161$ **35** $3m - 98 = -17$

36 Match each point on the graph with its coordinate from the list below.

$$-3.5, \ -2\tfrac{1}{2}, \ -1\tfrac{1}{2}, \ -0.5, \ 0, \ 1, \ 1.5, \ 2$$

37 Express the rational number 103.001 as $\dfrac{\text{an integer}}{\text{a natural number}}$.

38 Arrange the following numbers in order, from least to greatest.

$$\tfrac{2}{3} \quad -8 \quad \tfrac{3}{4} \quad 0.66 \quad -4 \quad -3.7 \quad 0$$

39 Approximate $5\sqrt{3} + 7\sqrt{3} - 18\sqrt{3}$ to the nearest hundredth.

40 If 2 is subtracted from a number and the difference is multiplied by 3, the result is 54. What is the original number?

41 Jim and his cousin Sue start running from the same point on a quarter-mile (1320-foot) oval track. Jim travels counterclockwise at 4.5 feet per second, and Sue travels clockwise at 3 feet per second. Let t represent the number of seconds they run.

  a Write an expression for the distance that Jim travels in t seconds.

  b Write an expression for the distance that Sue travels in t seconds.

  c Determine how far each of them has traveled after 10 seconds.

  d After how many seconds will Jim and Sue meet?

  e Determine how far Jim has traveled from his starting point when they meet for the second time.

In problems 42–47, evaluate each expression using matrices M and A.

$$M = \begin{bmatrix} 5 & -8 \\ -9 & 0 \end{bmatrix} \qquad A = \begin{bmatrix} -8 & -3 \\ 4 & -5 \end{bmatrix}$$

42 $M + A$ **43** $A + M$ **44** $A - M$

45 $M - A$ **46** MA **47** AM

In problems 48–50, solve each equation.

48 $|x_1| = 12$ **49** $|x_3| = 0$ **50** $|x_2| = -2$

51 Connie is paid a regular hourly wage of $12.75 per hour. She is paid time-and-a-half for any time she works after 8 hours per day.

  a How much did Connie earn if she worked 10 hours on Wednesday?
  b How many hours did Connie work if she earned $168.96 on Wednesday?

52 The perimeter of the rectangle is 36. Find the length and width of the rectangle.

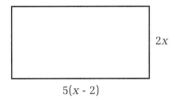

In problems 53–55, evaluate each expression if $(x_1, y_1) = (-3, 4)$ and $(x_2, y_2) = (5, -7)$.

53 $\dfrac{y_2 - y_1}{x_2 - x_1}$ **54** $\left(\dfrac{x_1 + x_2}{2}, \dfrac{y_1 + y_2}{2}\right)$

55 $\sqrt{(x_2 - x_1)^2 + (y_2 - y_1)^2}$

56 Refer to the figure.

  a If the perimeter is 382, solve for x.
  b Find the area of the figure.

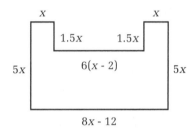

57 A number is chosen at random from the following set.

$$\left\{\tfrac{1}{3}, \tfrac{1}{2}, \tfrac{9}{10}, 1, 2, 2.5, 3, 8, 12\right\}$$

  a Determine the probability that the reciprocal of the chosen number is less than 1.
  b Determine the probability that the reciprocal of the chosen number is greater than or equal to 1.

58 Refer to the graph of precipitation in Seattle.

  a During which month does Seattle experience the most precipitation? The least precipitation?
  b On average, how much rain falls in September?
  c On average, how much precipitation falls in Seattle over the course of a year?
  d What percentage of the entire year's annual precipitation falls during December and January?

59 Find all real numbers with additive inverses that are equal to their multiplicative inverses.

1 A number is chosen at random from the following group.
$\frac{22}{7}$ $\sqrt{9}$ 0   123.45101114 . . .
Find the probability of the number's belonging to each set.
  a Natural numbers   **b** Rational numbers   **c** Real numbers

2 Determine whether the following statement is true Always, Sometimes, or Never: If x and y are real numbers and $x \neq y$, there is a real number between x and y.

3 Solve the equation $16(x - 4) + (-12x) = -10 + (-13)$ for x.

4 Simplify the expression $6x^2 - (8x - 9x^2) + x$.

5 Determine whether $\dfrac{(-4.5)^5 (2.7)^2}{(-2.8)^{32}}$ is positive, negative, or zero.

6 Rita begins at -14 on the number line. She moves 8 units to the right and then 10 units to the left. She then moves m units to the right and ends up at 26. Find m.

In problems 7–9, find the opposite of the reciprocal.
7 2   **8** $-\frac{2}{3}$ **9** 0.125

10 Find the value of y.
$$\begin{bmatrix} 3 & -5 \\ -4 & -2 \end{bmatrix}\begin{bmatrix} -6 \\ 8 \end{bmatrix} = \begin{bmatrix} x + 3 \\ x + y \end{bmatrix}$$

11 Is $\{-3, 1, 0, 1, 3\}$ closed under subtraction? Under division? Why or why not?

12 Refer to the graph.
  a Find the total number of points scored by Bill, Al, and Robert.
  b Find the average number of points scored by the five players.

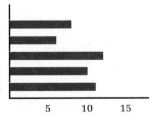

Points scored against S. Kore High

In problems 13 and 14, graph each inequality.
13 $x > -3$ **14** $2.3 \geq x$

PUZZLES AND CHALLENGES

1 Continue each pattern.

 a 1, 1, 2, 3, 5, 8, 13, . . .

 b 12, 1, 1, 1, 2, 1, . . .

 c O, T, T, F, F, S, . . .

2 Replace each letter with a unique digit to make the multiplication problem correct.

$$\begin{array}{r} A\ B\ C\ D\ E \\ \times\qquad 4 \\ \hline E\ D\ C\ B\ A \end{array}$$

3 Find a common English word that contains all five vowels in alphabetical order.

4 Explain the rule for the following number arrangement.

8,   5,   4,   9,   1,   7,   6,   3,   2,   0

5 Someone in the law firm of Smith, Ross, and Vincent has been embezzling funds. The police have taken the following statements. Exactly one statement is true.

Smith: Vincent did it.

Ross: I didn't do it.

Vincent: Smith lied when she said I did it.

Who was the guilty party?

6 Interpret each of the following.

 a MOMANON

 b MYSELF I'M

 c WHO'S
    FIRST

 d IEIEIECEIIEIEIEIECEICEIIEIE

 e WATER
    SWIMMING

 f WEAR
    LONG

 g THAT

 h BJAOCKX

4 WORKING WITH EQUATIONS

S tructures grow, shrink, shiver, and breathe. In cool weather, the huge steel cables of a suspension bridge contract, making the arch of the bridge's central span steeper. In high winds, the bridge may act like an airplane wing, causing the deck to twist and bow outward.

Measuring the health of huge structures such as bridges can be as complex as finding the cause of a person's illness. Diagnostic engineers use techniques such as radar to "see" a structure's reinforcing bars, just as physicians use X-rays to diagnose a person's physical problem. Engineers may also send sound waves into the concrete to check for cracks, empty spaces, or places where segments have failed to bond with one another. Once a structural problem is found, the engineer can prescribe an appropriate cure.

4.1 EQUATIONS WITH VARIABLES ON BOTH SIDES

Objective

After studying this section, you will be able to

■ Solve equations with a variable term on both sides

Part One: Introduction

A Variable Term on Both Sides

In equations such as $3x - 5 = 2x + 12$, the variable term appears on both sides of the equation. A strategy for solving equations like $3x - 5 = 2x + 12$ is to change the problem to one where the variable term is only on one side. This is a type of equation you know how to solve.

Example

Solve $3x - 5 = 2x + 12$.

By subtracting 2x from each side, you will get an equation with the variable term only on one side, an equation you know how to solve.

Add 5 to both sides

$$3x - 5 = 2x + 12$$
$$3x - 5 - 2x = 2x + 12 - 2x$$
$$x - 5 = 12$$
$$\underline{+ 5 \qquad\qquad + 5}$$
$$x = 17$$

Check

Left Side	Right Side
$3x - 5$	$2x + 12$
$= 3(17) - 5$	$= 2(17) + 12$
$= 51 - 5$	$= 34 + 12$
$= 46$	$= 46$

If $x = 17$, the sides are equal, so the answer checks.

Example

The perimeter of a deck is 8x + 84.

a Write an equation for the perimeter of the deck.
b Solve your equation for x.

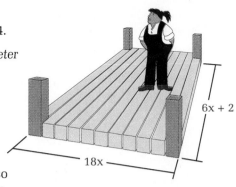

6x + 2

18x

The perimeter is 8x + 84. It is also 2(6x + 2) + 2(18x), so an equation for the perimeter is
Simplify the right side
Combine like terms
Subtract 8x from each side

$$8x + 84 = 2(6x + 2) + 2(18x)$$
$$8x + 84 = 12x + 4 + 36x$$
$$8x + 84 = 48x + 4$$
$$8x + 84 - 8x = 48x + 4 - 8x$$

$$84 = 40x + 4$$

Subtract 4 from each side

$$\frac{-4 \qquad\qquad -4}{80 = 40x}$$

Divide both sides by 40

$$\frac{80}{40} = \frac{40x}{40}$$

$$2 = x$$

Check

Left Side	Right Side
8x + 84	2(6x + 2) + 2(18x)
= 8(2) + 84	= 2[6(2) + 2] + 2[18(2)]
= 16 + 84	= 2(14) + 2(36)
= 100	= 28 + 72
	= 100

If x = 2, the sides are equal, so the solution checks.

Part Two: Sample Problems

Problem 1 Solve for z if 4.1z − 56.8 = 6.2 − 4.5z.

Solution We will isolate the variable on one side of the equation.

$$4.1z - 56.8 = 6.2 - 4.5z$$

Add 4.5z to both sides

$$\frac{+ 4.5z \qquad\qquad + 4.5z}{8.6z - 56.8 = 6.2}$$

Add 56.8 to both sides

$$\frac{+ 56.8 + 56.8}{8.6z = 63}$$

Divide both sides by 8.6

$$\frac{8.6z}{8.6} = \frac{63}{8.6}$$

$$z \approx 7.3$$

We rounded this answer to the nearest tenth because that was the degree of accuracy of the other numbers in the problem.

Problem 2 Solve for x_1 if $24 - 2x_1 = 7x_1 + 11x_1 - (3x_1 + 10)$.

Solution We will isolate the variable on one side of the equation. First we need to find the opposite of $(3x_1 + 10)$. The opposite of a quantity is the opposite of each term in the quantity.

$$24 - 2x_1 = 7x_1 + 11x_1 - (3x_1 + 10)$$
$$24 - 2x_1 = 7x_1 + 11x_1 - 3x_1 - 10$$
$$24 - 2x_1 = 15x_1 - 10$$

Add 2x to both sides
$$\underline{+\,2x_1 \qquad\qquad +\,2x_1}$$
$$24 \qquad\quad = 17x_1 - 10$$

Add 10 to both sides
$$\underline{+10 \qquad\qquad\qquad +10}$$
$$34 \qquad\quad = 17x_1$$

Divide both sides by 17
$$\frac{34}{17} = \frac{17x_1}{17}$$
$$2 = x_1$$

Be sure to check.

Problem 3 Solve for y if $3y^2 - 12y - 4 = 5y + 3y^2$.

Solution

$$3y^2 - 12y - 4 = 5y + 3y^2$$

Subtract $3y^2$ from both sides
$$\underline{-\,3y^2 \qquad\qquad\qquad -\,3y^2}$$
$$-12y - 4 = 5y$$

Add 12y to both sides
$$\underline{+\,12y \qquad\qquad +\,12y}$$
$$-4 = 17y$$

Divide both sides by 17
Because no directions are given, we round to two decimal places.
$$\frac{-4}{17} = \frac{17y}{17}$$
$$-0.24 \approx y$$

Check
A calculator is useful for this check. Enter

4 $\boxed{+/-}$ $\boxed{\div}$ 17 $\boxed{=}$ $\boxed{\text{STO}}$

This sequence stores the most accurate approximation for y in the calculator's memory, allowing us to find the most accurate approximations for the left and right sides of the equation.

Left Side
$3y^2 - 12y - 4$

Enter 3 $\boxed{\times}$ $\boxed{\text{RCL}}$ $\boxed{x^2}$ $\boxed{-}$ 12 $\boxed{\times}$ $\boxed{\text{RCL}}$ $\boxed{-}$ 4 $\boxed{=}$

The display shows -1.010380623.

Right Side
$5y + 3y^2$

Enter 5 $\boxed{\times}$ $\boxed{\text{RCL}}$ $\boxed{+}$ 3 $\boxed{\times}$ $\boxed{\text{RCL}}$ $\boxed{x^2}$ $\boxed{=}$

The display shows -1.010380623.

If $y = \frac{-4}{17}$, the sides are equal, so it checks.

Part Three: Exercises and Problems

Warm-up Exercises

Solve problems 1 and 2 by following the steps indicated.

1 Solve $2x + 10 = 5x - 14$.

  I subtract 2x from each side
  II add 14 to each side
  III divide each side by the coefficient of x

2 Solve $7(3 - 2x) = 8 - (4x - 9)$.

  I simplify each side
  II add 4x to each side
  III subtract 21 from each side
  IV divide each side by the coefficient of x

In problems 3–8, solve for x.

3 $16x - 83 = 9x - 160$
5 $4x + 6 - 2x = x + 7$
7 $12x + 4(x - 12) = 0$

4 $3x = 2x - 6$
6 $6.5x = 3.2x + 9.9$
8 $3.5x + 8 = 2.1x - 4$

9 Describe the length of $\overline{AB}$ in two different ways. Then solve for x.

In problems 10–12, write an equation for each diagram, and solve for x.

10

11

12

Problem Set

13 Describe the steps that you would need to solve the equation $9.5x + 8.7 = 11.2 - 1.4x$. Do not solve it.

14 Solve the equation in problem 13.

15 Check to see that $\frac{3}{4}$ solves $4x^2 = 6 - 5x$ by substituting $\frac{3}{4}$ for x. If you use a calculator, store $\frac{3}{4}$ as a decimal.

In problems 16–24, solve each equation.

16 $3.4x = 2.1x + 3.9$
19 $4x_1 - 6 = 2x_1$
22 $-74 + 12x = 23x + 47$

17 $-6 + 4x = 5x$
20 $6(2x - 3) = 30$
23 $7.6x - 3.2 = 12.5x$

18 $3x + 3 + x = x + 5$
21 $-5(x - 7) = 45$
24 $3y - 4 = 2y - 5$

25 A number added to 6 gives twice the number. Find the number.

26 The cost of a shirt is $11.93. The sales tax is 6.5%. Find the amount of tax and the total bill for the shirt.

In problems 27–30, simplify each expression and solve each equation.

27 $3x - 6x = 12 - 18$

28 $8x - (3x + 7) - 5$

29 $2.7x - 3.2x = 14.6 - 3$

30 $3(x + 5) + 2(4x - 3)$

31 Write an expression for Geraldo's height. He was 44 inches tall five months ago and has grown i inches each month since.

In problems 32–34, solve each equation.

32 $5y + 7 = 3y - 15$

33 $-2x_1 + 5 = 3x_1 - 10$

34 $4a + 20 - a = a + 12$

35 Solve the equation $x - 3a = 7a$ for x.

36 Find the values of a and b if
$(3a + 7, b - 9) = (-a - 19, 2b - 7.75)$.

In problems 37 and 38, find the two values of x that satisfy each equation.

37 $|x| = 9$

38 $x^2 = 81$

39 Gus Cedar wants to build a railing around his new deck. The perimeter of the deck is 6x.

  a Use the information given in the diagram to write an equation for the perimeter of the deck.
  b Solve your equation from part **a** for x.
  c Find the numerical values of the length and the width of the deck.
  d Find the numerical value of the perimeter of the deck.

In problems 40 and 41, choose from $\{-20, -14, -9, -4, 0, 4, 9, 14, 20\}$ to solve each equation.

40 $|x + 8| = 12$

41 $x^2 = 36 - 5x$

42 One kite starts at 200 feet off the ground and rises at the rate of 6 feet per second. A second kite starts at 100 feet off the ground and rises at the rate of 9 feet per second. Let t be the number of seconds the kites rise.

  a Write an expression for the height of each kite after t seconds.
  b How high is each kite after 24 seconds?
  c When are the kites at exactly the same height?

In problems 43–46, solve each equation.

43 $6.5y_1 = 12y_1 - 25 + 4.1y_1$

44 $9y - 2 - 2y + 135 = 0$

45 $18w + 3\frac{3}{4}w - 6 = -12w + 38.2$

46 $3 \cdot \text{Fred} + 9 = 12 \cdot \text{Fred} - 11$

47 Complete the table of values for $y = -3x + 8$ and graph the equation on a coordinate plane.

x	-3	-2	-1	0	1	2	3	4
y								

48 Simplify $-(4.2)^3 - \left(3.7 - \dfrac{12.4}{6.8 - 3.0}\right)$.

49 Use the equation $3x - 5y = 48$.

   a If $x = 0$, find y.

   b If $y = 0$, find x.

In problems 50–52, use the formula for the area of a triangle, $A = \frac{1}{2}bh$.

50 Given $b = 7.3$ and $h = 9.1$, find A.

51 Given $A = 98.6$ and $b = 12.8$, find h.

52 Given $A = 25\frac{1}{2}$ and $h = 17$, find b.

In problems 53 and 54, solve for x.

53 $4x - 2(3x - 7) = 12$

54 $-7(4 - x) = 28$

In problems 55–60, solve each equation.

55 $4.2w + w + 4.3 = 8.1 + 4.2w - 3.8$

56 $76.4n + 92.7 = 169.1n$

57 $-9.7x - 12.5 = 4.6 + 5.4x - 17.1$

58 $x(2x - 3) = 0$

59 $7.2y - 37.6 = 98.4 + 4.5y - 60.8$

60 $x^2 - 5.3x = 0$

In problems 61 and 62, solve for x. Give an exact value for each solution.

61 $18x + 5y = 12x - 18$ if $y = 4$

62 $10x - 18 = 3x + 5w$ if $w = -2$

63 For the equation $3x + 19 = x + y$, if y is randomly selected from $\{5, 10, 15, 20, 25, 30\}$, find the probability that x will be negative.

64 Use rectangle ABCD.

   a Find the length of $\overline{AB}$.

   b Find the length of $\overline{BC}$.

   c Find the perimeter of rectangle ABCD.

   d Find the area of rectangle ABCD.

   e Find the ratio of BC to AB.

65 A truck costs $1400 more with a diesel engine than with a gasoline engine. Both engines will get 8 miles to a gallon of fuel. If diesel fuel costs $0.93 a gallon and gasoline costs $1.03 a gallon, after how many miles of driving will the difference in fuel costs offset the difference in engine costs?

SPECIAL EQUATIONS

Objectives

After studying this section, you will be able to
- Identify equations that have no solutions
- Identify equations that are identities
- Identify equal matrices

Part One: Introduction

Equations That Have No Solutions

Solving equations with the variable on both sides can have surprising results. Here is an example.

Example *Can AB = CD?*

A |———————— x ————————| B

If AB = CD, then

$$
\begin{array}{rl}
x = & x + 11 \\
-x & -x \\
\hline
0x = & 11 \\
0 = & 11
\end{array}
$$

C |———— $x + 11$ ————| D

When we try to solve for x, the result is the false statement $0 = 11$. There is no solution to this equation, so AB cannot equal CD.

Equations That Are Identities

Let's look at another equation with a surprising solution.

Example *Solve $6x - 3 = 10x - 9 + 6 - 4x$.*

$$
\begin{array}{rl}
6x - 3 = & 10x - 9 + 6 - 4x \\
6x - 3 = & 6x - 3 \\
-6x & -6x \\
\hline
-3 = & -3
\end{array}
$$

After combining like terms, we see that the left side and the right side are identical. When we try to solve for x, the result is the true statement $-3 = -3$. Any real number is a solution to the equation.

An *identity* is an equation that is always true. Solving an identity always results in a true statement, and any real number is a solution to an identity. For example, $x + 3 = x + 3$ is an identity.

Equal Matrices

Two matrices are **equal matrices** if they have the same number of rows and columns and if each element of one matrix is equal to the corresponding element of the other matrix.

Example Solve for a, b, c, and d.

$$\begin{bmatrix} a & b+2 \\ 10 & c-5 \end{bmatrix} = \begin{bmatrix} 6 & -8 \\ 2d & 19 \end{bmatrix}$$

Since corresponding elements must be equal, $a = 6$, $b + 2 = -8$, $10 = 2d$, and $c - 5 = 19$. When we solve for each variable, the results are $a = 6$, $b = -10$, $c = 24$, and $d = 5$.

Part Two: Sample Problems

Problem 1 Find (x, y).

$$\begin{bmatrix} -2(x-3) & 12 \\ -14 & 3y-(y-2) \end{bmatrix} = \begin{bmatrix} -10 & 12 \\ -14 & 2(y+1) \end{bmatrix}$$

Solution The matrices are equal, so we can write these equations.

$$\begin{array}{ll}
-2(x-3) = -10 & 3y - (y-2) = 2(y+1) \\
-2x + 6 = -10 & 3y - y + 2 = 2y + 2 \\
\underline{-6-6} & 2y + 2 = 2y + 2 \\
-2x = -16 & \underline{-2y-2y} \\
\dfrac{-2x}{-2} = \dfrac{-16}{-2} & 2 = 2 \\
x = 8 & \underline{-2-2} \\
& 0 = 0
\end{array}$$

Therefore, $(x, y) = (8, \text{any real number})$.

Problem 2 *Bill has twice as many dimes as nickels. Sam has as many quarters as Bill has nickels. Both have the same amount of money. How many nickels does Bill have?*

Solution Let n = the number of nickels that Bill has.
$2n$ = the number of dimes that Bill has.
n = the number of quarters that Sam has.

Each nickel is worth 5 cents, each dime 10 cents, and each quarter 25 cents. Bill has $5n + 10(2n)$ cents, and Sam has $25n$ cents. These amounts are equal.

$$5n + 10(2n) = 25n$$
$$5n + 20n = 25n$$

This equation is an identity

$$25n = 25n$$

Since n is the number of nickels that Bill has, the answer must be that Bill can have any nonnegative, whole number of nickels.

Problem 3   *Find all values of x such that the perimeters of the two triangles are equal.*

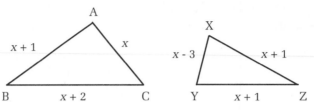

Solution   First we add the lengths of the 3 sides of each triangle.

Perimeter of triangle ABC   **Perimeter of triangle XYZ**

$$x + (x + 1) + (x + 2) = (x + 1) + (x + 1) + (x - 3)$$

$$
\begin{array}{rcl}
3x + 3 = & & 3x - 1 \\
- 3x & & - 3x \\
\hline
3 = & & -1
\end{array}
$$

Because there is no solution to the equation, no value of x will make the perimeters of the triangles equal.

Problem 4   *In 1987 Apollo Senior High School had 3260 students and was losing 70 students annually. In that same year, Gemini High School had 1640 students and was gaining 65 students per year.*

a *Let t be the number of years since 1987. Write expressions for the number of students at Apollo High School after t years and at Gemini High School after t years.*
b *Write an equation stating that after t years the schools will have the same number of students. Solve the equation for t.*
c *In what year will the schools have the same number of students?*

Solution   **a** Apollo loses 70t students in t years, so the number of students enrolled after t years is 3260 − 70t. Gemini gains 65t students in t years, so the number of students enrolled after t years is 1640 + 65t.

b
$$
\begin{array}{rcl}
3260 - 70t = & & 1640 + 65t \\
+ 70t & & + 70t \\
\hline
3260 = & & 1640 + 135t \\
- 1640 & & - 1640 \\
\hline
-1620 = & 135t \\
\end{array}
$$

$$\frac{1620}{135} = \frac{135t}{135}$$

$$12 = t$$

Be sure to check your answer.
Each school will have the same number of students in 12 years.

c From part **b** we know that the high schools will have the same number of students in 12 years. Since 1987 + 12 = 1999, each school will have the same number of students in 1999.

Part Three: Exercises and Problems

Warm-up Exercises

In problems 1–6, solve each equation.

1 $9x - 4 = 11x + 32$

2 $x + 7 = x$

3 $3x - 8 = 8 - 3x$

4 $9m + 7 = 3(3m - 2)$

5 $3x + 13 = x + 9$

6 $12 + 5x = 12 - 5x$

7 Mr. Later shipped some packages to his father, C.U. If the total bill was $11.64, what was the shipping price per pound?

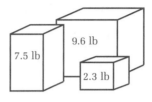

U.S.P.O.

7.5 lb $_____

9.6 lb $_____

2.3 lb $_____

Total $11.64

In exercises 8–11, solve for x.

8 $3x - 3 = 6x + 3 - 3x$

9 $4x - (2x - 3) = 2(x - 3) + 3$

10 $975x - 597 = 759x + 597$

11 $\frac{5}{6}x - 8 = \frac{1}{6}x + 10$

In problems 12 and 13, write an equation and solve for x. Check your answers.

12

13 Angle A measures 44°.

$(3x + 20)°$

A

14 Find the values of x, y, and z.

$[3x \quad 9 - y \quad 4z] = [x + 20 \quad y + 3 \quad 2(3z + 1)]$

Problem Set

15 Find the value in cents of

a 6 nickels and two dimes

b n nickels and 8 dimes

c 7 quarters and d dollars

16 Find the value in cents of

a 4 dimes and 7 quarters

b n nickels and 5 half-dollars

c d dimes and q quarters

17 Find a, b, and c.

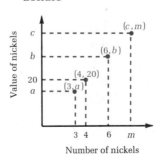

18 Solve for x.

a $3x + 2 = 3x + 2$

b $8x + 5 = 10x + 5 - 2x$

c

Problem Set, *continued*

In problems 19–22, solve for *x*.

19 $1993x + 3991 = 9319x - 9913$

20 $\frac{1}{3}x + 4 = \frac{1}{2}x - \frac{1}{6}x$

21 $839x - 462 = 635x + 445$

22 $\frac{7}{8}x - 5 = \frac{9}{8}x - \frac{1}{4}x + 5$

In problems 23 and 24, solve for *a*, *b*, *c*, and *d*.

23 $\begin{bmatrix} 2a & 6 \\ 3c & 8 \end{bmatrix} = \begin{bmatrix} 10 & b \\ -6 & 4+d \end{bmatrix}$

24 $\begin{bmatrix} 2b & 3c \\ a-4 & d+5 \end{bmatrix} = \begin{bmatrix} 18.2 & 27 \\ 12.3 & -32 \end{bmatrix}$

25 Use the equation $x = x + 1$.

    a Solve for x.

    b The statement LET X = X + 1 is frequently used in the BASIC computer language. The statement is interpreted as "Let the value stored for x be replaced by that value plus 1." Does the computer view X = X + 1 in "LET X = X + 1" as an equation?

26 If AB = CD, what is the length of $\overline{AB}$?

    $\vdash$ 3.4x $\dashv\vdash$ 3.7x $\dashv\vdash$———14.8———$\dashv$ $\vdash$ 5.8 $\dashv\vdash$———————7.1x———————$\dashv$

    A   B C   D

27 Use the equation $2x - 3y = 12$.

    a Find the missing values in (?, 0) and (0, ?).

    b Graph the equation on a coordinate plane by drawing a line through the points found in part **a**.

28 The sum of $\frac{1}{2}$ and its reciprocal is a number.

    a Find the number.

    b Find the reciprocal of the number.

29 A number increased by 70% of the number is 51. Find the number.

30 Wally works 2 hours a day as a waiter. He keeps track of his tips by using two graphs.

    a What is the largest amount Wally has earned in tips in 1 day?

    b What is the percentage increase in tips from day 1 to day 5?

    c Why doesn't the line in Graph II ever go down?

    d A cumulative graph like Graph II is called an ogive. Copy Graph II and complete it for the last 3 days.

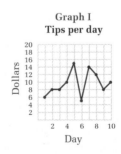

Graph I
Tips per day

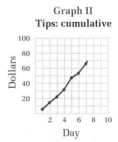

Graph II
Tips: cumulative

31 Neptune Junior High School has 1520 students, but its student population is declining by 40 students each year. Pioneer Junior High School has 1150 students, but its student population is increasing by 28 students each year. When will the two schools have the same number of students?

32 Evaluate $\dfrac{3x^2 - 4xy + 2y^2}{-x\sqrt{2xy}}$ if $x = -2$ and $y = -3$.

33 The sum of a number and its opposite is 5. Find the number.

34 Find the area of the circle. Approximate the answer to the nearest hundredth.

In problems 35–38, simplify each expression and solve each equation.

35 $9.3x - 2(1.6x - 3.5)$

36 $9.3x - 2.5 + 3.6x + 9.2$

37 $14 - (2n + 5) = -2n + 9$

38 $(n - 4)(n + 2) = 0$

39 Find the area of the rectangle for each value of a.

  a $a = 5$

  b $a = 10$

  c $a = 15$

  d What pattern did you notice in parts **a**, **b**, and **c**?

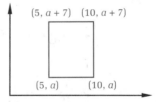

In problems 40–42, name the property illustrated.

40 $7x + 5 + 2x = 7x + 2x + 5$ **41** $3x - 4x = (3 - 4)x$ **42** $4x + (-4x) = 0$

In problems 43–45, graph each inequality on a number line.

43 $x > -5.7$ **44** $y \le -9$ **45** y is positive

46 Jim has the same number of dimes as Jack has quarters. Jim has twice as many nickels as dimes. He also has 5 times as many pennies as dimes. Jim and Jack have the same amount of money. How much does each have?

In problems 47–50, solve for x.

47 $3x - 5.2x = 1.9x - 4.1x - 7$ **48** $6x - 2.4x + 8 = 12.7x$

49 $6x - 4.8 + 12 = 9.65x + 7.2 - 3.65x$ **50** $3x - 1 = 16x - 12x$

51 Solve for x and y if $(2x - 3.4x, 6y + 7) = (13 + 5x, 3y - 2)$.

In problems 52 and 53, solve for x_2.

52 $x_2 = 4x_2 - 5$ **53** $3.1x_2 = 7.9x_2 - 4.8x_2$

Problem Set, *continued*

54 Solve for a, b, c, and d.

$$\begin{bmatrix} -(a-3) & b(b-4) \\ 3c & 8 \end{bmatrix} + \begin{bmatrix} 10 & 0 \\ -6 & 4+d \end{bmatrix} = \begin{bmatrix} a & 0 \\ 3c & 0 \end{bmatrix}$$

55 Chip's Computer Repair charges $50 for a service call plus $83 per hour. Byte's Computer Repair has a $100 service charge plus a $78 per hour charge. Ethan estimated how long it would take to repair his computer and discovered that the cost would be the same whether he called Chip or Byte. What was Ethan's estimate of the repair time?

56 If c is selected at random from $\{0, 5, 10, 15\}$, what is the probability that the area of the rectangle is 48?

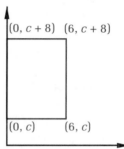

In problems 57 and 58, find the average (mean) for each set.

57 $\{5.8, 13.4, 28.6, 31.2, 43.5\}$

58 $\{-6, -4, -3, 3, 4, 6\}$

59 The perimeters of the rectangles are equal.

a Find x.
b Find the width and length of each rectangle.

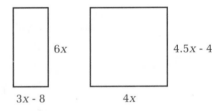

60 Refer to the graph, which represents weekly sales rankings among word processors for a 20-week period.

a Explain why the numbers on the vertical axis decrease.
b Give examples of ways to represent more clearly the information displayed in the graph.

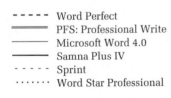

- - - - Word Perfect
══════ PFS: Professional Write
─────── Microsoft Word 4.0
─────── Samna Plus IV
- - - - Sprint
· · · · · · Word Star Professional

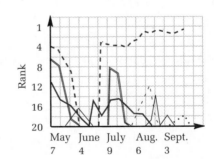

61 The perimeter of a triangle with sides x, x + 1, and x + 3 is the same as the perimeter of a rectangle with sides 0.5x + 2 and x. Find the lengths of the sides of the figures.

62 Solve for a, b, c, and d.

$$\begin{bmatrix} 2a - 3 & 5b \\ \frac{1}{2}c & c \end{bmatrix} = \begin{bmatrix} a + 1 & b \\ 3c + 8 & d + 8 \end{bmatrix}$$

DANGER! BRIDGE AHEAD
Lou Petulla inspects aging bridges

Early one July morning in 1983, drivers on the Mianus River Bridge in Greenwich, Connecticut, were startled to hear what sounded like an explosion and to feel the bridge shudder alarmingly beneath them. Suddenly, a 100-foot section of the bridge collapsed and plunged 70 feet to the river below, killing three motorists who were trapped under water.

The report that followed the tragedy stated that more than 100,000 bridges in the United States had structural problems. As more and more bridges approach the end of their useful lives, the work of civil engineers like Lou Petulla of Oil City, Pennsylvania, becomes increasingly important. One of Petulla's jobs as a bridge and highway engineer with the Pennsylvania Turnpike Commission is to inspect aging bridges and make safety recommendations. This work involves mathematics and a high degree of precision.

Petulla explains that the maximum weight a bridge can hold at a single point (*p*) depends on the material used in building the bridge and the moment of inertia (*i*), or the way the material is distributed. A steel I-beam, for example, may have an overall stress allowance (*S*) of 20,000 pounds per square inch and a moment of inertia of 145. The length of the I-beam in inches is *l*, and its depth in inches is *d*. These variables are related by the formula $S = \frac{pld}{8i}$. For the I-beam shown,

$$20,000 = \frac{p(168)(10)}{8(145)} \approx 1.45p$$

$$p = 13,793 \text{ lb}$$

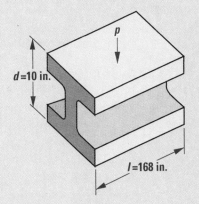

d = 10 in.

l = 168 in.

"This is the maximum point-load we could allow anywhere on this beam," explains Petulla. "If there were a chance that a passing truck, say, might cause that limit to be exceeded, we would have two choices: turn the truck away, or close the bridge."

4.3 | THE DISTRIBUTIVE PROPERTY IN EQUATIONS

Objectives

After studying this section, you will be able to
- Decide when to use the Distributive Property in solving equations
- Solve matrix equations

Part One: Introduction

Choosing the Distributive Property

You can often use the Distributive Property of Multiplication over Addition or Subtraction to simplify either side or both sides of an equation. It is important to decide when to distribute and when other methods could be used to simplify an expression.

Example   *Solve $2(x + 4) - 14 = -5(x - 3)$ for x.*

Use the Distributive Property of Multiplication over Addition or Subtraction

$$2(x + 4) - 14 = -5(x - 3)$$

$$2x + 8 - 14 = -5x + 15$$

Combine like terms

$$2x - 6 = -5x + 15$$

Add 6 to both sides

$$\begin{array}{rcl} & +6 & +6 \\ \hline 2x & = & -5x + 21 \end{array}$$

Add 5x to both sides

$$\begin{array}{rcl} +5x & & +5x \\ \hline 7x & = & 21 \end{array}$$

$$x = 3$$

Check

Left Side	Right Side
$2(x + 4) - 14$	$-5(x - 3)$
$= 2(3 + 4) - 14$	$= -5(3 - 3)$
$= 2(7) - 14$	$= -5(0)$
$= 14 - 14$	$= 0$
$= 0$	

If $x = 3$, the sides are equal, so the solution is $x = 3$.

Example   *Find the value of w in the hexagon.*

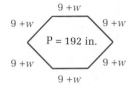

9 + w, 9 + w, 9 + w, P = 192 in., 9 + w, 9 + w, 9 + w

164 | Chapter 4   Working with Equations

An equation is $192 = 6(9 + w)$.

We could first apply the Distributive Property of Multiplication over Addition. But another approach to solving this problem would be to first divide both sides of the equation by 6 (remember $\frac{6}{6} = 1$).

$$192 = 6(9 + w)$$

Divide both sides by 6
$$\frac{192}{6} = \frac{6(9 + w)}{6}$$
$$32 = 9 + w$$

Subtract 9 from both sides
$$\begin{array}{r} -9 \quad -9 \\ \hline 23 = w \end{array}$$

The solution is $w = 23$ in. Be sure to check.

Solving Matrix Equations

In earlier lessons, you developed many skills for working with matrices. Now you can use these skills to solve *matrix equations*.

Example *Solve for* (x, y).

$$\begin{bmatrix} 3 & x \\ y & -1 \end{bmatrix} \cdot \begin{bmatrix} -4 \\ 2 \end{bmatrix} = \begin{bmatrix} 15 \\ 9 \end{bmatrix}$$

Multiply the matrices on the left.

$$\begin{bmatrix} 3(-4) + x(2) \\ y(-4) + (-1)(2) \end{bmatrix} = \begin{bmatrix} 15 \\ 9 \end{bmatrix}$$

Now we have two matrices that are equal, so corresponding elements must be equal.

$$\begin{array}{ll} 3(-4) + x(2) = 15 & \qquad y(-4) + (-1)(2) = 9 \\ -12 + 2x = 15 & \qquad\qquad -4y - 2 = 9 \\ 2x = 27 & \qquad\qquad\qquad -4y = 11 \\ x = \frac{27}{2} \text{ or } 13.5 & \qquad\qquad\qquad y = \frac{11}{-4} \text{ or } -2.75 \end{array}$$

The solution is $(x, y) = (13.5, -2.75)$.

Part Two: Sample Problems

Problem 1 *Solve for w if $10(w + 3) + 3(w + 3) = 39$.*

Solution Notice that $10(w + 3)$ and $3(w + 3)$ are like terms.

$$10(w + 3) + 3(w + 3) = 39$$

Combine like terms
$$13(w + 3) = 39$$

Divide both sides by 13
$$\frac{13(w + 3)}{13} = \frac{39}{13}$$
$$w + 3 = 3$$

Subtract 3 from both sides
$$\begin{array}{r} -3 \quad -3 \\ \hline w = 0 \end{array}$$

The solution is $w = 0$. Be sure to check.

Problem 2   The top scorer of the Hoopsters made 11 goals (2 points each) and 5 free throws (1 point each). The top scorer of the Netters made 13 goals and 2 free throws. Which team's top scorer scored more points, the Hoopsters' or the Netters'?

Solution   Matrix multiplication is an excellent way to set up and solve the problem.

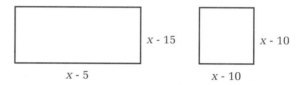

Multiplying the matrices on the left side, we get

$$\begin{bmatrix} 11(2) + 5(1) \\ 13(2) + 2(1) \end{bmatrix} = \begin{bmatrix} 22 + 5 \\ 26 + 2 \end{bmatrix} = \begin{bmatrix} 27 \\ 28 \end{bmatrix} = \begin{bmatrix} \text{top-scoring Hoopster} \\ \text{top-scoring Netter} \end{bmatrix}$$

The Netters' top scorer scored more points.

Problem 3   For what values of x will the rectangle and square have the same perimeter?

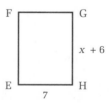

x - 15   x - 10

x - 5   x - 10

Solution   Unlike the terms in Sample Problem 1, $2(x - 5)$ and $2(x - 15)$ are not like terms. We will use the Distributive Property.

Perimeter of Rectangle   Perimeter of Square

$$2(x - 5) + 2(x - 15) = 4(x - 10)$$
$$2x - 10 + 2x - 30 = 4x - 40$$
$$4x - 40 = 4x - 40$$

This is an identity, so the equation makes a true statement for all values of x. Since this problem involves geometric figures, the lengths of the sides must be positive. Therefore, x can be any number greater than 15. The solution can be written as $x > 15$.

Part Three: Exercises and Problems

Warm-up Exercises

1 Solve $10(w + 3) = 30$ and check your solution.

2 Solve $3(x - 1) + 2(x - 1) = 15$.

3 The area of rectangle EFGH is 63. What is the numerical value of the perimeter?

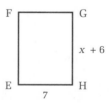

F   G

x + 6

E   H

7

In problems 32 and 33, evaluate each expression if $a = 5$, $b = 10$, and $c = 4$.

32 $\dfrac{-b + \sqrt{b^2 - 4ac}}{2a}$

33 $\dfrac{-b - \sqrt{b^2 - 4ac}}{2a}$

34 Solve for x and y.

$$\begin{bmatrix} x & 3 \\ 4 & 2y \end{bmatrix} \cdot \begin{bmatrix} 3 \\ 2 \end{bmatrix} = \begin{bmatrix} -9 \\ 21 \end{bmatrix}$$

In problems 35–37, write an algebraic expression for each quantity.

35 If a book has p pages with an average of w words per page, what is the number of words in the book?

36 If pencils cost p cents per dozen, what is the cost of 3 pencils?

37 Bill is b years old, and his brother Al is 6 years older. What was Al's age 3 years ago?

38 The two rectangles have equal perimeters. Find the length and the width of each rectangle.

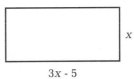
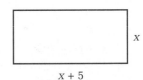

$3x - 5$ $x + 5$

In problems 39 and 40, solve for x and y.

39 $\begin{bmatrix} 4 & y - 3 \\ x + 5 & 10 \end{bmatrix} \cdot \begin{bmatrix} 4 \\ -3 \end{bmatrix} = \begin{bmatrix} -6 \\ -2 \end{bmatrix}$

40 $\begin{bmatrix} 2x + 3 & 9 \\ 17 & y - 4 \end{bmatrix} \cdot \begin{bmatrix} 13 \\ -5 \end{bmatrix} = \begin{bmatrix} 84 \\ 176 \end{bmatrix}$

In problems 41–44, solve for the unknown.

41 $5(t + 2) = 3(t - 2) - (t + 1)$

42 $12(n + 6) - 11(n + 6) = 7n$

43 $3.57(2.6x - 11.3) = -11.3(3.4x + 9.8)$

44 $12.3(2z - 5) = 11.6(3z - 2)$

45 The following matrix equation is used to evaluate the earnings of Matt and Marie. Matt worked 10 hours at Joe's Grill and 5 hours at the Park District. Marie worked 6 hours at Joe's and 7 hours at the Park District.

	Hours at Joe's	Hours at Park District		Hourly Rates		
Matt	10	5	$\cdot$	3.80	=	Matt's salary
Marie	6	7		4.20		Marie's salary

Use matrix multiplication to find Matt's and Marie's salaries.

46 The perimeter of the triangle is equal to the perimeter of the square. Find the lengths of the sides of the triangle and the length of a side of the square.

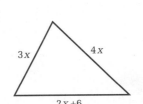

Red Demon Spoons
$0.69 each

Zulu Poppers
$1.25 each

Pepp's Snippers
$1.49 each

47 At Joe Grubb's Tackle and Bait Shop, Red Demon Spoons sell for
$0.69 each, Zulu Poppers sell for $1.25 each, and Pepp's Snippers
sell for $1.49 each. The table shows the purchases of four people.

Customer	Red Demon Spoons	Zulu Poppers	Pepp's Snippers
C. Bass	7	4	9
Brooke Trout	4	3	8
Wally Pike	2	1	3
Sue Shi	9	2	4

a Write a matrix multiplication problem to determine the bill for
each person.
b Calculate the bill for each person.

48 Find the values for a and b.

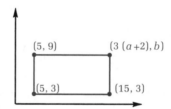

$(5, 9)$ $(3\,(a+2), b)$

$(5, 3)$ $(15, 3)$

In problems 49 and 50, solve for x and y.

49 $\begin{bmatrix} x & 3 \\ x & y \end{bmatrix} \cdot \begin{bmatrix} 1 \\ 2 \end{bmatrix} = \begin{bmatrix} 8 \\ 12 \end{bmatrix}$

50 $\begin{bmatrix} 2 & 3 \\ 5 & 7 \end{bmatrix} \cdot \begin{bmatrix} x \\ 4 \end{bmatrix} = \begin{bmatrix} y \\ y+1 \end{bmatrix}$

51 If a car travels at 35 miles per hour, it takes 30 minutes longer to
cover a given distance than it does at 45 miles per hour.

a Let t be the number of hours traveled at 45 miles per hour.
Find t.
b How far does the car travel?

In problems 52 and 53, find all values of x.

52 $x^2 = 49$

53 $x^2 = 60$ (nearest thousandth)

54 The reciprocal of a number is added to the reciprocal of 3 to
obtain the reciprocal of 2. Find the number.

4.4 | RATE PROBLEMS

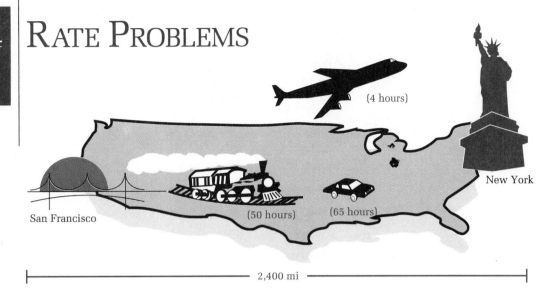

(4 hours)

New York

San Francisco

(50 hours)   (65 hours)

2,400 mi

Objective

After studying this section, you will be able to
- Solve rate problems

Part One: Introduction

Rate Problems

You can find total distance traveled by multiplying the rate of travel
by the time spent traveling. Similarly, you can multiply the rate of
work by the time spent working to find the total amount of work
completed. This relationship between rate and time will be helpful
to you in solving the following problems.

Example *The freshman class at Hardy High School decides to sell box lunches
to earn money for the spring dance. Ms. Garland's class, group 1, can
make 10 box lunches per hour. Mr. Rooney's class, group 2, makes 15
box lunches per hour. Group 2 starts making box lunches 2 hours after
group 1 starts making them. Let t be the number of hours that group 1
spends making box lunches.*

  a *Write an expression for each of the following.*

    i *The number of box lunches group 1 makes*

They make 10 box lunches
per hour for *t* hours   10*t*

ii *The number of hours group 2 makes box lunches*

Group 2 began making box
lunches 2 hours after group 1 $t - 2$

iii *The number of box lunches group 2 makes*

They made 15 box lunches
per hour but started 2 hours
later $15(t - 2)$

iv *The total number of box lunches made*

The total number of box
lunches made by both groups $10t + 15(t - 2)$

b *If 120 box lunches are ordered, how long must group 1 work?*

The total box lunches made must
be enough to fill the orders

$$
\begin{aligned}
10t + 15(t - 2) &= 120 \\
10t + 15t - 30 &= 120 \\
25t - 30 &= 120 \\
+\,30\quad &\ \ +30 \\
\hline
25t &= 150 \\
t &= 6
\end{aligned}
$$

Combine like terms
Add 30 to both sides

Group 1 must make box lunches for 6 hours.

c *How many box lunches will each group make?*

Ms. Garland's class makes $10(6) = 60$ box lunches.
Mr. Rooney's class makes $15(6 - 2) = 15(4) = 60$ box lunches.

Part Two: Sample Problems

Problem 1

Phineas Frog and Tiny Toad live 1000 hops apart. They each leave
home at the same time and travel toward each other. Phineas's speed
is 50 hops per minute. Tiny's speed is 65 hops per minute. The hops
are of equal length. Let t be the time they have been traveling.

a Write an expression for each of the following.

  i The distance that Phineas hops in t minutes
  ii The distance that Tiny hops in t minutes
  iii The distance that both travel in t minutes

b After 7 minutes, how many hops will Phineas have traveled?

c After 9 minutes, how many hops will Tiny have traveled?

d How long will it be before Phineas and Tiny meet?

Solution

a distance = rate · time

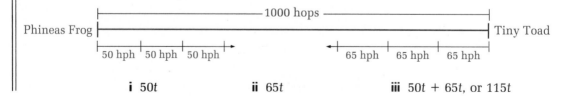

  i $50t$ **ii** $65t$ **iii** $50t + 65t$, or $115t$

b Phineas has traveled $50t = 50(7) = 350$ hops.
c Tiny has traveled $65t = 65(9) = 585$ hops.
d The combined number of hops is 1000.

$$115t = 1000$$

Divide both sides by 115

$$\frac{115t}{115} = \frac{1000}{115}$$

It will take about 8.70 minutes before they meet.

$$t \approx 8.70$$

Problem 2   *One jet travels at 400 miles per hour. Another travels at 600 miles per hour. The jets start from the same point and travel in the same direction, but the slower jet starts 2 hours earlier. How long will it be before the faster jet overtakes the slower one?*

Solution   Let t = the time the faster jet has traveled.
$t + 2$ = the time the slower jet has traveled with a 2-hour head start.

rate · time = distance ($r \cdot t = d$)
    $600t$ = distance traveled by the faster jet
$400(t + 2)$ = distance traveled by the slower jet

When the faster jet overtakes the slower jet, their distances traveled are equal.

$$600t = 400(t + 2)$$
$$600t = 400t + 800$$
$$200t = 800$$
$$t = 4$$

The jets will have traveled the same distance when the faster jet has traveled 4 hours.

Or, we can solve the problem using logic. Since the slower jet had a 2-hour head start, it had a head start of $400(2) = 800$ miles. The faster jet travels 600 miles per hour, so it gains 200 miles on the slower jet every hour. The faster jet can make up the 800 miles in 4 hours.

Part Three: Exercises and Problems

Warm-up Exercises

1 T.P. Gunn's altitude in his jet is 30,000 feet. He is descending at 25 feet per second. Five seconds later, his brother Peter is flying at 1000 feet and begins climbing at 4 feet per second. Let t be the number of seconds T.P. descends.

a Write an expression for each of the following.
  i The number of seconds Peter has been ascending
  ii T.P.'s altitude after t seconds
  iii Peter's altitude after t seconds
b Write an equation that shows that the two planes are at the same altitude after t seconds.
c Solve for t in the equation in part **b.**
d What is the altitude at the time found in part **c?**

2 George can swim 2 lengths per minute. Jack can swim 6 lengths per minute. If George starts swimming at noon and Jack starts at 1:00 P.M., at what time will Jack have swum as many lengths as George?

Problem Set

3 Terri, who makes 43 egg rolls per hour, starts at 8:00 A.M. Her sister Suzie, who makes 53 egg rolls per hour, starts at 10:00 A.M. Let t be the number of hours that Terri has been making egg rolls.

    a Write an expression for the number of egg rolls each has made after t hours.

    b How many egg rolls have been made if both stop working at 3:00 P.M.?

    c Write an equation showing that Terri and Suzie make the same number of egg rolls.

    d At what time of day have they made the same number of egg rolls? (Solve the equation from part **c** for t and convert to time of day.)

Terri   **Suzie**

4 Earl worked 20 hours last week. If he had earned $0.50 an hour more but had worked only 18 hours, he would have earned the same amount. How much per hour does Earl earn?

In problems 5–8, simplify each expression and solve each equation.

5 $3x - 5(2x + 3) - 6$ **6** $6(2x - 3) - 6 = 4(x + 6)$

7 $3(2y + 5) = 34 - 7y$ **8** $4.3(2x - 7.6) + 5.3x - 6.5$

9 Solve for a, b, c, and d.

$$2\begin{bmatrix} 2a & b + 3 \\ -3c & 6 - d \end{bmatrix} = \begin{bmatrix} -52 & 16 \\ 12 & 18 \end{bmatrix}$$

In problems 10 and 11, solve for y_1.

10 $-4y_1(2 - y_1) = 0$ **11** $y_1^2 + 27y_1 = 0$

12 In a two-boat sailing race, one boat, Windsprite, rounds the final buoy and sails straight for the finish line at 12.0 knots. Exactly 4 minutes after Windsprite rounds the final buoy, the other boat, Porpoise, reaches that point and heads for the finish line at 12.7 knots. Windsprite reaches the finish line 49 minutes after rounding the last buoy. Who wins the race?

In problems 13–16, solve for x.

13 $11.5(2x - 6) = 4(3.5x + 12)$ **14** $4(3 - 5x) + 10x = 5(3 - 2x)$

15 $6(2 - 3x) = 5(x + 4)$ **16** $3(5 - 2x) = 4(3x - 5)$

17 The area of rectangle A in square centimeters is the same as the perimeter of square B in centimeters. Find the dimensions of A and B.

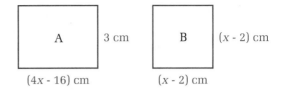

A   3 cm

(4x - 16) cm

B   (x - 2) cm

(x - 2) cm

18 Paul picked a number. He multiplied the number by 5, added 3, multiplied that result by 7, and ended up with 91. What number did Paul pick?

19 The wrestling team, for its annual fundraiser, sells boxes of grapefruit for $8 per box. Li sells 34 boxes per hour. Sam sells 6 boxes per hour. Tony sells 14 boxes per hour. Sam starts selling at 8:00 A.M., Tony at 9:00 A.M., and Li at 2:00 P.M. They sell until the team practice later that day. Let t be the number of hours that Sam sells boxes of grapefruit.

  a Write expressions for each of the following.
    i The number of boxes that Sam sells
    ii The number of boxes that Tony sells
    iii The number of boxes that Li sells
    iv The number of boxes sold by all three
  b If the team practice were at 5:00 P.M., how many boxes would they have sold? How much money would they have made?
  c Write an equation stating that 403 boxes were sold before the team practice. Then solve it for t.
  d Use your answer from part **c** to find the time of the team practice.

20 Evaluate $-x^2 + \dfrac{34 - x}{x} - 14x$ if $x = -2$.

21 At a NASCAR racetrack, the distance per lap is 2 miles. Lou Lambert drives his car at a constant rate of 160 miles per hour. Ralph Redding drives his car at a constant rate of 170 miles per hour. How long will it take before Ralph gains 2 laps in relation to Lou?

22 At World-Wide Widgets, Willie's wild widget machine makes 150 widgets per hour, but 8% are defective. Woody's wonderful widget maker makes 120 widgets per hour, with 3% defective. Let x be the number of hours each machine runs.

  a Write expressions for the number of widgets produced by Willie's machine and by Woody's machine.
  b Write expressions for the number of defective widgets produced by Willie's machine and by Woody's machine.
  c Write expressions for the numbers of good widgets produced by Willie's machine and by Woody's machine.
  d If each machine works for 5 hours, what is the total number of good widgets produced by the widget machines?

Problem Set, *continued*

23 The graph shows the sources of income for a public television station.

   a What percentage of income comes from the Corporation for Public Broadcasting?

   b What percentage of income comes from viewers?

   c If the station's total annual income is $15,000,000, what amount of the income comes from grants?

2% Other
6% Grants
7% CPB
23% Production Contracts
62% Viewer Subscriptions

24 If $5(x - 2) + y(3 + x) = 14$ and $y = 8$, find x.

25 A bagger with 2 years' experience at the Main Street Supermarket started work at 8:00 A.M. A cashier with 3 years' experience started at 10:00 A.M. They finished at the same time and earned the same amount that day. How many hours did each work? (Round to the nearest hundredth of an hour.)

Experience	Cashier	Bagger
1 year	7.50	6.25
2 years	8.25	6.75
3 years	8.90	7.20

26 The matrices below compare points scored by two football players. The first matrix shows that Lou makes 82% of his field goals and 90% of his extra points. Sly makes 78% of his field goals and 99% of his extra points. The second matrix shows that 3 points are awarded for each of x field goals and 1 point is awarded for each of y extra points. If $(x, y) = (27, 45)$, which kicker would be expected to score more points?

$$
\begin{array}{cc}
 & \begin{array}{cc} \textbf{Field} & \textbf{Extra} \\ \textbf{Goals} & \textbf{Points} \end{array} & \begin{array}{c} \textbf{Points} \\ \textbf{Awarded} \end{array} & & \begin{array}{c} \textbf{Points} \\ \textbf{Scored} \end{array}
\end{array}
$$

$$
\begin{array}{c} \text{Lou the Toe} \\ \text{Sly the Foot} \end{array}
\begin{bmatrix} 82\% & 90\% \\ 78\% & 99\% \end{bmatrix}
\begin{bmatrix} 3x \\ 1y \end{bmatrix}
=
\begin{bmatrix} \text{Lou} \\ \text{Sly} \end{bmatrix}
$$

In problems 27–30, simplify each expression and solve each equation.

27 $\frac{2}{3}(6x - 9) + \frac{4}{5}(10x + 20)$

28 $3(x^2 - 8) = 123$

29 $6.35(3y - 5.6x) - 0.04\left(x - \frac{y}{2}\right)$

30 $4(3x - 5) + 42 = 2(6x + 11)$

31 Solve for p and q.

$$
\begin{bmatrix} p & 7 \\ 2 + q & q \end{bmatrix}
\begin{bmatrix} 3 \\ 5 \end{bmatrix}
=
\begin{bmatrix} 2 \\ -30 \end{bmatrix}
$$

32 If $(x, y) = (3, 4)$ and the perimeter of the figure is 70, find z. (Hint: The figure is not drawn to scale.)

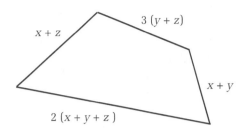

33 Richard has 15 more dimes than quarters and 10 more nickels than dimes. He has a total of $7.95. How many of each type of coin does he have?

34 Timmy had an average score of 66% on 4 tests. What score must he get on the next test to raise his average to 70%?

35 Complete the table of values for $y = |x - 2|$, and graph the equation on the coordinate plane.

x	−5	−4	−3	−2	−1	0	1	2	3	4	5
y											

36 Orville Wright was out bicycle riding with his brother Wilbur. Orville stopped to fix a flat tire. Wilbur continued at 10 miles per hour. After 30 minutes, Orville had fixed the flat, and he rode off at 12 miles per hour in pursuit of Wilbur. In how many hours did Orville catch up to Wilbur?

37 A city block is in the shape of a rectangle 800 feet by 600 feet, as shown. R.E. Lee starts at point A, running toward point B at a rate of 4.4 feet per second. After R.E. has run for 2 minutes, his sister Sara, who is at point D, starts after R.E. by running toward point A at the rate of 5.1 feet per second. They continue running around the block until Sara catches R.E.

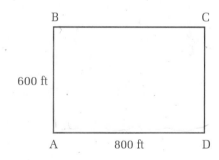

a How many seconds does it take for Sara to catch up to R.E.?
b At what point on the block does Sara catch up to R.E.?

38 At the Quality Cookie Company, the cookie ovens are used from 8:00 A.M. to 6:00 P.M. and produce 3000 cookies per hour. The packaging machine can package 4000 cookies per hour and also stops exactly at 6:00 P.M. At what time should the packaging machine be turned on so that all cookies are packaged and the machine never waits for cookies?

EQUATIONS WITH ABSOLUTE VALUES OR SQUARED QUANTITIES

Objectives

After studying this section, you will be able to
- Solve equations involving absolute values
- Describe solutions to equations as solution sets
- Solve equations by finding the square root of each side

Part One: Introduction

Absolute Values

As you learned in Chapter 3, the absolute value of a number is that number's distance from zero on the number line. If $|x| = 17$, for example, the solutions are $x = 17$ or $x = -17$ because both 17 and -17 are 17 units from zero on the number line.

Example   *Solve for x if $|x + 5| = 8$.*

We can illustrate the equation by this number line. The quantity $x + 5$ must be 8 units from zero.

$x + 5 = 8$ or $x + 5 = -8$
   $x = 3$ or $x = -13$

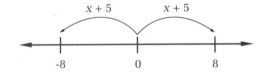

Check
Check both solutions in the original equation.

Left Side	**Right Side**
$\lvert x + 5 \rvert$	$= 8$
$= \lvert 3 + 5 \rvert$	
$= \lvert 8 \rvert$	
$= 8$	

Left Side	**Right Side**
$\lvert x + 5 \rvert$	$= 8$
$= \lvert -13 + 5 \rvert$	
$= \lvert -8 \rvert$	
$= 8$	

If $x = 3$ or $x = -13$, the sides are equal, so the answer checks.

Example   *Solve $|2x| = 8$ for x.*

We can illustrate the equation by this number line. The quantity $2x$ must be 8 units from zero.

$2x = 8$ or $2x = -8$
   $x = 4$ or $x = -4$

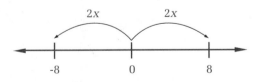

Be sure to check both solutions in the original equation.

Solution Sets

Many equations, such as absolute value equations, have more than one solution. Set notation is a useful way to list these solutions.

Example   *Solve* $|x| = 5$ *for x.*

The two solutions, 5 and -5, are written as $\{-5, 5\}$.

Example   *Solve* $|x| = -5$ *for x.*

There are no real number solutions since the absolute value of x cannot be negative. The solution set is written as $\{\ \}$. Such a set, one with no members, is called the **empty set.**

Example   *Solve* $|x| = x$ *for x.*

The solutions are 0 and all positive numbers. The solution set is written as $\{x : x \geq 0\}$, which is read "the set of all numbers x such that x is greater than or equal to zero."

Example   *Solve* $x + |-5| = x + 5$ *for x.*

If we simplify $|-5|$ to 5 we get $x + 5 = x + 5$, which is an identity. All values of x make a true statement. We write the solution set as $\{x : x \in \mathcal{R}\}$, which is read "the set of all numbers x such that x is an element of the set of real numbers."

Squared Quantities

We can solve an equation like $x^2 = 25$ by using inverse operations and absolute value.

Example   *Solve* $x^2 = 25$ *for x.*

We know that $(-5)^2$ and $(5)^2 = 25$. Therefore, the solution set of the equation is $\{-5, 5\}$. We can also solve $x^2 = 25$ using inverse operations. The inverse operation of squaring is finding the **square root.**

$$x^2 = 25$$

Take the square root of each side $\sqrt{x^2} = \sqrt{25}$

If we define $\sqrt{x^2}$ to be $|x|$, $|x| = 5$

the result is an absolute value
equation that has both a positive and
a negative solution. $x = 5 \text{ or } x = -5$

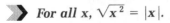 **For all x, $\sqrt{x^2} = |x|$.**

Example   *Solve* $(x + 5)^2 = 45$ *for x.*

$$(x + 5)^2 = 45$$

Take the square root of each side $\sqrt{(x + 5)^2} = \sqrt{45}$
Since $\sqrt{x^2} = |x|$, we know that
$\sqrt{(x + 5)^2} = |x + 5|$ $|x + 5| \approx 6.71$

$x + 5 \approx 6.71 \text{ or } x + 5 \approx -6.71$

Solve the absolute value equation $x \approx 1.71 \text{ or } x \approx -11.71$

Problem 1   *Solve $2|9 - x_1| = 26$ for x_1.*

Solution   The equation contains an absolute value quantity that we will first isolate.

$$2|9 - x_1| = 26$$

Divide both sides by 2

$$\frac{2|9 - x_1|}{2} = \frac{26}{2}$$

Solve the absolute value equation

$$|9 - x_1| = 13$$

$$
\begin{array}{ccccc}
9 - x_1 = & 13 & \text{or} & 9 - x_1 = & -13 \\
-9 & & & -9 & \\
\hline
-x_1 = & 4 & \text{or} & -x_1 = & -22 \\
x_1 = & -4 & \text{or} & x_1 = & 22
\end{array}
$$

The solution set is $\{-4, 22\}$.

Problem 2   *A right triangle contains an angle of 90°. The side opposite the right angle is called the **hypotenuse**. The other sides are called **legs**.*
*The **Pythagorean Theorem** states: for any right triangle,*
$(\text{leg } L_1)^2 + (\text{leg } L_2)^2 = (\text{hypotenuse})^2$.
Use the Pythagorean Theorem to find the length of the hypotenuse, $\overline{AC}$, in right triangle ABC.

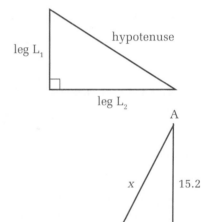

Solution   We can substitute the lengths of sides $\overline{BC}$ and $\overline{AB}$ into the following equation.

$(BC)^2 + (AB)^2 = (AC)^2$

$$(8)^2 + (15.2)^2 = x^2$$
$$64 + 231.04 = x^2$$
$$295.04 = x^2$$

Take the square root of each side

$$\sqrt{295.04} = \sqrt{x^2}$$
$$17.2 \approx |x|$$
$$x \approx 17.2 \text{ or } x \approx -17.2$$

There are two solutions to the equation. However, x is the length of a side of a triangle, so -17.2 is not a possible answer. The length of $\overline{AC}$ is about 17.2.

Part Three: Exercises and Problems

Warm-up Exercises

In problems 1–6, solve for x.

1

$x + 5$ $x + 5$

-13   0   13

2

$3x$ $3x$

-15   0   15

3

$x - 4$ $x - 4$

-9   0   9

4 $x^2 = -25$

5 $(x - 2)^2 = 25$

6 $(x + 1)^2 = 49$

7 In triangle ABC, what is the length of the leg labeled x? (Hint: Use the Pythagorean Theorem.)

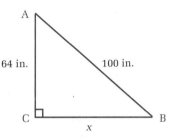

A

64 in.   100 in.

C   x   B

Problem Set

In problems 8–11, solve for x.

8 $\left|\frac{1}{2}x\right| = 8$

9 $|x| = -7$

10 $|-4| - x = 10$

11 $|12|x = 15$

12 Twice the absolute value of a number is 8. Find the solution set.

In problems 13–21, find the solution set of each equation.

13 $|y + 3| = 11$

14 $6|x + 1| = 48$

15 $|x_2 - 3| = 17$

16 $|2x - 1| = 9$

17 $3|5a| = 30$

18 $|y| = y$

19 $-2|x + 1| = -28$

20 $|y| = -y$

21 $-2|3x| = -16$

22 The graph shows the daily profits of Tony's Lemonade Stand.

  a What is Tony's average profit?

  b How many days were the profits above average?

  c Draw another graph to show the total profit accumulated each day.

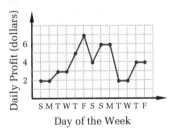

Daily Profit (dollars)

6

4

2

S M T W T F S S M T W T F

Day of the Week

In problems 23–26, evaluate each square root.

23 $\sqrt{4^2}$

24 $\sqrt{0^2}$

25 $\sqrt{(-5)^2}$

26 $\sqrt{-5^2}$

In problems 27–30, simplify each expression and solve each equation.

27 $9(x - 11) = 4(x + 4)$

28 $3.5 = 6 - (4 - 11x)$

29 $9(x - 2.5) + 4(x + 3.75)$

30 $8(3.4 - 2.1x) - 3(5.1x + 3.2)$

Problem Set, *continued*

31 Jamie can solve 2 equations per minute. Mackey can solve 3 equations per minute. If Jamie starts working at 10:00 A.M. and Mackey starts working at noon, at what time will Mackey have solved as many equations as Jamie?

In problems 32 and 33, solve for x.

32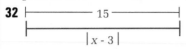

33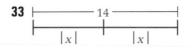

In problems 34–42, solve for x.

34 $x^2 = 1.96$ **35** $2x^2 = 8$ **36** $\sqrt{x^2} = 36$

37 $\sqrt{x^2} = 0$ **38** $x^2 = 46$ **39** $x^2 = -36$

40 $(x - 3)^2 = 144$ **41** $2|x + 3| = 28$ **42** $3|x - 4| = 6$

43 The sum of the absolute value of a number and 8 is 15. Find the solution set.

In problems 44–46, find the solution set of each equation.

44 $(x + 3)^2 = 36$ **45** $(x - 6)^2 = 0$ **46** $(2x - 6)^2 = 4$

47 If the absolute value of the difference between x and 5 is 9, what is x?

48 If a number is selected at random from $\{-6, -3, -2, -1, 0, 1, 2, 3, 6\}$, what is the probability that it is a solution of $x^2 = |5x + 6|$?

49 A 25-foot ladder is to touch a wall at a point 20 feet above the ground. How far away from the wall should the foot of the ladder be placed?

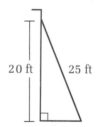
20 ft   25 ft

50 Mary Thon and Howie Runs compete in a 5-kilometer (5000-meter) race. Mary starts 4 minutes after Howie. If the race ends in a tie and if Howie runs 250 meters per minute, what is Mary's rate?

51 Solve for p and q.

$$\begin{bmatrix} p & 4 \\ 2p & q \end{bmatrix} \cdot \begin{bmatrix} 3 \\ 5 \end{bmatrix} = \begin{bmatrix} 8 \\ 6 \end{bmatrix}$$

52 Find x if the area of the rectangle is 64.

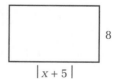
8

$|x + 5|$

In problems 53–55, graph each inequality on a number line.

53 $x \geq 6$ **54** $x - 4 \leq 5$ **55** $2x > -4$

56 If $(|x + 3|, y) = (7, 2)$, find x and y.

57 The area of the small square is 49. Find the area of the shaded region.

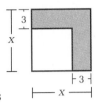

In problems 58–60, graph each set of numbers on a number line.

58 All positive integers less than or equal to 7.5
59 All integers whose squares are less than 20
60 All real numbers whose squares are less than 20

61 Find the length of the road to the nearest tenth of a mile.

24.6

62 If $(x_1, y_1) = (-3, 4)$ and $(x_2, y_2) = (19, -38)$, find (x_m, y_m) for

$$(x_m, y_m) = \left(\frac{x_1 + x_2}{2}, \frac{y_1 + y_2}{2} \right).$$

63 Find the length of each line segment.

a $\overline{PQ}$
b $\overline{QR}$
c $\overline{PR}$

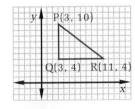

In problems 64–69, simplify each expression and solve each equation.

64 $|x| + 3|x| = 14$ **65** $\sqrt{x} = 9$ **66** $x^2 = 9$
67 $|x| = 9$ **68** $3x_1 - 9y + 11(y - 2x_1)$ **69** $3|x| + 6|x|$

70 What property is illustrated? If $x(x - 3) = 0$, then $x = 0$ or $x - 3 = 0$.

In problems 71–73, solve for x.

71 $\sqrt{(x - 2)^2} = 36$ **72** $\sqrt{(x - 2)^2} = 0$ **73** $\sqrt{(x - 2)^2} = -5$

74 The absolute value of the difference of a number and 7 is 15. Find the solution set.

Problem Set, *continued*

75 Franco and Page are on opposing football teams. Franco gets the ball at his team's 20-yard line and runs for a touchdown. When Franco reaches his own 40-yard line, Page runs after him from Franco's 20-yard line. Franco runs 7 yards per second, and Page runs 8 yards per second. Will Page catch Franco before he scores the touchdown? If so, on what yard line?

In problems 76–81, solve each equation.

76 $\sqrt{(x-3)^2} + 2|x-3| = 27$

77 $|3x - 5| + 27 = 36$

78 $2|y - 3| - 4|y - 3| = -24.5$

79 $|x| = |x| - 2$

80 $\sqrt{x^2} + 3\sqrt{x^2} = 4|x|$

81 $2|x - 3| + 5|x - 3| = 7x - 21$

WOMEN IN MATHEMATICS
It all started with Pythagoras

Pythagoras of Samos is one of history's most celebrated mathematicians. You probably know his famous theorem about the length of the sides of right triangles. The school he founded over 2500 years ago in southern Italy laid the foundation for all of later mathematics.

What is not so well known is that Pythagoras was the first important figure in history to recognize women as the equals of men in mathematics. He brought 28 women into his school, including his wife Theano, who wrote brilliantly on mathematics, physics, medicine, and child psychology. After her husband's death, Theano and two of her daughters took over the school and started several others.

Pythagorean schools prospered for over a century. Pythagoras influenced the great philosopher Plato, who brought women into his own schools in Athens. There women made important contributions in mathematics, philosophy, and a host of other areas.

The Pythagoreans studied the numbers 1, 3, 6, 10, 15 . . . , which they called "triangular" numbers. Can you tell why? What are the next five triangular numbers?

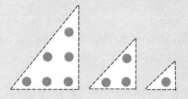

MORE EQUATIONS WITH ABSOLUTE VALUES OR SQUARED QUANTITIES

Objective

After studying this section, you will be able to
- Solve more interesting equations

Part One: Introduction

More Interesting Equations

We can use the familiar strategies of isolating the absolute value term, combining like terms, and applying the definition $\sqrt{x^2} = |x|$ when we solve equations with absolute values or squared quantities.

Example   *Solve each equation.*

a $|n| + 14.2 = 17.5$ **b** $5(w + 3)^2 + 10 = 30$

Our strategy is to isolate the quantity that contains the variable.

a

$$|n| + 14.2 = 17.5$$

Subtract 14.2 from each side $\underline{\quad -14.2 \quad -14.2\quad}$

Solve the absolute value equation $|n| \qquad = \quad 3.3$

$$n = 3.3 \text{ or } n = -3.3$$

The solution set is {3.3, −3.3}. Be sure to check the solutions.

b

$$5(w + 3)^2 + 10 = 30$$

Subtract 10 from each side $\underline{\quad\quad\quad -10 \quad -10\quad}$

$$5(w + 3)^2 \quad = \quad 20$$

Divide each side by 5 $$\frac{5(w + 3)^2}{5} = \frac{20}{5}$$

$$(w + 3)^2 = 4$$

Take the square root of both sides $$\sqrt{(w + 3)^2} = \sqrt{4}$$

$$|w + 3| = 2$$

Solve the absolute value equation $w + 3 = 2 \text{ or } w + 3 = -2$

$$w = -1 \text{ or } \qquad w = -5$$

The solution set is {−1, −5}.

Part Two: Sample Problems

Problem 1   Solve each equation.

    a $3|2y - 3| + 2|2y - 3| = 35$ **b** $|x| + 3(|x| - 2) = 4|x| - 6$

Solution   Our strategy will be to combine like terms.

a

$$3|2y - 3| + 2|2y - 3| = 35$$

Combine like terms $5|2y - 3| = 35$

Divide both sides by 5 $\dfrac{5|2y - 3|}{5} = \dfrac{35}{5}$

                        $|2y - 3| = 7$

Solve the absolute value equation

$$2y - 3 = 7 \text{ or } 2y - 3 = -7$$
$$\underline{+3 \quad +3} \qquad \underline{+3 \quad +3}$$
$$2y \quad = 10 \qquad 2y \quad = -4$$
$$y = 5 \qquad\qquad y = -2$$

The solution set is $\{-2, 5\}$. Be sure to check both solutions.

b

$$|x| + 3(|x| - 2) = 4|x| - 6$$
$$|x| + 3|x| - 6 = 4|x| - 6$$

Combine like terms $4|x| - 6 = 4|x| - 6$

This is an identity. Therefore, the equation is a true statement for any value of x. The solution set is $\{x : x \in \mathfrak{R}\}$.

Problem 2   Solve $|x + 4| = x - 2$.

Solution   Since this equation contains an absolute value quantity, either:

$$
\begin{array}{lll}
x + 4 = \quad x - 2 & & x + 4 = -(x - 2) \\
\underline{-x \qquad\quad -x} & \text{or} & x + 4 = -x + 2 \\
\qquad 4 = \quad -2 & & \underline{+x \qquad\quad +x} \\
& & 2x + 4 = \qquad 2 \\
& & \underline{\quad\; -4 \qquad -4} \\
& & 2x \quad = \quad -2 \\
& & x = -1
\end{array}
$$

The first equation has no solution, and the second equation gives us an apparent solution of -1. Let's check it.

Check

Left Side	Right Side
$|x + 4|$	$x - 2$
$= |-1 + 4|$	$= -1 - 2$
$= |3|$	$= -3$
$= 3$	

If $x = -1$, the sides are not equal, so the answer does not check. This equation has no solution. The solution set is the empty set, $\{\ \}$.

    An apparent solution that does not check is called an **extraneous solution** of the equation. In Sample Problem 2, the number -1 is an extraneous solution of the original equation.

Part Three: Exercises and Problems

Warm-up Exercises

In problems 1–6, solve each equation.

1 $|x - 3| + 4 = 8$

2 $|2y + 7| - 3 = 5$

3 $(2c - 1)^2 - 4 = 21$

4 $(x + 9)^2 + 2 = 146$

5 $3(x - 2)^2 + 4(x - 2)^2 = 252$

6 $4|x + 3| - 2|x + 3| = 114$

Problem Set

In problems 7–10, solve for **y**.

7 $|y - 5| = 7$ **8** $|5 - y| = 7$ **9** $|5| - y = 7$ **10** $5 - |y| = 7$

In problems 11–14, evaluate each expression for $a = -2$, $b = 8$, $c = 10$, and $d = 41$.

11 a^b **12** $(-1)^d$ **13** $\sqrt{c^2 - b^2}$ **14** $\dfrac{a^5 c^3}{b^2}$

In problems 15–17, solve each equation.

15 $3|z| + 4|z| = 21$ **16** $-6|p| = -30$ **17** $14 - 2|r| = 8$

p

In problems 18 and 19, solve for **x**.

18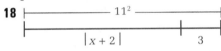

19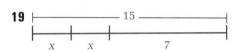

20 Find x if x is 12 units from 0 on a number line.

21 Find y if y is $|-5|$ units from 0 on a number line.

In problems 22–24, solve for **x**.

22 $4|x - 5| - 3|x - 5| = 11$

23 $|x + 6| + 2|x + 6| + 3|x + 6| = 18$

24 $7|x| = 8 + 5|x|$

25 Find the probability that an integer selected at random from $\{-4, -3, -2, -1, 0, 1, 2, 3, 4\}$ is within 3 units of 1.5 on the number line.

 26 If $(x_1, y_1) = (9, -3.4)$, $(x_2, y_2) = (-6.2, 15)$, and $m = \dfrac{y_2 - y_1}{x_2 - x_1}$, find m.

27 Find the value of y for the rectangle with a perimeter of 100.

$P = 100$ 7

$|2y - 3|$

Problem Set, *continued*

28 From 9:00 A.M. to noon, Pete travels west at 35 miles per hour. He stops one hour for lunch. He then continues driving west until 5:00 P.M. He travels a distance of 325 miles. What is Pete's average rate of travel in the afternoon?

In problems 29–31, solve for t.

29 $|t - 8| = 0$ **30** $|t| - |8| = 0$ **31** $t - |8| = 0$

32 A number added to the absolute value of the number is equal to 6. Find the number.

33 Find the value of x.

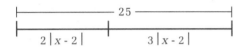

34 A number added to twice the absolute value of the number is equal to 6. Find the number.

35 The distance on the number line between x and 0 is less than 4 units. List all possible integer values of x.

36 Cal Lector has a coin collection containing some interesting older coins. The buffalo nickels are worth $0.75 each, the Mercury dimes are worth $0.85 each, and the Indian-head pennies are worth $0.45 each. He has the same number of nickels as he has dimes, and he has 5 fewer pennies than he has nickels. The total value of the coin collection is $26.45. Find the number of each type of coin in the collection.

37 The salaries of various types of engineers having various levels of experience at Micro Fish's Engineering, Inc., are shown in the matrix.

	Electrical	**Chemical**	**Civil**
1st Year	25,100	25,800	26,200
2nd Year	27,400	28,000	29,300
3rd Year	31,200	32,400	33,150

  a How much does a chemical engineer earn in the first 2 years at Micro Fish's?

  b How much more will a beginning civil engineer have earned than a beginning electrical engineer after each has worked at Micro Fish's for a period of 3 years?

  c Micro Fish's gives a 7% raise to all engineers. Write the new salary matrix.

38 For the equation $y = |x + 3|$, complete the table of values and graph the equation.

x	-6	-5	-4	-3	-2	-1	0	1
y								

In problems 39–42, graph each inequality on a number line.

39 $x > -5$ **40** $y \le 3.5$

41 All real numbers that are greater than or equal to -3.5 and less than -2.

42 All real numbers that are greater than -5 and that are also less than -6

43 The graph shows some items from the 1985 U.S. federal budget. Total expenses for 1985 were approximately $946 billion.

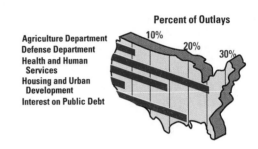

Percent of Outlays

Agriculture Department
Defense Department
Health and Human Services
Housing and Urban Development
Interest on Public Debt

a About how much was spent on defense?

b How much went to pay interest on the public debt?

c If the government paid around 9% interest per year on the debt, estimate the total debt in 1985.

In problems 44–46, solve for k.

44 $|2k - 5| = 13$ **45** $|2k| - 5 = 13$ **46** $|2k| - 5 = |13|$

47 The distance on the number line between x and -5 is 7 units. Find all possible values of x.

48 How far is it from point A to point C by way of point B?

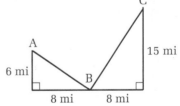

49 Find the coordinates of any point(s) 8 units from point B(2, 3) on a horizontal line drawn through point B.

In problems 50–52, graph each inequality on a number line.

50 $|x| < 5$ **51** $x^2 > 9$ **52** $x < -2$ or $x > 3$

53 Graph point P(-5, 2) on the Cartesian coordinate system. Find the coordinates of the 4 points 7 units from P on the vertical and the horizontal lines through P.

54 If $y = (x - 2)^2 + 7$ and $y = 11$, then solve for x.

Problem Set, *continued*

55 The rectangle has an area of 48.

   a Find the value of a.

   b Find the length of a diagonal of the rectangle.

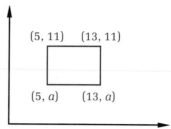

In problems 56–59, simplify each expression and solve each equation.

56 $9x_1 - 3(x_2 - 4x_1)$

57 $14.7(3.5y - 9) + 7(4.3 - 7.35y)$

58 $18|x - 5| - 36 = 0$

59 $4x(3x - 69) = 0$

60 Refer to the circle and the square in the coordinate system.

   a Find the ratio of the area of the circle to the area of the square. Express your answer to the nearest thousandth.

   b What percentage of the area of the square is the area of the circle? Express your answer to the nearest thousandth.

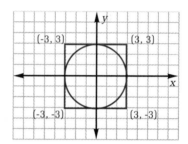

   c A point is selected at random from the set of all points that have x-coordinates and y-coordinates between -3 and 3. Find the probability that the point is in the circle.

61 Use a coordinate system.

   a Draw the four points A, B, C, and D if each point is a solution to $(|x|, |y|) = (2, 3)$.

   b Find the perimeter of the rectangle ABCD.

In problems 62 and 63, solve for x.

62 $\dfrac{|x|}{x} = 1$

63 $|x| = |x + 2|$

64 Rosie and Joe are riveters at Treetop Airlines. Every hour Rosie installs 1200 rivets and Joe installs 1450 rivets. Each day Joe starts riveting 2 hours later than Rosie. They quit at the same time.

   a If Rosie works 8 hours each day, what is the total number of rivets both riveters will install in a day?

   b An airplane requires 73,200 rivets. How many days will it take for both Rosie and Joe working together to completely rivet one airplane?

SURVEY PROJECTS

Objective

After studying this section, you will be able to
- Collect, graph, and interpret data

These projects will give you the opportunity to collect your own data. You can graph the data by using one of the methods you studied in Section 3.8 and then interpret the results.

1 Listen to a radio station that specializes in music. Determine how many minutes in one hour are actually spent playing music. Several people should keep track of this time systematically for a week. Then try to answer the following questions.

  a Is as much time spent playing music from 8:00 A.M. to 9:00 A.M. as from 4:00 P.M. to 5:00 P.M.? As from 8:00 P.M. to 9:00 P.M.?

  b Does the amount of time spent playing music vary from day to day through the week?

  c Find how the nonmusic time is used. How is it divided among commercials, disc jockey chatter, news, and phone calls from listeners?

  d Determine the best way to communicate your results. Will a graph make it easier for people to understand your data? If so, what kind of graph will be most effective?

  e Compare your results with those of groups who surveyed competing stations.

2 Take a survey to determine which of four TV shows is the most popular. What conclusions can you draw?

3 Take a survey to determine how much TV your classmates watch on a daily basis. Draw a bar graph to represent your findings. You will have to figure out ways to collect the data. Someone else might do the same thing for a group of adults and compare the two graphs.

  Here are some questions for you to consider before you begin.

  a How can you be sure your information is accurate?

  b Do you expect that the results will be the same from one week to the next, or will there be some variation? Why?

  c Will the results depend on what month it is? Why?

  d Is it necessary to keep track of all 7 days, or will the results be the same from one day to the next?

CHAPTER SUMMARY

CONCEPTS AND PROCEDURES

After studying this chapter, you should be able to
- Solve equations that have a variable on both sides (4.1)
- Identify equations that have no solutions and those that are identities (4.2)
- Identify equal matrices (4.2)
- Use the Distributive Property of Multiplication over Addition or Subtraction to solve equations (4.3)
- Solve matrix equations using matrix multiplication (4.3)
- Solve rate problems (4.4)
- Solve equations involving absolute values and squared quantities (4.5, 4.6)
- Describe solutions to equations as solution sets (4.5)
- Use the Pythagorean Theorem (4.5)
- Collect, graph, and interpret data (4.7)

VOCABULARY

empty set (4.5)   identity (4.2)
equal matrices (4.2)   legs (4.5)
extraneous solution (4.6)   Pythagorean Theorem (4.5)
hypotenuse (4.5)

SYMBOLS

{ }   empty set
$\{x : x \geq 0\}$ the set of all numbers such that x is greater than or equal to zero
$\{x : x \in \mathcal{R}\}$ the set of all numbers such that x is an element of the set of real numbers

REVIEW PROBLEMS

In problems 1–4, solve each equation.

1 $3x + 5 = 2x - 9$

2 $4x_2 - 3 = 12x_2 - 9.8$

3 $4(y - 7) = 3(y + 2)$

4 $-4.6(2x - 5) + 7 = 2(5x + 9)$

In problems 5–7, solve for x.

5 $|3 + x| = 7$

6 $|3| + x = 7$

7 $3 + |x| = 7$

8 Find x if the area of the rectangle is 120.

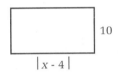

In problems 9 and 10, solve for a, b, c, and d.

9 $\begin{bmatrix} a^2 & |b| \\ \sqrt{c} & d \end{bmatrix} = \begin{bmatrix} 36 & 36 \\ 36 & 36 \end{bmatrix}$

10 $\begin{bmatrix} 3a + 8 & 5b \\ -2c & 4d - 12 \end{bmatrix} = \begin{bmatrix} a - 90 & b + 30 \\ c - 15 & 0 \end{bmatrix}$

11 Find all ordered pairs (x, y) such that x and y are even integers and their product is 12.

12 The sum of -4 and the square of a number is 21. Find the number.

13 Given AB = CD, find x.

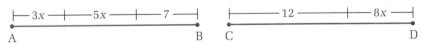

14 Alice and Betsy are writing invitations to Cathy's wedding. Alice starts at 8:00 A.M., and Betsy starts at 10:00 A.M. Alice writes 20 invitations per hour, and Betsy writes 25.

   a How many invitations will be ready by noon?
   b If they need 355 invitations, at what time will they finish?
   c If they continue, at what time will Betsy have prepared as many invitations as Alice?

Review Problems, *continued*

15 Find x for the line segment.

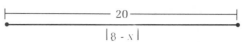

16 Multiply.

$$3 \begin{bmatrix} 4 & 2 \\ -5 & -6 \end{bmatrix} \begin{bmatrix} 2 \\ -3 \end{bmatrix}$$

17 Calculate the probability that a number chosen at random from $\{-4, 0, 2, 4, 6\}$ is a solution of $|x - 2| = 2 - x$.

 18 Find the distance from Midville to Summertown.

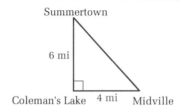

In problems 19–22, solve for **x**.

19 $(x + 3)^2 - 6 = 43$

20 $\sqrt{x^2} = 18$

21 $4|x - 4| = 8$

22 $3|x| + 5|x| = 32$

In problems 23–26, evaluate each expression if **x = 9** and **y = 4**.

23 $x^2 + y^2$

24 $(x + y)^2$

25 $\sqrt{x + y}$

26 $\sqrt{x} + \sqrt{y}$

 In problems 27–29, simplify each expression. Round each answer to the nearest tenth.

27 $(3.7)^3 - (4.6)(1.7)$

28 $\dfrac{2.9}{7.5(8.3)^2}$

29 $\sqrt{4^3 - (-5)^3}$

In problems 30–33, simplify each expression and solve each equation.

30 $3(x - 6) + 12(2x - 7)$

31 $|3x - 19| + 19 = 32$

32 $4(x - 5) = 5(x - 4) - x$

33 $5|x - 5| + 6|x - 5| - 3|x - 5| = 40$

34 The perimeter of the rectangle is 10.

a Find all possible values for x.

b Use the answers from part **a** to find all possible lengths of $\overline{AB}$.

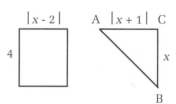

In problems 35–38, solve for **x**.

35 $\sqrt{x} + 7 = 16$

36 $3\sqrt{x^2} - 4|x| = 12$

37 $3(2x - 4) - (4x - 3) = 2x - 9$

38 $(x - 3)^2 + 5 = 12$

In problems 39–44, determine whether each is true Always, Sometimes, or Never.

39 $|x| = x$

40 $\sqrt{x^2} = |x|$

41 $\sqrt{x^2} = -x$

42 $|x| = -x$

43 $|x| < x$

44 $|x| > x$

45 Refer to the rectangle ABCD.

   a Write the coordinates of point D in terms of a.

   b Find the lengths of $\overline{AB}$ and $\overline{BC}$.

   c How long, to the nearest tenth, is the diagonal $\overline{AC}$?

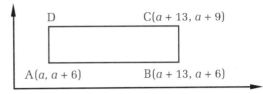

46 A shark can swim 15 feet per second, and a tuna can swim 13.5 feet per second. The tuna has a 7-second head start.

   a How close will the shark be to the tuna after 30 seconds?

   b Find the time it will take the shark to catch the tuna.

   c Find the distance the shark travels before catching the tuna.

47 Jay Lee and E. Claire work for King Donuts. Each hour, Jay makes 150 donuts, and E. Claire makes 120 donuts. Jay starts making donuts 1.5 hours after E. Claire starts.

   a If E. Claire makes donuts for 7 hours, how many donuts were made by both if they stopped at the same time?

   b If a total of 1502 donuts were made, how many hours, to the nearest tenth, did Jay work?

48 The perimeter of figure ABCDEF is 26.

   a Find x.

   b Find the length of diagonal $\overline{BD}$.

   c Find the area of the figure.

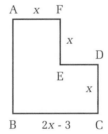

In problems 49 and 50, solve for x.

49 $\sqrt{(2.4 - x)^2} = 17.695$

50 $-12.26 = -4(x - 7.69)^2$

51 Spike Spoke and Frank Brake entered a 200-mile bicycle race. Both started on the 0.25-mile track at the same time and the same place. Spike traveled 20 miles per hour, and Frank traveled 19.5 miles per hour. Halfway through the race Spike's bicycle broke down, and he stopped for 0.5 hour to have it fixed. He then continued racing.

   a Who won the race?

   b How many laps was the loser behind the winner?

   c What is the most time that Spike could have taken to fix his bike and still have won the race?

CHAPTER TEST

1 Solve for x.

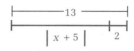

In problems 2–5, find the solution set.

2 $|2x - 1| = 9$

3 $\sqrt{x} = 4$

4 $\sqrt{2x + 3} = 9$

5 $3(x + 4) = 2(x + 6) + x$

6 Data Publishers has two printers. Printer A prints 300 pages per hour, and Printer B prints 275 pages per hour. On a job totaling 19,000 pages, how long must Printer B run to complete the job if Printer A runs 12 hours?

In problems 7 and 8, find the solution set.

7 $4(x + 1) = 2x + (2x + 1)$

8 $2(5 + 3x) = 3(2 + 5x)$

9 Geri had an average of 80% on four tests. What score must she get on the next test to raise her average to 83%?

In problems 10 and 11, solve for *t*.

10 $2|4t - 5| + |4t - 5| = 45$

11 $(t + 3)^2 + 12 = 98$

In problems 12 and 13, solve for *y*.

12 $5y^2 + 19y - 45 = 5y(y + 2)$

13 $3y + 2 = 4y - (5 - 2y)$

14 Solve for p and q.

$$\begin{bmatrix} 12p + 8 & 6q + 3 \\ 1 & p - q \end{bmatrix} = \begin{bmatrix} 20 & 3 \\ p + q & 1 \end{bmatrix}$$

15 If y is randomly selected from $\{-7, -5, -3, -1, 1, 3, 5, 7\}$, what is the probability that the figure is a square?

16 Solve for x and y.

$$\begin{bmatrix} 2x + 1 & 5 \\ 6 & y \end{bmatrix} \begin{bmatrix} 1 \\ -2 \end{bmatrix} = \begin{bmatrix} 21 \\ 15 \end{bmatrix}$$

PUZZLES AND CHALLENGES

1 Mr. Germany, Mr. America, and Mr. Brazil recently went on vacations to Germany, to America, and to Brazil. If exactly one of the following statements is true, who went where?

  i *Mr. Brazil went to Germany.*
  ii *Mr. Brazil did not go to America.*
  iii *Mr. Germany did not go to America.*
  iv *Mr. Germany did not go to Brazil.*

2 Two trains are 100 miles apart. They head toward each other, with the first train going 15 miles per hour and the second train going 10 miles per hour. On the front of the first train there is a fly which flies at thirty miles per hour. Just as the trains head toward each other, the fly leaves the first train and flies toward the second train. When it gets to the second train, it turns and flies back to the first train, then turns and flies to the second train, and so on, until the trains crash. At the time the trains crash, how far has the fly flown?

3 In this addition problem, each letter stands for a unique digit. If A = 3 and M = 4, complete the addition problem.

```
    S  A  M
 +  H  A  S
 ---------
 S  L  I  D
```

4 Interpret each cryptic clue.

a Famous psychologist holds one with less weight. (8)

b Different scuba men head most common letter. (7)

c Mixed-up hotel holds my first letter. I hate it. (6)

5 Interpret each expression.

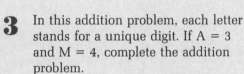

a
```
T  M
A  U
H  S
W  T
```

b ECNALG

c
```
D T S E
A     T
N     N
C E C O
```

5 WORKING WITH INEQUALITIES

Could a chimpanzee select a successful investment portfolio by throwing darts at the stock market listings in a newspaper? Surprisingly, the answer will be yes, if the Efficient Market Hypothesis proves to be correct.

The Efficient Market Hypothesis is only one of many mathematical models economists are now studying in an ongoing attempt to learn precisely how the stock market functions.

The Efficient Market Hypothesis is derived from the fact that the stock market is extremely quick to adjust to new information about individual stocks and the economy as a whole. According to the hypothesis, this speed may mean that no scheme for buying and selling stocks can consistently outperform a strategy of simply holding onto a group of securities that have been selected at random by an uninformed buyer, or even by a chimpazee.

5.1 SOLVING INEQUALITIES

Objectives

After studying this section, you will be able to
- Use the Addition and Subtraction Properties of Inequality
- Use the Multiplication and Division Properties of Inequality

Part One: Introduction

Addition and Subtraction Properties of Inequality

Solving inequalities is very similar to solving equations. The same strategies we used to solve equations can be used to solve inequalities.

What happens when the same number is added to both sides of an inequality?

$$
\begin{array}{r}
5 < 11 \\
+4 \quad +4 \\
\hline
9 < 15
\end{array}
$$

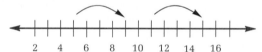

Adding 4 shifts both numbers 4 units to the right. The order of the sums remains the same as the order of the original numbers.

Let's see what happens when the same number is subtracted from both sides of an inequality.

$$
\begin{array}{r}
4 > -3 \\
-5 \quad -5 \\
\hline
-1 > -8
\end{array}
$$

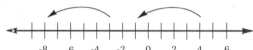

Subtracting 5 shifts both numbers 5 units to the left. The order of the differences is the same as the order of the original numbers.

The Addition and Subtraction Properties of Inequality

If the same number is added to or subtracted from both sides of an inequality, then the result is an inequality having the same order.

Example   Solve each inequality. (The solutions are given below.)

a $x + 7 < -4$

$$
\begin{array}{r}
x + 7 < -4 \\
-7 \quad -7 \\
\hline
x \quad\quad < -11
\end{array}
$$

b $9 \geq -14 + y$

$$
\begin{array}{r}
9 \geq -14 + y \\
+14 \quad +14 \\
\hline
23 \geq \quad\quad y
\end{array}
$$

We can express the solutions of an inequality in three ways:

- As an inequality
  $x < -11$ $y \leq 23$
- In set notation
  $\{x : x < -11\}$ $\{y : y \leq 23\}$
- As a graph on a number line

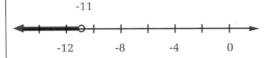

Multiplication and Division Properties of Inequality

What happens when both sides of an inequality are multiplied by the same positive number?

$$6 \quad > \quad -4$$
Is 2(6) greater than 2(−4)?
Yes, 12 $\quad > \quad$ −8.

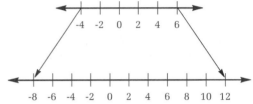

The number line shows that multiplying by 2 shifts the position of each number twice as far from zero as it was originally. The order of the products is the same as the order of the original numbers.

Now let's see what happens when both sides of an inequality are multiplied by the same negative number.

$$6 \quad > \quad -4$$
Is −2(6) greater than −2(−4)?
No, −12 $\quad < \quad$ 8.

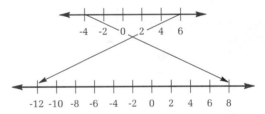

The number line shows that multiplying by −2 has two effects. It shifts the position of each number twice as far from zero as it was originally and it reverses the order of the inequality. The order of the products is the reverse of the order of the original numbers.

Now let's look at division.

$$-4 \quad < \quad -2 \qquad\qquad -4 \quad < \quad -2$$
Divide by 2. Is $\dfrac{-4}{2}$ less than $\dfrac{-2}{2}$?   Divide by −2. Is $\dfrac{-4}{-2}$ less than $\dfrac{-2}{-2}$?
Yes, −2 $\quad < \quad$ −1.   No, 2 $\quad > \quad$ 1.

The order of the inequality on the left remains the same. The order of the inequality on the right is reversed.

The pattern for division is the same as the pattern for multiplication because dividing by a number is the same as multiplying by the reciprocal of the number.

The Multiplication and Division Properties of Inequality

If both sides of an inequality are multiplied or divided by the same positive number, then the result is an inequality having the same order. If both sides of an inequality are multiplied or divided by the same negative number, then the result is an inequality having reversed order.

Example *Solve each inequality.*

a $\frac{1}{3}x \le 8$

$3\left(\frac{1}{3}x\right) \le 3(8)$

$x \le 24$

b $9 > -2y$

$\dfrac{9}{-2} < \dfrac{-2y}{-2}$

$-4.5 < y$

We can describe each solution as an inequality, using set notation or a graph.

$x \le 24$
$\{x : x \le 24\}$

$y > -4.5$
$\{y : y > -4.5\}$

Part Two: Sample Problems

Problem 1 *Solve and graph $4z + 5 \ge z$.*

Solution The order of the inequality remains the same

The order of the inequality is reversed

$$4z + 5 \ge z$$
$$\underline{-4z \qquad\quad -4z}$$
$$5 \ge -3z$$

$$\dfrac{5}{-3} \le \dfrac{-3z}{-3}$$
$$-1.\overline{6} \le z$$

The solution is $z \ge -1.\overline{6}$. The graph of the solution is as follows.

Problem 2 *Find the 2 smallest consecutive even integers whose sum is at least 51.*

Solution If we let $n =$ an even integer, then $n + 2 =$ the next even integer. If the sum of these two numbers is at least 51, the sum must be equal to or greater than 51.

$$n + (n + 2) \geq 51$$
$$2n + 2 \geq 51$$
$$\underline{ -2 \quad -2}$$
$$2n \quad \geq 49$$

The order of inequality remains
the same

$$\frac{2n}{2} \geq \frac{49}{2}$$

$$n \geq 24.5$$

The smallest even integer that is greater than 24.5 is 26. The next
even integer after 26 is 28. So 26 and 28 are the two smallest
consecutive even integers whose sum is at least 51.

Problem 3   *Find all values of x for which the perimeter is
at most 32.*

Solution   If the perimeter is at most 32, it is less than or equal to 32.

Write the inequality

$$2(x - 6) + 2x \leq 32$$
$$2x - 12 + 2x \leq 32$$
$$4x - 12 \leq 32$$
$$\underline{ +12 \quad +12}$$
$$4x \quad \leq 44$$

The order of the inequality remains
the same

$$\frac{4x}{4} \leq \frac{44}{4}$$

$$x \leq 11$$

Since the length of the side of a rectangle must be a positive number, x must be greater than 6. So, $x > 6$ and $x \leq 11$. This can be
written as $6 < x \leq 11$.

Part Three: Exercises and Problems

Warm-up Exercises

In problems 1–6, solve each inequality and graph the solution.

1 $x - 4 > 3$ **2** $y + 6 \leq 8$ **3** $3 > \frac{1}{2}x$

4 $-x > 4$ **5** $9 \leq 3x$ **6** $-2y < 6$

**In problems 7–10, express each of the following as an algebraic
inequality.**

7 A number is greater than or equal to 3.   **8** A number is less than $\frac{10}{3}$.

9    **10**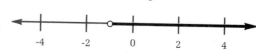

Problem Set

In problems 11–13, express each algebraic inequality as a complete sentence.

11 $4 > y$

12 $y < 4$

13 $-2 \le n$

In problems 14–19, solve each inequality and graph its solution set on a number line.

14 $5x + 18 \ge 43$

15 $-4y > 36$

16 $5(n - 3) < 135$

17 $3m - 4 \ge 4m + 5$

18 $98 \le 7(6 - 2n)$

19 $-3m < 57$

20 Find all values of x for which the perimeter is less than 37 inches.

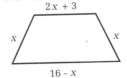

In problems 21–26, solve each inequality and express the solution set in set notation.

21 $15 - 3x < 2x$

22 $13 + x \ge 2x + 7$

23 $180 < 5x + 16$

24 $\frac{1}{3}x + 3 \le 91$

25 $2(2x - 5) > 90$

26 $6.2a > 5.6 - 9.1a$

In problems 27–30, write an inequality for each graph.

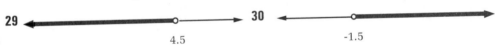

In problems 31–34, determine whether each statement is True or False if $a = 3$, $b = -2$, and $c = 6$.

31 $b^2 - 4ac < 0$

32 $0 < \frac{c}{a} + b$

33 $a(b + c) \ge ab + ac$

34 $a - b \le c$

35 Find all values of x for which the perimeter is at least 42 yards.

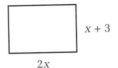

36 If a is selected at random from $\{-3, -2, -1, 0, 1, 2, 3\}$, find the probability that $a^2 - 2a - 3 < 0$.

37 Multiply the matrices.

$$\begin{bmatrix} 3 & -4 \\ -7 & 11 \end{bmatrix}\begin{bmatrix} -2 \\ -6 \end{bmatrix}$$

38 Write an inequality that describes the diagram. Then find all values of x that make the inequality true.

$3(x + 3)$ 5

39 If 30% of an integer is less than 43.3, find the largest possible integer for which this is true.

In problems 40–43, solve each inequality and graph its solution set.

40 $x < 2x + 5$ **41** $3x < -9$ **42** $-2 \leq 10 - 4z$ **43** $-x \leq -5$

44 Complete the table of values for $y = 3x - 7$ and then graph the equation.

x	-4	-3	-2	-1	0	1	2	3	4
y									

45 It is 405 miles from Bensonville to Dodgetown. Ham's car averages 21.3 miles per gallon of gasoline. Determine the least whole number of gallons of gasoline that Ham needs to make the trip.

46 Twice a number x exceeds 5 by at least 4. Find all possible values of x.

47 For the fraction $\dfrac{x}{2x - 5}$, find all values of x for which the numerator is less than the denominator.

In problems 48–51, solve each equation and simplify each expression.

48 $4(3x - 7) + \frac{1}{2}(8 - 6x) = 0$ **49** $3y(4y - 12) = 0$

50 $9 - (3 - 8y_2) - 5(y_2 + 3)$ **51** $y^2 - 4y = -3y$

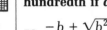

In problems 52 and 53, evaluate each expression to the nearest hundredth if $a = 2$, $b = 3$, and $c = -1$.

52 $\dfrac{-b + \sqrt{b^2 - 4ac}}{2a}$ **53** $\dfrac{-b - \sqrt{b^2 - 4ac}}{2a}$

54 Given the triangle, find the length of side x.

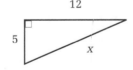

In problems 55–58, solve for x.

55 $|2x| = 10$ **56** $|x| - 8 = 17$ **57** $|x + 3| = 10$ **58** $x^2 = 36$

59 A natural number is less than the sum of its opposite and 8. Find all such numbers.

60 Find the 3 smallest consecutive integers whose sum is at least 89.

Problem Set, *continued*

61 You are given a number line.

    a How far apart are any two consecutive odd integers on this number line?

    b If n is an odd integer on this number line, find the next larger odd integer.

    c If n is an odd integer on this number line, find the next smaller odd integer.

    d If n + 3 is an even integer on this number line, find the next larger even integer.

In problems 62 and 63, write an inequality to describe each graph.

62

    -4   4

63

    -6   6

In problems 64–69, simplify each expression and solve each equation or inequality.

64 $-3(4x - 8) - (12 - 6x) \leq 0$

65 $-5(2x - 7) - 3(2x - 7) > -32$

66 $4x(3 - x) = 0$

67 $3x^2 + 2x \geq 3x^2 - 12$

68 $9(3 - 4x) - 3(3 - 4x)$

69 $12y - y^2 = 0$

70 A golf instructor received a $200 gift certificate. She used the certificate to buy two pairs of shoes at $45 each and as many golf balls as she could at $1.75 each. How many golf balls did she buy?

71 Write an inequality that describes the diagram. Then find all values of x that make the inequality true.

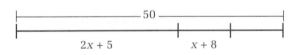

72 The sum of 2 consecutive odd integers is more than 145. Find the smallest pair of integers for which this is true.

73 Solve for x if 2x + 3y < 160 and y = 8; if y = x + 4.

74 Popular Video Rentals charted the number of tapes rented per day over several weeks.

    a On which days of the week are rentals slow?

    b On which days of the week are rentals brisk?

    c Give a possible reason for the variation in the number of rentals.

    d Suggest a way in which the manager might increase the number of rentals during the slower rental days.

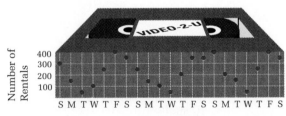

75 Steve and Liz have $12.50 to spend on lunch. Each buys 1 juice at $0.75, 1 salad at $1.59, and 2 hamburgers at $1.35 each. Let x be the number of orders of potatoes, costing $0.59 an order, that they can buy.

  a Write an expression for the total cost of lunch including x orders of potatoes.

  b Write an inequality that states that the total cost of both lunches is not more than the amount of money Steve and Liz have.

  c Determine how many orders of potatoes they can buy.

76 Solve for (x, y).

$$\begin{bmatrix} 3 & x \\ y & 5 \end{bmatrix} \begin{bmatrix} 4 \\ -2 \end{bmatrix} = \begin{bmatrix} 0 \\ 20 \end{bmatrix}$$

In problems 77 and 78, solve for x.

77 $3|2x - 2| + 2|2x - 2| = 20$ **78** $|x| + 8 = 6$

79 Find all pairs of natural numbers whose ratio is 3 to 4 and whose sum is less than 30.

80 Sally Forth leaves home at 8:00 A.M. and drives north at 45 miles per hour. Her friend Helen Dale leaves at 10:00 A.M. and heads north at 50 miles per hour. At what time will Helen catch up with Sally?

81 Solve for x if $|x - 3| + |3 - x| = 12$.

82 Set X contains four more elements than set Y. Determine how many elements set Y can contain if twice the number of elements in set X added to three times the number of elements in set Y is less than 160.

83 Find the area of square C.

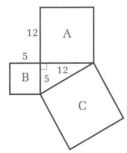

84 Assume that the denominator x of a fraction is greater than the numerator, $2x - 5$. Find all such fractions for which both the numerator and the denominator are positive integers.

USING INEQUALITIES

Objectives

After studying this section, you will be able to
- Use inequalities to classify angles
- Solve geometric problems involving inequalities

Part One: Introduction

Classifying Angles

There are many fields that use inequalities to solve problems. We can use equalities and inequalities to classify angles by measure.

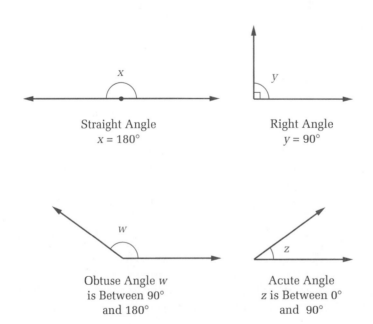

Straight Angle
$x = 180°$

Right Angle
$y = 90°$

Obtuse Angle w
is Between 90°
and 180°

Acute Angle
z is Between 0°
and 90°

Applications

We can name an angle by using a capital letter at its vertex, the point where the sides of an angle meet. We use the symbol $\angle$ instead of writing the word *angle*.

Example   *An angle is selected at random from this set.*

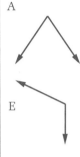
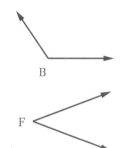
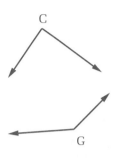
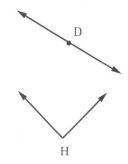

A

B

C

D

E

F

G

H

a *Determine the probability that it is an acute angle.*
The set contains 8 angles. $\angle A$ and $\angle F$ are acute angles, angles less than 90°. The probability is $\frac{2}{8}$, or $\frac{1}{4}$, or .25.

b *Determine the probability that it is a straight angle.*
The set contains 8 angles. $\angle D$ is a straight angle, an angle of 180°. The probability is $\frac{1}{8}$, or .125.

c *Determine the probability that it is an obtuse angle.*
The set contains 8 angles. $\angle B$, $\angle E$, and $\angle G$ are obtuse angles, angles greater than 90°. The probability is $\frac{3}{8}$, or .375.

d *Determine the probability that it is a right angle.*
The set contains 8 angles. $\angle C$ and $\angle H$ are right angles, angles of exactly 90°. The probability is $\frac{2}{8}$, or $\frac{1}{4}$, or .25.

Notice that the sum of the probabilities is 1. Why?

Part Two: Sample Problems

Problem 1   *If the measure of an angle is $5x + 40$, find the values of x for which the angle is acute.*

Solution   Since the angle must be acute, its measure must be greater than 0 and less than 90. We must solve two inequalities.

$$
\begin{array}{rl}
5x + 40 > & 0 \\
-40 \quad & -40 \\
\hline
5x \quad > & -40 \\
\dfrac{5x}{5} \quad > & \dfrac{-40}{5} \\
x > & -8
\end{array}
\qquad\qquad
\begin{array}{rl}
5x + 40 < & 90 \\
-40 \quad & -40 \\
\hline
5x \quad < & 50 \\
\dfrac{5x}{5} \quad < & \dfrac{50}{5} \\
x < & 10
\end{array}
$$

The angle with the measure $5x + 40$ will be acute if x is between -8 and 10. This can be expressed as $-8 < x < 10$.

Problem 2   Find x so that the area of the rectangle is less than 60.

$(16 - 2x)$

10

Solution   The area must be less than 60, and the lengths of the sides of the rectangle must be greater than 0. Therefore, we must solve two inequalities.

The first inequality is

$$\text{Area} < 60$$
$$10(16 - 2x) < 60$$

Distribute

$$160 - 20x < 60$$

Subtract 160 from each side

$$\underline{-160 \qquad\qquad -160}$$
$$-20x < -100$$

Divide by -20 (reverse the order)

$$\frac{-20x}{-20} > \frac{-100}{-20}$$
$$x > 5$$

The second inequality is

$$\text{Length of Side} > 0$$
$$16 - 2x > 0$$

Subtract 16 from each side

$$\underline{-16 \qquad\qquad -16}$$
$$-2x > -16$$

Divide by -2 (reverse the order)

$$\frac{-2x}{-2} < \frac{-16}{-2}$$
$$x < 8$$

For the rectangle above, the value of x must be less than 8 and greater than 5, or $5 < x < 8$.

Problem 3   Two angle measures are in the ratio 5 to 8. The sum of their measures is 78. Find the angle measures.

Solution   Since the two angle measures are in the ratio 5 to 8, we can express the angle measures as 5x and 8x. We know that $5x + 8x = 78$.

$$5x + 8x = 78$$
$$13x = 78$$
$$\frac{13x}{13} = \frac{78}{13}$$
$$x = 6$$

The angles measure 5(6), or 30, and 8(6), or 48.

Part Three: Exercises and Problems

Warm-up Exercises

In problems 1–8, classify the angle having the given measure.

1 97   **2** 42   **3** 90   **4** 180

5 2x if x = 30   **6** 2x if x = 45   **7** x − 10 if x = 90   **8** 2x + 5 if x = 50

9 The area of the rectangle must be less than 300. Which inequality or inequalities would you solve to find all possible values for x?

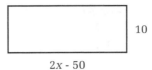

10

2x - 50

10 If the measure of an obtuse angle is 2y + 3, what are the possible values of y?

11 If the measure of an acute angle is 3x, what are the possible values of x?

Problem Set

12 If x = 12 and y = 8, find the measure and classification of each angle.

    a $\angle A = (90 + 3x)°$ **b** $\angle B = (5y - 3x)°$
    c $\angle C = (7x + 12y)°$ **d** $\angle D = (16x - y)°$

In problems 13–15, solve each inequality and graph the solution set.

13 $0 < 4x + 40$ **14** $4x + 40 < 90$ **15** $180 > 2x - 50$

16 The perimeter of the rectangle exceeds the perimeter of the triangle. Find all possible values of x.

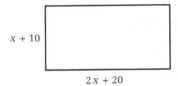

x + 10

2x + 20

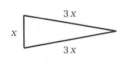

x

3x

3x

In problems 17 and 18, evaluate each expression.

17 $2(3^2 - 4.5) + \sqrt{49} - 8 \div 4$ **18** $(-3)^2 - (-3^2)$

19 Romeo and Juliet had a fight. Romeo drove off to the east in his Alfa Romeo at 50 miles per hour. Juliet rode west on her palomino at 6 miles per hour. When will they be 40 miles apart?

20 Rich had $1500 in his savings account. He then began depositing $755 every week. At the end of each month, Rich spends the interest. Let t be the number of weeks since he began making deposits.

    a Write an inequality stating that Rich's account has more than $10,000 and solve for t.
    b The federal government insures savings accounts up to $100,000. For how much longer will Rich's account be fully insured?

Problem Set, *continued*

In problems 21–26, simplify each expression and solve each equation or inequality.

21 $8(3 - x) > -4$

22 $4 - 3x - (6 - 5x)$

23 $|x| + 3 = 7$

24 $3x + 8 \leq 18 - 2x$

25 $2(3x + 5) = 8 - 6x$

26 $15 - |x| = 13$

27 Simplify the following.

$$-3 \begin{bmatrix} 3 & -4 \\ -9 & 11 \end{bmatrix} + \begin{bmatrix} -4 & 2 \\ -13 & 5 \end{bmatrix}$$

 28 The Speedy Rollers Paint Crew charges $18 per gallon for paint and $80 per hour for labor. If they use 22 gallons of paint and charge $1536, determine how many hours they worked.

In problems 29 and 30, the measure of ∠A is $3y + 8$.

29 Find y if ∠A is a right angle.

30 Find y if ∠A is a straight angle.

31 Find x if ∠B is 73°.

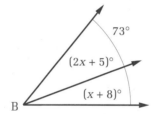

32 Three times the measure of an angle exceeds twice the measure of the same angle by 15. Find the measure of the angle.

33 Find x if the perimeter of the rectangle is greater than 140 and less than 600.

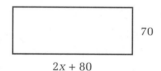

34 If the measure of x is selected at random from {10, 14, 18, 22, 26, 30}, what is the probability that ∠A is one of the following?

a Acute   **b** Right
c Obtuse   **d** Straight

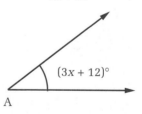

In problems 35–37, find the solution set of each inequality.

35 $2x - 4x < 10$

36 $4(3x + 2) \leq 8x + 12$

37 $-3(x + 5) > 30$

 38 Boomtown's population of 350,000 increases by 15,000 per year, and Ghostville's population of 200,000 decreases by 10,000 per year. In how many years will Boomtown's population be five times that of Ghostville?

39 Construct a table of values for $3x + 5y = 30$ using 0, 5, 10, 15, 20, and 25 for values of x. Then graph the equation.

40 Refer to the chart to answer the following questions.

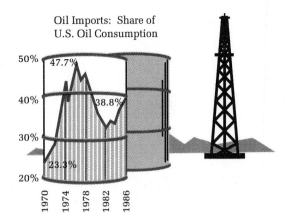

Oil Imports: Share of
U.S. Oil Consumption

    a Determine in which year imported oil was the greatest percentage of total U.S. oil consumption.

    b Determine in which year imported oil was the least percentage of total U.S. oil consumption.

    c Determine in which years imported oil was more than 40% of total U.S. oil consumption.

In problems 41–46, simplify each expression and solve each equation or inequality.

41 $4(3 - 6x) < -8(2 - 3x)$ **42** $18x + 45 > 0$ **43** $30 + 5(90 - x) = 100$

44 $2x^2 - 10x = 0$ **45** $x(3x - 7) - x(2x - 8)$ **46** $8(x - 3) - 5(x - 3) = 0$

In problems 47–49, determine whether each inequality is a True or a False statement if $(x_1, y_1) = (-4, 6)$.

47 $y_1 - 3x_1 > 15$ **48** $\frac{y_1}{x_1} < -2$ **49** $x_1{}^2 + y_1{}^2 \leq 75$

50 The measures of $\angle 1$ and $\angle 2$ are in the ratio 3 to 10. Find the angle measures and classify each angle.

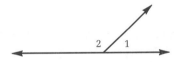

51 The water tower of Shermerville, Illinois, holding 500,000 gallons, springs a leak near the bottom of the tank, and water begins to drain at the rate of 15 gallons per hour.

    a Write an expression for the amount of water in the tank after t hours if no water is added to the tank.

    b Using t, write an inequality indicating that more than $\frac{1}{10}$ of the water has drained out of the tank. Solve the inequality.

52 An ordered pair (x, y) is randomly selected from the set $\{(-3, 4), (4, 5), (-2, 6), (4, -2), (0, 6)\}$. Find the probability that it is a solution for $x^2 + y^2 \leq 25$.

53 The measures of two angles are in the ratio 3 to 7. The sum of their measures is equal to the measure of a right angle. Find the angle measures.

54 The ratio of AB to BC is 5 to 3, and the ratio of BC to CD is 3 to 2. Find the length of $\overline{AD}$ if AB = 6.

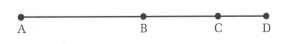

COMPOUND INEQUALITIES

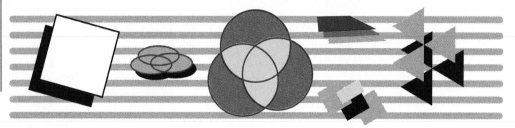

Objectives

After studying this section, you will be able to
- Find the intersection of sets
- Find the union of sets
- Solve compound inequalities

Part One: Introduction

Intersection of Sets

Let A be the set of all factors of 12: A = {1, 2, 3, 4, 6, 12}.
Let B be the set of all factors of 8: B = {1, 2, 4, 8}.
The intersection of sets A and B, A ∩ B, is the set of numbers that are both factors of 12 and factors of 8. This set is {1, 2, 4}.

A *Venn diagram* is one way to show the relationship between two or more sets. The shaded region shows the intersection of sets represented by A ∩ B. The *intersection* of set A and set B is the set of all elements that are in set A and in set B.

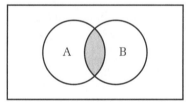

Example   *Graph 35 < x and x < 80 on a number line.*

First we graph 35 < x, and then we graph x < 80. The final graph shows the intersection (∩) of the first two graphs.

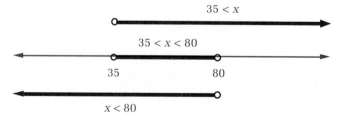

The intersection contains the numbers between 35 and 80, and the solution set may be written as {x : 35 < x < 80}.

Union of Sets

Let A be the set of positive multiples of 6 that are less than 25:
A = {6, 12, 18, 24}. Let B be the set of positive multiples of 8 that are
less than 25: B = {8, 16, 24}.

The union of sets A and B, represented
by A ∪ B, is the set of positive numbers less
than 25 that are multiples of 6 or multiples
of 8 or both. This set is {6, 8, 12, 16, 18, 24}.

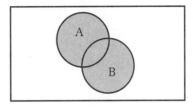

The *union* of set A and set B is the set
of all elements that are either in set A *or* in
set B or in both sets.

Example   *Graph x ≥ 6 or x ≤ −6 on a number line.*

First we graph x ≥ 6, and then x ≤ −6. The final graph shows the
union (∪) of the two graphs.

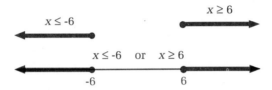

The union contains all numbers greater than or equal to 6 or less
than or equal to −6, and may be written as {x:x ≥ 6 or x ≤ −6}.

Compound Inequalities

When two inequalities are combined, the result is called a ***compound inequality.*** To solve a compound inequality, solve each inequality separately, and then find the union (∪) or the intersection
(∩) of the solution sets, whichever is indicated.

Example   *Solve for x if 3x − 15 < 36 and 3x − 15 > −36.*

$$3x - 15 < 36 \qquad \text{and} \qquad 3x - 15 > -36$$
$$\underline{+ 15 \quad + 15} \qquad\qquad\qquad \underline{+ 15 \quad + 15}$$
$$3x \quad < 51 \qquad\qquad\qquad 3x \quad > -21$$
$$\frac{3x}{3} < \frac{51}{3} \qquad\qquad\qquad \frac{3x}{3} > \frac{-21}{3}$$
$$x < 17 \quad \text{and} \qquad\qquad x > -7$$

Remember that *and* means intersection, so the solutions to the compound inequality are all numbers between −7 and 17, written
{x: −7 < x < 17}.
This is the graph of the solution set.

$$-7 < x < 17$$

Part Two: Sample Problem

Problem   *Write a compound inequality for each graph. Then write the solution as an intersection or union.*

a

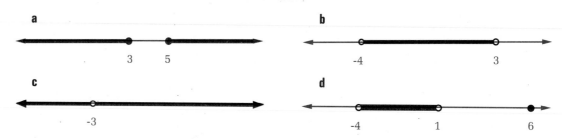

b

c

d

Solution   **Compound Inequality**   **Solution Set**

a $x \leq 3$ or $x \geq 5$ $\{x : x \leq 3\} \cup \{x : x \geq 5\}$

b $x > -4$ and $x < 3$ $\{x : x > -4\} \cap \{x : x < 3\}$
(also written as $-4 < x < 3$)

c $x > -3$ or $x < -3$ $\{x : x > -3\} \cup \{x : x < -3\}$
(also written as $x \neq -3$)

d $-4 < x < 1$ or $x = 6$ $\{x : -4 < x < 1\} \cup \{6\}$

Part Three: Exercises and Problems

Warm-up Exercises

In problems 1–4, match each compound inequality with the description of its solution set.

1 $x < 4$ or $x > 7$ **a**

2 $4 < x$ and $x < 7$ **b** $\{\ \}$
3 $x < 5$ or $x > 5$ **c** $\{x : x > 4\} \cap \{x : x < 7\}$

4 $x < 5$ and $x > 5$ **d**

In problems 5 and 6, give a compound inequality for each graph.

5   **6**

In problems 7 and 8, refer to the Venn diagram. List the elements of each intersection or union.

7 $A \cap B$
8 $(A \cup B) \cap C$

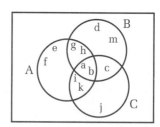

In problems 9–12, solve each compound inequality, describe the solution set, and draw the graph.

9 $12x - 13 \leq 59$ and $6x + 4 > -2$

10 $2x < -2$ or $\frac{1}{2}x \geq 3$

11 $5x - 9 < -4$ or $-3x + 2 < -16$

12 $4x + 31 \geq 11 - x$ and $2x \geq 3x + 1$

13 Radio stations WARP and WUFF are 100 miles apart. WARP has a broadcast range of 45 miles, and WUFF has a broadcast range of 28 miles. S.H. Uttle is biking from WARP to WUFF at a rate of 18 miles per hour. Let t be the number of hours S.H. has been biking.

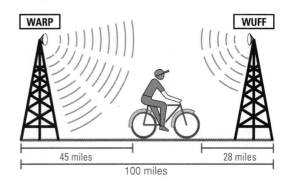

a Using t, write an inequality to indicate that S.H. is within listening range of WARP. Solve the inequality.

b Write an expression for S.H.'s distance from WUFF after biking for t hours.

c Using t, write an inequality to indicate that S.H. is within listening range of WUFF. Solve the inequality.

d Write a compound inequality to indicate when S.H. is in listening range of both WARP and WUFF during his bike trip.

Problem Set

In problems 14–22, graph each inequality on a number line.

14 $x \geq 15$

15 $3.5 > y$

16 $z \leq -5$

17 $\{x : x < 5\}$

18 $\{y : y \geq -2\}$

19 $\{x : -3.5 < x \leq 9.5\}$

20 $3 < x$ and $x \leq 5$

21 $x < -3$ or $x \geq 5$

22 $-8 < x < -3$

In problems 23 and 24, write compound inequalities to describe the union of the two sets and the intersection of the two sets.

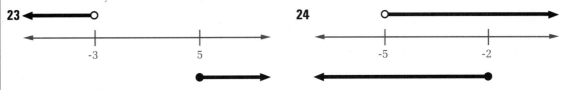

25 List all integers that are less than 5 units from 2.5 on the number line.

26 Radio stations WARM and KOOL are 175 miles apart. WARM has a broadcast range of 60 miles, and KOOL has a broadcast range of 65 miles. Ral Lee is biking from KOOL to WARM at 14 miles per hour. During what time range of the trip can Ral not listen to either station?

Problem Set, *continued*

27 Make two copies of the Venn diagram.

   a In one, shade the region that represents A ∩ B.

   b In the other, shade the region that represents A ∪ B.

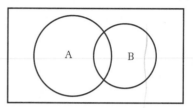

In problems 28 and 29, graph the solution of each compound inequality.

28 {x:x > 5} ∩ {x:3x ≤ 30}

29 {x:2x < −4} ∪ {x:x + 4 > 3}

30 If ∠C has a measure of 40 and ∠D measures 15% less than ∠C, find the measure of ∠D.

31 The miles per gallon for a car is the average number of miles it can be driven on 1 gallon of gasoline. For Honcho's car, the miles per gallon is always more than 22 but never above 31. If the car has an 11.3-gallon gasoline tank, what is the range for the number of miles the car can travel on 1 tank of gasoline?

32 Refer to the diagram.

   a Find all possible values of x if the measure of ∠A is more than 20 but less than 60.

   b Find all values of x if ∠A is an obtuse angle whose measure is less than 150.

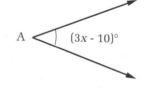

A $(3x - 10)°$

33 A museum hires students for part-time work at $4.25 an hour. Each student works from 15 to 25 hours per week. Find the range of weekly salaries for the students.

34 An airplane at 33,000 feet begins descending at 1200 feet per minute. A layer of clouds extends from an altitude of 24,000 feet down to 6000 feet. During what time interval of its descent is the airplane in the clouds?

35 Solve for x and y.

$$\begin{bmatrix} 6 & 2 \\ 3 & y \end{bmatrix}\begin{bmatrix} x \\ 4 \end{bmatrix} = \begin{bmatrix} 20 \\ -10 \end{bmatrix}$$

36 Find all values of x that will make the angle an obtuse angle.

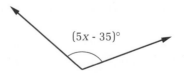

$(5x - 35)°$

37 Let A = {multiples of 8 between 5 and 50}. Let B = {multiples of 6 between 5 and 50}. List the elements of each set.

a A **b** B **c** A ∩ B **d** A ∪ B

In problems 38–41, solve each compound inequality, describe the solution set, and draw the graph.

38 $3y - 7 < y + 1$ or $y > -4y + 30$

39 $4x - 3 + 2x \leq 15$ and $-2 \leq x + 12$

40 $4x - 1 < 8x + 1$ and $3x + x + 1 < 7$

41 $4x - 2x < 7 - 2x$ or $5x > x + 7$

42 Graph the solution of $|x| < 5$ on a number line.

43 The cost of building a house is $35 per square foot. Write an expression for the cost of a house with x square feet. If a family can afford a house costing between $75,000 and $110,000, find the range of square feet of space they can have in their house.

MATHEMATICAL EXCURSION

BOOLEAN ALGEBRA

Can language be as exact as math?

During the nineteenth century, the English mathematician George Boole used mathematics to study logic. By changing language into symbols, he tried to create a rigorous system in which statements are examined for truth or falsity with mathematical exactness. The system, called Boolean algebra, has been used by philosophers and linguists who study the patterns of logical thought.

Whether or not a complex statement is true depends on the truth of its parts and the way they are combined. Let's look at a true statement and a false statement connected by the word *and*:

True	False	Combination
$8 \leq 10$	$6 \geq 19$	$8 \leq 10$ and $6 \geq 19$

We can see that both $8 \leq 10$ *and* $6 \geq 19$ cannot be true. This combination of these statements, called a conjunction, is false.

Now connect the statements with *or*: $8 \leq 10$ or $6 \geq 19$. This combination, called a disjunction, is true. If we represent conjunction with the symbol ∧ and disjunction with the symbol ∨, we can write that if p is true and q is false, then $p \wedge q$ is false but $p \vee q$ is true.

Can you complete the table? (Hint: Use some numerical statements for p and for q.)

p	q	$p \wedge q$	$p \vee q$
T	T		
T	F	F	T
F	T		
F	F		

ABSOLUTE VALUE AND OTHER INEQUALITIES

Objectives

After studying this section, you will be able to
- Use the distance method to solve absolute value inequalities
- Use the boundary algorithm to solve inequalities

Part One: Introduction

Distance Method of Solving Inequalities

You have already studied absolute value equations such as $|x - 4| = 6$. This equation means that $x - 4$ is 6 units from 0 on the number line.

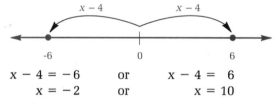

$$x - 4 = -6 \quad \text{or} \quad x - 4 = 6$$
$$x = -2 \quad \text{or} \quad x = 10$$

The solution set is $\{-2, 10\}$.

Absolute value inequalities often have solutions that are compound inequalities.

The inequality $|x - 4| < 6$ means that $x - 4$ is less than 6 units from 0 on the number line.

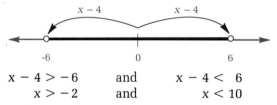

$$x - 4 > -6 \quad \text{and} \quad x - 4 < 6$$
$$x > -2 \quad \text{and} \quad x < 10$$

The solution set is $\{x: -2 < x < 10\}$.

The inequality $|x - 4| > 6$ means that $x - 4$ is more than 6 units from 0 on the number line.

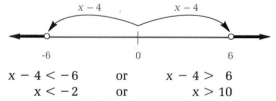

$$x - 4 < -6 \quad \text{or} \quad x - 4 > 6$$
$$x < -2 \quad \text{or} \quad x > 10$$

The solution set is $\{x: x < -2 \text{ or } x > 10\}$.

The Boundary Algorithm for Solving Inequalities

Another method for solving absolute value inequalities is the *boundary algorithm.* An *algorithm* is a step-by-step procedure for doing a specific task in a finite number of steps.

Four-Step Boundary Algorithm

1. **Find the boundary points by solving the corresponding absolute value equation.**

2. **Plot the boundary points on a number line.**

3. **Test the regions determined by the boundary points.**

4. **Graph the solution set of the absolute value inequality.**

Example

Solve for x if $|2x - 3| < 5$.

We can use the boundary algorithm.
Find the boundary points by solving the equation $|2x - 3| = 5$.

$$2x - 3 = -5 \qquad \text{or} \qquad 2x - 3 = 5$$
$$2x = -2 \qquad\qquad\qquad 2x = 8$$
$$x = -1 \qquad \text{or} \qquad x = 4$$

Plot the boundary points.

-1   4

Test a point from each of the three regions.

Region 1	Region 2	Region 3

-1   4

Let's choose -2, 0, and 6 as test values. We will test each value in $|2x - 3| < 5$.

Test Value	Left Side		Left Side < Right Side?	
-2	$|2(-2) - 3| = 7$		$7 < 5$?	No
0	$|2(0) - 3| = 3$		$3 < 5$?	Yes
6	$|2(6) - 3| = 9$		$9 < 5$?	No

Graph the solution by shading the region that contains 0. We leave the endpoints open, because the original inequality has the "less than" symbol ($<$). The endpoints would be closed if the original inequality used the "less than or equal to" symbol ($\leq$).

No   Yes   No

-1   4

The solution is $-1 < x < 4$.

Part Two: Sample Problems

Problem 1   *Solve for w if* $12 \geq |18 - 2w|$.

Solution   We can use the distance method. On the number line, the distance of $18 - 2w$ from 0 must be less than or equal to 12 units.

$$-12 \leq 18 - 2w \qquad \text{and} \qquad 18 - 2w \leq 12$$
$$-30 \leq -2w \qquad\qquad\qquad -2w \leq -6$$
$$15 \geq w \qquad \text{and} \qquad\quad w \geq 3$$

The solution is $3 \leq w \leq 15$.

Problem 2   *Solve for x if* $|x + 3| \leq 2x$.

Solution   We can use the boundary algorithm.

Find the boundary points by solving $|x + 3| = 2x$.

$$x + 3 = 2x \qquad \text{or} \qquad x + 3 = -2x$$
$$3 = x \qquad \text{or} \qquad\quad 3 = -3x$$
$$-1 = x$$

Checking these solutions, we find that 3 is the only solution of the original absolute value equation; -1 is an extraneous solution.

Plot the boundary points.

Test a point from each region. Let's choose -2, 0, and 4.

Test Value	Left Side	Right Side	Left Side $\leq$ Right Side?	
-2	$|-2 + 3| = 1$	$2(-2) = -4$	$1 \leq -4$?	No
0	$|0 + 3| = 3$	$2(0) = 0$	$3 \leq 0$?	No
4	$|4 + 3| = 7$	$2(4) = 8$	$7 \leq 8$?	Yes

Graph the solution set by shading the region that contains 4.

The solution is $x \geq 3$.

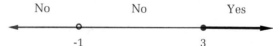

Problem 3   *Solve for x if* $(x - 2)(x + 3) \geq 0$.

Solution   We can use the boundary algorithm.

Find the boundary points by solving $(x - 2)(x + 3) = 0$. Use the Zero Product Property.

$$x - 2 = 0 \qquad \text{or} \qquad x + 3 = 0$$
$$x = 2 \qquad \text{or} \qquad x = -3$$

Plot the boundary points.

Test a point from each region. Let's choose -4, 0, and 4.

Test Value	Left Side	Left Side ≥ 0?
-4	$(-4-2)(-4+3) = 6$	Yes
0	$(0-2)(0+3) = -6$	No
4	$(4-2)(4+3) = 14$	Yes

Graph the solution set by shading the regions that contain -4 and 4.

The solution is $x \leq -3$ or $x \geq 2$.

Part Three: Exercises and Problems

Warm-up Exercises

In problems 1–6, describe what each statement means in terms of distance from 0 on the number line.

1 $|x| < 9$ **2** $|x + 3| = 5$ **3** $|x + 3| < 5$

4 $|x + 3| > 5$ **5** $|5 - 3x| \leq 14$ **6** $2|3x + 7| \leq 20$

In problems 7 and 8, find the boundary points.

7 $\left|7 + \frac{1}{2}x\right| < 9$ **8** $2|x + 3| \geq 10$

In problems 9 and 10, each graph gives the correct boundary points for the given inequality. Test the regions by choosing appropriate test values. Then describe the solution set.

9 $|2x + 7| > 11$ **10** $|2 - 4x| \leq 18$

11 Solve for x if $|x + 3| < 2x$.

12 If $3x$ is between 90 and 120, then x must be between _?_ and _?_.

Problem Set

In problems 13–18, solve for x.

13 $|x| > 2$ **14** $|x + 5| > 2$ **15** $|x - 1| \leq 3$

16 $|8x + 4| < 30$ **17** $|9x - 12| \geq 15$ **18** $|2x + 9| \leq -17$

19 If x is between 2 and 6, then $5x$ is between _?_ and _?_.

20 The sum of the measures of $\angle A$ and $\angle B$ is 125. Find the value of y.

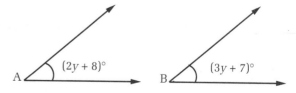

Problem Set, *continued*

21 If x is between 3 and 10, then 4x + 7 is between ___?___ and ___?___ .

In problems 22–24, solve for x and graph each solution on a number line.

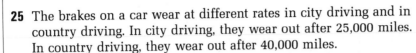

22 $|x + 8| = 3x$ **23** $\left|\frac{1}{2}x - 1\right| < 3$ **24** $\left|\frac{2}{3}x - 6\right| > 9$

25 The brakes on a car wear at different rates in city driving and in country driving. In city driving, they wear out after 25,000 miles. In country driving, they wear out after 40,000 miles.

  a If a car has been driven 10,000 miles in the country, determine how many miles the car can be driven in the city before the brakes wear out.

  b If a car has been driven 20,000 miles in the city, determine how many miles the car can be driven in the country before the brakes wear out.

  c A car has been driven 4000 miles in the city and 12,000 miles in the country. Determine how many more miles the car can be driven in the city if it is to go another 20,000 miles in the country before its brakes are replaced.

In problems 26–31, graph each solution on a number line.

26 x ≥ 5 and x < 10   **27** {x : x < −2} ∩ {x : x < 0}   **28** {x : −3 < x ≤ 5.5}

29 x > 4 and x > 7   **30** x ≠ −2   **31** x < −2 or x > −1

32 Find all values of x for which the diagram is possible.

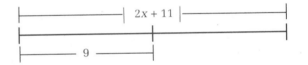

33 A 1990 model car gets between 13 and 18 miles per gallon of gasoline. If the tank holds 14 gallons, determine the range of distances the car can be driven on one tank of gasoline.

34 If 4x + 1 is between 17 and 45, then x must be between ___?___ and ___?___ .

In problems 35 and 36, write a compound inequality to describe each graph.

35

36

In problems 37 and 38, write an absolute value inequality to describe each graph.

37

38

39 If y_1 is randomly selected from $\{-8, -4, 0, 4, 8\}$, find the probability that y_1 is a solution of $|2y_1 - 3| < 9$.

 In problems 40 and 41, evaluate each expression for $a = -3$, $b = 6$, and $c = 5$. Round the answer to the nearest hundredth.

40 $\dfrac{-b + \sqrt{b^2 - 4ac}}{2a}$ **41** $\dfrac{-b - \sqrt{b^2 - 4ac}}{2a}$

In problems 42 and 43, write an absolute value inequality to describe each graph.

42
      -5   5
        43
            -8   8

In problems 44–46, simplify the expression and solve the equation and inequality.

44 $(4 - 6x^2) - 2(3 + x^2)$ **45** $|2x - 1| > 5$ **46** $\frac{2}{3}y = -18$

47 Determine whether each statement is True or False.
   a $|a + b| < |a| - |b|$ **b** $|a| + |b| \geq |a + b|$
   c $|a| \leq -a$ **d** $|a^2 + b^2| \leq a^2 + b^2$

48 If x is selected at random from $\{15, 25, 35, 45, 55\}$, find the probability that $\angle B$ is
   a Acute   **b** Right   **c** Obtuse

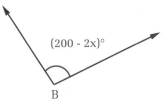
$(200 - 2x)°$
B

In problems 49–53, solve and graph each inequality.
49 $|x - 2| > 4$ **50** $-3|x - 4| > -15$ **51** $|x + 5| > x$
52 $-x + 6 \leq 10$ and $\frac{1}{2}x > 5$ **53** $8|2x - 1| - 5|2x - 1| > 12$

 54 Depending on the items sold, a sales representative earns a commission of 8% to 11% on each sale. Find the range of commissions possible on total sales of $8300.

55 Refer to $\angle P$ and $\angle Q$ to answer the following questions.
   a Find all values of x for which $\angle P$ is acute.
   b Find all values of x for which $\angle Q$ is obtuse.
   c For what values of x will both $\angle P$ be acute and $\angle Q$ be obtuse?

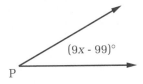
$(9x - 99)°$
P

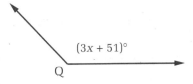
$(3x + 51)°$
Q

Problem Set, *continued*

56 If an element is randomly selected from the set of multiples of 3 between 15 and 78, what is the probability that the element is a multiple of 18?

57 The life expectancy of a ribbon for a popular brand of personal-computer printer is stated to be 3 million characters. The printer prints 160 characters per second.

   a Write an expression for the number of characters that can still be printed by this ribbon after x seconds of use on the printer.

   b Write an inequality that states that there are at least 80,000 characters of life left in the ribbon. Solve this inequality for x.

In problems 58–63, solve each inequality.

58 $x(x - 4) \leq 0$ **59** $x(x - 4)(x + 2) \geq 0$

60 $|2x - 5| \geq 2x$ **61** $|2x + 7| \leq 10$

62 $|x - 3| \leq |x + 7|$ **63** $x(x - 2)(x + 3)(x - 2) \leq 0$

64 Refer to the graph and find the values of x and y.

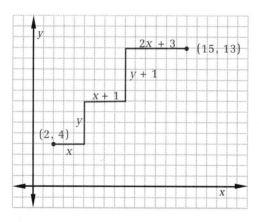

65 Find the ratio of the area of rectangle I to the area of rectangle II.

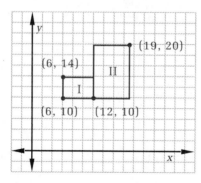

5.5 PROPERTIES OF INEQUALITY

Objectives

After studying this section, you will be able to
- Recognize and use the definitions of *less than* and *absolute value*
- Recognize and use the properties of order and inequality

Part One: Introduction

Definitions of *Less Than* and *Absolute Value*

The following definitions are formal statements of concepts you have already encountered.

Less than in the expression $a < b$ (a is less than b) means that there is a positive number c such that $a + c = b$.

The **absolute value** of a number, $|a|$, equals a if $a \geq 0$ and equals $-a$ if $a < 0$.

Properties of Order and Inequality

Below are formal statements of the main properties of order and inequality. These supplement the lists in Sections 2.6 and 3.7.

The Trichotomy Property
Given any two real numbers a and b, exactly one of the following is true: $a > b, a < b, a = b$.

The universal properties below apply to all real numbers.

Name of Property	Statement
Transitive Properties of Inequality	If $a > b$ and $b > c$, then $a > c$. If $a < b$ and $b < c$, then $a < c$.
Addition Properties of Inequality	If $a > b$, then $a + c > b + c$. If $a < b$, then $a + c < b + c$.
Subtraction Properties of Inequality	If $a > b$, then $a - c > b - c$. If $a < b$, then $a - c < b - c$.
Property of Squares of Real Numbers	For all real numbers a, $a^2 \geq 0$.

The following properties apply to inequalities.

Name of Property	Statement
Multiplication and Division Properties of Inequality (for positives)	If $a > b$ and $c > 0$, then $ac > bc$ and $\frac{a}{c} > \frac{b}{c}$.
	If $a < b$ and $c > 0$, then $ac < bc$ and $\frac{a}{c} < \frac{b}{c}$.
Multiplication and Division Properties of Inequality (for negatives)	If $a > b$ and $c < 0$, then $ac < bc$ and $\frac{a}{c} < \frac{b}{c}$.
	If $a < b$ and $c < 0$, then $ac > bc$ and $\frac{a}{c} > \frac{b}{c}$.
Inequality Properties of Reciprocals	If $a > 0$, then $\frac{1}{a} > 0$.
	If $a < 0$, then $\frac{1}{a} < 0$.
	If $a > 0$, $b > 0$, and $a > b$, then $\frac{1}{a} < \frac{1}{b}$.
	If $a > 0$, $b > 0$, and $a < b$, then $\frac{1}{a} > \frac{1}{b}$.
	If $a < 0$, $b < 0$, and $a > b$, then $\frac{1}{a} < \frac{1}{b}$.
	If $a < 0$, $b < 0$, and $a < b$, then $\frac{1}{a} > \frac{1}{b}$.
Inequality Properties of Opposites	If $a > 0$, then $-a < 0$.
	If $a < 0$, then $-a > 0$.

Part Two: Sample Problems

Problem 1　　*What property is illustrated by each statement?*

　　a *If* $3 > -4$ *and* $-4 > -4.5$, *then* $3 > -4.5$.
　　b *If* a *is not less than* b *and* $a \neq b$, *then* $a > b$.
　　c *If* $3 < 9$, *then* $4 < 10$.
　　d *If* $7 < 15$, *then* $-14 > -30$.
　　e *If* $6 > 5$, *then* $\frac{1}{6} < \frac{1}{5}$.
　　f *If* $-7 < 0$, *then* $-(-7) > 0$.
　　g *If* $-4 > -8$, *then* $-1 > -2$.

Solution　　**a** Transitive Property of Inequality
　　b Trichotomy Property
　　c Addition Property of Inequality
　　d Multiplication Property of Inequality (for negatives)
　　e Inequality Property of Reciprocals
　　f Inequality Property of Opposites
　　g Division Property of Inequality (for positives)

Problem 2   *Solve the inequality* $3 - 7x > -11$ *and give a reason for each step.*

Solution

	Steps	Reasons
a	$3 - 7x > -11$	Given
b	$(3 - 7x) - 3 > -11 - 3$	Subtraction Property of Inequality
c	$[3 + (-7x)] + (-3) > -11 + (-3)$	Difference Property
d	$(-7x + 3) + (-3) > -11 + (-3)$	Commutative Property of Addition
e	$-7x + [3 + (-3)] > -11 + (-3)$	Associative Property of Addition
f	$-7x + 0 > -14$	Additive Inverse Property
g	$-7x > -14$	Additive Identity Property
h	$\dfrac{-7x}{-7} < \dfrac{-14}{-7}$	Division Property of Inequality
i	$1x < 2$	Division
j	$x < 2$	Multiplicative Identity Property

Part Three: Exercises and Problems

Warm-up Exercises

In problems 1–6, name the property illustrated by each statement.

1 If $x < y$, then $2x < 2y$.

2 If $x > 0$, then $x \neq 0$.

3 If $-3 < 0$ and $0 < 8$, then $-3 < 8$.

4 If $3 > 2$, then $-6 < -4$.

5 If $x < 0$, then $-x > 0$.

6 If $-3 > -5$, then $\frac{-1}{3} < \frac{-1}{5}$.

7 Give a reason for each step in the solution of the inequality
$9 > 13 - 8x$.

    a $9 > 13 - 8x$

    b $9 - 13 > (13 - 8x) - 13$

    c $9 + (-13) > [13 + (-8x)] + (-13)$

    d $9 + (-13) > (-8x + 13) + (-13)$

    e $9 + (-13) > -8x + [13 + (-13)]$

    f $-4 > -8x + 0$

    g $-4 > -8x$

    h $\dfrac{-4}{-8} < \dfrac{-8x}{-8}$

    i $\frac{1}{2} < 1x$

    j $\frac{1}{2} < x$

Problem Set

8 Rectangles A and B have the same area. The length of A is greater than the length of B. Which rectangle has the greater width? What property justifies your answer?

Problem Set, *continued*

9 Make each statement correct. Use >, <, or =.

a $3(5)$ __?__ $3(2)$ **b** $-5(6)$ __?__ $-5(4)$ **c** $3(-7)$ __?__ $(-3)(7)$

d $(-5)^7$ __?__ 0 **e** $(-5)^8$ __?__ 0 **f** $-(-3)$ __?__ 0

10 Determine whether each statement is True or False.

a If $x > 1$, then $0 < \frac{1}{x} < 1$.   **b** If $x < -1$, then $\frac{1}{x} > 1$.

c If $x < 3$, then $x < 5$.   **d** If $x + 2 > 12$, then $2x > 20$.

e If $5(x - 3) > 0$, then $x > 3$.   **f** If $x - 5 < 0$, then $5 - x > 0$.

11 Rectangles A and B each have an area of 1 square meter.

a Find the width of rectangle A.
b Find the width of rectangle B.
c Which rectangle has the greater width?
d Name a property that explains your answer to part **c**.

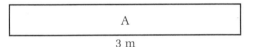

A

3 m

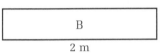

B

2 m

12 Charles, Lin, and Torry bowl together on Saturdays. Charles bowls worse than Lin. Charles usually beats Torry.

a Arrange the players from worst to best.
b What property justifies that Lin must bowl better than Torry?

13 Multiply the matrices.

$$\begin{bmatrix} -4 & 3.5 \\ 8 & \frac{1}{2} \end{bmatrix} \begin{bmatrix} -5 \\ 10 \end{bmatrix}$$

14 Determine the values of x that make the inequality $(x - 3)^2 \geq 0$ true.

15 Determine the values of x that make the inequality $(x + 2) \leq 0$ true.

16 Arrange the numbers in order from smallest to largest.

$$\frac{5}{6} \quad \frac{7}{8} \quad \frac{11}{12} \quad \frac{15}{18} \quad \frac{8}{9} \quad \frac{3}{4}$$

17 Refer to $\angle A$.

a Find x so that $\angle A$ is a straight angle.
b Find x so that $\angle A$ is a right angle.
c Find all values of x for which $\angle A$ will be an obtuse angle.
d Find all values of x for which $\angle A$ will be an acute angle.

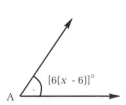

$[6(x - 6)]°$

A

In problems 18–20, for each pair of sets A and B find A ∪ B and A ∩ B.

18 $A = \{2, 4, 6, 8\}$, $B = \{1, 4, 9\}$

19 A = {1, 4, 7}, B = {2, 3, 5, 6, 8, 9}

20 A = {1, 4, 9, 16, 25, 36, 49, 64}, B = {1, 2, 4, 8, 16, 64, 128}

In problems 21–24, solve and graph.

21 $|2x - 1| > 8$

22 $|3x + 1| \leq x$

23 $-8 \leq y + 5$ and $8 - y > 10$

24 $-3x > 24$ or $x + 8 < 18$

25 Refer to the chart to answer the following questions.

   a Which counties have at most 30% of their land forested?

   b Find the number of square miles of forested land in county D.

   c Which counties have at least 120 square miles of forested land?

   d Could county H have less forested land than county G?

Total Land Area and Percent of Forested Land in Countries A - H in 1989

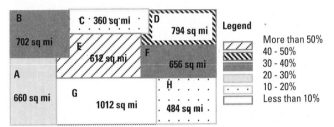

26 Determine whether each statement is True or False.

   a If $-2x > 6$, then $\frac{-2x}{-2} > \frac{6}{-2}$.

   b If $-5 < -3$, then $\frac{1}{-5} > \frac{1}{-3}$.

   c If $\frac{a}{x} < \frac{b}{x}$, then $a < b$.

   d If $\frac{1}{y} < 0$, then $y > 0$.

27 Determine whether each of the following makes a true statement for All values, Some values, or No values.

   a $(x - 3)^2 \geq 0$

   b $x + 5 > 5$

   c $(x + 2)^2 > x$

   d $(y - 3)^2 = (3 - y)^2$

   e $|a - b| = |b - a|$

   f $|x| = x$

   g $0 \geq |x|$

   h $\sqrt{x^2} = x$

   i $\sqrt{x^2} = |x|$

28 Solve the inequality $10 \leq 7 - 6x$ and justify each step.

29 Refer to ∠B.

   a Find all values of x for which the measure of ∠B will be between 60 and 105.

   b From the range found in part **a**, find all values of x for which ∠B will be obtuse.

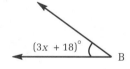

30 The gap between the tip and the electrode of a spark plug for a Stutz Bearcat automobile should be 0.035 of an inch with a tolerance of 0.002 inches. Let d be the actual gap of a Stutz Bearcat spark plug.

   a Write an inequality that states that the spark plug is gapped within tolerance.

   b Solve this inequality for the range of gaps d that are permissible.

Problem Set, *continued*

31 Solve the inequality $13x < 8x - 12$ and justify each step.

32 A Union 88 gasoline station receives a delivery of gasoline. The gasoline storage tank at the station can hold 10,000 gallons of gasoline. Before the delivery, the tank is 20% full. The tanker truck can pump 65 gallons per minute to the storage tank. Let t be the number of minutes the gasoline truck pumps gasoline to the storage tank.

    a Write an expression for the amount of gasoline in the storage tank at any time t during the delivery.

    b Write an inequality that represents that the storage tank is more than 75% full.

    c Find the range of times that the tank is more than 75% full by solving the inequality from part **b** for t.

    d Write an inequality that states that the storage tank is between 50% and 75% filled. Solve this inequality to find the range of times for which the condition exists.

33 If $a > b$ and $c > d$, determine whether each inequality makes a True or False statement.

    a $a + c > b + d$ **b** $a - c > b - d$ **c** $a - d > b - c$

    d $a - b > c - b$ **e** $a - c > b - c$ **f** $ac > bd$

34 A large bathtub contains 90 gallons of water. Bo has turned on the water so that it is running in at 6 gallons per minute. Unfortunately, he has left the drain open, removing 7.5 gallons of water per minute. Determine after how many minutes there will be 30 gallons of water remaining in the tub.

35 The radio station in Mudville has a broadcast range of 65 miles, and the radio station in Alantown has a broadcast range of 45 miles. The two stations are 170 miles apart. Casey leaves Mudville and drives at 35 miles per hour toward Alantown. Let t be the number of hours that Casey has been driving.

    a Write an inequality and solve it for the range of times that Casey is out of listening distance of the Mudville radio station.

    b Write an inequality and solve it for the range of times that Casey is out of listening distance of the Alantown radio station.

    c Find the range of times that Casey cannot listen to either radio station.

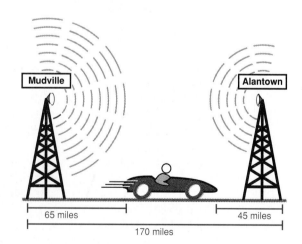

36 Determine whether each statement is True or False.

a If $\frac{3}{x} < x$, then $3 < x^2$.

b If $x < \frac{1}{x}$, then $x < 1$.

37 The following statement is written in BASIC.

`IF ABS(4X - 5) <= 12, THEN Y = 15 ELSE Y = 0.`

For what values of X will Y = 0?

PRESCRIPTION FOR FINANCIAL HEALTH

Eileen M. Sharkey advises early planning

A person who is concerned about his or her physical health might consult a doctor. A person who is concerned about his or her financial health might visit a certified financial planner. Eileen M. Sharkey, one of the nation's first and best-known financial planners, says, ''Our specialty is fiscal, rather than physical, planning. We help people organize and evaluate their financial objectives, then find strategies for achieving their goals with a minimum of risk.''

Ms. Sharkey points out that early planning for future needs is essential. ''Suppose you're 25 years old and you'd like to retire at 65 with $300,000 in the bank. You can do that by investing just $30 a month in a 12%-interest-bearing plan. If, however, you wait until you're 45, you'll need $300 a month. And beginning at 55, you'll need $1300 per month.''

A graduate of the University of London, Ms. Sharkey practices in Denver, where she also serves as president of the Institute of Certified Financial Planners. She has a thorough background in business mathematics but admits that the complexities of her field make it essential to work with a computer now. For moment-to-moment work at her desk, she finds a financial calculator indispensable.

The primary problem for a financial planner is to answer this question about each client: How much money must this person set aside today in order to have a planned amount at a specified time in the future? Here is a simple example of financial planning: you wish to deposit money in a savings account so that you will have $2000 a year from today. The interest you will get is 8%, compounded annually. How can you figure out how much money to deposit?

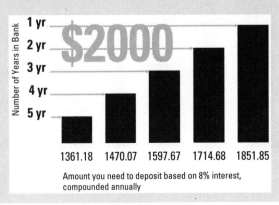

Amount you need to deposit based on 8% interest, compounded annually

CIRCLE GRAPHS, PICTOGRAPHS, AND ARTISTIC GRAPHS

Objectives

After studying this section, you will be able to
- Draw and interpret circle graphs
- Draw and interpret pictographs and artistic graphs

Circle Graphs

A circle graph, often called a pie graph, relates portions of data, represented by pie-shaped segments, to the total data, represented by the circle.

Problem   *A recent study for House of Pizza in Mathem City revealed that the following number of large pan pizzas were sold during a two-week period of time.*

Cheese only	241
Cheese and sausage	682
Cheese and pepperoni	316
Cheese, sausage, and mushrooms	297
Other combinations	348

  a *Determine the number of large pan pizzas sold during the two-week period.*
  b *Find the percentage of the total number of large pan pizzas represented by each of the five categories above.*
  c *Draw and label a circle graph for the data above.*

Solution   **a** $241 + 682 + 316 + 297 + 348 = 1884$

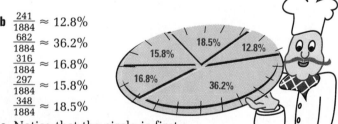

  b $\frac{241}{1884} \approx 12.8\%$
  $\frac{682}{1884} \approx 36.2\%$
  $\frac{316}{1884} \approx 16.8\%$
  $\frac{297}{1884} \approx 15.8\%$
  $\frac{348}{1884} \approx 18.5\%$

  c Notice that the circle is first divided into 20 equal sectors.
  Each sector is $\frac{1}{20}$ or 5% of the circle.

Pictographs and Artistic Graphs

A *pictograph* is a graph in which a picture represents a specified piece or amount of data. In this diagram, each picture represents 10 inhabitants per square mile.

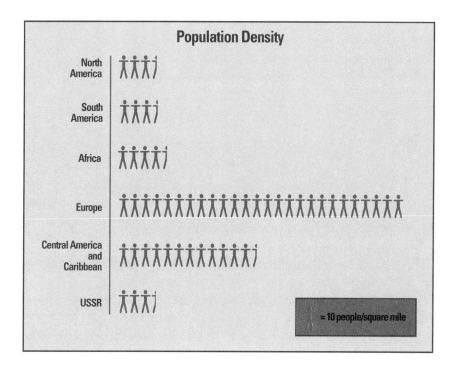

The diagrams below illustrate artistic representations of data. There is no one standard artistic form.

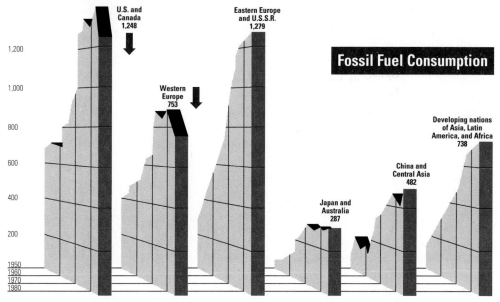

Carbon emissions: millions of metric tons in 1983   Used by permission from The Union of Concerned Scientists

Problem Set

1 Refer to the graph to answer the following questions.

   a Which company sold the most supercomputers?

   b What percentage of the total number of supercomputers sold did each of the five companies sell?

   c Which company sold 300% as many computers as Fujitsu?

Supercomputers: Worldwide Installations

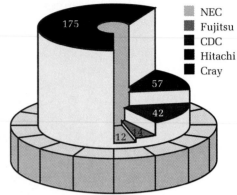

- NEC
- Fujitsu
- CDC
- Hitachi
- Cray

2 A local broadcast station obtains 48% of its income from advertising, 16% from investments, and 35% from donations. The remaining income comes from other sources. Draw a circle graph to illustrate the station's income according to source.

3 Two hundred students in a high school participate in four sports. The chart shows the number of students involved in each sport.

   a What percentage of students are involved in each sport?

   b If the school has 1050 students, and if the basketball, hockey, and swim teams all compete on the same night, what is the greatest number of student spectators each is likely to get?

4 Refer to the graph.

   a Which year had the most precipitation for January through March?

   b Which month consistently had the most precipitation year to year?

   c Which month had the lowest average precipitation from 1985 through 1987?

   d Based on the data given in the graph, could you predict the precipitation for January through March in 1988?

Average Total Precipitation in Chicago (inches)

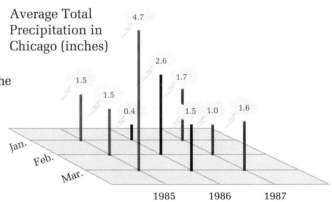

5 For each flavor of jellybean at the Nut and Candy Shop, the number of pounds sold was charted for one month.

a Determine, to the nearest tenth of a percent, the percentage of total sales represented by each flavor.

b Draw a circle graph to represent the percentage of total sales represented by each flavor.

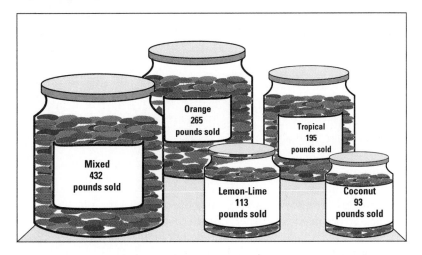

Orange
265
pounds sold

Tropical
195
pounds sold

Mixed
432
pounds sold

Lemon-Lime
113
pounds sold

Coconut
93
pounds sold

6 Plum Computer Company sold four models of computers in April.

Model	Number Sold	Unit Price
I	17,632	$ 395
II	14,140	$ 795
III	10,639	$1995
IV	4,487	$4350

a Draw a circle graph showing what proportion of total computers sold is represented by each model.

b Draw a circle graph showing what proportion of the total sales revenue is represented by each model.

7 The volumes shown by the graph indicate the growth in the number of Channel 77 viewers during three months.

a What is the ratio of viewers in February to viewers in January?

b What is the ratio of viewers in March to viewers in February?

c If the volume of the January TV is 1 cubic unit (1 × 1 × 1), what is the volume of the February TV?

d What is the volume of the March TV?

e What is the ratio of the February TV volume to the January TV volume?

f What is the ratio of the March TV volume to the February TV volume?

g Is this a fair pictograph? Why?

January: 6,000

February: 12,000

March: 24,000

CHAPTER SUMMARY

CONCEPTS AND PROCEDURES

After studying this chapter, you should be able to
- Solve inequalities using properties of inequality (5.1)
- Use inequalities to classify angles (5.2)
- Use inequalities to solve geometric problems (5.2)
- Determine the union and the intersection of sets (5.3)
- Solve compound inequalities (5.3)
- Use the distance method to solve absolute value inequalities (5.4)
- Use the boundary algorithm to solve inequalities (5.4)
- Apply the definitions of *less than* and *absolute value* (5.5)
- Use properties of order and inequality to solve inequalities (5.5)
- Draw and interpret circle graphs (5.6)
- Draw and interpret pictographs and artistic graphs (5.6)

VOCABULARY

acute angle (5.2)
algorithm (5.4)
boundary algorithm (5.4)
compound inequality (5.3)
intersection (5.3)
obtuse angle (5.2)

pictograph (5.6)
right angle (5.2)
straight angle (5.2)
union (5.3)
Venn diagram (5.3)
vertex (5.2)

PROPERTIES

Trichotomy Property
Transitive Properties of Inequality
Addition Properties of Inequality
Subtraction Properties of Inequality
Property of Squares of Real Numbers

Multiplication Properties of Inequality
Division Properties of Inequality
Inequality Properties of Reciprocals
Inequality Properties of Opposites

In problems 1–4, graph each inequality on a number line.

1 $x \geq -3.25$ **2** $-2 > y$ **3** $|x| \geq 2.5$ **4** $\{x: -5 < x < 1\}$

In problems 5 and 6, determine $A \cup B$ and $A \cap B$ for each pair of sets.

5 $A = \{2, 4, 6, 8, 10\}$
   $B = \{1, 4, 7, 10, 13\}$

6 $A = \{\text{negative integers}\}$
   $B = \{\text{whole numbers}\}$

7 Find all values of y for which the perimeter of the triangle will have the given value.

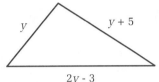

a 86   **b** 70
c Greater than 70   **d** Between 70 and 86

In problems 8–11, solve each inequality and graph the solution on a number line.

8 $-5x + 20 < -2$ **9** $-3z + 7 \leq -2z + 12$ **10** $2.5z + 3.7 \geq -23.8$ **11** $2 - 7(6) < -2x$

In problems 12 and 13, graph each inequality on a number line.

12 $-5 < x \leq 7$ **13** $x > -5$ and $x < 7$

14 Find (x, y) if $\begin{bmatrix} -2 & 3 \\ 6 & -1 \end{bmatrix} \begin{bmatrix} -5 \\ 4 \end{bmatrix} = \begin{bmatrix} x \\ y \end{bmatrix}$.

15 Metro's population was 680,000 in 1990. It is projected that the population will increase between 7% and 12% from 1990 to 2000. Find the range of projected populations for the year 2000.

16 If $(x, y) = (12, -5)$, identify each of the following as True or False and justify your answer.

a $x^2 + y^2 \geq 169$ **b** $3y - x < 0$ **c** $|x + y| = |x| + |y|$

17 Refer to the graph to answer the following questions.

a Write an inequality to describe the set graphed above the number line.
b Write an inequality to describe the set graphed below the number line.
c Write a compound inequality to describe the intersection of the two sets.

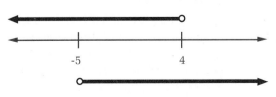

Review Problems, *continued*

18 Refer to the graph.

  a What percentage of Austria's forests had been damaged as of 1986?

  b Which countries had more than half of their forests damaged as of 1986?

  c Express the information at the bottom of the chart in graphical form.

  d If Hungary has more square kilometers of forest than does Finland, which country has more square kilometers of damaged forest? What property justifies your answer?

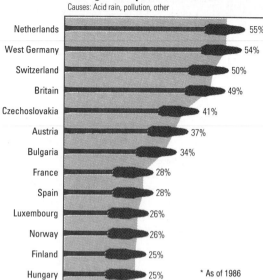

Damaged European Forest Areas*
Causes: Acid rain, pollution, other

Country	Percentage
Netherlands	55%
West Germany	54%
Switzerland	50%
Britain	49%
Czechoslovakia	41%
Austria	37%
Bulgaria	34%
France	28%
Spain	28%
Luxembourg	26%
Norway	26%
Finland	25%
Hungary	25%

* As of 1986

Belgium 16%, Poland 15%, Sweden 15%,
E. Germany 12%, Yugoslavia 5%, Italy 5%

In problems 19–22, simplify each expression and solve each equation and inequality.

19 $5(x - 3) = 2(2 - x)$

20 $-5(x - 3) < 20$

21 $12 - (10 - 6x) + 6(10 - 6x)$

22 $|2x + 7| = 21$

23 Jenny is older than her sister Beth but younger than her sister Mae. Arrange the three sisters in order from oldest to youngest. What property allows you to draw your conclusion?

In problems 24 and 25, solve each inequality. Graph each on a number line.

24 $x(x - 2)(x + 4) < 0$

25 $x^2 - 6x \geq 0$

In problems 26 and 27, write an algebraic inequality that describes each graph.

26

     -3   4

27

     -7   0

28 The measures of six angles are determined by evaluating the expression $25n + 30$ for the values of n in $\{1, 2, 3, 4, 5, 6\}$. One of the angles is chosen at random. What is the probability that the angle is an acute angle? A right angle? A straight angle? An obtuse angle?

In problems 29–32, solve each compound inequality. Graph each on a number line.

29 $18 - 5x \geq 3$ or $2(x - 3) \geq 20$

30 $x + 4 > 7$ and $x + 7 > 4$

31 $|x| > 4$

32 $4y + 2 \leq 10$ and $-4y - 2 \leq 10$

 33 Joan's test scores were 82, 93, and 84 on the first three 100-point tests. Determine what score Joan must earn on the fourth test to have an average of at least 90.

34 Find three consecutive even integers so that the sum of the third and three times the first equals four times the second.

35 Refer to the rectangle.

  a What are the restrictions on x?
  b If $x > 20$, then determine what we know about the values of y.
  c Find x if $y = x + 10$.

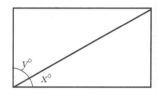

In problems 36–41, solve for x and graph each solution on a number line.

36 $7|x - 5| < 5|x - 5| + 14$

37 $|2x - 3| < x + 9$

38 $|x + 8| + |3x + 24| = 24$

39 $2|x - 15| + |15 - x| > 27$

40 $|x| + |-x| \leq 8$

41 $2|x - 5| - 7|x - 5| > |x - 5|$

 42 When Con Tractor decided to build a deck in his backyard, he calculated the cost to be $6 per square foot plus $75 for a building permit. His deck will be 14 feet wide and between 16 and 20 feet long. Average the costs of the smallest and largest possible decks to determine an estimate.

43 Refer to the angles.

  a Determine for what values of x both angles will have the same measure.
  b Determine for what values of x at least one of the angles will be acute.

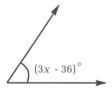 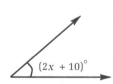

$(3x - 36)°$ $(2x + 10)°$

In problems 44–46, solve for x.

44 $\dfrac{x}{|x|} = 1$

45 $\dfrac{1}{x - 1} < 5$

46 $\dfrac{1}{x} \geq 3$

47 Rectangles I and II each have an area of 1 square inch. The length of I is 3 inches, while the length of II is 2 inches.

  a Find the width of I.
  b Find the width of II.
  c Determine which rectangle has the greater width.
  d Which property justifies your conclusion in part **c**?

CHAPTER TEST

In problems 1–3, solve each inequality and graph the solution set.

1 $4 - 3x < 9$ **2** $x + 5 < 11$ or $x - 3 \geq 6$ **3** $-3 < 2x + 3 \leq 21$

4 Name the property illustrated by each statement.
  a If $a > -b$ and $-b > -c$, then $a > -c$.
  b If $c \not< d$ and $c \neq d$, then $c > d$.
  c If $3 > 2$, then $\frac{1}{3} < \frac{1}{2}$.

5 Mr. and Mrs. Galavanting are taking a trip from Buffalo, New York, to Louisville, Kentucky, a distance of 545 miles. They travel at 55 miles per hour. Let t be the number of hours they have been traveling.
  a Write an expression for their distance from Louisville at any time t.
  b Write an inequality stating that they are within 95 miles of Louisville, and then solve it.

6 Find all values of y so that $3y - 6$ is an obtuse angle.

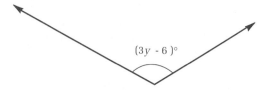

$(3y - 6)°$

In problems 7–9, solve each inequality and graph the solution set.

7 $7|2x + 4| - 3|2x + 4| > 15$
8 $|8x + 5| \geq 10$
9 $|x + 8| \leq 3x$

10 The manager of Country Estates Realty received a circle graph from the accounting department, describing the sales performance of her four salespersons during the month of March.
  a How much did Salesperson C sell?
  b Each salesperson receives a monthly salary of $1200, plus 1.25% commission on sales. How much did Salesperson C earn during March?

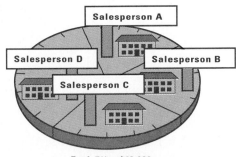

Salesperson A
Salesperson D
Salesperson B
Salesperson C

Each 5% = $43,200

PUZZLES AND CHALLENGES

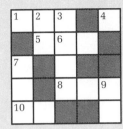

1 Complete the cross number square puzzle.

Across		Down	
1.	18	**2.**	5
4.	2	**3.**	65
5.	23	**4.**	2
8.	24	**6.**	15
10.	7	**7.**	28
		9.	8

2 In problems 1–3, a set of four words is given. From choices **a, b, c,** and **d,** pick the word that best fits with the given words.

1 why   are   you   tea

a eat   **b** sea   **c** ear   **d** yet

2 lid   mimic   mill   vivid

a mime   **b** medic   **c** divide   **d** mix

3 ate   won   for   too

a teen   **b** cause   **c** that   **d** duct

3 Remove six segments to leave two squares.

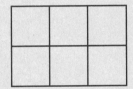

4 Carl is standing by the river with an 8-quart jug and a 5-quart jug. He needs to bring exactly 4 quarts back to his mother. Explain how he can measure out exactly 4 quarts.

6 | GRAPHING

R ogue waves materialize in an instant, wreak a moment of destructive havoc, then disappear as quickly and as mysteriously as they came. The largest rogue wave ever reliably measured towered 112 feet from crest to trough. That's a wall of water as high as an 11-story building. One example of the destructive power of these waves is the loss of the *Marques*. On June 3, 1984, this 117-foot, three-masted sailboat was struck by a rogue about 75 miles north of Bermuda and the ship sank in less than a minute.

Researchers believe that ocean currents and changes in seabed topography can contribute to the formation of rogue waves. Using mathematical models and computer-driven simulation devices, they hope to eventually predict when and where rogue waves are likely to appear.

TABLES, GRAPHS, AND EQUATIONS

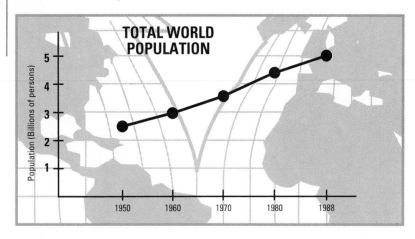

Objectives

After studying this section, you will be able to
- Construct graphs using tables and patterns
- Write equations from tables

Part One: Introduction

Graphing Using Tables and Patterns

Diagrams and pictures help build an understanding of relationships. You can study the picture of an equation, called a *graph,* to draw conclusions about that equation. Some equations can be graphed quickly using a pattern found in a table of values.

Example   *Make a table of values and graph $y = 3x + 2$.*

Let's try consecutive integer values for x and see whether we can find a pattern.

	+1	+1	+1	+1	+1	+1	+1	+1
x	−4	−3	−2	−1	0	1	2	3	4
y	−10	−7	−4	−1	2	5	8	11	14
	+3	+3	+3	+3	+3	+3	+3	+3

Notice that as x increases by 1, y increases by 3. Also, 3 is the coefficient of x in the equation $y = 3x + 2$.

We can use this pattern to sketch the graph of $y = 3x + 2$. If we start at $(-4, -10)$, we find another point on the graph by moving to the right 1 unit, increasing x by 1, and by moving up 3 units, increasing y by 3.

Continuing this same pattern, we find several points on the graph of
$y = 3x + 2$. To complete the sketch, we connect these points with a
straight line and use arrows to show that the line continues.

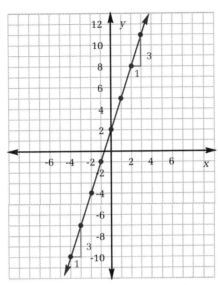
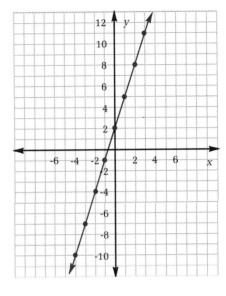

Example   *Make a table of values and graph $y = -2x + 8$.*

Let's try consecutive integer values for x and look for a pattern.

	+1	+1	+1	+1	+1	+1
x	**-3**	**-2**	**-1**	**0**	**1**	**2**	**3**
y	**14**	**12**	**10**	**8**	**6**	**4**	**2**
	-2	-2	-2	-2	-2	-2

Notice that as x increases by 1, y decreases by 2. Also, the coefficient of x in the equation $y = -2x + 8$ is -2.

We use this pattern to sketch the graph of $y = -2x + 8$. Choose any
point in the table, say (0, 8), and then repeatedly move 1 unit to the
right and 2 units down to graph additional points. Connect these
points with a straight line to sketch the graph of $y = -2x + 8$.

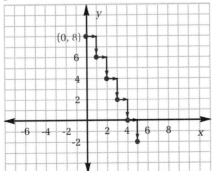
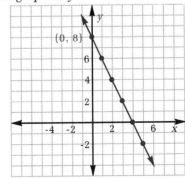

In these equations, written in the form $y = mx + b$, the coefficient of x gave us the pattern for the change in y-values. Now let's graph an equation of the form $y = mx + b$ where m is not an integer.

Example

Make a table of values and graph $y = \frac{2}{3}x - 5$.

We choose multiples of 3 for values of x so that the y-values are integers.

	$+3$	$+3$	$+3$	$+3$	$+3$	$+3$	
x	-9	-6	-3	0	3	6	9
y	-11	-9	-7	-5	-3	-1	1
	$+2$	$+2$	$+2$	$+2$	$+2$	$+2$	

Notice that as x increases by 3, y increases by 2. Also, the coefficient of x in the equation $y = \frac{2}{3}x - 5$ has 2 as its numerator and 3 as its denominator.

To graph this equation, choose any point in the table, say $(0, -5)$, and repeatedly move 3 units to the right and 2 units up in order to graph additional points. Connect these points with a straight line.

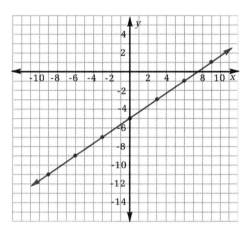

If we summarize what we have found, we see the following.

Equation	Change in y	Change in x	Coefficient of x
$y = 3x + 2$	3	1	3
$y = -2x + 8$	-2	1	-2
$y = \frac{2}{3}x - 5$	2	3	$\frac{2}{3}$

All three equations are in the form $y = mx + b$. It appears that m, the coefficient of x, describes the change in the y-values divided by the change in x-values. This can be stated as follows.

> $In\ y = mx + b,\ m = \dfrac{\text{change in } y}{\text{change in } x}.$

Writing an Equation from a Table

Let's use what we have learned and write an equation given a table of values.

Example   *Write an equation that represents the given table.*

x	-4	-3	-2	-1	0	1	2	3	4
y	-3	2	7	12	17	22	27	32	37

As the values of x increase by 1, the values of y increase by 5. From our earlier examples, we conclude that this table describes an equation of the form $y = mx + b$ where $m = \frac{5}{1}$, or 5, and $y = 5x + b$.

   Now we must find the value of b. Since any point in the table must make the equation true, choose one point, (0, 17), substitute the values in the equation, and solve for b.

$$y = 5x + b$$
$$17 = 5(0) + b$$
$$17 = b$$

An equation for this table is $y = 5x + 17$.

   We can use a different ordered pair to check that this is the correct equation. For example, if x = 3, then

$$y = 5(3) + 17$$
$$= 15 + 17$$
$$= 32$$

The answer checks.

Part Two: Sample Problems

Problem 1   Graph $y = \frac{-3}{5}x + 4$.

Solution   Let's make a table, using multiples of 5 for values of x.

x	-10	-5	0	5	10
y	10	7	4	1	-2

$$\frac{\text{change in } y}{\text{change in } x} = \frac{-3}{5}$$

Start at (0, 4) and repeatedly move 5 units to the right and 3 units down. Connect the points. Remember to put an arrow head at each end of the line.

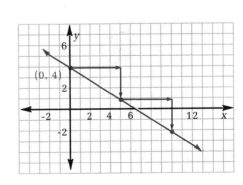

Problem 2   Write an equation of the line graphed.

Solution   From the graph, $\dfrac{\text{change in } y}{\text{change in } x} = \dfrac{1}{4}$,

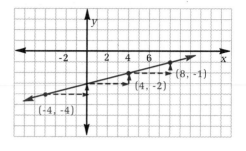

so $y = mx + b$ is $y = \frac{1}{4}x + b$.

Substitute any point on the graph, say $(8, -1)$, in the equation and solve for b.

$$y = \tfrac{1}{4}x + b$$
$$-1 = \tfrac{1}{4}(8) + b$$
$$-1 = 2 + b$$
$$-3 = b$$

An equation of the line is $y = \frac{1}{4}x - 3$.

Problem 3   Graph $y = x^2$.

Solution   Let's make a table of values.

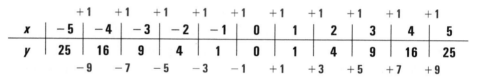

	+1		+1		+1		+1		+1		+1		+1		+1		+1		+1	
x	**−5**		**−4**		**−3**		**−2**		**−1**		**0**		**1**		**2**		**3**		**4**		**5**
y	**25**		**16**		**9**		**4**		**1**		**0**		**1**		**4**		**9**		**16**		**25**
		−9		−7		−5		−3		−1		+1		+3		+5		+7		+9	

Notice that the pattern in this table of values is very different from previous examples. The equation is not of the form $y = mx + b$. Since its graph is not a straight line, we describe it as nonlinear.

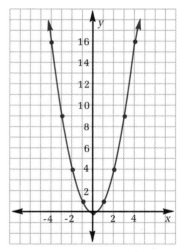

Part Three: Exercises and Problems

Warm-up Exercises

In problems 1–3, describe how you would move from one point to another on the graph of each equation.

1 $y = 2x - 3$ 　　　　　　　 **2** $y = \frac{2}{3}x + 5$ 　　　　　　　 **3** $y = \frac{-1}{4}x - 3$

In problems 4–6, make a table and graph each equation.

4 $y = 2x + 1$ 　　　　　　　 **5** $y = -x$ 　　　　　　　 **6** $y = -\frac{2}{3}x - 4$

7 Write an equation that describes the table.

x	− 2	− 1	0	1	2
y	2	8	14	20	26

8 Write an equation of the line graphed.

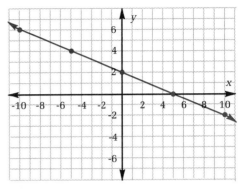

9 Fill in the missing values, assuming that the ordered pairs lie along a line.

x	− 3	− 2	− 1	0	1	3
y	− 7	− 3	1		9	41

10 List 4 possible values for x and y in the diagram and sketch a graph.

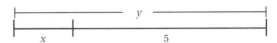

Problem Set

In problems 11–14, make a table of values and graph each equation.

11 $y = 2x + 6$

12 $y = \frac{1}{2}x + 6$

13 $y = -5x + 2$

14 $y = -2x - 5$

15 If one of the points (0, 1), (1, 3), (2, 5), (3, 7), (4, 9), or (5, 12) is randomly selected, what is the probability that it lies on the graph of $y = 2x + 1$?

In problems 16–19, write an equation for each table of values.

16

x	− 5	− 4	− 3	− 2	− 1	0	1	2	3	4	5
y	− 40	− 30	− 20	− 10	0	10	20	30	40	50	60

17

x	− 5	− 4	− 3	− 2	− 1	0	1	2	3	4	5
y	65	57	49	41	33	25	17	9	1	− 7	− 15

18

x	− 5	− 4	− 3	− 2	− 1	0	1	2	3	4	5
y	5	4	3	2	1	0	− 1	− 2	− 3	− 4	− 5

19

x	− 5	− 4	− 3	− 2	− 1	0	1	2	3	4	5
y	− 20	− 17	− 14	− 11	− 8	− 5	− 2	1	4	7	10

Problem Set, *continued*

20 If one of the equations below is selected at random, what is the probability that its graph passes through the point with coordinates (1, 5)?

$y = \frac{1}{5}x$ $y = 5x$ $y = \frac{2}{5}x + 3$ $y = x$

$y = -5x$ $y = x + 4$ $y = -\frac{5}{3}x + \frac{20}{3}$ $y = -\frac{9}{2}x - \frac{1}{2}$

21 Find all values of p for which point C is located to the right of point B.

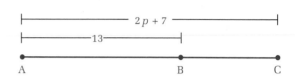

22 From the graph, calculate

  a The lengths of $\overline{AB}$ and $\overline{BC}$
  b The ratio of BC to AB
  c The lengths of $\overline{CD}$ and $\overline{DE}$
  d The ratio of DE to CD
  e The ratio of EF to AF

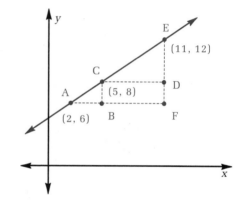

In problems 23 and 24, solve each inequality and graph each solution on a number line.

23 $18 < 12 - 4x$

24 $3(5 + x) - 7x \geq x$

25 Refer to the graph of the right triangle.

  a Find the coordinates of point $H(x_1, y_1)$.
  b Use the Pythagorean Theorem to find the distance from point P(1, 2) to point T(6, 10). Approximate your answer to the nearest tenth.

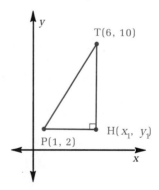

26 Write the equivalent form of the equation that results from adding $-5x$ to both sides of $5x + y = 12$.

27 Unfortunately, Laura's cat ate all but two scraps of her homework problems on graphing lines. Fortunately, both were parts of the same problem. She determined that $(8, -2)$ had been plotted on the graph. She also found part of the table used to make the graph. Fill in the rest of the table, using 6 additional number pairs, and redraw the graph for her.

x	0	1					
y	14	12					

28 Refer to the diagram.

a Find the coordinates of point B and complete the table.

b Write an equation for the table.

	A	B				
x	4					
y	12					

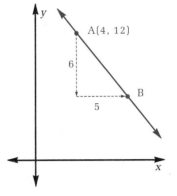

In problems 29 and 30, write an equation for each table of values.

29

x	-16	-14	-12	-10	-8	-6	-4	-2	0	2
y	-21	-18	-15	-12	-9	-6	-3	0	3	6

30

x	-4	-3	-2	-1	0	1	2	3	4	5
y	16	9	4	1	0	1	4	9	16	25

31 Ziggy is a mutant robot. At the command "walk," he takes three steps straight ahead, turns left, takes another two steps, faces right again, and stops. The command module that controls Ziggy's movements looks like a coordinate system, with Ziggy at the origin, facing the positive x-axis. Each step corresponds to a one-integer move on the coordinate system. For example, after one command to walk, Ziggy will end up at $(3, 2)$.

a If Ziggy is given the command to walk four times, list the four stopping points.

b Willie has figured out how to make Ziggy walk backward, but Ziggy still follows the same pattern. If he is back at the origin and is told to walk backward three times, list his stopping points.

c Suppose Ziggy is placed on the point $(0, 4)$, again facing in the same direction as the positive x-axis (directly to the right). If Ziggy is given the command to walk four times, list the four stopping points.

Problem Set, *continued*

In problems 32–34, sketch the graph of each equation.

32 $y = -3x$ 　　　　**33** $y = \frac{2}{5}x - 3$ 　　　　**34** $y = -\frac{4}{3}x$

35 Copy and complete the table of values for $y = 3x - 5$ and graph
the equation.

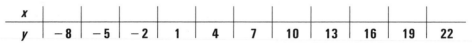

x										
y	-8	-5	-2	1	4	7	10	13	16	19	22

36 Make a table of values and graph the equation $y = x^2 + 1$.

37 Solve the equation for x and y.

$$\begin{bmatrix} 3 & 5 \\ -4 & 1 \end{bmatrix} \cdot \begin{bmatrix} x \\ 2 \end{bmatrix} = \begin{bmatrix} 22 \\ y \end{bmatrix}$$

38 Plot the points on a coordinate system and write an equation for
the table of values.

x	-3	-1	1	3	5	7	9	11	13
y	-19	-14	-9	-4	1	6	11	16	21

In problems 39 and 40, solve each inequality.

39 $12 < |3x + 5|$ 　　　　**40** $|x + 5| \geq x$

41 Refer to the diagram.

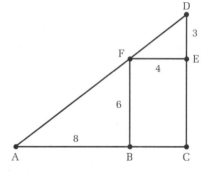

  a Use the slope and the Pythagorean
    Theorem to find the length of each
    segment.
    i $\overline{AF}$ 　**ii** $\overline{FD}$ 　**iii** $\overline{AD}$
  b From your answers to part **a**, do you
    think that $\overline{AD}$ is a straight line?
  c Calculate each ratio.
    i $\dfrac{BF}{BA}$ 　**ii** $\dfrac{DE}{EF}$ 　**iii** $\dfrac{DC}{AC}$

42 An airplane at 30,000 feet begins to descend at 25 feet per
second. Let x be the number of seconds of descent.

  a Let h be the height of the plane above the ground after x
    seconds. Write an equation to describe the relationship
    between h and x.
  b Sketch a graph of the airplane's height h above the ground for
    varying values of x in seconds.
  c Find x when the plane is 5000 feet above the ground.
  d Find the height of the plane 120 seconds after it starts its
    descent.

43 Refer to the graphed line.

  a Find the coordinates of point D and point E.

  b Write an equation of the line.

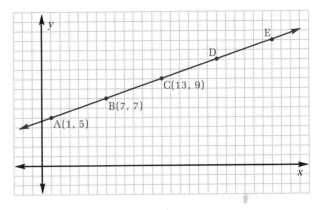

44 Every year, sea turtles return to a certain group of islands to lay eggs. A large number of scientists and volunteers count the baby turtles that hatch, working hard to spot nearly every baby turtle. Here are their findings over a six-year period.

Year	1983	1984	1985	1986	1987	1988
Number of turtles	3260	3190	3120	3050	2980	2910

  a Draw a graph of the data.

  b Write an equation that represents the data.

  c What do you predict will be the number of sea turtles hatching in 1989?

  d Scientists have determined that if the number of baby turtles declines below 2000, the population will be in danger of extinction. If nothing changes, in what year will that happen?

45 Fencing for the sides and the back of a rectangular yard costs $1.50 per meter. Fencing for the front of the yard costs $2.00 per meter.

  a Let W represent the width (sides) of the yard. Let L represent the length (front and back) of the yard. Write an equation for the cost, C, to fence a yard that is W meters by L meters.

  b Copy and complete the width/length table for the total cost of the fence. Write your answer as a 5 × 5 matrix.

  c Ian wants his yard to be in one of the rectangular shapes from the table and has only $220 to spend on fencing. What choices does Ian have for the dimensions of his yard?

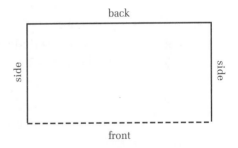

	Length				
Width	20	25	30	35	40
10					
15					
20					
25					
30					

46 If $(-3, 6)$ is a point on the graph for the equation in the form $y = 2x + b$, find b.

Problem Set, *continued*

In problems 47–49, copy and complete the table of values for each equation and sketch a graph of each.

x	−8	−6	−4	−2	0	2	4	6	8
y									

47 $y = x^2 + 4$ **48** $y = |x + 4|$ **49** $y = |x - 4|$

50 Refer to the table of values.

x	−4	−3	−2	−1	0	1	2	3	4	5
y	4	3	2	1	0	1	2	3	4	5

  a If the table is extended so y = 23, what is x?
  b If the table is extended so x = −1994, what is y?
  c Write an equation that represents the values in the table.

51 Consider the table of values.

x	0	1	2	3	4	5	6
y	1	2	4	8	16	32	64

  a Find y if x = 10.
  b If y = 256, find x.
  c Try to guess the equation for the table.

52 A 6-ounce can of frozen juice costs $0.89. Assume the same cost per ounce for other size cans of frozen juice.

Ounces	3	6	12	18	24	32
Cost in Cents		89				

  a Fill in the table.
  b What is the cost per ounce of frozen juice?
  c Write an equation that will give the cost, y, of x ounces of frozen juice.

53 The table of values was created by following a pattern.

x	1	2	3	5	8	13				
y	2	3	5	8	13	21				

  a Determine a logical rule for completing the table.
  b Plot the points given in the table on a coordinate system. Do they lie on a line?
  c Can you find an equation for this table? (Hint: It is unlikely that you will be able to come up with an equation for the table. It involves a famous set of numbers called the Fibonacci sequence.)

<table>
<tr><td>6.2</td><td></td></tr>
</table>

SLOPE-INTERCEPT FORM OF AN EQUATION

Objectives

After studying this section, you will be able to
- Identify the slope and y-intercept of a line whose equation is written in the form $y = mx + b$
- Interpret the slope of a line in three ways

Part One: Introduction

Equations of the Form $y = mx + b$

In the last section you learned that a linear equation written in the form $y = mx + b$ has a straight line as its graph. Let's look more closely at the constants m and b and how each affects the graph.

$y = mx + b$	Value of b	If $x = 0$, then	Point on Line
$y = 3x + 2$	2	$y = 2$	(0, 2)
$y = -2x - 3$	-3	$y = -3$	(0, -3)
$y = \frac{3}{5}x + 1$	1	$y = 1$	(0, 1)

You can see that if an equation is written in the form $y = mx + b$, then $y = b$ when $x = 0$. Therefore, (0, b) is always a point on the line. The graphs below show that each line intersects the y-axis at the point (0, b).

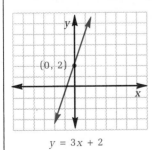

$y = 3x + 2$

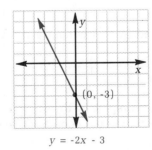

$y = -2x - 3$

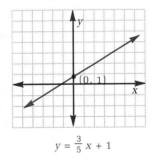

$y = \frac{3}{5}x + 1$

In the equation $y = mx + \boldsymbol{b}$, $\boldsymbol{b}$ is called the **y-intercept.** The point at which the line intersects the y-axis, (0, $\boldsymbol{b}$), is also called the y-intercept.

Example   *Find the point where the graph of y = 2x − 9 crosses the y-axis.*

Let x = 0 and solve for y.

y = 2x − 9
y = 2(0) − 9
y = −9

The graph of y = 2x − 9 crosses the y-axis at the point (0, −9).

The chart summarizes how we can find additional points on a graph of the equation y = mx + b by using the value of m.

Equation	Value of *m*	Change in *y* / Change in *x*	To Graph
y = 3x + 2	3	$\frac{3}{1}$	Move 1 unit to the right, then move three units up.
y = −2x − 3	−2	$\frac{-2}{1}$	Move 1 unit to the right, then move two units down.
y = $\frac{3}{5}$x + 1	$\frac{3}{5}$	$\frac{3}{5}$	Move 5 units to the right, then move 3 units up.

The value of ***m*** in the equation y = ***m***x + b is called the ***slope*** of the line. The slope of a line indicates how rapidly y rises or falls as the values of x change. A linear equation written in the form y = mx + b is in the ***slope-intercept form.*** This form works well with graphing calculators.

Interpreting the Slope of a Line

We will determine the slope of a line in three different ways, depending on whether we are graphing a line, writing an equation for a line that is already graphed, or applying the concept of slope to a rate-of-change problem.

You will find the first interpretation of slope especially useful when graphing a line from its equation.

 Slope is the value of m in an equation that is written in the form y = mx + b.

Example   *Sketch the graph of y = 3x + 1.*

Since the equation is in the form y = mx + b, we know that the slope is 3 and the y-intercept is 1. Begin by plotting (0, 1). From this point, move 1 unit to the right and 3 units up. Use this pattern to graph several points. Then connect these points with a line.

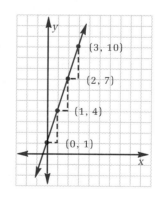

The second interpretation is helpful in writing an equation of a line when its graph is given.

> **Slope is the $\dfrac{\text{change in } y}{\text{change in } x}$ when moving from one point to another on the graph of a line.**

Example *Write an equation of the line in the graph.*

The y-intercept is -1

and $\dfrac{\text{change in } y}{\text{change in } x} = \dfrac{2}{3}$.

So an equation is $y = \frac{2}{3}x - 1$.

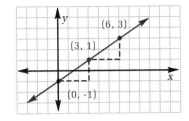

The third interpretation is most useful when interpreting slope as a rate of change in problem solving.

> **Slope is the rate of change in y when the change in x is 1.**

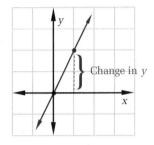

Example *An airplane 30,000 feet above the ground begins descending at the rate of 2000 feet per minute. Assuming the plane continues at the same rate of descent, how long will it be before it is on the ground?*

Let the y-axis represent the height in feet above the ground and the x-axis represent time in minutes. The y-intercept is (0, 30,000). The slope is $\dfrac{\text{change in height}}{1 \text{ minute of time}}$ or -2000 feet per minute.

An equation of the descent is $y = -2000x + 30,000$.

The plane is on the ground when the height y is 0.

$$0 = -2000x + 30,000$$
$$2000x = 30,000$$
$$x = 15$$

The plane is on the ground in 15 minutes.

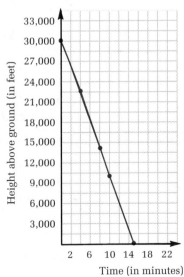

The point (15, 0), at which the graph crosses the x-axis, is called the **x-intercept** of the graph.

Part Two: Sample Problems

Problem 1 Graph the equation $y = \frac{-3}{4}x + 5$.

Solution The y-intercept is (0, 5), and the slope is $\frac{-3}{4}$.

Start at (0, 5) and repeatedly move 4 units to the right and 3 units down. Connect the points with a line.

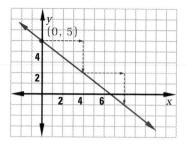

Problem 2 Graph the equation $y = x$.

Solution The equation $y = x$ can be written as $y = 1x + 0$. The y-intercept is (0, 0), and the slope is $\frac{1}{1}$.

Start at (0, 0) and repeatedly move 1 unit to the right and 1 unit up. Connect the points with a line.

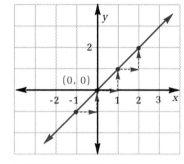

Problem 3 Graph the equation $2y = 4.6 - 7.8x$.

Solution Put the equation into the form $y = mx + b$.

$$2y = \quad 4.6 - 7.8x$$
$$y = \quad 2.3 - 3.9x$$
$$y = -3.9x + 2.3$$

The y-intercept is (0, 2.3), and the slope is $\frac{-3.9}{1}$.

Start at (0, 2.3) and repeatedly move 1 unit to the right and 3.9 units down. Then draw a line to connect the points.

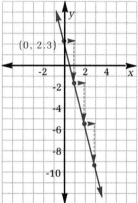

Part Three: Exercises and Problems

Warm-up Exercises

In problems 1 and 2, find the slope and the y-intercept and write an equation of each line.

1

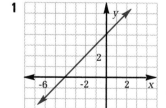

2

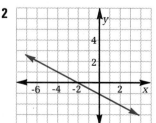

In problems 3 and 4, find the slope and y-intercept of each line and draw its graph.

3 $y = \frac{9}{5}x + 1$ **4** $y = -x$

In problems 5 and 6, find the slope of each line.

5

6
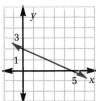

7 Write an equation of the line that has the same slope as $y = 3x + \frac{8}{9}$ and the same y-intercept as $y = -5x - 1$.

8 What is the slope of $y = x + 2$?

In problems 9 and 10, graph the equation.

9 $y = -\frac{4}{5}x + 3$ **10** $y = -3x$

Problem Set

In problems 11–16, find the slope and the y-intercept and graph each equation.

11 $y = 3x + 8$ **12** $y = 2 - 7x$ **13** $y = -4x$

14 $y = \frac{2}{5}x - 3$ **15** $y = x + 5.4$ **16** $y = x$

In problems 17–18, find the slope and the y-intercept and write an equation of each line.

17
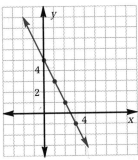

18
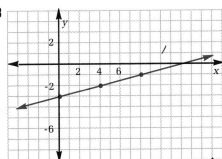

In problems 19 and 20, use each table of values to determine the slope of each line.

19

x	−5	−4	−3	−2	−1	0	1	2	3	4	5
y	−24	−19	−14	−9	−4	1	6	11	16	21	26

20

x	−15	−11	−7	−3	1	5	9	13	17	21	25
y	26	23	20	17	14	11	8	5	2	−1	−4

Problem Set, *continued*

21 Find all values of x such that the total length of the line segment is greater than 177.

$3x + 2$ $x + 1$

In problems 22–25, solve each equation and each inequality.

22 $3(5 - x) = 39$

23 $2 - 4x \le 3x - 2$

24 $x + 19 = 2x - (x - 19)$

25 $-12 > |x + 5|$

26 Refer to the diagram of rectangle ABCD.

  a Find the slope of $\overline{BD}$.
  b Find the coordinates of point C.
  c Find the coordinates of point A.
  d Find the slope of $\overline{AC}$.

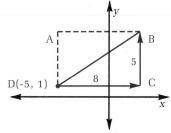

In problems 27 and 28, find three other points on the line containing the given point and having the given slope.

27 Point = $(-937, 799)$, slope = 73

28 Point = $(5, 2)$, slope = $\frac{13}{8}$

29 The following BASIC program will give 10 ordered pairs for any linear equation, given a point and the slope.

```
10 REM Linear equation table maker
20 PRINT "Enter the coordinates, separated by a
      comma, of any point on the line: ";
30 INPUT X1, Y1
40 PRINT "Enter the numerator and denominator of
      the slope separated by commas: ";
50 INPUT N,D
60 REM Print out 10 ordered pairs
70 PRINT "(";X1;",";Y1;")"
80 FOR C = 1 TO 9
90 REM Move to next point
100 LET X1 = X1 + D
110 LET Y1 = Y1 + N
120 PRINT "(";X1;",";Y1;")"
130 NEXT C
140 END
```

Use the program to generate a table of 10 values for each point-slope pair below. Based on the explanation, what do x and y represent?

Point	Slope	Explanation
a (1, 0.25)	0.20	First-class postage
b (32, 0)	$\frac{5}{9}$	Celsius/Fahrenheit conversion
c (15, 211)	$-\frac{3}{5}$	Aerobic pulse rate vs. age

30 Given the table of values, what are the patterns of change in x and in y? What is the slope, $\dfrac{\text{change in y}}{\text{change in x}}$?

x	−2	−1.5	−1	−0.5	0	0.5	1	1.5	2	2.5
y	7	4	1	−2	−5	−8	−11	−14	−17	−20

In problems 31–34, find the slope and y-intercept of each linear equation.

31 $3y = 6x - 9$

32 $5x = 2y - 4$

33 $y - \frac{2}{3}x - 6 = 0$

34 $4x - 2y = 10$

35 Find the y-intercept of a line that has slope 2 and passes through (4, 16).

36 Graph $y = 0.7x + 5$ and $y = -2.6x - 5$ on the same coordinate plane. To the nearest tenth, find the point of intersection of the two lines.

37 Refer to the line segment PQ.
a Find the coordinates of 2 points with integer coordinates on the line segment.
b If x increases by 2, what is the change in y?
c If x increases by 1, what is the change in y?
d Find the slope of $\overline{PQ}$.
e Find the coordinates of the point where the line segment crosses the y-axis.
f Write an equation for $\overline{PQ}$.

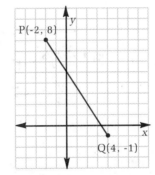

38 Solve for x and y.
$$\begin{bmatrix} 3 & 11 \\ 1 & y \end{bmatrix} \cdot \begin{bmatrix} x \\ 1 \end{bmatrix} = \begin{bmatrix} 31 \\ 7 \end{bmatrix}$$

39 If $x = y + 4$, solve $3y + 4x = 18$ for x and y.

40 Point P has coordinates (1, 4), and point Q has coordinates (11, 9). A turtle is at point P, facing up. Write three LOGO commands to move the turtle to point Q. (Hint: FD*n* and BK*n* move forward *n* steps and back *n* steps; RT*n* and LT*n* turn right *n* degrees and left *n* degrees.)

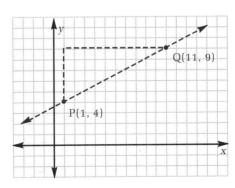

Problem Set, *continued*

41 Assume that $y = 3x + 5$.

 a Graph the equation.
 b Draw a line through (2, 2) that is parallel to the line $y = 3x + 5$.
 c Write an equation of the parallel line.

42 An airplane is flying at an altitude of 32,000 feet. The pilot is instructed to drop to 25,000 feet within the next mile of travel relative to the ground. (Hint: One mile is 5280 feet.)

 a Draw a sketch, to scale, of the plane's projected path.
 b How many feet will the airplane descend as it travels one foot relative to the ground?
 c What will the plane's altitude be after it has traveled 660 feet relative to the ground?
 d If the plane continues at the same rate of descent, how far will it have traveled relative to the ground when it is 11,000 feet above the ground?

43 If $3x + 2y = 18$, solve for y in terms of x.

44 If $3x + 2y = 18$, solve for x in terms of y.

45 Ziggy, the mutant robot from problem 31 in Section 6.1, is at point (3, 5). He is facing eastward in the direction of the positive x-axis. If Ziggy starts walking, which of the following points would be stopping points?

 a (15, 13)   **b** (27, 20)   **c** (5, 8)
 d (303, 205)   **e** (33, 25)   **f** (60, 45)

46 Given the information in the diagram, find the area of rectangles PQRS, PCDS, and ASRB.

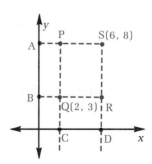

47 A line has an equation $y = -3x + b$. If b is selected from $\{-6, -3, 0, 3, 6\}$, what is the probability that the graph of this line will pass through exactly two quadrants? (The axes are not considered to be in any quadrant.)

THE GEOMETRY OF SLOPE

Objectives

After studying this section, you will be able to
- Determine slopes of different lines
- Use the slope formula

Part One: Introduction

Slopes of Different Lines

Just as the slope of a hill is the rate at which the height changes as you walk forward, the slope of a line is the rate at which the value of y changes as the value of x increases.

The slope is shown for each line in the diagram.

Lines that slant upward from left to right have a positive slope. The steeper the slant of a line with a positive slope, the greater the numeric value of the slope. Lines that slant downward from left to right have a negative slope. The steeper the slant of a line with a negative slope, the smaller the numeric value of the slope.

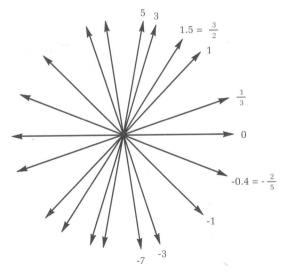

What happens when you graph $y = \frac{1}{3}x - 2$ and $y = \frac{1}{3}x + 4$ on the same coordinate system?

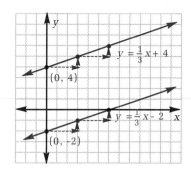

Since the lines have the same slope but different y-intercepts, the lines are parallel.

The Slope Formula

How can we determine the slope of a line without knowing its equation? If we try an example, we can come up with a general rule.

Example   *Determine the slope of the line that passes through the points $(-2, 4)$ and $(3, -5)$.*

Plot the points on a coordinate system and determine the $\dfrac{\text{change in } y}{\text{change in } x}$ from point to point.

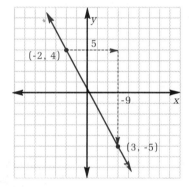

To move from $(-2, 4)$ to $(3, -5)$, we must move 5 units to the right and 9 units down. Therefore, the slope of the line is $\frac{-9}{5}$ or $-\frac{9}{5}$. In this case,

$$\frac{\text{change in } y}{\text{change in } x} = \frac{(-5) - 4}{3 - (-2)}$$
$$= \frac{-9}{5} = -\frac{9}{5}.$$

In the example above, we found the change in y by subtracting the y-coordinates of the two points. We found the change in x by subtracting the x-coordinates in the same order. This method leads to the slope formula, a fourth way of interpreting slope.

 The slope for the line containing points (x_1, y_1) and (x_2, y_2) is $\dfrac{y_2 - y_1}{x_2 - x_1}$.

Example   *Find the slope of the line that passes through $(3, 9)$ and $(-6, -4)$.*

Let $(x_1, y_1) = (3, 9)$ and $(x_2, y_2) = (-6, -4)$.

$$\text{Slope} = \frac{y_2 - y_1}{x_2 - x_1}$$
$$= \frac{(-4) - 9}{(-6) - 3}$$
$$= \frac{-13}{-9}$$
$$= \frac{13}{9}$$

Would the slope be different if we had chosen (x_1, y_1) to be $(-6, -4)$ and (x_2, y_2) to be $(3, 9)$?

$$\text{Slope} = \frac{y_2 - y_1}{y_2 - x_1}$$

$$= \frac{9 - (-4)}{3 - (-6)}$$

$$= \frac{13}{9}$$

Because the result is the same, it does not matter in which order we pick the points.

Part Two: Sample Problems

Problem 1 *Write an equation of the line in the diagram.*

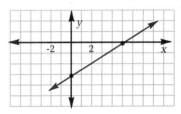

Solution In the diagram, we can see that the y-intercept is -3. If we select two points on the graph, we determine that the slope of the line is $\frac{3}{5}$. An equation of the line is $y = \frac{3}{5}x - 3$.

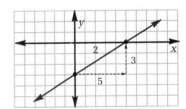

Problem 2 *An equation for line L_1 is $y = -\frac{2}{3}x + \frac{9}{5}$, and line L_2 passes through the points $(-3, 8)$ and $(6, 14)$. Determine whether the two lines are parallel.*

Solution We need to determine whether the lines have the same slope. The slope of L_1 is $-\frac{2}{3}$, the value of the coefficient of x in the slope-intercept form of the equation. The slope of L_2 is

$$\frac{y_2 - y_1}{x_2 - x_1} = \frac{14 - 8}{6 - (-3)} = \frac{6}{9} = \frac{2}{3}.$$

Because the slopes of the lines are not the same, the lines are not parallel.

Problem 3   *Determine whether the points (3, 5), (5, 8), and (13, 21) lie on the same line. (This is the same as asking whether the three points are **collinear**.)*

Solution   We can plot the points and try to connect them with a line. From the drawing, it looks as though the points might be collinear, but to be more accurate we must verify our answer algebraically. If the points are really collinear, the slope will be the same for all the pairs of points.

Let's try (3, 5) and (5, 8).

$$\text{Slope} = \frac{8 - 5}{5 - 3} = \frac{3}{2} = 1.5$$

Now let's try (5, 8) and (13, 21).

$$\text{Slope} = \frac{21 - 8}{13 - 5} = \frac{13}{8} = 1.625$$

Because the slopes are different, the three points must be noncollinear, not on the same line.

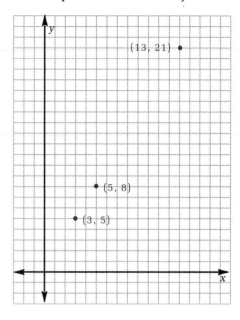

Problem 4   *Determine the point at which the line y = 3x + 4 crosses the x-axis.*

Solution   The point at which any line crosses the x-axis has a y-coordinate of 0, so let y = 0 and solve for x.

$$y = 3x + 4$$
$$0 = 3x + 4$$
$$-4 = 3x$$
$$\frac{-4}{3} = x$$

The point at which the graph of y = 3x + 4 crosses the x-axis is $\left(\frac{-4}{3}, 0\right)$. The x-intercept of the line is $\frac{-4}{3}$.

Part Three: Exercises and Problems

Warm-up Exercises

1 Which of the lines below has the smallest slope? (Assume all axes have the same scale.)

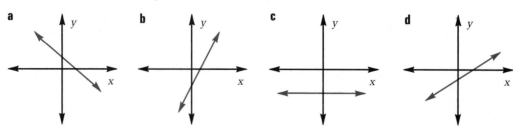

2 Find the slope of the line that passes through (3, 7) and (8, 15).

3 Find the slope of the line in the diagram.

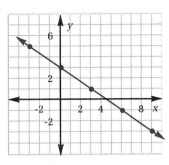

4 Is the line through (−3, 8) and (−1, 5) parallel to the line $y = -1.5x - 8$?

5 Determine whether (−21, 12), (−2, 1), and (20, −10) are collinear.

6 Find the point at which $y = -2x + 3$ crosses the x-axis.

Problem Set

In problems 7–10, find the slope of the line with each pair of points.

7 (3, 5) and (−1, 9)   **8** (2.6, 4.9) and (−3.2, 5.6)

9 (7, 5) and (10, 5)   **10** (−2, 4) and (−2, 7)

11 Determine which lines are parallel to $y = -\frac{3}{2}x + 5$.

   a $3x + 2y = 7$ **b** $3x - 2y = 4$
   c $3x + 2y = 5$ **d** The line through (−9, 7) and (12, 5)

12 Draw a horizontal line through (5, −2) and a vertical line through (−1, 4). Determine the point at which the lines intersect.

13 Describe the steps necessary to get from A to B, B to C, C to D, and so on.

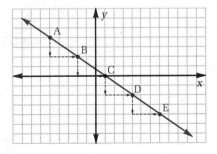

14 Consider the points A(1, 2), B(2, 5), C(3, 8), and D(4, 10).

   a If 3 of the points are chosen at random, what is the probability that they are collinear?
   b If 2 of the points are chosen at random, what is the probability that they are collinear?

Problem Set, *continued*

In problems 15 and 16, say whether the points are collinear.

15 $(0, -7)$, $(5, 13)$, and $(-3, -19)$ **16** $(0, 4)$, $(-3, 6)$, and $(6, 10)$

17 Refer to the line PT.

    a Find the change in x going from P to Q, Q to R, and R to S.

    b Find the change in y going from P to Q, Q to R, and R to S.

    c Find the ratio $\dfrac{\text{change in } y}{\text{change in } x}$.

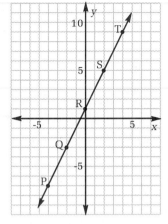

18 Find the slope of the line that passes through $(4, 2)$ and has an x-intercept of 7.

19 A line has a slope of 3. One of the points on the line is $(2, -3)$. Another point on the line is $(5, p)$. Find p.

20 Find the value of n so that the points $(2, 5)$, $(7, n)$, and $(9, -6)$ are collinear.

21 Determine which of the following points is not a solution to the equation $y = 4x + 5$.
$(-3, -7)$, $(-2, -3)$, $(0, 5)$, $(1, 8)$, $(2, 13)$, $(3, 17)$

22 The Fahrenheit temperature increases $\frac{9°}{5}$ for every $1°$ change in the Celsius temperature. Find the change in Fahrenheit temperature if the Celsius temperature increases by $20°$. Find the change in the Fahrenheit temperature if the Celsius temperature decreases by $30°$. If the Fahrenheit temperature increases by $45°$, by how many degrees does the Celsius temperature increase?

23 Imagine yourself walking on a Cartesian coordinate system. Begin at $A(0, 0)$ and walk east 8 units. Name this point B. Then walk north 4 units and name this point C. Walk west 3 units and name this point D. Give the coordinates of points B, C, and D. Then find the slopes of $\overline{AB}$, $\overline{BC}$, $\overline{CA}$, and $\overline{DA}$.

24 Find the slope of the line through the origin and $(-2, 8)$.

25 If, in going from one point on a line to another, the change in x is -12 and the change in y is 3, what is the slope of the line?

26 Graph the line that passes through $(-4, -2)$ with slope -3.

27 Find the slope of the line with x-intercept 7 and y-intercept 4.

28 Find the value of k so that the line through $(2, k)$ and $(5, 9)$ is parallel to each of the following lines.

a $-2x + y = 6$ **b** $y = 4x + 1$

29 In a presentation to the stockholders, the vice-president for sales displayed the graph at right. "As you can see," she told them, "our sales have taken off since the introduction of the new products in May." Why should her claim be questioned?

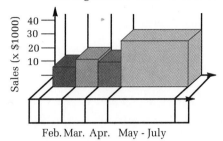
Amalgamated Retailers, Inc.

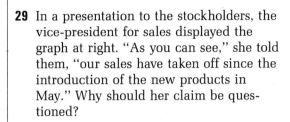
Feb. Mar. Apr. May - July

30 A line has a slope of 9. One of the points on the line is $(-2, p)$. Another point on the line is $(2, 2p + 1)$. Determine the value of p.

31 A road sign says that for the next 4 miles the road descends at a 6% grade, that is, it descends 6 feet for every 100 feet traveled. If a car next to that sign is 9468 feet above sea level initially, how many feet above sea level will the car be when it reaches the end of the 4 miles?

32 The points $A(1, 4)$, $B(2, 6)$, $C(0, 10)$, and $D(-1, 1)$ are consecutive vertices of a quadrilateral ABCD. Find the slopes of the diagonals. (Hint: Draw a picture of ABCD with its diagonals.)

33 Although the data graphed in the diagram are not collinear, the points seem to conform to a line. Use a ruler to find a line that contains the maximum number of the points. Write an equation for the line that you found.

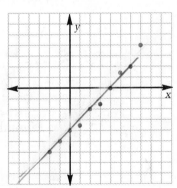

In problems 34–37, write an equation of each line.

34 A line with slope of -3 and y-intercept of 10

35 A line passing through $(6, 0)$ with y-intercept of 2

36 A line containing points $(1, 4)$ and $(2, 7)$

37 A line passing through the origin and parallel to $y = 2x + 6$

38 Find the values of q if the slope of the line through $(2, 11)$ and $(5, |q|)$ is 4.

Problem Set, *continued*

39 Refer to the diagram.
  a Find the slopes of $\overline{BC}$ and $\overline{AB}$.
  b What is the relationship of their slopes?
  c What type of angle is $\angle ABC$?

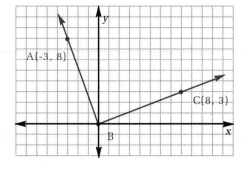

In problems 40 and 41, write an equation of each line described.

40 A line is parallel to $y = 4x - 5$ with y-intercept of -9.
41 A line is parallel to a diagonal of a square with vertices A(1, 3), B(1, 5), C(3, 5), and D(3, 3). The line contains the point (0, 3) and has a positive slope.

MATHEMATICAL EXCURSION

THE GEOMETRY OF BILLIARDS
Another kind of applied mathematics

Unlike the game of pool, the game of three-cushion billiards uses a table that has no pockets. A player must shoot a cue ball so that it strikes three cushions of the table and another ball before hitting a third ball.

To be successful at this game, it is very helpful to know geometry and to have plenty of practice. It is also a big help to know how to use the table marks called "diamonds."

The system can be very complicated, but here's a simple example: Suppose the cue ball is at position 60 (circled in the diagram). A player wants the ball to hit the lower cushion last, at diamond 10.

$$60 - 10 = 50$$

The way to do this is to aim at diamond 50 on the upper cushion. See what happens!

Now, for each of the following, tell which upper-cushion diamond a player should aim at, and sketch the path of the ball.

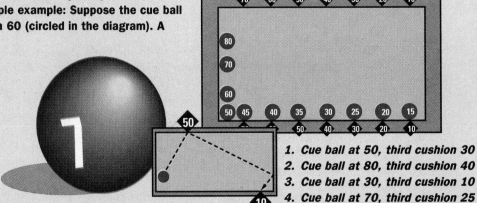

1. Cue ball at 50, third cushion 30
2. Cue ball at 80, third cushion 40
3. Cue ball at 30, third cushion 10
4. Cue ball at 70, third cushion 25

OTHER FORMS OF LINEAR EQUATIONS

Objectives

After studying this section, you will be able to
- Graph equations of the form $y = b$
- Graph equations of the form $x = a$
- Graph equations in the general linear form $Ax + By = C$

Part One: Introduction

Equations of the Form $y = b$

You have seen how to draw the graph of $y = mx + b$ without making a table. Now we will look at graphs of equations in forms other than $y = mx + b$.

Let's look at the graph of an equation written in the form $y = b$ and draw some conclusions.

Example   *Graph the equation $y = 3$.*

Since $0 \cdot x = 0$, we can rewrite $y = 3$ in the slope-intercept form as $y = 0x + 3$. Now we can make a table of values and plot the points.

x	-2	-1	0	1	2
y	3	3	3	3	3

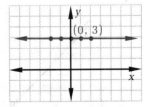

The graph of $y = 3$ is a horizontal line that intersects the y-axis at $(0, 3)$.

What is the slope of $y = 3$? In the table above, we see that no matter what value is chosen for x, the value of y is always 3. The $\dfrac{\text{change in y}}{\text{change in x}}$ is always 0, so the slope of the line must be 0.

We can also find the slope by using the slope formula. Choose any 2 points on the graph, say $(1, 3)$ and $(-2, 3)$, and evaluate the slope.

$$m = \frac{3 - 3}{-2 - 1} = \frac{0}{-3} = 0$$

Referring to the equation $y = 0x + 3$, the coefficient of x is 0, so the slope of $y = 3$ must be 0.

In general, the graph of an equation written in the form $y = b$ is a horizontal line that intersects the y-axis at $(0, b)$. The slope of any horizontal line is 0.

Equations of the Form $x = a$

Let's study the graph of an equation written in the form $x = a$ and draw some conclusions.

Example   *Graph the equation $x = 7$.*

An equation of the form $x = 7$ cannot be written in the $y = mx + b$ form. We can select any real number for y, but x must always be 7. Let's construct a table of values and plot the points.

x	7	7	7	7	7
y	-2	-1	0	1	2

The graph of $x = 7$ is a vertical line that intersects the x-axis at $(7, 0)$.

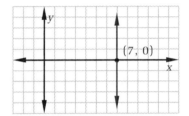

What is the slope of $x = 7$? From the table, $\dfrac{\text{change in } y}{\text{change in } x}$ always has a denominator of 0. Because we cannot divide by 0, we say that the slope is ***undefined.***

Using the slope formula, choose any two points on the graph, say $(7, 2)$ and $(7, -2)$.

$$\text{Slope} = \frac{-2 - 2}{7 - 7} = \frac{-4}{0}$$

The slope is, again, undefined.

In general, the graph of an equation written in the form $x = a$ is a vertical line that intersects the x-axis at $(a, 0)$. The slope of any vertical line is undefined.

Equations of the Form $Ax + By = C$

What if an equation is written as $Ax + By = C$, a form called the ***general linear form?*** Let's look at an example.

Example   *Graph the equation $5x + 3y = 30$.*

Method 1: The Slope-Intercept Method

Using the slope-intercept method, we can rewrite the equation in the $y = mx + b$ form. Then we can use the slope m and the y-intercept b to draw the graph.

$$5x + 3y = 30$$

$$\underline{-5x \qquad\quad -5x}$$

$$3y = -5x + 30$$

$$\frac{3y}{3} = -\frac{5x}{3} + \frac{30}{3}$$

$$y = -\frac{5}{3}x + 10$$

The slope is $-\frac{5}{3}$, and the y-intercept is (0, 10).

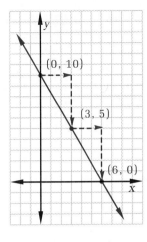

Method 2: The Intercepts Method

Using the intercepts method, we can find the x-intercept and the y-intercept. We can then plot these two points and connect them with a line.

To find the y-intercept, let x = 0 and solve for y.

$$5x + 3y = 30$$
$$5(0) + 3y = 30$$
$$3y = 30$$
$$y = 10$$

The y-intercept is (0, 10).

To find the x-intercept, let y = 0 and solve for x.

$$5x + 3y = 30$$
$$5x + 3(0) = 30$$
$$5x = 30$$
$$x = 6$$

The x-intercept is (6, 0).

We can now plot the points (0, 10) and (6, 0) on a coordinate system and connect them with a line.

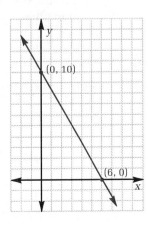

Part Two: Sample Problems

Problem 1   Graph the equation $y = \frac{9}{2}$.

Solution   The equation is in the form $y = b$. Its graph is a horizontal line with y-intercept $\left(0, \frac{9}{2}\right)$.

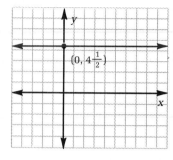

Problem 2   Graph the equation $x = -\sqrt{5}$.

Solution   The equation is in the form $x = a$. Its graph is a vertical line with x-intercept $\left(-\sqrt{5}, 0\right)$, or approximately $(-2.2, 0)$.

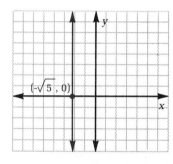

Problem 3   Graph the equation $7x - 3y = 22$.

Solution   The equation is in the form $Ax + By = C$. Let's use the intercepts method.

Let $x = 0$ and solve for y.

$$7x - 3y = 22$$
$$7(0) - 3y = 22$$
$$-3y = 22$$
$$y = -\frac{22}{3} \approx -7.3$$

The y-intercept is $(0, \approx -7.3)$.

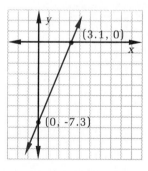

Let $y = 0$ and solve for x.

$$7x - 3y = 22$$
$$7x - 3(0) = 22$$
$$7x = 22$$
$$x = \frac{22}{7} \approx 3.1$$

The x-intercept is $(\approx 3.1, 0)$.

Plot the intercepts and draw the line.

Part Three: Exercises and Problems

Warm-up Exercises

In problems 1–3, graph each equation.

1 $x = -3$ **2** $y = 5$ **3** $5x + 10y = 10$

In problems 4–6, state the x-intercept and y-intercept.

4 $x = -2$ **5** $y = 3$ **6** $2x + 3y = 12$

7 List 3 points on ℓ and write its equation.

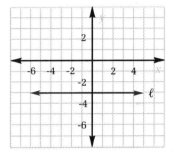

8 Find the point of intersection of the graphs of $x = 4$ and $y = 9$.

Problem Set

In problems 9–14, graph each equation.

9 $3x + 2y = 6$ **10** $3x + 2y = 12$ **11** $3x + 2y = -18$
12 $2x + 3y = 6$ **13** $6x + 9y = 18$ **14** $-2x - 3y = -6$

In problems 15 and 16, find the slope of each line.

15 The line passing through $(-8, 7)$ and $(-5, 6)$
16 A line parallel to the graph of $y = -7x + 4$

17 Write an equation for each of the four parallel lines pictured in the diagram.

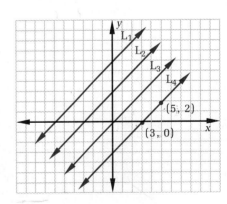

In problems 18–21, find the x-intercept of each line.

18 $y = 5x - 80$ **19** $5y - 2x = 17$ **20** $4x = 12 - y$
21 The line passing through $(0, 5)$ and $(-3, 0)$

22 Graph each equation on the same coordinate plane.

     a $2x + 3y = 36$ **b** $4x + 6y = 36$ **c** $6x + 9y = 36$

23 Solve for a and b if $(3a + 7, 8 - 3b) = (9 - 2a, 5b + 3)$.

Problem Set, *continued*

In problems 24–26, graph each equation.

24 $3x - 6y = 18$ **25** $y = -\frac{3}{4}x + 8$ **26** $4y - x = 10$

27 Triangle ABC is a right triangle.

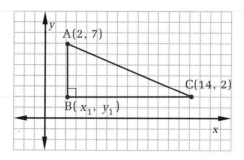

a What are the coordinates of vertex $B(x_1, y_1)$?
b What is the length of $\overline{AC}$?
c What is the slope of $\overline{AB}$?
d What is the slope of $\overline{BC}$?
e What is the slope of $\overline{AC}$?

28 Determine whether the graph of $5x - 4y = 60$ has the same y-intercept as the graph of $y = x + 12$.

29 Determine whether the point $(5, 7)$ lies on the line $y - 7 = \frac{2}{3}(x - 5)$.

In problems 30–32, rewrite each equation in slope-intercept form.

30 $2x + y = 9$ **31** $5x - 3y = 30$ **32** $6x - 5y = 0$

In problems 33 and 34, draw the graph of each line.

33 A line with an x-intercept of -7 and a slope of $\frac{3}{2}$

34 A line with an x-intercept equal to its y-intercept and containing the point $(1, 5)$

35 Find an equation of the line through point $(-3, 1)$ that is parallel to the line graphed in the diagram.

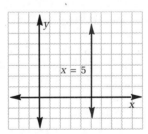

In problems 36–38, rewrite each linear equation in general linear form, $Ax + By = C$ where A, B, and C are integers.

36 $y = 5x - 3$ **37** $y = \frac{2}{3}x + 6$ **38** $3 - 2x = 4y$

39 Refer to the line $y = 10x + 3$.

a Determine where the graph of $x = -1$ crosses the line.
b Determine where the graph of $y = 7$ crosses the line.

40 The temperature at 6:00 A.M. is 27°F and is rising at the rate of $\frac{2}{9}°$ per minute. At what time will the thermometer read 41°F?

41 The slope of a line L_1 is 20% of the slope of $y = 30x - 6$. Find the slope of line L_1.

42 If Louis Pokes is riding his bicycle at 18 miles per hour, how far can he ride in 4.5 hours? What is his rate in feet per second?

In problems 43 and 44, find the slope of each line.

43 $y = \dfrac{2x - 12}{6}$

44 A line passing through $(-5, 9)$ and $(9, -5)$

45 Find the area of the rectangle formed by graphing the four equations $x = -3$, $y = -1$, $x = 5$, and $y = 6$.

In problems 46 and 47, determine whether the two given lines are parallel.

46 The line through $(-112, 345)$ and $(112, 569)$, and the line $y = x$

47 The line through $(-14, 7)$ and $(-10, 1)$, and the line with y-intercept 3 and x-intercept 2

In problems 48–50, rewrite each equation in slope-intercept form.

48 $-\sqrt{2}x + y = 9$ **49** $\frac{1}{2}x + \frac{1}{3}y = \frac{5}{6}$ **50** $y + 7 = \frac{2}{3}(x - 6)$

51 A balloon is being blown by the wind so that every second it rises 10 feet and travels horizontally 6 feet. The balloon is initially 150 feet directly above a lighthouse. Two minutes later, someone traveling in a plane spots the balloon.

How high above the lighthouse is the balloon at this point? How far horizontally has the balloon traveled from the lighthouse? Calculate both the length and the slope of an imaginary line joining the top of the lighthouse to the balloon when it is spotted.

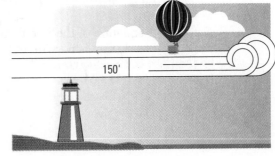

52 Let $x = 2t + 1$ and $y = 3t - 1$.

  a Complete the table of values.

  b Find $\dfrac{\text{change in } y}{\text{change in } x}$.

  c On a coordinate system, graph the line containing the ordered pairs (x, y).

  d Write an equation to describe the line graphed in part **c**.

  e Find the x-intercept of the graph.

  f Find the y-intercept of the graph.

t	x	y
-2		
-1		
0		
1		
2		
3		

Problem Set, *continued*

53 Given two points on a line, this program will give the slope of the line in fractional form and in decimal form.

```
10 REM Calculates slope given two points
20 REM Data entry section
30 PRINT "Enter X1 and Y1 separated by commas: ";
40 INPUT X1,Y1
50 PRINT "Enter X2 and Y2 separated by commas: ";
60 INPUT X2,Y2
70 REM Calculate numerator and denominator of
     slope
80 LET N = Y2 - Y1
90 LET D = X2 - X1
100 REM Check undefined slope
110 IF D = 0 THEN GOTO 160
120 REM Print out slope two ways
130 PRINT "Slope in fraction form = ";N;"/";D
140 PRINT "Slope in decimal form = ";N/D
150 GOTO 180
160 REM Print undefined slope
170 PRINT "SLOPE IS UNDEFINED"
180 END
```

Type the program in and save it. Use the program to find the slope of the line joining the points (7.2, $-$2.5) and (3.4, 7.6).

In problems 54 and 55, graph the equation or equations that result from solving each matrix equation.

54 $2\begin{bmatrix} x \\ 6 \end{bmatrix} + 3\begin{bmatrix} y \\ 4 \end{bmatrix} = 4\begin{bmatrix} -3 \\ 6 \end{bmatrix}$

55 $\begin{bmatrix} x & 7 \\ -6 & y \end{bmatrix} = 2\begin{bmatrix} -1 & 3.5 \\ -3 & 4.0 \end{bmatrix}$

56 ABCDE is a pentagon. If two of the diagonals of the pentagon are selected at random, what is the probability that both slopes are positive?

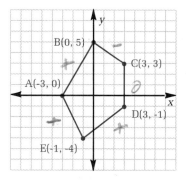

In problems 57–59, graph each equation.

57 $|y| = 2$ **58** $|x + 5| = 2$ **59** $|x - 3y| = 6$

60 The number of degrees in an obtuse angle is 9 more than 3 times the number of degrees in an acute angle. Find the range of possible acute angles.

6.5 | ONE MORE FORM OF A LINEAR EQUATION

Objectives

After studying this section, you will be able to
- Write an equation of a line in point-slope form
- Choose the most appropriate form of a linear equation for a given situation

Part One: Introduction

The Point-Slope Form

Consider the line that passes through $A(-3, 4)$ and $B(9, -7)$. Let $C(x, y)$ be any other point on this line. The slope of the line can be found by using points A and B or by using points A and C.

$$\text{Slope(AB)} = \frac{-7 - 4}{9 - (-3)} = \frac{-11}{12}$$

$$\text{Slope(AC)} = \frac{y - 4}{x - (-3)} = \frac{y - 4}{x + 3}$$

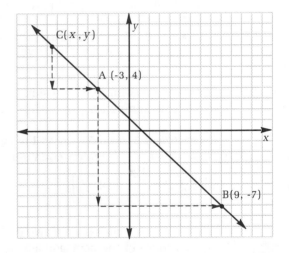

The slope of the line is the same for any two points on the line, so the slope determined by using points A and B will be equal to the slope determined by using points A and C.

$$\text{Slope(AC)} = \text{Slope (AB)}$$

$$\frac{y - 4}{x + 3} = \frac{-11}{12}$$

Multiply both sides of the equation by $(x + 3)$

$$(x + 3)\left(\frac{y - 4}{x + 3}\right) = \frac{-11}{12}(x + 3)$$

Simplify the expression on the left

$$y - 4 = \frac{-11}{12}(x + 3)$$

 This equation is in point-slope form, $y - y_1 = m(x - x_1)$ where (x_1, y_1) is a point on a line with slope m.

Example   Write an equation of the line that passes through $(-18, 6)$ with slope $\frac{9}{7}$.

We will use the point-slope form. Substitute $\frac{9}{7}$ for m, -18 for x_1, and 6 for y_1. The equation in point-slope form is $y - 6 = \frac{9}{7}(x + 18)$.

Three Forms of a Linear Equation

Having several forms of a linear equation is much more convenient than having just one form.

Let's summarize the forms of the linear equation and the best uses of each.

Form	Equation	Usefulness
Slope-Intercept	$y = mx + b$, m is slope b is y-intercept	Sketching graphs; finding slope, y-intercept of a line
Point-Slope	$y - y_1 = m(x - x_1)$, m is slope (x_1, y_1) any point on line	Writing an equation of a line, given one point and slope or two points on a line
General Linear	$Ax + By = C$ $A, B \neq 0$	Application problems; quickly finding x- and y-intercepts and drawing graph; writing equation of line with undefined slope

Remember that an equation will have the same graph no matter which form you use.

Part Two: Sample Problems

Problem 1   Find the slope and the y-intercept of the line with equation $5x - 7y = -12$.

Solution   Let's write the equation in the form $y = mx + b$ so that we can find the slope and the y-intercept.

$$5x - 7y = -12$$
$$\underline{-5x \qquad\qquad -5x}$$
$$-7y = -5x - 12$$
$$\frac{-7y}{-7} = \frac{-5x}{-7} + \frac{-12}{-7}$$
$$y = \frac{5}{7}x + \frac{12}{7}$$

The slope is $\frac{5}{7}$, and the y-intercept is $\frac{12}{7}$.

Problem 2   *Write an equation of the line that passes through* $(9, -2)$ *and* $(-7, -1)$.

Solution   To find an equation of a line, we need a point and the slope. Use the slope formula to compute the slope of the line.

$$\text{Slope} = \frac{y_2 - y_1}{x_2 - x_1} = \frac{-1 - (-2)}{-7 - 9} = \frac{1}{-16} = -\frac{1}{16}$$

Let's choose one of the points, $(9, -2)$, and use the point-slope form of an equation.

$$y - y_1 = m(x - x_1)$$
$$y - (-2) = -\tfrac{1}{16}(x - 9)$$
$$y + 2 = -\tfrac{1}{16}(x - 9)$$

We could have chosen the point $(-7, -1)$ instead of $(9, -2)$. Then we would have had this equation.

$$y + 1 = -\tfrac{1}{16}(x + 7)$$

Are the two equations really different? Look at Sample Problem 3.

Problem 3   *Write the slope-intercept form of the two equations in Sample Problem 2.*

Solution   Change each equation to $y = mx + b$ form.

$$y + 2 = -\tfrac{1}{16}(x - 9) \quad \text{or} \quad y + 1 = -\tfrac{1}{16}(x + 7)$$

$$
\begin{array}{ll}
y + 2 = -\tfrac{1}{16}x + \tfrac{9}{16} & \quad y + 1 = -\tfrac{1}{16}x - \tfrac{7}{16} \\
\underline{ -2 -2} & \quad \underline{ -1 -1} \\
y = -\tfrac{1}{16}x - \tfrac{23}{16} & \quad y = -\tfrac{1}{16}x - \tfrac{23}{16}
\end{array}
$$

When we write the equations in slope-intercept form, they are identical.

Problem 4   *Graph* $y - 2 = 3(x + 1)$.

Solution   The equation $y - 2 = 3(x + 1)$ is in the point-slope form. The slope is 3, and a point on the line is $(-1, 2)$.

Plot the point $(-1, 2)$ and then move right 1 unit and up 3 units. Repeat this pattern and connect the points with a line.

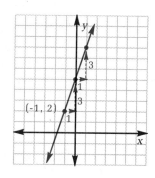

Part Three: Exercises and Problems

Warm-up Exercises

1 Write an equation of the line passing through $(-187, 593)$ and having slope $\frac{-77}{93}$.

2 Find the slope and y-intercept of the graph of $6x - 5y = 105$.

3 Sketch the graph of $y - 5 = \frac{2}{3}(x + 3)$.

4 Write an equation of the line.

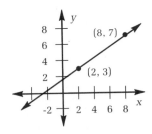

In problems 5–7, write an equation of the line that passes through each pair of points.

5 $(3, 4)$ and $(-2, 8)$ **6** $(6, 2)$ and $(-8, -2)$ **7** $(3, 0)$ and $(2, 0)$

In problems 8–10, name a point on the graph of each equation.

8 $y = 3x - 4$ **9** $3.4x + 5.8y = 21.6$ **10** $3(x - 4) = y + 1$

Problem Set

11 Find the slope of the line $y - 3 = 4(x + 2)$.

12 Write in the point-slope form an equation of the line having slope $-\frac{2}{3}$ and passing through point $(4, -6)$.

In problems 13–16, write each equation in the general linear form where A, B, and C are integers.

13 $y = 3x - 4$ **14** $y = \frac{2}{3}x - 3$
15 $y - 2 = 4(x + 5)$ **16** $3x = 2(y - 7)$

17 Write an equation of the line shown in the diagram.

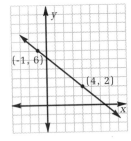

18 List four points on the line $y - 3 = \frac{2}{3}(x - 5)$.

In problems 19–22, write an equation of the line that passes through each pair of points.

19 $(-2, 3)$ and $(4, 7)$

20 $(-2, -4)$ and $(6, -5)$

21 $(5, 7)$ and $(12, 7)$

22 $(-3, 2)$ and $(-3, 5)$

23 Write an equation of the line with intercepts $(-2, 0)$ and $(0, 8)$.

24 Points $(3, 4)$ and $(-5, k)$ are on a line with a slope $\frac{-2}{3}$. What is the value of k?

25 The slope of a line is $\frac{2}{3}$ of its y-intercept. If the y-intercept is -4, write an equation of the line.

26 Refer to the right triangle ABC.

  a Write an equation of the line containing points A and B.

  b Write an equation of the line containing points B and C.

  c If the slope of $\overline{AC}$ is $\frac{3}{2}$, what is an equation of this line?

  d Find the coordinates of point C.

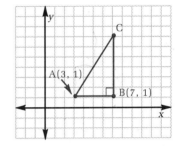

27 Write an equation of the line containing $(1974, 18.5)$ and $(1990, 29.9)$.

28 The points $(-8, 6)$ and $(4, 8)$ are on a line.

  a Write the point-slope form of an equation of this line using $(-8, 6)$ as the point.

  b Write the point-slope form of an equation of this line using $(4, 8)$ as the point.

  c Write each of the equations from part **a** and part **b** in slope-intercept form.

29 Franklin is out flying his kite. The slope of the string on the kite is $\frac{7}{3}$. If Franklin's hands are 4 feet above the ground and the kite is 300 feet horizontally from his hands, how high is the kite above the ground? How much string is there between the kite and his hands?

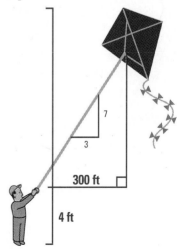

30 The slope-intercept form of the equation of a line is $y = \frac{3}{4}x + 2$. A point on this line is $(-4, -1)$. Using the given point, write an equation in point-slope form for this line.

31 Solve for x_1 if $|3x_1 + 5| \le 12$.

32 The vertices of a triangle have coordinates $A(-3, 4)$, $B(3, 4)$, and $C(0, 10)$. Write equations for $\overline{AC}$, $\overline{BC}$, and $\overline{AB}$.

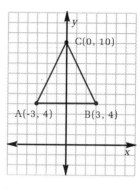

In problems 33 and 34, graph each equation.

33 $y + 8 = 1.25(x + 4)$ **34** $y - 4 = \frac{1}{2}(x - 3)$

35 Since 1962, researchers with the Perry Preschool Program in Ypsilanti, Michigan, have studied 100 children, half of whom attended preschool and half of whom did not. By age 19, big differences in academic and social skills were evident between the groups. Copy the double bar graph and use the data from the chart to complete the graph on the effects of preschool attendance.

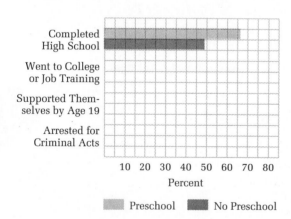

High Marks for Preschool

	Preschool	No Preschool
Completed High School	67%	49%
Went on to College or Job Training	38%	21%
Supported Themselves by Age 19	45%	25%
Arrested for Criminal Acts	31%	51%

Fortune; copyright 1988 Time, Inc. All Rights Reserved.

In problems 36–38, write an equation for each line.
36 A line that passes through points $(5, -4)$ and $(2, 2)$
37 A line with x-intercept 5 and y-intercept -7
38 A line that passes through $(3.5, 7.7)$ and $(0.5, 9.2)$

39 Refer to the graph.

   a Write an equation of the line using the
     point-slope form.

   b Write an equation of the line using the
     slope-intercept form.

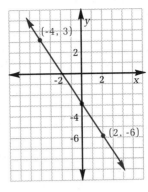

40 The point (2, 3) is on a line with slope 6. Find the y-intercept of
this line.

41 Refer to the diagram.

   a Find the area of the larger circle.

   b Find the area of the smaller circle.

   c Find the area of the shaded region.

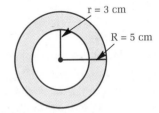

42 Find the points of intersection of the lines described by $|y| = 4$
and $x = 2$.

43 The intercept form of the equation of a line is written as

$\dfrac{x}{a} + \dfrac{y}{b} = 1$, where a is the x-intercept and b is the y-intercept.

For example, the equation $2x + 3y = 24$ (in the general linear

form) can be changed to $\dfrac{x}{12} + \dfrac{y}{8} = 1$ (the intercept form)

by multiplying both sides by $\dfrac{1}{24}$. The x-intercept is 12, and the
y-intercept is 8.

   a Let $3x + 5y = 60$.

     i Write the equation in the intercept form.

     ii Determine the x- and y-intercepts.

     iii Graph the line by using the intercepts.

     iv Find the slope of the line by using the intercepts.

   b Let $5x - 2y = 40$.

     i Write the equation in the intercept form.

     ii Determine the x- and y-intercepts.

     iii Graph the line by using the intercepts.

     iv Find the slope of the line.

Problem Set, *continued*

44 The following matrix equation is a compact way of representing two linear equations.

$$\begin{bmatrix} 2 & 3 \\ 5 & 1 \end{bmatrix} \begin{bmatrix} x \\ y \end{bmatrix} = \begin{bmatrix} 10 \\ 12 \end{bmatrix}$$

a Multiply the matrices to determine the equations.
b Graph the two equations on the same coordinate system.
c Determine the coordinates of the point of intersection.

CAREER PROFILE

WHERE HAVE ALL THE SARDINES GONE?
Richard Ford looks for answers

Monterey Bay, in California, was once home to great numbers of sardines, and the local economy depended heavily on sardine fishing. Then, a few decades ago, the sardine population dropped sharply, causing the economy to suffer huge losses.

What caused the sardine crash? "Overfishing was the main cause," explains Dr. Richard Ford, a professor of marine biology at San Diego State University. "But there were also natural changes in the ocean that favored the rise of the anchovy over the sardine." The question, like many questions about fish populations, has no precise answer. That doesn't bother Dr. Ford. "Uncertainty is one of the things that makes what I do interesting," he says. "And it leaves room for others to come along and find the answers."

Dr. Ford spends half his time teaching and half doing research on marine and fisheries ecology. He developed his love of the ocean as a child growing up in California. It was when he began keeping turtles in his back yard that he discovered his interest in marine biology.

Dr. Ford majored in zoology in college, earning a master's degree at Stanford University in the biology of fishes and a Ph.D. in oceanography at Scripps Institution of Oceanography. He has studied mathematics through calculus and uses math extensively. "Math is especially important for interpreting the research of others and for doing statistical analysis of my own data," he says.

To determine the health of a fish population, Dr. Ford may weigh a large number of individual fish and plot their weights against their ages, as shown in the graph. The slope of the line that most closely connects the points on the graph will indicate their rate of growth. The greater the slope, the healthier the population.

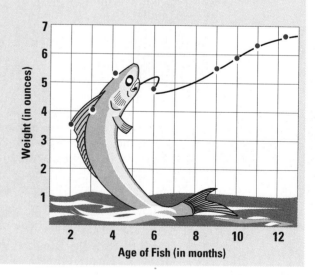

6.6 | NONLINEAR GRAPHING

Objectives

After studying this section, you will be able to
- Graph inequalities in two variables
- Graph absolute value equations in two variables
- Graph parabolas

Part One: Introduction

Graphing Inequalities

In Chapter 5, we used a four-step boundary algorithm to graph compound inequalities on a number line. To graph inequalities on the coordinate plane, we will use a similar procedure, a three-step boundary algorithm.

Three-Step Boundary Algorithm for Graphing Inequalities

1. **Graph** the boundary equation of the inequality.
   a If the inequality symbol is > or < , then the line is dashed.
   b If the inequality symbol is ≥ or ≤ , then the line is solid.

2. **Test** a point in each region determined by the boundary equation.

3. **Shade** the region where the point tested makes the inequality a true statement.

A graphing calculator or computer graphing software can be particularly helpful with nonlinear graphing. For example, you might use available technology to graph boundary equations quickly. If you have access to graphing tools, use them to experiment. As you work, watch for patterns.

Example   *Graph 3x + 7y < 20 on the coordinate plane.*

Graph the boundary equation $3x + 7y = 20$. Using the intercepts method, we find that the x-intercept is $\left(\frac{20}{3}, 0\right)$ and the y-intercept is $\left(0, \frac{20}{7}\right)$.

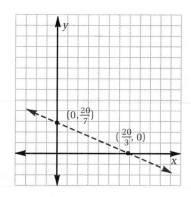

We used a dashed line because for the points on the line, $3x + 7y < 20$ is not a true statement.

Test a point on each side of the line. Let's try (0, 0) and (0, 6).

Left side	Right side		Left side	Right side
$3x + 7y$	< 20		$3x + 7y$	< 20
$= 3(0) + 7(0)$			$= 3(0) + 7(6)$	
$= 0$			$= 42$	

Since $0 < 20$, the point (0, 0) is a solution of the inequality.

Shade the entire region on the same side of the line as (0, 0). All points in the shaded region are solutions of the inequality.

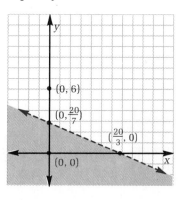

Graphing Absolute Value Equations

The graph of an absolute value equation or inequality is nonlinear. Look for patterns that might help you in your graphing.

Example   *Graph the equation $y = |x + 2|$.*

Make a table of values.

x	−4	−3	−2	−1	0	1	2	3	4
y	2	1	0	1	2	3	4	5	6

The y-values decrease as the x-values increase up to $x = -2$. As x increases beyond -2, the y-values also increase. When $x = -2$, the expression $x + 2$ equals 0. The point at which the y-values change from decreasing to increasing, $(-2, 0)$, is called the **vertex** of the graph. Many absolute value graphs are V-shaped.

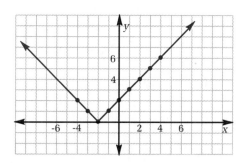

Graphing Parabolas

The graph of an equation that contains a squared variable term is also nonlinear. Again, construct a table and look for patterns to help you in your graphing.

Example   Graph the equation $y = (x - 2)^2 - 6$.

Make a table of values.

x	−2	−1	0	1	2	3	4	5	6
y	10	3	−2	−5	−6	−5	−2	3	10

The pattern is similar to the absolute value pattern. The y-values increase in either direction from x = 2. When x = 2, the expression $(x - 2)^2$ equals 0. The point (2, −6) is the vertex of the graph. This U-shaped curve is called a ***parabola.***

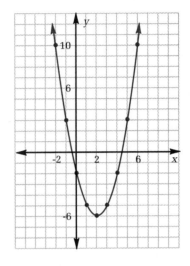

Part Two: Sample Problems

Problem 1   Graph the equation $y = |x - 1| + 4$.

Solution   The graph will be V-shaped. Make a table of values and graph the points.

x	−2	−1	0	1	2	3	4
y	7	6	5	4	5	6	7

The vertex occurs where x − 1, the expression within the absolute value bars, is zero. Because x − 1 = 0 when x = 1, the point (1, 4) is the vertex of the graph.

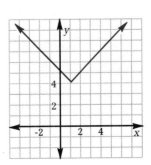

Problem 2   *Graph each inequality on the coordinate plane.*

        a $x \geq -4$ **b** $0 < y$

Solution   Use the three-step boundary algorithm to graph each inequality.

a Graph $x = -4$, using a solid line.

    Test a point in each region. Let's
try (0, 0) and (−10, 0). If $x = 0$,
the statement $x \geq -4$ is true, but
if $x = -10$, $x \geq -4$ is false.

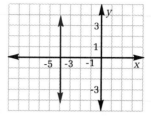

    Shade the region that includes (0, 0).

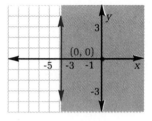

b Graph $y = 0$, using a dashed line.

    Test a point in each region. Let's
try (0, 5) and (0, −5). If $y = 5$,
$0 < y$ is true. If $y = -5$, $0 < y$ is
false.

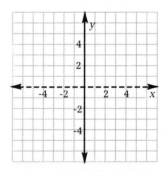

    Shade the region that includes (0, 5).

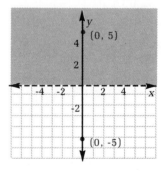

Problem 3   *Graph the inequality* $y < (x + 3)^2$.

Solution   Use the three-step boundary algorithm to graph the inequality.

Graph the equation $y = (x + 3)^2$, using a dashed line.
Make a table of values.

x	-6	-5	-4	-3	-2	-1	0
y	9	4	1	0	1	4	9

Because $x + 3 = 0$ when $x = -3$, the point $(-3, 0)$ is the vertex of the graph, and the graph is a parabola.

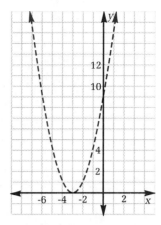

Test a point inside the U and one outside the U. Let's test $(0, 0)$ and $(-3, 2)$.

When we substitute $(0, 0)$ into the inequality, we get $0 < 9$, which is true. When we substitute $(-3, 2)$ into the inequality, we get $2 < 0$, which is false.

Shade the entire region outside the U shape because $(0, 0)$ makes the inequality true.

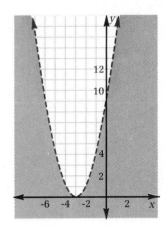

Part Three: Exercises and Problems

Warm-up Exercises

In problems 1–3, determine whether the graph of the boundary equation of each inequality is solid or dashed.

1 $y \le 3x + 2$ **2** $y > (x + 1)^2$ **3** $x \ge 7$

4 Will $(-3, 8)$ be shaded in the graph of $y > |x - 5|$?

5 Graph $x \le -2$ on the coordinate plane.

In problems 6 and 7, state the coordinates of the vertex.

6 $y = |x + 5| - 2$ **7** $y = (x - 3)^2 + 2$

In problems 8–10, graph each nonlinear equation.

8 $y = |x - 4|$ **9** $y = |x - 4| + 2$ **10** $y = (x - 4)^2 + 2$

11 Which equation represents the graph?

   a $y = |x - 8| - 3$
   b $y = |x + 8| - 3$
   c $y = |x - 8| + 3$
   d $y = |x + 8| + 3$

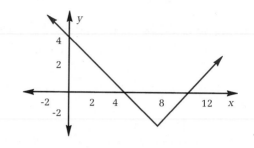

Problem Set

12 Decide which of the following test points make the inequality $y \leq \frac{1}{2}x + 4$ true and which make it false.

   a $(-2, 2)$ **b** $(-4, 2)$ **c** $(8, 4)$ **d** $(10, 14)$

13 Describe how the graphs of $y \leq 2x - 3$ and $y < 2x - 3$ differ.

14 Find a point that satisfies the inequality $y \geq x - 7$ but does not satisfy the inequality $y > x - 7$.

15 Solve for x and y.

$$\begin{bmatrix} 3 & -1 \\ 2 & y \end{bmatrix} \begin{bmatrix} x \\ 4 \end{bmatrix} = \begin{bmatrix} 7 \\ 12 \end{bmatrix}$$

In problems 16 and 17, copy and complete each table and graph each equation.

16 $y = x^2 - 7$

x	−2	−1	0	2	3
y					

17 $y = 2|x - 7| + 5$

x	−5	−1	7	11	15
y					

18 Which inequality does the graph represent?

   a $2x - 3y < 6$ **b** $2x - 3y \geq 6$
   c $2x - 3y > 6$ **d** $2x - 3y \leq 6$

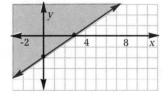

19 Graph the equation $y = (x - 3)^2 - 4$ and find the x- and y-intercepts of the graph.

20 If $y = 7$ and $y = |x| + 1$, find the value of x.

In problems 21–23, graph each on the coordinate plane.

21 $x = -5$ **22** $x > -5$ **23** $x < -5$

24 Graph the inequality $x > 3$ in three ways.

  a On a number line   **b** On the coordinate plane

  c On the x-axis of the graph in part **b**

In problems 25–28, graph each inequality.

25 $y > \frac{1}{2}x - 4$ **26** $3x + 2y \le 6$ **27** $y - 4 > \frac{-1}{4}(x - 3)$ **28** $y < 7.5$

29 Refer to the line segments in the diagram.

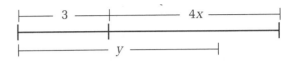

  a Write the inequality described by the diagram.

  b Graph the inequality from part **a**.

  c What particular restriction does the diagram impose on your graph?

30 Make a table of values and graph $y = |x - 2| + 1$.

31 Refer to the graph.

  a Find an equation of the boundary line.

  b Find an inequality.

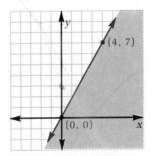

32 Given the equation $y = \sqrt{x + 5}$, for what values of x will y have a real number value?

33 The slope of a line is randomly chosen from $\{-4, 0, 2, -1\}$, and the y-intercept of the line is randomly chosen from $\{-5, 0, 3, -2\}$.

  a Find the probability that the line is horizontal.

  b Find the probability that the line passes through the origin.

  c Find the probability that the line passes through the first quadrant.

34 Triangle PQR can be represented by matrix M, where

$$M = \begin{bmatrix} 1 & 0 \\ 5 & 0 \\ 3 & 2 \end{bmatrix}.$$

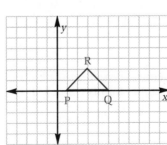

Copy the diagram. Multiply

$$M \cdot \begin{bmatrix} 0 & 1 \\ -1 & 0 \end{bmatrix}$$

and on the same axes graph the figure represented by the new matrix.

Problem Set, *continued*

35 Write equations of the lines L_1, L_2, and L_4, which are parallel to line L_3.

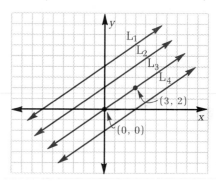

36 Find values of k so that the graphs of $y = |x + 2| + k$ and $y = (x + 2)^2 + 1$ intersect at exactly

    a Two points   **b** Three points   **c** Four points

37 Can you find values for a and k so that the graphs of $y = |x + a| + k$ and $y = x^2$ intersect at exactly at one point?

38 On the same coordinate axes, sketch the graphs of $y = \sqrt{x + 2}$ and $y = -\sqrt{x + 2}$.

39 Graph the inequality $y < (x - 3)^2$.

40 Sam graphed his weekly sales income over a 10-week period.

    a What was his maximum weekly income?
    b What was the range of his weekly income over the 10-week period?
    c Can we say that the point (3.5, 250) is on the graph?
    d Find Sam's average weekly income over the 10-week period.

Weekly Sales Income

In problems 41–43, graph each equation or inequality.

41 $|x| < 4$ **42** $y = \dfrac{1}{x - 2}$ **43** $|y| \geq 6$

44 A triangle is formed by points that satisfy both $y \geq |x| - 4$ and $y \leq 6$. Find the area of this triangle.

45 Refer to the intercept form of the equation of a line, $\dfrac{x}{a} + \dfrac{y}{b} = 1$, where a is the x-intercept and b is the y-intercept. (Hint: See problem **43** in Section 6.5.)

    a Write the equation of a line whose x-intercept is -4 and whose y-intercept is 10.
    b Rewrite the equation from part **a** in slope-intercept form.
    c What lines cannot have an intercept form? Why not?
    d Rewrite the equation $\dfrac{x}{a} + \dfrac{y}{b} = 1$ in slope-intercept form.
    e Rewrite the equation $y = \dfrac{3}{4}x - 2$ in intercept form.

46 The sum of the girth (distance around) and the height of a box must be less than 108 inches in order to be accepted by a parcel delivery firm. Make a graph of the girths and heights of boxes that would be acceptable.

47 You are given a table of values.

x	64	36	16	4	0
y	8	6	4	2	0

a Even though the y-values decrease by 2, the graph for this data is not a line with slope −2. Why not?

b Write an equation that relates x and y.

c The pattern suggests that the next pair in the table should be (−4, −2). Does this point fit your equation from part **b**?

HISTORICAL SNAPSHOT

A PROBLEM-SOLVING PLAN
George Pólya and the triumph of discovery

Have you ever wondered what it would be like to make a great discovery? According to Hungarian-born mathematician George Pólya (1887–1985), you know the feeling well, for you experience it every time you solve a problem, even a simple one. Pólya, who taught at Stanford University, believed that if you are curious about a problem and use your creativity to solve it in your own way, you will enjoy what he called "the triumph of discovery."

One of this century's most gifted mathematicians, Pólya enjoyed the triumph of discovery in a wide variety of fields, including probability, number theory, geometry, and combinatorics. But it was his investigations into the way that people solve problems that won him the greatest acclaim. In his classic book *How to Solve It*, published in 1945 and afterwards translated into 15 languages, he introduced the four-step problem-solving scheme taught almost universally today:

1. Understand the problem.
2. Devise a plan.
3. Carry out the plan.
4. Look back.

Experience the triumph of discovery by solving this problem from How to Solve It:

Suppose you found among your grandfather's papers a bill reading "For 72 turkeys, $_67.9_" (with the first and the last digit of the price faded to illegibility). What was the price per turkey paid by your grandfather?

CHAPTER SUMMARY

CONCEPTS AND PROCEDURES

After studying this chapter, you should be able to
- Make a table of values from an equation and use it to graph the equation (6.1)
- Write an equation from a table of values and from a graphed line (6.1)
- Find the slope and the y-intercept of a line whose equation is in the $y = mx + b$ form (6.2)
- Interpret the slope of a line in three ways (6.2)
- Find the slope of a line using the slope formula (6.3)
- Determine whether the slope of a line is positive or negative by its slant (6.3)
- Graph horizontal and vertical lines (6.4)
- Graph equations in the general linear form $Ax + By = C$ (6.4)
- Write an equation of a line in point-slope form (6.5)
- Choose the most appropriate form of a linear equation for a given situation (6.5)
- Graph inequalities in a coordinate plane using the three-step boundary algorithm (6.6)
- Graph absolute value equations in a coordinate plane (6.6)
- Graph a parabola using a table of values and patterns (6.6)

VOCABULARY

collinear (6.3)	point-slope form (6.5)	x-intercept (6.2)
general linear form (6.4)	slope (6.2)	y-intercept (6.2)
parabola (6.6)	slope-intercept form (6.2)	

AN IMPORTANT CONCEPT

You should be able to interpret the slope of a line in each of these ways.
- As m, the coefficient of x in the $y = mx + b$ form
- As $\dfrac{\text{change in } y}{\text{change in } x}$ on the graph of a line
- As a rate of change in y when the change in x is 1
- As $\dfrac{y_2 - y_1}{x_2 - x_1}$ when (x_1, y_1) and (x_2, y_2) are points on a line
- As a measure of the steepness of a line

REVIEW PROBLEMS

In problems 1–9, graph each equation or inequality.

1 $y = \frac{3}{4}x - 2$ **2** $x < 4$ **3** $y = 5$

4 $y = -2x + 3$ **5** $y - 6 = 2(x - 3)$ **6** $3x + 4y \le 24$

7 $y = 4x$ **8** $x = 5$ **9** $2y - 3 + y = 0$

10 Refer to the table of values.

x	−5	−4	−3	−2	−1	0	1	2	3	4
y	−14	−9	−4	1	6	11	16	21	26	31

  a Find the pattern of change in y-coordinates.
  b Find the slope and y-intercept of the line.
  c Write the slope-intercept form of the equation of the line.

11 Solve for p and q.

$$\begin{bmatrix} 4 & -2 \\ 3 & q \end{bmatrix} \begin{bmatrix} p \\ 6 \end{bmatrix} = \begin{bmatrix} 12 \\ -5 \end{bmatrix}$$

In problems 12–14, solve each equation or inequality.

12 $3x_1 + 5 < 12$ **13** $|2x_1 - 4| = 14$ **14** $2y > 5$

15 A client studying architectural plans of a room wants the length increased by 10% and the width decreased by 20%. Find the new dimensions.

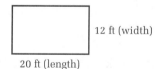

12 ft (width)

20 ft (length)

16 Use a large sheet of graph paper to do the following problem.

  a Mark the horizontal axis in degrees Fahrenheit from 0° to 220°, in multiples of 20.
  b Mark the vertical axis in degrees Celsius from 0° to 120°.
  c Plot the ordered pair for the freezing point of water. Water freezes at 32°F, or 0°C.
  d Plot the ordered pair for the boiling point of water. Water boils at 212°F, or 100°C.
  e Draw the line that connects the two plotted points. This allows you to convert from °F to °C.
  f Use the graph from part **e** to approximate your body temperature, 98.6°F, in degrees Celsius.
  g Convert 50°C to degrees Fahrenheit.
  h Find the slope of the graph.

Review Problems, *continued*

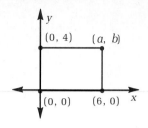

17 The vertices of a rectangle are given.

    a Find the coordinates (a, b).
    b Find the perimeter and the area.
    c Find the slopes of the diagonals.
    d Find the length of the diagonals.

18 The formula $h = 4000 + 250t$ gives the altitude or height h in meters of an airplane in terms of time t in seconds.

    a Determine the slope of this equation.
    b Graph the equation using t as the horizontal axis and h as the vertical axis.
    c What is the height of the plane at $t = 30$ seconds?
    d At what time is the plane 7000 meters high?

19 Find the slope of the line shown.

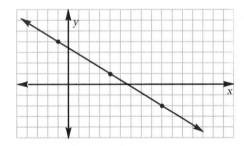

In problems 20–24, write an equation of each line.

20 A line with y-intercept $\frac{2}{3}$ and slope 6

21 A line with slope $\frac{-3}{8}$ and passing through the point $(7, -5)$

22 A line parallel to $y = -4x - 5$ and passing through $(0, 3)$

23 A line passing through points $(6, 3)$ and $(8, 17)$

24 A line parallel to $x = 5$ and passing through $(7, 6)$

25 Find y if the given points are collinear.

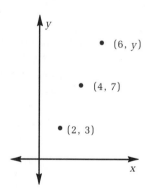

26 A point is selected at random from $\{(0, 6), (2, 0), (-3, 4), (-6, 0), (0, 0)\}$.

    a What is the probability that the point selected is on either the x-axis or the y-axis?
    b What is the probability that it is not on either axis?

27 Given the line $2x - 3y = 12$, find the x- and y-intercepts. Through which quadrants does the line pass?

28 Find the value of k so that the line containing points $(x_1, y_1) = (7, -5)$ and $(x_2, y_2) = (3, k)$ has a slope of 11.

29 Ziggy, the mutant robot, is back to his old pattern. (See problem 31 in Section 6.1.) At what point would Ziggy have to start in order to stop at point (23, 17)?

In problems 30 and 31, graph each pair of inequalities on the same coordinate plane.

30 $6x - 2y < 5$
$y < 4$

31 $y \le 2x - 7$
$y \ge |x| - 10$

32 Find k if $y = 5x + 7$ and $y = (2k + 1)x - 9$ are parallel lines.

33 Put the following equations in order of increasing slope.

a $y = \frac{2}{3}x - 6$ **b** $3x - 4y = 7$ **c** $6(x - 2) = 3(y + 5)$

34 Find the slope of a line if its x- and y-intercepts are additive inverses of each other.

35 A road starts at 900 feet above sea level. Its altitude rises 4 feet for every 100 feet of horizontal distance.

a Write a linear equation for the given information.
b Determine the altitude of a point in the road whose horizontal distance is 3200 feet from the start.
c The altitude of a point in the road is 1600 feet. How far is the point horizontally from the start of the road?

In problems 36–38, graph each equation or inequality.

36 $y = x^2 - 4$ **37** $y > x^2 - 4$ **38** $y = (x + 2)^2 - 3$

 39 The Lees bought a house in 1956 for $12,000. In 1988, they sold it for $125,000. Assume that the increase in value was constant over this period. Let $t = 0$ in 1956. Write an equation for the value V of the house at any time t. Determine its value in 1975. When was its value $75,562.50? Assuming the rate of increase remains constant, determine the house's value in the year 2001.

In problems 40 and 41, write an equation of each line.

40

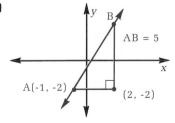

AB = 5
A(-1, -2)
(2, -2)
B

41

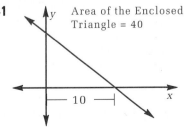

Area of the Enclosed Triangle = 40

10

CHAPTER TEST

1 Complete the table of values for the equation $y = 3x - 5$.

x										
y	−8	−5	−2	1	4	7	10	13	16	19

2 Write an equation for the table.

x	−3	−2	−1	0	1	2	3	4	5	6
y	18	14	10	6	2	−2	−6	−10	−14	−18

3 If a line passes through (4, 8) and its y-intercept is 3, what is the slope of the line?

4 Write an equation of the line in the graph.

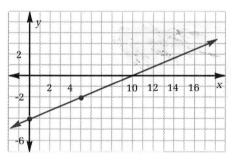

5 Find the value of k so that the line through $(-2, 5)$ and $(7, k)$ has a slope equal to each of the following.

a 8 **b** $\frac{-2}{3}$ **c** 0 **d** Undefined

In problems 6–9, graph each equation.

6 $y = \frac{4}{3}x - 2$ **7** $6x - 3y = 24$

8 $(y + 5) = 2(x - 1)$ **9** $7x = 10y - 6$

10 Gemini High School has a student population of 1640 students, which is increasing at a rate of 65 students per year. Find an equation that represents this information and sketch its graph.

11 Write an equation of the line passing through (1963, 82.7) with slope -0.5.

12 Graph the inequality.

13 Graph the equation $y = |x| - 2.5$.

PUZZLES AND CHALLENGES

1 One day, two brilliant mathematicians, Hamberg and Dodge, are walking down the street when Hamberg remarks that he does not know the ages of Dodge's three children. The following dialogue takes place.

Dodge:
   The product of their ages is 36.
Hamberg:
   I still don't know their ages.

Dodge:
   The sum of their ages is equal to the number on that red house across the street.
Hamberg:
   I still don't know their ages.
Dodge:
   Oh, yes, the oldest is visiting her grandmother.
Hamberg:
   Now I know.

What are the ages of Dodge's children?

2 Find the next logical row if the pattern is to be consistent.

```
                              1
                  1                    1
                  2                    1
        1         2         1          1
        1         1         1          2
1       3         1         2          2
        3                   1
1       3         1         1          2

                              1
                              1
                    1         1
                    2         1
                    1         2
                    2         2

                    1
                    1
                    2         1
                    1         2   1
```

3 You have ten stacks of half dollars. One entire stack is counterfeit. You know the weight of a genuine half dollar. You also know that each counterfeit half dollar weighs 0.5 gram more than a genuine coin. You have a very accurate scale that allows you to determine the exact weight of a stack of coins. Explain how it is possible to determine which stack is counterfeit using only one weighing.

4 A farmer, transporting a fox, a chicken, and a bag of corn, comes to a river. There is a ferry to cross the river, but it will hold at most two things: the farmer and one other. If the farmer leaves the chicken with the corn, the chicken will eat the corn. If the farmer leaves the chicken with the fox, the fox will eat the chicken. Explain how the farmer and his possessions can get across the river intact.

7 FORMULAS AND FUNCTIONS

According to a new theory of continental drift, Miami Beach, Florida, may again lie at the doorstep of West Africa one day in the future.

Because of the rise of molten material from the earth's mantle, the continents move a few centimeters a year on slablike plates. Scientists believe that this sliding motion caused the breakup of the supercontinent, Pangaea, 200 million years ago. Theoretically, at one time all the continents were joined together as components of this supercontinent.

The new theory postulates that Pangaea was only the most recent of a series of supercontinents that have split apart and reassembled during the past 2.6 billion years. If this theory of supercontinent cycles proves true, one day a new Pangaea will be formed.

WORKING WITH FORMULAS

$$F = \frac{9}{5}C + 32$$

Objectives

After studying this section, you will be able to
- Recognize formulas
- Write and evaluate formulas
- Use units with formulas

Part One: Introduction

What Is a Formula?

To solve a mathematical problem, it is often necessary to use formulas. A *formula* is an equation that states a general rule or principle in mathematical language or symbols.

Writing and Evaluating Formulas

Formulas can be used to solve a variety of problems.

Example   *Write a formula to express the number of feet f in m miles if there are 5280 feet in one mile.*

To find the number of feet in m miles, we multiply the number of miles, m, by 5280.

$f = m \cdot 5280$

Example   *The formula $F = \frac{9}{5}C + 32$ is used to convert Celsius temperature C to Fahrenheit temperature F. If the Celsius temperature is 20°, find the Fahrenheit temperature.*

$F = \frac{9}{5}C + 32$

$F = \frac{9}{5}(20) + 32$

$F = 36 + 32$

$F = 68$

The Fahrenheit temperature is 68°.

Input: $C = 20$

$F = \frac{9}{5}C + 32$

$F = \frac{9}{5}(20) + 32$

Output: $F = 68$

Note   The diagram above is an *input-output diagram.* The *inputs* are numbers substituted for variables. The *outputs* are the results.

Example *The formula $d = 16t^2$ is used to find the distance d in feet that an object falls in t seconds. Use the distance formula to find the time it takes an object to fall 64 feet.*

$$d = 16t^2$$
$$64 = 16t^2$$
$$4 = t^2$$
$$-2 = t \text{ or } 2 = t$$

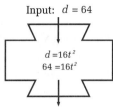

Input: $d = 64$

$d = 16t^2$
$64 = 16t^2$

Output: $t = 2$ or $t = -2$

In this example, the input has more than one output. The statement $t = -2$ or $t = 2$ can be written more concisely as $t = \pm 2$. This is read as "t equals positive 2 or negative 2." Note, however, that only $t = 2$ is a solution for this problem. The object falls 64 feet in 2 seconds.

Using Units in Formulas

Formulas are usually written in terms of certain units. Always be sure that the input variables have the correct units.

Example *The formula $i = prt$ is used to calculate the simple interest on a loan.*

i = the amount of interest in dollars,
p = the amount borrowed, called the principal, also in dollars,
r = the interest rate in percent charged per year, and
t = the time in years.

Calculate the simple interest on a loan of $600 at 11% annual interest for a period of 36 months.

Since the formula must have time in years, we convert 36 months to 3 years and substitute 3 for t. Notice we also changed the 11% to its decimal equivalent.

$i = prt$
$i = (600)(0.11)(3)$
$i = 198$

The interest is $198.

Example *Find the volume of a rectangular box if the length is 12 inches, the width is 24 inches, and the height is 1.5 feet.*

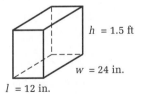

$h = 1.5$ ft
$w = 24$ in.
$l = 12$ in.

The formula for the volume of a rectangular box is $V = lwh$.

First, we must agree upon a common unit. If we use feet, we must change 12 inches to 1 foot and 24 inches to 2 feet. Then
$V = (1)(2)(1.5)$
$\quad = 3$
The volume of the box is 3 cubic feet.

Part Two: Sample Problems

Problem 1   Judge Tuff fines speeders $50 plus $3 for every mile per hour over the speed limit. Let *f* be the amount of the fine and *m* the number of miles per hour over the speed limit.

    a Write a formula that relates *f* and *m*.
    b How much was Roland Fast fined if he was caught driving 70 miles per hour in a 55-mile-per-hour zone?

Solution   **a** $f = 50 + 3m$
    b Roland was driving 15 miles per hour over the speed limit.

$$f = 50 + 3m$$
$$f = 50 + 3(15)$$
$$f = 95$$

The fine was $95.

Problem 2   Family Food Mart hires high school students to work part time. Baggers are paid $5.00 per hour and cashiers $5.25 per hour. The following table shows the hours worked last week.

Employee	Bagger Hours	Cashier Hours
Phil Jones	20	10
Amy Collins	12	5
Carmen Martinez	6	20
Steven Choi	15	8

    a Write a formula to calculate each employee's weekly wages.
    b Use the formula to calculate Carmen's total wages for the week.

Solution   **a** If W = weekly wages,
            B = hours worked as a bagger, and
            C = hours worked as a cashier,
    then $W = 5B + 5.25C$.
    b $W = 5(6) + 5.25(20)$
              $= 135$

Carmen earned $135. This problem can also be solved by matrix multiplication.

Problem 3   What values of k are not allowed in the formula $m = \dfrac{2000}{k^2 - 9}$?

Solution   Since the denominator cannot be zero, we determine the values of *k* that make $k^2 - 9 = 0$.

$$k^2 - 9 = 0$$
$$k^2 = 9$$
$$k = -3 \text{ or } k = 3$$

If $k = \pm 3$, the value of the denominator will be zero. Therefore, *k* cannot be ± 3.

Part Three: Exercises and Problems

Warm-up Exercises

1 Find A.

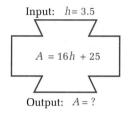

Input: $h = 3.5$

$A = 16h + 25$

Output: $A = ?$

2 What values of m are not allowed in the formula $a = \dfrac{m - 4}{m(m + 2)}$?

3 What is the simple interest on a loan of $525 at 12% interest for 6 months?

4 Write a formula for the perimeter P of each of the triangles shown below.

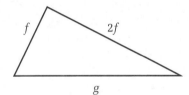
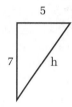

5 Write a formula to compute the slope of the line containing points (a, b) and (c, d).

In problems 6–8, write a formula for each.

6 The distance d in miles traveled in t hours at r miles per hour
7 The total value v in cents of n nickels and d dimes
8 The total value v in dollars of n nickels and d dimes

In problems 9–12, use the formula $F = \frac{9}{5}C + 32$ to convert each temperature.

9 0° Celsius to Fahrenheit
10 32° Fahrenheit to Celsius
11 37° Celsius to Fahrenheit
12 105° Fahrenheit to Celsius

13 The formula for the perimeter P of a 5-sided figure (known as a pentagon) is $P = a + b + c + d + e$. If $a = 10$, $b = 4$, $c = 8$, $d = 12$, and $e = 11$, use an input-output diagram to find the perimeter.

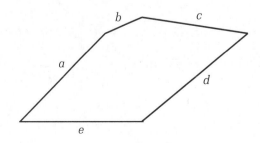

Problem Set

In problems 14–17, use the formula $t = \dfrac{x \pm y}{8}$ to compute values of t for the given input values of (x, y).

14 $(24, 40)$ **15** $(12, -4)$ **16** $(12, 0)$ **17** $(12, 4)$

18 Write a formula for the number of calories c burned by exercising h hours if 20 minutes burns 180 calories.

19 A long-distance phone call costs $2.35 for the first three minutes and $0.42 for each additional minute. Let c represent the cost of a call and m the number of additional minutes.
  a What formula relates m and c?
  b What is the total cost of a 5-minute phone call at these rates?

In problems 20 and 21, graph each on a coordinate plane.

20 $y = -\frac{2}{3}x + 5$ **21** $4x + 2y \le -12$

22 A record album costs $9.99, a compact disc costs $13.79, and a tape costs $11.49.
  a Write a formula to describe the total amount a of a bill for r record albums, c compact discs, and t tapes.
  b Use the formula from part **a** to compute the total bill for 5 records, 3 discs, and 7 tapes.
  c Use the formula from part **a** to compute the total bill for 8 records and 5 discs.
  d Rose had $400 to spend on tapes, discs, and records for her music club. She selected 12 records and 8 tapes. How many compact discs can she buy?

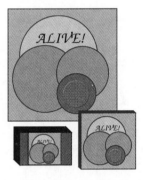

23 Simplify.

$$5\begin{bmatrix} 3 & -2 \\ -5 & -4 \end{bmatrix} - 5\begin{bmatrix} 3 & 4 \\ 2 & -8 \end{bmatrix}$$

24 Liz randomly selected a whole number from $\{1, 2, 3, \ldots, 40\}$ for the side of a square. What is the probability that the area of Liz's square is greater than 200?

In problems 25–27, the formula for the speed of sound v in feet per second through air at temperature t in Celsius is

$$v = \frac{1087\sqrt{273 + t}}{16.52}.$$

25 Find the speed of sound at $t = 0°$ Celsius.
26 Find the speed of sound at $t = 75°$ Fahrenheit.
27 Find the speed of sound at $t = -273°$ Celsius.

28 Use the formula $x = \dfrac{-b \pm \sqrt{b^2 - 4ac}}{2a}$ to determine the value of x if $a = 2$, $b = 5$, and $c = 3$.

In problems 29–31, find an equation of each line.

29 The line joining $(-5, 8)$, $(-1, 7)$, $(3, 6)$, and $(7, 5)$

30 The line with slope 7 and y-intercept $\frac{2}{3}$

31 The line with x-intercept -3 and y-intercept 8

32 Two angles have measures x and y. The sum of the measures of the angles is 180. Write a formula to express this relationship and solve the formula for y.

33 The wages for each Family Food Mart worker in Sample Problem 2 can be calculated using matrix multiplication. Write the two matrices you would multiply to find the employees' wages. Calculate the wages using matrix multiplication.

In problems 34 and 35, the area of a 6-sided polygon (a hexagon) is given by the formula $A = \frac{1}{2}aP$, where the apothem a is shown in the diagram and P is the perimeter of the figure.

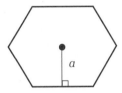

34 Find the area of a hexagon with each side 2 feet long and an apothem $\sqrt{3}$ feet long.

35 Find the length of a side of the hexagon if $a = 6\sqrt{3}$ centimeters and the area is $432\sqrt{3}$ square centimeters.

36 What inputs cannot be used in the following formulas if the output is v?

a $v = \dfrac{d}{t}$ **b** $v = \dfrac{t + 50}{t + 30}$ **c** $v = \dfrac{1000}{t^2 - 16}$ **d** $v = \dfrac{120x}{(x - 2)(x - 3)}$

In problems 37–41, use the formula $g \approx 0.2642L$ to relate liters L of gasoline to gallons g of gasoline.

37 If you buy 39 liters of gasoline, how many gallons do you buy?

38 If you buy 13.5 gallons of gasoline, how many liters do you buy?

39 If a liter of gasoline costs $0.31, how much change would you receive from a dollar after buying a gallon of gasoline?

40 If a gallon of gasoline costs $1.18, what is the cost of a liter of gasoline?

41 In Canada, gasoline costs $0.34 per liter in Canadian dollars. Each Canadian dollar is worth $1.10 in American money. Knight Rider's tank holds 40 gallons of gasoline. How much will it cost in American money to fill the tank in Canada?

In problems 42–44, use the formula $k \approx 1.609m$ to relate kilometers k per hour to miles m per hour.

42 Express 55 miles per hour as kilometers per hour.

43 In parts of France, the highway speed limit is 120 kilometers per hour. What is that speed limit in miles per hour?

Problem Set, *continued*

44 Most car speedometers show both units of measurement. Compare the number of kilometers per hour on a speedometer at the 50-miles-per-hour mark with the value given by the formula. Are they the same?

45 Avery selected two numbers from {2, 4, 8}. He used one for the radius of a cylinder and the other for the height. What is the probability that the volume of the cylinder will be greater than 95?

46 In March, the daily profits of a newly opened videotape store were recorded. Use the data shown to create a line graph.

Date	1st	5th	13th
Profit	$200	$700	$1700

   a Using the graph, what was the profit on March 3? On March 9?
   b Predict the profit on March 15.
   c If the profit on March 10 was really $1400, was the profit more or less than the amount shown on the graph?
   d On what date was the profit approximately $800?
   e At what rate (slope) were profits increasing (in dollars per day)?
   f Write an equation for profit P in terms of date d.

47 A circular ice rink is 40 yards in diameter. If the ice is $\frac{1}{2}$ inch thick, what is the volume of the ice on the rink?

48 Consider the equation $y = \sqrt{5 - x} + 3$.

   a What possible values can be chosen for x?
   b What is the smallest possible value for y?
   c Graph the equation using a table of values or a computer.

49 The height h reached by a rocket is estimated by the equation $h = 160t - 32t^2$, where h is measured in feet and time t is in seconds.

   a Does the rocket start at ground level?
   b What is the height of the rocket at $t = 0$, $t = 1$, $t = 2$, $t = 3$, $t = 4$, and $t = 5$?
   c For what values of t is $h = 0$?
   d Draw a graph relating h and t, using t as the horizontal axis.

In problems 50–52, the value v of a car after being owned for t years is given by the formula $v = 0.73^t \cdot$ (new car cost).

50 What is the present value of a car bought 5 years ago for $12,000?

51 What was the original cost of a car whose value is $2340 after 7 years?

52 If a car cost $15,000 initially and is now worth $2270, for how many years has the car been owned?

7.2 SPECIAL FORMULAS OF GEOMETRY

Objectives

After studying this section, you will be able to
- Use formulas of perimeter
- Use formulas of area
- Use formulas of volume
- Use formulas of analytic geometry

Part One: Introduction

Formulas of Perimeter

You have already solved many problems involving perimeter. To find the perimeter of a polygon, we add the lengths of all its sides. For circles, we calculate the perimeter by using the formula $C = \pi d$, where d is the diameter of the circle, or $C = 2\pi r$, where r is the radius of the circle. The perimeter of a circle is called its ***circumference.***

Example *Find the perimeter of each figure.*

a
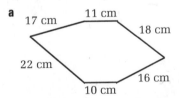

b
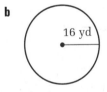

a The perimeter of the hexagon is $17 + 22 + 10 + 16 + 18 + 11 =$ 94 centimeters.

b We use the formula $C = 2\pi r$ to find the circumference of the circle. $C = 2\pi(16)$, or 32π, or approximately 100.53 yards.

Example *Find the length of a side of an equilateral triangle whose perimeter is 24 inches.*

By definition, an ***equilateral figure*** has all sides of equal length, so the length of each side of the triangle is $\frac{24}{3}$, or 8 inches.

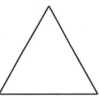

$P = 24$ in.

Formulas of Area

The formulas for area that we will use in this book are summarized below. Areas are always given in square units.

Triangle	Rectangle	Parallelogram	Square

$$A = \frac{bh}{2}$$

$A = bh$ or $A = lw$

$A = bh$

$A = s^2$

Trapezoid	Circle	Rectangular Box	Sphere

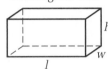

$$A = \frac{h(b_1 + b_2)}{2}$$

$A = \pi r^2$

Surface Area = $2lw + 2lh + 2wh$

Surface Area = $4\pi r^2$

Example　　　*Find the area of each figure.*

a

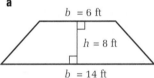

$b = 6$ ft

$h = 8$ ft

$b = 14$ ft

b

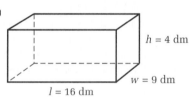

$h = 4$ dm

$w = 9$ dm

$l = 16$ dm

c

$r = 8$ in.

a We substitute 8 for h, 6 for b_1, and 14 for b_2 in the formula for the area of a trapezoid.

$$A = \frac{h(b_1 + b_2)}{2}$$
$$= \frac{8(6 + 14)}{2}$$
$$= 80 \text{ square feet}$$

b We substitute 16 for l, 9 for w, and 4 for h in the formula for the surface area of a rectangular box.

$$A = 2lw + 2lh + 2wh$$
$$= 2(16)(9) + 2(16)(4) + 2(9)(4)$$
$$= 488 \text{ square decimeters}$$

c We substitute 8 for r in the formula for the surface area of a sphere.

$$A = 4\pi r^2$$
$$= 4\pi(8)^2$$
$$= 256\pi$$
$$= 804.25 \text{ square inches}$$

Formulas of Volume

The formulas that follow are used to calculate volume, the space enclosed by a three-dimensional figure. Volume is always measured in cubic units.

Rectangular Prism

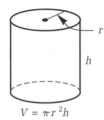

$$V = lwh$$

Pyramid

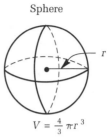

$V = (\frac{Bh}{3})$ where B
is the area of the base

Sphere

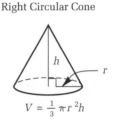

$$V = \frac{4}{3}\pi r^3$$

Right Circular Cylinder

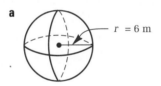

$$V = \pi r^2 h$$

Right Circular Cone

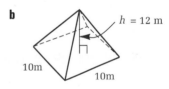

$$V = \frac{1}{3}\pi r^2 h$$

Example　　*Find the volume of each solid.*

a

$r = 6$ m

b

$h = 12$ m

10m　　10m

The base is a square.

a We substitute 6 for r in the formula for the volume of a sphere.

$V = \frac{4}{3}\pi r^3$

$= \frac{4}{3}\pi(6)^3$

$= 288\pi$

≈ 904.78 cubic meters

b Since B is the area of the square base, we substitute 100 for B and 12 for h in the formula for the volume of a pyramid.

$V = \dfrac{Bh}{3}$

$= \dfrac{(100)(12)}{3}$

$= 400$ cubic meters

Formulas of Analytic Geometry

Analytic geometry is the geometry of the coordinate plane. The formulas below will help you solve problems that relate to graphing on the plane.

Earlier, we discussed the Pythagorean Theorem, which describes the relationship between the lengths of the three sides of a right triangle.

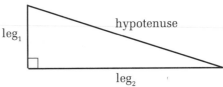

 The Pythagorean Theorem
$$(leg_1)^2 + (leg_2)^2 = (hypotenuse)^2$$

The Pythagorean Theorem is useful for finding the length of a line segment between two points on a plane.

Example   *Find the distance between points A(− 1, 2) and B(3, 5).*

Draw a horizontal line through point A and a vertical line through point B, labeling the point of intersection C.

From the graph we can see that the coordinates of C are (3, 2). The length of leg $\overline{AC}$ is 4, and the length of leg $\overline{BC}$ is 3. We can use the Pythagorean Theorem to find the distance from A to B.

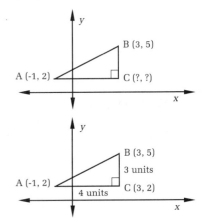

$$(hypotenuse)^2 = 4^2 + 3^2$$
$$= 16 + 9$$
$$= 25$$
$$hypotenuse \;\;= \pm 5$$

Since a distance must be positive, the distance between the points is 5.

We could have solved the problem above using the **distance formula.**

 The distance d between two points (x_1, y_1) and (x_2, y_2) is $d = \sqrt{(x_2 - x_1)^2 + (y_2 - y_1)^2}$.

Let's use the distance formula to find the distance between A(− 1, 2) and B(3, 5). Let $(− 1, 2) = (x_1, y_1)$ and $(3, 5) = (x_2, y_2)$.

$$d = \sqrt{[3 - (-1)]^2 + (5 - 2)^2}$$
$$= \sqrt{4^2 + 3^2}$$
$$= \sqrt{25}$$
$$= 5$$

Another important formula is used to find the coordinates of a point that is midway between two given points on a plane. This point is called the **midpoint.**

Example   *Find the coordinates of the midpoint of the line segment joining the points $(x_1, y_1) = (2, −8)$ and $(x_2, y_2) = (−10, −4)$.*

We find the coordinates of the midpoint of the line segment by first finding the average of the x-coordinates and then finding the average of the y-coordinates.

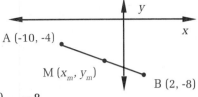

The average of the x-coordinates is $\dfrac{2 + (-10)}{2} = \dfrac{-8}{2} = -4$.

The average of the y-coordinates is $\dfrac{-8 + (-4)}{2} = \dfrac{-12}{2} = -6$.

The coordinates of the midpoint are $(-4, -6)$.

> **The coordinates (x_m, y_m) of the midpoint of the segment joining (x_1, y_1) and (x_2, y_2) are**
>
> $$(x_m, y_m) = \left(\dfrac{x_1 + x_2}{2}, \dfrac{y_1 + y_2}{2}\right).$$

Part Two: Sample Problems

Problem 1

Find the perimeter of the trapezoid shown in the diagram.

Solution

The lengths of the horizontal and vertical segments can be read from the graph. They are 6 units, 5 units, and 2 units. The length of the diagonal segment can be found by using the distance formula.

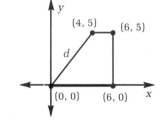

$$d = \sqrt{(4 - 0)^2 + (5 - 0)^2}$$
$$= \sqrt{16 + 25}$$
$$= \sqrt{41} \approx 6.40$$

The approximate perimeter is $6 + 5 + 2 + 6.40$, or 19.40 units.

Problem 2

M is the midpoint of segment AB. Find the coordinates of point B.

Solution

Let $(x_1, y_1) = (-4, -1)$ and $(x_m, y_m) = (3, 2)$. Then substitute the values into the midpoint formula.

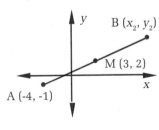

If $(x_m, y_m) = \left(\dfrac{x_1 + x_2}{2}, \dfrac{y_1 + y_2}{2}\right)$, then

$$x_m = \dfrac{x_1 + x_2}{2} \quad \text{and} \quad y_m = \dfrac{y_1 + y_2}{2}$$

$$3 = \dfrac{-4 + x_2}{2} \qquad\qquad 2 = \dfrac{-1 + y_2}{2}$$

$$6 = -4 + x_2 \qquad\qquad 4 = -1 + y_2$$

$$10 = x_2 \qquad\qquad\qquad 5 = y_2$$

The coordinates of point B are (10, 5).

Problem 3 Homer Owner has a corner lot. The city is assessing a fee of $55 per linear foot for installing sidewalks. How much will the city assess Homer?

Solution The frontage consists of one 100-foot straight section, a curved section that is one-fourth the circumference of a circle with a radius of 10 feet, and one 80-foot straight section. The total cost is found by multiplying the total number of linear feet by 55.

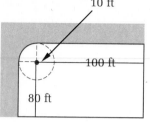

Cost = 55 · (the total number of feet of curb)

$$= 55\left[100 + 80 + \frac{1}{4}(2\pi)(10)\right]$$
$$= 55(100 + 80 + 5\pi)$$
$$\approx 10{,}763.94$$

The city will assess Homer $10,736.94.

Problem 4 Find the height h of a cylinder whose volume is 1000 cubic feet and whose radius is 8 feet.

Solution The formula is $V = \pi r^2 h$.

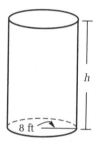

Substitute
$$1000 = \pi(8)^2 h$$
$$1000 = 64\pi h$$
$$\frac{1000}{64\pi} = h$$
$$\frac{125}{8\pi} = h, \text{ or } h \approx 4.97 \text{ feet}$$

Part Three: Exercises and Problems

Warm-up Exercises

1 Sketch a rectangle with vertices A(−4, 2), B(3, 2), C(3, −2), and D(−4, −2).

  a What is the midpoint of segment AD?
  b What is the length of diagonal BD?
  c What is the midpoint of diagonal AC?
  d What is the distance between points A and C?

2 The formula for the volume of a cylinder is $V = \pi r^2 h$.

  a If r = 3 centimeters and h = 5 centimeters, find V.
  b If V = 125.66 and r = 16, find h.

3 Rose Bud wants to buy topsoil for a vegetable garden. The garden consists of two sections that are each half circles with radii of 3 feet, connected by a square section that is 6 feet on a side. What is the area of the garden?

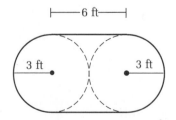

4 Find the average of Ted's bowling scores for the past month if his scores were 154, 167, 180, 216, 144, 191, 177, and 205.

In problems 5–7, find out how many calories Mary Thon burns in each run. She burns 350 calories per hour and can run 9.3 miles in an hour.

5 A 2.5-hour run **6** A 1-mile run **7** A 14-mile run

8 Find the area of the trapezoid. **9** Find the volume of the cone.

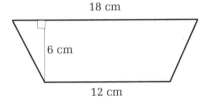

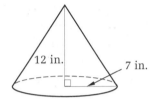

10 Find the slope of the line that passes through the points (4, 3) and (7, −1).

In problems 11 and 12, evaluate each expression for $a = 2$, $b = −3$, and $c = −2$.

11 $\sqrt{b^2 - 4ac}$ **12** $\dfrac{-b \pm 5}{4}$

Problem Set

In problems 13–15, find the distance between each pair of points.

13 (4, 2) and (8, 2) **14** (5, 14) and (5, 1) **15** (10, 26) and (3, 2)

In problems 16–18, solve for x.

16 $3x(x + 2) = 0$ **17** $x^2 = 64$ **18** $x^2 = 40$

19 What is the midpoint of the segment joining (−4, 3) and (6, −1)?

20 During February, Marcus earned money by baby-sitting. He charged \$2.50 per hour. The first week he worked 6 hours, the second week 14 hours, the third week 9 hours, and the fourth week 15 hours.
  a How many hours did he average per week?
  b What were his average weekly earnings?
  c What were his average daily earnings?

In problems 21 and 22, a line passes through the two points (−2, 5) and (4, 3).

21 Find the slope of the line.
22 Write an equation of the line.

Problem Set, *continued*

In problems 23 and 24, use the formula for the circumference of a circle.

23 If the radius of a circle is 10 meters, what is the circumference?

24 If the circumference of a circle is 45 centimeters, what is the radius?

In problems 25 and 26, refer to the diagram.

25 Find the volume of the box.

26 Find the total area of the six sides of the box.

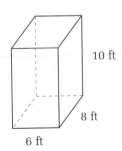

27 The sum of the measures of the two angles is 90. Find the measure of each angle.

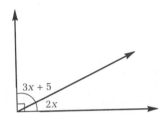

28 Find the output for x in the formula

$$x = \frac{-b \pm \sqrt{b^2 - 4ac}}{2a}$$ when the inputs

are $a = 1$, $b = 5$, and $c = 6$.

In problems 29–31, find the distance between each pair of points.

29 (7, 15) and (13, 7)   30 (2, 5) and (9, −10)   31 (−4, 3) and (7, −2)

32 By the end of the 1986–87 National Hockey League season, the record for the most games played was held by Gordie Howe, who played 1767 games. Gordie had played for 26 seasons. Find the average number of games he played each season.

33 Triangle GHI can be represented by a 3 × 2 matrix.

$$M = \begin{bmatrix} 1 & 0 \\ 5 & 0 \\ 3 & 1 \end{bmatrix}$$

   a Draw triangle GHI on a set of axes.

   b On the same axes, draw the figure represented by this matrix.

   $$M \cdot \begin{bmatrix} .7 & .7 \\ -.7 & .7 \end{bmatrix}$$

34 Find the values of p and q so that (−2, 5) is the midpoint of the segment joining points (p, p + q) and (p + 4, 3q + 6).

35 For what values of k will the slope of the line joining (12, 4) and (9, k) be negative?

36 If one of the numbers $\{-9, -7, -5, -3, -1, 1, 3, 5, 7, 9\}$ is chosen at random, what is the probability that it is a proper input for the formula $y = \sqrt{x^2 - 25}$?

37 Find the surface area of a sphere with a diameter of 10.5 meters.

38 Jill took 28 seconds to drive her race car once around the half-mile track. What is her speed in miles per hour?

39 A line passes through the point C(-2, 5) and the midpoint of the segment joining A(-4, -5) and B(6, 3).
  a Draw a picture of the problem described above.
  b Find the coordinates of M, the midpoint of AB.
  c Find the slope of the line through C and M.
  d Write an equation of the line that passes through C and M.

In problems 40 and 41, refer to the diagram.

40 Write a formula using x and y for the area of the shaded region.

41 Use your formula from problem **40** to find the shaded area if $x = 12$ feet and $y = 8$ feet.

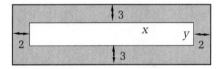

42 The village of Winnetbrook will pay 60% of the cost of replacing sidewalks in front of Mr. Subbia's home. The cost of replacing one piece of sidewalk is $62.50.
  a Mr. Subbia needs p pieces of sidewalk replaced. Write a formula for his total bill.
  b Use your formula from part **a** to determine Mr. Subbia's bill for replacing 16 pieces of sidewalk.

43 Con Tractor is hired to construct a roof with a pitch of $\frac{5}{12}$ across a 40-foot span.
  a What is the slope of the roof?
  b What is the height of the roof?
  c What is the length of the rafter (one of the two equal sides of the roof)?

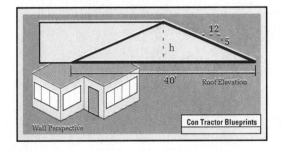

44 A(1, 4), B(3, 11), C(9, 11), and D(7, 4) are the vertices of a quadrilateral.
  a What type of quadrilateral is ABCD?
  b Find the midpoint of $\overline{AC}$.
  c Find the midpoint of $\overline{BD}$.

Problem Set, *continued*

45 Refer to the diagram.

  a Find the midpoint of $\overline{AB}$.

  b Find the coordinates of point C, which is $\frac{1}{4}$ of the way from A to B.

  c Find the coordinates of point D, which is $\frac{3}{4}$ of the distance from A to B.

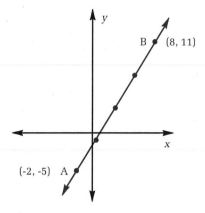

46 What is the volume of air in a spherical balloon that is 10 meters in diameter?

In problems 47 and 48, use Hero's formula to compute the area of a triangle whose sides are *a, b,* and *c* in length. The formula is
$$\text{Area} = \sqrt{s(s-a)(s-b)(s-c)} \text{ where}$$
$$s = \frac{a+b+c}{2}.$$

47

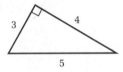

48

49 The Indianapolis Motor Speedway is a 2.5-mile oval. It has a front stretch, a back stretch, north and south short chutes, and 4 quarter-circular corners. Let x be the length of a short chute. The other sections are labeled in the diagram.

  a Find the lengths of the short chute, back stretch, and a corner.

  b Each corner is $\frac{1}{4}$ of a circle. Find the radius of that circle.

  c In a recent race, Rick Mears averaged 210 miles per hour along the back stretch. How many seconds did it take him to cover the back stretch?

  d The pole position for a recent race was won by averaging 206 miles per hour. How many seconds would it take the pole sitter to complete a full lap?

Indianapolis Motor Speedway

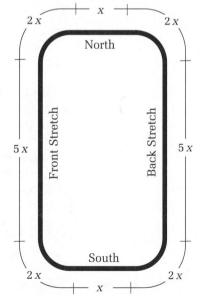

In problems 50–53, find the area of each figure.

50 6.7 cm 17 cm
15.2 cm

51 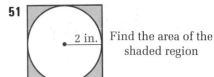 2 in. Find the area of the shaded region

52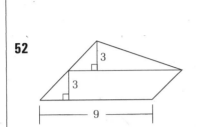
3
3
9

53
1
$\frac{7}{8}$ mi
$1\frac{1}{2}$ mi

USING THE QUADRATIC FORMULA

Objectives

After studying this section, you will be able to
- Recognize a quadratic equation
- Use the quadratic formula to solve quadratic equations

Part One: Introduction

What Is a Quadratic Equation?

An equation that can be written in the form

$$ax^2 + bx + c = 0$$

where a, b, and c are real numbers and a is not zero, is called a **quadratic equation** in x.

When you were studying techniques for solving equations, you learned how to solve some simple quadratic equations that had either b or c equal to zero. Let's review how to solve these equations.

Example *Solve each quadratic equation. (The solutions are given below.)*

a $2y^2 - 17 = 0$

In this quadratic equation,
$a = 2$, $b = 0$, and $c = -17$.
$$2y^2 - 17 = 0$$
$$2y^2 = 17$$
$$y^2 = 8.5$$
$$\sqrt{y^2} = \sqrt{8.5}$$
$$|y| = \sqrt{8.5}$$
$$y \approx \pm 2.92$$

b $3x^2 - 5x = 0$

In this quadratic equation,
$a = 3$, $b = -5$, and $c = 0$.
$$3x^2 - 5x = 0$$
$$x(3x - 5) = 0$$
$$x = 0 \text{ or } 3x - 5 = 0$$
$$3x = 5$$
$$x = 0 \text{ or } x = \frac{5}{3}$$

Working with the Quadratic Formula

The quadratic formula can be used to solve all types of quadratic equations. You will learn the proof of this formula in Chapter 11. The quadratic formula is stated in these terms.

⟫ *If $ax^2 + bx + c = 0$ and $a \neq 0$, then*

$$x = \frac{-b \pm \sqrt{b^2 - 4ac}}{2a}.$$

Example

Use the quadratic formula to solve each quadratic equation.

a $3x^2 - x - 2 = 0$

This equation is already in the form $ax^2 + bx + c = 0$. We determine the values of a, b, and c and input these values into the quadratic formula. In this equation, $a = 3$, $b = -1$, and $c = -2$.

$$x = \frac{-b \pm \sqrt{b^2 - 4ac}}{2a}$$

$$= \frac{-(-1) \pm \sqrt{(-1)^2 - 4(3)(-2)}}{2(3)}$$

$$= \frac{1 \pm \sqrt{1 + 24}}{6}$$

$$= \frac{1 \pm 5}{6}$$

$$x = \frac{1 + 5}{6} \text{ or } x = \frac{1 - 5}{6}$$

$$= \frac{6}{6} \quad \text{or} \quad = \frac{-4}{6}$$

$$= 1 \quad \text{or} \quad = \frac{-2}{3}$$

The solution set is $\left\{ 1, -\frac{2}{3} \right\}$.

b $x^2 = -2x - 3$

Rewrite the equation as $x^2 + 2x + 3 = 0$.
Then $a = 1$, $b = 2$, and $c = 3$.

$$x = \frac{-b \pm \sqrt{b^2 - 4ac}}{2a}$$

$$= \frac{-2 \pm \sqrt{2^2 - 4(1)(3)}}{2(1)}$$

$$= \frac{-2 \pm \sqrt{4 - 12}}{2}$$

$$= \frac{-2 \pm \sqrt{-8}}{2}$$

Since there is no real-number value for $\sqrt{-8}$, we can conclude that this quadratic equation has no real-number solutions.

Part Two: Sample Problems

Problem 1 A rectangle's length is 3 centimeters greater than its width, and its area is 200 square centimeters. Find the dimensions of the rectangle.

Solution Let x represent the length of the rectangle and x − 3 represent the width. Then x(x − 3) is the area of the rectangle.

$$x(x - 3) = 200$$
$$x^2 - 3x = 200$$
$$x^2 - 3x - 200 = 0$$

We can use the quadratic formula, inputting the values $a = 1$, $b = -3$, and $c = -200$.

$$x = \frac{-b \pm \sqrt{b^2 - 4ac}}{2a}$$

$$= \frac{-(-3) \pm \sqrt{(-3)^2 - 4(1)(-200)}}{2(1)}$$

$$= \frac{3 \pm \sqrt{9 + 800}}{2}$$

$$= \frac{3 \pm \sqrt{809}}{2}$$

$$\approx \frac{3 \pm 28.44}{2}$$

$$x \approx \frac{31.44}{2} \text{ or } x \approx \frac{-25.44}{2}$$

$$\approx 15.72 \text{ or } \approx -12.72$$

Since x represents the length of a rectangle, it must be positive, so x ≈ 15.72 and x − 3 ≈ 12.72. The length of the rectangle is about 15.72 centimeters, and the width is about 12.72 centimeters.

Problem 2 A girl on the roof of a building drops a tennis ball from a height of 29 feet above the ground. Determine how long it will take for the ball to hit the ground.

Solution The formula $d = 16t^2$ gives the distance d in feet that a ball falls in t seconds. This formula is a quadratic equation, but we can use square roots to solve it more quickly.

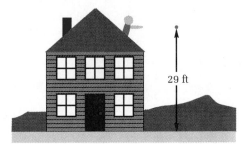

$$d = 16t^2$$
$$29 = 16t^2$$
$$\frac{29}{16} = t^2$$
$$\pm\sqrt{\frac{29}{16}} = t$$
$$\pm 1.35 \approx t$$

Since t must be positive, it will take approximately 1.35 seconds for the ball to reach the ground.

Problem 3   *Solve* $7.18x^2 - 19.14x + 11.35 = 0$ *for x.*

Solution   We will use the quadratic formula, inputting the values $a = 7.18$, $b = -19.14$, and $c = 11.35$.

$$x = \frac{-(-19.14) \pm \sqrt{(-19.14)^2 - 4(7.18)(11.35)}}{2(7.18)}$$

We can use a calculator to help us with the solution.

First we evaluate $\sqrt{(-19.14)^2 - 4(7.18)(11.35)}$ and store it in the calculator's memory.

19.14 $\boxed{\pm}$ $\boxed{x^2}$ $\boxed{-}$ 4 $\boxed{\times}$ 7.18 $\boxed{\times}$ 11.35 $\boxed{=}$ $\boxed{\sqrt{}}$ $\boxed{\text{STO}}$

The display should be $\boxed{6.353550189}$

Now we can calculate both solutions by using the quantity we stored in memory.

$\boxed{(}$ 19.14 $\boxed{+}$ $\boxed{\text{RCL}}$ $\boxed{)}$ $\boxed{\div}$ $\boxed{(}$ 2 $\boxed{\times}$ 7.18 $\boxed{)}$ $\boxed{=}$ ≈ 1.78

$\boxed{(}$ 19.14 $\boxed{-}$ $\boxed{\text{RCL}}$ $\boxed{)}$ $\boxed{\div}$ $\boxed{(}$ 2 $\boxed{\times}$ 7.18 $\boxed{)}$ $\boxed{=}$ ≈ 0.89

Note   Parentheses are used around the entire numerator and the entire denominator to ensure that the division will be done last.

The solution set is $\{\approx 1.78, \approx 0.89\}$.

Part Three: Exercises and Problems

Warm-up Exercises

In problems 1–3, determine the values of a, b, and c for each quadratic equation.

1 $-7 = -2x^2$ **2** $5x - 3 = 0$ **3** $2x = 3 - x^2$

4 Does the quadratic equation $2x^2 + 4x + 3 = 0$ have real-number solutions?

In problems 5–7, solve each quadratic equation.

5 $n^2 = 36$ **6** $x^2 - 2x = 0$ **7** $x^2 = -2x + 3$

Problem Set

8 Which of the following are quadratic equations?

   a $2x + 3y = 7$ **b** $2x^2 + 3x = 7$
   c $2x(x + 3) = 7$ **d** $2x^3 + 3x^2 + 5x = 7$

In problems 9–14, determine the values of a, b, and c.

9 $2x^2 + 5x - 9 = 0$ **10** $x^2 = 12x - 4$ **11** $-2x^2 + 4 = 5x$
12 $x^2 - 5x = 0$ **13** $x^2 + 12 = 0$ **14** $3x + 7 = 0$

Problem Set, *continued*

15 The product of two consecutive integers is 72. Find all such integers.

In problems 16–19, find the solution set for each equation.

16 $x^2 + 15x + 54 = 0$

17 $3x + 5x + 1 = 0$

18 $x^2 + 2x + 9 = 0$

19 $2x^2 + 5x - 3 = 0$

20 Refer to the diagram.

   a Find x.
   b Find $\angle ABD$.
   c Find $\angle DBC$.
   d Find the ratio of $\angle ABD$ to $\angle DBC$.

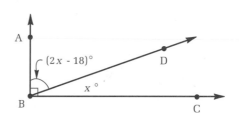

In problems 21–23, solve each equation. Do not use the quadratic formula.

21 $5x^2 - 80 = 0$

22 $7x^2 - 8x = 0$

23 $3x^2 + 15x = 0$

24 A farmer is building a fence around a rectangular plot of land x feet by y feet. The cost of ordinary fencing is $4 per foot. He will use fancier fencing costing $6 per foot on one of the longer sides, x feet in length.

   a Write a formula to determine the cost c of building the fence.
   b Determine the cost of the fencing if the dimensions of the plot of land are 100 feet by 60 feet.

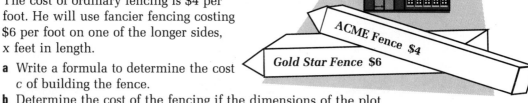

25 The area of the rectangle is 36. Find the dimensions of the rectangle.

26 Twice the square of n increased by 13 is equal to 0. Find all possible values of n.

27 Complete the table.

Quadratic equation	$ax^2 + bx + c = 0$	a	b	c
a $x^2 = 3x - 4$				
b $2x(x + 7) = 0$				
c $5x^2 = 45$				
d $3x(x + 4) = 5(3 - x)$				

28 The product of two consecutive integers is 1806. Find all such integers.

In problems 29–31, you are given points A(5, 12) and B(11, −6).
29 Find the distance from A to B.
30 Find the slope of line segment AB.
31 Find the midpoint of line segment AB.

In problems 32 and 33, use the formula $h = -16t^2 + 96t$, which gives the height h in feet of a projectile at time t seconds.
32 At what height is the projectile at $t = 2$ seconds?
33 At what times is the projectile 128 feet above the ground?

34 A bar graph in which the graph is cut off at the bottom is called a *truncated bar graph.* Sherman Shelby put this truncated bar graph into a newspaper ad to show that his product was more reliable than Brand X.

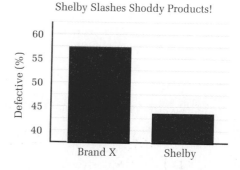

a Use a ruler to measure the heights of the bars for Brand X and the Shelby brand. The height of the Shelby-brand bar is what percentage of the height of the Brand X bar?

b Explain why this truncated graph is misleading.

In problems 35–38, find the solution set for each equation.
35 $x^2 + 5x + 6 = 0$ **36** $2x^2 - 11x + 15 = 0$
37 $x^2 - 9x = 0$ **38** $x^2 - 9 = 0$

39 On a computer enter the following BASIC program for solving quadratic equations in the form $ax^2 + bx + c = 0$.

```
10 INPUT a,b,c
20 LET x1 = (-b + sqr(b*b - 4*a*c))/(2*a)
30 LET x2 = (-b - sqr(b*b - 4*a*c))/(2*a)
40 PRINT x1,x2
50 END
```

a Use the program to solve each equation.
   i $3x^2 - 2x - 4 = 0$
  ii $x^2 + 5x = 0$
 iii $x^2 + 6x + 9 = 0$
 iv $x^2 + 5x + 12 = 0$

b Why did the program give two identical answers for equation **iii**?

c Why did the program "crash" when solving equation **iv**?

In problems 40–42, solve each equation.
40 $3x^2 - 13x - 100 = 0$
41 $x^2 + 4x = 2$
42 $w^2 + 6w + 14 = 0$

Problem Set, *continued*

43 If AB times BC is 168, find the length of $\overline{AC}$.

44 The formula $H = \frac{-1}{432}x^2 + 75$ is used to find the height H in feet of the arch of a bridge at a point x feet from the center of the bridge.

  a How high is the bridge at the center?
  b How long is the bridge?
  c Vertical bracing posts are placed every 60 feet along the bridge, starting from the center, as shown. What is the sum of the lengths of all the bracing posts (rounded to the nearest foot)?

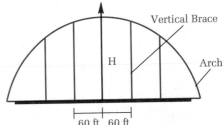

Vertical Brace

H

Arch

60 ft 60 ft

THE MATHEMATICS FOLLIES
Great mathematicians are human too

Even the greatest mathematicians have common human weaknesses. For some examples, we can look at the efforts of mathematicians to go beyond the quadratic formula to find general solutions to equations of degree higher than 2.

General Third-Degree Equation:
$$Ax^3 + Bx^2 + Cx + D = 0$$
General Fourth-Degree Equation:
$$Ax^4 + Bx^3 + Cx^2 + Dx + E = 0$$

In the early sixteenth century, the Italian Niccolo Fontana found a partial solution to the third-degree formula. Extremely possessive, he refused to tell anyone what it was! Another mathematician, Girolamo Cardan, convinced him to reveal it and then published it as his own. When one of Cardan's students solved the fourth-degree equation, Cardan stole that, too!

Almost 300 years passed with no major advances toward solving the fifth-degree equation and beyond. Then in 1832 Evariste Galois wrote out a brilliant proof that there is *no* general algebraic solution to equations higher than the fourth degree. A headstrong, impetuous man, he was killed the next day in a duel. One of the most promising mathematicians of his day, Galois was only 20 when he died.

Solve these third- and fourth-degree equations.

  1. $x^3 = 125$ *2.* $5x^3 - 320 = 0$
  3. $12x^4 = 12$ *4.* $9x^4 - 729 = 0$

Girolamo Cardan

LITERAL EQUATIONS

Objectives

After studying this section, you will be able to

- Recognize a literal equation
- Solve a literal equation

Part One: Introduction

What Is a Literal Equation?

Many equations and formulas, such as those used to calculate watts of electrical power in terms of volts and amperes, contain more than one variable.

In this section, you will solve equations for one variable in terms of the other variables without substituting any values. This process is referred to as solving a literal equation. A **literal equation** is an equation with two or more different variables.

Example   *Which of the following are literal equations?*

a $2x^2 - 3x + 7 = 0$ **b** $5x - 19 = \pi$
c $x_1 x_2 + 3 = 0$ **d** $V = \pi r^2 h$
e $ax + b = 0$ **f** $x - 5 = \sqrt{7}$

Equations **a**, **b**, and **f** are not literal equations because they contain only a single variable.

Equations **c**, **d**, and **e** are literal equations because each has at least two different variables.

Solving Literal Equations

Literal equations are useful in computer programming. For example, if we want a computer program to calculate the height H of several boxes given the volume V, the length L, and the width W, we can solve the formula $V = LWH$ for H in terms of the other variables.

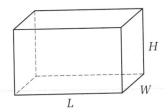

$$V = LWH$$
$$\frac{V}{LW} = H$$

Divide both sides by *LW*

Now we can use this formula in a computer program to find the height *H* of any rectangular box.

```
10 PRINT "Enter values for V, L, and W, separated by
   commas";
20 INPUT V, L, W
30 LET H = V/(L*W)
40 PRINT "The value of H is approximately", H
```

Example   *The formula A = p + prt represents the total value A, after t years, of a savings bond purchased for p dollars at an interest rate of r percent per year.*

a *Solve for r.*

$$A = p + prt$$

Subtract p from both sides
$$A - p = prt$$

Divide both sides by pt
$$\frac{A - p}{pt} = \frac{prt}{pt}$$

Simplify
$$\frac{A - p}{pt} = r$$

b *Solve for p.*

$$A = p + prt$$

Use the Distributive Property of Multiplication over Addition
$$A = p(1 + rt)$$

Divide both sides by (1 + rt)
$$\frac{A}{(1 + rt)} = \frac{p(1 + rt)}{(1 + rt)}$$

Simplify
$$\frac{A}{1 + rt} = p$$

c *Use the formula for r to determine the rate of interest that must be paid in order for a $750 bond to mature to $1000 in 30 months.*

$$r = \frac{A - p}{pt}$$

Substitute 1000 for A, 750 for p, and 2.5 for t(30 months = 2.5 years)

$$= \frac{1000 - 750}{750(2.5)}$$

$$= \frac{250}{1875}$$

$$\approx 0.1333$$

The interest rate is approximately 13.33%.

Part Two: Sample Problems

Problem 1   *Solve for the positive value of a in the formula $c^2 = a^2 + b^2$.*

$$c^2 = a^2 + b^2$$

Solution   Subtract b^2 from both sides $c^2 - b^2 = a^2$

Take the square root of each side $\sqrt{c^2 - b^2} = |a|$

$$a = \pm\sqrt{c^2 - b^2}$$

Since we want a positive value for a, $a = \sqrt{c^2 - b^2}$.

Problem 2   *While working in the school science lab, Bart Beame made the observations shown in the diagrams below. D_1 and D_2 are distances measured from the fulcrum of the lever, and M_1 and M_2 are masses in like units.*

Find the value of D_1.

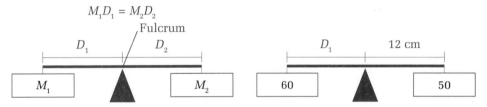

Solution   Using the formula, we replace M_1 by 60, D_2 by 12, and M_2 by 50.

$$M_1D_1 = M_2D_2$$
$$60D_1 = 50(12)$$
$$60D_1 = 600$$
$$D_1 = 10 \text{ cm}$$

Problem 3   *Put the equation $Ax + By = C$ into slope-intercept form. What are the slope and the y-intercept of the line?*

Solution $Ax + By = C$

$$By = -Ax + C$$
$$y = \frac{-Ax}{B} + \frac{C}{B}$$

The slope is $\frac{-A}{B}$, and the y-intercept is $\frac{C}{B}$.

Part Three: Exercises and Problems

Warm-up Exercises

1 Solve $ax + 2y + c = 9$ for y.

2 Solve for x_2 if $x_1y_1 = x_2y_2$.

3 Determine the value of y in the diagram.

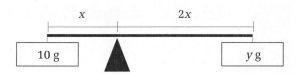

In problems 4–6, solve each quadratic equation.

4 $x^2 = 17$ **5** $3x^2 = 27$ **6** $x^2 + 5x = 0$

In problems 7–9, use the formula $W = V \cdot A$ (watts = volts · amps).

7 Write the formula for amps in terms of V and W.

8 Write the formula for volts in terms of A and W.

9 Find the voltage of a circuit if it can produce 15,000 watts of power at an amperage of 68 amps.

In problems 10–12, use the formula $PV = nRT$.

10 Solve for P.   **11** Solve for R.   **12** Solve for n.

Problem Set

13 Solve $A = 2lw + 2lh + 2wh$ for w.

14 Find x.

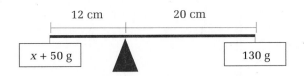

15 Solve for r in the formula $d = rt$.

16 Solve the literal equation $A = \dfrac{h(b_1 + b_2)}{2}$ for h.

In problems 17–19, solve each literal equation for *t*.

17 $d = rt$ **18** $d = 16t^2$ **19** $i = prt$

20 To convert Celsius temperature C to Fahrenheit temperature F, use the formula $F = \frac{9}{5}C + 32$. Solve this formula for C and find the Celsius temperature if the Fahrenheit temperature is 23°.

21 The volume of a cone is represented by the formula $V = \frac{1}{3}\pi r^2 h$. Solve the formula for h and find the height h of a cone with a volume of 56.55 cubic centimeters and a radius of 3 centimeters.

22 The formula for the area of a trapezoid is $A = \dfrac{h(b_1 + b_2)}{2}$. Solve the formula for b_1 and find base b_1 of a trapezoid whose area is 12.5 square inches, whose base b_2 is 4 inches, and whose height h is 5 inches.

23 A diagonal has been drawn in the rectangle.
  a Write a formula to relate x and y.
  b Solve the formula from part **a** for y.
  c Describe the relationship between x and y.

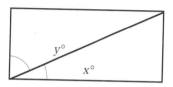

In problems 24–27, solve each literal equation for x.

24 $P = 2x + 2y$

25 $A = \dfrac{x_1 + x_2 + x}{3}$

26 $V = \pi x^2 h$

27 $F = \dfrac{mGx}{r^2}$

28 The absolute value of the difference of twice a number and 5 is 17. Find the number.

29 Solve $A_v = \dfrac{x_1 + x_2 + x_3 + x_4}{4}$ for x_4. If Max scored 88, 91, and 86 on his first three tests, what score does he need on the fourth test to average 90?

In problems 30–33, find the determinant of each matrix. The formula for the determinant of the 2-by-2 matrix

$$M = \begin{bmatrix} a & b \\ c & d \end{bmatrix}$$

is $\det(M) = a \cdot d - b \cdot c$.

30 $\begin{bmatrix} 8 & 4 \\ 3 & 5 \end{bmatrix}$

31 $\begin{bmatrix} 6 & -2 \\ 3 & 2 \end{bmatrix}$

32 $\begin{bmatrix} -5 & 7 \\ 2 & 3 \end{bmatrix}$

33 $\begin{bmatrix} -4 & 5 \\ -8 & 10 \end{bmatrix}$

34 Refer to the graph.
  a On what date did the Dow Jones average exhibit the greatest variation? What was the variation?
  b On which dates was the closing average up from the previous day's closing average?
  c On which dates was the closing average the same as the previous day's closing average?
  d On how many days did the Dow Jones average vary by more than 100 points?
  e On what dates was the closing average of the Dow higher than the high of the previous day?

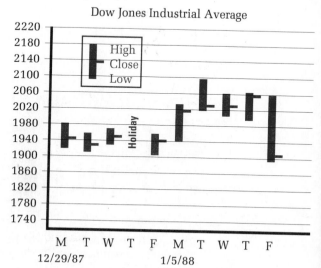

Dow Jones Industrial Average

35 When the radius of a circle is increased by 5, its area is increased by 32π. Find the radius of the original circle.

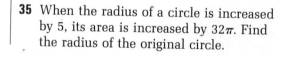

Problem Set, *continued*

In problems 36–39, find the slope and the y-intercept for each linear equation.

36 $3x + 2y = 7$ **37** $6x - 5y = -11$

38 $-2x + y = 14$ **39** $2y - 5x = 10$

40 The formula $N = (1.10)^T \cdot C$ is used to determine the appreciated value of a house, where C is the original cost of the house, T is the number of years since the house was built, and N is the current value of the house.

a Solve the equation for C.

b Complete line 20 in the following BASIC program by writing your solution to part **a** in BASIC form.

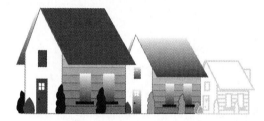

```
10 INPUT N,T
20 LET C =
30 PRINT C
40 END
```

c Calculate the original cost of a house built in 1954 and valued at $60,000 in 1989.

d Calculate the original cost of a house built in 1937 and valued at $135,000 in 1989.

e Calculate the original cost of a house built in 1962 and valued at $175,000 in 1989.

In problems 41 and 42, refer to the diagram.

41 Find all values of k that satisfy the given diagram.

42 What are the possible slopes of AB?

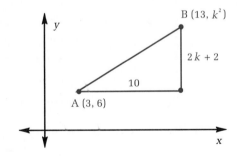

43 The square of a given negative number is 3 more than 4 times the number. Find the number.

44 A ball is thrown upward from the ground at a speed of 96 feet per second. Its distance above the ground is given by the formula $d = -16t^2 + 96t$, where d is measured in feet and t is time measured in seconds.

a When does the ball come back to the ground?

b At what time(s) is the ball 100 feet above the ground?

c At what time(s) is the ball 144 feet above the ground?

d Is the ball ever 200 feet above the ground? Why or why not?

FUNCTIONS AND RELATIONS

Objectives

After studying this section, you will be able to
- Define a relation
- Define a function
- Identify the natural domain of a function or relation

Part One: Introduction

What Is a Relation?

You are already familiar with the concept of an ordered pair. Now you will be introduced to what many consider the most important concept in all of mathematics, functions.

First, let's look at the concept of a relation by using examples.

Example   *Use the formula $d = 16t^2$.*

    a *Give the set of ordered pairs (t, d) that results when t is chosen from the input set $\{0, 1, 4, 16\}$ to compute d.*

    b *Give the set of ordered pairs (d, t) that results when d is chosen from the input set $\{0, 1, 4, 16\}$ to compute t.*

The set of ordered pairs can be represented in a table.

a The equation $d = 16t^2$ is already solved for d.

Input set for t:
$\{0, 1, 4, 16\}$

t	0	1	4	16
d	0	16	256	4096

b Solve the equation for t.
$$d = 16t^2$$
$$t = \pm\sqrt{\frac{d}{16}}$$

Input set for d:
$\{0, 1, 4, 16\}$

d	0	1	4	16
t	0	$\pm\frac{1}{4}$	$\pm\frac{1}{2}$	± 1

A second way to represent the set of ordered pairs is by using an input-output diagram.

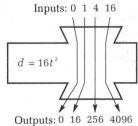

a   Inputs: 0 1 4 16

$d = 16t^2$

Outputs: 0 16 256 4096

b   Inputs: 0 1 4 16

$t = \pm\sqrt{\frac{d}{16}}$

Outputs: 0 $\frac{1}{4}$ $-\frac{1}{4}$ $\frac{1}{2}$ $-\frac{1}{2}$ 1 -1

A third way to represent the set of ordered pairs is by mapping.

a Input Set for t: Output Set for d: **b** Input Set for d: Output Set for t:

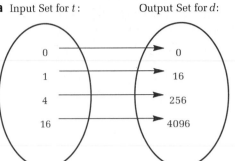
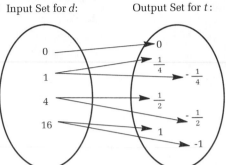

a In all three representations, the set of ordered pairs is $\{(0, 0), (1, 16), (4, 256), (16, 4096)\}$.

b In all three representations, the set of ordered pairs $\{(0, 0), \left(1, \frac{1}{4}\right), \left(4, \frac{1}{2}\right),$ $(16, 1), \left(1, -\frac{1}{4}\right), \left(4, -\frac{1}{2}\right), (16, -1)\}$.

Each of the sets above is a **relation.** A **relation** is a set of ordered pairs.

Example   Write the relation for $y = |x - 3|$ if

a the input set for x is $\{1, 3, 5.\}$

b the input set for y is $\{1, 3, 5.\}$

a If x = 1, then y = 2.
If x = 3, then y = 0.
If x = 5, then y = 2.
The relation is
$\{(1, 2), (3, 0), (5, 2)\}$.

b If y = 1, then x = 2 or x = 4.
If y = 3, then x = 0 or x = 6.
If y = 5, then x = −2 or x = 8.
The relation is
$\{(2, 1), (4, 1), (0, 3), (6, 3), (−2, 5), (8, 5)\}$.

What Is a Function?

Let's look again at the diagrams at the top of the page. We formed two different relations by using the input set $\{0, 1, 4, 16\}$ first for t and then for d.

Input Set for t: Output Set for d: Input Set for d: Output Set for t:

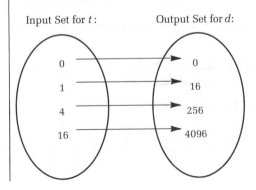
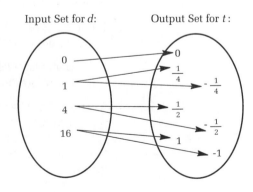

In the first diagram, each input is paired with exactly one output. When this happens, we say the relation is a function.

In the second diagram, some inputs are paired with more than one output. In this case, the relation is not a function.

A *function* is a relation in which each input is paired with exactly one output.

The set of all inputs is called the *domain* of the function or relation. The set of all outputs is called the *range* of the function or relation.

Example   *Which of the following relations are functions?*

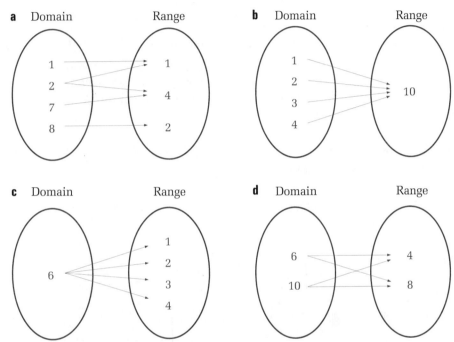

The only function pictured is **b**. In **b**, each domain element is paired with exactly one range element.

In **a**, the domain element 2 is paired with range elements 1 and 4, so the relation is not a function.

In **c**, the domain element 6 is paired with 1, 2, 3, and 4, so the relation is not a function.

In **d**, the domain elements 6 and 10 are paired with both 4 and 8, so the relation is not a function.

In diagram **b** above, each input is paired with the same output, 10. This type of function is called a *constant function.*

If we say "y is a function of x," we mean that when the inputs are for x and the outputs are for y, the pairs (x, y) form a function.

Similarly, if we say "x is a function of y," we mean that when the inputs are for y and the outputs are for x, the pairs (x, y) form a function.

Example   *Refer to the relation {(1, 2), (2, 3), (3, 4), (5, 4)}.*

> **a** *Is y a function of x?*
> The x's are the inputs. Each x is paired with only one y, so y is a function of x.
>
> **b** *Is x a function of y?*
> The y's are the inputs. The input 4 is paired with both 5 and 3, so x is not a function of y.

The Natural Domain of a Function or Relation

The *natural domain* of a function or relation is the largest possible set of inputs for which the function or relation has meaning.

Example   *Find the natural domain of each relation if the x's are the input values.*

> **a** $y = 10x$, *where y is the value, in cents, of x dimes*
> Since x is the number of dimes, x must be a whole number. The domain is {0, 1, 2, 3, . . .}.
>
> **b** $y = \frac{6}{x}$
> The domain is the set of all real numbers except 0. We cannot divide by 0.
>
> **c** $y = \sqrt{2x - 3}$
> In order to evaluate the square root, the quantity $2x - 3$ must be nonnegative. Therefore, we solve the inequality $2x - 3 \geq 0$.
>
> | | |
> |---|---|
> | | $2x - 3 \geq 0$ |
> | Add 3 to each side | $2x \geq 3$ |
> | Divide each side by 2 | $x \geq 1.5$ |
>
> The domain is {x:x ≥ 1.5}.
>
> **d** $y = 3x - 8$
> The domain is the set of all real numbers, since an output y is possible for any input x.

Part Two: Sample Problems

Problem 1   Let $y = x^2$.

> **a** *Is y a function of x?*   **b** *Is x a function of y?*

Solution   **a** Yes. Any number used as an input for x yields exactly one output for y.
b No. For example, if the input for y is 4, there are two outputs for x, namely 2 and −2.

Problem 2   Let $y = x^2$.

> **a** *If x is the input variable, what is the natural domain?*
> **b** *If y is the input variable, what is the natural domain?*

Solution **a** Any number can be input for x. The domain is $\{x : x \in \mathcal{R}\}$.

b In order to get an output for x, we must have a nonnegative input for y. The domain is $\{y : y \geq 0\}$.

Problem 3 Let $y < 2x$.

a *If x is the input variable, what is the natural domain?*
b *Is y a function of x?*

Solution **a** For any real-number input for x, a meaningful value can be found for y. The domain is $\{x : x \in \mathcal{R}\}$.

b No. Suppose the input for x were 3. Then 5 and 4 would be only two of the many outputs for y.

Part Three: Exercises and Problems

Warm-up Exercises

In problems 1–3, identify the natural domain of each relation if x is the input variable.

1 $y = \sqrt{1 - x}$ **2** $y = \dfrac{1}{x^2 - 9}$ **3** $y = 2x + 7$

In problems 4–6, determine whether x is a function of y or y is a function of x.

4 $\{(2, 3), (2, 1), (1, 4)\}$

5

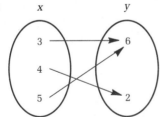

6

x	0	3	−1	6	2
y	6	4	−1	3	6

7 Let $y = \dfrac{4}{x}$.

a What is the natural domain if x is the input variable?
b Is y a function of x?

8 Explain why all functions are relations but not all relations are functions.

Problem Set

9 Let $y^2 = 4x$. Find the outputs if the inputs are the given values of x.

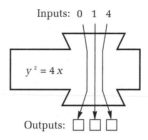

10 Find the outputs if the inputs are the given values of x.

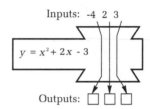

11 Which of the following relations are functions?

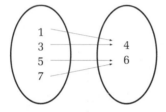 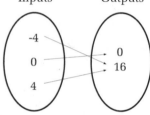

a Inputs   Outputs   **b** Inputs   Outputs   **c** Inputs   Outputs

12 Let $y = \sqrt{x}$.

   a What is the natural domain if y is the input variable?

   b Is x a function of y?

13 Is y a function of x?

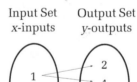

Input Set   Output Set
x-inputs   y-outputs

In problems 14–17, solve each literal equation for ℓ.

14 $P = 2\ell + 2w$ **15** $V = \ell wh$ **16** $\ell + \ell w = s$ **17** $\sqrt{\ell} = t$

18 The chart contains sets of values for p and q.

   a Is q a function of p?

   b Is p a function of q?

p	2	3	8	11	15
q	5	7	0	−1	−4

In problems 19–21, the first element of each ordered pair is the input value. Does the set describe a function? Why or why not?

19 {(5, 2), (5, 7), (9, 12), (12, 9)}   **20** {(0, 1), (2, 4), (3, 9), (8, 14)}   **21** {(0, 1), (2, 1), (3, 1), (4, 1)}

22 Steve Darby is having a party for the chess team after the state tournament. He figures the cost of soft drinks to be $1.69 per eight-pack plus $0.10 deposit per bottle. He also needs ice at $1.80 per bag.

 a Write a formula to find the cost C if he buys p eight-packs and i bags of ice.

 b Find the cost C if Steve buys 7 eight-packs of soft drinks and 2 bags of ice.

23 Solve $2p^2 = 4p + 3$ for p.

In problems 24–26, the input variable is x. What is the natural domain of each function?

24 $y = \frac{4}{x}$ **25** $y = \sqrt{x - 4}$ **26** $y = \frac{2x}{x(x - 3)}$

27 Solve for x if $y = 0$. $y = x^2 - 4x + 3$

In problems 28–30, refer to the table.

28 Copy and complete the table for $SUM = DIE_1 + DIE_2$.

29 Use the table to determine the probability that $SUM = 7$.

30 Use the table to determine the probability that SUM is a prime number.

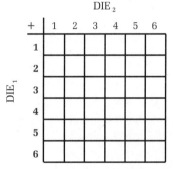

31 For the relation $x = 5y^2$, the input for x is 125.

 a What is the range for y?

 b Is x a function of y?

32 For the equation $y = x^3$, if the domain for x is the set $\{1, 2, 3, 4\}$, is y a function of x?

33 Solve $ax + b = cx + d$ for x.

34 There are 4 quarts in a gallon. Write a formula to describe the number of quarts Q in G gallons. What is the natural domain of G?

In problems 35 and 36, determine the natural domain for each function of x.

35 $y = \sqrt{2x - 6}$ **36** $y = \frac{4x}{x^2 - 4}$

Problem Set, *continued*

37 Find x if AD = x^2, AB = 3x, BC = 4x, and CD = 8.

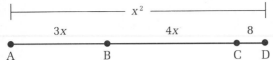

In problems 38 and 39, a line contains the point $(-7, 4)$ and has slope $-\frac{2}{3}$.

38 Write an equation of the line in point-slope form.

39 Write an equation of the line in slope-intercept form.

40 Solve $7x - 8y = 17$ and $y = 4$ for x.

41 For delivery of a first-class letter, the post office charges $0.25 for the first ounce and $0.20 for each additional ounce or fraction thereof.

   a If the input value is the number of ounces that the letter weighs and the output is the cost of mailing the letter, is this relation a function?

   b If the input value is the cost of mailing the letter and the output is the weight of the letter, is this relation a function?

42 The graph represents a relation in which x is the input variable and y is the output variable.

   a What is the domain?
   b What is the range?
   c Is y a function of x?

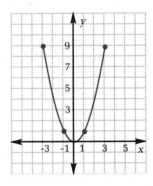

43 The average of five grades for Stu Figueroa is 91.8, and the average of six grades is 86.5. What grade did Stu get on his sixth test?

44 A rectangle is divided into four smaller rectangles.

   a Copy the diagram and label each of the four distinct rectangles with its area.
   b Write four formulas for the area of the whole rectangle.

45 If the input variable for q comes from {1, 3, 5, 7} and $|p| = q$, is p a function of q? Why or why not?

In problems 46 and 47, use the fact that the weight of water is approximately 62.5 pounds per cubic foot.

46 Write a formula to calculate the weight x of the water in any rectangular box whose dimensions are measured in feet.

47 Find the weight of water in a rectangular aquarium 2 feet long, 1 foot wide, and 9 inches high.

48 Suppose that one of the relations below is picked at random. Determine the probability of the following.

$$x = y + 3 \qquad y = x^2 \qquad x = |y| \qquad y = \frac{6}{x} \qquad x^2 = |y|$$

a y is a function of x

b x is a function of y

49 Let E, F, G, and H be midpoints.

a Find the coordinates of midpoints E, F, G, and H.

b Find the midpoint of $\overline{EG}$.

c Find the midpoint of $\overline{FH}$.

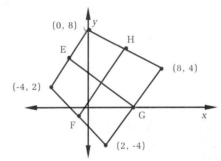

In problems 50–52, find the natural domain of each function of x.

50 $y = \dfrac{\sqrt{3x - 8}}{\sqrt{25 - x^2}}$

51 $y = \dfrac{-12}{\sqrt{12.7 - x^2}}$

52 $y = \dfrac{6}{|x|^5 - 32}$

53 The ratio of the sides of a rectangle is 5:1. If the area is 100, what are the dimensions of the rectangle?

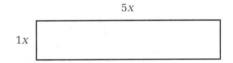

In problems 54 and 55, the horizontal axis is the input axis, and the vertical axis is the output axis. Give the input variable and the output variable as well as the domain and range.

54

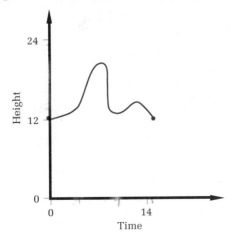

55

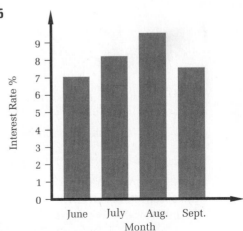

FUNCTION NOTATION AND GRAPHING

Objectives

After studying this section, you will be able to
- Use function notation
- Graph functions

Part One: Introduction

Function Notation

The notation $f(x) = x^2$, read "The function f of x is x squared," is an example of *function notation*. It indicates that $y = x^2$ describes a function if x is the input value. It is common to use f to name a function, but other letters, such as g or h, may be used.

Function notation is also used to indicate that an output value is to be calculated for a given input value. For example, $f(5)$ is mathematical shorthand for "the value of the output when the input value is 5."

Example   *If $f(x) = x^2$, what is $f(5)$?*

For the function $f(x) = x^2$, we will calculate the output when the input is 5 by substituting 5 for x.

$$f(x) = x^2$$
$$f(5) = 5^2$$
$$= 25$$

Input: $x = 5$

$f(x) = x^2$

$f(5) = (5)^2$

Output: $f(5) = 25$

We read $f(5) = 25$ as "f of 5 is 25."

Example   *Let $y = \pm\sqrt{x}$. Is $g(x) = \pm\sqrt{x}$ a valid statement?*

Remember, $g(x)$ can be used only if $y = \pm\sqrt{x}$ is a function when the input value is x. For each positive input value of x, we obtain two output values of y, so y is not a function of x. Therefore, we cannot write $g(x) = \pm\sqrt{x}$.

The input variable is referred to as the *independent variable* of the function because we have the freedom to choose its value. The output variable is referred to as the *dependent variable,* since its value depends on our choice for the input value.

Graphing

Graphing functions is identical to graphing equations. Traditionally, the horizontal axis is the **input,** or domain, **axis,** and the vertical axis is the **output,** or range, **axis.**

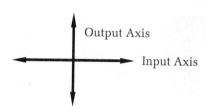

Example   Graph $f(t) = 3t + 2$.

Since t is the input variable, input values for t will be located on the horizontal axis, and output values of $f(t)$ will be located on the vertical axis.

$f(t) = 3t + 2$ is a linear equation. The slope is 3, and the $f(t)$-intercept is 2.

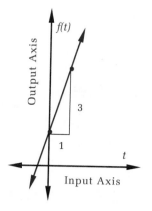

Part Two: Sample Problems

Problem 1   Graph $f(x) = (x - 1)^2$, *if the domain is all real numbers.*

Solution   Make a table of values, graph the points, and then draw a smooth curve.

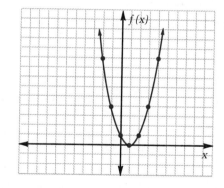

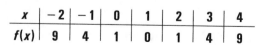

x	−2	−1	0	1	2	3	4
f(x)	9	4	1	0	1	4	9

Problem 2   Let $f(x) = x^2 + 5$. *Find x so that* $f(x) = 41$.

Solution
$$f(x) = x^2 + 5 \text{ and } f(x) = 41$$
$$x^2 + 5 = 41$$
$$x^2 = 36$$
$$x = \pm 6$$

The solution set for x is $\{6, -6\}$.

Problem 3   Let $g(x) = 2x - 11$. *Evaluate the function g for each input value.*

a $g(4)$ **b** $g(5a)$ **c** $g(a + 3)$

Solution $g(x) = 2x - 11$

a $g(4) = 2(4) - 11$, so $g(4) = -3$
b $g(5a) = 2(5a) - 11$, so $g(5a) = 10a - 11$
c $g(a + 3) = 2(a + 3) - 11$, so $g(a + 3) = 2a - 5$

Part Three: Exercises and Problems

Warm-up Exercises

In problems 1–4, $f(x) = 3$ and $g(x) = 2x + 1$. Evaluate the following.

1 $g\left(\sqrt{3}\right)$ **2** $f(-2)$ **3** $f(2a)$ **4** $f(a^2 - 1)$

In problems 5 and 6, give the natural domain of each function.

5 $f(x) = \sqrt{x - 1}$ **6** $h(x) = \dfrac{x}{|x - 4|}$

7 Graph $f(x) = x^2 - 2$.

Problem Set

In problems 8–10, let $f(x) = 2x + 7$. Evaluate.

8 $f(3)$ **9** $f(-4)$ **10** $f(-3.5)$

In problems 11–13, graph each function. Use the horizontal axis as the input axis.

11 $f(x) = 3x - 4$ **12** $g(x) = x^2 + 1$ **13** $h(x) = -3$

 14 The formula for the volume of a cylinder is $V = \pi r^2 h$. Find the volume of the cylinder shown.

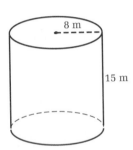

In problems 15 and 16, use the function $f(t) = 12t + 37$.

15 Find $f(7)$.   **16** Find t so that $f(t) = 109$.

In problems 17 and 18, solve each literal equation.

17 Solve $PV = nRT$ for T.   **18** Solve $F = \dfrac{gm_1 m_2}{r^2}$ for g.

 19 A line segment is drawn on a graph.

    a Find the midpoint of $\overline{AB}$.
    b Find the length of $\overline{AB}$.
    c Find the slope of $\overline{AB}$.
    d Find the length of the segment from A to the midpoint of $\overline{AB}$.

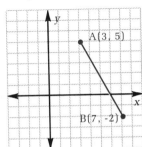

20 Solve the equation $2y^2 = 3y - 1$ for y, using the quadratic formula.

21 Refer to the equation $y = \sqrt{4x - 8}$.

    a If x is the input variable, what is the natural domain?
    b Is y a function of x?

22 Refer to the function $f(x) = 3x + 4$.

   a Find $f(5)$.   **b** Find $f(4)$.

   c Find $f(9)$.   **d** Does $f(4) + f(5) = f(9)$?

23 Refer to the equation $y = 4x^2 + 1$.

   a Is $f(x) = 4x^2 + 1$ a valid statement?

   b If x is the input variable, what is the natural domain?

24 Use the diagrams below to answer the questions.

i

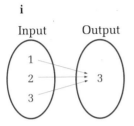

ii

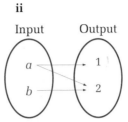

   a What is the domain of each of the relations shown?

   b What is the range of each of the relations shown?

   c Is relation **i** a function? Is relation **ii** a function? Give a reason why or why not in each case.

   d Which of the functions is a constant function?

25 Refer to the diagram. If $f(x) = 3x - 4$, $AB = f(7)$, and $BC = f(9)$, what is the length of $\overline{AC}$?

In problems 26 and 27, simplify each expression and solve each equation.

26 $4x(x - 2) = 3(4 - x)$ **27** $4x(x - 2) - 3(4 - x)$

28 Multiply.

$$\begin{bmatrix} 3 & -4 \\ -2 & 1 \end{bmatrix} \begin{bmatrix} 6 \\ -5 \end{bmatrix}$$

29 The Ring-a-Ling Phone Company bills monthly charges of $8.20 for phone line maintenance, $1.25 per phone, and $0.05 per unit for calls.

   a Write a formula for the monthly bill b in terms of the number of phones p and the number of units u used that month.

   b Find the average monthly bill for a family that has 3 phones and uses an average of 1,579 units per month.

In problems 30–32, solve each equation for k.

30 $2k^2 = 60$ **31** $3k^2 - 12k = 0$ **32** $k^2 = 4k + 12$

Problem Set, *continued*

In problems 33 and 34, use $f(x) = 3x + c$ and $f(4) = 7$.

33 Find the value of c.

34 Find $f(-8)$.

35 Refer to the graph. The horizontal axis represents the domain elements, and the vertical axis represents the range elements.

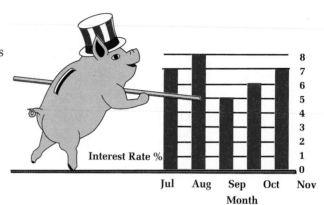

a What are the domain elements?
b What are the range elements?
c What does each domain element represent?
d What does each range element represent?

36 Find the entries for the matrix if $f(x) = \dfrac{|x|}{x}$.

$$\begin{bmatrix} f(2) & f(-3) \\ f(5) & f(7) \end{bmatrix}$$

37 Let $f(x) = 19x - 11$ and $g(x) = 17x + 83$. Find x so that $f(x) = g(x)$.

38 Refer to the table.

x	1	2	3	4	5	6	7	8
$f(x)$	1	8	27	64				

a Look for a pattern and find the missing range elements.
b Write the function as a set of ordered pairs whose first members are the values of x.
c Write a formula for this function.

39 The Mudville Exponents baseball team won 75, 87, 93, and 84 games in the past 4 seasons. How many games must they win this season in order for their 5-year average to be at least 90 wins per season?

40 Let $f(x) = 2x^2 + x$ and $g(x) = -2(x - 1)$. Find all values of x such that $f(x) = g(x)$.

41 Let $f(x) = 2^x$.

a Use a calculator to find $f(0)$, $f(0.5)$, $f(1)$, $f(1.5)$, $f(2)$, $f(2.5)$, and $f(3)$.
b Graph the data found in part **a**, using the horizontal axis as the input axis. Connect the points with a smooth curve.

42 Graph $f(x) = (x - 1)^2$ if the domain is the set of all real numbers.

In problems 43 and 44, solve for y.

43 $3y^2 + 2y = 8$

44 $f(y) = 7y^2 + 14y$ and $f(y) = 0$

In problems 45 and 46, refer to the diagram.

45 Find the cost of tiling the floor of the room shown if each tile is a 12-inch square and the cost of one tile is $1.19.

46 Suppose a new baseboard (edging around the walls of the room) is also installed, at a cost of $2 per linear foot. Find the cost of the baseboard.

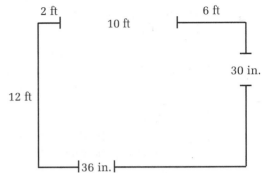

In problems 47 and 48, $f(x) = x^2$ and $g(x) = 2x + 1$.

47 Find $f(11)$ and $g(25)$.

48 Find $g(t^2)$.

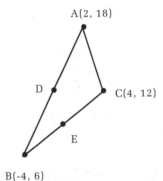

In problems 49–52, refer to the diagram.

49 Find the coordinates of the midpoints D and E.

50 Find the distance from D to E.

51 Find the distance from A to C.

52 Find the ratio of DE to AC.

53 Solve for (x, y).

$$\begin{bmatrix} x & -4 \\ 0 & 8 \end{bmatrix} \begin{bmatrix} x \\ 2 \end{bmatrix} = \begin{bmatrix} 8 \\ y \end{bmatrix}$$

54 The triangle at the right can be represented by

$$\begin{bmatrix} 0 & 0 \\ 3 & 0 \\ 1.5 & 2 \end{bmatrix} \cdot T$$

Which matrix represents T?

a $\begin{bmatrix} 1 & 0 \\ 0 & -1 \end{bmatrix}$

b $\begin{bmatrix} -1 & 0 \\ 0 & -1 \end{bmatrix}$

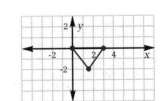

In problems 55 and 56, find the natural domain of each function.

55 $f(x) = \sqrt{|x - 3|}$

56 $f(x) = \sqrt{\dfrac{6}{x^2 - 4}}$

In problems 57–59, $f(4x) = 12x - 7$.

57 Find $f(1)$.

58 Find $f(16.5)$.

59 Find $f(a)$.

Problem Set, *continued*

In problems 60 and 61, use the function $f(t) = t^2 + 5t - 7$.

60 Find t so that $f(t) = -1$.   **61** Find $f(k + 3)$.

In problems 62–65, $f(x) = 3x - 5$ and $g(x) = x + 1$. (Hint: Problems 64 and 65 are examples of composition of functions, in which one function uses the output of another function as its input.)

62 Find $f(3)$.   **63** Find $g(-2)$.
64 Find $f[g(-2)]$.   **65** Find $g[f(3)]$.

66 Let $f(t) = 6t$ and $g(t) = t^2 + 5$.

   a Find $g[f(2)]$.

   b Find $f[g(2)]$.

   c Is composition of functions commutative?

MATHEMATICAL EXCURSION

MIRRORS REVEAL THE STARS
How telescopes work

The telescope was invented by Dutch eyeglass maker Hans Lippershey in 1608. Lippershey's design is called a *refractor*. Light from the sky is collected by the objective lens (B) and magnified by the eyepiece (A). Today, small telescopes are often built on this principle. However, most of the world's largest telescopes are *reflectors*. In a reflector, a parabolically curved mirror is attached at one end of a tube (E). The parabolic shape causes all light rays from the sky to focus at a single point (F). A small, flat mirror placed at point F reflects the light to the eyepiece through a hole in the side of the telescope.

   Reflectors have great advantages over refractors. They are cheaper, plagued with fewer optical defects, and, because they can be supported from underneath, can be built much larger than refractors.

   Focusing all light at a single point of a parabolic mirror can be used in reverse to produce flashlights and headlights. When a light source is located in front of parabolic reflectors, light strikes the reflector surface and is sent outward in parallel rays, achieving maximum brightness and distance.

   What other instruments are built on the principles of refraction and reflection?

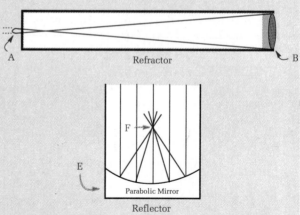

Refractor

Reflector

MEAN, MODE, AND MEDIAN

Objective

After studying this section, you will be able to
- Determine mean, mode, and median

Measures of Central Tendency

Data analysis often involves finding quantities that represent the data. The **mean, mode,** and **median** are three such quantities. They are called **measures of central tendency** because they are ways to describe the center of a set of data.

The data below represent the number of boxes of grapefruit sold by 15 jazz-band members as part of a school fund-raiser.

4	19	0	38
24	11	12	2
17	13	5	4
6	4	19	

We organize the data from smallest to largest.

0	4	12	19
2	5	13	24
4	6	17	38
4	11	19	

The principal asked the band director to find the average number of boxes sold. The band director calculated that the total number of boxes sold was 178. She then divided by 15 (the number of jazz-band members) to find the average number of boxes sold per member.

$$\frac{\text{Total number of boxes sold}}{\text{Number of jazz-band members}} = \frac{178}{15} = 11\frac{13}{15} \approx 11.9$$

The average obtained by dividing the sum of a set of terms by the number of terms is called the **mean** of the data.

The band director noticed that the number 4 occurred among the data the greatest number of times. The number that occurs the greatest number of times is called the **mode** of the data.

The band director could have given a third type of average for the data by choosing the number 11. This number is the middle number of the data and is called the **median.** Since the total number of data values is an odd number, there are as many values greater than the median as there are values less than the median. When there is an even number of data values, the median is defined to be the mean of the two middle numbers.

Problem

The data below represent the scores Stu Dent earned for nine labs in chemistry.

10, 7, 5, 5, 6, 8, 9, 10, 5

a Determine the mean, mode, and median for the nine lab scores.
b Determine the new mean, mode, and median if Stu earned a 10 on the next lab.

Solution

a We first arrange the data from smallest to largest.

5, 5, 5, 6, 7, 8, 9, 10, 10

The sum of the nine lab scores is 65.

$$\text{Mean} = \frac{\text{Total of lab scores}}{\text{Number of labs}} = \frac{65}{9} = 7\frac{2}{9} \approx 7.2$$

Since 5 appears most often, 5 is the mode. The median (middle score) is 7.

b The data for the ten lab scores are

5, 5, 5, 6, 7, 8, 9, 10, 10, 10

The sum of the scores is 75.

$$\text{Mean} = \frac{\text{Total of lab scores}}{\text{Number of labs}} = \frac{75}{10} = 7.5$$

The scores 5 and 10 appear the most often and the same number of times. The data are bimodal with the modes being 5 and 10.

There is an even number of data values, so there are two middle scores, 7 and 8. To find the median, we determine the mean of the two middle scores. The mean of 7 and 8 is 7.5, so the median is 7.5.

In the example, both the median and the mean represented the typical data value better than the mode. Whenever all three measures of central tendency differ, it will be your task to decide which is the most appropriate one to use.

Problem Set

1 In a survey of Newtonville residents, people were asked their income. Their responses were $35,000, $61,000, $19,000, $480,000, $22,000, $29,500, $16,500, $13,000, $35,000, and $23,000.

a Arrange the data from smallest to largest.
b Find the median income.
c Find the mean income.
d What income is the mode?
e The mean is larger than all but one of the data values. Why is this the case? Is it fair to conclude that the mean represents the typical income?
f Which measure of central tendency best represents the data?

2 The mean of a set of three numbers is 18, and the median is 12. The difference between the smallest and largest numbers is 20. Find the largest of the three numbers.

3 The salaries of five employees in a company are $12,000, $18,000, $14,000, $16,000, and $80,000.

a Find the mean and median of the salaries.
b Is the mean or the median a better measure of central tendency for the data? Why?
c Find the new salaries if each employee is given an 8% raise.
d Find the mean and median of the new salaries.

4 The data below represent Eric's daily sales totals during a 10-day work period as an employee of Roxie's Record Ranch. Eric earns a base salary of $20 a day and a commission of 2% on his sales.

Sales: $160, $240, $130, $420, $360, $110, $190, $120, $280, $670

a Find the mean and median of the sales total.
b List the amount of commission he made each day.
c Find the mean and median of the sales commission data.
d Explain how you could obtain the answers for part **c** by using the answers to part **a.**
e List Eric's daily earnings.
f Find the mean and median of the data representing his daily earnings.

5 The figure represents the number of books sold at a school bookstore during the first week of the semester.

a Find the total sales.
b Find the number of books sold.
c Find the mean selling price per book.

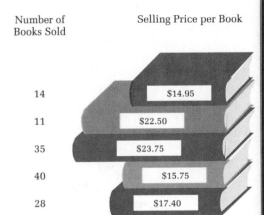

Number of Books Sold

Selling Price per Book

14     $14.95

11     $22.50

35     $23.75

40     $15.75

28     $17.40

6 During a bridge match, Charles kept track of the number of clubs he was dealt in each 13-card hand. The numbers of clubs were 3, 4, 4, 3, 2, 0, 6, 3, 4, 3, 1, 5, 4, 7, 1, 3, 3, 2, and 3.

a Find the mean number of clubs per hand.
b Find the mode of the data.
c Find the median of the data.
d Why are all these numbers 3 or near 3?

CHAPTER SUMMARY

CONCEPTS AND PROCEDURES

After studying this chapter, you should be able to
- Recognize formulas (7.1)
- Write and evaluate formulas (7.1)
- Use appropriate units with formulas (7.1)
- Find perimeters, areas, and volumes of geometric figures (7.2)
- Use the distance and midpoint formulas of analytic geometry (7.2)
- Solve quadratic equations using the quadratic formula (7.3)
- Recognize literal equations (7.4)
- Solve literal equations (7.4)
- Define a relation (7.5)
- Define a function (7.5)
- Identify the natural domain of a function or relation (7.5)
- Use function notation (7.6)
- Graph functions (7.6)
- Determine mean, mode, and median (7.7)

VOCABULARY

circumference (7.2)	independent variable (7.6)	mode (7.7)
constant function (7.5)	input (7.1)	natural domain (7.5)
dependent variable (7.6)	input axis (7.6)	output (7.1)
domain (7.5)	input-output diagram (7.1)	output axis (7.6)
equilateral figure (7.2)	literal equation (7.4)	quadratic equation (7.3)
formula (7.1)	mean (7.7)	range (7.5)
function (7.5)	median (7.7)	relation (7.5)
function notation (7.6)		

FORMULAS

Quadratic
$$x = \frac{-b \pm \sqrt{b^2 - 4ac}}{2a}$$

Distance
$$d = \sqrt{(x_2 - x_1)^2 + (y_2 - y_1)^2}$$

Midpoint
$$(x_m, y_m) = \left(\frac{x_1 + x_2}{2}, \frac{y_1 + y_2}{2} \right)$$

REVIEW PROBLEMS

1 If $a = 3$, $b = 4$, and $c = -5$, what is the value of x in the formula $x = \dfrac{-b \pm \sqrt{b^2 - 4ac}}{2a}$?

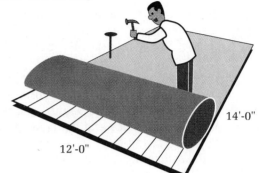

In problems 2–4, refer to the figure.

2 Find the area in square feet.

3 Find the area in square yards.

4 Carpet, padding, and installation costs $17.75 per square yard. Find the cost to carpet the room.

14'-0"

12'-0"

5 Find the surface area of a sphere with a radius of 8 millimeters.

6 Write a formula in the form $y = \underline{\ ?\ }$ for the data.

x	−2	−1	0	1	2	3	4	5
y	−0.5	−1	—	1	0.5	$0.\overline{3}$	0.25	0.2

7 Solve for a, b, c, and d.

$$\begin{bmatrix} 3a & -b \\ 0 & 12 \end{bmatrix} + \begin{bmatrix} 4 & -3 \\ \dfrac{c}{5} & d \end{bmatrix} = \begin{bmatrix} 16 & b \\ -30 & 7 \end{bmatrix}$$

In problems 8 and 9, use the formula $i = p + prt$.

8 Solve for p.　　　　　　**9** Solve for r.

10 Solve $A = \dfrac{h(b_1 + b_2)}{2}$ for h.

11 In a game, Carlton accumulated the numbers of colored markers shown. Each marker has the following value.

Red—1 point　　　　Orange—25 points
Green—5 points　　　White—50 points
Yellow—10 points

　a Find Carlton's point total.
　b Find the mean value of his markers.
　c Find the median value of his markers.

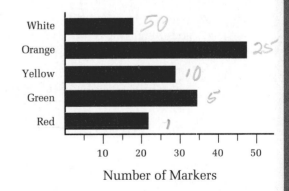

Number of Markers

Review Problems, *continued*

12 Refer to the diagram.

   a Is this relation a function?
   b Write a formula for this relation.

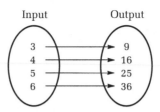

 In problems 13–15, use the formula for the volume of a sphere,
$V = f(r) = \frac{4}{3}\pi r^3$.

13 Find $f(10)$.

14 Find $f(16.2)$.

15 What is the natural domain of r?

In problems 16 and 17, graph each function of t. Use the horizontal axis for values of t and the vertical axis for values of $f(t)$.

16 $f(t) = \frac{2}{3}t + 4$ **17** $f(t) = t^2 - 2$

18 For each of two line segments, point A is one endpoint, and point M is the midpoint. Find O, the other endpoint, for each line segment.

A	M	O
(4, 5)	**(− 2, 7)**	
(− 1, 6)	**(4, − 3)**	

In problems 19 and 20, find the natural domain for each function.

19 $f(x) = \sqrt{x^2 - 9}$ **20** $h(x) = \dfrac{\sqrt{2x - 12}}{x^2 - 144}$

21 Find the product of the two matrices if $f(x) = x^2$ and $g(x) = 3x - 4$.

$$\begin{bmatrix} f(2) & f(3) \\ f(-1) & f(-6) \end{bmatrix} \begin{bmatrix} g(4) \\ g(-6) \end{bmatrix}$$

In problems 22–24, $f(x) = 7x + 4$ and $g(x) = |x - 3|$. Evaluate each expression.

22 $f(2)g(2)$ **23** $f(-3) + g(-3)$ **24** $g(t + 9)$

 25 The cost of a taxi ride is $1.60, plus $1.50 per mile and an additional charge of $0.05 per minute while the meter is running.

   a Write a formula for the cost c if the meter runs m minutes and the trip is d miles.

   b Find the cost of a taxi ride if it takes 30 minutes to make the trip and the distance is 6.4 miles.

In problems 26–29, solve each equation.

26 $5x^2 - 6x + 1 = 0$ **27** $3(4x^2 - 2x) = 6(2x^2 - 5)$

28 $30x = 2x^2 + 72$ **29** $x(x + 4) = 20$

30 For the equation $h^2 + k^2 = 25$, the input for h is $\{3, -3, 4, -4, 0\}$. Write the relation as a set of ordered pairs (h, k).

In problems 31 and 32, find the distance between the two given points. Then find the midpoint of the segment connecting them.

31 $(4, 5)$ and $(-3, -2)$ **32** $(4, -2)$ and $(-13, -5)$

33 A ball is dropped from the top of a building 145 feet high. Its distance above the ground is given by the formula $d = 145 - 16t^2$ (d in feet, t in seconds).

a At what time does the ball hit the ground?
b At what time is the ball 50 feet in the air?

In problems 34–36, use the formula for earned run average (ERA) for baseball pitchers, ERA $= \frac{9r}{I}$, where r = earned runs allowed and I = innings pitched.

34 Gopher Jones pitched $72\frac{2}{3}$ innings and allowed 66 earned runs. Compute his ERA.

35 Sudden Sam Jones had an ERA of 2.44 and pitched $44\frac{1}{3}$ innings. How many runs did he allow?

36 Solve the ERA formula for r.

37 A particle moves on a curve described by $f(t) = \sqrt{t^2 - 4}$. Find the natural domain of this function.

38 Ralph and Timothy are acrobats and work on a piece of equipment that is like a teeter-totter. If Ralph weighs 150 pounds and Timothy weighs 100 pounds, how far must Ralph sit from the fulcrum to balance if Timothy is 6 feet from the fulcrum?

In problems 39 and 40, use the function $f(b) = b^2 + 6b + 7$.
39 Find b so that $f(b) = -1$. **40** Find w so that $f(2w) = 3$.

In problems 41–45, let $f(x) = x^2 + 5x - 7$ and $g(x) = x + 1$.
41 Find x so that $f(x) = g(x)$.
42 Find $g(4x)$.
43 Find x so that $f(x) = g(4x)$.
44 Find $g(k + 3)$.
45 Find k so that $g(k + 3) = 2g(k)$.

In problems 46–49, find the solution set for each equation.
46 $\frac{1}{3}x^2 - 2x - \frac{1}{2} = 0$
47 $x(x - 12) = 2(x - 12)$
48 $\sqrt{38} - \sqrt{20}x + \sqrt{2}x^2 = 0$
49 $(x + 2)^2 + 5(x + 2) + 6 = 0$

7 CHAPTER TEST

1 Solve for x if $5ax - 2b = 3c$.

2 Refer to the diagram.

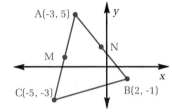

  a Find M, the midpoint of $\overline{AC}$.
  b Find N, the midpoint of $\overline{AB}$.
  c Write an equation of the line that passes through M and N.

In problems 3–6, solve each quadratic equation.

3 $3x^2 - 15x = 0$

4 $2x^2 - 4x - 5 = 0$

5 $n^2 - 17 = 64$

6 $x^2 = -2x + 3$

7 The salaries of 6 employees in a company are $18,000, $14,500, $12,000, $80,000, $14,000, and $18,000.

  a Find the mean salary.
  b Find the median salary.

8 Give the natural domain of $f(x) = \dfrac{4}{|x| - 2}$.

9 Penny Wise has only nickels and dimes in her pocket. She has a total of $1.25.

  a Using n for nickels and d for dimes, write a formula to represent this.
  b If Penny has three times as many nickels as dimes, how many of each does she have?

10 If $f(x) = 5x - 17$ and $g(x) = -2x + 3$, what is $f(2) - g(3)$?

11 Let $\{(2, 5), (3, 4), (4, 5), (6, 8)\}$ be a set of ordered pairs (x, y).

  a Is x a function of y?
  b Is y a function of x?

12 Find the value of x so that the perimeter and area of the rectangle will have the same numerical value.

PUZZLES AND CHALLENGES

1 How many rectangles can you find in each figure?

2 In a cafeteria survey of 100 students, it was found that
 50 students had pickles on their burgers,
60 students had mustard on their burgers,
 70 students had ketchup on their burgers,
20 students had pickles and mustard on their burgers,
 25 students had pickles and ketchup on their burgers,
45 students had mustard and ketchup on their burgers, and
 10 students had pickles, mustard, and ketchup on their burgers.

What percentage of the students had either ketchup or mustard on their burgers?

3 a It is possible to draw twelve different shapes using 5 squares. Three of the shapes are shown below. Draw the other nine shapes.

b Use the twelve different shapes to form a 10 × 6 rectangle.

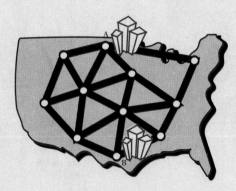

4 The map shows where cities, represented by dots (o), are joined by roads, represented by lines (▬). If Mathman always travels southward, how many routes can he choose from when driving from A to B?

8 SYSTEMS OF EQUATIONS

Once limited to studying the night sky, astronomers now are focusing on the dynamic processes that made our universe what it is. To understand these processes, astronomers are increasingly dependent on supercomputers—machines that can perform several hundred million calculations each second.

Before supercomputers, astronomers were limited to observations and limited calculations to test a theory. By running mathematical models on a supercomputer, astronomers are able to simulate cosmic events in great detail. They can "watch" galaxies develop and grow. Astronomers can test their ideas about black holes and even "see" hot gases circulating deep within a fiery star. Supercomputer simulations enable astronomers to test their theories about the universe more completely than ever before.

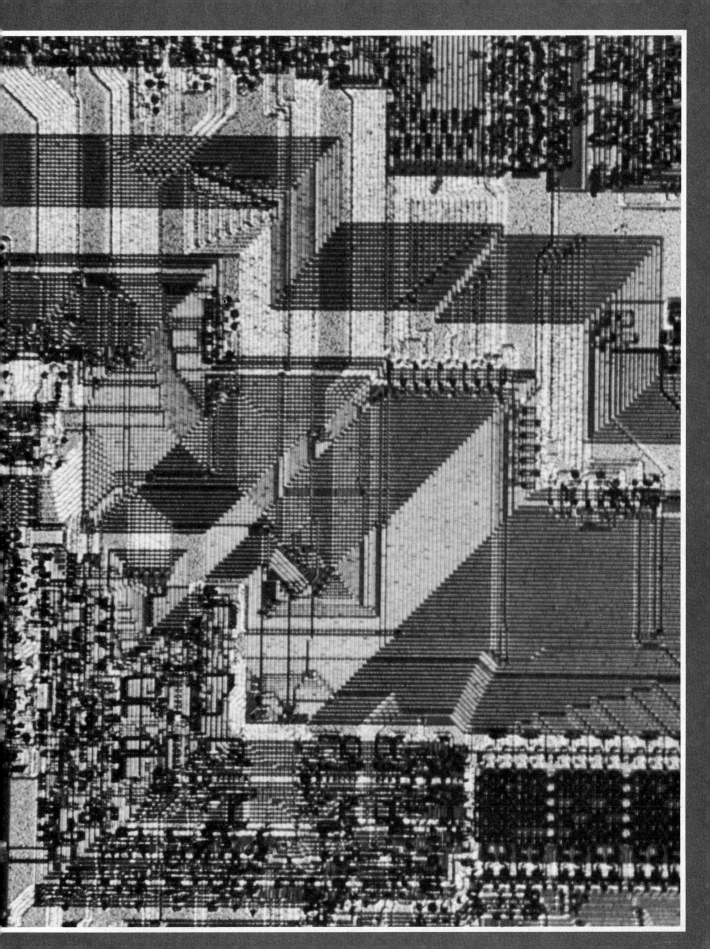

8.1 SOLVING SYSTEMS OF EQUATIONS BY GRAPHING

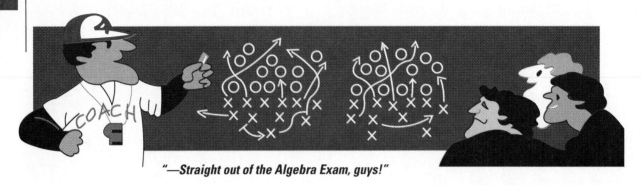

"—Straight out of the Algebra Exam, guys!"

Objectives

After studying this section, you will be able to
- Recognize a system of equations
- Solve a system by graphing
- Solve word problems by graphing

Part One: Introduction

What Is a System of Equations?

Members of a football team, computers linked in a network, and components of an automobile engine all function as part of a system. In this section, you will learn how equations can function as part of a system.

Now we will see how a ***system of equations*** is two or more equations with the same variables. The equations in a system are often referred to as ***simultaneous equations.*** In this text a brace, {, is used to show a system.

A ***linear system*** is a system of two or more linear equations. A ***nonlinear system*** is one in which at least one of the equations has a graph that is not a straight line.

A linear system equivalent to the two equations $y = 3x - 4$ and $y = x$

$$\begin{cases} y = 3x - 4 \\ y = x \end{cases}$$

A nonlinear system equivalent to the two equations $3x + 2y = 4$ and $y = x^2$ (the nonlinear equation is $y = x^2$)

$$\begin{cases} 3x + 2y = 4 \\ y = x^2 \end{cases}$$

To solve a system of equations means to determine all the ordered pairs of real numbers that simultaneously satisfy all the equations of the system.

Graphing to Solve Systems

One method of solving a system of two equations is to graph both equations of the system on the same set of coordinate axes and then look for the points (ordered pairs) where the graphs intersect.

Let's look at an example of a system we are to solve.

Example   *Solve the system.*

$$\begin{cases} 2x + 3y = 12 \\ y = 3x - 7 \end{cases}$$

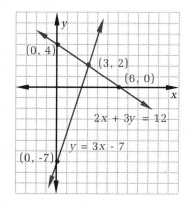

Although we have not solved systems of equations before, we have graphed two lines on the same coordinate plane. Let's try that strategy.

To graph $2x + 3y = 12$, we use the x-intercept $(6, 0)$ and the y-intercept $(0, 4)$.

Since the equation $y = 3x - 7$ is in slope-intercept form, we use the slope 3 and the y-intercept $(0, -7)$ to graph it. The graphs intersect at the point $(3, 2)$.

Remember that every point on the line represents an ordered pair that satisfies the equation of the line. If there is a point where the two lines intersect, that point will satisfy both equations at the same time and will be the solution to the system. Systems of equations that have a solution are called **consistent.** For this system, the solution is the ordered pair $(3, 2)$. We can check by substituting $(3, 2)$ into each equation. If you have access to a graphing calculator, you can use it to verify the solution.

Check

$2x + 3y = 12$ $y = 3x - 7$

Left Side	**Right Side**		**Left Side**	**Right Side**
$2(3) + 3(2)$	$= 12$		2	$= 3(3) - 7$
$= 6 + 6$				$= 9 - 7$
$= 12$				$= 2$

In both equations, the sides are equal, so the answer checks.

Solving Word Problems by Graphing

In order to solve word problems, it is important to understand what the problem states and what you need to find. If you need to find two things and the problem gives you two pieces of information, you can solve the problem by considering it as a system and graphing it.

To solve by graphing, we need to decide what to use for ordered pairs and what the two lines represent. Let's look at an example.

| Example | Jason and Carlos live 10 miles apart. They leave their houses at the same time to meet each other partway. Jason walks at a rate of 2 miles per hour, and Carlos jogs at a rate of 5 miles per hour. When will they meet? How far are they from Jason's house when they meet? |

We are to answer two questions: How long before Jason and Carlos meet (time), and how far from Jason's house do they meet (distance)? We know two pieces of information: Jason's rate is 2 miles per hour and Carlos's rate is 5 mile per hour.

For ordered pairs we use (time, distance from Jason's house). If we can find two ordered pairs for each person, we can draw a line that represents Jason's travel and a line that represents Carlos's travel. Then we can see where the lines intersect.

At time zero, Jason is at home.   (0, 0)

At 1 hour, Jason has walked 2 miles.   (1, 2)

We can use these ordered pairs to draw one line.

At time zero, Carlos is 10 miles from Jason's house.   (0, 10)

After 2 hours, Carlos has jogged 10 miles (5 miles per hour) and has arrived at Jason's house.   (2, 0)

We can use these ordered pairs to draw a second line.

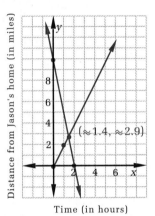

The two graphs intersect at approximately (1.4, 2.9). The two boys meet after approximately 1.4 hours and about 2.9 miles from Jason's home.

Part Two: Sample Problems

| Problem 1 | Determine which of the ordered pairs (0, 3), (2, 4), and (4, 5) are solutions to the system. |

$$\begin{cases} y = |x - 1| + 2 \\ y = 0.5x + 3 \end{cases}$$

| Solution | An ordered pair that is a solution will make both equations true statements. We substitute each ordered pair into each equation. |

The ordered pairs (0, 3) and (4, 5) are solutions.

Pair	First Equation	Second Equation	Result
(0, 3)	$3 = |0 - 1| + 2$	$3 = 0.5(0) + 3$	A solution
(2, 4)	$4 \neq |2 - 1| + 2$	$4 = 0.5(2) + 3$	Not a solution
(4, 5)	$5 = |4 - 1| + 2$	$5 = 0.5(4) + 3$	A solution

Problem 2   *Solve the system by graphing.*

$$\begin{cases} f(x) = |x| \\ g(x) = \frac{1}{2}x + 3 \end{cases}$$

Solution   The function $g(x) = \frac{1}{2}x + 3$ is linear and in slope-intercept form.

The function $f(x) = |x|$ is nonlinear, so we use a table of values.

x	−4	−3	−2	−1	0	1	2	3	4	5	6
f(x)	4	3	2	1	0	1	2	3	4	5	6

It appears that there are two solutions to the system, $(-2, 2)$ and $(6, 6)$. Check to be sure.

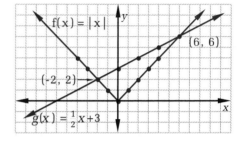

Problem 3   *A hot-air balloon at 500 feet begins rising at the rate of 120 feet per minute. A second hot-air balloon, at 1500 feet, begins descending at the rate of 200 feet per minute. When will the balloons be at the same height? What is this height?*

Solution   We are asked to find both the time when the balloons are at the same height and what height this is. We have two pieces of information: the height and rising rate of one balloon and the height and descending rate of the other balloon.

For ordered pairs, we can use (time, height).

At time zero, one balloon is at 500 feet, (0, 500).
After 1 minute, this balloon will have risen 120 feet, to 620 feet, (1, 620).
We can use the ordered pairs to draw a line.

At time zero, the other balloon is at 1500 feet, (0, 1500).
After 1 minute, this balloon will have descended 200 feet, to 1300 feet, (1, 1300).
We can use the ordered pairs to draw a line.

The lines intersect at approximately (3.1, 875), so after approximately 3.1 minutes the balloons are 875 feet above the ground. Check the answer.

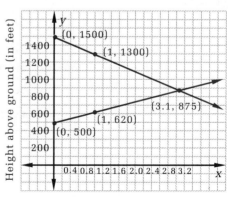

Time (in minutes)

Part Three: Exercises and Problems

Warm-up Exercises

In problems 1–3, determine whether $(2, -4)$ is a solution to the system. If so, determine whether it is the only solution.

1 $\begin{cases} 3x + 2y = -2 \\ 2x - 3y = 16 \end{cases}$
2 $\begin{cases} y = -x - 2 \\ y = x^2 - 8 \end{cases}$
3 $\begin{cases} y = -|x + 2| \\ y = -x^2 \end{cases}$

In problems 4–6, graph each system to find the solution(s) and check. State whether the system is linear or nonlinear.

4 $\begin{cases} y = \frac{2}{3}x - 4 \\ 2x + y = 4 \end{cases}$
5 $\begin{cases} y = x^2 \\ y = x + 2 \end{cases}$
6 $\begin{cases} y = \frac{1}{3}x + \frac{4}{3} \\ y = |x| \end{cases}$

7 Paula has $1.50 in nickels and dimes. The total number of coins she has is 18. How many of each type of coin does she have?

Problem Set

In problems 8–10, determine whether each system is linear or nonlinear. For each one that is nonlinear, indicate which equation or equations make it so.

8 $\begin{cases} y = 2x - 1 \\ 3x = y - 2 \end{cases}$
9 $\begin{cases} x = 6 \\ y = -2 \end{cases}$
10 $\begin{cases} y = x^2 - 4 \\ y = 2^x \end{cases}$

11 Refer to the figure. Solve for x.

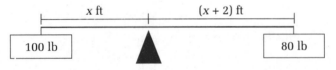

12 Rich counts out $61 in one-dollar and five-dollar bills. He has 17 bills in all. How many one-dollar bills does he have? How many five-dollar bills does he have?

13 Find the point at which the horizontal line with equation $y = 9$ intersects the graph.

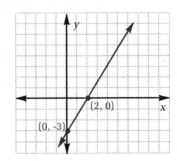

14 Find 2 numbers that add up to 22 if one number is 8 more than the other.

15 Use the ordered pairs A(-1, -5), B(4, 5), C(6, -1), and D(-4, 4).
   a Graph these points on the coordinate plane.
   b Connect points A and B with a straight line. Connect points C and D with a straight line.
   c Find where the two lines intersect.

16 Find the perimeter of the trapezoid.

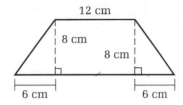

In problems 17 and 18, multiply.

17 $\begin{bmatrix} 3 & 5 \\ 2 & -1 \end{bmatrix}\begin{bmatrix} 4 \\ 3 \end{bmatrix}$ **18** $\begin{bmatrix} 3 & 5 \\ 2 & -1 \end{bmatrix}\begin{bmatrix} x \\ y \end{bmatrix}$

19 Danny and his sister Deanne are 24 miles apart. They start biking toward each other. Danny rides at a rate of 8 miles per hour, and Deanne rides at a rate of 12 miles per hour. How long will it be before they meet? How far will each have traveled?

In problems 20 and 21, solve each system by graphing. Check your answers.

20 $\begin{cases} x = 4 \\ y = 5 \end{cases}$ **21** $\begin{cases} y = 2x - 3 \\ y = x - 2 \end{cases}$

22 How heavy is each weight?

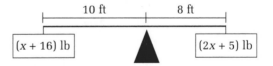

23 A hot-air balloon rises from the ground at 120 feet per minute. At the same time that the first balloon leaves the ground, a balloon at 2500 feet begins descending at 75 feet per minute. When are the balloons at the same height above the ground? What is the common height of the balloons?

24 If one of the systems is chosen at random, what is the probability that (5, -2) is a solution of the system?
   a $\begin{cases} -8x + 5y = -50 \\ 2x + 7y = -4 \end{cases}$ **b** $\begin{cases} x = 5 \\ y = x - 2 \end{cases}$
   c $\begin{cases} y = |x - 2| - 5 \\ y = -2 \end{cases}$ **d** $\begin{cases} y = x^2 - 20 \\ y = -x + 3 \end{cases}$

Problem Set, *continued*

25 The sum of two numbers is 120. Their difference is 10. Let x represent the larger of the numbers and y the smaller.

    a Write a system using x and y.

    b Guess a solution to the system and then check your guess.

26 Refer to the graph.

    a What percentage does each tick mark represent?

    b Which grade was most common?

    c About what percentage of the students received a B?

    d About how many students received an A?

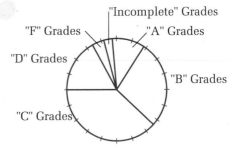

1600 Mathematics Grades Issued
at End of the Third Grading Period

27 It costs $0.0375 per square centimeter to put a ceramic coating on a wooden sphere. How much will it cost to coat a sphere that has a radius of 3 centimeters?

In problems 28 and 29, solve by graphing.

28 $\begin{cases} y = \frac{3}{4}x - 2 \\ x = 4 \end{cases}$
        29 $\begin{cases} 2x + 3y = 12 \\ \quad\quad y = \frac{2}{3}x + 8 \end{cases}$

30 Find the point where the diagonals of the rectangle intersect.

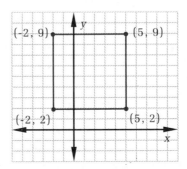

In problems 31–33, for each equation in the system, make a table of values as shown. Use your tables to find a solution for each system.

x	− 3	− 2	− 1	0	1	2	3
y							

31 $\begin{cases} y = 2x \\ y = x + 1 \end{cases}$
    32 $\begin{cases} \quad\quad y = -2x \\ x + y = 2 \end{cases}$
    33 $\begin{cases} y = 3 \\ y = 3x + 6 \end{cases}$

34 Use the formula $e = ir$ to find the voltage e needed to operate an electric heater that draws a current i of 8.5 amperes and has a resistance r of 11.8 ohms.

In problems 35–37, solve each system by graphing. Make a table for each nonlinear function. Check your answers.

35 $\begin{cases} f(x) = |x| \\ g(x) = 4 \end{cases}$ **36** $\begin{cases} y = x^2 + x \\ y = x + 4 \end{cases}$ **37** $\begin{cases} f(x) = x^2 \\ g(x) = x + 2 \end{cases}$

38 The cost of a microcomputer that is new now will decrease according to the formula $c = \dfrac{2000}{2^t}$, where c is the cost of the computer after t years. A. Hacker has no money at $t = 0$ years and saves \$150 per year. How soon can he afford the computer, and what will he have to pay for it?

In problems 39–42, solve each equation.

39 $2x^2 - 6x - 8 = 0$ **40** $x - 7 = -6x$ **41** $3x^2 - 4x + 1 = 0$ **42** $x^2 - 12x + 4 = 0$

43 After t days, the number n of bacteria in a culture is $n = 1240 \cdot 3^t$. Find n for each given value of t.

  a 120 hours   **b** 2 weeks

44 Refer to the figures.

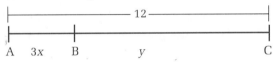 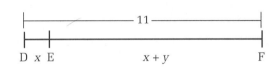

  a Write a system from the diagrams.
  b Solve the system by graphing.
  c What is the ratio of AB to EF?

45 Solve the system by graphing. If you have access to a graphing calculator, you may want to use it.

$$\begin{cases} y = 0.75x + 4 \\ y = \tfrac{2}{3}x - 3 \end{cases}$$

46 The perimeter of the rectangle is the same as the perimeter of the square. The unknown side of the rectangle is 3 units more than the side of the square.

  a Write a system of equations.
  b Solve the system.
  c Find the area of each figure.

47 Solve for (x, y).

$$\begin{bmatrix} 3 & x \\ y & -5 \end{bmatrix} \begin{bmatrix} 2 \\ 6 \end{bmatrix} = \begin{bmatrix} 12 \\ x \end{bmatrix}$$

48 If a 7-sided polygon is equiangular, find the sum of the angles. Then find the exact measure of each angle.

Problem Set, *continued*

49 The change in population of Rattlesnake Gulch since 1980 is best approximated by the function $p(t) = 310(1.2)^t$, where t is the number of years after January 1980 and $p(t)$ is the population of the town after that number of years.

a Copy and complete the table.

t	0	1	2	3	4	5	6
$p(t)$	310						

b Graph $p(t) = 310(1.2)^t$, using the horizontal axis as time and the vertical axis as population.

c Refer to the graph to find out when the population in Rattlesnake Gulch reached 1000.

d Refer to the graph to approximate the number of people in Rattlesnake Gulch in June of 1984.

50 Find the determinant of each matrix if the determinant of a 2-by-2 square matrix is defined as:

$$\text{Det} \begin{bmatrix} a & b \\ c & d \end{bmatrix} = ad - bc$$

a $\begin{bmatrix} 2 & 4 \\ 5 & 7 \end{bmatrix}$ **b** $\begin{bmatrix} -2 & -3 \\ 4 & 5 \end{bmatrix}$ **c** $\begin{bmatrix} 1 & 1 \\ 1 & 1 \end{bmatrix}$ **d** $\begin{bmatrix} 6 & 4 \\ 3 & 2 \end{bmatrix}$

51 Solve the system by graphing. (Hint: Use the following values of x to make a table for the first equation: $-3, -2, -1, -0.5, -0.2,$ $-0.1, 0.1, 0.2, 0.5, 1, 2, 3$.)

$$\begin{cases} f(x) = \dfrac{1}{2x} \\ g(x) = 2x \end{cases}$$

52 An arch has an equation of the form $h = ax^2 + b$ where h is the height of the arch above the ground and x is the horizontal distance in meters from the center of the arch. The letters a and b stand for constants. When $x = 0$, the height of the arch is 40 meters, and when $x = 300$, the height of the arch is 0 meters.

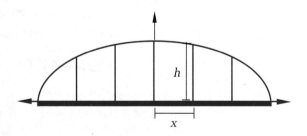

a Find the values of a and b.

b For what x value is the height of the arch 25 meters?

53 Fill in the elements of the matrix so that the matrix equation is equivalent to the system.

$$\begin{bmatrix} & \\ & \end{bmatrix} \begin{bmatrix} x \\ y \end{bmatrix} = \begin{bmatrix} 35 \\ 50 \end{bmatrix} \qquad \begin{cases} 3x + 2y = 35 \\ 2x + y = 20 \end{cases}$$

54 Determine which of the linear systems will not have a single ordered pair for a solution. Then find the determinant of the first matrix in each system. There is a relationship between the determinant of a system's matrix and the nature of the solutions. Can you guess this relationship?

a $\begin{bmatrix} 4 & 8 \\ 3 & 6 \end{bmatrix} \begin{bmatrix} x \\ y \end{bmatrix} = \begin{bmatrix} 2 \\ 4 \end{bmatrix}$
b $\begin{bmatrix} 1 & 5 \\ 2 & 7 \end{bmatrix} \begin{bmatrix} x \\ y \end{bmatrix} = \begin{bmatrix} -1 \\ 4 \end{bmatrix}$

c $\begin{bmatrix} -6 & -5 \\ -2 & 5 \end{bmatrix} \begin{bmatrix} x \\ y \end{bmatrix} = \begin{bmatrix} 4 \\ -5 \end{bmatrix}$
d $\begin{bmatrix} 1 & 3 \\ 2 & -1 \end{bmatrix} \begin{bmatrix} x \\ y \end{bmatrix} = \begin{bmatrix} 4 \\ -5 \end{bmatrix}$

THE LANGUAGE OF SPACE SCIENCE

Palmer Dyal puts math to work in moon research

"It's the language of the business" is how Dr. Palmer Dyal describes the value of mathematics to space science. Dr. Dyal is the assistant director of space research at the NASA Ames Research Center in Mountain View, California, where for more than two decades he has been making valuable contributions to space science. In 1972 Dr. Dyal was awarded NASA's Medal for Exceptional Scientific Achievement.

Dr. Dyal earned his Ph.D. in nuclear physics at the University of Illinois. Before joining NASA, he worked for the Atomic Energy Commission. He has an extensive background in mathematics. "There's nothing in math that we can't use in our research," he says. Algebra? "We use it all the time." Systems of equations? "Absolutely." To illustrate, he describes an experiment he conducted to find the iron content of the moon.

Two magnetometers left on the moon by *Apollo 15* and *Apollo 16* astronauts measured the magnetic fields at two sites (M_{15T} and M_{16T}). A magnetometer in the *Explorer 35* satellite orbiting the moon measured the strength of Earth's magnetic field (M_e). The magnetic field measured by each surface magnetometer represented the sum of the moon's field at the site (M_{15T} or M_{16T}) and Earth's field.

$$M_{15T} = M_e f(i) + M_{15}$$
$$M_{16T} = M_e f(i) + M_{16}$$

Because Earth's field is affected by the moon's iron content, it is multiplied by $f(i)$, a function of the iron, in each equation.

The two equations have six unknowns. The experiment was conducted twice more, resulting in two additional equations each time. With six equations in six variables at his disposal, Dr. Dyal was able to solve for $f(i)$. Now he could calculate the moon's iron content, $9.0 \pm 4.7\%$. It was this work that led to his NASA medal.

Earth's Field   Field at the Moon

Explorer 35   Apollo LSM

LSM = Lunar Surface Module

MORE ABOUT LINEAR SYSTEMS

Objectives

After studying this section, you will be able to
- Recognize special cases of linear systems
- Solve single-variable problems on the plane

Part One: Introduction

Special Cases of Linear Systems

You need to be able to recognize and solve certain types of linear systems. In this section, you will learn about two special cases of linear systems. You will also learn how to set up a system to solve some single-variable equations.

Do all linear systems intersect in exactly one point? Consider the next two examples.

Example   *Solve the system by graphing.*

$$\begin{cases} y = \frac{1}{3}x - 2 \\ x - 3y = 6 \end{cases}$$

The first equation is in slope-intercept form. Let's rewrite the second equation in the same form before graphing.

First equation

$y = \frac{1}{3}x - 2$

Second equation

$x - 3y = 6$

$-3y = -x + 6$

$y = \frac{1}{3}x - 2$

The equations of the system are identical! Any point that solves the first equation will also solve the second equation. All points on the line are therefore solutions of the system. We call such a system ***dependent.*** This system is also consistent. Recall that consistent systems have one or more solutions. In set notation, the solution can be written as

$$\left\{(x, y) \mid y = \tfrac{1}{3}x - 2\right\}$$

It is read as "The solution is the set of all ordered pairs (x, y) such that they satisfy $y = \frac{1}{3}x - 2$."

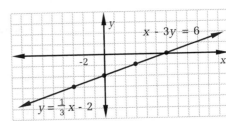

Example   *Solve the system by graphing.*

$$\begin{cases} f(x) = 2x - 5 \\ g(x) = 2x + 3 \end{cases}$$

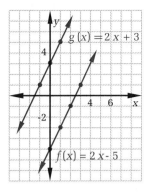

Both functions are in the slope-intercept form, so we use that information to quickly draw the graphs.

The graphs are parallel! There is no point of intersection. We call such a system of equations ***inconsistent.*** Inconsistent systems have no solutions.

Can we predict that a system is inconsistent before graphing? In this example the slope, 2, is the same for each function, but the y-intercepts, -5 and 3, are different. These are the characteristics of a linear system with no solution.

Solving Single-Variable Problems on the Plane

For equations in a single variable that are complex, looking at the equation as a system is a helpful technique. To introduce the procedure, let's look at a simple equation.

Example   *Solve* $2x + 3 = x - 1$ *for x.*

We write the equation as a system by setting each side of the equation equal to y.

$$\begin{cases} y = 2x + 3 \\ y = x - 1 \end{cases}$$

Graphing this system, we find the solution is $(-4, -5)$. Since our original problem has only one variable, x, we need only the x-coordinate, -4. Let's check -4 in the original equation.

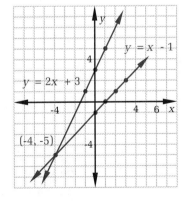

$$2x + 3 = x - 1$$
$$2(-4) + 3 = -4 - 1$$
$$-8 + 3 = -5$$
$$-5 = -5$$

If $x = -4$ the sides are equal, so the answer checks. Therefore, the solution is -4.

This system is consistent and ***independent.*** In an independent system, not every ordered pair that satisfies one equation will satisfy the other.

Example

Solve $|x + 2| = -|x| + 10$ for x.

We can rewrite the equation as a system.

$$\begin{cases} y = |x + 2| \\ y = -|x| + 10 \end{cases}$$

We make a table for each of these equations and graph the system, using the data from the tables.

$y = |x + 2|$

x	-4	-3	-2	-1	0
y	2	1	0	1	2

$y = -|x| + 10$

x	-2	-1	0	1	2
y	8	9	10	9	8

Possible solutions are $(x, y) = (-6, 4)$ and $(x, y) = (4, 6)$, so $x = -6$ or $x = 4$. Check -6 and 4 in the original problem.

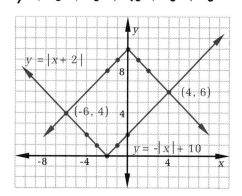

Part Two: Sample Problems

Problem 1

Solve $(x - 4)^2 = -\frac{3}{2}x + 16$ for x.

Solution

We can rewrite the equation as a system. $\begin{cases} f(x) = (x - 4)^2 \\ g(x) = -\frac{3}{2}x + 16 \end{cases}$

To graph $f(x)$, we make a table.

x	1	2	3	4	5	6	7
$f(x)$	9	4	1	0	1	4	9

We can graph $g(x)$ using the slope-intercept method.

The x-coordinates of the points of intersection are $x = 6.5$ and $x = 0$. Check these results.

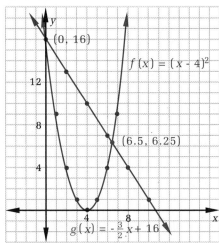

Problem 2   Solve the linear system. $\begin{bmatrix} -1 & 2 \\ 3 & -6 \end{bmatrix}\begin{bmatrix} x \\ y \end{bmatrix} = \begin{bmatrix} 8 \\ -18 \end{bmatrix}$

Solution   First, we multiply the matrices on the left. $\begin{bmatrix} -1x + 2y \\ 3x - 6y \end{bmatrix} = \begin{bmatrix} 8 \\ -18 \end{bmatrix}$

From the equality of matrices, we write a system of equations.

$$\begin{cases} -1x + 2y = 8 \\ 3x - 6y = -18 \end{cases}$$

Equation	x-intercept	y-intercept
$-1x + 2y = 8$	-8	4
$3x - 6y = -18$	-6	3

The graphs are parallel. There is no solution to the system.

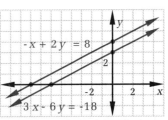

Summary

We can classify linear systems of two equations in two variables as consistent or inconsistent.

- A *consistent* system of equations is a system that has one or more solutions.

- A consistent system can be *independent.* The equations of an independent system have exactly one solution. The graphs of the equations are two straight lines that intersect in a single point.

- A consistent system can be *dependent.* The equations of a dependent system have every point on the line as solutions. The graphs of the equations are the same line.

- An *inconsistent* system has no solutions. The graphs of the equations are two parallel lines.

Part Three: Exercises and Problems

Warm-up Exercises

1 Convert the system to nonmatrix form.

$$\begin{bmatrix} 3 & 4 \\ -1 & 2 \end{bmatrix}\begin{bmatrix} x \\ y \end{bmatrix} = \begin{bmatrix} 7 \\ -3 \end{bmatrix}$$

2 Convert the linear system to matrix form.

$$\begin{cases} 4x - y = 7 \\ 3x = 2y - 5 \end{cases}$$

In problems 3 and 4, use matrix multiplication to determine whether (3, 5) is a solution to the system.

3 $\begin{bmatrix} 2 & -1 \\ 4 & -3 \end{bmatrix} \begin{bmatrix} x \\ y \end{bmatrix} = \begin{bmatrix} 1 \\ -3 \end{bmatrix}$ **4** $\begin{cases} 4x + 2y = 22 \\ 3x - y = -4 \end{cases}$

In problems 5–7, classify each system as consistent or inconsistent. If the system is consistent, classify it as dependent or independent.

5 $\begin{cases} y = 3x + 4 \\ y = 3x + 6 \end{cases}$ **6** $\begin{cases} 3x + 2y = 8 \\ y = \frac{-3}{2}x + 4 \end{cases}$ **7** $\begin{cases} y = x + 7 \\ 4x - y = -4 \end{cases}$

Problem Set

8 Find the point of intersection of the lines $x = 3$ and $y = -2x + 7$.

In problems 9–11, solve each system.

9 $\begin{cases} y = 2x - 3 \\ y - 2x = 7 \end{cases}$ **10** $\begin{cases} y = 0.5x - 4 \\ 2y = x - 8 \end{cases}$ **11** $\begin{cases} y = x + 4 \\ y = \frac{1}{2}x - 3 \end{cases}$

12 Determine whether $(-3, 4)$ is a solution to the system.

$\begin{bmatrix} 2 & 5 \\ 3 & -4 \end{bmatrix} \begin{bmatrix} x \\ y \end{bmatrix} = \begin{bmatrix} 14 \\ -25 \end{bmatrix}$

13 A small plane travels 120 miles per hour with no wind. On a particular day, there is a tail wind blowing at 20 miles per hour. How long will a 200-mile trip take?

14 If two of the lines L_1, L_2, L_3, and L_4 are randomly selected, what is the probability that the system they form will be inconsistent?

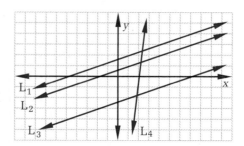

15 Solve the equation $x + 3 = |2x|$ by graphing $f(x) = x + 3$ and $g(x) = |2x|$.

16 Refer to the diagram.

a Write a system for the diagram.
b Solve the system from part **a**.
c Check your solution on the diagram.

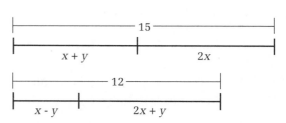

17 Fourteen liters of a mixture were spilled during a laboratory experiment. Sixty percent of the mixture was chemical A. Determine how many liters of chemical A were lost due to spillage?

In problems 18–21, classify each system as consistent or inconsistent. If the system is consistent, determine whether it is dependent or independent.

18 $\begin{cases} x + y = 3 \\ \quad\ x = 3 - y \end{cases}$

19 $\begin{cases} -4x + 2y = -3 \\ \ \ 4x - 2y = 5 \end{cases}$

20 $\begin{cases} y = \frac{4}{3}x + 3 \\ 3 = 4x - 3y \end{cases}$

21 $\begin{cases} y = -3 \\ x = 6 \end{cases}$

22 Refer to the nonlinear system.
$$\begin{cases} f(x) = |x - 2| + 5 \\ f(x) = (x + 3)^2 - 10 \end{cases}$$

a Consider the first function.
  i Determine the vertex of the graph.
  ii Make a table.
  iii Draw the graph.
b Consider the second function.
  i Determine the vertex of the graph.
  ii Make a table.
  iii Draw the graph on the same set of axes as the graph in part **a**.
c Find the points of intersection.
d Write the solution set to $|x - 2| + 5 = (x + 3)^2 - 10$.

In problems 23 and 24, write each linear system in matrix form.

23 $\begin{cases} -4x + 2y = -3 \\ \ \ 6x - 2y = \ \ 12 \end{cases}$

24 $\begin{cases} x = 7 \\ y = -2 \end{cases}$

In problems 25 and 26, write the system of equations that corresponds to each matrix equation.

25 $\begin{bmatrix} 3 & 7 \\ 5 & -4 \end{bmatrix} \begin{bmatrix} x \\ y \end{bmatrix} = \begin{bmatrix} 17 \\ 33 \end{bmatrix}$

26 $\begin{bmatrix} 1 & 4 \\ -6 & 0 \end{bmatrix} \begin{bmatrix} x \\ y \end{bmatrix} = \begin{bmatrix} 7 \\ 11 \end{bmatrix}$

27 If $y = 3x + 4$ and $x = 5$, evaluate $3x + 4y$.

28 If $y = 2x - 1$ and $3x + y = 39$, solve for y.

29 If $|x| = 8$ and $y = 8x - 12$, find all values for y.

30 James has 8 United States coins totaling exactly $0.80.

a How many different combinations of coins could he have?
b What is the probability that a given combination of coins has at least one quarter?

In problems 31–34, solve each equation.

31 $x^2 = 4x + 21$

32 $x = 3x - 12$

33 $5x + 9 = 3(3 + 2x) - x$

34 $x(x + 2) = 4(4 + 2)$

Problem Set, *continued*

35 Janice mixed 12 pounds of cashews that cost $6.50 per pound with 16 pounds of peanuts that cost $3.25 per pound. She intended to sell the mixture at her store.

  a How many pounds of the mixture did she have?
  b How much money was the mixture worth?
  c How much should she charge per pound of nut mixture in order to make a profit?

In problems 36 and 37, solve each system.

36 $\begin{bmatrix} 1 & -2 \\ 1 & -1 \end{bmatrix}\begin{bmatrix} x \\ y \end{bmatrix} = \begin{bmatrix} 6 \\ 5 \end{bmatrix}$
          37 $\begin{bmatrix} 5 & 8 \\ -1 & 0 \end{bmatrix}\begin{bmatrix} x \\ y \end{bmatrix} = \begin{bmatrix} 12 \\ -4 \end{bmatrix}$

38 A pharmacist mixed 40 milliliters of a 30% iodine solution with 60 milliliters of a 40% iodine solution. What percentage of the mixture is iodine?

39 The perimeter of rectangle A is 16, and the perimeter of rectangle B is 8.

  a Write a system for the data presented in the figure.
  b Solve the system.

40 Solve $|x + 2| = -|x| + 6$ for x.

41 Indigo Industries pays its workers $6.80 per hour and $1\frac{1}{2}$ times this amount for overtime. Use matrix multiplication to determine the wages for the four workers listed below.

Name	Number of Hours at Regular Pay	Number of Hours at Overtime Pay
Sam Smith	32	0
Toni Gonzales	40	12
Susan Chang	40	6
Trevor Jones	40	11

42 Let $f(x) = x^2 + 5x - 6$. Find all inputs for x that result in a zero output.

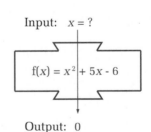

Input: x = ?

$f(x) = x^2 + 5x - 6$

Output: 0

43 Find the values of k so that the line through (4, k) and (2, k + 1) has a slope greater than 4.

44 If $y = 3x + 1$, $z = 3x - 4$, and $3x + y + z = 99$, find the numerical value of x.

45 The areas of the square and rectangle shown are equal.

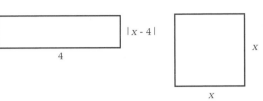

   a Write an equation reflecting the above statement.

   b Solve this equation by using a system and graphing.

46 The equation for the height h of an airplane in feet after t minutes is $h = 5000 - 150t$. The equation for the height h of another airplane in feet after t minutes is $h = 1000 + 50t$. When will the two airplanes be at the same height above the ground? What is their common height at that time?

In problems 47 and 48, find the determinant of the first matrix of the system and solve the system.

47 $\begin{bmatrix} 3 & 2 \\ \frac{3}{2} & 1 \end{bmatrix} \begin{bmatrix} x \\ y \end{bmatrix} = \begin{bmatrix} 4 \\ 2 \end{bmatrix}$

48 $\begin{bmatrix} 2 & -1 \\ 2 & -3 \end{bmatrix} \begin{bmatrix} x \\ y \end{bmatrix} = \begin{bmatrix} 0 \\ 8 \end{bmatrix}$

49 Solve for x by guessing. For part **a** give one answer. For part **b** give two answers.

   a $\sqrt{x + 5} = \sqrt{3x - 3}$

   b $\sqrt{2x - 1} = \sqrt{x - 1} + 1$

50 In the following system, let $\frac{1}{a}$ be replaced by x, and let $\frac{1}{b}$ be replaced by y.

$$\begin{cases} \dfrac{1}{a} + \dfrac{1}{b} = \dfrac{5}{6} \\ \dfrac{1}{a} - \dfrac{1}{b} = \dfrac{1}{6} \end{cases}$$

   a Solve for (x, y) by graphing.

   b Solve for (a, b).

51 Solve $x^2 = (x - 2)^2$ for x.

52 Solve the system.

$$\begin{cases} y = (x - 2)^2 + 3 \\ y = |x - 2| + 3 \end{cases}$$

53 Let max {a, b, c} be the maximum value of a, b, or c. Graph $f(x) = \max \{x^2, 3, x + 5\}$.

54 Solve the system. (Hint: Make a table of values for each equation, using x values from -5 to 5.)

$$\begin{cases} x^2 + y^2 = 25 \\ |x| + |y| = 5 \end{cases}$$

SOLVING SYSTEMS OF EQUATIONS USING THE SUBSTITUTION METHOD

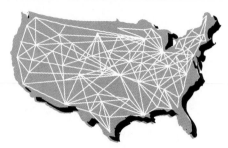

Objectives

After studying this section, you will be able to
- Use substitution to solve linear systems
- Use substitution to solve nonlinear systems

Part One: Introduction

Often systems of equations can be solved efficiently and more exactly without graphing. In this section, we develop a method that will enable you to solve systems of equations algebraically.

Example   *Solve the system.*

$$\begin{cases} y = \frac{1}{2}x + 5 \\ 2x + y = 7 \end{cases}$$

We can solve the system by graphing.

$y = \frac{1}{2}x + 5$

The slope is $\frac{1}{2}$. The y-intercept is 5.

$2x + y = 7$

The x-intercept is $3\frac{1}{2}$. The y-intercept is 7.

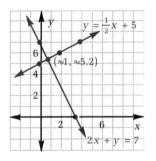

But these graphs do not intersect at a point with integer coordinates, making the intersection difficult to read. It appears to be approximately (1, 5.2). Let's check to be sure.

Check

$y = \frac{1}{2}x + 5$			$2x + y = 7$	
Left Side	**Right Side**		**Left Side**	**Right Side**
5.2	$= 0.5(1) + 5$		$2(1) + 5.2$	$= 7$
	$= 5.5$		$= 7.2$	

In both equations, the left and right sides are not equal, so the answer does not check.

The answer is close, but close is often not good enough. If you have access to a graphing calculator, use it to solve the system. Then check the answer. You will see that we still need a procedure that will give a more precise answer.

Linear System Substitutions

Let's look again at our example.

Example   *Solve the system.*

$$\begin{cases} y = \frac{1}{2}x + 5 \\ 2x + y = 7 \end{cases}$$

The first equation is solved for y, so we can substitute $\frac{1}{2}x + 5$ for the value of y in the second equation. Then $2x + y = 7$ becomes $2x + \frac{1}{2}x + 5 = 7$.

Now this equation has only one variable, and we can solve for x.

$$\mathbf{2.5x + 5 = 7}$$
$$\mathbf{2.5x = 2}$$
$$\mathbf{x = 0.8}$$

To find the y-coordinate, substitute 0.8 for the value of x in the first equation.

$y = \frac{1}{2}x + 5$ becomes $y = \frac{1}{2}(0.8) + 5$
$$= 0.4 + 5$$
$$= 5.4$$

By this method, (x, y) = (0.8, 5.4). Let's check again.

Check

$y = \frac{1}{2}x + 5$ $2x + y = 7$

Left Side   Right Side   **Left Side   Right Side**
5.4 $= 0.5(0.8) + 5$ $2(0.8) + 5.4$ $= 7$
               $= 5.4$ $= 7$

In both equations, the left and right sides are equal, so the answer checks. The exact solution is (x, y) = (0.8, 5.4).

The method we used to solve for the point of intersection is called the ***substitution method.*** Our strategy was to obtain an equation with only one variable. Keep this important idea in mind as you work through the chapter.

Nonlinear System Substitutions

The substitution method can also be used to solve problems in which one or both of the equations are nonlinear.

Example   *Solve the system.*

$$\begin{cases} y = |x - 2| \\ y = 2x \end{cases}$$

Let's substitute 2x for the value of y in the first equation.

$y = |x - 2|$ becomes $2x = |x - 2|$
$$-2x = x - 2 \text{ or } 2x = x - 2$$
$$-3x = -2 \quad \text{ or } \quad x = -2$$
$$x = \frac{2}{3} \quad \text{ or } \quad x = -2$$

Each value for x has a corresponding value of y. So we substitute each x into the second equation.

$x = \frac{2}{3}$ $x = -2$

$y = 2x$ becomes $y = 2\left(\frac{2}{3}\right)$ $y = 2x$ becomes $y = 2(-2)$

$\qquad\qquad = \frac{4}{3}$ $\qquad\qquad = -4$

It appears that there are two solutions, $(x, y) = \left(\frac{2}{3}, \frac{4}{3}\right)$ and $(x, y) = (-2, -4)$.

We must check both possible solutions.

Check

$y = |x - 2|$ $y = 2x$

Left Side	**Right Side**	**Left Side**	**Right Side**
$\frac{4}{3}$	$= \left|\frac{2}{3} - 2\right|$	$\frac{4}{3}$	$= 2\left(\frac{2}{3}\right)$
	$= \left|-\frac{4}{3}\right|$		$= \frac{4}{3}$
	$= \frac{4}{3}$		

For this solution, the sides are equal, so the answer checks.

Check

Left Side	**Right Side**	**Left Side**	**Right Side**
-4	$= |-2 - 2|$	-4	$= 2(-2)$
	$= |-4|$		$= -4$
	$= 4$		

For this solution, the sides are not equal, so the answer does not check. The only correct solution to the system is $\left(\frac{2}{3}, \frac{4}{3}\right)$.

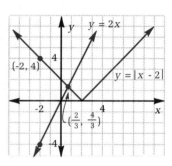

With nonlinear systems, apparent solutions will not always be actual solutions. Recall that an apparent solution that does not actually check in the equations is called an extraneous solution. The only way to determine whether a solution is extraneous is to check all possible solutions in the original equations. The graph of the two equations has only one point of intersection.

Part Two: Sample Problems

Problem 1   *Solve the system.*

$$\begin{cases} 2x + 3y = 7 \\ x + 4y = 9 \end{cases}$$

Solution   First we solve one of the equations for x or y so we can substitute into the other equation. It seems quicker to solve the second equation for x.

$x + 4y = 9$

$\qquad x = -4y + 9$

Remember our strategy. We can substitute the value $-4y + 9$ for x into the other equation of the system in order to obtain an equation with a single variable.

The use of parentheses reminds us to use the Distributive Property of Multiplication over Addition.

$$2x + 3y = 7$$
$$2(-4y + 9) + 3y = 7$$
$$-8y + 18 + 3y = 7$$
$$-5y + 18 = 7$$
$$-5y = -11$$
$$y = 2.2$$

Now we substitute 2.2 for y in the second equation.

$$x = -4y + 9 \quad \text{becomes} \quad x = -4(2.2) + 9$$
$$= 0.2$$

The solution to the system is $(x, y) = (0.2, 2.2)$. Be sure to check.

Problem 2   *Allan is 20 years older than his cousin Chip. In 3 years, Allan will be twice as old as Chip. How old are Allan and Chip now?*

Solution   Let a = Allan's present age
and c = Chip's present age.

Then $a + 3$ = Allan's age in 3 years
and $c + 3$ = Chip's age in 3 years.

Now, Allan is 20 years older than Chip. In 3 years, Allan will be twice as old as Chip.

$$a = 20 + c$$
$$a + 3 = 2(c + 3)$$

The first equation $a = 20 + c$ is solved for a, so substitute the value $20 + c$ for a in the second equation.

$$a + 3 = 2(c + 3)$$
$$20 + c + 3 = 2(c + 3)$$
$$23 + c = 2c + 6$$
$$23 = c + 6$$
$$17 = c$$

Now substitute 17 for c in the first equation.

$$a = 20 + c$$
$$= 20 + 17$$
$$= 37$$

Allan is 37 years old, and Chip is 17 years old.

Part Three: Exercises and Problems

Warm-up Exercises

In problems 1–3, solve each system by the substitution method.

1 $\begin{cases} 2x + 3y = 28 \\ \quad\quad x = 2y - 7 \end{cases}$ **2** $\begin{cases} 3x + y = 12 \\ 2x + 3y = 1 \end{cases}$ **3** $\begin{cases} y = 3x \\ y = x^2 - 4 \end{cases}$

4 Liz Bean is 18 years older than Bob Bean. In 5 years, Liz will be twice as old as Bob. How old is each now?

5 At a recent basketball game, a total of 21,270 tickets were sold. Some were $2 tickets, and some were $4 tickets. The total revenue was $69,380. How many of each type of ticket were sold?

6 The area of the rectangle is y. The perimeter of the rectangle is y + 4. Solve for x and y.

Problem Set

In problems 7–12, solve each system by the substitution method and check.

7 $\begin{cases} y = 2x \\ 3x + y = 10 \end{cases}$

8 $\begin{cases} 3x - 2y = 2 \\ y = 2x + 6 \end{cases}$

9 $\begin{cases} y = x^2 \\ y = 4 \end{cases}$

10 $\begin{cases} y = |x| \\ y = 2 \end{cases}$

11 $\begin{cases} y = x^2 \\ y = 2x + 8 \end{cases}$

12 $\begin{cases} x = -2y + 5 \\ 3x - 4y = -15 \end{cases}$

13 Celia works in a candy shop. A customer wants 3 pounds of candy priced at $4 per pound mixed with $2\frac{1}{2}$ pounds of candy priced at $3.50 per pound. Find the value of the mixture. How much is the mixture worth per pound?

In problems 14 and 15, solve each system by the substitution method. Approximate answers to the nearest tenth.

14 $\begin{cases} x - 6y = 12 \\ 3x - 7y = -5 \end{cases}$

15 $\begin{cases} 4x - y = 15 \\ -2x + 3y = 12 \end{cases}$

16 Jim Shu runs at a rate of 14.4 miles per hour, while Hi Topps runs in the same direction at a rate of 12.8 miles per hour. If they have been running for 20 minutes, how far has each run? If they begin to run at the same time and from the same place, how far apart will they be after 10 minutes?

In problems 17–20, solve each system by the substitution method and check.

17 $\begin{cases} y = |x + 3| \\ y = 4 \end{cases}$

18 $\begin{cases} y = |x| + 5 \\ y = 3 \end{cases}$

19 $\begin{cases} y = 2x \\ y = |x| \end{cases}$

20 $\begin{cases} y = |2x - 3| \\ y = 10 \end{cases}$

In problems 21–24, solve each system by the substitution method.

21 $\begin{cases} 3x + 4y = 6 \\ \quad\quad y = 2x + 7 \end{cases}$

22 $\begin{cases} \quad x = 4y - 5 \\ x + 2y = 19 \end{cases}$

23 $\begin{cases} y = 36 \\ y = (x - 2)^2 \end{cases}$

 24 $\begin{cases} y = x^2 + 5 \\ y = 3x + 10 \end{cases}$

 25 Which is greater, the area of a square with an 8-inch side or the area of a circle with a 5-inch radius?

26 Tina's dad is twenty years older than Tina. Eight years ago, half of Tina's age was 7. How old is Tina's dad?

In problems 27 and 28, evaluate for $a = 3$.

27 $a^5 \cdot a^7$

28 a^{12}

29 The Roll'n'Rocks group gives 3 performances at Municipal Stadium. They are paid $15 for each ticket sold plus a flat fee of $100,000 for each performance. If the stadium seats up to 65,000 people per performance, then what is the range of money they can earn for the 3 performances?

30 A small plane travels 120 miles per hour with no wind. One day it encountered a head wind of 15 miles per hour. How long did a 210-mile trip take that day?

31 Use matrix multiplication to check whether $(-2, 4)$ solves the system.

$$\begin{cases} \quad 8x + 5y = \quad 4 \\ -3x + 2y = 14 \end{cases}$$

32 Use the formula $r_t = \dfrac{r_1 r_2}{r_1 + r_2}$ to find r_t if $r_1 = 60$ ohms and $r_2 = 40$ ohms.

In problems 33–36, solve each system by the substitution method.

33 $\begin{cases} \quad x + 2y = 6 \\ 3x - 5y = -26 \end{cases}$

34 $\begin{cases} 4x - y = 12 \\ 5x + 3y = \quad 1 \end{cases}$

35 $\begin{cases} 2x - 5y = 16 \\ \quad 6x + y = -16 \end{cases}$

36 $\begin{cases} 11(r_p - r_w) = 1155 \\ \quad 7(r_p + r_w) = 1155 \end{cases}$

37 The perimeter of square B equals y, the length of a side of rectangle A. The perimeter of the rectangle is 44. Find x and y.

Problem Set, *continued*

38 Solve the system by the substitution method and check.

$$\begin{cases} 3x + y = 7 \\ \quad\ y = |x| \end{cases}$$

39 If the 10-pound weight in the figure is increased by 30%, then the 10-foot length must be decreased by what percentage to keep the lever in balance?

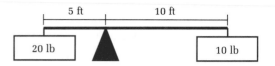

40 Solve the system.

$$\begin{bmatrix} 1 & 0 \\ -2 & 3 \end{bmatrix}\begin{bmatrix} x \\ y \end{bmatrix} = \begin{bmatrix} 6 \\ -5 \end{bmatrix}$$

41 Determine A if the rectangle can be represented by the product

$$\begin{bmatrix} -1 & 0 \\ -1 & 2 \\ 2 & 2 \\ 2 & 0 \end{bmatrix} \cdot A$$

   a 2

   b $\begin{bmatrix} 0 & 1 \\ -1 & 0 \end{bmatrix}$

   c $\frac{3}{2}$

   d $\begin{bmatrix} 3 & -2 \\ 2 & 3 \end{bmatrix}$

In problems 42 and 43, solve each system by using substitution. Approximate answers to the nearest thousandth.

42 $\begin{cases} 4x + 5y = -5 \\ -x + 7y = 13 \end{cases}$ **43** $\begin{cases} 2x + 3y = -7 \\ 5x - \ y = 12 \end{cases}$

44 Reggie has a car that can use gasohol. His car uses a mix of 1 gallon of alcohol to every 4 gallons of gasoline. He pays $1.10 per gallon for gasoline and only $0.40 per gallon for alcohol. His tank holds 20 gallons.

   a How much money does Reggie save per tankful?
   b His car gets 24 miles per gallon on gasohol, but it gets 28 miles per gallon on plain gasoline. Does he really save as much as his cost per gallon suggests?
   c How much does Reggie really save or lose on one tank of gasohol?

45 A balloon at 500 feet begins rising at the rate of 2 feet per second. A blimp at 10,000 feet begins descending at the rate of 4 feet per second. When will the balloon and the blimp be at the same height? What is this equal height?

46 For her inboard motor, Elaine must mix gasoline and oil in the ratio of 12 to 1.

   a If Elaine has 4 quarts of oil, how much gasoline should she buy?

   b If she has only 15 gallons of gasoline, how much oil should she buy?

   c If she buys 15 gallons of gasoline, how much of the mixture will she be putting in the tank?

47 The perimeter of the triangle and the perimeter of the rectangle are equal.

   a Let P = perimeter. Write an equation for P in each figure.

   b Write a single equation and solve it for x.

   c Find the numerical value of P.

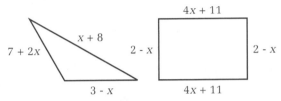

48 A room is 18 feet long, 15 feet wide, and 8 feet high. Find the total area of walls and ceiling after 80 square feet is subtracted to allow for doorways and windows. How many quarts of paint will be needed to paint the room if 1 quart covers 100 square feet?

49 The area of the trapezoid is 100 square centimeters.

   a Find x.

   b For what values of y will the two bases be the same?

   c For what values of y will the top base be longer than the bottom base?

   d Find the range of possible values for y.

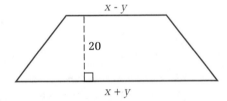

50 Solve the system by the substitution method and check.

$$\begin{cases} \dfrac{1}{x} = 7 - \dfrac{1}{y} \\[2mm] \dfrac{3}{x} - \dfrac{1}{y} = 1 \end{cases}$$

51 D, E, and F are midpoints of $\overline{BC}$, $\overline{AC}$, and $\overline{AB}$, respectively.

   a Find the coordinates of D, E, and F.

   b Using the point-slope form of the equation of a line, write the equations of $\overline{AD}$, $\overline{BE}$, and $\overline{CF}$.

   c For each pair of equations in part **b**, find the point of intersection.

   d What is wrong with the diagram?

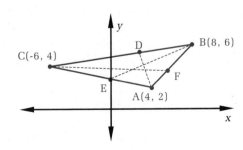

Problem Set, *continued*

52 Determine values of a and b that make the system dependent.
$$\begin{cases} y = (2a + b)x + a - b \\ y = (a - b)x + 14 \end{cases}$$

53 There are four points $(1, 9)$, $(9, 10)$, $(5, 1)$, and $(-3, 0)$ in the coordinate plane. A line is drawn through 2 of the points. A second line drawn through the remaining 2 points crosses the first line. Find the coordinates of the point of intersection.

54 The perimeter of the square equals y, the length of a side of the right triangle. Find the sides of the triangle to the nearest thousandth.

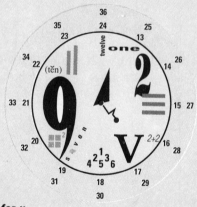

55 The variable f represents a function of x so that $f(x + y) = f(x) + f(y)$ for every pair of real numbers x and y. Find the numerical value of $f(0)$.

MATHEMATICAL EXCURSION

CLOCK ARITHMETIC
An everyday use of math

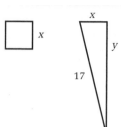

The equation $8 + 5 = 1$ seems clearly to be wrong. It is, in fact, correct in a system of mathematics called *clock arithmetic*. The system is used every day to tell time. What time is it 8 hours after 5 o'clock? The answer is 1 o'clock.

Clock arithmetic is an example of a *modular system*. The clock system of numbers consists of only the whole numbers from 1 to 12. Other numbers greater than 12 can be converted to clock numbers by adding or subtracting multiples of 12.

As an example: $37 = 37 - 3(12) = 1$. Thus, if it is 12 o'clock now, 37 hours from now a clock will look exactly the same as it will look only 1 hour from now. In modular arithmetic, we write this equation as $37 \equiv 1(\text{Mod } 12)$. This means that 37 is equivalent to 1 in the modular 12 system.

Solve for x.

1. $18 \equiv x(\text{mod } 12)$
2. $29 \equiv x(\text{mod } 12)$
3. $77 \equiv x(\text{mod } 12)$
4. $199 \equiv x(\text{mod } 12)$
5. $-15 \equiv x(\text{mod } 12)$
6. $100 \equiv x(\text{mod } 12)$
7. $37 \equiv x(\text{mod } 9)$
8. $55 \equiv x(\text{mod } 2)$

Find all solutions in the modular 12 system. Some of these problems may have more than one solution.

9. $3x \equiv 3(\text{mod } 12)$
10. $5x \equiv 4(\text{mod } 12)$
11. $2x \equiv 11(\text{mod } 12)$
12. $7x \equiv 1(\text{mod } 12)$
13. $4x \equiv 8(\text{mod } 12)$
14. $9x + 5 \equiv 2(\text{mod } 12)$

THE MULTIPLICATION-ADDITION ALGORITHM AND THE COMPUTER

Objectives

After studying this section, you will be able to
- Use the Multiplication-Addition Algorithm to solve linear systems of equations
- Use a BASIC program to solve systems of equations

Part One: Introduction

Linear Systems and the Multiplication-Addition Algorithm

Solving systems of equations can have a number of practical applications. A computer solves numerous systems to generate the image produced by a CAT scan. You will find out how this is done later in this section.

The substitution method can always be used to solve systems of equations, but it is not always the quickest, most straightforward way. Let's look at another method of solving systems of equations.

Example   *Solve the system.*

$$\begin{cases} 4x - y = 16 \\ 3x + y = 12 \end{cases}$$

Remember that our strategy for solving systems is to obtain one equation with one variable. Let's see what happens if we add the two equations.

The y terms are opposites and add to zero. We have one equation with one variable.

$$\begin{array}{r} 4x - y = 16 \\ \underline{3x + y = 12} \\ 7x + 0y = 28 \\ x = 4 \end{array}$$

We can substitute 4 for x in either original equation. Let's substitute in the first equation.

$$4x - y = 16 \quad \text{becomes} \quad \begin{aligned} 4(4) - y &= 16 \\ 16 - y &= 16 \\ -y &= 0 \\ y &= 0 \end{aligned}$$

The solution to the system is $(x, y) = (4, 0)$. Check to be sure.

Example

Write a system of equations represented by the diagram. Use the Multiplication-Addition Algorithm to solve the system.

The system of equations represented by the diagram is

$$\begin{cases} 3x = 2 + 2y \\ 2x + y = 13 \end{cases}$$

In this problem, we need to rewrite the first equation so that both variables are on the same side of the equation.

$$\begin{cases} 3x = 2 + 2y \\ 2x + y = 13 \end{cases} \quad \text{becomes} \quad \begin{cases} 3x - 2y = 2 \\ 2x + y = 13 \end{cases}$$

Notice that adding the equations would not result in one equation with one variable, because neither the x-terms nor the y-terms are opposites. The y-terms will be opposites if each side of the second equation is multiplied by 2. What property permits this?

First, we multiply $2x + y = 13$ by 2.

$$\begin{cases} 3x - 2y = 2 \\ 2(2x + y = 13) \end{cases} \quad \text{becomes} \quad \begin{cases} 3x - 2y = 2 \\ 4x + 2y = 26 \end{cases}$$

Now we can add the two equations.

$$
\begin{aligned}
3x - 2y &= 2 \\
4x + 2y &= 26 \\
\hline
7x + 0y &= 28 \\
7x &= 28 \\
x &= 4
\end{aligned}
$$

Then we substitute 4 for x in either original equation to find *y*.

$$
3x - 2y = 2 \quad \text{becomes} \quad
\begin{aligned}
3(4) - 2y &= 2 \\
12 - 2y &= 2 \\
-2y &= -10 \\
y &= 5
\end{aligned}
$$

The solution to the system is $(x, y) = (4, 5)$. We check the solution in each equation of the system.

Check

$3x = 2 + 2y$

Left Side	Right Side
$3(4)$	$= 2 + 2(5)$
$= 12$	$= 2 + 10$
	$= 12$

$2x + y = 13$

Left Side	Right Side
$2(4) + 5$	$= 13$
$= 8 + 5$	
$= 13$	

If $(x, y) = (4, 5)$ in both equations, the sides are equal, so the answer checks.

Example   *Solve the matrix equation.*

$$\begin{bmatrix} 7 & 3 \\ -4 & 5 \end{bmatrix} \begin{bmatrix} x \\ y \end{bmatrix} = \begin{bmatrix} 33 \\ -39 \end{bmatrix}$$

The matrix equation above is equivalent to this system.

$$\begin{cases} 7x + 3y = 33 \\ -4x + 5y = -39 \end{cases}$$

Adding the two equations will not give us one equation with one variable, and multiplying either equation by any integer will not make the x-terms or the y-terms opposites. If we multiply the first equation by 4 and the second equation by 7, then the x-terms will be opposites.

First, we multiply $7x + 3y = 33$ by 4 and $-4x + 5y = -39$ by 7.

$$\begin{cases} 4(7x + 3y = 33) \\ 7(-4x + 5y = -39) \end{cases} \quad \text{becomes} \quad \begin{cases} 28x + 12y = 132 \\ -28x + 35y = -273 \end{cases}$$

The x-terms are now opposites, so we can add.

$$\begin{array}{r} 28x + 12y = 132 \\ -28x + 35y = -273 \\ \hline 0x + 47y = -141 \\ 47y = -141 \\ y = -3 \end{array}$$

Now we substitute -3 for y in either original equation. Let's use the second equation this time.

$$-4x + 5y = -39 \quad \text{becomes} \quad \begin{array}{r} -4x + 5(-3) = -39 \\ -4x - 15 = -39 \\ -4x = -24 \\ x = 6 \end{array}$$

The solution to the system is $(x, y) = (6, -3)$. Be sure to check.

Let's summarize the steps used in these examples.

The Multiplication-Addition Algorithm

1. *Arrange* the equations with like terms in columns.

2. If necessary, make either the x-terms or the y-terms opposites by *multiplying* each term of one or both equations by an appropriate number.

3. *Add* the resulting equations and *solve* for the remaining variable.

4. *Substitute* the value obtained in step 3 in either original equation and *solve* for the other variable.

5. *Check* your answer.

These steps are referred to as the ***Multiplication-Addition Algorithm.***

Equations and BASIC

If all problems in linear systems were limited to two variables, a computer method would be unnecessary. However, in business, engineering, and medicine, it is common to solve systems with 10 to 10,000—or even more—variables.

An example of a computer application to linear systems is Computerized Axial Tomography, or CAT scanning, in medicine. In this process, X-rays are sent through a section of the body and mathematically reconstructed into a three-dimensional image. The scanner moves around the body, one degree at a time, until it has moved 180 degrees. For every degree, 160 separate pieces of information are generated, for a total of 160(180), or 28,800, equations in 28,800 variables. The computer solves this system and produces the three-dimensional image that helps doctors diagnose and evaluate medical problems.

To solve a system, a computer uses a method, called the **Row Reduction Algorithm,** that applies exactly the same process to every problem. The following program in BASIC uses the Row Reduction Algorithm to solve any consistent, independent system in two variables. It assumes that the system is arranged in the form

$$a_1x + a_2y = a_3$$
$$b_1x + b_2y = b_3$$

where a_1, a_2, a_3, b_1, b_2, and b_3 are constants and $a_1 \neq 0$.

```
10   REM     Row Reduction Algorithm for Two-Variable
             Linear Systems
20   REM     ----------------- Step 1 -----------------
30   REM     --- Data Entry for a(1),a(2),a(3),b(1), ---
                  b(2),b(3)
40   PRINT   "Enter a(1), a(2), and a(3) separated by
             commas.";
50   INPUT   a(1),a(2),a(3)
60   PRINT   "Enter b(1), b(2), and b(3) separated by
             commas.";
70   INPUT   b(1),b(2),b(3)
80   IF      a(1) =0 THEN 280
90   REM     ----------------- Step 2 -----------------
100  REM     ----- Multiply first equation by the -----
                  reciprocal of a(1)
110  LET     a(2) = a(2) / a(1)
120  LET     a(3) = a(3) / a(1)
130  REM     ----------------- Step 3 -----------------
140  REM     ---- Multiply first equation by [-b(1)] ----
150  REM     ---- Add results to the second equation ----
160  LET     b(2) = b(2) + a(2) * [-b(1)]
170  LET     b(3) = b(3) + a(3) * [-b(1)]
```

```
180 REM      --------------- Step 4 ----------------
190 REM      -------------- Solve for y -------------
200 IF       b(2) = 0 THEN 280
210 LET      y = b(3) / b(2)
220 REM      --------------- Step 5 ----------------
230 REM      -- Substitute for y in first equation and --
             solve for x
240 LET      x = a(3) - a(2) * y
250 PRINT    "The solution is (" ; x ; "," ; y ; ")"
260 GOTO     300
270 REM      --------- Error Message Section ---------
280 PRINT    "Your system doesn't have a solution that"
290 PRINT    "is a single ordered pair, or a(1) is zero."
300 END
```

If you have access to a computer, enter this program and try it on the previous example. You may need to enter the variables with capital letters.

Part Two: Sample Problems

Problem 1

A small airplane travels a distance of 1155 miles from Fargo, North Dakota, to Cheyenne, Wyoming, and returns. Because of a head wind, the trip to Cheyenne takes 11 hours. The return trip with the same wind as a tail wind takes 7 hours. Find the speed of the plane with no wind and find the speed of the wind.

Solution

Let r_p = the rate of the plane with no wind and
r_w = the rate of the wind.

Then $r_p - r_w$ = rate of the plane going to Cheyenne, and
$r_p + r_w$ = rate of the plane returning to Fargo.

Since distance = rate · time $(d = rt)$, we have

$$\begin{cases} 1155 = (r_p - r_w) \, 11 \text{ going to Cheyenne} \\ 1155 = (r_p + r_w) \, 7 \text{ returning to Fargo} \end{cases}$$

First, we divide the first equation by 11 and the second by 7.

$$\begin{cases} 1155 = (r_p - r_w)11 \\ 1155 = (r_p + r_w)7 \end{cases} \quad \text{becomes} \quad \begin{cases} 105 = r_p - r_w \\ 165 = r_p + r_w \end{cases}$$

Now we add.

$$270 = 2r_p$$
$$135 = r_p$$

By substituting 135 for r_p in $r_p + r_w = 165$, we see that $r_w = 30$.

The rate of the plane with no wind is 135 miles per hour, and the rate of the wind is 30 miles per hour.

Problem 2   *Paul has several nickels and quarters in his bank. He has a total of 41 coins, and their total value is $5.45. How many coins of each type does Paul have in his bank?*

Solution   Let q = the number of quarters in Paul's bank.
Let n = the number of nickels in Paul's bank.

There are 41 coins in all. $q + n = 41$
The amount of money is $5.45. $25q + 5n = 545$

Let's use our computer program to find the solution.

```
Enter a(1), a(2), a(3) separated by commas.    1,1,41
Enter b(1), b(2), b(3) separated by commas.    25,5,545
(17, 24)
■
```

The boldface entries are our responses to the computer prompts, and the answer is (17, 24). This means that Paul has 17 quarters and 24 nickels.

Part Three: Exercises and Problems

Warm-up Exercises

In problems 1–3, by what number would you multiply each equation of each system to eliminate the *x*-terms? The *y*-terms? Use the Multiplication-Addition Algorithm to solve each system.

1 $\begin{cases} x + 2y = 4 \\ 3x - y = 7 \end{cases}$

2 $\begin{cases} 4x - 5y = 9 \\ 3x + 2y = -4 \end{cases}$

3 $\begin{cases} 3y = 4x - 9 \\ 2x - 3y = 4 \end{cases}$

4 William wants to make 40 pounds of a mixture of nuts by combining peanuts selling for $2.40 per pound with cashews selling for $3.20 per pound. If the mixture is to sell for $2.70 per pound, how many pounds of each type of nut should William use in the mixture?

5 The perimeter of the triangle is 22. The perimeter of the rectangle is 34.

  a Write a system of equations to represent the diagrams.
  b Solve for x and y.

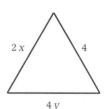

In problems 6 and 7, use the computer program to solve each system.

6 $\begin{cases} 7.25x + 3.25y = 25.75 \\ 3x + 2y = 12 \end{cases}$

7 $\begin{bmatrix} 4.2 & 7.9 \\ -6.8 & 2.4 \end{bmatrix} \begin{bmatrix} x \\ y \end{bmatrix} = \begin{bmatrix} 12.6 \\ -1.4 \end{bmatrix}$

Problem Set

In problems 8–10, use the Multiplication-Addition Algorithm to solve each system.

8 $\begin{cases} 3x + 4y = 10 \\ x - 5y = -3 \end{cases}$
9 $\begin{cases} 4x + 2y = -10 \\ 3x + y = -6 \end{cases}$
10 $\begin{cases} 3x + 4y = 18 \\ 4x - 5y = -7 \end{cases}$

11 If 12 pencils cost $1, determine how much 30 pencils cost.

12 Nina is six years older than her brother Ramon. Three years ago, she was twice as old as Ramon. How old is each now?

In problems 13 and 14, use the Multiplication-Addition Algorithm to solve each system.

13 $\begin{cases} 3x + 2y = 7 \\ 9x + 6y = 21 \end{cases}$
14 $\begin{cases} -x + 4y = 12 \\ 2x - 8y = 6 \end{cases}$

15 Paula has $8 in nickels and dimes. All together she has 100 coins. How many of each type of coin does she have?

In problems 16 and 17, use the Multiplication-Addition Algorithm to solve each system.

16 $\begin{bmatrix} 3 & 1 \\ 7 & -2 \end{bmatrix}\begin{bmatrix} x \\ y \end{bmatrix} = \begin{bmatrix} 8 \\ -3 \end{bmatrix}$
17 $\begin{bmatrix} 3 & -4 \\ 4 & 2 \end{bmatrix}\begin{bmatrix} x \\ y \end{bmatrix} = \begin{bmatrix} -17 \\ 4 \end{bmatrix}$

18 Jorge has 5 times as many quarters as dimes. He has 180 coins in his collection. How many coins of each type does he have?

19 Refer to the diagram.

    a Find the coordinates of the midpoints A and B.

    b Find the slopes of $\overline{AB}$ and $\overline{CD}$.

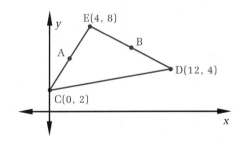

20 Superman takes off after Lex Luthor, who is 125 miles away. Flying to capture Lex takes Superman 210 seconds with a tail wind. The return trip takes 215 seconds because the same wind is now a head wind. How fast would Superman fly with no wind? What is the speed of the wind?

In problems 21–23, solve by any method.

21 $\begin{cases} x + 5y = 10 \\ y = x + 8 \end{cases}$
22 $\begin{bmatrix} 1 & 4 \\ -2 & -3 \end{bmatrix}\begin{bmatrix} x \\ y \end{bmatrix} = \begin{bmatrix} 7 \\ 6 \end{bmatrix}$
23 $\begin{cases} 3x - 5y = 23 \\ 2x + 4y = -14 \end{cases}$

Problem Set, *continued*

24 Mrs. Lincoln mixes two brands of coffee to make 15 pounds of a mixture selling for $4.78 per pound. She will mix Monson Coffee, selling at $3.90 per pound, with Valley Brothers Coffee, selling at $5.75 per pound. How many pounds of each type of coffee should she use in the mixture?

In problems 25–27, use the computer program to solve each simple system. Check your answers manually.

25 $\begin{cases} x + y = 10 \\ x - y = 6 \end{cases}$

26 $\begin{cases} 2x + 3y = 11 \\ 3x + 4y = 16 \end{cases}$

27 $\begin{cases} x + 0y = 5 \\ 0x + y = 3 \end{cases}$

28 $\angle CFD$ and $\angle DFE$ are complementary, and $\angle AFE$ is a straight angle. Find x and y.

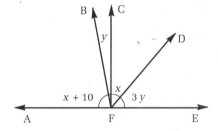

29 A real-estate agent, Stella Jones, told a potential client that the average income in Glenmont was over $38,000. Later, when the city council was proposing a higher tax rate, Stella claimed that the average income was only $20,000. Technically, Stella is not lying in either case. Explain.

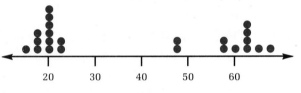

Income (x $1000) in Glenmont

In problems 30–32, solve each system.

30 $\begin{cases} 2x + 5y = 31 \\ x - 2y = -7 \end{cases}$

31 $\begin{cases} x - y = 7 \\ 2x + y = -1 \end{cases}$

32 $\begin{cases} 5x - 2y = -2 \\ 2x - 3y = 8 \end{cases}$

33 Approximate the solution to the nearest whole number.
$\begin{cases} 2001x + 1984y = 20{,}772 \\ 1492x + 1776y = 16{,}993.6 \end{cases}$

34 The BASIC program in this section works only on systems that have a single ordered pair for a solution. Predict what the BASIC program will do if you enter a linear system that has many solutions or no solutions.

In problems 35 and 36, use the computer program to solve each system.

35 $\begin{cases} 0.7x - 0.2y = 1.2 \\ 3.5x + 2.7y = -4.8 \end{cases}$

36 $\begin{cases} 0.6x - 3.2y - 4.5 = 0 \\ -0.3x + 2.9y + 4.8 = 0 \end{cases}$

37 Try the BASIC program on this system, which has no solution. Explain why the problem has no solution.

$$\begin{cases} 3x - y = 12 \\ 3x - y = 14 \end{cases}$$

38 Solve the system. Approximate your answer to the nearest hundredth.

$$\begin{cases} \sqrt{2}x + \sqrt{5}y = \sqrt{8} \\ \sqrt{6}x + \sqrt{15}y = \sqrt{21} \end{cases}$$

39 Try the BASIC program on this system, which has many ordered-pair solutions. Explain why the problem has many solutions.

$$\begin{cases} 3x - y = 12 \\ 6x - 2y = 24 \end{cases}$$

40 Refer to the diagram.

a Express a in terms of x.
b Express b in terms of x.
c Find a and b if $b = 4a$.

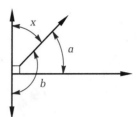

In problems 41–43, solve each system.

41 $\begin{cases} 2y = 10 \\ x + 2y = 11 \end{cases}$ **42** $\begin{cases} 5x - 2y - 11 = 0 \\ 2x + 3y + 7 = 0 \end{cases}$ **43** $\begin{cases} x - 3y = 7 \\ -2x + 6y = -14 \end{cases}$

44 The perimeter of the triangle is 26 centimeters. If the equal sides were doubled, the perimeter would be increased by 16. What are the dimensions of the triangle?

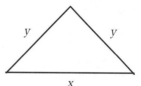

45 Ernie is able to deliver 1000 advertising pamphlets from the local store in 6 hours, while it takes Ernestine 8 hours to deliver 1000 pamphlets. They work together for 2 hours. After the 2 hours, what fraction of the 1000 pamphlets has each delivered? What fraction have they delivered together?

46 Solve for (x, y).

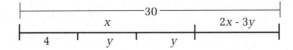

47 A chemist needs 1 liter of 7% hydrochloric-acid solution (7% acid and 93% water). She has 2% hydrochloric-acid solution and 9% hydrochloric-acid solution already mixed in 1-liter containers on her laboratory shelf. How much of each solution should she mix with the other to obtain the 1 liter of 7% solution?

Problem Set, *continued*

48 A printing press prints 3000 copies per hour. If the press begins at 8:00 A.M. and finishes its run at 1:30 P.M. the same day despite a $1\frac{1}{2}$-hour breakdown, how many copies are printed?

49 A box kite is rising from the ground at 4 feet per second, and a dragon kite is descending from 700 feet at 2 feet per second. When will the kites be at the same height above the ground? What is that equal height?

50 Solve by the substitution method.
$$\begin{cases} x^2 + y^2 = 25 \\ \quad\quad y = 3x \end{cases}$$

51 Vanna needs to wash her dresses. The local laundromat charges $1.10 to wash each load and $0.65 to dry each load. Vanna needs to wash and dry 20 loads of dresses. She has just the right amount of money, all in nickels and quarters. If Vanna has a total of 300 coins, how many coins of each type does she have?

In problems 52 and 53, solve each system.

52 $\begin{cases} 4(x - 3) + 12(y - 6) = 14 \\ -7(x + 2) + 6(y - 3) = -5 \end{cases}$

53 $\begin{cases} 4x + 12y = 14 \\ -7x + 6y = -5 \end{cases}$

54 Zap Electric charges $75 for a service call plus $45 for installing each electrical outlet. Short Circuit Electric charges $48 for the service call and $49.50 for each outlet installed. If the bill for a given service call would have been the same from each company, how many outlets were installed?

55 A sink has two faucets, A and B, and a drain, C. The drain empties the sink at the same rate that faucet A fills the sink. If drain C is closed and both faucets are turned on, the sink is filled in 5 minutes. If faucet A is turned off, faucet B is on, and drain C is open, the sink is filled in 20 minutes. Find the rates at which faucets A and B fill the sink.

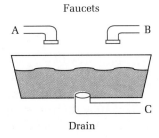

56 The sum of the reciprocals of two numbers is 14. The difference of their reciprocals is 4. Find the numbers.

In problems 57–59, solve by any method.

57 $\begin{bmatrix} 1 & 1 \\ 1 & -1 \end{bmatrix} \begin{bmatrix} x^2 \\ y^2 \end{bmatrix} = \begin{bmatrix} 25 \\ 25 \end{bmatrix}$

58 $\begin{cases} f(x) = x^2 + 2 \\ g(x) = -x + 8 \end{cases}$

59 $\begin{cases} y = |x| \\ y = |x + 3| \end{cases}$

8.5 | SOLVING SYSTEMS OF INEQUALITIES BY GRAPHING

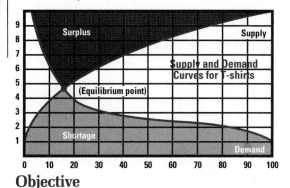

Objective

After studying this section, you will be able to
- Solve systems of inequalities by graphing

Part One: Introduction

Graphing Systems of Inequality

A *system of inequalities* is a system involving two or more inequalities instead of equations. Systems of inequalities often have an infinite number of solutions. Therefore graphing, rather than using an algebraic approach, is a better method for solving a system of inequalities. We use a graph to represent the solutions to a system of inequalities because it is impossible to list all of them. The set of points shared by the graphs of the inequalities represents the solution set of the system.

Example *Solve the system.*

$$\begin{cases} y < 3x + 1 \\ -x - 2y \le 6 \end{cases}$$

We need to graph each inequality. The boundary equation of the first inequality is $y = 3x + 1$, which is in slope-intercept form. This equation's graph will therefore be a line with a slope of 3 and a y-intercept of 1. We draw the graph using a dashed line, since the inequality symbol means "less than."

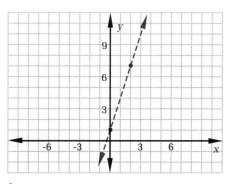

The graph divides the coordinate plane into two regions. By choosing a point from each region and testing its coordinates in the inequality, we can determine which region is the graph of the inequality. We usually choose points with integral coordinates, known as *lattice points.* Let's try $(-5, 0)$ and $(5, 0)$.

Point $(-5, 0)$
Left Side   Right Side

Left Side	Right Side
y	$< 3x + 1$
0	$< 3(-5) + 1$
0	< -14

Point $(5, 0)$
Left Side   Right Side

Left Side	Right Side
y	$< 3x + 1$
0	$< 3(5) + 1$
0	< 16

Only the point $(5, 0)$ solves the inequality, so we shade the entire region that contains that point. Pick several points in the shaded region and check that they satisfy the inequality.

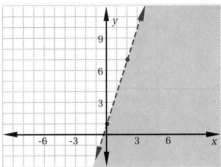

To graph the second inequality, we first solve for y, obtaining $y \geq \frac{-1}{2}x - 3$. We graph this inequality as we did the first one. This time the boundary line should be solid since the inequality is "equal to or less than." Again we choose test points to determine where to shade. Let's choose $(-6, -3)$ and $(6, 0)$.

Point $(-6, -3)$
Left Side   Right Side

Left Side	Right Side
y	$\geq \frac{-1}{2}x - 3$
-3	$\geq \frac{-1}{2}(-6) - 3$
-3	≥ 0

Point $(6, 0)$
Left Side   Right Side

Left Side	Right Side
y	$\geq \frac{-1}{2}x - 3$
0	$\geq \frac{-1}{2}(6) - 3$
0	≥ -6

Since $(6, 0)$ is the point that satisfies the inequality, we shade the region containing that point, to the right of and above the line.

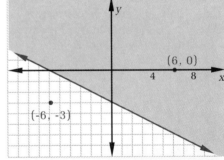

To solve the system, we graph the two inequalities on the same coordinate plane. It is helpful to use a different color for each graph.

The solution set of the system is the intersection of the two graphs. Pick a point from this region and check to see that it satisfies both inequalities in the system.

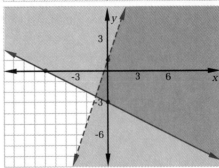

Part Two: Sample Problem

Problem   *Solve the system.* $\begin{cases} |x| < 4 \\ y \geq (x - 2)^2 \end{cases}$

Solution   For $|x| < 4$, the boundary equation is $|x| = 4$. This means that $x = 4$ or $x = -4$. The boundaries of the graph will be two dashed vertical lines separating the coordinate plane into three regions. We might suspect that the region to be shaded is the one between the lines. Let's test a point in each region—$(-8, 0)$, $(0, 0)$, and $(8, 0)$.

Point $(-8, 0)$
Left Side		Right Side
$|x|$	$<$	4
$|-8|$	$<$	4
8	$<$	4

Point $(0, 0)$
Left Side		Right Side
$|x|$	$<$	4
$|0|$	$<$	4
0	$<$	4

Point $(8, 0)$
Left Side		Right Side
$|x|$	$<$	4
$|8|$	$<$	4
8	$<$	4

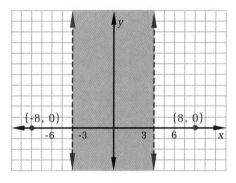

Since $0 < 4$, we shade between the two dashed vertical lines.

For $y \geq (x - 2)^2$ the boundary equation is $y = (x - 2)^2$. Its graph should be a parabola. Let's make a table of values.

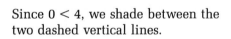

x	−1	0	1	2	3	4	5
y	9	4	1	0	1	4	9

Now we can draw the graph. The curve is solid and separates the coordinate plane into regions inside the parabola and outside the parabola. Let's test one point from each region.

Inside Point $(2, 4)$
Left Side	Right Side
y	$\geq (x - 2)^2$
4	$\geq (2 - 2)^2$
4	$\geq \quad 0$

Outside Point $(0, 0)$
Left Side	Right Side
y	$\geq (x - 2)^2$
0	$\geq (0 - 2)^2$
0	$\geq \quad 4$

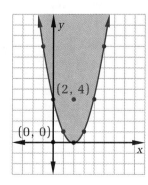

First, we shade the region inside the parabola.

The solutions to the system are the points of intersection of the two graphs. Check a point in this region to be sure.

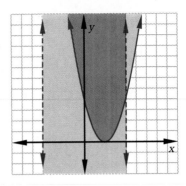

Part Three: Exercises and Problems

Warm-up Exercises

1 Look at the graph of the system.

$$\begin{cases} y = -\frac{3}{2}x + 6 \\ y = \frac{1}{2}x + 1 \end{cases}$$

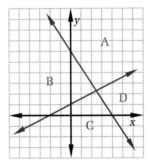

a Which regions satisfy
$y \le \frac{-3}{2}x + 6$?

b Which regions satisfy
$y \ge \frac{1}{2}x + 1$?

c Which region satisfies both inequalities?

2 Determine which of the points $(1, 1)$, $(5, 0)$, $(2, -3)$, and $(0, 0)$ satisfy the system.

$$\begin{cases} x + y < 6 \\ 2x - y \ge 4 \end{cases}$$

In problems 3 and 4, solve each system of inequalities by graphing.

3 $\begin{cases} y > \frac{1}{2}x + 3 \\ y \le -\frac{2}{3}x + 1 \end{cases}$
  4 $\begin{cases} y > |x + 4| \\ y \le \frac{1}{2}x + 1 \end{cases}$

Problem Set

5 Determine which of the points $(0, 0)$, $(12, 0)$, $(12, 12)$, $(0, 12)$, $(0, 6)$, $(-12, 0)$, $(0, -12)$, and $(5, 5)$ satisfy the system.

$$\begin{cases} x + y > 10 \\ \phantom{x + {}} y < 2x + 1 \end{cases}$$

6 It took Jack 20 minutes to drive 17 miles. How many miles could Jack cover in 90 minutes at the same average speed?

7 Determine whether $(5, -4)$ is a solution to the system.

$$\begin{cases} y < |x| \\ y \ge -x \end{cases}$$

8 Evaluate $(x + 2)^6$ if $x = 3$.

In problems 9–11, solve each system of inequalities by graphing.

9 $\begin{cases} x < 3 \\ y > 4 \end{cases}$ **10** $\begin{cases} x - 4y > 8 \\ 2x + y < 7 \end{cases}$ **11** $\begin{cases} y \le \frac{3}{4}x + 5 \\ 2x + 3y \le 12 \end{cases}$

12 Find the probability that a point selected at random from $\{(5, 1), (1, 5), (-1, 5), (-5, 1), (-5, -1), (-1, -5), (1, -5), (5, -1)\}$ lies in the solution set of the following system.
$\begin{cases} y \ge x \\ y < 5x \end{cases}$

13 The Acme Pencil Company uses a formula to predict the daily profit (in cents) to be expected from the production of n cases of pencils. The formula is $p(n) = 25n - 300$. How many cases must Acme produce per day to make a profit ($p > 0$)? If Acme produces between 100 and 200 cases of pencils per day, what is the expected range of daily profit?

14 Solve for x and y.
$$\left(\begin{bmatrix} 1 & 0 \\ 0 & 1 \end{bmatrix} + \begin{bmatrix} 1 & 2 \\ 0 & 3 \end{bmatrix} \right) \begin{bmatrix} x \\ y \end{bmatrix} = \begin{bmatrix} 12 \\ -16 \end{bmatrix}$$

15 Demosthenes, the Marble King, has 18 marbles in his pocket. At least 1 is a steelie; the rest are agates. He has at least 4 more agates than steelies. How many different combinations of agates and steelies might he have? What are these combinations?

In problems 16–19, solve each system by the most appropriate method.

16 $\begin{cases} 3x + 2y = 10 \\ 2x - 4y = 28 \end{cases}$ **17** $\begin{cases} 2x + 12 = 48 \\ x + 3y = 33 \end{cases}$

18 $\begin{cases} -2.5x + 8.9y = 4.9 \\ 2.7x - 3.4y = 12.2 \end{cases}$ **19** $\begin{cases} y^2 = 5y + 6 \\ x^2 + x = 0 \end{cases}$

20 Let $f(x) = x + 3$ and $g(x) = x^2 + 1$.
  a Copy and complete the table.
  b Determine which of the values of x in the table make $f(x)$ and $g(x)$ equal.

x	-2	-1	0	1	2
$f(x)$					
$g(x)$					

In problems 21 and 22, solve each system by graphing.

21 $\begin{cases} y = x + 1 \\ x - 4y < 8 \end{cases}$ **22** $\begin{cases} y < 5 \\ x = 4 \end{cases}$

23 Jane has only nickels and dimes in her pocket. She has at least $2 and at most $3. What are the possible combinations of coins that she can have?

Problem Set, *continued*

In problems 24 and 25, write a formula for each given rule.

24 The electrical power p in watts is equal to the current i multiplied by the voltage e.

25 The displacement d of a piston equals the area a times the stroke s.

26 The perimeter of rectangle A is at least 16, and the perimeter of rectangle B is at most 10.

    a Find the possible values of x and y.
    b State the assumptions you must make to solve this problem.

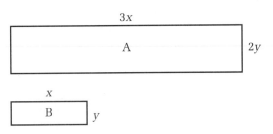

In problems 27–29, solve each system by graphing.

27 $\begin{cases} y < x \\ y \geq -x \end{cases}$
        28 $\begin{cases} y \leq \frac{1}{2}x + 3 \\ y < -2x - 1 \end{cases}$
        29 $\begin{cases} y > 3 \\ y \leq \frac{2}{3}x + 5 \end{cases}$

30 Solve for (x, y) if $y = |x - 2| - 3$ and $y = -4$.

In problems 31–34, solve each system by graphing.

31 $\begin{cases} 4x - 2y < 6 \\ y > \frac{3}{4}x - 3 \end{cases}$
        32 $\begin{cases} x < 3 \\ 3x + 2y \leq 8 \end{cases}$

33 $\begin{cases} y > 4 \\ y \leq \frac{2}{3}x + 5 \end{cases}$
        34 $\begin{cases} -2x + 4y \leq 12 \\ x - 3y > 7 \end{cases}$

35 Solve for n if $\dfrac{1}{n} = a + b$.

36 The sum of two whole numbers is at most 10. Determine the probability that one of the numbers is zero. (Hint: Let x = one whole number and y = the other whole number. Write an appropriate system of three inequalities. Then graph the system and look at the lattice points.)

In problems 37–39, solve each system by graphing.

37 $\begin{cases} y \leq \frac{3}{5}x + 2 \\ y \leq \frac{3}{5}x - 1 \end{cases}$
        38 $\begin{cases} x < 3 \\ x > 5 \end{cases}$
        39 $\begin{cases} y \geq -\frac{2}{3}x + 4 \\ y < -\frac{2}{3}x - 1 \end{cases}$

40 Penny deposits \$450 in a bank account paying $5\frac{1}{4}\%$ interest per year. How long must Penny leave her money in the bank in order to earn at least \$50 in interest?

In problems 41–44, evaluate each expression to the nearest thousandth if $a = 3$ and $b = 4$.

41 $\sqrt{a} + \sqrt{b}$ **42** $\sqrt{a + b}$

43 $\sqrt{ab}$ **44** $\sqrt{a}\,\sqrt{b}$

45 The sum of the digits of a two-digit number is 8. Find all possible products of the two digits.

46 Find all integer inputs x so that the output is less than 6.

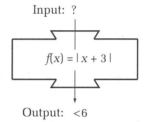

In problems 47–49, solve each literal equation for *t*.

47 $d = rt$ **48** $d = \frac{1}{2}gt^2$ **49** $a = p + prt$

50 Solve the system to three decimal places.
$$\begin{cases} \frac{1}{7}x + \frac{1}{11}y = \frac{1}{13} \\ \frac{1}{5}x + \frac{1}{25}y = \frac{1}{125} \end{cases}$$

51 Refer to the system.
$$\begin{cases} 2a + 5b = -4 \\ 3a - 5b = 19 \end{cases}$$

    a Solve the system.

    b Find (x, y) if $a = \dfrac{1}{x}$ and $b = \dfrac{1}{y}$.

52 The triangle inequality rule says that in any triangle the sum of two sides of the triangle must be greater than the third side of the triangle. If the perimeter of the triangle shown is at most 30, and if the sides must be positive integers, what are the possible values of x?

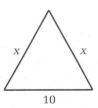

53 Graph the solutions to the system.
$$\begin{cases} y \le x \\ 3x + 2y \le 12 \\ x \ge -2y + 4 \end{cases}$$

In problems 54 and 55, solve each system by graphing.

54 $\begin{cases} |x| + |y| \le 5 \\ y \ge x \end{cases}$ **55** $\begin{cases} x^2 + y^2 \le 25 \\ y \ge x \end{cases}$

CHAPTER SUMMARY

CONCEPTS AND PROCEDURES

After studying this chapter, you should be able to
- Recognize a system of equations (8.1)
- Solve a system of equations by graphing (8.1)
- Solve word problems by graphing (8.1)
- Characterize a system as consistent and dependent, consistent and independent, or inconsistent (8.2)
- Solve single-variable problems on the plane (8.2)
- Solve systems of equations by substitution (8.3)
- Solve systems of equations by the Multiplication-Addition Algorithm (8.4)
- Solve systems of equations by using a BASIC program for row reduction (8.4)
- Solve systems of inequalities by graphing (8.5)

VOCABULARY

consistent system (8.1)
dependent system (8.2)
inconsistent system (8.2)
independent system (8.2)
lattice point (8.5)
linear system (8.1)
Multiplication-Addition Algorithm (8.4)

nonlinear system (8.1)
Row Reduction Algorithm (8.4)
simultaneous equations (8.1)
substitution method (8.3)
system of equations (8.1)
system of inequalities (8.5)

SYSTEMS AND THEIR SOLUTIONS

A consistent linear system has at least one solution. A consistent system is independent if it has only one solution (so that the graph of the system is two intersecting lines). A consistent system is dependent if it has an infinite number of solutions (so that the graph of the system is two coincident lines).

An inconsistent linear system has no solutions. The graph of the system is two parallel lines.

A system can be solved by a computer program, graphing, substitution, or the Multiplication-Addition Algorithm.

REVIEW PROBLEMS

1 Solve the system by graphing.

$$\begin{cases} y = -x + 8 \\ y = 3x + 4 \end{cases}$$

2 Write the system as a matrix equation.

$$\begin{cases} 2x + 3y = 11 \\ -5x + 8y = 7 \end{cases}$$

3 Tom is 5 years older than Jerry. In 2 years, Jerry will be three-fourths as old as Tom. Find their ages now.

In problems 4–6, classify each system as consistent or inconsistent. If the system is consistent, classify it as dependent or independent.

4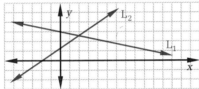

5 $\begin{cases} 2x - y = 6 \\ -6x + 3y = -18 \end{cases}$

6 $\begin{cases} y = 3x + 7 \\ y = 3x - 11 \end{cases}$

7 Norton has at most 6 more vests than Ralph, but he has at least 1 more than twice as many vests as Ralph. How many vests could Norton have?

In problems 8–13, solve each equation or system.

8 $\begin{cases} y = x - 7 \\ 2x = -1 + 7y \end{cases}$

9 $|x + 1| = 3x - 1$

10 $\begin{cases} \sqrt{7}x + \sqrt{3}y = 15 \\ \sqrt{11}x - \sqrt{5}y = 8 \end{cases}$

11 $\begin{cases} -4x + 5y = -36 \\ 5x - 3y = 32 \end{cases}$

12 $\begin{cases} 0.162x - 0.315y = 11.462 \\ 0.782x + 0.916y = 43.857 \end{cases}$

13 $\begin{cases} y \geq 2x - 3 \\ 2x - 5y < 10 \end{cases}$

14 Solve the matrix equation.

$$\begin{bmatrix} 2 & 3 \\ 6 & -5 \end{bmatrix} \begin{bmatrix} x \\ y \end{bmatrix} = \begin{bmatrix} 11 \\ -23 \end{bmatrix}$$

15 Buck invested $1992. He invested some at 9.34% and the rest at 8.57%. The interest earned at the end of the year was $181.59. How much did he invest at 9.34%?

Review Problems, *continued*

16 Refer to the diagram.

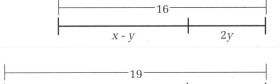

  a Write a system.
  b Solve the system in part **a.**
  c Check your solution on the diagram.

17 A fishing charter charges $350 for a full-day fishing trip and $225 for each half-day fishing trip. The crew work for 20 days out of the month. They need to make at least $7560 a month to make a fair profit. How many full-day trips and how many half-day trips should be scheduled in order to make the necessary profit?

18 Use the function $f(x) = |x - 2| + 4$.

  a Compute $f(-3)$.   **b** Compute $f(10)$.
  c Compute $f(12.5)$.   **d** Compute $f(-22)$.

In problems 19–22, solve by any method.

19 $\begin{cases} x^2 + y^2 = 18 \\ \quad\quad y = x \end{cases}$ **20** $\begin{cases} y = x^2 + 4 \\ y = x + 10 \end{cases}$

21 $\begin{bmatrix} 1 & 2 \\ 1 & 1 \end{bmatrix} \begin{bmatrix} \frac{1}{x} \\ \frac{1}{y} \end{bmatrix} = \begin{bmatrix} 4 \\ 3 \end{bmatrix}$ **22** $\begin{cases} \frac{1}{x} + \frac{1}{y} = -2 \\ \frac{1}{x} = \frac{1}{y} + 16 \end{cases}$

23 Find the value of k so that the system is inconsistent.

$$\begin{cases} y = (k + 3)x + 7 \\ y = 2kx + 13 \end{cases}$$

24 Solve $x^3 - 1 = 3x + 2$ for x.

25 Find x and y if the area of the shaded region is 66.

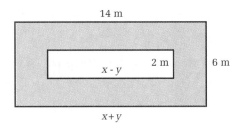

26 Mr. Ramirez, a plumber, charges $32 for a service call plus $45 per hour to do the work. His cousin, also a plumber, charges $40 for a service call plus $43 per hour to do the work. Let c be the cost billed by each cousin for the plumbing job they did together and let t be the number of hours they worked.

  a Write a system of equations involving c and t.
  b Solve the system.

27 Solve the system by graphing both functions on the coordinate plane. Copy and complete the table for each nonlinear function. Check your answer(s).

$$\begin{cases} f(x) = 2^x \\ g(x) = 0.5x + 3 \end{cases}$$

x	-6	-4	-2	0	2	4	6
$f(x)$							
$g(x)$							

28 The Big Fizz Soda Company has two bottling machines. One machine is 20% faster than the second. If the two machines together can fill 9000 soda bottles per hour, how many soda bottles per hour can each machine fill?

29 Refer to the diagram.

   a Find the volume of the cone.
   b Find the volume of the cylinder.
   c Find the ratio of the volume of the cylinder to the volume of the cone.

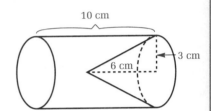

In problems 30 and 31, solve each system.

30 $\begin{cases} \frac{1}{\pi}x - \pi y = -7 \\ \pi x + \frac{1}{\pi}y = 7 \end{cases}$

31 $\begin{cases} \frac{1}{2.31}x - \frac{3}{3.71}y = 14.49 \\ \frac{3}{2.31}x + \frac{7}{3.71}y = 34.78 \end{cases}$

32 Henry and Jane go to Al's Cafe. They have a maximum of $10 to spend. Each sandwich costs $1.45, and each side order costs $0.89. If they want to purchase at least two of each item, what combinations of sandwiches and side orders can they buy?

33 The following data was gathered on a 10-gram mass of a radio-active substance.

Time (years)	0	5	10	15	20	25
Mass (grams)	10	8.7	7.6	6.6	5.7	5.0

   a Draw a smooth graph, using time in years for the horizontal axis and mass in grams for the vertical axis.
   b Assuming the pattern continues, determine approximately how much of the substance will remain after 50 years.
   c If 4.2 grams remain, determine approximately how many years have passed.

34 The triangle shown in the figure is spun around line L. Find the volume of the cone formed.

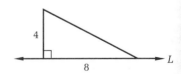

In problems 35–38, solve each system by graphing.

35 $\begin{cases} |y| > 5 \\ |x| < 4 \end{cases}$

36 $\begin{cases} y < |x| - 3 \\ y \le -x^2 \end{cases}$

37 $\begin{cases} y \ge (x - 3)^2 \\ |y - 2| < 2 \end{cases}$

38 $\begin{cases} y \le -|x| + 3 \\ y \ge (x + 2)^2 \end{cases}$

8

CHAPTER TEST

1 Solve by graphing.
$$\begin{cases} y = |x| - 3 \\ y = -\frac{1}{2}x - 1 \end{cases}$$

2 Tom is 4 years older than Jerry. In 2 years, Jerry will be half as old as Tom. Find their ages now.

In problems 3–6, solve the systems by any method.

3 $\begin{cases} x^2 + y^2 = 25 \\ \quad y = 3x \end{cases}$ **4** $\begin{cases} -2x + 4y \le 12 \\ \quad x - 3y > 7 \end{cases}$ **5** $\begin{cases} y \ge |x| - 3 \\ v \le -|x| + 5 \end{cases}$ **6** $\begin{cases} 4x + 2y = 10 \\ \quad y = -2x - 10 \end{cases}$

7 A box kite is rising from the ground at 5 feet per second, and a dragon kite is descending from 800 feet at 2 feet per second. When will the kites be at the same height? What is that height?

8 The perimeter of the rectangle is 225. The three angles in the triangle add to 180. Solve for (x, y).

9 Tickets to a recent high-school basketball game cost $1.50 for students and $2.50 for adults. Six hundred tickets were sold, and the total revenue was $1020. How many students and how many adults attended the game?

10 The perimeter of the triangle is y. The perimeter of the rectangle is 36. Solve for x and y.

In problems 11–12, classify each system as consistent or inconsistent. If the system is consistent, classify it as either dependent or independent.

11 $\begin{cases} x - 4y = -5 \\ y = \frac{1}{4}x + 3 \end{cases}$ **12** $\begin{bmatrix} 2 & 3 \\ -4 & -6 \end{bmatrix} \begin{bmatrix} x \\ y \end{bmatrix} = \begin{bmatrix} 7 \\ -14 \end{bmatrix}$

PUZZLES AND CHALLENGES

1 Ten billiard balls all look and feel the same, but one of them is heavier or lighter than the others. A balance scale is used to weigh the billiard balls. In exactly three weighings, using only billiard balls, how can you determine which ball has the different weight and whether it is heavier or lighter than the others?

2 Sharpe Buyer went to buy a new stereo priced at $491.30. "I'll wait until it goes on sale," Sharpe mused. Later, the price was $289. "I'll still wait," she decided. On two more occasions, the prices were $170 and $100, respectively. She finally bought the stereo when it had been reduced again, at a rate consistent with the earlier reduction. What did she pay?

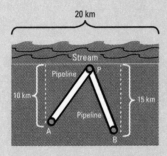

20 km

3 Two towns, A and B, are located as shown on the diagram. A water pumping station, P, is to be built to furnish both towns with water from the stream. Where should the pumping station be placed along the stream to minimize the length of the pipeline?

4 Sara's home address is made up of the five digits shown in the figure, but not necessarily in the order given. When the middle number of Sara's address is subtracted from the product of the number formed by the first two digits and the number formed by the last two digits, the result is a number with digits that are all the same. Also, the number formed by the first two digits is smaller than the number formed by the last two digits. What is Sara's home address?

5 A piece of cheese is in the shape of a cube. How can you cut the cheese into two pieces with a single cut so that the two new surfaces created by the cut are perfect hexagons?

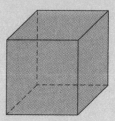

9 EXPONENTS AND RADICALS

We speak with many voices. Each word we utter is made up of a complex array of separate sounds. Our vocal cords begin the process with a simple frequency pulse. As this sound travels outward through our mouth and nasal cavities, many new frequencies are generated. What we hear is the composite effect created by these different sounds.

The instrument most often used to study the patterns of speech frequency is the sound spectrograph. The spectrograph translates speech into a picture. The top diagram shows the frequency analysis of the phrase *algebra is fun and exciting.* The vertical scale represents frequency in kilocycles per second (kHz). The diagram shows those frequency components that were present at each instant when the phrase was spoken. The louder components appear as the darker areas or lines of the diagram.

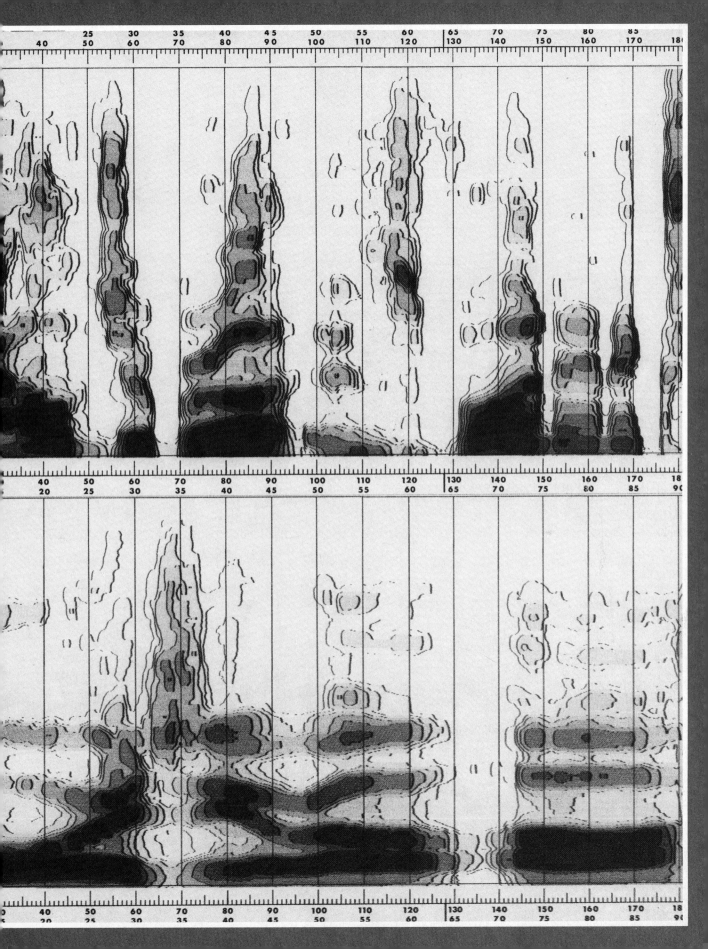

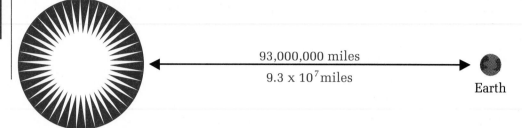

9.1 LARGE NUMBERS

Sun

93,000,000 miles
9.3×10^7 miles

Earth

Objectives

After studying this section, you will be able to
- Use scientific notation for large numbers
- Compute with scientific notation on a calculator
- Identify the coefficient, the base, and the exponent of a term

Part One: Introduction

Scientific Notation for Large Numbers

Just as abbreviations are used to save space and time when writing long words, scientific notation is used to write very large or very small numbers more efficiently.

There is an old Persian tale that as a reward for inventing the game of chess, the inventor asked the ruler of Persia for 1 grain of rice on the first square of the chessboard, 2 grains on the second square, 4 grains on the third square, 8 grains on the fourth square, and so on until all 64 squares of the chessboard were filled. Let's calculate the amount of rice on each square.

Square	Grains of Rice
1	1
2	2
3	$4 = 2^2$
4	$8 = 2^3$
5	$16 = 2^4$
10	$512 = 2^9$
20	$524,288 = 2^{19}$
21	$1,048,576 = 2^{20}$
30	$536,870,912 = 2^{29}$

The number of grains of rice increases very quickly. In fact, the only reasonable way to represent such large numbers is to use *exponents*. For example, on the sixty-fourth square there are 2^{63} grains of rice. If you evaluate this number with a calculator using the $\boxed{y^x}$ key, the display will read $\boxed{9.223372037 \quad 18}$. What does this display mean?

When answers become too large for the calculator's display, they are automatically converted to scientific notation. A number is written in *scientific notation* if it is written as the product of a number having one nonzero digit to the left of the decimal point and the number 10 raised to a power. In scientific notation, × is used to show multiplication.

$$9.223372037 \times 10^{18}$$
$$= 9.223372037 \times 1{,}000{,}000{,}000{,}000{,}000{,}000$$
$$= 9{,}223{,}372{,}037{,}000{,}000{,}000$$

You can multiply by 10^{18} quickly by moving the decimal point 18 places to the right. Scientific notation is a compact way of representing very large numbers.

Example   *In the 1980 U.S. census, the population was given as 226,545,805. Since it is not possible to be so precise, it is reasonable to say that there were about 227 million people in the United States. Express 227 million in scientific notation.*

$$227{,}000{,}000$$
$$= 2.27 \times 100{,}000{,}000$$
$$= 2.27 \times 10^{8}$$

Using A Calculator with Scientific Notation

All scientific calculators allow you to enter numbers in scientific notation. The keys most commonly used to enter the power of 10 are $\boxed{\text{EEX}}$, $\boxed{\text{EE}}$, or $\boxed{\text{EXP}}$. We will use the second form in this book.

Example   *Evaluate* $(-3.57 \times 10^{12})(6.02 \times 10^{23})$.

Using a calculator, we enter the following.

$$3.57 \quad \boxed{\pm} \quad \boxed{\text{EE}} \quad 12 \quad \boxed{\times} \quad 6.02 \quad \boxed{\text{EE}} \quad 23 \quad \boxed{=}$$

The display should be $\boxed{-2.14914 \quad 36}$
Remember, calculators do not display the 10. The display shows the exponent of the 10. The approximate answer is -2.15×10^{36}.

Coefficient, Base, and Exponent

In -2.15×10^{36}, the -2.15 is called the *coefficient,* the 10 is called the *base,* and the 36 is called the *exponent.*

Similarly, in the expression $5x^{7}$, the 5 is called the *coefficient,* the x is the *base,* and the 7 is the *exponent.*

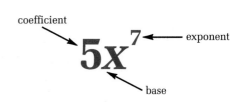

Example   *Write an expression with coefficient 4.57, base 10, and exponent 17.*

The answer is 4.57×10^{17}. (This is in scientific notation.)

Part Two: Sample Problems

Problem 1   Write each number in scientific notation.

   a 3,570,000   **b** −2.34   **c** −980.35

Solution   **a** 3.57×10^6 **b** -2.34×10^0 **c** -9.8035×10^2

Problem 2   Write each number without using powers of 10.

   a 2.103×10^7 **b** -7.3987019×10^4

Solution   **a** We move the decimal point 7 places to the right.
   21,030,000
   b We move the decimal point 4 places to the right.
   −73,987.019

Problem 3   Multiply or divide as indicated.

   a $(2^3)(2^4)$ **b** $\dfrac{-3.76 \times 10^{34}}{8.23 \times 10^{16}}$

Solution   **a** $(2^3)(2^4) = (2 \cdot 2 \cdot 2)(2 \cdot 2 \cdot 2 \cdot 2)$
   $= 2^7$
   $= 128$
   b Using a calculator, we enter the following.

   3.76 $\boxed{\pm}$ $\boxed{\text{EE}}$ 34 $\boxed{\div}$ 8.23 $\boxed{\text{EE}}$ 16 $\boxed{=}$

   The result displayed is $\boxed{\text{−4.568651276} \quad \text{17}}$. A reasonable approximation is -4.57×10^{17}.

Problem 4   Make a table for $y = 2^x$ and then graph the equation.

Solution   We use the $\boxed{y^x}$ key to find approximate values for y.

   For instance, to compute $2^{-1.5}$,

   2 $\boxed{x^y}$ 1.5 $\boxed{\pm}$ $\boxed{=}$ is entered.

   The display shows $\boxed{\text{0.35355339}}$,

   which rounds to 0.35.

   As we complete the rest of the table,
   we note that the values of 2^x are
   always positive, even when the exponent is negative.

   We refer to the table to plot the
   points on a graph and draw the
   curve for $y = 2^x$.

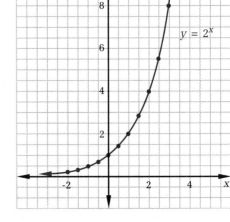

x	−2	−1.5	−1	−0.5	0	0.5	1	1.5	2	2.5	3
y	0.25	0.35	0.5	0.71	1	1.41	2	2.83	4	5.66	8

Problem 5   Homer J. Ernmore deposits $8500 in the bank, where the interest rate is 8% per year. How much money will he have at the end of 9 years?

Solution   We use the formula $a = p(1 + r)^t$, where
a is the amount of money at the end of t years;
p is the initial amount, or principal;
r is the rate of interest; and
t is the number of years.

$$a = 8500(1 + 0.08)^9$$
$$= 8500(1.08)^9$$
$$\approx 8500(1.9990046)$$
$$\approx 16{,}991.54$$

After 9 years, there will be approximately $16,991.54 in the bank.

Part Three: Exercises and Problems

Warm-up Exercises

1 In chemistry, a quantity called a mole contains approximately 6.02×10^{23} particles of a substance. This number is referred to as Avogadro's number. Express it without using a power of ten.

In problems 2–4, express each number in scientific notation.

2 32,400   **3** 62.5   **4** 1.7643

In problems 5–7, simplify each expression.

5 $2^5 \cdot 2^5$ **6** $2^5 + 2^5$ **7** $(2 + 2)^5$

8 Study the pattern and find a and b.

In problems 9–12, identify the coefficient, base, and exponent of each term.

9 a^4 **10** $3x$ **11** 3.25×10^{12} **12** $-7 \cdot 5^{3 \cdot 4}$

Problem Set

In problems 13–15, write each number in scientific notation.

13 345.98   **14** 186,000   **15** 18.9

In problems 16–18, write each number without using a power of ten.

16 2.73×10^6 **17** 8.975423×10^4 **18** 2.6×10^1

Problem Set, *continued*

In problems 19–22, solve for _n_.

19 $10^n = 1000$ **20** $4^n = 64$ **21** $2^n = 64$ **22** $5^n = 125$

In problems 23–30, simplify each expression.

23 $3^4 \cdot 3^5$ **24** 3^9 **25** $4^2 \cdot 4^8$ **26** 4^{10}

27 $3^2 + 4^2$ **28** $(3 + 4)^2$ **29** $7^5 + 6^5$ **30** $(7 + 6)^5$

In problems 31–33, determine whether each statement is True or False.

31 $(3 \cdot 5)^4 = 3^4 \cdot 5^4$ **32** $(3 + 5)^4 = 3^4 + 5^4$ **33** $2^4 \cdot 2^5 = 2^{20}$

34 Make a table of values and graph the equation $y = 3^x$.

35 Find the ratio of the volume of the smaller cube to the volume of the larger cube.

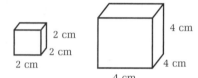

In problems 36–39, solve each equation and simplify each expression.

36 $3^5 n + 4^2 n - \sqrt{16n}$ **37** $(3.2 \times 10^4)y = 2.67 \times 10^5$

38 $1.5 - 8.2(4 - 11.6x) + 9.2^3 - 3.4x$ **39** $15.4 - 8.2^2 p = 3.5(p + 1.3)$

40 Arrange the following eight numbers in order from smallest to largest.

7.3×10^{15} 9.7×10^{14} 3.2×10^{16} 83.7×10^{14}

$9.\overline{6} \times 10^{14}$ $7.\overline{3} \times 10^{15}$ 3.23×10^{16} 10^{15}

In problems 41 and 42, evaluate each expression.

41 $(4.32 \times 10^8)(7.98 \times 10^3)$ **42** $\dfrac{4.29 \times 10^8}{-8.63 \times 10^3}$

43 Find the area of the rectangle.

3.49 x 10⁴ units

6.42 x 10⁶ units

44 Kelvyn was hired to wash windows at \$40 a day. Hopps was hired to dry windows according to the following plan: \$0.01 for the first day, \$0.02 for the second day, \$0.04 for the third day, and so on, with each day doubling the amount earned on the previous day. After 20 days, they both quit. Who earned more money? How much more?

In problems 45–48, if $x = 3.5$ and $y = 6$, evaluate each expression.

45 $x^3 \cdot x^4$ **46** x^7 **47** $y^5 \cdot y^8$ **48** y^{13}

In problems 49–51, if $x = -2$ and $y = 5$, evaluate each expression.

49 $(x + y)^2$ **50** $x^2 + y^2$ **51** $x^2 + 2xy + y^2$

52 Write an expression with coefficient -3.5, base x_1, and exponent 4.

 53 Refer to the triangle. Find the value of d.

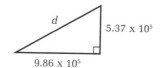

54 Graph the three equations on a single set of axes.

  a $y = 4^x$ **b** $y = 3^x$ **c** $y = 2^x$

55 Solve $2^x = 3x - 1$ by graphing.

 56 Light travels about 186,000 miles per second. How many miles does light travel in a year? (This distance is called a light-year.)

 In problems 57–59, simplify each expression.

57 $\dfrac{(3.42 \times 10^3)^4}{(8.21 \times 10^2)^3}$ **58** $\dfrac{(10^4)^5}{5^4 \cdot 2^5}$ **59** $\dfrac{(3^4)^5}{3^4 \cdot 3^5}$

60 A lily pad on a pond doubles in size every day. At the end of the fiftieth day, it entirely covers the pond. On which day did it cover half the pond?

61 One pair of opposite sides of a square is increased by 20 percent, and the other pair is decreased by 20 percent. By what percentage did the area of the square change?

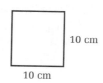

In problems 62 and 63, evaluate each expression and express your answer in scientific notation.

62 $(5.31 \times 10^{12})(2.43 \times 10^{12})$ **63** $(2.4 \times 10^3)^5$

 64 Lindi deposited $1500 in a savings account. How much money will she have at the end of 6 years if the bank pays a simple interest rate of $8\frac{1}{2}\%$ per year?

In problems 65–68, evaluate each expression if $p = 6$ and $q = 4$.

65 $p(p + q)$ **66** $p^2 + pq$ **67** $3(p + q)$ **68** $3p + 3q$

In problems 69 and 70, find the slope of a line containing the given points.

69 $(-3, 6)$ and $(11, 2)$ **70** $(2.35 \times 10^6, 8.51 \times 10^4)$ and $(4.71 \times 10^6, 9.47 \times 10^4)$

Problem Set, *continued*

71 Find the probability that a number selected at random from $\{4.2 \times 10^3, -6.2 \times 10^6, 1.26 \times 6^{10}, 0.8 \times 10^0, 10^8 \times 4.67\}$ is written in scientific notation.

In problems 72–75, evaluate each expression if $x = 2$ and $y = 4$.

72 x^3 **73** 3^x **74** x^y **75** y^x

In problems 76 and 77, evaluate each expression.

76 $\dfrac{8^3 + 6^3}{8^2 + 6^2}$ **77** $\dfrac{8^3 \cdot 6^3}{8^2 \cdot 6^2}$

78 Determine the ratio of the volumes of the cones.

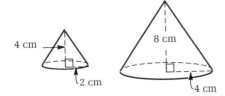

79 Rich plans to invest some money for 6 years at a rate of 9% simple interest per year. How much must he invest in order to have $20,000 after 6 years?

In problems 80 and 81, simplify each expression and write your answer in scientific notation.

80 $3.2 \times 10^{12} + 9.7 \times 10^{12}$ **81** $8.34 \times 10^{15} - 4 \times 10^{16}$

82 We know that 18 grams of water has 6.02×10^{23} molecules. If a glass contains 250 grams of water, how many molecules of water are in the glass?

83 The opposite angles of the quadrilateral are equal in measure. Solve for (x, y).

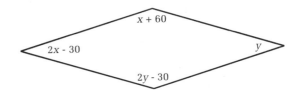

84 Solve for y if $y^2 + 3.5y + 1.5 = 0$.

85 A geometric sequence is a sequence of numbers in which each term is computed from the previous term by multiplying by the same number, for instance: 2, 6, 18, 54, 162, and so on. Find the next four terms in each geometric sequence.

a 1, 2, 4, 8, 16, . . .   **b** $\dfrac{1}{2}, \dfrac{1}{4}, \dfrac{1}{8}, \dfrac{1}{16}, \cdots$

c 100, 50, 25, 12.5, . . .   **d** 1, -3, 9, -27, . . .

9.2 MULTIPLICATION PROPERTIES OF EXPONENTS

Objectives

After studying this section, you will be able to
- Use the multiplication properties of exponents
- Multiply a polynomial by a monomial

Part One: Introduction

Multiplication Properties of Exponents

Let's consider the following example.

Example   *Multiply* $3^4 \cdot 3^7$.

Method 1
$$3^4 \cdot 3^7 = 81 \cdot 2187$$
$$= 177,147$$

Method 2
$$3^4 \cdot 3^7 = (3 \cdot 3 \cdot 3 \cdot 3)(3 \cdot 3 \cdot 3 \cdot 3 \cdot 3 \cdot 3 \cdot 3)$$
$$= 3^{11}$$
$$= 177,147$$

Notice that $3^4 \cdot 3^7 = 3^{11}$ and that $4 + 7 = 11$. This illustrates the Multiplication Property of Exponents.

The Multiplication Property of Exponents

$$a^m \cdot a^n = a^{m+n}$$

When we multiply two numbers with the same base, we add the exponents. The base remains the same.

Example   *Simplify each expression. (The solutions are given below.)*

a $y^4 \cdot y^3 \cdot y^9$

$$y^4 \cdot y^3 \cdot y^9 = y^{4+3+9}$$
$$= y^{16}$$

b $x^{12}y^3x^5y^{11}$

$$x^{12}y^3x^5y^{11} = x^{12}x^5y^3y^{11}$$
$$= x^{12+5} \cdot y^{3+11}$$
$$= x^{17}y^{14}$$

Example   *Evaluate* $(3^5)^4$.

Method 1
$$(3^5)^4 = (243)^4$$
$$= 3,486,784,401$$

Method 2
$$(3^5)^4 = (3^5)(3^5)(3^5)(3^5)$$
$$= (3 \cdot 3 \cdot 3 \cdot 3 \cdot 3)(3 \cdot 3 \cdot 3 \cdot 3 \cdot 3)(3 \cdot 3 \cdot 3 \cdot 3 \cdot 3)(3 \cdot 3 \cdot 3 \cdot 3 \cdot 3)$$
$$= 3^{20}$$
$$= 3,486,784,401$$

Note that $(3^5)^4 = 3^{20}$ and $5 \cdot 4 = 20$. This illustrates a property that is often referred to as the Power to a Power Property.

The Power to a Power Property

$$\left(a^m\right)^n = a^{mn}$$

When we raise a power to a power, we multiply the exponents. The base remains the same.

Example   *Find the volume of the cube.*

$V = (x^4)^3$

   $= x^{12}$

Example   *Simplify each expression. (The solutions are given below.)*

a $(3 \cdot 5)^4$

   $(3 \cdot 5)^4 = (15)^4$

        $= 50{,}625$

b $3^4 \cdot 5^4$

   $3^4 \cdot 5^4 = (3 \cdot 3 \cdot 3 \cdot 3)(5 \cdot 5 \cdot 5 \cdot 5)$

        $= 81 \cdot 625$

        $= 50{,}625$

Notice that $(3 \cdot 5)^4 = 3^4 \cdot 5^4$. This illustrates the Distributive Property of Exponentiation over Multiplication.

The Distributive Property of Exponentiation over Multiplication

$$(ab)^n = a^n b^n$$

An exponent distributes over multiplication.

Example   *Simplify each expression. (The solutions are given below.)*

a $(2x)^7$

   $(2x)^7 = 2^7 x^7$

       $= 128x^7$

b $(3x^4 y^2)^5$

   $(3x^4 y^2)^5 = 3^5 \cdot (x^4)^5 \cdot (y^2)^5$

           $= 243x^{20} y^{10}$

Be careful! Many students try to apply the Distributive Property of Exponentiation over Multiplication when quantities in parentheses are added or subtracted. For instance, they think that $(x + y)^2 = x^2 + y^2$. But this is not true. Let's see what happens when we evaluate each expression for $x = 3$ and $y = 5$.

$$(x + y)^2 = (3 + 5)^2 \qquad x^2 + y^2 = 3^2 + 5^2$$
$$= 8^2 \qquad\qquad\qquad = 9 + 25$$
$$= 64 \qquad\qquad\qquad = 34$$

Since each expression has a different value, $(x + y)^2 \neq x^2 + y^2$. In other words, exponentiation does not distribute over addition (or subtraction). In the next chapter you will see that $(x + y)^2 = x^2 + 2xy + y^2$. Check this by evaluating each expression for $x = 3$ and $y = 5$.

Multiplying Polynomials by Monomials

A *monomial* is a real number, a variable, or the product of real numbers and variables.

These are monomials:

$9 \qquad x \qquad 13xym \qquad \frac{2}{3}x^2ym^7 \qquad \sqrt{2}x^2$

These are not monomials:

$x + y \qquad \frac{x}{y} \qquad -3 - 4x \qquad \sqrt{x}$

A *polynomial* is a monomial, a sum of monomials, or a difference of monomials.

These are polynomials:

$3xy \qquad 3x^4 + 9xy^2 \qquad -\frac{2}{3}y^4m - 11y^2 + 7 - 9x \qquad x^2 - 4x + 5$

This is not a polynomial:

$\dfrac{3x^2 - 5}{2x}$

Example *Find the area of the rectangle.*

$3x^4$ [rectangle]

$5x^7 - 9x^3 - 7x + 2$

We use the Distributive Property of Multiplication over Addition and Subtraction and the properties of exponents to multiply the polynomial by the monomial.

$$A = 3x^4(5x^7 - 9x^3 - 7x + 2)$$
$$= (3x^4)(5x^7) - (3x^4)(9x^3) - (3x^4)(7x) + (3x^4)(2)$$
$$= 15x^{11} - 27x^7 - 21x^5 + 6x^4$$

Part Two: Sample Problems

Problem 1 *Simplify each expression.*

a $(1.46 \times 10^5)^3$
b $(-1.5x^4y)^5$
c $(3x)^4x^8 + (5x^2)^6$

Solution **a** $(1.46 \times 10^5)^3 = (1.46)^3(10^5)^3$
$$= 3.112136 \times 10^{15}$$
$$\approx 3.11 \times 10^{15}$$

b $(-1.5x^4y)^5 = (-1.5)^5(x^4)^5(y)^5$
$$= -7.59375x^{20}y^5$$
$$\approx -7.6x^{20}y^5$$

c $(3x)^4x^8 + (5x^2)^6 = (3)^4(x)^4x^8 + (5)^6(x^2)^6$
$$= 81x^4x^8 + 15{,}625x^{12}$$
$$= 81x^{12} + 15{,}625x^{12}$$
$$= 15{,}706x^{12}$$

Problem 2 Evaluate each expression.

a $(3.5 \times 10^5)(4.17 \times 10^8)$ **b** $(2x^3y^5)^7(-5xy^2)^5$

Solution **a** $(3.5 \times 10^5)(4.17 \times 10^8) = (3.5)(4.17)(10^5)(10^8)$
$$= 14.595 \times 10^{13}$$

In scientific notation we write 1.4595×10^{14}. We round this to 1.46×10^{14}.

b $(2x^3y^5)^7(-5xy^2)^5 = (2)^7(x^3)^7(y^5)^7(-5)^5(x)^5(y^2)^5$
$$= 128x^{21}y^{35}(-3125)x^5y^{10}$$
$$= (128)(-3125)x^{21}x^5y^{35}y^{10}$$
$$= -400{,}000x^{26}y^{45}$$

In scientific notation we write $(-4 \times 10^5)x^{26}y^{45}$.

Problem 3 The Pacific Ocean has a surface area of approximately 1.66×10^8 square kilometers.

a How many square meters of surface area does the Pacific Ocean have?
b If the average depth of the Pacific Ocean is about 4.03×10^3 meters, what is the approximate volume of water in the Pacific Ocean in cubic meters?

Solution **a** We need to convert square kilometers to square meters.

$$1 \text{ kilometer} = 1000 \text{ meters}$$
$$1 \text{ kilometer} \times 1 \text{ kilometer} = 1000 \text{ meters} \times 1000 \text{ meters}$$
$$1 \text{ square kilometer} = 1{,}000{,}000 \text{ square meters}$$
$$= 10^6 \text{ square meters}$$

The surface area of the Pacific Ocean is about $(1.66 \times 10^8)(10^6) = 1.66 \times 10^{14}$ square meters.

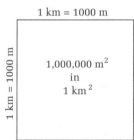

b To find the volume of water, we multiply the surface area by the average depth.

$$\text{Volume} = (1.66 \times 10^{14})(4.03 \times 10^3)$$
$$\approx 6.69 \times 10^{17}$$

There are approximately 6.69×10^{17} cubic meters of water in the Pacific Ocean.

Part Three: Exercises and Problems

Warm-up Exercises

In problems 1–5, simplify each expression.

1 $y^5 \cdot y^8 \cdot y^3$ **2** $(a^3)^3$ **3** $(5x^3y)^2$
4 $x_1{}^3x_2{}^4$ **5** $2^7 \cdot 5^7$

6 Multiply $3x^2(2x^4 - 6x^3 + 5x^2 - 2)$.

In problems 7–12, determine whether each statement is True or False. Explain why.

7 $(2a + b)^2 = 4a^2 + b^2$ **8** $x^3 + x^3 = x^6$

9 $(-3xy^2)^3 = -3x^3y^5$ **10** $(2x^2y)^4 = 16x^8y^4$

11 $2 \cdot 5^4 = 10^4$ **12** $(a + b)^2 = (ab)^2$

13 Find an expression for the area of the rectangle.

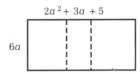

Problem Set

In problems 14–16, simplify each expression.

14 $x^3 \cdot x^5$ **15** $(x^3y^5)(-y^7x)$ **16** $(3xy^2)(-2x^4y^3)(-xy)$

In problems 17 and 18, solve for x.

17 $3^4 \cdot 3^5 = 3^x$ **18** $4^5 \cdot 4^x = 4^{13}$

In problems 19–21, if $p = -2$ and $q = 4$, evaluate each expression.

19 $(p + q)^2$ **20** $p^2 + q^2$ **21** $p^2 + 2pq + q^2$

22 Indicate whether each of the following is a polynomial. If not, explain why not.

a $x^3 - \dfrac{2}{3}x^2 + 2$ **b** $3 - t + t^5 - t^7$ **c** 4

d $5y + 3$ **e** $3x^2 - \dfrac{2}{x}$ **f** 2^x

In problems 23–25, apply a property of exponents to each expression. Then use scientific notation to approximate the answer to three decimal places.

23 $(2^6)^9$ **24** $(3 \times 10^4)^5$ **25** $6^8 \cdot 6^{12}$

26 Find the area of the rectangle if the areas of the squares are 9 square meters and 16 square meters.

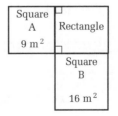

In problems 27–29, simplify each expression.

27 $(y^3)^5$ **28** $(-2k^3)^5$ **29** $(x^3y^5)(-x^4y^6z^3)$

30 A light-year is equal to about 6×10^{12} miles. Alpha Centauri, the nearest star to us other than the sun, is about 4 light-years from Earth.

a Determine how many miles Alpha Centauri is from Earth.

b If you went by rocket ship to Alpha Centauri at one million miles per hour, how long would it take you? Express your answer in both hours and years.

In problems 31 and 32, multiply.

31 $2x^3(3x^5 + 98x^3 - 14x^2 - 42)$

32 $-3y(-4y^3 - 6y^2 + 5y + 4)$

33 A nanosecond is one billionth of a second. On computers, the speed at which one piece of data can be retrieved from memory is 150 nanoseconds. How many pieces of data can be retrieved from memory in an hour?

In problems 34 and 35, solve each system.

34 $\begin{cases} 2x + 3y = 4 \\ 5x - 4y = 33 \end{cases}$

35 $\begin{cases} y = 3x + 5 \\ 2x + 3y = 59 \end{cases}$

36 A sandwich that costs $1.40 today will increase in cost due to inflation. E. Conn O'Mist determined that the cost c of the sandwich in t years can be estimated by the formula $c = 1.4(1 + 0.05)^t$.

a Estimate the cost of the sandwich in 10 years.

b Estimate the cost of the sandwich in 100 years.

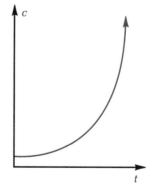

In problems 37–40, evaluate each expression if $x_1 = 5$.

37 $3x_1^4$

38 $x_1^2 + x_1^2$

39 $-3x_1^4$

40 $(5x_1)^3$

In problems 41 and 42, simplify each expression.

41 $(3x^2y)^4$

42 $(a^5b^2)^3(a^2b)^4$

In problems 43 and 44, solve for n.

43 $(3^4)^5 = 3^n$

44 $(2^5)^8 = 2^{4n}$

45 Pedro is twice as old as Maria. In 6 years the sum of their ages will be 57. How old is Maria now? How old is Pedro?

46 Let x = 7.

a Evaluate $3x^4$.   **b** Evaluate $(3x)^4$.

c Explain why the answers in parts **a** and **b** are different.

In problems 47–50, simplify each expression.

47 $\dfrac{20^5}{10^5}$ **48** 2^5 **49** $\dfrac{18^7}{6^7}$ **50** 3^7

51 The table lists approximate uses of rural land in the United States in 1980. Construct a circle graph to convey the information. Don't forget to allow for "Other" land use not specified.

Rural land use	Area (× 1000 acres)
Total	1,412,011
Crop Land	420,994
Pasture	132,356
Range Land	405,914
Forest	393,197

52 Evaluate expressions **a–d** below.

a $(-3)^4$ **b** -3^4 **c** $(-3)^5$ **d** -3^5

e Explain why parts **c** and **d** have the same result but parts **a** and **b** have different results.

In problems 53–56, simplify each expression.

53 $-3x^9$ **54** $(-3x)^4$ **55** $-(4x)^3$ **56** $(-2x)(-3x)$

In problems 57–65, simplify each expression.

57 $5x^3 + 8x^3$ **58** $3x^4 \cdot 4x^5$ **59** $(4x)^2 + 4x^2$

60 $4x(2x)^5$ **61** $(-4x^2)^3(2xy)$ **62** $(4x^2)^3 \cdot (3x)^5 \cdot 7(x^2)^3$

63 $(-3.7 \times 10^5)^3$ **64** $(2.3 \times 10^5)^3$ **65** $(-4x^4y^3z^6)^2$

66 The number of different bridge hands that can be dealt is approximately 6.35×10^{11}. What is the probability that you will be dealt a hand of 13 cards all of the same suit, if there are 4 suits and a total of 52 cards in the deck of cards used for bridge?

67 Determine how many 3-by-$1\frac{1}{2}$-inch tickets can be printed on a piece of cardboard measuring 30 by 24 inches.

Problem Set, *continued*

68 Determine whether each statement is True or False. Explain.

    a $3^4 \cdot 3^5 = 3^{20}$ **b** $a^{bc} = a^b \cdot a^c$ **c** $x^3 y^3 = xy^3$

In problems 69–74, use a calculator to evaluate each expression if $x = 1.7$.

69 $x \cdot x \cdot x \cdot x \cdot x \cdot x \cdot x \cdot x \cdot x \cdot x \cdot x \cdot x$ **70** $3(x^2)^4$

71 $x + x + x + x + x + x + x$ **72** $8x^3 + 7x^3$

73 $(4x)^3 \cdot (4x)^5$ **74** $x^2(3x^2 + 4x + 5)$

75 There are approximately 20 drops of water in 1 cubic centimeter of water. Approximate the number of drops of water in a swimming pool 50 meters long and 30 meters wide and with an average depth of 2 meters.

76 Evaluate $(13^5)^7 - 13^{35}$.

77 Study the pattern and find a, b, c, and d.

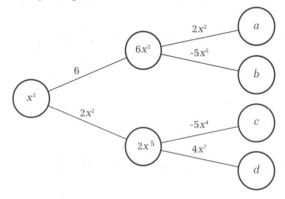

In problems 78 and 79, if $a = 3$ and $b = -2$, determine whether each statement is True or False.

78 $(a + b)^2 = a^2 + b^2$ **79** $(a - b)^2 = a^2 - 2ab + b^2$

80 The circumference of Earth is approximately 25,000 miles. If roughly $\frac{2}{3}$ of Earth is covered by ocean, what is the approximate land area of Earth in square miles? What is the approximate volume of Earth in cubic feet?

In problems 81–83, simplify each expression.

81 $8x(2x^2 + 5x + 4) + 5(4x^2 - 6x^3 - 2x)$

82 $(3x)^4(5x^2 + 2x + 5)$

83 $(3x + 2x)(4x^2 + 5x + 6)$

84 If $y = \frac{1}{2}$ and $(2x_1 y)^3 = 3^3$, solve for x_1.

In problems 85–87, evaluate each expression if $x = -4$.

85 $[(3x)^2]^4$ **86** $(5 + x)^2$ **87** $(x^2 + 3x^2)^5$

In problems 88–90, simplify each expression.

88 $(3xy)^4(2x^2y^3)^5$ **89** $(-3.7x^2y^3)^3$ **90** $(7xy^2)^3(-3x)^5$

91 A number chosen at random from {0, 1, 2, 3, 4, 5, 6, 7, 8, 9} is cubed. Find the probability that the number and the units digit of the cube of the number are the same.

92 Determine whether each of the following sequences is geometric. (Hint: Refer to the definition of *geometric sequence* given on page 422.)

a 1, 4, 16, 64, . . .   **b** 1, 4, 9, 16, 25, . . .
c 25, 5, 1, 0.2, . . .   **d** 3, 7, 11, 15, . . .
e $x, x^2, x^3, x^4, . . .$ **f** $x, x^2, x^4, x^8, . . .$

93 Refer to the diagram. The sum of the volumes of the two boxes is numerically equal to the area of the top of Box I. Find the value of $a + b$.

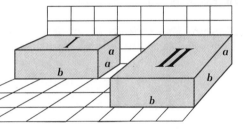

94 In August of 1987, it rained 9.26 inches in Northbrook, Illinois, in a 14-hour period. One cubic inch of rain contains about 320 raindrops. The town of Northbrook encompasses 25 square miles of land. Approximate the number of drops of rain that fell on Northbrook in that 14-hour period.

95 On most scientific calculators there is a factorial key $\boxed{x!}$ For instance, $5! = 5 \cdot 4 \cdot 3 \cdot 2 \cdot 1 = 120$. Try this key on a calculator.

a Compute 8!.
b Verify by multiplying $8 \cdot 7 \cdot 6 \cdot 5 \cdot 4 \cdot 3 \cdot 2 \cdot 1$.
c Approximate the value of $\dfrac{45!}{18! \ 27!}$.
d Find the largest value of n for which your calculator will give an answer for $n!$.

96 If one of the digits 1, 2, 3, 4, 5, 6, 7, 8, 9, 0 is randomly selected, find the probability that it is the units digit of the square of some integer.

97 Find the slope of the line containing the points $(2.35 \times 10^6, 8.51 \times 10^4)$ and $(4.71 \times 10^6, 9.47 \times 10^4)$.

9.3 | Division Properties of Exponents

Objectives

After studying this section, you will be able to
- Use the division properties of exponents
- Divide a polynomial by a monomial

Part One: Introduction

Division Properties of Exponents

The process of simplifying $\frac{9}{12}$ involves the following steps.

$$\frac{9}{12} = \frac{3 \cdot 3}{3 \cdot 4} = \frac{3}{3} \cdot \frac{3}{4} = 1 \cdot \frac{3}{4} = \frac{3}{4}$$

We can use the same procedure to simplify algebraic fractions.

Example *Simplify each expression. (The solutions are given below.)*

a $\dfrac{3xy}{6y}$

$$\frac{3xy}{6y} = \frac{3y \cdot x}{3y \cdot 2}$$

$$= \frac{3y}{3y} \cdot \frac{x}{2}$$

$$= 1 \cdot \frac{x}{2}$$

$$= \frac{x}{2}$$

b $\dfrac{8x^2z}{12xy}$

$$\frac{8x^2z}{12xy} = \frac{4x \cdot 2xz}{4x \cdot 3y}$$

$$= \frac{4x}{4x} \cdot \frac{2xz}{3y}$$

$$= 1 \cdot \frac{2xz}{3y}$$

$$= \frac{2xz}{3y}$$

Now let's simplify a fraction whose numerator and denominator contain quantities with the same base.

Example *Simplify $\dfrac{5^9}{5^3}$.*

$$\frac{5^9}{5^3} = \frac{5 \cdot 5 \cdot 5 \cdot 5 \cdot 5 \cdot 5 \cdot 5 \cdot 5 \cdot 5}{5 \cdot 5 \cdot 5}$$

$$= \frac{5 \cdot 5 \cdot 5}{5 \cdot 5 \cdot 5} \cdot \frac{5 \cdot 5 \cdot 5 \cdot 5 \cdot 5 \cdot 5}{1}$$

$$= 1 \cdot 5^6$$

$$= 5^6$$

Notice that $\dfrac{5^9}{5^3} = 5^6$ and $9 - 3 = 6$. This example illustrates the Division Property of Exponents.

The Division Property of Exponents

If $a \neq 0$, then $\dfrac{a^m}{a^n} = a^{m-n}$.

When we divide two numbers with the same base, we subtract the exponents. The base remains the same.

Example   *Simplify each expression. (The solutions are given below.)*

a $\dfrac{2x^{12}}{4x^7}$ b $\dfrac{2^{10}}{2^6}$

$\dfrac{2x^{12}}{4x^7} = \dfrac{2x^{12-7}}{4}$ $\dfrac{2^{10}}{2^6} = 2^{10-6}$

$= \dfrac{1x^5}{2}$ $= 2^4$

$= \dfrac{x^5}{2}$ $= 16$

What do we do in a situation such as $\dfrac{x^5}{x^9}$, where the exponent in the denominator is larger than the exponent in the numerator? If we apply the division property and subtract the exponents, we get x^{-4}. In Section 9.4, you will study more about negative exponents. For now, here are two other ways to do the problem.

Method 1

$\dfrac{x^5}{x^9} = \dfrac{x \cdot x \cdot x \cdot x \cdot x}{x \cdot x \cdot x \cdot x \cdot x \cdot x \cdot x \cdot x \cdot x}$

$= \dfrac{x \cdot x \cdot x \cdot x \cdot x}{x \cdot x \cdot x \cdot x \cdot x} \cdot \dfrac{1}{x \cdot x \cdot x \cdot x}$

$= 1 \cdot \dfrac{1}{x^4}$

$= \dfrac{1}{x^4}$

Method 2

$\dfrac{x^5}{x^9} = \dfrac{1}{x^{9-5}}$

$= \dfrac{1}{x^4}$

We know that exponentiation distributes over multiplication. Does exponentiation distribute over division? Let's use the expression $\left(\dfrac{2}{5}\right)^8$.

$\left(\dfrac{2}{5}\right)^8 = \dfrac{2}{5} \cdot \dfrac{2}{5} \cdot \dfrac{2}{5} \cdot \dfrac{2}{5} \cdot \dfrac{2}{5} \cdot \dfrac{2}{5} \cdot \dfrac{2}{5} \cdot \dfrac{2}{5} = \dfrac{2^8}{5^8}$

The preceding example illustrates the following property.

The Distributive Property of Exponentiation over Division

If $b \neq 0$, then $\left(\dfrac{a}{b}\right)^n = \dfrac{a^n}{b^n}$.

Exponentiation distributes over division.

Example   Simplify $\left(\dfrac{2x}{y}\right)^5 \left(\dfrac{y}{xz}\right)^3$.

$$\left(\frac{2x}{y}\right)^5 \left(\frac{y}{xz}\right)^3 = \left(\frac{2^5 x^5}{y^5}\right)\left(\frac{y^3}{x^3 z^3}\right)$$

$$= \frac{2^5 x^5 y^3}{y^5 x^3 z^3}$$

$$= \frac{32 x^{5-3}}{y^{5-3} z^3} = \frac{32 x^2}{y^2 z^3}$$

Dividing a Polynomial by a Monomial

To divide a polynomial by a monomial, we must divide each term of the polynomial by the monomial term.

Example   Simplify each expression.

a $\dfrac{10x^5 - 4x^8 - 6x^4}{-2x^3}$ **b** $\dfrac{x^3 y^2 + xy - y^4}{xy^2}$

We separate each fraction into three fractions with the same denominator. Then we use the properties of exponents to simplify.

a $\dfrac{10x^5 - 4x^8 - 6x^4}{-2x^3} = \dfrac{10x^5}{-2x^3} - \dfrac{4x^8}{-2x^3} - \dfrac{6x^4}{-2x^3}$

$$= -5x^{5-3} - (-2x^{8-3}) - (-3x^{4-3})$$

$$= -5x^2 - (-2x^5) - (-3x^1)$$

$$= -5x^2 + 2x^5 + 3x$$

b $\dfrac{x^3 y^2 + xy - y^4}{xy^2} = \dfrac{x^3 y^2}{xy^2} + \dfrac{xy}{xy^2} - \dfrac{y^4}{xy^2}$

$$= x^{3-1}\left(\frac{y^2}{y^2}\right) + \frac{x}{x}\left(\frac{1}{y^{2-1}}\right) - \frac{y^{4-2}}{x}$$

$$= x^2 + \frac{1}{y} - \frac{y^2}{x}$$

Part Two: Sample Problems

Problem 1   Simplify each expression.

a $\dfrac{18^7}{9^7}$ **b** $\dfrac{14(2x)^3 y^5}{28x^7 y^3}$

Solution   **a** $\dfrac{18^7}{9^7} = \left(\dfrac{18}{9}\right)^7$ **b** $\dfrac{14(2x)^3 y^5}{28x^7 y^3} = \dfrac{7 \cdot 2 \cdot 2^3 x^3 y^5}{7 \cdot 2 \cdot 2x^7 y^3}$

$$= 2^7 \qquad\qquad\qquad\qquad = \frac{2^{3-1} y^{5-3}}{x^{7-3}}$$

$$= 128 \qquad\qquad\qquad\qquad\quad = \frac{4y^2}{x^4}$$

Problem 2 *Simplify each expression.*

a $\dfrac{4 \cdot 3}{4}$ b $\dfrac{x \cdot y}{x}$ c $\dfrac{4 + 3}{4}$ d $\dfrac{x + y}{x}$

Solution

a $\dfrac{4 \cdot 3}{4}$

$= \dfrac{4}{4} \cdot 3$

$= 1 \cdot 3$

$= 3$

b $\dfrac{x \cdot y}{x}$

$= \dfrac{x}{x} \cdot y$

$= 1 \cdot y$

$= y$

c $\dfrac{4 + 3}{4}$

$= \dfrac{4}{4} + \dfrac{3}{4}$

$= 1 + \dfrac{3}{4}$

$= 1\dfrac{3}{4}$ or $\dfrac{7}{4}$

d $\dfrac{x + y}{x}$

$= \dfrac{x}{x} + \dfrac{y}{x}$

$= 1 + \dfrac{y}{x}$

Multiplication in the numerator is different from addition in the numerator. Addition terms are not factors, so you cannot "cancel."

Problem 3 *The distance light travels in one year, called a light-year, is approximately 5.88×10^{12} miles.*
  a *How far does light travel in one second?*
  b *The distance from Earth to the sun is about 9.3×10^{7} miles. How long does it take light to travel from the sun to Earth?*

Solution We use units to help us solve the problem.

a $\dfrac{365 \text{ days}}{1 \text{ year}} \cdot \dfrac{24 \text{ hours}}{1 \text{ day}} \cdot \dfrac{60 \text{ min}}{1 \text{ hour}} \cdot \dfrac{60 \text{ sec}}{1 \text{ min}} = \dfrac{3.1536 \times 10^{7} \text{ sec}}{1 \text{ year}}$

$\dfrac{\dfrac{5.88 \times 10^{12} \text{ miles}}{1 \text{ year}}}{\dfrac{3.1536 \times 10^{7} \text{ sec}}{1 \text{ year}}} \approx \dfrac{1.86 \times 10^{5} \text{ miles}}{1 \text{ sec}}$

So, light travels approximately 1.86×10^{5} miles per second.

b Since distance = rate · time, time $= \dfrac{\text{distance}}{\text{rate}}$

Time $= \dfrac{9.3 \times 10^{7} \text{ miles}}{\dfrac{1.86 \times 10^{5} \text{ miles}}{1 \text{ sec}}} \approx 4.97 \times 10^{2}$ sec

It takes about 497 seconds, or about 8 minutes and 17 seconds, for light to travel from the sun to Earth.

Part Three: Exercises and Problems

Warm-up Exercises

In problems 1–4, simplify each expression.

1 $\dfrac{3x^{5}}{12x^{5}}$ **2** $\dfrac{4a^{3}b^{8}}{2ab^{10}}$ **3** $\dfrac{b + 3}{b}$ **4** $\dfrac{2^{2}}{2^{4}}$

5 Evaluate each expression if $x = -2$. Then answer part **c**.

a $\dfrac{5x^{4} - 10x^{3}}{5x}$ **b** $x^{3} - 2x^{2}$ **c** Explain your results in parts **a** and **b**.

Problem Set

In problems 6–8, write each fraction in its simplest form.

6 $\dfrac{12x^2y^3}{8xy}$

7 $\dfrac{6x^4ym}{12xy^5m^2}$

8 $\dfrac{(2f)^3 3f^4}{4f^2}$

In problems 9–11, evaluate $\dfrac{a^5}{a^3}$ for the given value.

9 $a = 5$

10 $a = 2$

11 $a = 10$

In problems 12–14, let $f(x) = \dfrac{x}{2^6}$.

12 Find $f(2^{10})$.
13 Find $f(2^6)$.
14 Find $f(2^4)$.

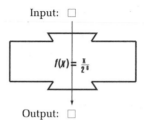

Input: ☐

$f(x) = \frac{x}{2^6}$

Output: ☐

In problems 15–18, simplify each expression.

15 $\dfrac{(3x^2y)^4}{9x^5y^6}$

16 $\left(\dfrac{3x}{9x^2}\right)^3$

17 $\dfrac{-2.5xy^2}{-5x^3y}$

18 $\dfrac{9^7x^4z}{-9^9x^2z^4}$

19 A giant cube, 8 feet by 8 feet by 8 feet, was made out of small cubes. In parts **a–c**, determine how many small cubes were used if the length of each side of a small cube has the given measure.

    a 2 feet   **b** 6 inches   **c** w feet

In problems 20–23, evaluate each expression if $a = 2$ and $b = 3$.

20 $\dfrac{a^5}{a^4}$

21 $\dfrac{b^{10}}{b^{12}}$

22 $\dfrac{ab^3}{a^2b^2}$

23 $\dfrac{(ab)^{13}}{(ab)^{11}}$

24 A microprocessor chip is capable of handling virtual memory of up to 2^{64} bytes. Write this number in scientific notation.

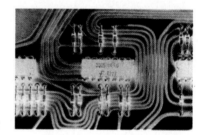

25 For each of the following, determine whether the expression is equal to $(2^5)^4$. Explain.

    a $(32)^4$ **b** 2^{20} **c** 2^9 **d** $2^5 \cdot 2^4$

In problems 26–28, simplify each expression.

26 $\dfrac{4x^2y^3z}{2xy^5z^9}$

27 $\dfrac{(-2.5x^4)}{(2.5x^2)^2}$

28 $\dfrac{9^7}{18^8}$

29 To evaluate 2^{-1} on a calculator, use the key sequence [2] [y^x] [1] ☐ $\pm$ ☐ $=$ ☐. Then evaluate 2^{-2}, 5^{-2}, and 10^{-3}.

30 Find the combined principal and interest on $500 invested at 8% interest per year after the given number of years. Use the memory key on your calculator to save time.

   a 1 year   **b** 5 years   **c** 100 years

In problems 31 and 32, divide.

31 $\dfrac{60x^5 - 18x^3 + 24x^2 + 30x}{6x}$ **32** $\dfrac{8a^3 - 4a^2 + 10a - 12}{-2a}$

33 The speed of sound in air is about 7.42×10^2 miles per hour. How many seconds will pass from the time lightning strikes until thunder is heard 0.8 miles away?

In problems 34 and 35, evaluate each expression.

34 $\dfrac{3 \cdot 5}{5}$ **35** $\dfrac{3 + 5}{5}$

In problems 36–38, evaluate each expression.

36 $\frac{1}{3} \div 3$ **37** $4 \div \frac{1}{4}$ **38** $\frac{1}{4} \div 4$

39 The speed of light is about 6.696×10^8 miles per hour.

   a Find the speed of light in feet per second.
   b Find the number of seconds in one year.
   c Find the distance, in feet, light travels in one year.

In problems 40–42, simplify each expression.

40 $\dfrac{-7x^2(2x)^4}{-3(xy)^5}$ **41** $\dfrac{(3x^2y)(-2x)^3}{(16xy^2)^4}$ **42** $\dfrac{(-2.5 \times 10^3)^5}{(3.2 \times 10^4)}$

43 Arrange the numbers in order from smallest to largest.

   $(3.2 \times 10^3)^4$ $(3.2 \times 10^5)^2$ $(3.2 \times 10^6)^2$ $(3.2 \times 10^2)^5$

44 Find the length of the base b.

                      Area = $18x^2 + 16$ $2x$

                               b

45 Solve the matrix equation for (x, y).

$$\begin{bmatrix} x & x + 3 \\ 2x + 1 & x - 2 \end{bmatrix} \begin{bmatrix} 2x \\ 3 \end{bmatrix} = \begin{bmatrix} 74 \\ 7y \end{bmatrix}$$

Problem Set, *continued*

46 How many times must you add 10^{-10} to itself to get 10^{20}?

47 In 1950, it was estimated that the population of the world was 2.5 billion and that there were 5×10^{14} wheat plants. Determine how many wheat plants per person there were in 1950.

48 Let $x = 2$ and $y = 3$.
  a Evaluate $(x + y)^2$.   **b** Evaluate $x^2 + y^2$.   **c** Evaluate $x^2 + 2xy + y^2$.
  d Which expressions in parts **a–c** are equivalent?

49 In a class-action lawsuit, the courts ordered an electric company to credit its customers $560 million dollars. Find the average credit per customer if the company has 1.8 million customers.

50 Find side s if the volume of the box is a^{18} cubic units.

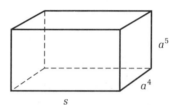

In problems 51 and 52, simplify.

51 $\dfrac{2(x_2 + 3x_1)^3 + 6(x_2 + 3x_1)^2}{x_2 + 3x_1}$

52 $\dfrac{(x_1 + 2x_2 + 3x_3)^6}{(x_1 + 2x_2 + 3x_3)^5}$

53 The relationship between mass and energy is expressed by the equation $E = mc^2$, in which E is energy in ergs, m is mass in grams, and c is the speed of light. The speed of light is about 3.00×10^{10} centimeters per second. Suppose 5.630 grams of mass are converted to energy in an atomic reaction.

  a Find the energy released in ergs.
  b Find the energy released in foot-pounds if
    1 foot-pound $\approx 1.356 \times 10^2$ ergs.

54 Find all integer values of x so that $\dfrac{x^3 + 5x^2 + 7x + 15}{x}$ is an integer.

55 Find side s and the volume and surface area of the cube.

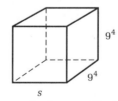

56 Judy invested $10,000 at 9.5% interest at the end of 1982. Find the year in which her original investment doubled.

57 Solve $5^{2x} = 5^3 \cdot 5^x$ for x.

9.4 NEGATIVE AND ZERO EXPONENTS

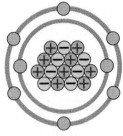

ATOMIC
MASS
UNIT = 1u = 1.660 x 10^{-27} kg

Objectives

After studying this section, you will be able to
- Simplify expressions with negative and zero exponents
- Use scientific notation for small numbers

Part One: Introduction

Negative and Zero Exponents

Let's take a close look at the pattern. In each case, decreasing the exponent by 1 gives the same result as dividing by the base, 4.

$$4^3 = 64$$
$$4^2 = 16$$
$$4^1 = 4$$
$$4^0 = 1$$
$$4^{-1} = \frac{1}{4}, \text{ or } \frac{1}{4^1}$$
$$4^{-2} = \frac{1}{16}, \text{ or } \frac{1}{4^2}$$
$$4^{-3} = \frac{1}{64}, \text{ or } \frac{1}{4^3}$$

We can see that 4^3 and 4^{-3} are reciprocals because 64 and $\frac{1}{64}$ are reciprocals. We can also see that 4^2 and 4^{-2}, and 4^1 and 4^{-1} are reciprocals. This pattern illustrates the following.

> ➤ *If $a \neq 0$, then $a^{-m} = \frac{1}{a^m}$, and $\frac{1}{a^{-m}} = a^m$.*

We can also see from the pattern that $4^0 = 1$.

> ➤ *If $a \neq 0$, then $a^0 = 1$. Any number, except 0, raised to the zero power is 1.*

Example   *Simplify $\frac{x^5}{x^5}$ if $x \neq 0$.*

Method 1

$$\frac{x^5}{x^5} = \frac{x \cdot x \cdot x \cdot x \cdot x}{x \cdot x \cdot x \cdot x \cdot x}$$
$$= 1$$

Method 2

$$\frac{x^5}{x^5} = x^{5-5}$$
$$= x^0$$
$$= 1$$

Example   *Simplify* $x^{-3} \cdot x^3$ *if* $x \neq 0$.

Method 1

$$x^{-3} \cdot x^3 = \frac{1}{x^3} \cdot x^3$$

$$= \frac{x^3}{x^3}$$

$$= 1$$

Method 2

$$x^{-3} \cdot x^3 = x^{-3+3}$$

$$= x^0$$

$$= 1$$

Example   *Simplify each expression.*

a $\dfrac{2x^3}{-6x^7}$ **b** $\dfrac{x^5}{x^{-4}}$

a Method 1

$$\frac{2x^3}{-6x^7} = \frac{1}{-3x^{7-3}}$$

$$= \frac{1}{-3x^4}$$

Method 2

$$\frac{2x^3}{-6x^7} = \frac{1x^{3-7}}{-3}$$

$$= \frac{x^{-4}}{-3}$$

b Method 1

$$\frac{x^5}{x^{-4}} = x^5 \cdot \frac{1}{x^{-4}}$$

$$= x^5 \cdot x^4$$

$$= x^9$$

Method 2

$$\frac{x^5}{x^{-4}} = x^{5-(-4)}$$

$$= x^{5+4}$$

$$= x^9$$

In part **a,** each method produced a different form of the same answer. Either form is acceptable.

Scientific Notation for Small Numbers

The mass of a single atom of hydrogen is about $\dfrac{1}{6.02 \times 10^{23}}$ grams. The value of this extremely small number is approximately 0.00000000000000000000000166 when written as a decimal. Let's write this number in scientific notation.

$$\frac{1}{6.02 \times 10^{23}} = \frac{1}{0.602 \times 10^{24}} \approx \frac{1.66}{10^{24}} = 1.66 \times 10^{-24}$$

Comparing the scientific notation form of the number with the approximate decimal form, you can see that the -24 as the power of 10 means that the decimal point is to be moved 24 spaces to the left to obtain the decimal value of the number.

Example   *Express the number* 3.2098×10^{-5} *in decimal notation.*

We move the decimal point 5 places to the left.

$$3.2098 \times 10^{-5} = 0.000032098$$

Example   *Express the decimal 0.003234 in scientific notation.*

We reverse what we did in the previous example. We move the decimal point 3 places to the right and adjust the power of 10.

$$0.003234 = 3.234 \times 10^{-3}$$

Example   *Evaluate* $\dfrac{3.09 \times 10^{-4}}{9.36 \times 10^{-5}}$.

Method 1

Enter 3.09 $\boxed{\text{EE}}$ 4 $\boxed{\pm}$ $\boxed{\div}$ 9.36 $\boxed{\text{EE}}$ 5 $\boxed{\pm}$ $\boxed{=}$ on a scientific calculator. The result is approximately 3.301.

Method 2

$$\frac{3.09 \times 10^{-4}}{9.36 \times 10^{-5}} = \frac{3.09}{9.36} \times 10^{-4 - (-5)}$$
$$\approx 0.3301 \times 10^{1}$$
$$\approx 3.301$$

Part Two: Sample Problems

Problem 1   *Simplify each expression.*

a $\left(\dfrac{2x^0}{3y^{-3}}\right)^{-4}$
     b $\dfrac{-3x^{-5}y^{-3}z}{6x^{-3}y^{-5}z^{-2}}$

Solution

a $\left(\dfrac{2x^0}{3y^{-3}}\right)^{-4} = \left(\dfrac{2}{3y^{-3}}\right)^{-4}$

$= \dfrac{2^{-4}}{3^{-4}(y^{-3})^{-4}}$

$= \dfrac{2^{-4}}{3^{-4}y^{12}}$

$= \dfrac{3^4}{2^4y^{12}}$

$= \dfrac{81}{16y^{12}}$ or $\dfrac{81y^{-12}}{16}$

b $\dfrac{-3x^{-5}y^{-3}z}{6x^{-3}y^{-5}z^{-2}} = \dfrac{-1x^3y^5z \cdot z^2}{2x^5y^3}$

$= \dfrac{-y^{5-3}z^{1+2}}{2x^{5-3}}$

$= \dfrac{-y^2z^3}{2x^2}$ or $\dfrac{-x^{-2}y^2z^3}{2}$

⌨ **Problem 2**   *The Sahara is a desert about 16,896,000 feet long and about 5,808,000 feet wide, and its sand is on the average 12 feet deep.*

a *Find the volume, in cubic feet, of sand in the Sahara.*
b *The volume of a single grain of sand is approximately* 1.3×10^{-9} *cubic feet. How many grains of sand make up the Sahara?*

Solution

a Volume $= lwh$

$\approx (1.6896 \times 10^7)(5.808 \times 10^6)(12)$
$\approx 117.758 \times 10^{13}$
$\approx 1.17758 \times 10^{15}$

The volume of sand in the Sahara is about 1.18×10^{15} cubic feet.

b Number of grains of sand $= \dfrac{\text{volume of sand}}{\text{volume per grain}}$

$\approx \dfrac{1.18 \times 10^{15}}{1.3 \times 10^{-9}}$
$\approx 9.1 \times 10^{23}$

There are approximately 9.1×10^{23} grains of sand in the Sahara.

Part Three: Exercises and Problems

Warm-up Exercises

In problems 1–4, evaluate each expression.

1 $4^3 \cdot 4^{-5}$

2 4^0

3 $\dfrac{9.3 \times 10^4}{2 \times 10^7}$

4 3^{-2}

In problems 5–8, simplify each expression.

5 $\dfrac{2x^{-3}}{4x^2}$

6 $\dfrac{6x^{-3}y^4z}{9x^2y\,z^{-2}}$

7 $\left(\dfrac{3x^5y^0}{6x^{-2}y^{-3}}\right)^2$

8 $\dfrac{(a+b)^{-3}}{(a+b)^{-4}}$

9 Write 0.00359 in scientific notation.

10 Write 2.43×10^{-5} without a power of 10.

11 Express the area of the triangle in scientific notation.

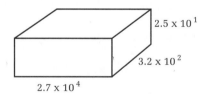

Problem Set

12 Arrange the numbers from smallest to largest.

$2.1 \times 10^{-3} \qquad -4.3 \times 10^4 \qquad 10^{-2} \qquad 7.31 \times 10^2$

In problems 13–16, evaluate each expression if $p = 5$.

13 $\dfrac{p^6}{p^3}$

14 $\dfrac{p^4}{p^6}$

15 $\dfrac{p^3 \cdot p^5}{p^5}$

16 $\dfrac{p}{p^5}$

In problems 17–19, simplify each expression.

17 7^0

18 $(-3.5)^0(4.7)$

19 $(4^3)(4^{-3})$

20 Find the volume of the box.

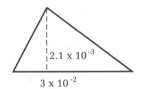

In problems 21–23, simplify.

21 $\dfrac{x^5}{x^{-3}}$

22 $\dfrac{y^{-4}}{y^3}$

23 $\dfrac{a^3b^{-7}}{a^{-3}b^4}$

In problems 24–26, express each number in scientific notation.

24 0.003401

25 0.32109

26 3.98

27 Determine whether each of the following expressions is between 0 and 0.01.

a 4.37×10^{-3} **b** 1.67×10^{-2} **c** 8.61×10^{-1} **d** 5.87×10^{-4}

In problems 28–30, write each number without a power of 10.

28 9.32×10^{-4} **29** 4.03×10^{-1} **30** 3.67×10^{0}

31 The population p of Mythical City t years from now can be approximated by using the formula $p = 1{,}200{,}000 \cdot (1.02)^{t}$. What is the present population? (Hint: Let $t = 0$.) What will the population be in 10 years?

In problems 32–39, simplify each expression.

32 $(12x)^{4}$ **33** $12(x + x)^{6}$ **34** $-4(3x)^{5}$ **35** $2(-4x)^{6}$

36 $x \cdot x$ **37** $\dfrac{(6x^{2}y^{3})^{4}}{(2xy^{2})^{3}}$ **38** $\dfrac{-9a^{3}b^{-8}}{-24ab^{9}}$ **39** $\dfrac{(7x^{2}y^{-4})^{0}}{12^{-2}x^{-3}y^{-4}}$

In problems 40–43, evaluate each expression.

40 0^{5} **41** 0^{1} **42** 4^{0} **43** 2^{0}

44 The cube shown is to be covered with colored tiles. Determine the number of tiles that will be needed if each tile has the given dimensions.

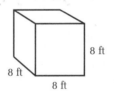

8 ft

8 ft

8 ft

a 2 feet by 2 feet **b** 6 inches by 6 inches
c w feet by w feet **d** w inches by w inches

In problems 45 and 46, evaluate without using a calculator.

45 $(4 \times 10^{6})(2 \times 10^{4})$ **46** $\dfrac{9.6 \times 10^{7}}{1.2 \times 10^{3}}$

In problems 47–49, find each missing number.

47 $3^{8} \cdot (\quad) = 3^{24}$ **48** $(\quad)^{5} = 8^{10}$ **49** $(8)^{5}(\quad)^{5} = 24^{5}$

In problems 50–52, simplify.

50 $(3x^{-1}y^{-2})^{3}$ **51** $\dfrac{(3x^{2})^{-2}}{xy^{-2}}$ **52** $\dfrac{(2x)^{-1}y^{-3}}{-4x^{2}y^{-4}}$

In problems 53–55, solve for x.

53 $x^{0} = 1$ **54** $x^{1} = 1$ **55** $1^{x} = 1$

56 Solve for (x, y).

$$\begin{bmatrix} 2 \times 10^{3} & 10^{4} \\ 10^{1} & 2 \times 10^{2} \end{bmatrix}\begin{bmatrix} 10^{5} \\ 3 \times 10^{4} \end{bmatrix} = \begin{bmatrix} x \\ y \end{bmatrix}$$

Problem Set, *continued*

In problems 57–59, solve for *n*.

57 $(2^5)(2^n) = 2^{12}$

58 $(x^n)^4 = x^{-12}$

59 $\dfrac{x^4}{x^{12}} = x^n$

60 Evaluate each expression.

    a $\sqrt{36}$ **b** $\sqrt{9}$ **c** $\sqrt{4}$ **d** $3 \cdot 2$

61 The rate 18 feet per second can be expressed as the fraction
$\dfrac{18 \text{ feet}}{1 \text{ second}}$. Use fractions to simplify each of the following.

    a (18 feet per second) · (60 seconds per minute)
    b (40 miles per hour) · (1 hour per 60 minutes)

In problems 62–64, evaluate each expression.

62 $\left(\dfrac{1}{2}\right)^{-3}$ **63** $\left(\dfrac{2}{3}\right)^2$ **64** $\left(\dfrac{3}{2}\right)^{-2}$

65 In a given year the United States Veterans Administration Life Insurance Program provides \$211.5 billion for 7.3 million policy holders. Find the mean coverage per policy holder.

In problems 66–69, solve for *x*.

66 $3^x = 1$ **67** $3^x = 3$ **68** $3^x = \dfrac{1}{9}$ **69** $3^x = -3$

70 Refer to the diagram.

    a Write the formula to find the surface area of the box in terms of *a*.
    b Find the surface area if $a = 3.14 \times 10^4$ millimeters.
    c Find *a* if the surface area of the box is 5.2×10^9 square millimeters.

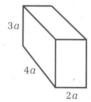

In problems 71–73, simplify.

71 $\left(\dfrac{4x^2}{y}\right)^{-3}$ **72** $2^{-1} + 3^{-1}$ **73** $\dfrac{4(x+y)^{-1}}{3(x+y)^{-2}}$

In problems 74 and 75, solve for *x* in terms of *a*.

74 $3ax + 2ax = 15a^2 + 30a$ **75** $4ax - 12a = 2a^2$

76 Use a calculator and the formula $xy = 1$ to complete the table.

x	10^4	10^3	10^2	10^1	10^0	10^{-1}	10^{-2}	10^{-3}	10^{-4}
y									

In problems 77 and 78, solve for x.

77 $2^{-4} \cdot x = 2^6$

78 $\left(3^{-1}\right)^{-2}x + 1 = 0$

79 Determine the area of the largest triangle pictured.

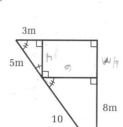

80 A number is chosen at random from {0, 1, 2, 3, 4, 5, 6, 7, 8, 9} and is raised to the fifth power. Find the probability that the number and the units digit of the fifth power of the number are the same.

In problems 81 and 82, graph each equation.

81 $y = \left(\dfrac{1}{2}\right)^x$

82 $y = 2^{-x}$

83 Solve for x if $3^x = 27 \cdot 3^{2x}$.

84 Solve the system for (x, y).
$$\begin{cases} 3^x = 2^y \\ 2^x = 3^y \end{cases}$$

85 Refer to the diagram.
  a Write a formula for the cylinder's volume in terms of a.
  b Find the volume of the cylinder if $a = 2$.
  c Find the volume of the cylinder if $a = 3$.
  d Find the ratio of the volumes of the cylinders in parts **b** and **c**.

86 Try to figure out what the "log" function, [log], on a calculator does.

  a Enter each of the following and record the result.

  i 100,000 [log]　　　　**ii** 10,000 [log]

  iii 1000 [log]　　　　　**iv** 100 [log]

  v 0.01 [log]　　　　　　**vi** 0.001 [log]

  b Find the pattern in part **a** and then, without a calculator, try to find the log of each of the following.
  i 1,000,000　　　　**ii** 0.000001
  iii 0.1　　　　　　　**iv** 1

  c Use a calculator to find the log of 32 to the nearest tenth. Try to figure out how to interpret this result.

SIMPLIFYING RADICALS

Objectives

After studying this section, you will be able to
- Identify terms used with radicals
- Use properties to simplify radicals
- Add and subtract radicals

Part One: Introduction

Terminology

The square root symbol $\sqrt{}$ is also called a radical sign. An expression in the form $\sqrt{a}$ is a **radical expression.** The number under the radical sign, such as the 5 in $\sqrt{5}$, is called the **radicand.**

All positive numbers have both a positive and a negative square root. For the positive root of x, we write $\sqrt{x}$, and for the negative root of x, we write $-\sqrt{x}$. For example, $\sqrt{36} = 6$ and $-\sqrt{36} = -6$.

Properties Used in Simplifying Radicals

What conclusion can you draw from the following problems?

$$\sqrt{4 \cdot 9} \qquad \sqrt{4} \cdot \sqrt{9} \qquad\qquad \sqrt{16 \cdot 4} \qquad \sqrt{16} \cdot \sqrt{4}$$
$$= \sqrt{36} \qquad = 2 \cdot 3 \qquad\qquad = \sqrt{64} \qquad = 4 \cdot 2$$
$$= 6 \qquad\quad = 6 \qquad\qquad\quad = 8 \qquad\quad = 8$$

Notice that $\sqrt{4 \cdot 9} = \sqrt{4} \cdot \sqrt{9}$ and $\sqrt{16 \cdot 4} = \sqrt{16} \cdot \sqrt{4}$. These examples illustrate the Distributive Property of Square Root over Multiplication.

The Distributive Property of Square Root over Multiplication

If $a \geq 0$ and $b \geq 0$, then $\sqrt{ab} = \sqrt{a} \cdot \sqrt{b}$.

We can use the Distributive Property of Square Root over Multiplication to rewrite a radical term so that the radicand does not have any factors that are perfect squares. Let's use $\sqrt{18}$ as an example.

The largest factor of 18 that is a perfect square is 9.	$\sqrt{18} = \sqrt{9 \cdot 2}$
Apply the Distributive Property of Square Root over Multiplication	$= \sqrt{9}\,\sqrt{2}$
Take the square root of 9	$= 3\sqrt{2}$

A radical term is written in ***standard radical form*** when it is written as the product of a number and a radical with a radicand that contains no perfect square factors.

Example   *Write $\sqrt{300}$ in standard radical form.*

$$\sqrt{300} = \sqrt{4}\,\sqrt{75}$$
$$= 2\sqrt{75}$$

Continue, because this radicand still contains a perfect square factor, 25

$$= 2\sqrt{25}\,\sqrt{3}$$
$$= 2 \cdot 5\sqrt{3}$$
$$= 10\sqrt{3}$$

Adding and Subtracting Radicals

Radical terms with the same radicands are ***like radical terms.*** We combine like radical terms by adding or subtracting their coefficients.

Example   *Find the length of $\overline{AB}$.*

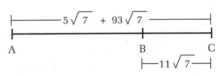

Combine like radical terms.

$$5\sqrt{7} + 93\sqrt{7} - 11\sqrt{7} = 87\sqrt{7}$$

Example   *Simplify $8\sqrt{3} + 7\sqrt{5} - 11\sqrt{3} + 2\sqrt{5}$.*

Combine like radical terms.

$$8\sqrt{3} + 7\sqrt{5} - 11\sqrt{3} + 2\sqrt{5} = 8\sqrt{3} - 11\sqrt{3} + 7\sqrt{5} + 2\sqrt{5}$$
$$= -3\sqrt{3} + 9\sqrt{5}$$

Example   *Add $\sqrt{50} + \sqrt{18}$.*

Let's put each term into standard radical form and combine like radical terms.

$$\sqrt{50} + \sqrt{18} = \sqrt{25}\sqrt{2} + \sqrt{9}\sqrt{2}$$
$$= 5\sqrt{2} + 3\sqrt{2}$$
$$= 8\sqrt{2}$$

Example   *Determine whether $\sqrt{a + b} = \sqrt{a} + \sqrt{b}$ makes a True or False statement for all values of a and b.*

Let's try $a = 16$ and $b = 9$.

Left Side	**Right Side**
$\sqrt{a + b}$	$\sqrt{a} + \sqrt{b}$
$= \sqrt{16 + 9}$	$= \sqrt{16} + \sqrt{9}$
$= \sqrt{25}$	$= 4 + 3$
$= 5$	$= 7$

For $a = 16$ and $b = 9$, the sides are not equal. We see that $\sqrt{a + b} \neq \sqrt{a} + \sqrt{b}$. Square root does not distribute over addition.

Part Two: Sample Problems

Problem 1 Approximate $\sqrt{2}\ \sqrt{5}\ \sqrt{7}$ to the nearest thousandth.

Solution To compute more efficiently, first apply the Distributive Property of Square Root over Multiplication. Then use a calculator to find the square root of the product.

$$\sqrt{2}\ \sqrt{5}\ \sqrt{7} = \sqrt{70}$$
$$\approx 8.367$$

Problem 2 Find length x in the right triangle. Give your answer in standard radical form.

Solution Use the Pythagorean Theorem.

$$x^2 + 6^2 = 8^2$$
$$x^2 + 36 = 64$$
$$\underline{-36 \qquad -36}$$
$$x^2 \quad = 28$$
$$\sqrt{x^2} \quad = \sqrt{28}$$
$$|x| \quad = \sqrt{4}\ \sqrt{7}$$
$$x \quad = \pm 2\sqrt{7}$$

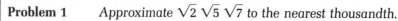

The length must be positive, so $x = 2\sqrt{7}$.

Problem 3 Multiply. Give the answer in standard radical form.

a $\left(5\sqrt{6}\right)^2$ b $\sqrt{3}\left(\sqrt{3} + \sqrt{6}\right)$

Solution

a $\left(5\sqrt{6}\right)^2 = 5\sqrt{6} \cdot 5\sqrt{6}$ b $\sqrt{3}\left(\sqrt{3} + \sqrt{6}\right) = \sqrt{3}\ \sqrt{3} + \sqrt{3}\ \sqrt{6}$
$= 25\sqrt{36}$ $= \sqrt{9} + \sqrt{18}$
$= 25 \cdot 6$ $= 3 + \sqrt{9}\sqrt{2}$
$= 150$ $= 3 + 3\sqrt{2}$

Square root and squaring are inverse operations. If you take the square root of a number and then square it, the result is the original number. Therefore, $(\sqrt{7}^2) = 7$.

Part Three: Exercises and Problems

Warm-up Exercises

In problems 1–4, evaluate each expression.

1 $\sqrt{9 + 16}$ **2** $\sqrt{9} + \sqrt{16}$ **3** $\sqrt{12^2 + 5^2}$ **4** $\sqrt{12^2} + \sqrt{5^2}$

In problems 5–8, simplify each expression.

5 $\sqrt{2}\left(\sqrt{2} + \sqrt{6}\right)$ **6** $9\sqrt{3} + 4\sqrt{3} - 3\sqrt{5}$

7 $\sqrt{20} + \sqrt{75}$ **8** $\dfrac{\sqrt{16}}{\sqrt{9}} \cdot \sqrt{27}$

In problems 9–12, write each term in standard radical form.

9 $\sqrt{20}$ **10** $\sqrt{90}$ **11** $\sqrt{14}$ **12** $\sqrt{800}$

13 Solve for x.

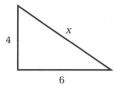

Problem Set

In problems 14–16, express each radical term in standard radical form.

14 $\sqrt{36}$ **15** $\sqrt{28}$ **16** $\sqrt{15}$

In problems 17–20, write each expression in standard radical form.

17 $\sqrt{64} + \sqrt{36}$ **18** $\sqrt{64 + 36}$

19 $\sqrt{2}\left(\sqrt{3} + \sqrt{8}\right)$ **20** $\sqrt{3}\left(\sqrt{6} + \sqrt{30}\right)$

In problems 21 and 22, simplify each expression.

21 $3\sqrt{4} + 8\sqrt{9} + 15\sqrt{16}$ **22** $5\sqrt{6} - \sqrt{24} + \sqrt{54}$

23 Refer to the triangle. Express each answer in standard radical form.

   a Find the area of the triangle.
   b Find the length of the hypotenuse.

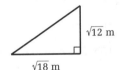

In problems 24–30, predict each answer.

24 $\sqrt{0.49}$ **25** $\sqrt{0.049}$ **26** $\sqrt{0.0049}$ **27** $\sqrt{0.00049}$

28 $\sqrt{0.0000049}$ **29** $\sqrt{0.00000049}$ **30** $\sqrt{0.00000000049}$

31 Refer to the diagram.

   a Write the perimeter of the rectangle in standard radical form.
   b Find the area of the rectangle.

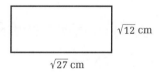

32 The legs of a right triangle are 5 and $\sqrt{11}$. Find the length of the hypotenuse.

33 Lefty can throw a baseball at a speed of 95 miles per hour.

   a How fast is this in miles per second?
   b The distance from the pitcher to the batter is 60 feet 6 inches. How long does it take the ball to get to the batter after it leaves Lefty's hand? (Hint: There are 5280 feet in a mile.)

Problem Set, *continued*

In problems 34 and 35, solve for x.

34 $3x = \left(4\sqrt{2}\right)\left(3\sqrt{2}\right)$

35 $\sqrt{2}\left(3\sqrt{2} + x\right) = 6 - 4\sqrt{2}$

In problems 36–38, solve for x.

36 $\sqrt{2}x = \sqrt{8}$

37 $-\sqrt{3}x = \sqrt{12}$

38 $\sqrt{10}x = \sqrt{30}$

39 Find the area of the shaded region if the radii of the circles are $\sqrt{12}$ and $\sqrt{48}$.

In problems 40 and 41, simplify each expression.

40 $\left(\sqrt{11}\right)^2 - \left(\sqrt{6}\right)^2 + \left(\sqrt{3}\right)^2$

41 $\left[\left(\sqrt{7}\right)^2 - \left(\sqrt{2}\right)^2\right]^2$

In problems 42–45, approximate to the nearest hundredth.

42 $\dfrac{1}{\sqrt{7}}$

43 $\dfrac{\sqrt{7}}{7}$

44 $\sqrt{5}\,\sqrt{3}\,\sqrt{11}$

45 $\dfrac{1}{\sqrt{5}}$

In problems 46 and 47, express each answer in scientific notation.

46 $\dfrac{\left(\sqrt{32} \times 10^8\right)}{\left(\sqrt{8} \times 10^2\right)}$

47 $\left(\sqrt{1.21} \times 10\right)^2$

48 The area of a square is 120 square inches. Find the exact length of each side in standard radical form.

49 Refer to the diagram. Express the answers in standard radical form.

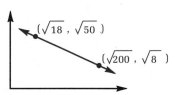

a Find the slope of the line passing through the points shown.
b Find an equation of the line.

In problems 50 and 51, determine whether the first expression is less than, greater than, or equal to the second expression.

50 $\sqrt{17^2 - 15^2} \ ? \ \sqrt{17^2} - \sqrt{15^2}$

51 $\sqrt{\sqrt{9} + \sqrt{16}} \ ? \ \sqrt{9} + \sqrt{16}$

52 Find the midpoint of the segment joining $\left(-4\sqrt{2}, 3\right)$ and $\left(-8\sqrt{2}, -9\right)$.

53 Find the probability that the value of a number selected at random from $\{\sqrt{13}, \sqrt{7}, \sqrt{21}, \sqrt{11}, \sqrt{19}, \sqrt{29}\}$ is between 3 and 4.

In problems 54 and 55, multiply and simplify, using only the rules for multiplying radicals. Do these without a calculator.

54 $\dfrac{10}{\sqrt{5}} \cdot \dfrac{\sqrt{5}}{\sqrt{5}}$

55 $\dfrac{\sqrt{20}}{\sqrt{3}} \cdot \dfrac{\sqrt{3}}{\sqrt{3}}$

In problems 56 and 57, express in standard radical form.

56 $\sqrt{15}\,\sqrt{10}\,\sqrt{14}\,\sqrt{21}$

57 $\sqrt{5}\,\sqrt{15} + \sqrt{10}\,\sqrt{30}$

58 Solve for (x, y).

$$\begin{bmatrix} 1 & 1 \\ 4 & -1 \end{bmatrix} \begin{bmatrix} x \\ y \end{bmatrix} = \begin{bmatrix} \sqrt{2} \\ 14\sqrt{2} \end{bmatrix}$$

 59 Complete the table for $y = \sqrt{x - 2}$ and graph.

x	1	2	3	4	5	6	7
y							

In problems 60–62, express in standard radical form.

60 $\left(2\sqrt{18}\right)^2$

61 $-2\sqrt{98}$

62 $\left(4\sqrt{2}\right)\left(6\sqrt{3}\right)\left(\sqrt{18}\right)$

63 Hero's Formula states that the area of a triangle equals $\sqrt{s(s - a)(s - b)(s - c)}$ where s is the semiperimeter of the triangle, $s = \dfrac{a + b + c}{2}$, and a, b, and c are the lengths of the sides of the triangle. In parts **a–c**, find the area of the triangle with the given side. Express your answers both in standard radical form and as a decimal correct to two decimal places.

   a 8, 9, and 11   **b** 16, 18, and 22   **c** 4, 9, and 7

64 Solve $x^2 + 6x - 6 = 0$.

65 Find (x, y, z, a).

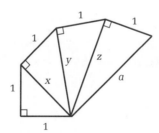

66 Solve the system.

$$\begin{cases} \sqrt{3}x + \sqrt{5}y = \sqrt{15} \\ \sqrt{27}x - \sqrt{20}y = \sqrt{375} \end{cases}$$

In problems 67–69, solve for x.

67 $\sqrt{x} = x^2$

68 $\sqrt{(x - 2)^2} = 4$

69 $\dfrac{1}{\sqrt{(x + 5)^2}} = 4$

RATIONALIZING

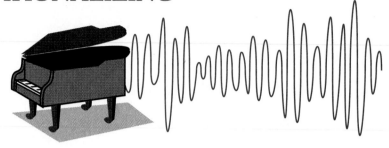

$$\frac{f}{f'} = \frac{\sqrt{D'}}{\sqrt{D}}$$

LAW OF DENSITIES OF STRINGS

Objectives

After studying this section, you will be able to
- Use the Distributive Property of Square Root over Division
- Rationalize denominators and numerators

Part One: Introduction

Distributive Property of Square Root over Division

Let's analyze the following examples.

$$\sqrt{\frac{4}{9}} = \sqrt{\left(\frac{2}{3}\right)^2} \qquad\qquad \frac{\sqrt{4}}{\sqrt{9}} \qquad\qquad \sqrt{\frac{16}{25}} = \sqrt{\left(\frac{4}{5}\right)^2} \qquad\qquad \frac{\sqrt{16}}{\sqrt{25}}$$

$$= \frac{2}{3} \qquad\qquad\qquad = \frac{2}{3} \qquad\qquad\qquad = \frac{4}{5} \qquad\qquad\qquad = \frac{4}{5}$$

Notice that $\sqrt{\frac{4}{9}} = \frac{\sqrt{4}}{\sqrt{9}}$ and that $\sqrt{\frac{16}{25}} = \frac{\sqrt{16}}{\sqrt{25}}$. These examples illustrate the Distributive Property of Square Root over Division.

The Distributive Property of Square Root over Division

If $a \geq 0$ and $b > 0$, then $\sqrt{\dfrac{a}{b}} = \dfrac{\sqrt{a}}{\sqrt{b}}$.

Example   *Simplify each expression. (The solutions are given below.)*

a $\sqrt{\dfrac{36}{121}}$

$$\sqrt{\frac{36}{121}} = \frac{\sqrt{36}}{\sqrt{121}}$$

$$= \frac{6}{11}$$

b $\dfrac{\sqrt{50}}{\sqrt{2}}$

$$\frac{\sqrt{50}}{\sqrt{2}} = \sqrt{\frac{50}{2}}$$

$$= \sqrt{25}$$
$$= 5$$

Rationalizing Denominators and Numerators

Recall from arithmetic that you can multiply a fraction by 1 without changing the value. For example, the result of $\frac{3}{5} \cdot 1$ is $\frac{3}{5}$. This idea forms the basis for rationalizing. *Rationalizing* is the process of changing a radical denominator or numerator to an integer without changing the value of the fraction.

Let's rationalize the denominator of $\dfrac{\sqrt{5}}{\sqrt{2}}$. (Remember, $\dfrac{\sqrt{2}}{\sqrt{2}} = 1$.)

$$\frac{\sqrt{5}}{\sqrt{2}} \cdot 1 = \frac{\sqrt{5}}{\sqrt{2}} \cdot \frac{\sqrt{2}}{\sqrt{2}} = \frac{\sqrt{10}}{\sqrt{4}}$$

$$= \frac{\sqrt{10}}{2}$$

Thus $\dfrac{\sqrt{5}}{\sqrt{2}}$ and $\dfrac{\sqrt{10}}{2}$ have the same value.

➤ **To rationalize, multiply the fraction by a radical form of 1 that will make the appropriate radicand a perfect square.**

Example

Rationalize each denominator. (The solutions are given below.)

a $\dfrac{1}{\sqrt{3}}$

$$\frac{1}{\sqrt{3}} = \frac{1}{\sqrt{3}} \cdot \frac{\sqrt{3}}{\sqrt{3}}$$

$$= \frac{\sqrt{3}}{\sqrt{9}}$$

$$= \frac{\sqrt{3}}{3}$$

b $\dfrac{6\sqrt{3}}{\sqrt{8}}$

$$\frac{6\sqrt{3}}{\sqrt{8}} = \frac{6\sqrt{3}}{\sqrt{8}} \cdot \frac{\sqrt{2}}{\sqrt{2}}$$

$$= \frac{6\sqrt{6}}{\sqrt{16}}$$

$$= \frac{6\sqrt{6}}{4}$$

$$= \frac{3\sqrt{6}}{2}$$

Example

Rationalize each numerator. (The solutions are given below.)

a $\dfrac{3\sqrt{2}}{2}$

$$\frac{3\sqrt{2}}{2} \cdot \frac{\sqrt{2}}{\sqrt{2}} = \frac{3\sqrt{4}}{2\sqrt{2}}$$

$$= \frac{3(2)}{2\sqrt{2}}$$

$$= \frac{3}{\sqrt{2}}$$

b $\dfrac{\sqrt{5}}{10}$

$$\frac{\sqrt{5}}{10} \cdot \frac{\sqrt{5}}{\sqrt{5}} = \frac{\sqrt{25}}{10\sqrt{5}}$$

$$= \frac{5}{10\sqrt{5}}$$

$$= \frac{1}{2\sqrt{5}}$$

Part Two: Sample Problems

Problem 1 The length of one leg of a right triangle is $\frac{1}{2}$ centimeter, and the length of the hypotenuse is 1 centimeter. Find the length of the other leg.

Solution Use the Pythagorean Theorem. Let x represent the length of the other leg.

$$\left(\frac{1}{2}\right)^2 + x^2 = 1^2$$

$$\frac{1}{4} + x^2 = 1$$

$$x^2 = \frac{3}{4}$$

$$|x| = \sqrt{\frac{3}{4}}$$

$$x = \pm \frac{\sqrt{3}}{\sqrt{4}}$$

$$x = \pm \frac{\sqrt{3}}{2}$$

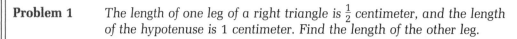

Since x is the length of a leg of a triangle, it must be positive, so the exact length of the other leg of the triangle is $\frac{\sqrt{3}}{2}$ centimeter.

Problem 2 Rewrite in standard radical form.

$$\sqrt{24} + \sqrt{6} + \frac{\sqrt{18}}{\sqrt{3}}$$

Solution

$$\sqrt{24} + \sqrt{6} + \frac{\sqrt{18}}{\sqrt{3}} = \sqrt{4}\,\sqrt{6} + \sqrt{6} + \sqrt{\frac{18}{3}}$$

$$= 2\sqrt{6} + \sqrt{6} + \sqrt{6}$$

$$= 4\sqrt{6}$$

Part Three: Exercises and Problems

Warm-up Exercises

In problems 1 and 2, simplify.

1 $\sqrt{\dfrac{16}{49}}$

2 $8 \cdot \sqrt{\dfrac{25}{4}}$

In problems 3–5, rationalize each denominator.

3 $\dfrac{21}{\sqrt{3}}$

4 $\dfrac{\sqrt{8}}{\sqrt{2}}$

5 $\dfrac{15}{\sqrt{15}}$

In problems 6–8, rationalize each numerator.

6 $\dfrac{\sqrt{2}}{3}$ **7** $\dfrac{5\sqrt{3}}{6}$ **8** $\dfrac{\sqrt{9}}{15}$

In problems 9 and 10, simplify each expression.

9 $\dfrac{2\sqrt{20}}{3} - \dfrac{\sqrt{15}}{\sqrt{3}}$ **10** $\sqrt{8} + \sqrt{50} - \dfrac{\sqrt{96}}{\sqrt{3}}$

11 Find lengths x and y.

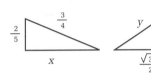

Problem Set

In problems 12–15, rationalize each denominator or numerator.

12 $\dfrac{1}{\sqrt{5}}$ **13** $\dfrac{\sqrt{3}}{2}$ **14** $\dfrac{4}{\sqrt{6}}$ **15** $\dfrac{2\sqrt{3}}{9}$

16 Arrange the numbers in size from smallest to largest.

$(0.5)^2$ $\sqrt{0.49}$ $\sqrt{\dfrac{16}{25}}$ 0.8 6.4×10^{-2}

In problems 17 and 18, simplify.

17 $\sqrt{2} + \dfrac{4}{\sqrt{2}} + \sqrt{\sqrt{64}}$ **18** $2\sqrt{2}\left(\dfrac{3}{\sqrt{2}} + \sqrt{2}\right)$

19 Find x.

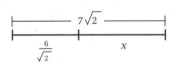

In problems 20 and 21, solve for x.

20 $\sqrt{2}\left(x + 3\sqrt{2}\right) = 18$ **21** $2\sqrt{2}x + 5 = 27$

In problems 22–25, simplify each fraction.

22 $\dfrac{\sqrt{18}}{\sqrt{2}}$ **23** $\sqrt{\dfrac{18}{2}}$ **24** $\dfrac{\sqrt{6x^2}}{\sqrt{2x}}$ **25** $\dfrac{\sqrt{12a^5}}{\sqrt{2a^{-3}}}$

In problems 26 and 27, simplify each expression.

26 $3x^2(4x^3 + 5x^2 - 6x - 9)$ **27** $\dfrac{8x^5 + 4x^4 + 12x^3 - 18x^2}{4x}$

Problem Set, *continued*

In problems 28 and 29, solve for x.

28 $3\sqrt{2} = \sqrt{2}(x - 4)$ **29** $\sqrt{2}x(3\sqrt{2}x - 6) = 0$

30 The lengths of the legs of a right triangle are each 5 centimeters. Find the length of the hypotenuse.

In problems 31 and 32, write each expression in standard radical form.

31 $\dfrac{\sqrt{10}}{\sqrt{40}} \cdot \dfrac{\sqrt{32}}{\sqrt{2}}$ **32** $\dfrac{\sqrt{12}}{\sqrt{6}} + \sqrt{20} - \sqrt{4}$

In problems 33 and 34, find the x- and y-intercepts of each line.

33 $\sqrt{3}x + \sqrt{5}y = \sqrt{30}$ **34** $-x\sqrt{7} + y\sqrt{2} = \sqrt{42}$

35 The area of a square is 12 square centimeters. Find its perimeter.

In problems 36 and 37, write each expression in standard radical form.

36 $\dfrac{3}{\sqrt{2}} + \dfrac{5}{\sqrt{2}}$ **37** $2\sqrt{3} + \sqrt{18} + 2\sqrt{27} - \dfrac{8}{\sqrt{2}}$

38 The sum of the areas of the two smaller circles is equal to the area of the largest circle, and the indicated numbers are all radii. Find r.

In problems 39–41, rationalize each numerator.

39 $\dfrac{\sqrt{8}}{4}$ **40** $\dfrac{\sqrt{2}}{\sqrt{32}}$ **41** $\dfrac{x\sqrt{3}}{\sqrt{5}}$ (x is an integer)

In problems 42–45, use a calculator to compute.

42 $\sqrt{0.49}$ **43** $\sqrt{4.9}$ **44** $\sqrt{49}$ **45** $\sqrt{490}$

46 Find the value of x in standard radical form.

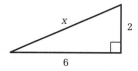

In problems 47–50, solve for x.

47 $\sqrt{2}x + 2\sqrt{8}x = \sqrt{75}$ **48** $\left(\sqrt{2}\right)^2 x + \left(\sqrt{3}\right)^2 x = 50$

49 $\left(\sqrt{7}\right)^2 x - x = 42$ **50** $3\sqrt{2} + \sqrt{2}x = 2\sqrt{2}$

51 Solve for x.

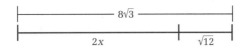

52 Is $x = 4$ a solution of $\sqrt{x + 5} + \sqrt{x} = 5$?

53 Solve for (x, y).

$$\begin{bmatrix} \sqrt{2} & \sqrt{3} \\ 2\sqrt{2} & -\sqrt{3} \end{bmatrix} \begin{bmatrix} x \\ y \end{bmatrix} = \begin{bmatrix} 6 \\ 9 \end{bmatrix}$$

54 The area of square S_1 is 18. The area of square S_2 is 24. Find the area of square S_3.

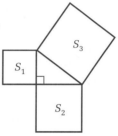

In problems 55 and 56, solve for x in standard radical form. Graph each solution set on a number line.

55 $|x + \sqrt{3}| < \sqrt{75}$

56 $|\sqrt{2}x + \sqrt{8}| \geq \sqrt{98}$

In problems 57–62, find y in standard radical form for each value of x.

57 $x = 1$

58 $x = 2$

59 $x = 3$

60 $x = 4$

61 $x = 5$

62 $x = 6$

63 A baseball diamond is a square with sides 90 feet in length. Determine the exact distance from home plate to second base along a straight line.

64 Determine how many of the small squares can fit inside the large square with no overlapping.

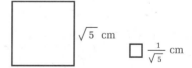

In problems 65 and 66, use the formula $A = \dfrac{s^2\sqrt{3}}{4}$, in which A is the area of an equilateral triangle and s is the length of each side.

65 Find the area of an equilateral triangle in which each side is $\sqrt{48}$.

66 Find the area of an equilateral triangle with a perimeter of $\sqrt{48}$.

67 Give a counterexample to show that $\sqrt{ab} = \sqrt{a} \cdot \sqrt{b}$ is not always true.

Problem Set, *continued*

68 The area of the rectangle is 6 square meters, and the perimeter of the rectangle is $8\sqrt{2}$ meters. Solve for x.

69 Solve for x.

$$\begin{bmatrix} \sqrt{2} & \sqrt{3} \\ \sqrt{3} & \sqrt{2} \end{bmatrix} \begin{bmatrix} x \\ y \end{bmatrix} = \begin{bmatrix} 5 \\ 2\sqrt{6} \end{bmatrix}$$

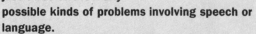

CAREER PROFILE

MARCI LAUREL, SPEECH AND LANGUAGE PATHOLOGIST

The ability of people to communicate with one another is one of humankind's most precious gifts. Because the ability may seem natural and effortless, it is easy to take for granted. Yet speech and language disorders are surprisingly common among all populations of people. Stuttering, difficulties with articulation, and symbolism disorders like aphasia are just three of the many possible kinds of problems involving speech or language.

Marci Laurel is a pathologist who works with children as young as ten months of age to correct their problems with speech and language. When testing children, Ms. Laurel listens to the way they produce sounds and assesses how easy it is to understand their speech. Certain sounds, for example, *s*, *l*, and *r*, are particularly hard for young children to say. When Ms. Laurel suspects a disorder, she administers tests to judge the severity of the problem and, if treatment is warranted, to decide what type of treatment to use. Later, the results of the tests can be used as a baseline against which to judge the child's progress.

Ms. Laurel makes frequent use of mathematics in her work. "A background in statistics is very important, both for understanding research done by others and for analyzing my own results," she says. "And since hearing is closely associated with speaking, familiarity with the physics and mathematics of the science of acoustics is very useful."

Ms. Laurel suffered a mild speech disorder herself as a child. That and the influence of several people she admired led her to choose speech pathology as a career. She did undergraduate work at the University of Florida, then continued at the university to obtain her master's degree in speech and language pathology.

RADICAL EQUATIONS

Objectives

After studying this section, you will be able to
- Solve radical equations
- Identify extraneous solutions of radical equations

Part One: Introduction

Radical Equations

In Chapter 2, you learned how to solve an equation by applying the same operation to both sides of the equation. We will now use this method to solve radical equations. Remember that squaring is the inverse of taking a square root.

Example *Write an equation and solve for x.*

a

b

After writing an equation to describe the diagram, our strategy will be to isolate the radical on one side of the equation and then square both sides of the equation.

a
$$\sqrt{x} + 4 = 7$$
$$\underline{\quad -4 \quad\quad -4\quad}$$
$$\sqrt{x} = 3$$
$$\left(\sqrt{x}\right)^2 = 3^2$$
$$x = 9$$

b
$$\sqrt{x-3} = 12$$
$$\left(\sqrt{x-3}\right)^2 = 12^2$$
$$x - 3 = 144$$
$$\underline{\quad +3 \quad\quad +3\quad}$$
$$x = 147$$

Let's check these solutions.

Check

Left Side	Right Side
$\sqrt{x} + 4$	$= 7$
$= \sqrt{9} + 4$	
$= 3 + 4$	
$= 7$	

If $x = 9$, the sides are equal, so the answer checks.

Left Side	Right Side
$\sqrt{x - 3}$	$= 12$
$= \sqrt{147 - 3}$	
$= \sqrt{144}$	
$= 12$	

If $x = 147$, the sides are equal, so the answer checks.

Extraneous Solutions

Be careful! When squaring both sides of a radical equation and then solving, you must be cautious. You may obtain results that are not actually solutions of the original equation.

Example   *Solve each equation for x.*

a $\sqrt{x} = -3$

$\sqrt{x} = -3$

b $\sqrt{2x - 1} + 7 = 4$

$$\sqrt{2x - 1} + 7 = 4$$
$$\underline{\hspace{1.5cm} -7 \quad -7}$$
$$\sqrt{2x - 1} \quad = -3$$

In both equations, the square root is equal to a negative number, which cannot be true for any real value of x. Neither equation has a real solution. What if we proceeded to solve each equation?

$$\left(\sqrt{x}\right)^2 = (-3)^2$$
$$x = 9$$

$$\left(\sqrt{2x - 1}\right)^2 = (-3)^2$$
$$2x - 1 = 9$$
$$\underline{\hspace{0.5cm} +1 \quad +1}$$
$$2x \quad = 10$$
$$x \quad = 5$$

Let's check these apparent solutions in the original equations to see if they are actual solutions.

Check

Left Side	Right Side
$\sqrt{x}$	$= -3$
$= \sqrt{9}$	
$= 3$	

If $x = 9$, the sides are not equal, so the answer does not check.

Left Side	Right Side
$\sqrt{2x - 1} + 7$	$= 4$
$= \sqrt{2(5) - 1} + 7$	
$= \sqrt{9} + 7$	
$= 3 + 7$	
$= 10$	

If $x = 5$, the sides are not equal, so the answer does not check.

In both cases, the apparent solution did not check. Such solutions are called *extraneous.* Once again we see that it is critical to check all answers.

Part Two: Sample Problems

Problem 1   *Solve $\sqrt{y} + \sqrt{y} = 168$ for y.*

Solution

$$\sqrt{y} + \sqrt{y} = 168$$

Add like radical terms
$$2\sqrt{y} = 168$$

Divide each side by 2
$$\sqrt{y} = 84$$

Square each side
$$\left(\sqrt{y}\right)^2 = 84^2$$
$$y = 7056$$

Remember to check the solution in the original equation.

Problem 2   *Solve* $\sqrt{3x + 4} = x$ *for x.*

Solution   We square both sides, since the radical is already isolated.

$$\sqrt{3x + 4} = x$$
$$\left(\sqrt{3x + 4}\right)^2 = x^2$$
$$3x + 4 = x^2$$

This is a quadratic equation. We can put it in the form $ax^2 + bx + c = 0$ and use the quadratic formula.

$0 = x^2 - 3x - 4$, so $a = 1$, $b = -3$, and $c = -4$.

$$x = \frac{-b \pm \sqrt{b^2 - 4ac}}{2a}$$
$$= \frac{-(-3) \pm \sqrt{(-3)^2 - 4(1)(-4)}}{2(1)}$$
$$= \frac{3 \pm \sqrt{25}}{2}$$
$$= \frac{3 \pm 5}{2}$$

So two possible solutions are $x = 4$ and $x = -1$.

Check

Left Side	**Right Side**		**Left Side**	**Right Side**
$\sqrt{3x + 4}$	$= x$		$\sqrt{3x + 4}$	$= x$
$= \sqrt{3(4) + 4}$	$= 4$		$= \sqrt{3(-1) + 4}$	$= -1$
$= \sqrt{16}$			$= \sqrt{1}$	
$= 4$			$= 1$	

If $x = 4$, the sides are equal, so the answer checks.

If $x = -1$, the sides are not equal, so the answer does not check.

The only solution to the radical equation is $x = 4$.

Problem 3   *Solve* $\sqrt{4x + 8} = \sqrt{3x + 13}$ *for x.*

Solution

$$\sqrt{4x + 8} = \sqrt{3x + 13}$$
$$\left(\sqrt{4x + 8}\right)^2 = \left(\sqrt{3x + 13}\right)^2$$

$$
\begin{array}{rcr}
4x + 8 = & 3x + 13 \\
-3x & -3x \\
\hline
x + 8 = & 13 \\
-8 & -8 \\
\hline
x = & 5
\end{array}
$$

Check

Left Side	**Right Side**
$\sqrt{4x + 8}$	$= \sqrt{3x + 13}$
$= \sqrt{4(5) + 8}$	$= \sqrt{3(5) + 13}$
$= \sqrt{28}$	$= \sqrt{28}$

If $x = 5$, the sides are equal, so the answer checks.

Part Three: Exercises and Problems

Warm-up Exercises

In problems 1–4, describe the first step in solving each equation.

1 $\sqrt{y} + 4 = 14$

2 $\sqrt{3x - 4} = \sqrt{7}$

3 $\sqrt{x + 2} + \sqrt{x + 2} = 5$

4 $10\sqrt{x} = 50$

In problems 5–7, solve each equation. Be sure to check for extraneous solutions.

5 $\sqrt{x} + 5 = 3$

6 $\sqrt{2x + 3} = x$

7 $\sqrt{x + 2} + \sqrt{x + 2} = 5$

8 Find the value of x.

Problem Set

In problems 9–12, solve each equation for x_1.

9 $\sqrt{x_1} = 15$

10 $\sqrt{x_1} + 2 = 15$

11 $\sqrt{x_1 + 2} = 15$

12 $\sqrt{x_1 - 2} = 15$

In problems 13–15, solve each equation.

13 $\sqrt{a} = 12$

14 $\sqrt{2x - 3} = 9$

15 $\sqrt{y} - 3 = 5$

16 For each of the following, determine whether the equation is an identity.

a $3x \cdot 5x = 15x^2$ **b** $3x \cdot 5x = 15x$ **c** $x \cdot x = 2x$

d $x \cdot x = x^2$ **e** $x + x = x^2$ **f** $3x + 5x = 8x^2$

In problems 17–19, solve for x_1 if $y_1 = 36$.

17 $\sqrt{x_1 + y_1} = 5$

18 $\sqrt{x_1 y_1} = 5$

19 $\sqrt{x_1} - \sqrt{y_1} = 5$

20 Find x if the distance between the points $(x, 6)$ and $(0, 2)$ is 5.

In problems 21–24, solve each equation and write each expression in standard radical form.

21 $\sqrt{a} = \sqrt{9}$

22 $\sqrt{a} + \sqrt{9}$

23 $\sqrt{y + 1} + \sqrt{y + 1} = 24$

24 $\sqrt{3}\left(\sqrt{3} + \sqrt{12}\right)$

25 Find the value of x if the perimeter of the rectangle shown is 44.

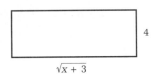

26 Solve $\sqrt{x^2 - 5x + 6} = \sqrt{12}$ for x.

27 In 1987, there were 5132 accidents on the Kennedy Expressway in Chicago.

  a Determine the average number of accidents per day.

  b About 3% of all automobile accidents result in a fatality. If this percentage is accurate, how many fatal accidents might there have been on the Kennedy in 1987?

In problems 28–30, determine whether each statement is True or False if $a = 4$ and $b = -3$.

28 $(a + b)^2 = a^2 + b^2$

29 $(a + b)^2 = a^2 + 2ab + b^2$

30 $a^2 - b^2 = (a + b)(a - b)$

In problems 31 and 32, simplify.

31 $\dfrac{4\sqrt{2}}{3} \cdot \dfrac{12}{5\sqrt{2}} \cdot \dfrac{25}{8}$

32 $\dfrac{\sqrt{10} + \sqrt{6}}{\sqrt{2}}$

33 Find the value of x if the perimeter of the rectangle shown is 26.

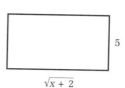

$\sqrt{x + 2}$ 5

In problems 34–37, solve for x.

34 $\sqrt{x^2 - 49} = 8$

35 $\sqrt{x^2 - 49} = \sqrt{8}$

36 $\sqrt{x^2 + 49} = 8$

37 $\sqrt{x^2 + 49} = \sqrt{8}$

In problems 38–40, simplify each expression and solve each equation.

38 $\sqrt{28} + \sqrt{63}$

39 $\sqrt{x^4} + \sqrt{9x^2}$

40 $\dfrac{\sqrt{x^4}}{\sqrt{x^2}} = \sqrt{36}$

41 Find the value of y if the slope of the line through the points $\left(5, \sqrt{y}\right)$ and $(4, 1)$ is 12.

42 Solve for x.

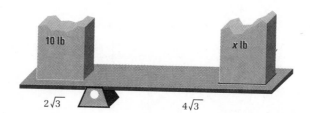

In problems 43–46, solve for x.

43 $\sqrt{3x} + 4\sqrt{27}x = 26\sqrt{24}$

44 $\sqrt{8x - 8} = 4$

45 $\sqrt{6x - 5} = x$

46 $\sqrt{x^2 - 36} + 6 = 2$

Problem Set, *continued*

47 Determine the natural domain of the function $f(x) = \sqrt{2x + 6}$.

48 Find the ratio of $\sqrt{18}$ to $\sqrt{8}$.

49 Find the ratio of the square of $\sqrt{18}$ to the square of $\sqrt{8}$.

50 Compute the area and the perimeter of the rectangle.

6.4 x 10⁴ cm

4.7 x 10⁴ cm

51 Find the area of the triangle whose base is $\sqrt{50}$ and whose height is $\sqrt{24}$.

52 Mr. Vandenberg was grading papers but forgot his problem sheet. He pulled out the paper of his perfect student. Her answers are given below. If she got all the answers correct, determine what the problems might have been.

    a $2\sqrt{3}$ **b** $5\sqrt{2}$ **c** $4\sqrt{5}$ **d** $-2\sqrt{7}$

53 Multiply $\left(-\sqrt{2} + \sqrt{6} - \sqrt{a}\right)\sqrt{18}$ and write your answer in standard radical form.

54 The pendulum formula, $p = 2\pi\sqrt{\frac{l}{g}}$, can be used to find the period p of a pendulum (the time it takes for the pendulum to swing back and forth once).

    a Find the period if $l = 1$ meter and $g = 9.8$ meters per square second.

    b Find the length (l) of the pendulum if $p = 3$ seconds and $g = 9.8$ meters per square second.

55 Find the value of x.

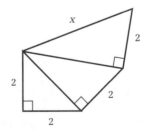

56 Solve $4\left(\sqrt{x - 3} - 5\right) = 2\sqrt{x - 3}$ for x.

57 The distance between the midpoint of the line segment with endpoints $(3, -5)$ and $(5, 7)$ and the point with coordinates $(x, 6)$ is 5. Find x.

58 Refer to the diagram.

    a Write a formula for the volume of the cone in terms of a.

    b Find the volume if $a = 4.67 \times 10^3$.

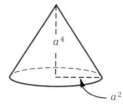

59 Find the length of the hypotenuse of the triangle represented by the matrix.

$$\begin{bmatrix} -\sqrt{2} & 0 \\ 3\sqrt{2} & 0 \\ 3\sqrt{2} & 6\sqrt{2} \end{bmatrix}$$

60 Find the ratio of the area of the triangle to the area of the entire rectangle.

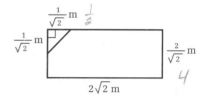

In problems 61 and 62, solve for x.

61 $3x - 19\sqrt{x} - 14 = 0$

62 $x + 2\sqrt{x} - 15 = 0$

63 Find the smallest positive integer N so that $N \cdot \sqrt{40}$ will be greater than 100.

64 A fast-food franchise has restaurants located in cities A, B, and C. The franchise intends to build a food warehouse in town W_1, W_2, or W_3. Where should the warehouse be built if the sum of the distances from A, B, and C to the warehouse is to be a minimum?

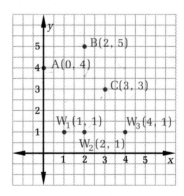

65 Solve $x^4 - 3x^2 - 28 = 0$ for x.

In problems 66–68, solve for x.

66 $2^x \cdot 4^x \cdot 8^x = 64$

67 $5^x \cdot 3^x = \dfrac{4^x}{2^{2x}}$

68 $2^{x^2 - 3x} = 1$

69 A rapid-transit train spends 1 minute at each station. The time of the trip from each station to the next is 4 minutes. If it takes 1 hour and 14 minutes from the time the train leaves the first station until it arrives at the last station, how many stations are there?

OTHER ROOTS AND FRACTIONAL EXPONENTS

Objectives

After studying this section, you will be able to
- Evaluate roots other than square roots
- Evaluate expressions containing fractional exponents
- Use a calculator to evaluate roots

Part One: Introduction

Other Roots

The expression $\sqrt[3]{125}$ means
"the number that, when raised to the third power, is 125."
Since $5^3 = 125$, the number is 5. Therefore, we write $\sqrt[3]{125} = 5$,
read "the third (cube) root of 125 is 5."

The 3 in the expression $\sqrt[3]{125}$ is called the **root index** and
indicates the root we are to find. When no root index is given, it is
understood to be the square root. Let's take a look at problems
involving other roots.

Example   *Evaluate each expression.*

    a $\sqrt[4]{16}$ **b** $\sqrt[5]{-32}$ **c** $\sqrt[3]{1.728}$

    a $\sqrt[4]{16} = 2$ because $2 \cdot 2 \cdot 2 \cdot 2 = 16$, or $2^4 = 16$.

    b $\sqrt[5]{-32} = -2$ because $(-2)(-2)(-2)(-2)(-2) = -32$, or $(-2)^5 = -32$.

    c $\sqrt[3]{1.728} = 1.2$ because $(1.2)(1.2)(1.2) = 1.728$, or $(1.2)^3 = 1.728$.

Fractional Exponents

Recall the Power to a Power Property, $(a^m)^n = a^{mn}$. We will use this
property to explain what a fractional exponent indicates. Let's evaluate the two expressions below.

$$\left(3^{\frac{1}{2}}\right)^2 = 3^{\left(\frac{1}{2}\right)(2)} \qquad\qquad \left(\sqrt{3}\right)^2 = \sqrt{3} \cdot \sqrt{3}$$
$$= 3^1 \qquad\qquad\qquad\qquad = \sqrt{9}$$
$$= 3 \qquad\qquad\qquad\qquad\quad\; = 3$$

In each case, we squared a positive number and got the same result.
This means that the two numbers we squared must be equal. In

other words, $3^{\frac{1}{2}} = \sqrt{3}$. Finding the square root of a number is the same as raising the number to the power $\frac{1}{2}$.

> If $x \geq 0$, and m is a positive integer, then $\sqrt[m]{x} = x^{\frac{1}{m}}$.

Example   *Evaluate each expression. (Solutions are given below.)*

a $169^{\frac{1}{2}}$

$$169^{\frac{1}{2}} = \sqrt{169}$$
$$= 13$$

b $\left(25^{\frac{1}{4}}\right)^2$

$$\left(25^{\frac{1}{4}}\right)^2 = 25^{\left(\frac{1}{4}\right)(2)}$$
$$= 25^{\frac{1}{2}}$$
$$= \sqrt{25}$$
$$= 5$$

Using A Scientific Calculator

You have used a calculator to compute with exponents, and by using fractional powers, you can also use it to do calculations with roots.

Example   *Evaluate $\sqrt[4]{75}$ to the nearest thousandth.*

We will use the root key, either $\boxed{y^{1/x}}$ or $\boxed{\sqrt[x]{y}}$, to approximate $\sqrt[4]{75}$ on the calculator. When we enter 75 $\boxed{y^{1/x}}$ 4 $\boxed{=}$, the display shows

$\boxed{2.942830956}$

The answer to the nearest thousandth is 2.943.

Note   Your calculator may not have a $\boxed{y^{1/x}}$ key. Since you know that $\frac{1}{4} = 0.25$, you can use the $\boxed{y^x}$ key instead. Enter 75 $\boxed{y^x}$ 0.25 $\boxed{=}$

Part Two: Sample Problems

Problem 1   *Write $\sqrt[3]{16}$ in standard radical form.*

Solution   Because the root index is 3, we now need to look for perfect cubes, or "third powers," instead of perfect squares.

$$\sqrt[3]{16} = \sqrt[3]{8} \cdot \sqrt[3]{2}$$
$$= 2\sqrt[3]{2}$$

Problem 2   *Solve $\sqrt[3]{x} = -7$ for x.*

Solution   We can find x by cubing (raising to the third power) both sides of the equation.

$$\sqrt[3]{x} = -7$$
$$\left(\sqrt[3]{x}\right)^3 = (-7)^3$$
$$x = -343$$

Check
Since $(-7)(-7)(-7) = -343$, $\sqrt[3]{-343} = -7$.

Problem 3 *The volume of a cube is 17. Find the length of each edge of the cube, rounded to the nearest hundredth.*

e

Solution To find the edge, we use the formula for volume of a cube.

$$V = e^3$$
$$17 = e^3$$
$$\sqrt[3]{17} = \sqrt[3]{e^3}$$
$$\sqrt[3]{17} = e$$
$$2.57 \approx e$$

Use a calculator to approximate $\sqrt[3]{17}$

Each edge of the cube is about 2.57 units long.

Part Three: Exercises and Problems

Warm-up Exercises

In problems 1–3, evaluate each expression.

1 $\left(4^3\right)^{\frac{1}{3}}$ **2** $\left(9^{\frac{1}{2}}\right)^4$ **3** $\left(729^{\frac{1}{2}}\right)^{\frac{1}{3}}$

In problems 4–6, evaluate each expression.

4 $\sqrt[3]{-27}$ **5** $\sqrt[4]{-16}$ **6** $\sqrt[3]{1.331}$

7 Evaluate to the nearest hundredth.
   a $\sqrt[4]{12}$ **b** $\sqrt[3]{75}$

8 Find the volume of the cube.

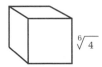

$\sqrt[6]{4}$

Problem Set

9 Find the next number in the pattern.
   $1, \sqrt{2}, 2, \sqrt{8}, 4$

In problems 10–13, approximate to the nearest thousandth.

10 $\sqrt[4]{20}$ **11** $16^{0.2}$ **12** $1024^{0.1}$ **13** $\sqrt[3]{8}$

In problems 14 and 15, simplify.

14 $3\sqrt{2}\left(\sqrt{2} + 4\right) - \sqrt{3}\left(2\sqrt{3} - \sqrt{6}\right)$ **15** $\sqrt{28} - 2\sqrt{63} - 4\sqrt{7}$

16 Walter needed repairs on his truck. The parts cost $500, and labor was $40 per hour. If the total cost of repairs was $720, how many hours of labor were spent on the truck?

17 Find the slope of the line that contains the points with coordinates $\left(5, 8\sqrt{2}\right)$ and $\left(3, 4\sqrt{2}\right)$.

In problems 18–20, write in standard radical form.

18 $\sqrt[4]{32}$

19 $\dfrac{\sqrt[3]{48}}{\sqrt[3]{3}}$

20 $\sqrt[3]{54}$

21 Arrange the numbers in order from smallest to largest.

$8\sqrt{2}$ $6\sqrt{3}$ $4\sqrt{5}$ $4\sqrt{6}$ 10

   128   *108*   *80*   *96*   *100*

In problems 22 and 23, write each expression in standard radical form.

22 $-\sqrt[3]{24} + 5\sqrt[3]{3} + \sqrt[3]{3}$

23 $(x^2 + y^2)\sqrt[3]{5} + (x^2 - y^2)\sqrt[3]{5}$

24 Refer to the diagram.

  a Find each side of the triangle if $x = 4\sqrt{2}$.

  b Find the area of the triangle.

In problems 25–27, solve each equation.

25 $\sqrt[4]{x} = 3$

26 $\sqrt[3]{3x + 1} = -2$

27 $\sqrt[5]{y + 3} = -1$

28 If $y = 64^{\frac{1}{x}}$, make a table of values for x and y. Use $x = 2$ to $x = 8$. Sketch the graph.

In problems 29–31, solve for x.

29 $\sqrt[3]{x} = 4$

30 $\sqrt[3]{x} + 2 = 4$

31 $\sqrt[3]{2x + 3} + 5 = 4$

In problems 32–35, the volume of a cube is given. Find the length of each edge of the cube.

32 216 cm^3

33 80 m^3

34 $x^6 \text{ cm}^3$

35 $8y^3 \text{ in.}^3$

In problems 36–38, graph each equation.

36 $y = \sqrt{x}$

37 $y = \sqrt[3]{x}$

38 $y = \sqrt[4]{x}$

39 Find all numbers that are equal to their square root.

40 Find all numbers that are equal to their cube root.

In problems 41–43, find the value of *n*.

41 $\sqrt[3]{2} \cdot \sqrt[3]{5n} = \sqrt[3]{30}$

42 $\dfrac{\sqrt[3]{18}}{\sqrt[3]{3}} = \sqrt[3]{3n}$

43 $\sqrt[3]{n} = 2\sqrt[3]{2}$

Problem Set, *continued*

In problems 44–46, solve for *x*.

44 $16^x = 4$ **45** $10^x = 10{,}000$ **46** $100{,}000^x = 100$

In problems 47–49, use a calculator to evaluate each expression.

47 $4^{\frac{1}{3}}$ and $64^{\frac{1}{9}}$ **48** $5^{\frac{1}{2}}$ and $25^{\frac{1}{4}}$ **49** $32^{\frac{1}{5}}$ and $1024^{\frac{1}{10}}$

50 Refer to the diagram.

  a If $AB = 8$, find the length of a side of the cube.

  b Find the volume of the cube.

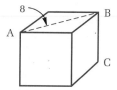

51 Arrange the numbers in order from smallest to largest.

$\sqrt[3]{15}$ $2\sqrt[3]{2}$ $3\sqrt[3]{2}$ $2\sqrt[3]{3}$

52 Make a table of values for $y = 2.1^x$ and graph.

In problems 53–60, write each number as a power of 10.

53 100

54 10,000,000,000

55 100,000

56 1,000,000,000,000,000

57 0.001

58 0.00000000001

59 0.000001

60 0.000000000000000001

61 Your calculator probably has a key with the word "log" written on it. Enter numbers from problems **53–60** in the calculator, hitting the log key after each entry. Record the displayed numbers. (Hint: You will need to enter some of the numbers in scientific notation.)

62 The volume of a hemisphere is 288π cubic centimeters. Find the radius of the hemisphere.

In problems 63–65, write each expression in standard radical form with the denominator rationalized.

63 $\sqrt[3]{2}\ \sqrt[3]{4}$ **64** $\sqrt[3]{3}\left(\sqrt[3]{9} + 3\sqrt[3]{72}\right)$ **65** $\dfrac{\sqrt[3]{6}}{\sqrt[3]{4}}$

66 For what positive integers *n* will $\sqrt[n]{-100}$ be negative?

67 Find the area of the equilateral triangle with sides of each given length. Use the formula for the area of an equilateral triangle,

$A = \dfrac{s^2\sqrt{3}}{4}$, in which *s* is the measure of each side of the triangle.

  a 12   **b** $4\sqrt{3}$ **c** $\sqrt{2}$

68 Refer to the diagram.

    a Which cube has the greater volume?

    b Which cube has the greater surface area?

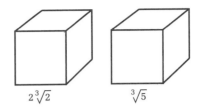

$2\sqrt[3]{2}$ $\sqrt[3]{5}$

69 The formula for the volume of a regular tetrahedron (triangular pyramid) with edge length e is $V = \dfrac{e^3\sqrt{2}}{12}$. For each given volume of a regular tetrahedron, find the exact length of the edge and then evaluate the length to the nearest hundredth.

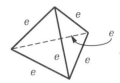

    a $V = \frac{27\sqrt{2}}{12}$

    b $V = 150\sqrt{2}$

    c $V = 300$

HISTORICAL SNAPSHOT

WARTIME CODE BROKEN
Alan Turing reveals the "Enigma"

In 1940, during World War II, German forces bombed the British mainland and patrolled British waters. All German intelligence was encoded on the Enigma, a complex machine capable of generating 105,456 different letter combinations. When the British intercepted a message, they saw only a meaningless jumble of letters.

Alan Turing, a competitive cross-country runner, is shown finishing second in a race in England.

The British began a deciphering project under the leadership of the brilliant mathematician Alan Turing, who had already made significant progress in the development of computers, then in their infancy. Turing's team built a machine called the Bombe, which unscrambled the Enigma's combinations. In February 1941 the British intercepted a German message. Turing fed it into the Bombe and got this in return:

FROM: ADMIRAL COMMANDING U-BOATS ESCORT FOR U69 AND U107 WILL BE AT POINT 2 ON MARCH 1 AT 0800 HOURS

Turing had cracked the code! The Bombe became one of Britain's greatest weapons, helping to bring about the eventual defeat of Germany.

Some codes are far easier to crack than the Enigma's. A fairly simple code is one based on letter frequencies. Each letter in a coded message stands for another letter. The letter *E* is used most often in English, followed in order by *T, R, I, N, O, A, S, D, L, C, H, F, U, P, M, Y, G, W, V, B, X, K, Q, J,* and *Z*. Can you decipher this message?
MLUK LB EMLKBP PMHLB RKK PKKPKMPEPPKM

SCATTERGRAMS

Objective

After studying this section, you will be able to
- Draw a scattergram and calculate the equation of a fitted line

Lines of Best Fit and Scattergrams

When data are collected and plotted as points on a coordinate system, the result is called a **scattergram.** Real data rarely fit an equation exactly. Often, however, data follow a pattern that can be described mathematically.

Year	Height (in inches)
1948	78.0
1952	80.3
1956	83.25
1960	85.0
1964	85.75
1968	88.24
1972	87.75
1976	88.5
1980	92.75
1984	92.5

In the scattergram of high-jump statistics for the Olympic Games, we see that the height of the winning jump tends to increase in each Olympiad. Furthermore, that increase appears to be linear. The points closely follow an imaginary line, the **line of best fit,** or the **regression line.**

It is possible to determine the line of best fit; many calculators can do it. In this book, however, we will not go through statistical methods. You can often achieve good results by using a ruler and guessing where the line should go. The following example illustrates an algebraic method for determining a **fitted line,** an approximation of a line of best fit.

Problem 1 *Refer to the Olympic high-jump statistics.*

  a *Find an equation of a fitted line.*
  b *Predict the winning height in 1992.*

Solution

a To find two points of a fitted line, we divide the data into two groups. The first group of data will be for 1948–1964; the second, for 1968–1984. For each group, we calculate the mean of the years and the mean of the heights.

Group 1
Mean of years
$$\frac{1948 + 1952 + 1956 + 1960 + 1964}{5} = 1956$$

Mean of heights
$$\frac{78.0 + 80.3 + 83.25 + 85.0 + 85.75}{5} = 82.46$$

The representative point for Group 1 is (1956, 82.46).

Group 2
Mean of years
$$\frac{1968 + 1972 + 1976 + 1980 + 1984}{5} = 1976$$

Mean of heights
$$\frac{88.24 + 87.75 + 88.5 + 92.75 + 92.5}{5} \approx 89.95$$

The representative point for Group 2 is (1976, 89.95).

Now we plot the two points on a graph and draw the line through them. Then we use the two points to calculate the slope of the line. Finally we choose one of the points to write the point-slope form of the equation of the line.

$$m = \frac{89.95 - 82.46}{1976 - 1956} \approx 0.37$$

An equation of the line is
$y - 82.46 = 0.37(x - 1956)$.

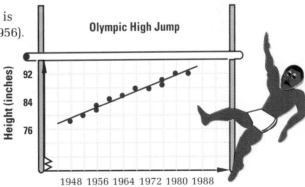

Olympic High Jump

b To predict the winning height in 1992, we substitute 1992 for x in the equation and solve for y.

$$y - 82.46 = 0.37(1992 - 1956)$$
$$y - 82.46 = 13.32$$
$$y = 95.78$$

So, the winning height in 1992 will probably be about 96 inches. Checking our answer against the graph, we see that the line passes very close to (1992, 96).

Problem 2   *Estimate the line of best fit for the scattergram.*

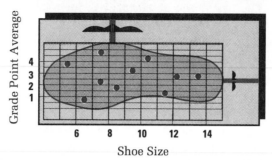

Grade Point Average

Shoe Size

Solution   Because these data do not follow a linear pattern, it is not appropriate to fit a line to the points. This makes sense, because there is probably no relationship between shoe size and grade-point average.

Problem Set

1 The graph represents the average yearly heating bill for a one-bedroom apartment in the Greatview apartment complex during the first 6 years the complex was in operation.

a Write an equation of a line through (1, 250) and (6, 305).

b Find the projected average yearly costs for years 7 and 8.

c Write an equation of a line through (2, 260) and (5, 290).

d Use the equation from part **c** to find the projected average yearly heating costs for years 7 and 8.

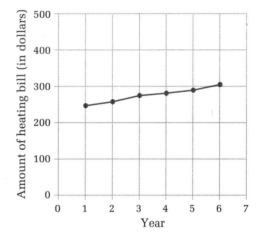

Amount of heating bill (in dollars)

Year

2 Roy was listening to a cricket outside his window. He noticed that the number of times the cricket chirped per minute was related to the temperature. He gathered the following data over a 12-day period.

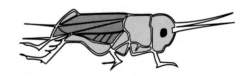

Temp. (in °F)	50	55	52	68	60	58	73	75	72	80	64	56
Chirps per min.	40	60	48	116	80	76	135	140	125	160	98	64

a Make a scattergram with temperature on one axis and the number of chirps per minute on the other.

b About how many times would a cricket chirp per minute at the following temperatures?
i 90°F   **ii** 40°F

3 Use the equation $y - 82.46 = 0.37(x - 1956)$ from the example at the beginning of this section. What does the equation suggest would have been the winning high jump in 1700 if the Olympic Games had been held then?

4 Use the data shown in the table.

x	2	5	6	9	11	13	16	17	22
y	1	2	3	5	6	5	7	9	10

a Make a scattergram for the data.

b Estimate the line of best fit for the data.

c Use the fitted line to estimate the value of y if x = 26.

5 Refer to the data.

a Plot a scattergram of longevity versus speed for the given animals.

b Estimate the line of best fit for the given data.

Animal	Average Longevity (in years)	Average Running Speed (in mph)
Pig	10	11
Cat	11	30
Lion	10	50
Horse	22	47
Dog	11	45
Chicken	7	9
Fox	9	42
Rabbit	7	35
Deer	12	30
Bear	23	30
Elephant	35	25
Squirrel	8	12

6 The table lists the winning distances for the women's Olympic shot put from 1948 to 1980.

a Make a scattergram of the data.

b Find an equation of a fitted line.

c What does your equation predict as the winning distance in 1984?

d The actual winning distance was about 20.5 meters. Give possible explanations for the discrepancy between your prediction in part **c** and the actual performance.

Year	Distance (in meters)
1948	13.75
1952	15.28
1956	16.59
1960	17.32
1964	18.14
1968	19.61
1972	21.03
1976	21.16
1980	22.41

7 The data represent the results of a study done by some university students, involving the amounts of cholesterol and fat found in fast foods served in the university cafeteria.

a Draw a scattergram.

b Draw a fitted line.

c Write an equation for the fitted line.

d Estimate the amount of fat in a food containing 45 grams of cholesterol.

Food	Cholesterol (mg)	Fat (g)
A	10	8
B	10	12
C	15	13
D	18	17
E	23	19
F	26	27
G	31	29
H	38	33

CHAPTER SUMMARY

CONCEPTS AND PROCEDURES

After studying this chapter, you should be able to
- Use scientific notation (9.1, 9.4)
- Use a calculator for operations involving scientific notation (9.1, 9.4)
- Identify the parts of an exponential term (9.1)
- Use multiplication and division properties of exponents (9.2, 9.3, 9.6)
- Multiply and divide a polynomial by a monomial (9.2, 9.3)
- Simplify expressions containing negative and zero exponents (9.4)
- Identify terms that refer to radicals (9.5)
- Simplify radical expressions (9.5)
- Add and subtract like radical terms (9.5)
- Rationalize numerators and denominators (9.6)
- Solve radical equations (9.7)
- Identify extraneous solutions of radical equations (9.7)
- Evaluate roots of higher orders (9.8)
- Evaluate expressions containing fractional exponents (9.8)
- Draw a scattergram and calculate the equation of a fitted line (9.9)

VOCABULARY

base (9.1)
coefficient (9.1)
exponent (9.1)
extraneous solution (9.7)
fitted line (9.9)
index (9.8)
like radical terms (9.5)
line of best fit (9.9)
monomial (9.2)

polynomial (9.2)
radical (9.5)
radicand (9.5)
rationalizing (9.6)
regression line (9.9)
scattergram (9.9)
scientific notation (9.1)
standard radical form (9.5)

PROPERTIES

Multiplication Property of Exponents
Power to a Power Property
Distributive Property of Exponentiation over Multiplication
Division Property of Exponents
Distributive Property of Exponentiation over Division
Distributive Property of Square Root over Multiplication
Distributive Property of Square Root over Division

9 | REVIEW PROBLEMS

1 Solve for the value of x in standard radical form.

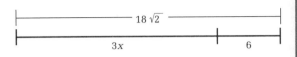

2 Find the slope and the y-intercept of the graph of $10^{18}x + 10^6y = 10^{34}$.

In problems 3–6, simplify.

3 2^4x^4 **4** $-2x^4$ **5** $(2x)^4$ **6** $(-2x)^4$

7 Find the value of r if the volume of the cylinder is 400 cubic meters.

In problems 8–10, evaluate to three decimal places.

8 $3\sqrt{5}$ **9** $\sqrt{5} + 2\sqrt{5}$ **10** $\sqrt{9} \cdot \sqrt{5}$

11 If two of the numbers in set A are picked at random, what is the probability that they are equal?

$$A = \left\{ \frac{\sqrt{2 + \sqrt{3}}}{2}, \frac{\sqrt{6} - \sqrt{2}}{4}, \frac{\sqrt{2 + \sqrt{3}}}{2}, \frac{\sqrt{6} + \sqrt{2}}{2} \right\}$$

In problems 12–14, determine whether each statement is True or False.

12 $2^5 2^3 = 4^8$ **13** $\dfrac{d_2^{\,3}}{d_2^{\,6}} = d_2^{\frac{1}{2}}$ **14** $c_2^{\,3} \cdot c_3^{\,4} = c_5^{\,7}$

In problems 15–18, solve for g.

15 $g^2 = 36$ **16** $2^g = 1$ **17** $2^g = \frac{1}{2}$ **18** $2^g = 0.25$

In problems 19–22, simplify.

19 $2x^2(3x^2 - 5x - 12)$ **20** $12x(3x - 5) - 6x(2x - 4)$

21 $\dfrac{12x^2 - 24x - 8}{4x}$ **22** $5^0x^2 + 7x^2$

Review Problems, *continued*

In problems 23–26, evaluate.

23 $\dfrac{5^9}{5^3}$ **24** 5^6 **25** $\dfrac{4^{12}}{4^7}$ **26** 4^5

In problems 27–30, evaluate each expression for $x = 4$ and $y = -2$.

27 $x^2 \cdot x^3$ **28** $(x^2)^3$ **29** $(xy)^3$ **30** $(-4y)^3$

31 If one of the following is selected at random and evaluated, what is the probability that it equals $\sqrt{32}$?

a $\sqrt{16} + \sqrt{16}$ **b** $3\sqrt{2} + \sqrt{2}$ **c** $\sqrt{8} + \sqrt{8}$

d $\sqrt{30} + \sqrt{2}$ **e** $\dfrac{\sqrt{64}}{\sqrt{2}}$ **f** $2\sqrt{8}$

32 The volume of a sphere is 288π cubic centimeters. Find the radius of the sphere.

33 Solve the system for (x, y).

$$\begin{cases} \dfrac{1}{\sqrt{2}}x + \sqrt{2}y = 3\sqrt{2} \\ \dfrac{-1}{\sqrt{2}}x + \sqrt{2}y = -5\sqrt{2} \end{cases}$$

In problems 34–36, solve for x.

34 $x^{\frac{1}{3}} = 8$ **35** $x^3 = 8$ **36** $x^2 = 8$

37 Find the area of the trapezoid.

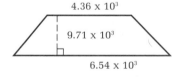

38 The table shows how much money Americans spent eating out.

a Draw a scattergram.
b Draw a fitted line.
c What would the graph predict for 1990? Is this an accurate prediction?

Year	Billions Spent
1982	104
1983	111
1984	118
1985	124
1986	131
1987	145

Source: Nielson *Review of Retail Grocery Store Trends*

In problems 39–41, find all values of x that make the statement true.

39 $\sqrt{x} + \sqrt{x} = 8$ **40** $\dfrac{\sqrt{x}}{4} = 9$ **41** $\sqrt{x} + 11 = 10$

42 The formula for the volume of a regular tetrahedron (triangular pyramid) is $V = \frac{e^3\sqrt{2}}{12}$, in which e is the edge length. Given each edge length, find the exact value of the volume in standard radical form, and then round to the nearest hundredth.

a $e = 4$ **b** $e = 2.5$ **c** $e = \sqrt[3]{6}$

In problems 43–45, solve for n.

43 $2\sqrt{5} = \sqrt{n}$ **44** $-5|n| = -\sqrt{n}$ **45** $y^2\sqrt{3} = \sqrt{n}$

46 If the distance between $(-2, 4)$ and $(x, 5)$ is $\sqrt{106}$, find x.

In problems 47–49, solve for x.

47 $\sqrt{(-3)^2} = x$ **48** $\left(\sqrt{5}\right)^2 = x$ **49** $\sqrt{x^2} = 5$

50 Refer to the diagram to find the value of x. Is it easier to use radicals or a calculator to do this problem?

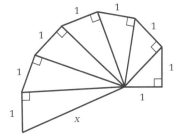

51 A hard disc in a microcomputer can store 40 megabytes of data. One megabyte is 1000K, and one K is 2^{10} bytes. How many bytes of data can the hard disc store? If each byte stores one character (for example, a letter, a space, or a punctuation mark) and there are an average of 4400 characters on a page of a book, how many book pages can be stored on this hard disc?

52 Use a calculator to complete the tables of values for $f(x) = 10^x$ and $g(x) = \log(x)$.

x	0	1	2	3	4	5	6
f(x)							

x	10^0	10^1	10^2	10^3	10^4	10^5	10^6
g(x)							

53 The sum of the x- and y-intercepts of the graph of $5x + 3y = k$ is $32\sqrt{5}$. Find the length of the line segment joining the x- and y-intercepts.

1 Arrange the numbers in order from least to greatest.

$52{,}000 \qquad 4.9 \times 10^4 \qquad 4.9 \times 10^5 \qquad 9.837 \times 10^3 \qquad 0.000977$

In problems 2–5, determine whether each statement is True or False.

2 $2^{17} + 2^{17} = 2^{18}$

3 $\sqrt{a^2 - b^2} = a - b$

4 $\dfrac{\sqrt{a}}{\sqrt{b}} = \sqrt{\dfrac{a}{b}}$

5 $\begin{bmatrix} \sqrt{18} & \sqrt{84} \\ 4\sqrt{3} & \sqrt{2} + \sqrt{18} \end{bmatrix} = \begin{bmatrix} 3\sqrt{2} & 2\sqrt{21} \\ \sqrt{48} & \sqrt{32} \end{bmatrix}$

In problems 6–9, solve for x.

6 $2^x 2^{x+3} = 8^6$

7 $1776^x = 1$

8 $x^{-2} = 9$

9 $\sqrt{x^2} = 9$

10 Find the ratio of the volume of the smaller cone to the volume of the larger cone.

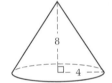

11 From the data below, predict the value of p if $v = 5$.

v	0.5	1.0	1.8	2.5	2.7	3.3	4.0	4.4
p	350	290	270	280	230	230	180	175

12 The area of the rectangle is 6. Find the length and the width.

In problems 13–15, evaluate each expression without using a calculator. Write the result in scientific notation.

13 $\sqrt{4.9 \times 10^9}$

14 $3.2 \times 10^{12} + 9.7 \times 10^{12}$

15 $\dfrac{4.2 \times 10^{-2}}{3 \times 10^5}$

In problems 16 and 17, rationalize the denominator.

16 $\dfrac{5 + \sqrt{12}}{\sqrt{3}}$

17 $\dfrac{1}{5 + \sqrt{7}}$

18 Find the value of r to the nearest tenth if the volume of the cylinder is 500 cubic meters.

PUZZLES AND CHALLENGES

1 In problems a and b, what phrase does each word puzzle suggest?

a STANDING
A MISS

b SEARCH

SEARCH

2 In problems **a** and **b**, interpret each cryptic clue. The number in parentheses is the number of letters in the word.

a First half of equation and end of radical are the same. (5)

b Capacity of solid is loud. (6)

3 Explain the rule for the following number arrangement.

8, 5, 4, 9, 1, 7, 6, 3, 2, 0

4 Complete parts **a–e** to find the result.

a Choose a 3-digit number with all the digits different.
b Reverse the order of the digits.
c Subtract the smaller number from the larger number.
d Reverse the order of the digits of the difference you found in part c.
e Add the numbers from parts **c** and **d**.

5 Starting at the top and moving down, how many ways can you spell ALGEBRA?

```
          A
        L   L
      G   G   G
    E   E   E   E
      B   B   B
        R   R
          A
```

6 In problems **a–d**, evaluate each of the following.

a 11^0
b 11^1
c 11^2
d 11^3

7 Use your answers from problems 6a–d to predict 11^4.

10 POLYNOMIALS

When an X-ray beam is passed through a crystal, the ray scatters in many directions. One of the ways scientists have devised to show the ray's distinctive pattern is as a series of dots on a strip of photographic film. This diffraction pattern, as it is called, contains an enormous quantity of information that describes the makeup of the crystal's molecules.

Biochemists have begun to use diffraction patterns in order to study the three-dimensional organization of highly complex molecules called macromolecules. These macromolecules typically consist of thousands of atoms and are a part of life processes.

An X-ray diffraction analysis of macromolecules is no simple matter even for today's highest-speed computers. Usually, several months are required in order to solve, refine and display a macromolecule's structure in three dimensions.

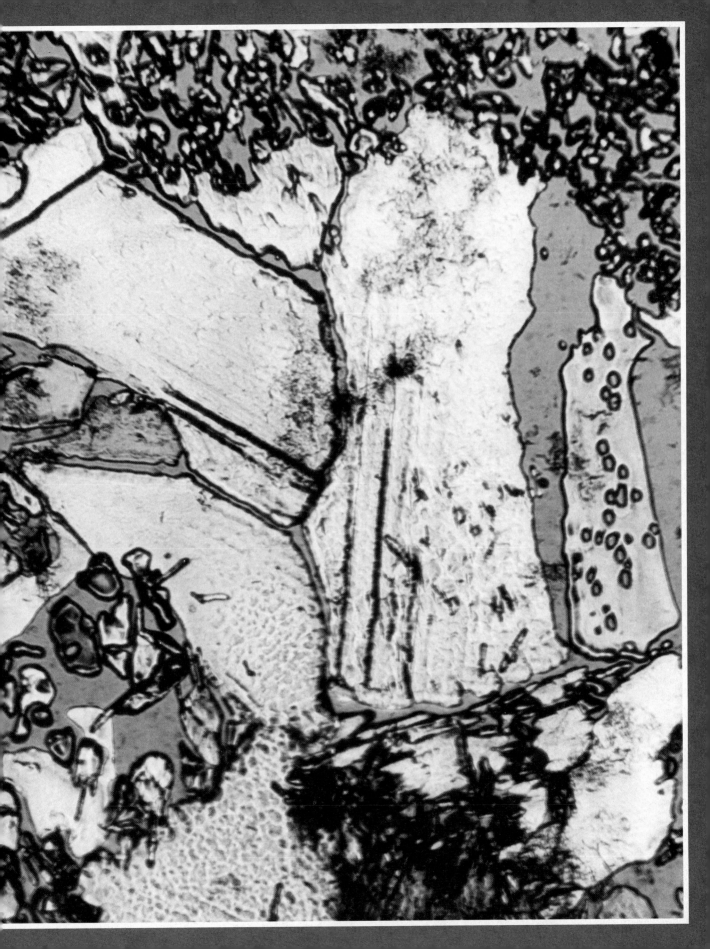

ANATOMY OF A POLYNOMIAL

Objectives

After studying this section, you will be able to
- Identify polynomial expressions
- Classify polynomials

Part One: Introduction

Polynomial Expressions

Recall from Chapter 9 that a monomial is a real number, a variable, or a product of real numbers and variables. Let's look at the monomial $-1.75x^8y^4z$.

The **coefficient** of a monomial is the numerical factor. The coefficient of $-1.75x^8y^4z$ is -1.75.

The **degree of a monomial** is the sum of the exponents of the variables. The degree of $-1.75x^8y^4z$ is 13 because the sum of the exponents 8, 4, and 1 is 13.

Remember that a polynomial expression is either a monomial or a sum or difference of monomial terms. Now let's look at the polynomial $9x^3 + 13x - 8x^7 + x^4 - 30$.

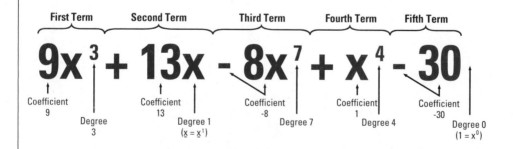

The **degree of a polynomial** is the largest of the degrees of the individual terms. The degree of $9x^3 + 13x - 8x^7 + x^4 - 30$ is 7. The terms of the above polynomial can be rearranged in ascending order of powers as $-30 + 13x + 9x^3 + x^4 - 8x^7$ or in descending order of powers as $-8x^7 + x^4 + 9x^3 + 13x - 30$.

The coefficient of the first term of a polynomial written in descending order is called the *leading coefficient*. The leading coefficient of $3x^4 - 5x^2 - 7x + 8$ is 3.

Classifying Polynomials

Polynomials can be classified by number of terms or by degree. Polynomials with one term are monomials. Polynomials with two terms are called *binomials*, and those with three terms are called *trinomials*.

Example	Number of Terms	Class by Terms	Degree	Class by Degree
12	1	monomial	0	constant
$2y$	1	monomial	1	linear
$3x - 4$	2	binomial	1	linear
$x^2 - 5x + 4$	3	trinomial	2	quadratic
$4x^3 - 2x^2 + x - 5$	4	polynomial	3	cubic

Part Two: Sample Problems

Problem 1 *Refer to the polynomial* $-7x^2y^3 - 4xy + 25$.

    a *Give the degree of the polynomial.*
    b *Classify the polynomial by the number of terms it has.*
    c *Evaluate the polynomial if* $x = -3$ *and* $y = 5$.

Solution **a** The degree of a term with more than one variable is the sum of the exponents of the variables.

The degree of the first term is 5.
The degree of the second term is 2.
The degree of the third term is 0.

Since the degree of the polynomial is the highest degree of any monomial term, the degree of the polynomial is 5.

    b The polynomial is a trinomial because it has three terms.

    c $-7x^2y^3 - 4xy + 25$
      $= -7(-3)^2(5)^3 - 4(-3)(5) + 25$
      $= -7(9)(125) + 12(5) + 25$
      $= -7875 + 60 + 25$
      $= -7790$

Problem 2 *Multiply* $3xy^2(5x^2 + 2xy - 9xy^2 - 15y^7)$.

Solution $3xy^2(5x^2 + 2xy - 9xy^2 - 15y^7)$
    $= (3xy^2)(5x^2) + (3xy^2)(2xy) - (3xy^2)(9xy^2) - (3xy^2)(15y^7)$
    $= 15x^3y^2 + 6x^2y^3 - 27x^2y^4 - 45xy^9$

Problem 3   *Refer to the expression* $((x + 3)x - 7)x + 2$.

a *Evaluate the expression if* $x = 5.2$.
b *Write the expression in polynomial form.*
c *Evaluate the polynomial if* $x = 5.2$.

Solution   The expression $((x + 3)x - 7)x + 2$ is called the **nested form** of the polynomial. This is a convenient form for evaluating a polynomial using a calculator or computer.

a $((x + 3)x - 7)x + 2$
$= ((5.2 + 3)5.2 - 7)5.2 + 2$
This is a nice problem to do on a calculator.
First we store 5.2 in the memory by entering 5.2 $\boxed{\text{STO}}$
Then we evaluate the expression.

$\boxed{\text{MR}}$ $\boxed{+}$ 3 $\boxed{=}$ $\boxed{\times}$ $\boxed{\text{MR}}$ $\boxed{-}$ 7 $\boxed{=}$ $\boxed{\times}$ $\boxed{\text{MR}}$ $\boxed{+}$ 2 $\boxed{=}$

The display is $\boxed{187.328}$

b $((x + 3)x - 7)x + 2$
$= (x^2 + 3x - 7)x + 2$
$= x^3 + 3x^2 - 7x + 2$

c $x^3 + 3x^2 - 7x + 2$
$= 5.2^3 + 3(5.2)^2 - 7(5.2) + 2$
$= 140.608 + 81.12 - 36.4 + 2$
$= 187.328$

Using the nested form to evaluate a polynomial is more efficient because it usually takes fewer calculator keystrokes and because it takes less computing time.

Part Three: Exercises and Problems

Warm-up Exercises

In problems 1–8, match the polynomials in the left column with the descriptions on the right. An item in the left column may match several entries on the right.

1 $15x^2 - 3x^4 + 2x + 7 - x^3$ **a** quadratic
2 $3x^3 - 2x - 4$ **b** binomial
3 $x^2 - 9$ **c** linear
4 $12x - 4x^3$ **d** trinomial
5 $5x^2 - xy - 4y^2$ **e** cubic binomial
6 -27 **f** quadratic trinomial
7 $4x^2$ **g** monomial
8 $6 - 5x$ **h** fourth-degree polynomial
   i constant

Problem Set

In problems 9–12, determine which expressions are polynomials.

9 $xy^{10} - x^5y^8 + 2y^{12}$ **10** $2\sqrt{x} + 5x^2 - 14$

11 $\frac{3}{4}y + \frac{13}{3}y^2 + \sqrt{2}y - 7$ **12** $3x^{2.5} - 5x^{1.5} + 4x^{.05} + 10$

13 Multiply $12x(x^3 - 4x + x^2 - 1)$ and write the product in ascending order of powers.

In problems 14–17, give the degree and coefficient of each monomial.

14 $-15x^2yz^5$ **15** $\frac{2}{3}x^6yzw$ **16** $\frac{5x^2}{8}$ **17** $\frac{x}{2}$

18 Represent $\angle ABC$ in terms of x.

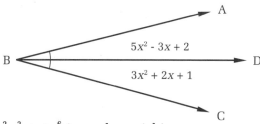

19 The expression $8x^2y^5 - 12x^3y - x^2y^3 + 4x^6$ is a polynomial in x and y.

a How many terms does it have?
b What is the degree of each term?
c What is the degree of the polynomial?

20 If a term of the expression $3x^{2.5} + \frac{3}{x^2} + 7x + 15x - 7 + 2^x$ is selected at random, what is the probability that the term is a monomial?

21 Write a polynomial expression in descending order for the area of $\triangle ABC$.

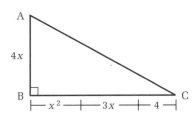

In problems 22 and 23, multiply.

22 $6x^2y(4x^2y^2 - 3xy + 5)$ **23** $-10.5xy(7.6x^2y^4 + 3.4xy^2)$

24 What numbers can be substituted for $\square$ and $\triangle$ so that $3x^5 + 12x^2 + x + 2$ means $3x^5 + 12x^2 + \square x^\triangle + 2$?

In problems 25–28, solve each equation or system of equations.

25 $\sqrt{5x} = 20$ **26** $\begin{cases} 3x - 2y = 22 \\ 2x + \ y = 3 \end{cases}$

27 $3x(2x + 17) = 0$ **28** $3x - (2x + 17) = 0$

Problem Set, *continued*

29 If $g(x) = x^3 - 5x + 15$, what are $g(1)$, $g(-2)$, and $g\left(\sqrt{5}\right)$?

30 If $P(t) = 2^t$, what are $P(0)$, $P(5)$, and $P(-3)$?

31 Solve the polynomial equation $y = x^2 - 9x - 50$ for x if $y = 0$.

In problems 32 and 33, evaluate each trinomial for $x = -4$, $y = 7$, and $z = -2$.

32 $3x^2 - yz + 5z^3$ **33** $45.7 + 3.5y - 6.2y^2$

In problems 34–36, write each expression as a polynomial in descending order of powers of x.

34 $8x^2 - 3x^3 + 11x + 17x^3 - 7x^2 + x - x^2 + 6$
35 $(3x^2 - 2x + 7)6x^3$ **36** $((4x - 3)x + 6)x + 10$

37 Refer to the diagrams.

| Point C is the vertex of the graph. | Point D is the vertex of the graph. | Point E is the vertex of the graph. |

a Which point is the vertex of graph FGH?
b What do you think the word *vertex* means?

38 Write the expression $((x - 3)x + 5)x - 7$ in polynomial form. Then evaluate the polynomial for $x = 2.5$.

In problems 39–44, evaluate each expression if $x = 9$.

39 $(x + 2)(x + 4)$ **40** $(x - 7)(x + 7)$ **41** $(x + 3)(x + 3)$
42 $(x - 2)(x - 2)$ **43** $x^2 - 49$ **44** $x^2 + 9$

In problems 45 and 46, make a table of values and graph each.

45 $y = x^2$ **46** $y = -x^2$

47 The diagram shows a rectangle with width $5x$ and length $x^3 + 3x^2 + 2x + 4$. The area is $5x(x^3 + 3x^2 + 2x + 4)$. The area can also be represented as the sum of the areas of the smaller rectangles. Compute the areas of the remaining three small rectangles and add to find the area of the entire rectangle.

48 Write the polynomial $5x^2 + 6x + 8$ in nested form. Then find the value of the expression if $x = -4$.

49 Refer to the line AE.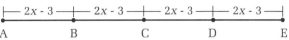

$\vdash$ 2x - 3 $\dashv\vdash$ 2x - 3 $\dashv\vdash$ 2x - 3 $\dashv\vdash$ 2x - 3 $\dashv$

A   B   C   D   E

a Write a binomial to describe the length of $\overline{AE}$.
b Write a monomial to describe the length of $\overline{AE}$.

In problems 50 and 51, simplify each expression.

50 $7y(4y + 1) + 5y(4y + 1)$ **51** $4wz^3(w^2z - 3w) + z^2(w^2z - 3w)$

52 Write two equivalent expressions to describe the volume of the rectangular box.

$3x$

$2x$

$x^2 - 10x$

In problems 53 and 54, make a table of values and graph each function.

53 $f(x) = (x - 3)^2$ **54** $g(x) = (x - 3)^2 + 2$

55 Copy the diagram. Compute the area of the rectangle in two ways.

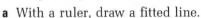

$2x^3 + 3x^2 + 7x + 5$

	$2x^3$	$3x^2$	$7x$	5
$2x$	$4x^4$	$6x^3$	$14x^2$	$10x$
3	$6x^3$	$9x^2$	$21x$	15

$2x + 3$

56 The factored form of $5y + 30$ is $5(y + 6)$. The multiplied form of $5(y + 6)$ is $5y + 30$. Write the factored form of each polynomial.

a $21 - 14x$ **b** $55x + 33$ **c** $x^2 + 3x$

57 On your own paper, trace the graph of mean passenger-car efficiency.

a With a ruler, draw a fitted line.
b What does your line predict as the average efficiency in 1990?

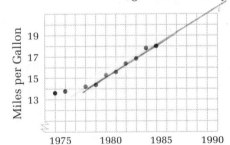

U.S. Mean Passenger-Car Efficiency

58 One of the factors of $5xy^2$ is $5xy$. List the other eleven factors of $5xy^2$.

In problems 59 and 60, solve for x.

59 $(3^x)^{x - 5} = 1$ **60** $\left(\dfrac{7^{4x - 5}}{7^{2x - 5}}\right)^{x - 7} = 1$

61 Solve $x(3x - 8) = 3x^2 - 2(x - 36)$ for x.

ADDITION AND SUBTRACTION OF POLYNOMIALS

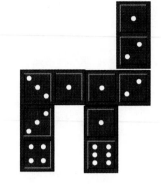

Objective

After studying this section, you will be able to
■ Add or subtract polynomials

Part One: Introduction

Addition and Subtraction of Polynomials

Recall from Chapter 2 that like terms contain the same variables to the same powers.

Like Terms	Unlike Terms
$23x^5y^2$ and $4y^2x^5$	$10x$ and $10x_1$
$2.5A^3B$ and $-42A^3B$	$5x^3y^2$ and $3x^2y^3$

Like terms are combined by adding or subtracting their coefficients. The powers of the variables do not change. To add polynomials, combine their like terms.

Example   Add $(23x^4 - 3x^2 - 15) + (7x^4 + x^3 + 3x^2 + 11)$.

$$(23x^4 - 3x^2 - 15) + (7x^4 + x^3 + 3x^2 + 11)$$
$$= 23x^4 - 3x^2 - 15 + 7x^4 + x^3 + 3x^2 + 11$$

$$= 30x^4 - 3x^2 - 15 + x^3 + 3x^2 + 11$$

$$= 30x^4 + x^3 - 3x^2 - 15 + 3x^2 + 11$$

$$= 30x^4 + x^3 + 0x^2 - 15 + 11$$

$$= 30x^4 + x^3 - 4$$

Example   Subtract $(5x^2 - 3x + 2) - (2x^2 - 5x + 7)$.

To subtract polynomials, be very careful to "distribute" the subtraction by changing the sign of each coefficient of the polynomial being subtracted.

$$(5x^2 - 3x + 2) - (2x^2 - 5x + 7)$$
$$= 5x^2 - 3x + 2 - 2x^2 + 5x - 7$$
$$= 3x^2 + 2x - 5$$

Part Two: Sample Problems

Problem 1 *Simplify* $(5x^3 + x^2 - 4)\,3x^2 - 5x(x^3 - 3x)$.

Solution We use the Distributive Property of Multiplication over Addition or Subtraction.

$$(5x^3 + x^2 - 4)\,3x^2 - 5x(x^3 - 3x)$$
$$= (5x^3)3x^2 + (x^2)3x^2 + (-4)\,3x^2 + (-5x)(x^3) + (-5x)(-3x)$$
$$= 15x^5 + 3x^4 - 12x^2 - 5x^4 + 15x^2$$
$$= 15x^5 - 2x^4 + 3x^2$$

Problem 2 *Subtract.*

$$\begin{array}{r} 5x^2 - 13x - 25 \\ -(3x^2 + 4x - 10) \end{array}$$

Solution

$$\begin{array}{r} 5x^2 - 13x - 25 \\ -(3x^2 + 4x - 10) \end{array} \qquad \text{Change signs} \qquad \begin{array}{r} 5x^2 - 13x - 25 \\ -3x^2 - 4x + 10 \\ \hline 2x^2 - 17x - 15 \end{array}$$

Problem 3 *Refer to the rectangle.*
a *Write a polynomial expression to represent the area of the shaded region of the rectangle.*
b *Use this expression to compute the area of the shaded region if $x = 5.7$ meters.*

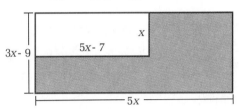

Solution The area of the shaded region equals the area of the large rectangle minus the area of the small rectangle.

a Area of large rectangle $\quad 5x(3x - 9)$, or $15x^2 - 45x$
Area of small rectangle $\quad x(5x - 7)$, or $5x^2 - 7x$
Area of the shaded region $\quad (15x^2 - 45x) - (5x^2 - 7x)$
$$= 15x^2 - 45x - 5x^2 + 7x$$
$$= 10x^2 - 38x$$

b
$$10x^2 - 38x$$
$$= 10(5.7)^2 - 38(5.7)$$
$$= 324.9 - 216.6$$
$$= 108.3$$

The area of the shaded region is 108.3 square meters.

Part Three: Exercises and Problems

Warm-up Exercises

1 Simplify.
$(x^5 - 4x^3 - 19) - (3x^5 + 11x^4 - 5x^3) + (8x^4 - x^3 - 2x^2 + 15)$

2 Subtract $9 - x^3 + 2x^2 - 4x$ from $7x^3 + 6x^2 + 2$.

In problems 3–5, determine whether the terms are like terms.

3 7 and 7x
4 $-6m^3n^2$ and $-6m^2n^3$
5 $4a^2b^4$ and $-4a^2b^4$

Problem Set

In problems 6–8, add or subtract as indicated.

6 $(6x - 5) + (8 - 14x)$

7 $(7x + 3y - 4z) - (9y - 6x + z)$

8 $(y^3 + 4y^2 - 5y + 12) + (6y - 4y^2 - 7y^3)$

9 Find the length of segment BC.

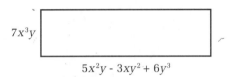

In problems 10–12, simplify.

10 $8x + 3x$

11 $8x \cdot 3x$

12 $x^8 \cdot x^3$

13 Write a formula in polynomial form for the area of the rectangle.

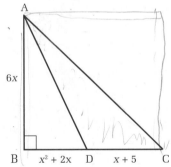

$7x^3y$

$5x^2y - 3xy^2 + 6y^3$

14 If one of these expressions is selected at random, what is the probability that it is a polynomial?

a $2x^3 - 5x^2 - 3|x| + 7$

b $5xy^2z^3w^4$

c 33

d $\frac{3}{x^2} + \frac{4}{x} + \frac{2}{3}$

15 Add the matrices.

$$\begin{bmatrix} x^2 + 3x & 5x \\ 14x & 3x^2 + 5 \end{bmatrix} + \begin{bmatrix} x^2 - 3x & 7 \\ -9 + x & -3x^2 + 10 \end{bmatrix}$$

16 Refer to the diagram.

a Write a polynomial expression to represent the area of $\triangle ABC$.

b Write a polynomial expression to represent the area of $\triangle ABD$.

c Write a polynomial expression to represent the area of $\triangle ADC$.

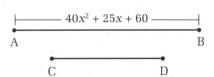

17 The expression $ax^4 + bx^3 + cx^2 + dx + e$ is a fourth-degree polynomial in x. Find a, b, c, d, and e for the polynomial $x^2 - x^3 - 8 + 5x^4$.

18 Simplify $(x^2 + 5x + 21) + (4x^2 - 7x - 16) - (3x^2 - 4x + 10)$.

19 The length of $\overline{CD}$ is 60% of the length of $\overline{AB}$. Write an expression to describe CD.

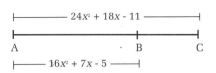

In problems 20–22, make a table of values and graph each.

20 $y = |x|$ **21** $y = 2|x|$ **22** $y = \frac{1}{3}|x|$

23 Solve for (p, q).
$$\begin{cases} 2p + 6q = 5 \\ 3p - 4q = 14 \end{cases}$$

24 Write the polynomial that describes the measure of $\angle ABC$.

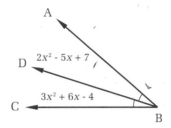

25 Give the coefficient and degree of the monomial $(2x)(-3y^2)$.

In problems 26–28, perform the indicated operation.

26 $(-3x)^4$ **27** $-(3x)^4$ **28** $(-3x) \cdot 4$

29 Refer to the diagram.
  a Find the area of each region in the diagram.
  b Use the diagram and multiply $(4x + 2)(5x + 3)$.

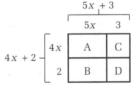

In problems 30–33, simplify each expression and solve each equation or inequality.

30 $9(x - 7) - 4(x + 5) = 3$ **31** $(9x - 7) - (4x + 5) = 3$
32 $9x - 7 - 4x + 5 - 3$ **33** $9x - 7 \leq 4(x + 5) - 3$

34 Subtract $7x^3 + 2x^2 - 6x + 3$ from $8x^2 - x + 4$.

35 If the area of the shaded region is 47 square meters, what is x?

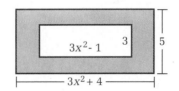

In problems 36–38, write each expression as a monomial, if possible.

36 $x^3 + x^3$ **37** $x^3 \cdot x^3$ **38** $x^3 + 3$

39 Subtract $(x^2 - 8x - 10) - (11 + 6x - 15x^2)$.

40 Copy the multiplication diagram and fill in the missing terms.

Problem Set, *continued*

41 Evaluate $(((x + 7)x - 7)x + 7)x - 7$ for $x = 7$.

In problems 42 and 43, subtract.

42
$$\begin{array}{r} 4x^2 - 6x + 11 \\ -(2x^2 - 6x + 3) \\ \hline \end{array}$$

43
$$\begin{array}{r} -15x^3 + 4x^2 - 10x - 14 \\ -(3x^3 + 4x - 4) \\ \hline \end{array}$$

44 Solve $3x(x + 5) = 3x^2 + 9x - 30$ for x.

45 Refer to the figure to find the areas of the following.

   a The shaded rectangles
   b The unshaded rectangles
   c The entire figure

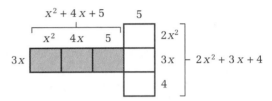

46 Evaluate $((3x - 2.7)x + 4.8)x + 7.5$ if $x = 8.25$.

47 Refer to the rectangle.

   a Find the perimeter of the rectangle.
   b Find the area of the rectangle.
   c For what value of x will the numerical value of the perimeter equal the numerical value of the area?

48 A manufacturer finds that the profit for producing and selling x radar units is $43x - x^2$ dollars. For what values of x between 40 and 50 will the manufacturer make a profit?

49 Find AB in terms of x and y.

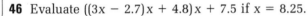

50 Given $(3x + 4)x + (3x + 4)5$.

   a Use the Distributive Property of Multiplication over Addition or Subtraction to obtain a product of binomials.
   b Solve $(3x + 4)x + (3x + 4)5 = 0$.

51 Find the values of x and y for which both levers are in balance.

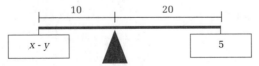

52 What is the difference between the circumference of the larger circle and the circumference of the smaller circle?

In problems 53 and 54, multiply.

53 $3x^3 \cdot 5x^5 \cdot x$

54 $4x \cdot 3x^2 \cdot (x^2 - 4x + 2)$

55 A package of Bippy mixed seeds produces 40% red flowers and 60% white flowers. Of these flowers, 30% will be tall, and 70% will be short.

  a Copy the matrix and fill it in to show what percentage of the flowers will be tall and red, short and red, tall and white, and short and white.

  b Suppose a package has 150 seeds. Use scalar multiplication on your matrix to find the number of each type of seed.

	40% Red	60% White
30% Tall	12%	18%
70% Short	28%	42%

In problems 56 and 57, solve for x.

56 $\dfrac{4^{3x^2 - 5x}}{4^{2x^2 - 7x}} = 1$

57 $3^{x^2 - 6x} \cdot 3^{-x^2 - 4x + 5} = 1$

58 Find the values of a, b, and c so that $a(2x^2 + bx + 12) = cx^2 + 24x + 36$.

MATHEMATICAL EXCURSION

PRIME NUMBER GENERATORS
The search for a perfect formula

One of the unsolved problems of mathematics is how to find a formula that will generate only prime numbers. An excellent, but not perfect, prime generator was discovered by the Swiss mathematician Leonard Euler. Euler's formula, $p = n^2 + n + 41$, produces a prime number for every value of n from $n = 1$ through $n = 39$. Then, suddenly, it breaks down.

  If $n = 40$ then $p = 1681$ or 41×41.
  If $n = 41$ then $p = 1763$ or 41×43.

Since $p = n^2 + n + 41$ is a polynomial, let's use trinomial factoring to understand what happens when $n = 40$.

$$n = 40, \ p = (40)^2 + 40 + 41$$
$$= 40(40 + 1) + 41$$
$$= 40(41) + 41$$
$$= 41(40 + 1)$$
$$= 41(41)$$

1. Show that $p = n^2 + n + 91$ is not prime for $n = 90$ and $n = 91$.
2. Find a whole number value of n so that $p = 5n^2 + 3n + 71$ is not prime.

10.3 MULTIPLICATION OF POLYNOMIALS

Objectives

After studying this section, you will be able to
- Multiply polynomials
- Multiply binomials

Part One: Introduction

Multiplying Polynomials

Multiplying two polynomials is an important application of the Distributive Property of Multiplication over Addition or Subtraction.

Multiplication of Two Polynomials	
	$(2x+6)(3x^2+5x+7)$
Think	$(\quad)(3x^2+5x+7)$ The symbol ( ) represents any quantity. In this case it represents $(2x+6)$.
Distribute	$(\quad)3x^2 + (\quad)5x + (\quad)7$
Substitute	$(2x+6)3x^2 + (2x+6)5x + (2x+6)7$
Distribute again	$= 2x \cdot 3x^2 + 6 \cdot 3x^2 + 2x \cdot 5x + 6 \cdot 5x + 2x \cdot 7 + 6 \cdot 7$
	$= 6x^3 + 18x^2 + 10x^2 + 30x + 14x + 42$
Combine like terms	$= 6x^3 + 28x^2 + 44x + 42$

When we multiplied the binomial (2 terms) by the trinomial (3 terms), the product had 6 terms before we combined like terms. Each term of the binomial was multiplied by each term of the trinomial. This suggests a shorter method.

To use the ***short multiplication method,*** multiply each term of one polynomial by each term in the other polynomial. It is helpful to vertically align the like terms of the products.

$$(2x + 6)(3x^2 + 5x + 7) = 6x^3 + 10x^2 + 14x$$
$$\underline{\phantom{6x^3 + {}} 18x^2 + 30x + 42}$$
$$6x^3 + 28x^2 + 44x + 42$$

Example   *Multiply* $(7x - 12)(4x + 9)$.

We use the short multiplication method.

$$(7x - 12)(4x + 9) = 28x^2 + 63x$$
$$\underline{\qquad\qquad - 48x - 108}$$
$$= 28x^2 + 15x - 108$$

Multiplying Binomials

When you multiply two binomials, you find various patterns of products. Look for these patterns as you multiply binomials.

Example   *Multiply the binomial expressions. (The solutions are given below.)*

    a $(x^2 - 5)(2x - 9)$ **b** $(3x - 7)(5x + 2)$ **c** $(2x - 3)(2x + 3)$

We use the short multiplication method.

$(x^2 - 5)(2x - 9)$	$(3x - 7)(5x + 2)$	$(2x - 3)(2x + 3)$
$= 2x^3 - 9x^2$	$= 15x^2 + 6x$	$= 4x^2 + 6x$
$\underline{\quad - 10x + 45}$	$\underline{\quad - 35x - 14}$	$\underline{\quad - 6x - 9}$
$2x^3 - 9x^2 - 10x + 45$	$15x^2 - 29x - 14$	$4x^2 \qquad - 9$
No terms combine.	Two terms combine.	Two terms add to 0.

Example   *What is the x term in the product of* $(11x + 4)(5 - 6x)$?

The x term results from adding two products:
$(11x)(5) = 55x$ and $(4)(-6x) = -24x$. So, the x term of the product is $31x$, since $55x + (-24x) = 31x$.

Part Two: Sample Problems

Problem 1   *Simplify the expression* $(2x - 3)(5x - 8) - (x + 7)(4x - 1)$.

Solution   We recall the order of operations. When we multiply the two pairs of binomials, we keep the product of the second pair in parentheses. We will distribute the subtraction sign later.

$$(2x - 3)(5x - 8) - (x + 7)(4x - 1)$$
$$= 10x^2 - 16x - 15x + 24 - (4x^2 - x + 28x - 7)$$
$$= 10x^2 - 31x + 24 - (4x^2 + 27x - 7)$$
$$= 10x^2 - 31x + 24 - 4x^2 - 27x + 7$$
$$= 6x^2 - 58x + 31$$

Problem 2   *Solve the equation* $(x + 15)(2x - 5) = 0$.

Solution   We use the Zero Product Property.

$$x + 15 = \quad 0 \quad \text{or } 2x - 5 = 0$$
$$x = -15 \text{ or} \qquad 2x = 5$$
$$x = 2.5$$

The solution set is $\{-15, 2.5\}$.

Problem 3   Write an expression for the area of the entire rectangle. Use polynomial form.

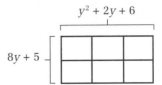

Solution   We can solve this problem in either of two ways.

Method 1

We add the areas of the six small rectangles.

$$\begin{aligned}\text{Area} &= 8y^3 + 16y^2 + 48y \\ &\quad\ \ + \ \ 5y^2 + 10y + 30 \\ &= 8y^3 + 21y^2 + 58y + 30\end{aligned}$$

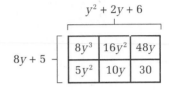

Method 2

Multiply the length and width.

$$\begin{aligned}\text{Area} &= (8y + 5)(y^2 + 2y + 6) \\ &= 8y^3 + 16y^2 + 48y \\ &\qquad\qquad\ 5y^2 + 10y + 30 \\ &= 8y^3 + 21y^2 + 58y + 30\end{aligned}$$

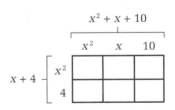

Problem 4   Multiply each pair of expressions.

a $\left(3 - \sqrt{5}\right)\!\left(3 + \sqrt{5}\right)$ **b** $\left(4\sqrt{2} - 7\right)\!\left(\sqrt{2} - 2\right)$

Solution   These are products of binomials.

a $\left(3 - \sqrt{5}\right)\!\left(3 + \sqrt{5}\right)$

$$\begin{aligned}&= 9 + 3\sqrt{5} - 3\sqrt{5} - \left(\sqrt{5}\right)^2 \\ &= 9 \qquad\ + 0 \quad\ - 5 \\ &= 4\end{aligned}$$

b $\left(4\sqrt{2} - 7\right)\!\left(\sqrt{2} - 2\right)$

$$\begin{aligned}&= 4\sqrt{4} - 8\sqrt{2} - 7\sqrt{2} + 14 \\ &= 4 \cdot 2 - 15\sqrt{2} + 14 \\ &= 22 - 15\sqrt{2}\end{aligned}$$

Part Three: Exercises and Problems

Warm-up Exercises

1 Copy the diagram and use it to multiply $(x + 4)(x^2 + x + 10)$.

In problems 2–5, multiply.

2 $(8a - 3b)(a + b)$ **3** $\left(\sqrt{3} + 1\right)\!\left(\sqrt{5} + 1\right)$

4 $-4x^2(3x^2 - 4x + 1)$ **5** $(4p + q)(4p - q)$

In problems 6 and 7, solve for x.

6 $(x + 1)(x - 3) = 4$ **7** $x(x - 2) = -6$

Problem Set

8 Make a diagram to illustrate $(4x + 7)(5x + 2)$. Then use the diagram to find the product.

In problems 9–17, multiply the binomials.

9 $(x + 5)(x - 3)$ **10** $(4 + m)(8 - m)$ **11** $(x - 4)(x - 9)$

12 $(x + 2y)(2x + y)$ **13** $(x - 4)(x - 6)$ **14** $(N + 5)(6 - N)$

15 $(x + 4)(x - 9)$ **16** $(x_1 + x_2)(x_1 - x_2)$ **17** $(x_1 - x_2)(x_1 - x_2)$

18 Refer to the rectangle.

   a Write an expression for the area of the rectangle.

   b Write this expression in polynomial form.

In problems 19–22, find all pairs of integers that have the given product.

19 -5 **20** 17 **21** 12 **22** 20

23 Refer to the rectangle.

   a If P = perimeter, write an equation for the diagram shown using P and x.

   b If $P = 40$, find x.

24 Simplify the expression $(3x + 1)(4x - 2) - (2x - 3)(4x + 5)$.

25 Find the missing value if $(x + 5)(x + \underline{\ ?\ }) = x^2 + 7x + 10$.

26 Determine the values of x for which $\angle ABC$ is a right angle.

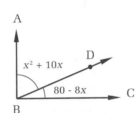

In problems 27 and 28, solve for x.

27 $(x - 4)(2x + 3) = 0$ **28** $x(2x + 1) = 0$

29 Multiply $\left(\sqrt{3} + 1\right)\left(\sqrt{3} + 1\right)$ using the square shown.

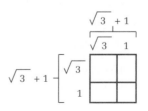

30 If $y = (x + 4)^2 - 16$ and $y = 0$, find x.

Problem Set, *continued*

31 Find the missing value if $(x + 6)(x + \underline{\ ?\ }) = x^2 + 2x - 24$.

In problems 32–34, make a table of values and graph each equation.

32 $y = x^2$ **33** $y = 2x^2$ **34** $y = \frac{1}{3}x^2$

In problems 35–37, multiply and watch for patterns.

35 $(x - 3)(x + 3)$ **36** $(x + 3)(x + 3)$ **37** $(x + 8)^2$

In problems 38–40, copy the diagram and fill in the missing values.

38   **39** 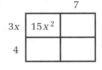   **40**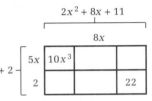

In problems 41 and 42, rewrite each problem, filling in the blanks.

41 $3(\underline{\ ?\ }x + \underline{\ ?\ }y^2 - \underline{\ ?\ }) = 6x + 15y^2 - 30$

42 $x^3(\underline{\ ?\ } + \underline{\ ?\ } + \underline{\ ?\ }) = x^6 + x^4 + x^3$

43 Use the diagram to find the x^2-term.

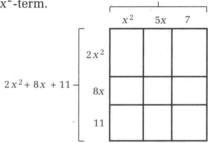

44 Two binomials are multiplied and the product is $x^2 + Ax + 12$, in which A is an integer. What are the six values of A that could result from the factors given?

a $(x + 3)(x + 4)$ **b** $(x + 2)(x + 6)$ **c** $(x + 1)(x + 12)$
d $(x - 3)(x - 4)$ **e** $(x - 2)(x - 6)$ **f** $(x - 1)(x - 12)$

45 The base of a square is increased by 10 and the height is decreased by 6, yet the area remains unchanged.

a Write expressions for the areas of the square and the resulting rectangle.
b Write an equation relating the areas.
c Solve the equation from part **b**, and use the result to find the area of the original square.

46 Find three consecutive integers if the product of the first and third integers is one less than the square of the second integer.

10.4 | SPECIAL MULTIPLICATIONS

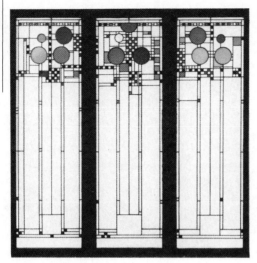

Objectives

After studying this section, you will be able to
- Recognize the difference of squares pattern
- Recognize the perfect square trinomial pattern
- Interpret geometric models

Part One: Introduction

The Difference of Squares Pattern

In this section, you will see two types of binomial multiplication that have interesting and useful patterns. Here is one type of binomial multiplication.

- $(x - 5)(x + 5) = x^2 + 5x - 5x - 25 = x^2 - 25$
- $(3x + 4y)(3x - 4y) = 9x^2 - 12xy + 12xy - 16y^2 = 9x^2 - 16y^2$
- $(\square + \triangle)\,(\square - \triangle) = \square^2 - \square\triangle + \square\triangle - \triangle^2 = \square^2 - \triangle^2$

  sum   difference   **difference of squares**

> $(\square + \triangle)\,(\square - \triangle) = \square^2 - \triangle^2$

The product of two binomials that are the sum and difference of the same two terms is the ***difference of their squares.***

Now you can quickly multiply binomials that fit the above pattern by writing the difference of squares.

Example   *Multiply $(7y - 9x)(7y + 9x)$.*

This expression fits the pattern. The product is the difference of the squares of $7y$ and $9x$.

$(7y - 9x)(7y + 9x)$
$= (7y)^2 - (9x)^2$
$= 49y^2 - 81x^2$

The Perfect-Square-Trinomial Pattern

You can see another pattern when you square a binomial. To square a binomial, you multiply a binomial by itself.

- $(y + 7)^2 = (y + 7)(y + 7) = y^2 + 7y + 7y + 49 = y^2 + 14y + 49$
- $(y - 7)^2 = (y - 7)(y - 7) = y^2 - 7y - 7y + 49 = y^2 - 14y + 49$

The examples above suggest the following:

- $(x - 5)^2 = (x - 5)(x - 5) = x^2 \mathbf{- 5x - 5x} + 25 = x^2 - 10x + 25$
- $(3x + 2y)^2 = (3x + 2y)(3x + 2y) = 9x^2 \mathbf{+ 6xy + 6xy} + 4y^2$
  $= 9x^2 + 12xy + 4y^2$
- $(\square + \triangle)^2 = (\square + \triangle)(\square + \triangle) = \square^2 \mathbf{+ \square\triangle + \square\triangle} + \triangle^2$
  $= \square^2 + 2\square\triangle + \triangle^2$
- $(\square - \triangle)^2 = (\square - \triangle)(\square - \triangle) = \square^2 \mathbf{- \square\triangle - \square\triangle} + \triangle^2$
  $= \square^2 - 2\square\triangle + \triangle^2$

The square of a binomial is a trinomial that is the sum of
- the square of the first term
- twice the product of the two terms
- the square of the second term

> $(\square + \triangle)^2 = \square^2 + 2\square\triangle + \triangle^2$ *and* $(\square - \triangle)^2 = \square^2 - 2\square\triangle + \triangle^2$

The resulting trinomials are called *perfect square trinomials.*

Example *Multiply* $(3x + 5)^2$.

The pattern for squaring a binomial is
$(\text{first term})^2 + 2(\text{first term})(\text{second term}) + (\text{second term})^2$.

$(3x + 5)^2$
$= (3x)^2 + 2(3x)(5) + (5)^2$
$= 9x^2 + 30x + 25$

Example *Is* $x^2 - 12x + 36$ *a perfect square trinomial?*

Check the pattern to see if $x^2 - 12x + 36$ is the square of a binomial.

The first term is the square of x.
The second term is $2(x)(-6)$, or $-12x$.
The third term is the square of (6).

Yes; the trinomial is $(x - 6)^2$.

Geometric Interpretations

A geometric model can illustrate binomial products that are perfect square trinomials or the difference of squares.

Example *Multiply* $(3x + 2)^2$.

This diagram is a visual model for squaring $(3x + 2)^2$.

Notice that 6x occurs twice and that there are two perfect squares, $9x^2$ and 4. The diagram illustrates that $(3x + 2)^2 = 9x^2 + 12x + 4$.

Example

Multiply $(A + B)(A - B)$.

The shaded region is $A^2 - B^2$ (large square minus small square).

Rearrange the shaded pieces to form a rectangle with the area $(A + B)(A - B)$.

This illustrates that $(A + B)(A - B) = A^2 - B^2$.

Part Two: Sample Problems

Problem 1

Rationalize the denominator.

$$\frac{11}{5 - \sqrt{3}}$$

Solution

Let's multiply the fraction by $\dfrac{\sqrt{3}}{\sqrt{3}}$ and see what happens.

$$\frac{11}{5 - \sqrt{3}} \cdot \frac{\sqrt{3}}{\sqrt{3}} = \frac{11\sqrt{3}}{5\sqrt{3} - 3}$$

This does not rationalize the denominator.
The difference of squares technique will help. Let's multiply the numerator and denominator by $5 + \sqrt{3}$. The binomials $5 - \sqrt{3}$ and $5 + \sqrt{3}$ are *conjugates*—that is, the only difference is the sign of one term.

$$\frac{11}{5 - \sqrt{3}}$$

To multiply by $\dfrac{5 + \sqrt{3}}{5 + \sqrt{3}}$ is to multiply by 1

$$= \frac{11}{5 - \sqrt{3}} \cdot \frac{5 + \sqrt{3}}{5 + \sqrt{3}}$$

The product of $5 + \sqrt{3}$ and $5 - \sqrt{3}$ is the difference of squares

$$= \frac{11(5 + \sqrt{3})}{(5)^2 - (\sqrt{3})^2}$$

$$= \frac{11(5 + \sqrt{3})}{25 - 3}$$

$$= \frac{11(5 + \sqrt{3})}{22}$$

$$= \frac{5 + \sqrt{3}}{2}$$

By multiplying the denominator by its conjugate, we have rationalized the denominator.

Problem 2   *Multiply* $4x - (x + 5)(x - 5)$ *and simplify.*

Solution   Following the order of operations, we must first multiply and then subtract.

$$4x - (x + 5)(x - 5)$$
$$= 4x - (x^2 - 25)$$
$$= 4x - x^2 + 25$$
$$= -x^2 + 4x + 25$$

Problem 3   *Supply the missing term that will make each trinomial a perfect square trinomial.*

        a $x^2 + 18x + \underline{\ ?\ }$ **b** $y^2 \underline{\ ?\ } + 169$

Solution   **a** $x^2 + 18x + \triangle^2 = (x + \triangle)^2$
        The middle term of $(x + \triangle)^2$ is $2x\triangle$, and $2x\triangle = 18x$, so $\triangle = 9$.
        Since 9^2 is 81, the missing term is 81.
        The perfect square trinomial is $x^2 + 18x + 81$.
        b $y^2 \underline{\ ?\ } + 169 = (y \pm \triangle)^2$
        Since $\triangle^2 = 169$, $\triangle = \pm 13$. The two possibilities are $\triangle = 13$ or
        $\triangle = -13$.
        $(y + 13)^2 = y^2 + 26y + 169$ or $(y - 13)^2 = y^2 - 26y + 169$. The
        missing term is either $+26y$ or $-26y$.

Problem 4   *Find a quadratic equation whose solutions are -4 and 2.*

Solution   We will work backwards using the Zero Product Property.

$$x = -4 \text{ or } x = 2$$
$$x + 4 = 0 \text{ or } x - 2 = 0$$
$$(x + 4)(x - 2) = 0$$
$$x^2 + 2x - 8 = 0$$

Part Three: Exercises and Problems

Warm-up Exercises

In problems 1–3, multiply.

  1 $(5x + 9y)^2$ **2** $(7y^5 + 1)(7y^5 - 1)$ **3** $(7x - 3)(3x + 7)$

In problems 4 and 5, supply the missing term that will make each trinomial a perfect square trinomial.

  4 $4y^2 + 12y + \underline{\ ?\ }$ **5** $x^2 \underline{\ ?\ } + 225$

  6 Rationalize the numerator.
    $\dfrac{\sqrt{3} - 4}{3}$

  7 Find a quadratic equation whose solutions are -3 and $\frac{5}{2}$.

Problem Set

In problems 8–10, multiply using the difference-of-squares pattern.

8 $(x - 2)(x + 2)$ **9** $(y + 7)(y - 7)$ **10** $(2x - 3)(2x + 3)$

11 Write an expression for each of the following.

   a The sum of the terms $5y$ and $2a$.
   b The difference of the terms $5y$ and $2a$.
   c The difference of the squares of $5y$ and $2a$.

In problems 12–14, multiply using the perfect-square-trinomial pattern.

12 $(x + 6)(x + 6)$ **13** $(x + 10)^2$ **14** $(2x + 5)^2$

15 The figure is a square made up of four regions.

   a Copy the figure and find the area of each region.
   b Which of the smaller regions are also squares?
   c Which regions have the same area?
   d Find the area of the largest square.

$x + 4$

	x	4
x	I	II
4	III	IV

$x + 4$

In problems 16–21, multiply.

16 $(x + 10)(x - 7)$ **17** $(x - 13)(x + 13)$ **18** $(2x - 7)(2x + 3)$
19 $(5 - x)(5 + x)$ **20** $-4x^3(3x^3 - 6x + 2)$ **21** $(R + r)(R - r)$

In problems 22–24, supply the missing term that will make each trinomial a perfect square trinomial.

22 $y^2 + 14y +$ _?_ **23** x^2 _?_ $+ 144$ **24** $y^2 - 20y +$ _?_

25 Find the quadratic equation with solutions of 6 and -7.

In problems 26 and 27, solve for x.

26 $(x - 6)(x - 1) = 0$ **27** $(x - 6)(x - 1) = 24$

28 Express AB in terms of x and y.

$\longmapsto 2x + 3y \longmapsto x - y \longmapsto 5y - x \longmapsto$
A   C   D   B

29 Which expression describes the area of the shaded region?

   a $\pi(R + r)(R - r)$ $\pi(R^2 - r^2)$
   b $\pi R^2 - \pi r^2$
   c $\pi(R^2 - r^2)$

30 Divide $\dfrac{4a^3 + 8a^2 - 16a}{-2a}$

Problem Set, *continued*

31 What two binomial factors have the product $y^2 - 49$?

32 The sum of two numbers is $\sqrt{200}$. The difference of the two numbers is $\sqrt{800}$. Find the two numbers.

33 Refer to the diagram of the rectangle.
  a What restrictions does the diagram impose on x?
  b Find x if the perimeter is 90.
  c Find the restrictions on x if the perimeter is, at most, 200.

$x + 42$

$3x - 12$

In problems 34–39, multiply.

34 $(x - 5)(x + 5)$ **35** $(x + 5)(x + 5)$ **36** $(3x - y)(2x - 4y)$
37 $(x + 5)(x^2 - 5x + 25)$ **38** $(3w + 8)(3w - 8)$ **39** $(4x + 5)(5x + 4)$

In problems 40–42, use the properties of exponents to simplify each expression.

40 $(3.2)^3(3.2)^5$ **41** $[(3.2)^2]^4$ **42** $(3.2)(10^4)^3$

43 The base of a square is increased by 6 inches, and the height is decreased by 6 inches. The resulting area is 64 square inches. What was the area of the original square?

x

x

x

In problems 44 and 45, make a table of values and graph each equation.

44 $y = x^2 + 3$ **45** $y = x^2 - 3$

In problems 46–48, rationalize each denominator or numerator.

46 $\dfrac{10}{\sqrt{5}}$ **47** $\dfrac{11}{5 - \sqrt{3}}$ **48** $\dfrac{3 + \sqrt{5}}{7}$

In problems 49 and 50, copy each chart and fill in the blanks.

49

	___	___
$3x$	$6x^2$	___
8	___	72

50

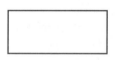

		$2x$	___
$4x$	$8x^3$	___	___
5	___	___	5

51 The product of two consecutive odd integers is 35. Find the integers.

In problems 52–54, rationalize each denominator and express each answer in standard radical form.

52 $\dfrac{\sqrt{2}}{3 + \sqrt{2}}$

53 $\dfrac{15}{\sqrt{7} - 2}$

54 $\dfrac{\sqrt{12}}{5 - \sqrt{3}}$

55 Find the area of the figure.

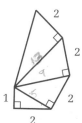

10.5 | FACTORING

Objectives

After studying this section, you will be able to
- Recognize factors of an expression
- Identify common factors
- Use factoring to solve equations

Part One: Introduction

Factoring an Expression

Factoring can help you look at an expression or equation in a different form. It can also be helpful in solving equations. To *factor* an expression means to write it as a product of two or more expressions, called *factors*.

Example   Does $x^2 - 7x + 12$ *factor into* $(x - 4)(x - 3)$?

We can check by multiplying the factors.

$(x - 4)(x - 3)$
$= x^2 - 3x - 4x + 12$
$= x^2 - 7x + 12$

So $x^2 - 7x + 12$ does factor into $(x - 4)(x - 3)$.

Finding factors is sometimes a matter of trial and error. For simple expressions there are procedures that we can follow.

Common Factors

To multiply $2(3x + y + 4) = 6x + 2y + 8$, we use the Distributive Property. This process can be reversed by factoring.

Example   Factor $6x + 2y + 8$.

Look for a *common factor* that is contained in all terms of the expressions. In this case, 2 is a common factor. We use the Distributive Property to factor a 2 from each term.

$6x + 2y + 8 = 2(3x) + 2(y) + 2(4)$
$\qquad\qquad\quad = 2(3x + y + 4)$

Example *Factor $3xy^2 + 15xy - 9x$.*

We use the Distributive Property to factor out the common factor $3x$.

$$3xy^2 + 15xy - 9x$$
$$= 3x(y^2) + 3x(5y) - 3x(3)$$
$$= 3x(y^2 + 5y - 3)$$

We can always check the result of factoring by multiplying.

When we say factor we mean factor *completely,* until no further factoring is possible. In the previous example we might have factored using different common factors.

$$3xy^2 + 15xy - 9x = 3(xy^2 + 5xy - 3x)$$
$$3xy^2 + 15xy - 9x = x(3y^2 + 15y - 9)$$
$$3xy^2 + 15xy - 9x = 3x(y^2 + 5y - 3)$$

Only the last factored form is completely factored. Why are the first two equalities not factored completely?

Solving Equations

Some equations can be solved by factoring and applying the Zero Product Property.

Example *Solve $x^2 + 17x = 0$ for x.*

Factor $x^2 + 17x$ and then apply the Zero Product Property.

$$x^2 + 17x = 0$$
$$x(x + 17) = 0$$
$$x = 0 \text{ or } x = -17$$

The solution set is $\{0, -17\}$.

Example *Solve $(6x^2 - 14x)(x + 13) = 0$ for x.*

We will completely factor the first binomial and then use the Zero Product Property.

$$(6x^2 - 14x)(x + 13) = 0$$
$$2x(3x - 7)(x + 13) = 0$$
$$2x = 0 \text{ or } 3x - 7 = 0 \text{ or } x + 13 = 0$$
$$x = 0 \text{ or } \quad 3x = 7 \text{ or } \quad x = -13$$
$$x = \frac{7}{3}$$

The solution set is $\left\{0, \frac{7}{3}, -13\right\}$.

Part Two: Sample Problems

Problem 1 *Rewrite each of the following expressions.*

a *Write the indicated product $10a(2a + b^2)$ as a sum.*
b *Write the sum $42k^3 + 14k$ as an indicated product.*

Solution **a** $10a(2a + b^2) = 20a^2 + 10ab^2$ (a sum)
b $42k^3 + 14k = 7k(6k^2 + 2)$ (a product)

Problem 2 Solve $32x^3 + 45x^2 = 5x^2$.

Solution Before we can use the Zero Product Property, one side of the equation must be zero.

$$32x^3 + 45x^2 = 5x^2$$

Subtract $5x^2$
$$\underline{\ -5x^2 \quad -5x^2}$$
$$32x^3 + 40x^2 = 0$$

Factor
$$8x^2(4x + 5) = 0$$
$$8x^2 = 0 \text{ or } 4x + 5 = 0$$
$$x^2 = 0 \text{ or } \quad 4x = -5$$
$$x = 0 \text{ or } \quad x = \tfrac{-5}{4}, \text{ or } -1.25$$

The solution set is $\{0, -1.25\}$. Check your answers in the original problem.

Problem 3 Refer to the polynomial $7x - 5x^2 + 12 + x^3$.

 a Put the polynomial into nested form. (See Sample Problem 3 in Lesson 10.1.)
 b Evaluate the polynomial for $x = -0.0052$.

Solution **a** To put this polynomial into nested form, follow the steps listed in the table.

Putting a Polynomial into Nested Form	
Put the polynomial in descending order of powers	$7x - 5x^2 + 12 + x^3$ $= x^3 - 5x^2 + 7x + 12$
Factor an x out of all x–terms	$= (x^2 - 5x + 7)x + 12$
Within the parentheses, factor an x out of all x–terms	$= ((x - 5)x + 7)x + 12$

In higher-degree polynomials, we continue this process until the entire nest is formed.

 b We use the nested form and the calculator to evaluate the polynomial for $x = -0.0052$. We first store -0.0052 in memory.

0.0052 $\boxed{\pm}$ $\boxed{\text{STO}}$

Then we enter the following.

1 $\boxed{\times}$ $\boxed{\text{RCL}}$ $\boxed{-}$ 5 $\boxed{=}$ $\boxed{\times}$ $\boxed{\text{RCL}}$ $\boxed{+}$ 7 $\boxed{=}$ $\boxed{\times}$ $\boxed{\text{RCL}}$ $\boxed{+}$ 12 $\boxed{=}$

The result should be approximately 11.9635.

The nested form, also called *Horner's form,* is very useful in saving computer time. The repeated (recursive) pattern of the evaluation requires only addition and multiplication.

Part Three: Exercises and Problems

Warm-up Exercises

In problems 1 and 2, factor each expression.

1 $-18a^4b^2 + 12a^3b^3 - 24a^2b$

2 $6x^3y - 9x^2y^3 + 12xy$

In problems 3 and 4, solve for x.

3 $2x^2 + 3x = 0$

4 $5x^3 + 8x^2 = 6x^2$

5 Express the polynomial $2x^3 - 3x + x^2 - 1$ in nested form.

Problem Set

In problems 6–11, determine the common factor in each expression.

6 $7x^2 - 28x$

7 $2x^7 + 6x^6 - 5x^4 + 13x^3$

8 $9x^2y - 12x^2$

9 $22x^2 - 77x - 33$

10 $2xy + 5y$

11 $-8y^2 + 16y$

12 Write the area of the rectangle as a sum.

$$10a$$

$$5a + b$$

In problems 13–16, factor out all common factors in each expression.

13 $16x^2 + 12x$

14 $12x^3y^2 - 18xy^4$

15 $25x^3 + 75x^2 + 25x$

16 $28x^4 - 7x^3$

17 Does $x^2 - 5x - 14$ factor into $(x + 7)(x - 2)$?

18 Multiply $8x(3x^2 - 2x + 1)$.

19 Factor $24x^3 - 16x^2 + 8x$.

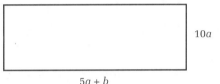

20 Multiply $(x + 5)(x + 3)$.

21 Factor $x^2 + 8x + 15$.

In problems 22–27, factor each expression.

22 $15x^2 - 30x - 10$

23 $14x - 21x^2 - 7x^3$

24 $7x^3 + 35x + 7$

25 $x^5 - x^4 + 3x^3 + 2x^2$

26 $x^3y + 3x^2y^2 + xy^3$

27 $2x^2y + 8xy + 2y$

28 If you factor the common factor 3x out of $6x^2 - 30x$, is the expression factored completely? Explain.

Problem Set, *continued*

29 Write the sum $8x^2 + 20x + 16$ as an indicated product.

30 Find the missing values in the multiplication diagram.

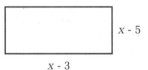

$$6x^2y \quad \boxed{\begin{array}{c|c|c} 18x^3y & 30x^5y^2 & -12x^2y \end{array}}$$

with ? ? ? above the three boxes.

31 Write the product $2c^3(4c + 5)$ as a sum.

In problems 32 and 33, solve for x.

32 $6x(9x - 15) = 0$

33 $(x - 7)(x + 7) = 0$

34 Solve the following system.

$$\begin{cases} y = 2x + 1 \\ 3x - 5y = 2 \end{cases}$$

35 Find a quadratic equation that has $\{-8, 3\}$ as its solution set.

36 Let $f(x) = (x - 5)^2 - 9$.

   a Find $f(5)$, $f(4)$, and $f(6)$.   **b** Find x if $f(x) = 0$.   **c** Find x if $f(x) = -9$.

37 The area of a rectangle is $16x^2 + 12x$. The length of the rectangle is $4x$. Find the height.

In problems 38 and 39, use a calculator to evaluate each expression for $x = 7.41$.

38 $(x + 3)x + 9$

39 $((x + 5)x + 8)x - 6$

40 Find x if the area of the rectangle is 15 square centimeters.

$$x - 5$$
$$x - 3$$

41 Let $(x + 3)(x - 3) = 0$.

   a Multiply the binomials and solve for x.
   b Use the Zero Product Property to solve the equation.

42 The height in feet $h(t)$ of a ball at t seconds is given by $h(t) = -16t^2 + 96t$.

   a What is the height of the ball at $t = 0$?
   b What is the value of $h(t)$ if the ball is at ground level?
   c When is the ball at this height again?

In problems 43–45, multiply.

43 $(a + 6)^2$ **44** $(b - 8)(b + 8)$ **45** $(c + 2d)(c - 2d)$

In problems 46–48, factor.

46 $a^2 + 12a + 36$ **47** $b^2 - 64$ **48** $c^2 - 4d^2$

49 Solve for x so that the lever is in balance.

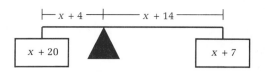

In problems 50–53, solve.

50 $7x^2(5x + 24) = 0$ **51** $3x^3 - 12x^2 = 0$

52 $(3y + 2)(2y - 17) = 0$ **53** $x^2 - 5x = x^3 + 4x^2 - 5x$

In problems 54 and 55, evaluate each expression for $x = -2.5$.

54 $((x + 4.8)x - 8.4)x - 1.3$ **55** $x^3 + 4.8x^2 - 8.4x - 1.3$

In problems 56–59, write each polynomial in nested form. Then evaluate for $x = 0.076$.

56 $5x^2 - 6x + 7$ **57** $2x^3 + 3x + 15$

58 $4x^3 + 12x^2 - 3x - 9$ **59** $x^3 + 5x^2 + 3x + 4$

60 Find x if the area of the triangle is 24x square meters.

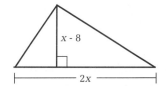

In problems 61–63, write a quadratic equation with the given solutions.

61 5 and -7 **62** 0 and 9   **63** 6 and 6

64 Find the value of B in each middle term of each product.

    a $(x - 1)(x - 9) = x^2 + Bx + 9$
    b $(x - 3)(x - 3) = x^2 + Bx + 9$
    c $(x + 1)(x + 9) = x^2 + Bx + 9$

65 Solve for (x, y).

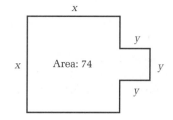
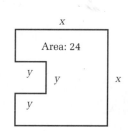

66 Find the cubic equation whose solutions are $\frac{3}{4}$, -3, and 3.

FACTORING TRINOMIALS

Objectives

After studying this section, you will be able to
- Factor trinomials with a leading coefficient of 1
- Recognize trinomials that cannot be factored

Part One: Introduction

Trinomials with a Leading Coefficient of 1

In order to develop a strategy for factoring, let's take another look at binomial multiplication.

$$\begin{array}{lll} & \textbf{First} & \textbf{Middle} & \textbf{Last} \\ & \textbf{Term} & \textbf{Term} & \textbf{Term} \end{array}$$

$$(x + 3)(x + 5) = x^2 + (5 + 3)x \quad + (3)(5) \quad = x^2 + 8x + 15$$
$$(x - 3)(x + 5) = x^2 + [5 + (-3)]x + (-3)(5) = x^2 + 2x - 15$$
$$(x + a)(x + b) = x^2 + (a + b)x \quad + (a)(b)$$

You can see that the last term in the trinomial is the product of the second terms of the binomials. The coefficient of the middle term is the sum of the second terms of the binomials. These observations are the key to factoring trinomials with a leading coefficient of 1.

Example   *Factor $x^2 + 7x + 10$.*

A check for common factors reveals that there are no common factors other than 1. So let's try to factor this trinomial into two binomials.

We need two numbers with a product of 10 and a sum of 7. The two numbers are 2 and 5.

The expression $x^2 + 7x + 10$ factors into $(x + 2)(x + 5)$.
We can check this answer by multiplying.

Example   *Factor $y^2 - 13y + 22$.*

Since there are no common factors other than 1, let's try to factor this trinomial into two binomials.

We need two numbers with a product of 22 and a sum of -13. Because we need a positive product and a negative sum, both numbers must be negative. The two numbers are -11 and -2.

The expression $y^2 - 13y + 22$ factors into $(y - 11)(y - 2)$.
We can check this answer by multiplying.

Example   Factor $x^2 - 8x - 20$.

We need two numbers with a product of -20 and a sum of -8. Because the product is negative, one of the numbers must be positive, and the other must be negative. Let's list the pairs of factors of -20.

Factors	Sum of Factors
$-1, 20$	19
$-2, 10$	8
$-4, 5$	1
$4, -5$	-1
$2, -10$	-8
$1, -20$	-19

The sum of the numbers 2 and -10 is -8, so we can factor $x^2 - 8x - 20$ into $(x + 2)(x - 10)$.

Some Trinomials That Do Not Factor

Can all trinomials be factored? Let's work through the example.

Example   Factor $x^2 + 5x - 4$.

We list the factors of -4 and look for a pair whose sum is 5.

Factors	Sum
$-1, 4$	3
$-2, 2$	0
$-4, 1$	-3

None of the pairs of factors add up to 5. This trinomial doesn't factor, which means that it does not factor into polynomials with terms that are integer coefficients.

Part Two: Sample Problems

Problem 1   Find the solution set for $x^2 - 11x - 12 = 0$.

Solution   Our strategy will be to factor the trinomial and then use the Zero Product Property. We can use -12 and 1 to factor the trinomial.

$$x^2 - 11x - 12 = 0$$
$$(x - 12)(x + 1) = 0$$
$$x - 12 = 0 \text{ or } x + 1 = 0$$
$$x = 12 \text{ or } \quad x = -1$$

The solution set is $\{12, -1\}$.

Problem 2   Factor $3x^2 - 45x + 42$.

Solution   We first look for common factors.

$$3x^2 - 45x + 42$$

There is a common factor of 3 $\quad = 3(x^2 - 15x + 14)$

We can use -1 and -14 to factor $\quad = 3(x - 1)(x - 14)$

Problem 3 The area of the shaded region is 31 square centimeters.

a Write an expression to represent the area of the shaded region.

b Write an equation that indicates that the area of the shaded region is 31 square centimeters.

c Find the numerical area of the square with side x.

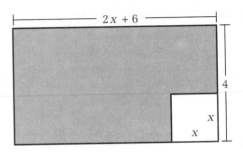

Solution The area of the shaded region is the area of the rectangle minus the area of the square.

a The area of the rectangle is $4(2x + 6)$.
   The area of the square is x^2.
   The area of the shaded region is
   $4(2x + 6) - x^2$, or $8x + 24 - x^2$.

b The equation is $4(2x + 6) - x^2 = 31$, or $8x + 24 - x^2 = 31$.

c To solve a quadratic equation, we first make one side equal to 0.

$$8x + 24 - x^2 = 31$$
$$0 = x^2 - 8x + 7$$
$$0 = (x - 7)(x - 1)$$
$$x - 7 = 0 \text{ or } x - 1 = 0$$
$$x = 7 \text{ or } \quad x = 1$$

If $x = 7$, the side of the square would be longer than the side of the rectangle. Therefore, 7 is not a possible answer. The only possible value for x is 1. So the area of the square is 1 square centimeter.

Problem 4 Solve $x^2 - 1 = 2x$ for x.

Solution Rearrange the equation and use the Zero Product Property.

$$x^2 - 1 = 2x$$
$$x^2 - 2x - 1 = 0$$

The only possible factors of -1 are 1 and -1, but the sum of 1 and -1 is 0. Even though the trinomial cannot be factored, we can use the quadratic formula to solve the equation.

In $x^2 - 2x - 1 = 0$, $a = 1$, $b = -2$, and $c = -1$.

$$x = \frac{-b \pm \sqrt{b^2 - 4ac}}{2a}$$

$$= \frac{2 \pm \sqrt{(-2)^2 - 4(1)(-1)}}{2 \cdot 1}$$

$$= \frac{2 \pm \sqrt{8}}{2}$$

$$= \frac{2 \pm 2\sqrt{2}}{2}$$

$$= 1 \pm \sqrt{2}$$

$$\approx 2.41 \text{ or } x \approx -0.41$$

Part Three: Exercises and Problems

Warm-up Exercises

In problems 1–3, completely factor each trinomial.

1 $x^2 - x - 12$ **2** $2x^2 + 14x + 12$ **3** $3x^2 - 21x + 24$

In problems 4–6, solve for *x*.

4 $x^2 + 8x = -16$ **5** $x^2 + 3 = 2x$ **6** $2x - 4 = -x^2$

Problem Set

In problems 7–9, find the middle term of each product.

7 $(x + 9)(x + 4)$ **8** $(x + 9)(x - 4)$ **9** $(x - 9)(x + 4)$

In problems 10 and 11, factor.

10 $x^2 + 7x + 12$ **11** $x^2 + 12x + 11$

12 The area of the rectangle is 24 square feet. Find the sum of *l* and *w* if both are whole numbers.

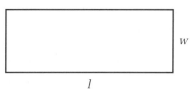

In problems 13 and 14, factor.

13 $3x^2 + 21$ **14** $x^3 + 33x^2$

In problems 15 and 16, solve using the Zero Product Property.

15 $(5 - 2x)(3x + 8) = 0$ **16** $4x - 3x^2 = 0$

In problems 17–20, factor.

17 $x^2 + 8x + 7$ **18** $x^2 - 8x + 7$ **19** $x^2 - 6x - 7$ **20** $x^2 + 6x - 7$

21 Multiply $(3x - 20)(x + 5)$.

22 Factor $3x^2 - 5x - 100$.

23 For what values of x are the perimeters of the triangle and the square equal?

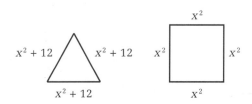

24 Solve for (x, y).
$$\begin{cases} 3x + 4y = 15 \\ x = 2y - 5 \end{cases}$$

Problem Set, *continued*

In problems 25–30, factor.

25 $x^2 - 19x + 18$ **26** $x^2 - 17x - 18$ **27** $x^2 - 9x + 18$
28 $x^2 + 7x - 18$ **29** $x^2 + 11x + 18$ **30** $x^2 + 3x - 18$

In problems 31–33, factor out -1. Then write the expression in descending order of powers.

31 $-x^2 - 5x + 9$ **32** $4 - 3x$ **33** $3x - 2x^2 - 7$

34 Two lines are perpendicular if they form a right angle. Find the values of x for which segments AB and BC are perpendicular if $\angle ABC = x^2 - 13x$.

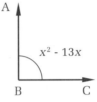

In problems 35–37, factor completely.

35 $5 - 4x - x^2$ **36** $2x - 3 + x^2$ **37** $-x^2 - 6x - 8$

In problems 38 and 39, solve each inequality and graph the solution on a number line.

38 $|x - 3| > 7$ **39** $-4x + 5 > 7$

40 Form a rectangle, using the four pieces shown. Find the dimensions of the rectangle. Then find the area of the rectangle.

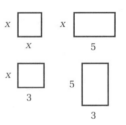

In problems 41–43, multiply.

41 $3x(x^2 - 5x - 11)$ **42** $5(x - 3)(x + 4)$ **43** $2x(x - 7)^2$

In problems 44–46, factor completely.

44 $3x^2 - 24x - 27$ **45** $5x^3 + 30x^2 + 40x$ **46** $x^3 - 10x^2 + 25x$

47 Solve for (x, y).

In problems 48 and 49, solve for x.

48 $(4^x)^{x+1} = 4^{20}$ **49** $\dfrac{9^{x^2 - 10x}}{9^{3x}} = 9^{-42}$

In problems 50 and 51, evaluate each expression if $x = -16.42$.

50 $(x - 17.43)x - 11.87$

51 $((x + 5)x - 13)x + 27$

In problems 52 and 53, write each polynomial in nested form.

52 $x^2 + 5x + 12$

53 $x^3 + 3x^2 + 7x + 11$

54 Find x if the area of the shaded region is 16 square meters.

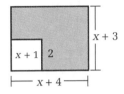

In problems 55 and 56, write a quadratic equation with the given solutions.

55 -7 and 9

56 0 and 3

57 Copy and complete the table of the binomial factors of $x^2 + qx - 16$ if q has the given values.

	q	Binomial Factors
a	0	(_?_)(_?_)
b	-6	(_?_)(_?_)
c	15	(_?_)(_?_)
d	-8	(_?_)(_?_)

In problems 58–60, write each expression in simplest form.

58 $3x^4 \cdot (2x)^5$

59 $\dfrac{4x^8}{x^4 + x^4}$

60 $\dfrac{(x^3)^4}{x^3}$

In problems 61 and 62, solve for x.

61 $x^2 - 15x + 54 = 0$

62 $7x^4 + 14x^3 - 105x^2 = 0$

63 Copy and complete the table of the binomial factors of $x^2 + 3x + p$ if p has the given values.

	p	Binomial Factors
a	2	(_?_)(_?_)
b	-4	(_?_)(_?_)
c	-10	(_?_)(_?_)
d	-18	(_?_)(_?_)

64 Find x if the area of the shaded region is 48π square inches.

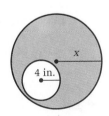

Problem Set, *continued*

In problems 65–70, factor.

65 $x^2 - 13x + 40$ **66** $x^2 - 3x - 40$ **67** $x^2 + 14x + 40$

68 $x^2 + 6x - 40$ **69** $x^2 + 39x - 40$ **70** $x^2 - 18x - 40$

71 Find (x, y) if $\angle ABC$ is three times as great as $\angle CBD$.

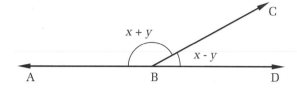

In problems 72–74, factor.

72 $x^3 + 18x^2 - 40x$ **73** $10x^2y - 15xy + 5y$ **74** $-x^2 + 8x - 16$

75 If b is randomly selected from $\{-25, -23, -14, -11, -10, -5, -2, 0, 2, 5, 10, 11, 14, 23, 25\}$, what is the probability that $x^2 + bx + 24$ can be factored?

76 Refer to the right triangle and solve for x.

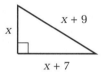

In problems 77–79, factor.

77 $5x - x^2 - 4$ **78** $2x^2 - 13x$ **79** $2x^2 - 8x + 6$

80 If $x^2 + 7x + P = (x + A)(x + B)$ and A, B, and P are whole numbers, what is the greatest possible value of P?

81 Find x if the volume of the box is 315 cubic meters.

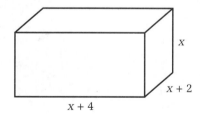

82 Solve for x and y.
$$\begin{bmatrix} x^2 & 3x \\ y^2 & y \end{bmatrix}\begin{bmatrix} 1 \\ 5 \end{bmatrix} = \begin{bmatrix} -14 \\ 14 \end{bmatrix}$$

83 Use the Zero Product Property to solve for x.
$(x + 2)(x^2) + (x + 2)(3x) + (x + 2)(-4) = 0$

84 Solve $x(3x - 5) = 5x - (35 - x^2)$ for x.

85 Solve $(ax + 8c)(3ax - d) = 0$ for x.

86 Given the following, find $\angle BCF$.

$\angle ABC = \angle BCD$
$\angle ABC = 2x + 10$
$\angle BCD = 5y + 46$
$\angle EBC = 3y + 70$

87 Multiply $\left(x + \sqrt{32}\right)\left(x - \sqrt{8}\right) = x^2 + ax + b$ to find a and b.

88 Factor $x^3 - 6x^2 - 4x + 24$.

89 Solve $x^3 - 6x^2 - 4x + 24 = 0$.

CAREER PROFILE

CREATIVE APPLICATIONS OF CHEMISTRY
Paul Gillette finds new uses for plastics

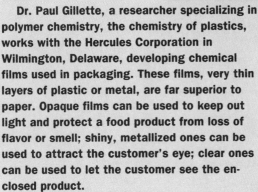

The applications of chemistry in our daily lives are almost endless. It is obvious that products such as cleaning fluids and synthetic fibers are produced by chemical means. Other applications are not so obvious. For example, food-packaging materials that appear to be made of paper are often produced by very complex chemical processes.

Dr. Paul Gillette, a researcher specializing in polymer chemistry, the chemistry of plastics, works with the Hercules Corporation in Wilmington, Delaware, developing chemical films used in packaging. These films, very thin layers of plastic or metal, are far superior to paper. Opaque films can be used to keep out light and protect a food product from loss of flavor or smell; shiny, metallized ones can be used to attract the customer's eye; clear ones can be used to let the customer see the enclosed product.

In high school, Dr. Gillette had a keen interest in both chemistry and mathematics. The creative possibilities of chemistry attracted him: "I saw chemistry as a field where you were encouraged to tinker and to create things on your own." Chemistry also permitted him to make extensive use of mathematics: "It's the applications of math that interest me. Everything in math can be put to use."

Dr. Gillette majored in chemistry and math in college and earned his Ph.D. in macromolecular science.

Dr. Gillette works in industry, so he must know not only how well a film works but also how much it costs. As an example of Dr. Gillette's work, suppose a manufacturer wants to layer a package in gold film. Chemists measure the thickness of films in angstrom units. There are 254 million angstroms in 1 inch. If the film is 500 angstroms thick and the price of gold is $400 per ounce, the cost of one square foot of film will be $1.28.

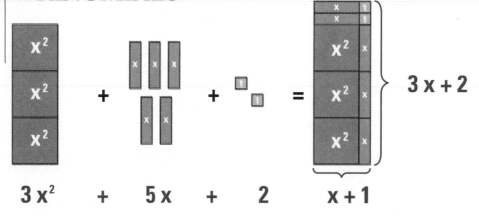

10.7 | More About Factoring Trinomials

$$3x^2 + 5x + 2 \qquad x+1$$

Objectives

After studying this section, you will be able to
- Factor a trinomial when the leading coefficient is not 1
- Use the computer to factor

Part One: Introduction

Leading Coefficients Other Than 1

In Section 10.6 we factored $ax^2 + bx + c$ where $a = 1$. The following examples will help you develop a strategy for factoring trinomials when the leading coefficient is not 1.

Example   *Factor $5x^2 - 16x + 12$.*

We need to look at all possible factors of the first and last terms. The last term is positive, so both factors of the last term have the same sign. Since the middle term is negative, both factors of the last term are negative.

Possible Factors of First Term	**Possible Factors of Last Term**
1x, 5x	$-3, -4$ or $-4, -3$
	$-2, -6$ or $-6, -2$
	$-1, -12$ or $-12, -1$

Which combination of possible factors gives a correct middle term?

Possible Factors	**Middle Term**
$(x - 3)(5x - 4)$	$-4x - 15x = -19x$
$(x - 4)(5x - 3)$	$-3x - 20x = -23x$
$(x - 2)(5x - 6)$	$-6x - 10x = -16x$ ⟵

The third combination of possible factors gives a middle term of $-16x$, so $5x^2 - 16x + 12$ factors as $(x - 2)(5x - 6)$.

Example   *Factor $2x^2 + 5x - 3$.*

Since the last term is negative, the factors of the last term are opposite in sign.

Possible Factors of First Term	**Possible Factors of Last Term**
1x, 2x	1, -3 or -1, 3
	-3, 1 or 3, -1

Possible Factors	**Middle Term**
$(x + 1)(2x - 3)$	$-3x + 2x = -1x$
$(x - 1)(2x + 3)$	$3x - 2x = 1x$
$(x - 3)(2x + 1)$	$x - 6x = -5x$
$(x + 3)(2x - 1)$	$-x + 6x = 5x$

The fourth combination of possible factors gives a middle term of 5x, so $2x^2 + 5x - 3$ factors as $(x + 3)(2x - 1)$.

Example   *Factor $14x^2 - 35x - 21$.*

$$14x^2 - 35x - 21$$

Check for common factors $\qquad = 7(2x^2 - 5x - 3)$

Refer to previous example for
possible combinations of factors $\qquad = 7(x - 3)(2x + 1)$

Helpful Hints for Factoring

1. Write the trinomial in descending order of powers.

2. Take out any common factors. If the leading coefficient is negative, factor out the negative common factor.

3. If the leading coefficient of a trinomial is 1, find two numbers whose product is the last term and whose sum is the middle term.

4. If the leading coefficient is not 1, find factors of the first term, find factors of the last term, and try all possible combinations until you find the correct middle term.

   a. If the last term is positive, both factors of the last term have the same sign as the middle term.

   b. If the last term is negative, one factor of the last term is positive and one is negative.

Using the Computer to Factor

Factoring is a process that depends on repeated trial and error. For this reason it is often helpful to use a computer. The following BASIC program will quickly check possible factorings of a trinomial until a correct one is found or until all possibilities have been checked. The program requires the following.

- Common factors have been removed.
- The trinomial is of the form $ax^2 + bx + c$.
- The value of a is positive.

```
 10 PRINT "Enter a, b, and c separated by commas: ";
 20 INPUT A,B,C; REM DATA ENTRY
 30 IF    A <= 0 OR C = 0 THEN GOTO 390
 40 REM    Set subtraction mode if constant term C < 0
 50 LET    CF = 1
 60 IF    C < 0 THEN CF = -1
 70 LET    C = ABS(C)
 80 REM    Set to negative mode if signs are - then +
 90 LET    BF = 1
100 IF    B<0 AND C>0 THEN BF = -1
110 REM    Find a factor of the leading coefficient
120 FOR    I = 1 TO SQR(A)
130 IF    A/I <> INT(A/I) THEN 360
140 LET    F1 = I
150 LET    F2 = A/I
160 REM    Find a factor of the constant term
170 FOR    J = 1 TO SQR(C)
180 IF    C/J <> INT(C/J) THEN 350
190 LET    L1 = J
200 LET    L2 = C/J
210 REM    Check for correct factors
220 IF    F1 * L1 + CF * F2 * L2 <> B * BF THEN 250
230 PRINT "(";F1;"x + ";CF*BF*L2;")(";F2;"x + ";BF*L1;")"
240 GOTO    400
250 IF    F2 * L2 + CF * F1 * L1 <> B * BF THEN 280
260 PRINT "(";F2;"x + ";CF*BF*L1;")(";F1;"x + ";BF*L2;")"
270 GOTO    400
280 IF    F1 * L2 + CF * F2 * L1 <> B * BF THEN 310
290 PRINT "(";F1;"x + ";CF*BF*L1;")(";F2;"x + ";BF*L2;")"
300 GOTO    400
310 IF    F2 * L1 + CF * F1 * L2 <> B * BF THEN 350
320 PRINT "(";F2;"x + "; CF*BF*L2;")(";F1;"x + ";BF*L1;")"
330 GOTO    400
340 REM    If factors don't check, keep searching
350 NEXT    J
360 NEXT    I
370 PRINT "The trinomial can't be factored over the integers."
380 GOTO    400
390 PRINT "Leading coefficient not positive or constant term = 0."
400 END
```

Now you can run the program to factor $36x^2 - 37x - 48$.

```
Enter a, b, and c separated by commas.
36, -37, -48
(9x - 16)(4x + 3)
```

Part Two: Sample Problems

Problem 1   Factor $-24x^3 - 78x^2 - 18x$.

Solution   The expression is in descending
order.

$$-24x^3 - 78x^2 - 18x$$

The common factor is $-6x$.

$$= -6x(4x^2 + 13x + 3)$$

Now, $4x^2$ can factor into $4x \cdot 1x$ or $2x \cdot 2x$. The last term can factor
into $3 \cdot 1$ or $1 \cdot 3$. Let's try $4x$ and $1x$ first.

Possible Factors	Middle Term
$(4x + 3)(x + 1)$	$7x$
$(4x + 1)(x + 3)$	$13x$

We need $13x$ as a middle term, so $-24x^3 - 78x^2 - 18x$ factors into
$-6x(4x + 1)(x + 3)$.

Problem 2   *The height h of a toy rocket t seconds
after launching is determined by the
formula $h(t) = -16t^2 + 112t$.*

a *Find the height of the rocket 2.5
seconds after launching.*
b *After how many seconds is the
rocket 196 feet above the ground?*
c *When will the rocket hit the
ground?*

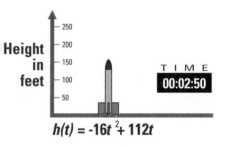

$h(t) = -16t^2 + 112t$

Solution   **a** Let $t = 2.5$.
$h(2.5) = -16(2.5)^2 + 112(2.5)$
$h(2.5) = -100 + 280$
$h(2.5) = 180$

The rocket is 180 feet above the ground after 2.5 seconds.
b Let $h(t) = 196$ and solve for t.
$h(t) = -16t^2 + 112t$
$196 = -16t^2 + 112t$
$0 = -16t^2 + 112t - 196$
$0 = -4(4t^2 - 28t + 49)$
$0 = -4(2t - 7)(2t - 7)$ Both binomial factors are the same.
$0 = 2t - 7$
$7 = 2t$
$3.5 = t$

The rocket is 196 feet above the ground after 3.5 seconds.
c The rocket will reach the ground when height $h(t) = 0$.

$$h(t) = -16t^2 + 112t$$
$$0 = -16t^2 + 112t$$
$$0 = -16t(t - 7)$$
$$-16t = 0 \quad \text{or} \quad t - 7 = 0$$
$$t = 0 \quad \text{or} \quad t = 7$$

Since $t = 0$ represents launch time, $t = 7$ must be landing time. The
rocket will hit the ground 7 seconds after launch.

Problem 3 Factor $6x^2 - 35x + 25$.

Solution The expression is in descending order.
There are no common factors.
Now check for possible factors and combinations of factors.

Possible Factors of First Term	Possible Factors of Last Term	Possible Factors	Middle Term
3x, 2x	$-1, -25$	$(3x - 1)(2x - 25)$	$-77x$
	$-5, -5$	$(3x - 5)(2x - 5)$	$-25x$
	$-25, -1$	$(3x - 25)(2x - 1)$	$-53x$
6x, 1x	$-1, -25$	$(6x - 1)(x - 25)$	$-151x$
	$-5, -5$	$(6x - 5)(x - 5)$	$-35x$ ←——
	$-25, -1$	$(6x - 25)(x - 1)$	$-31x$

Since $-35x$ is the middle term that we need, $6x^2 - 35x + 25$
factors into $(6x - 5)(x - 5)$.

Part Three: Exercises and Problems

Warm-up Exercises

In problems 1–3, completely factor each trinomial.

1 $6x^2 + 11x + 4$ **2** $8x^2 + 10x - 3$ **3** $12x^2 - 4x - 8$

4 Write a quadratic equation that has -4 and $\frac{1}{2}$ as solutions.

5 Solve $3r^2 = 4(2r - 1)$ for r.

Problem Set

In problems 6–9, factor each trinomial.

6 $2x^2 + 5x + 3$ **7** $2x^2 + 7x + 3$ **8** $2x^2 - 7x + 3$ **9** $2x^2 - 5x - 3$

10 The trinomial $3x^2 + Px + 4$ can be factored, and P represents an integer. Find the possible values of P.

11 Factor the trinomial $7x^2 - 17x + 6$.

12 The perimeter of triangle ABC is
13 meters. Find the length of the shortest side.

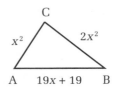

In problems 13 and 14, solve each equation by factoring.
13 $3x^2 + 13x + 10 = 0$
14 $2x^2 + 13x - 24 = 0$

15 A number n squared, less 3 times the number, is 40. Find the number.

In problems 16–19, factor each trinomial.

16 $6x^2 - 11x - 35$ **17** $2x^2 - 9x + 10$

18 $3x^2 + 14x - 24$ **19** $2x^2 - 11x + 12$

In problems 20–23, multiply each binomial.

20 $(3x - 5)(3x + 5)$ **21** $(y - 13)(y + 13)$

22 $(2x + 7)(2x - 7)$ **23** $(y - 4)(y + 4)$

24 Factor the trinomial $10z^2 + z - 3$.

25 The area of square I added to the area of square II equals the area of square III. Find x.

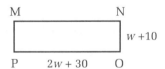

In problems 26 and 27, factor each trinomial.

26 $x^3 + 6x^2 + 8x$ **27** $x^3 - 5x^2 - 6x$

In problems 28 and 29, multiply.

28 $(r - 6)^2$ **29** $(2v + 9)^2$

30 The area of rectangle MNOP is 100 square meters. Find the dimensions of the rectangle.

M   N

$w + 10$

P $2w + 30$ O

31 Solve the system.
$$\begin{cases} 2x - 3y = 14 \\ x + y = -13 \end{cases}$$

In problems 32–35, factor each trinomial completely.

32 $-4x^3 - 10x^2 + 6x$ **33** $18x^2 - 120x - 42$

34 $8x^2 + 12x - 140$ **35** $30x^2 + 115x + 100$

In problems 36–38, evaluate each expression if $x = 3$ and $y = -5$.

36 $x^3 + y^3$ **37** $(x + y)^3$ **38** $x^3 + 3x^2y + 3xy^2 + y^3$

In problems 39–41, factor each polynomial.

39 $x^3 + 2x^2 + x$ **40** $z^4 - 12z^3 + 36z^2$ **41** $\pi R^2 h + 2\pi R h$

Problem Set, *continued*

42 Find a if the slope of the line through $(5, 4)$ and $(9, a)$ is -10.

In problems 43–46, factor each quadratic. (Hint: You may wish to use the computer program given in this section.)

43 $12m^2 - 19m - 21$ **44** $120n^2 - 13n - 12$

45 $70p^2 - 81p - 36$ **46** $289q^2 - 256$

47 Let $f(x) = x^2 - 15x$.

   a Find x so that $f(x) = 0$.   **b** Find x so that $f(x) = 16$.

In problems 48 and 49, write a quadratic equation that has the given solutions.

48 0 and -2 **49** -10 and -10

50 Refer to the diagram.

   a Fill in the missing values.

   b Write an expression for the total area.

   c Find the values of x for which the total area can also be represented by $12x + 48$.

In problems 51 and 52, factor each polynomial.

51 $12m^2 + 16m - 28$ **52** $-15x^2 + 20x + 35$

In problems 53–56, solve for x.

53 $2x^2 = 9(x - 1)$ **54** $3x^2 + 4x = 15$

55 $x(4x + 7) = 2$ **56** $2x^3 + 3x^2 - 27x = 0$

In problems 57 and 58, factor each trinomial.

57 $2x^2 + 7x - 3$ **58** $4x^2 + 9$

59 The sides of a rectangle are $(2x + 7)$ and $(2x + 3)$. The area is 12 square meters. Find the value of x and find the perimeter of the rectangle.

In problems 60–62, factor each trinomial.

60 $15y^2 - 78y + 72$ **61** $15y^2 + 66y + 72$ **62** $15y^2 - 21y - 72$

63 Solve for (x, y).

$$\begin{cases} y = x^2 \\ y - 2x = 8 \end{cases}$$

64 Find all possible values of P in $x^2 - 10x + P = (x - A)(x - B)$ if P, A, and B are whole numbers.

65 The area of the rectangle is 20 square meters. Find the dimensions of the rectangle.

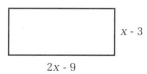

66 Let $f(x) = 3x^2 - 28x$.
  a Find x if $f(x) = 0$.　　**b** Find x if $f(x) = -9$.

In problems 67 and 68, factor each trinomial.

67 $9v^2 + 6v + 1$　　　　**68** $49v^2 + 14v + 1$

69 Find x if the area of the shaded region is 25 square inches.

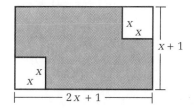

70 The height in feet $h(t)$ of a Fourth of July starburst rocket t seconds after launching is given by the function $h(t) = -16t^2 + 176t$.

  a What is the height of the rocket after 2 seconds?
  b The rocket explodes at a height of 384 feet. How many seconds have gone by since its launch? Explain your result.
  c If the rocket does not explode, how many seconds after its launch will it hit the ground?

In problems 71–73, factor each trinomial.

71 $12z^2 + 101z - 35$　　　**72** $12z^2 - 23z - 35$　　　**73** $12z^2 - 16z - 35$

 74 Solve $6x^4 - 11x^2 + 5 = 0$ for x.

75 The volume of the box is 108 cubic centimeters. Find the dimensions of the box.

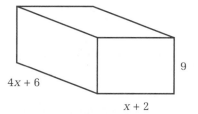

76 Where does the graph of the equation $y = 6x^2 - x - 7$ intersect the x-axis?

In problems 77–79, factor each polynomial.

77 $361y^2 - 961$　　　R **78** $21x^2 + 17x + 45$　　　P **79** $50 - 12x^2 - x$

FACTORING SPECIAL POLYNOMIALS

Objectives

After studying this section, you will be able to

- Factor the difference of squares
- Factor perfect square trinomials
- Use the process of completing the square to write perfect square trinomials

Part One: Introduction

Factoring the Difference of Squares

We can use the difference of squares multiplication pattern to factor a binomial that is the difference of two squares.

$$\square^2 - \triangle^2 = (\square + \triangle)(\square - \triangle)$$

Example *Factor the following expressions. (The solutions are given below.)*

a $x^2 - 49$

This is a difference of squares pattern.

$x^2 - 49$
$= (x)^2 - (7)^2$
$= (x + 7)(x - 7)$

b $36y^2 - 16$

A common factor is 4.

$36y^2 - 16$
$= 4(9y^2 - 4)$
$= 4[(3y)^2 - (2)^2]$
$= 4(3y + 2)(3y - 2)$

c $w^2 + 25$

This is a sum of squares, not a difference. This binomial cannot be factored over the integers.

Factoring Perfect Square Trinomials

By recognizing the perfect square pattern, you will be able to factor the following trinomials quickly.

$$\square^2 + 2\square\triangle + \triangle^2 = (\square + \triangle)^2 \qquad \square^2 - 2\square\triangle + \triangle^2 = (\square - \triangle)^2$$

Example *Factor the following expressions. (The solutions are given below.)*

a $x^2 - 10x + 25$

$x^2 - 10x + 25$
$= x^2 - 2(x)(5) + 5^2$
$= (x - 5)(x - 5)$
$= (x - 5)^2$

b $9y^2 + 30y + 25$

$9y^2 + 30y + 25$
$= (3y)^2 + 2(3y)(5) + 5^2$
$= (3y + 5)(3y + 5)$
$= (3y + 5)^2$

c $y^2 - 5y - 36$

This trinomial does not fit the pattern.

If the trinomial does not fit the pattern exactly, we must go back to the general strategy for factoring in Section 10.7. The trinomial in part **c** can be factored as $y^2 - 5y - 36 = (y - 9)(y + 4)$.

Completing the Square

In the following example, you will fill in a term so that each resulting trinomial will be a perfect square trinomial. This process is known as *completing the square.*

Example *Find the missing term that will make the trinomial a perfect square. Then factor the trinomial. (The solutions are given below.)*

a $9y^2 \underline{\quad ? \quad} + 64$
$9y^2 \underline{\quad ? \quad} + 64$
$= (3y)^2 \pm 2(3y)(8) + 8^2$

The missing term is $\pm 48y$.

$9y^2 + 48y + 64 = (3y + 8)^2$
$9y^2 - 48y + 64 = (3y - 8)^2$

b $x^2 - 16x + \underline{\quad ? \quad}$
$x^2 - 16x + \underline{\quad ? \quad}$
$= x^2 - 2x(8) + 8^2$

The missing term is 64.

$x^2 - 16x + 64 = (x - 8)^2$

Part Two: Sample Problems

Problem 1 *Factor the following expressions.*

a $3x^2 - 300$ **b** $x^2 + 18x + 81$

Solution **a** $3x^2 - 300 = 3(x^2 - 100) = 3(x + 10)(x - 10)$

b $x^2 + 18x + 81 = x^2 + 2(x)(9) + (9)^2 = (x + 9)^2$

Problem 2 *Use the chart to help complete the square on each trinomial.*

a $9x^2 + 12x + \underline{\quad ? \quad}$ **b** $25y^2 + \underline{\quad ? \quad} + 81$

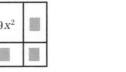 

Solution **a** We know that $9x^2 = (3x)^2$ and $12x = 6x + 6x$. Notice that a $6x$ is located in each of the equal regions in the following chart. The top and side dimensions that yield these products are also shown.

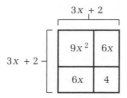

The missing square term is 4, so the perfect square trinomial is $9x^2 + 12x + 4$.

b Since $25y^2 = (5y)^2$ and $81 = (9)^2$, each term fits into one of the square regions. The top and side dimensions can be labeled. The two missing terms are equal and are the product of $5y$ and 9.

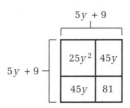 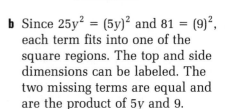

The missing terms are each $45y$, so the perfect square trinomial is $25y^2 + 90y + 81$.

Part Three: Exercises and Problems

Warm-up Exercises

In problems 1–6, factor each polynomial.

1 $y^2 - 121$ **2** $y^2 - 2y + 1$ **3** $3x^2 + 12$

4 $x^2 + 10x + 16$ **5** $4y^2 - 16$ **6** $4x^2 + 4x + 1$

In problems 7 and 8, fill in the blank to complete the square.

7 $16x^2 + 24x \underline{\quad ? \quad}$ **8** $25x^2 \underline{\quad ? \quad} + 9$

Problem Set

In problems 9–12, find the middle term of each perfect square trinomial.

9 $(y + 5)^2 = y^2 \underline{\quad ? \quad} + 25$ **10** $(t - 12)^2 = t^2 \underline{\quad ? \quad} + 144$

11 $(2x + 3)^2 = 4x^2 \underline{\quad ? \quad} + 9$ **12** $(3w + 2z)^2 = 9w^2 \underline{\quad ? \quad} + 4z^2$

In problems 13–15, find the last term of each perfect square trinomial.

13 $r^2 - 14r \underline{\quad ? \quad}$ **14** $s^2 - 20s \underline{\quad ? \quad}$ **15** $t^2 + 24t \underline{\quad ? \quad}$

In problems 16–21, factor each polynomial.

16 $x^2 + 18x + 81$ **17** $m^2 - 81$ **18** $t^2 + 14t + 49$

19 $p^2 - 18p + 81$ **20** $r^2 + 81$ **21** $x^2 - 36y^2$

22 Find x if the perimeter of the rectangle is 46 centimeters.

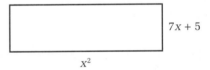

$7x + 5$

x^2

In problems 23–25, find the middle term in each perfect square trinomial.

23 $d^2 \underline{\quad ? \quad} + 49$ **24** $y^2 \underline{\quad ? \quad} + 64$ **25** $z^2 \underline{\quad ? \quad} + 9$

In problems 26 and 27, solve each inequality and graph the solution on a number line.

26 $|x - 2| < 5$ **27** $|x + 2| \geq 7$

In problems 28–33, determine which are perfect square trinomials.

28 $r^2 + 6r + 9$ **29** $t^2 + 6t + 36$ **30** $3m^2 + 16m + 64$

31 $49c^2 - 42c + 9$ **32** $s^2 - 4s - 4$ **33** $x^2 + 12x - 36$

In problems 34–36, factor each polynomial.

34 $81 - w^2$ **35** $121 - 25z^2$ **36** $2v^2 - 72$

37 Solve for (x, y).
$$\begin{cases} 5(x - y) = 25 \\ 3(x + y) = 27 \end{cases}$$

In problems 38 and 39, calculate mentally.

38 $(1.3 \times 10^{-15})^2$

39 $\sqrt{1.21 \times 10^{16}}$

In problems 40–43, factor each expression completely.

40 $6x^2 + 29x + 35$

41 $4x^2 - 64$

42 $3x^2 + 9x + 6$

43 $16x^2 + 56x + 49$

44 How many small blocks are necessary to form the large block?

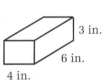

3 in.

6 in.

4 in.

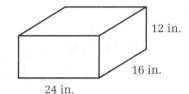

12 in.

16 in.

24 in.

In problems 45–47, factor each trinomial into binomial square factors.

45 $x^2 + 2xy + y^2$

46 $w^2 + 4w + 4$

47 $y^2 + 8y + 16$

In problems 48 and 49, solve each equation by factoring.

48 $25b^2 - 40b + 16 = 0$

49 $121r^2 + 66r + 9 = 0$

In problems 50 and 51, simplify.

50 $(4x^2)^3 + (3x^3)^2$

51 $\dfrac{x^3 - 2x^2 + x}{x}$

In problems 52 and 53, solve each equation.

52 $(x - \underline{\ ?\ })^2 = x^2 - \underline{\ ?\ }x + 49$

53 $4y^2 + \underline{\ ?\ }y + 25 = (2y + \underline{\ ?\ })^2$

54 Complete the square on the trinomial $25x^2 + 30x + \underline{\ ?\ }$. Then fill in the chart.

$25x^2$

55 Begin with the equation $y = x^2 + 8x$.

a Add 16 to both sides of the equation.
b Factor the right side of the equation from part **a**.
c Solve for y by subtracting 16 from both sides.
d Make a table and graph the equation from part **c**.

In problems 56–58, factor each polynomial.

56 $x^2 - 100$

57 $w^2 + 13w + 36$

58 $z^2 - 16$

Problem Set, *continued*

59 Solve the equation $(2x - 7)(x + 6) = 0$.

60 Write a quadratic equation that has -7 and 7 as solutions.

In problems 61–63, determine which are perfect square trinomials.

61 $2y^2 - 8y + 16$ **62** $x^2 + 12x + 36$ **63** $169q^2 - 182q + 49$

64 Complete the square on the trinomial $16y^2 \underline{} + 25$.

65 Begin with the equation $f(x) = x^2 - 10x$.
  a Add 25 to both sides of the equation.
  b Factor the perfect square trinomial on the right side of the equation from part **a**.
  c Solve for $f(x)$ in the equation from part **a** by subtracting 25 from both sides.

In problems 66–69, simplify each expression and solve each equation.

66 $x(x + 1) - 2x^2 + (x + 5)(x + 1)$ **67** $4(x - 3) + 5(2x - 7) = 16 - 2x$

68 $2x(x + 5) = x(x + 3)$ **69** $y(y + 2) - y^2 = 16$

In problems 70–72, solve for x.

70 $(7^{3x + 4})^{3x} = 7^{-4}$ **71** $\dfrac{4^{x^2 + 6x}}{4^{-9}} = 1$ **72** $(8^x)^{x - 4} = (8^4)^{4 - x}$

73 Find x if the area of the trapezoid is 78 square centimeters.

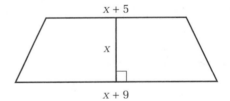

In problems 74–79, factor each polynomial.

74 $x^2 - 64$ **75** $z^2 - 16z + 64$ **76** $r^2 + 64$

77 $2x^3 - 18x$ **78** $s^2 - 16s - 64$ **79** $8x^2 + 2x - 15$

80 Find a if the slope of the line segment is greater than 10.

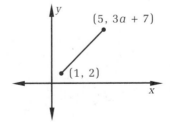

81 Factor the right side of the equation $y = x^2 - 6x + 9$. Make a table of values and then graph the equation.

82 Find x if $y = (x - 3)^2 - 36$ and $y = 0$.

83 Find x if $y = |x - 3| - 6$ and $y = 0$.

84 Find a if the perimeter of rectangle ABCD is 44 meters.

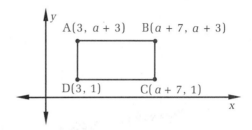

In problems 85 and 86, write each expression in nested form.

85 $x^3 - 6x^2 + 7x + 9$

86 $x^3 - 5x^2 + 7$

In problems 87–89, solve each equation.

87 $36 - b^2 = 0$

88 $4v^2 - 36 = 0$

89 $(4w + 5)^2 = 0$

In problems 90 and 91, graph each solution.

90 $y \le 2x - 7$

91 $y = |x - .4| + 2$

In problems 92 and 93, factor each polynomial completely.

92 $16x^4 - 81$

93 $x^4 - 8x^2 + 16$

94 Solve the equation $z^4 - 21z^2 - 100 = 0$.

95 Find s if the area of the shaded region is 85 square centimeters.

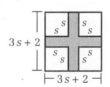

In problems 96 and 97, factor each polynomial as the difference of two squares.

96 $4x^2 - 13$

97 $6x^2 - 7y^2$

98 At $t = 0$ seconds, Vicki stood on the roof of a building and threw a ball in the air. The height in feet $h(t)$ of the ball at t seconds is given by the formula $h(t) = -16t^2 + 96t + 56$.

a How tall is the building? (Hint: $t = 0$.)
b When is the ball at its highest point?
c To what height does the ball travel?
d When does the ball strike the ground?

CHAPTER SUMMARY

CONCEPTS AND PROCEDURES

After studying this chapter, you should be able to
- Identify polynomial expressions (10.1)
- Classify polynomials (10.1)
- Add polynomials (10.2)
- Subtract polynomials (10.2)
- Multiply polynomials (10.3)
- Multiply binomials (10.3)
- Recognize the difference of squares pattern (10.4)
- Recognize the perfect square trinomial pattern (10.4)
- Interpret geometric models (10.4)
- Recognize factors of an expression (10.5)
- Identify common factors (10.5)
- Solve quadratic equations by factoring (10.5)
- Factor trinomials with a leading coefficient of 1 (10.6)
- Recognize trinomials that cannot be factored (10.6)
- Factor trinomials with a leading coefficient not equal to 1 (10.7)
- Use a computer program to factor trinomials (10.7)
- Factor the difference of squares (10.8)
- Factor perfect square trinomials (10.8)
- Use the process of completing the square to write perfect square trinomials (10.8)

VOCABULARY

binomial (10.1)
completing the square (10.8)
conjugates (10.4)
degree of a monomial (10.1)
degree of a polynomial (10.1)
difference of squares (10.4)
factor (10.5)

Horner's form (10.5)
leading coefficient (10.1)
nested form (10.1)
perfect square trinomial (10.4)
short multiplication method (10.3)
trinomial (10.1)

In problems 1 and 2, simplify each expression.

1 $4x(x - 2) + 6x^2 + 8x + 5$

2 $7x(x + 8) + 4(x)(x + 8) - 6x^2 + 2x$

In problems 3–5, classify each polynomial by the number of terms.

3 $3xy^2$ **4** $9x^4 - 6x^2 + 4x$ **5** $7x + 2y$

In problems 6 and 7, multiply.

6 $6x(3x^2 - 4)$ **7** $5x^2(9x + 6)$

8 If a number is selected at random from $\{0, 1, 5, 14, 25, 36, 49, 66, 81, 90, 100\}$, what is the probability that the number is a perfect square?

9 Refer to the rectangle made of smaller rectangles A, B, C, and D.

   a Find the area of each small rectangle.
   b Multiply $(x + 4)(3x + 2)$.

In problems 10 and 11, multiply.

10 $(3x + 12)(x^2 + 4x - 3)$ **11** $(2x - 4)(x + 3)$

In problems 12 and 13, write each expression as a product.

12 $3x^2(x^2 - 5x + 7) + 7x(x^2 - 5x + 7) - 9(x^2 - 5x + 7)$

13 $(x + 3)(x - 3) - (9 - x^2)$

In problems 14–19, factor each expression.

14 $9x^2 + 18x$ **15** $9x^2y + 6xy^2$ **16** $x^2 - 10x + 25$

17 $9 - 4k^2$ **18** $Fred^2 - Sue^2$ **19** $4x^3 - 40x^2 + 100x$

In problems 20 and 21, solve each equation.

20 $(x - 7)(x + 3) = 0$ **21** $x^2 - 4x = 32$

22 Write a quadratic equation that has -5 and 11 as solutions.

Review Problems, *continued*

In problems 23 and 24, factor each expression.

23 $2x^2 - x - 3$ **24** $5y^2 + 7y + 2$

25 Find two consecutive odd integers whose product is 3363.

In problems 26 and 27, supply the missing term so that each expression is a perfect square trinomial.

26 $x^2 + 16x + \underline{\ \ ?\ \ }$ **27** $x^2 + \underline{\ \ ?\ \ } + 9$

In problems 28–30, multiply.

28 $(2x - 5)(3x + 7)$ **29** $2x(x - 1)(x + 3)$ **30** $(8x - 5y)^2$

In problems 31–33, factor each polynomial.

31 $2x^2 - 5x + 3$ **32** $8x^2 + 25x + 3$ **33** $4x^2 - 25$

34 If x is an even integer, what is the sum of the next three consecutive even integers?

35 Let $f(x) = ((x + 3)x + 4)x + 8$.
    a Find $f(-3)$.   **b** Find $f(0)$.

36 Solve $(9x - 3)(4x + 2) = 0$ for x.

37 Simplify $2x^2(2x^2 - 3x + 1) - 4x(x^3 - 2x^2 + x - 7)$.

 38 What polynomial is 20% of $40x^2 - 20x + 5$?

In problems 39–44, factor each polynomial.

39 $x^2 - 13x + 40$ **40** $3x^2 - 60x + 300$ **41** $x^2 - 6x - 40$

42 $6x^2 - 30x - 36$ **43** $35y^2 - 140y$ **44** $2x^3 - 8x$

45 The volume of the box is 270 cubic centimeters. Find the value of x.

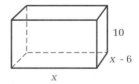

In problems 46–53, simplify each expression and solve each equation.

46 $(2x^2)^3(-3x^2)$ **47** $x(x + 3) - (x^2 - 7)$ **48** $(x + 2)(x + 1) - x(x + 3)$

49 $x^2 + 9 = -10x$ **50** $x(x + 1) + 2(x + 1) = 0$ **51** $9x^2 = 16$

52 $(5x + 1)^2 - 5(x + 1)$ **53** $4x(x - 3) = 4(x - 3)$

54 Solve $6x^2 - 5x + 1 \geq 0$ for x.

55 Given x = 4.31, evaluate $(x + 9)x - 3$.

56 Find the value of x.

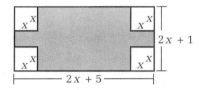

In problems 57 and 58, write each expression in nested form.

57 $x^2 - 7x + 11$ **58** $x^3 + 5x^2 + 11x - 9$

In problems 59–61, multiply.

59 $\left(\sqrt{5} + 2\right)\left(\sqrt{5} - 2\right)$ **60** $\left(\sqrt{5} + \sqrt{3}\right)\left(\sqrt{5} - \sqrt{3}\right)$ **61** $\left(\sqrt{6} + \sqrt{2}\right)\left(\sqrt{6} + \sqrt{2}\right)$

62 The area of the shaded region is 53 square centimeters. Find the value of x.

63 Suppose B and C are integers. Find all possible integer values of A in $x^2 + Ax + 14 = (x + B)(x + C)$.

64 The square of a number is 96 more than 10 times the number. Find the number.

65 What is the x^2-term of the product $(9x^2 - 3x + 5)(x^2 + 2x + 1)$?

In problems 66–69, completely factor each expression.

66 $(x + 1)x^2 + (x + 1)x + (x + 1)(-2)$ **67** $x^2(x^2 - 4) - 9(x^2 - 4)$
68 $x^3 - 4x^2 + 3x$ **69** $x^4 - 2x^2 + 1$

In problems 70 and 71, solve each inequality.

70 $x^2 - 8x + 16 > 0$ **71** $x^3 - 6x^2 - 7x \geq 0$

72 Write a quadratic equation whose solutions are $-\frac{1}{2}$ and $\frac{3}{4}$.

73 The average of the polynomials $x^2 + 2x + 1$, $3x^2 - 3x + 4$, and $2x^2 - 11x - 5$ is 6. Find the value of x.

74 What should appear in the blank to make the expression $x^2 + 9x + \underline{\quad?\quad}$ a perfect square trinomial?

1 Simplify.

$(x^3 + 5x^2 + 21x) + (4x^2 - 7x - 16) - (3x^2 - 4x + 10)$

In problems 2–5, multiply or divide.

2 $(2x + 11)(2x - 11)$

3 $(3x^2 + 10x + 7) \div (3x + 7)$

4 $(10x + 5)(2x^2 - 6x + 3)$

5 $(6x^3 - 5x - 38) \div (x - 2)$

6 Find the area of a square with side $5x - 2$.

7 Refer to the square.

  a Find the value of K.

  b Find the length of a side.

x^2	$5x$
$5x$	K

In problems 8–10, find the solution set.

8 $y(y + 3)(2y - 5) = 0$

9 $3x^2 + x = 4$

10 $2r^2 + 7r + 3 = 4 - 2r^2 - r$

11 Given the areas within the square, write a binomial multiplication problem to represent the total area.

$9x^2$	$15x$
$15x$	25

In problems 12–15, factor each expression.

12 $x^2 - 2x - 15$

13 $20z^3 + 70z^2 + 30z$

14 $x^2 + 7x + 2$

15 $r(r - 3) - 4(r - 3)$

16 Graph on a number line the solution set of $x^2 - 2x - 15 < 0$.

17 If one expression is chosen from those below, what is the probability of each of the following?

$5x^3y - 14y$ $3x^2 - 4x - 12$ $7 + r^3$

$2x + 3y - 7z$ $\dfrac{x^2}{8} + \dfrac{y^2}{6}$ $\dfrac{5 - x}{x^2}$ $\dfrac{x^2 + 5x + 4}{x + 1}$

  a It is a polynomial with degree 4.

  b It is a binomial.

  c It is not a polynomial.

PUZZLES AND CHALLENGES

1 Study the following pattern and write the product of $(H + T)^4$ and $(H + T)^5$.

$$(H + T)^0 = \boxed{1}$$

$$(H + T)^1 = \boxed{1}\ H + \boxed{1}\ T$$

$$(H + T)^2 = \boxed{1}\ H^2 + \boxed{2}\ HT + \boxed{1}\ T^2$$

$$(H + T)^3 = \boxed{1}\ H^3 + \boxed{3}\ H^2T + \boxed{3}\ HT^2 + \boxed{1}\ T^3$$

$$(H + T)^4 =$$

$$(H + T)^5 =$$

2 Find all integer values of y so that $\dfrac{6}{y + 2}$ is an integer.

3 If $x^2 + y^2 = 14$ and $(x + y) = 5$, what is $(x - y)$? (Hint: Compare $(x - y)^2$ to $(x + y)^2$.)

4 Simplify $(x - a)(x - b)(x - c) \cdot \ldots \cdot (x - z)$.

5 Find all integer values of x so that $\dfrac{x^2 - 2x + 3}{x - 2}$ is an integer.

6 Use the diagram to express the volume of the cube as a polynomial. (Hint: $V = (a + b)^3$.)

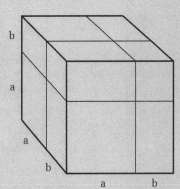

11 | QUADRATICS

Scientists will soon scan the heavens for signals from extraterrestrial life forms. Beginning in 1992 and continuing through 1998, NASA plans to look for possible signals from nearly 800 stars known to be somewhat similar to our sun. In addition, a less detailed survey of the entire sky is planned.

Sensitive radiotelescope receivers have been designed to listen selectively to 14 million separate frequency bands. The receivers will be linked with the dish-shaped antennas of NASA's spacecraft-tracking Deep Space Network and with other, larger radiotelescopes.

These receivers will enable researchers to weed out those identifiable signals produced by natural sources such as pulsars as well as signals produced on Earth such as radio-frequency interference.

GRAPHING THE PARABOLA

Objectives

After studying this section, you will be able to
- Graph equations of the form $y = x^2$
- Graph equations of the form $y = (x - h)^2 + k$
- Compare the absolute value graph and the parabola

Part One: Introduction

The Graph of $y = x^2$

Let's make a table of values for the simple function $f(x) = x^2$ and then look for patterns.

Differences
in x-values

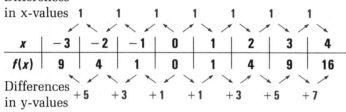

x	-3	-2	-1	0	1	2	3	4
$f(x)$	9	4	1	0	1	4	9	16

Differences
in y-values $+5$ $+3$ $+1$ $+1$ $+3$ $+5$ $+7$

Starting from $x = 0$, as the x-values increase by 1, the y-values increase in a pattern of 1, 3, 5, 7, ... As the x-values decrease by 1, the y-values follow the same pattern.

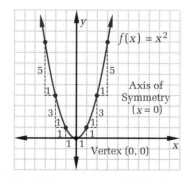

This pattern helps us quickly sketch a U-shaped curve, the graph of the parabola. Or, you may want to sketch the graph of $f(x) = x^2$ using a graphing calculator.

Throughout this chapter, the x-values in tables will increase or decrease by 1 from a point called the **vertex.**

The vertex of this parabola is its lowest, or minimum, point. Parabolas can also be "upside down," in which case the vertex is the highest, or maximum, point. The *axis of symmetry* of a parabola is a line that divides the graph into halves that are mirror images of each other. The axis always passes through the vertex.

For the graph of $f(x) = x^2$, the coordinates of the vertex are $(0, 0)$. The axis of symmetry is the y-axis, which has the equation $x = 0$.

Graphing $y = (x - h)^2 + k$

Let's look at other examples of functions with graphs that are parabolas.

Example   *Graph the function $f(x) = (x - 2)^2 + 3$.*

We center the table at $x = 2$ because $(x - 2)^2 = 0$ if $x = 2$.

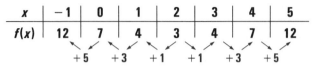

x	-1	0	1	2	3	4	5
$f(x)$	12	7	4	3	4	7	12

The shape of this parabola is identical to the graph of $f(x) = x^2$. In the function $f(x) = (x - 2)^2 + 3$, the $(x - 2)^2$ indicates a shift of 2 units to the right. The $+3$ tells us that the parabola is shifted up 3 units. So, the coordinates of the vertex are $(2, 3)$, and the equation of the axis of symmetry is $x = 2$.

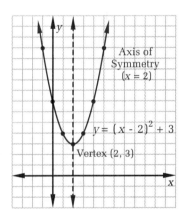

An equation tells us a great deal about a function and its graph. This information is summarized in the table.

Equation	Vertex	Axis of Symmetry
$y = x^2$	$(0, 0)$	$x = 0$
$y = (x + 3)^2$	$(-3, 0)$	$x = -3$
$y = (x - 2)^2 + 3$	$(2, 3)$	$x = 2$
$y = (x - h)^2 + k$	(h, k)	$x = h$

The Absolute Value Graph and the Parabola

Do we see the same change in an absolute value graph that we see in a parabola? The following example shows how a function containing an absolute value can be graphed.

Example   Graph $f(x) = |x - 3| + 5$.

Since $|x - 3| = 0$ if $x = 3$, we center the table at $x = 3$.

x	0	1	2	3	4	5	6
$f(x)$	8	7	6	5	6	7	8

+1   +1   +1   +1   +1   +1

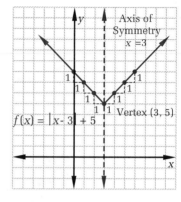

The vertex is at (3, 5), and the axis of symmetry is x = 3. The pattern of change in y-values is +1, +1, +1, . . . , which forms a V-shaped graph.

The pattern of change is not the same for the graph of a parabola as for the graph of an absolute value function. The following table summarizes what we have found.

Parabola	**Absolute Value Graph**
For an equation of the form $y = (x-h)^2 + k$, **where** h **and** k **are constants,** ■ **The vertex is** (h, k). ■ **The axis of symmetry is** $x = h$. ■ **The graph has a U-shape with a pattern of** +1, +3, +5, +7, ...	**For an equation of the form** $y = |x-h| + k$, **where** h **and** k **are constants,** ■ **The vertex is** (h, k). ■ **The axis of symmetry is** $x = h$. ■ **The graph has a V-shape with a pattern of** +1, +1, +1, ...
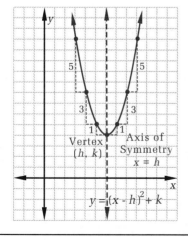	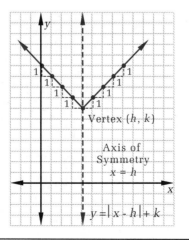

Part Two: Sample Problems

Problem 1 For each equation, give the coordinates of the vertex and the equation of the axis of symmetry. Then describe the shape of the graph and give the equation for the graph it resembles.

a $y = (x - 2)^2 + 3$
b $y = x^2 - 4$
c $y = |x - 6| - 3$
d $y = |x| + 4$
e $y = (x + 5)^2$

Solution We need to have the equations fit the form
$y = (x - h)^2 + k$ or $y = |x - h| + k$.
Remember that $x^2 = (x - 0)^2$ and $|x| = |x - 0|$.

	Vertex	Axis of Symmetry	Shape of Graph	Graph it Resembles
a	$(2, 3)$	$x = 2$	U	$y = x^2$
b	$(0, -4)$	$x = 0$	U	$y = x^2$
c	$(6, -3)$	$x = 6$	V	$y = |x|$
d	$(0, 4)$	$x = 0$	V	$y = |x|$
e	$(-5, 0)$	$x = -5$	U	$y = x^2$

Problem 2 Quickly sketch each graph.

a $y = (x - 2)^2 - 4$
b $f(x) = |x + 3| + 1$

Solution

a The vertex is $(2, -4)$.
The axis of symmetry is $x = 2$. The graph is U shape.
The graph has a $+1, +3, +5, \ldots$ pattern.

b The vertex is $(-3, 1)$.
The axis of symmetry is $x = -3$. The graph is V shape.
The graph has a $+1, +1, +1, \ldots$ pattern.

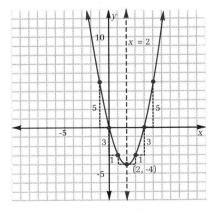

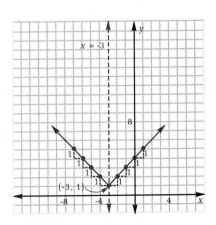

Problem 3   *Refer to the figure.*

a *Write an equation for the total area of the figure using the variable A for the area.*

b *Graph the equation (label the horizontal axis x and vertical axis A), and identify the coordinates of the vertex. Write the equation of the axis of symmetry.*

c *What is the least possible value of A, the area of the figure?*

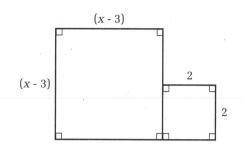

Solution   We can write the equation for the total area by adding the areas of the two squares.

a The area A can be represented as $A = (x - 3)^2 + 4$.

b The vertex is (3, 4), and the axis of symmetry is $x = 3$.

c The least possible area, A, is at the lowest point on the graph, the vertex, (x, A). The smallest area is 4. When $x = 3$, the length of the side of the large square is 0, and the area is 4, the area of the small square.

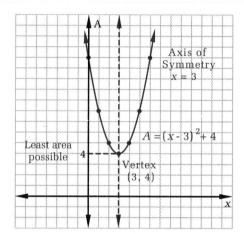

Problem 4   *Use the function $f(x) = x^2 - 6x + 9$ for the following.*

a *Factor the perfect square trinomial and rewrite the original function using the factored form.*

b *Find the coordinates of the vertex and the equation of the axis of symmetry of the parabola.*

Solution   Since the coefficient of the middle term of the trinomial is -6, the factored term is $(x - 3)$.

a The function is $f(x) = (x - 3)^2$.

b The vertex is (3, 0), and the axis of symmetry is $x = 3$.

Part Three: Exercises and Problems

Warm-up Exercises

In problems 1–3, identify a) the vertex, b) the equation of the axis of symmetry, and c) the shape of the curve.

1 $y = (x - 2)^2 + 4$ **2** $y = |x - 2| - 3$ **3** $y = (x + 3)^2 - 4$

4 Sketch each graph.

a $f(x) = (x + 1)^2$ **b** $f(x) = (x - 1)^2 + 2$ **c** $y = |x - 1| + 2$

In problems 5 and 6, graph each equation.

5 $y = (x + 4)^2 - 5$ **6** $y = |x - 3| - 4$

In problems 7 and 8, give the equation of each graph.

7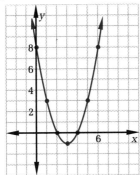

8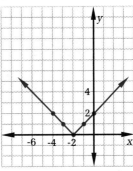

Problem Set

9 Refer to the equation $y = (x - 3)^2 + 5$.

   a Find y if $x = 3$.   **b** Find y if $x = 6$.   **c** Find y if $x = 0$.

In problems 10–13, find the vertex and the axis of symmetry.

10 $y = (x - 4)^2 + 5$ **11** $y = (x + 5.4)^2 - 3.2$
12 $y = x^2 - 9$ **13** $y = x^2$

14 Refer to the equation $y = (x - 2)^2 + 5$.

   a Find x if $y = 14$.   **b** Find x if $y = 5$.   **c** Find x if $y = 9$.

15 Sketch each function.

   a $f(x) = (x - 3)^2$ **b** $f(x) = x^2 - 5$ **c** $f(x) = (x - 3)^2 - 5$

In problems 16–21, find the vertex and the axis of symmetry.

16 $y = x^2 - 5$ **17** $y = |x - 2|$ **18** $y = (x - 2)^2$
19 $y = (x + 5)^2 - 4$ **20** $y = |x| + 3$ **21** $y = (x + 3)^2 + 2$

In problems 22–24, sketch the graph.

22 $y = |x - 3|$ **23** $y = |x| - 5$ **24** $y = |x - 3| - 5$

25 Find the slope of the line containing the points $(8, -3)$ and $(-5, 9)$.

In problems 26 and 27, write each expression in standard radical form.

26 $\sqrt{20} + \sqrt{45}$ **27** $\frac{4}{\sqrt{2}} + \sqrt{18}$

28 Write an equation to represent the diagram. Then sketch a graph of this equation. If $x = 12$, how long is $\overline{AB}$?

$$A \;|\underset{(x+3)^2}{\underline{\quad\quad\quad\quad}}\; \overset{y}{|} \;\underset{5}{\underline{\quad\quad\quad}}\;| B$$

Problem Set, *continued*

29 Write an equation of the form $y = |x - h| + k$ for a graph with a vertex of $(-2, 5)$ and an axis of symmetry of $x = -2$.

30 Write an equation of the form $y = (x - h)^2 + k$ for a graph with a vertex of $(6, 4)$ and an axis of symmetry of $x = 6$.

In problems 31–34, solve each equation and simplify each expression.

31 $3(x + 4) - 4 = 2(4x - 6)$

32 $(2xy^2)^3 - 14y^3(x - x^3y^3)$

33 $9x + 4(x - 3) + 6x + 9$

34 $(x + 4)(x + 7) = 0$

35 Write an equation in the form $y = (x - h)^2 + k$ for the parabola shown.

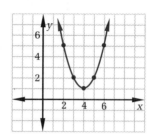

36 Solve for (x, y).
$$\begin{cases} 4x + 9y = 10 \\ 2x - 3y = 20 \end{cases}$$

37 A long-distance telephone call costs $0.65 for the first 3 minutes and $0.20 for each additional minute. If Hubert paid $17.45 for a call, how long was the call?

38 Write an equation of the form $y = |x - h| + k$ if the axis of symmetry and the vertex are the same as those for $y = (x - 4)^2 + 7$.

In problems 39–41, simplify each expression.

39 $x^8 \cdot x^7$

40 $(y^5)^3 \cdot y^7$

41 $\dfrac{2^{10}}{2^{12}}$

In problems 42–44, factor each trinomial.

42 $x^2 + 9x + 20$

43 $6x^2 + 8xy + 10zx$

44 $x^2 - 10x + 25$

45 The area of a circle is given by $A = \pi r^2$. Complete the following table and use the information to sketch a graph.

r	0	1	2	3	4	5
A						

46 Write the equation that corresponds to the table.

x	−5	−4	−3	−2	−1	0	1
y	5	0	−3	−4	−3	0	5

47 Solve for (x, y) by graphing on a single set of axes.
$$\begin{cases} y = x^2 \\ y = |x| \end{cases}$$

48 Write the equation $y = x^2 - 8x + 16$ in the factored form $y = (x - h)^2$ and graph the equation.

49 For $y = (x - 2)^2 + 4$, find the value of y if $x = 0$.

50 For $y = (x - 2)^2 - 9$, find the values of x if $y = 0$.

51 The height in meters h of a kite is a function of time in seconds t. This function is $h(t) = (t - 5)^2 + 45$, and $t \geq 0$.
  a How far above the ground is the kite when $t = 15$ seconds?
  b At what time is the kite at its lowest point?
  c What is the kite's lowest height above the ground?
  d Graph the equation.

52 The figure at the right is a square.
  a What equation is represented by the diagram? Rewrite it in the form $y = (x - h)^2 + k$.
  b Graph the parabola from part **a**.
  c What significance does the vertex of the parabola have in relationship to the square?

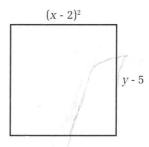

53 Find the values of k so that the slope of the line through $(5, 7)$ and $(3, |k|)$ is equal to 3.

54 Find 25% of the polynomial $16x^2 - 8x + 12$.

55 Multiply.
$$\begin{bmatrix} 5x & x + 2 \\ x & x + 6 \end{bmatrix} \begin{bmatrix} x \\ x - 3 \end{bmatrix}$$

In problems 56–58, factor.

56 $2x^2 - 5x - 12$ **57** $y^2 - 16x^2$ **58** $x^2 + 9x - 12$

59 A parabola has the form $y = (x - h)^2 + k$ and passes through $(0, 6)$ and $(-3, 21)$. Find its equation.

60 The figure at the right is a square.
  a What equation is represented by the diagram?
  b Graph the parabola given by the equation in part **a**.
  c What two points (x, y) on the graph would give the square an area of 16?

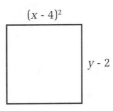

Problem Set, *continued*

In problems 61–63, graph each equation.

61 $y = \sqrt{x}$ **62** $y = \sqrt{x - 2}$ **63** $y = \sqrt{x - 2} + 4$

In problems 64 and 65, write the equation that represents each figure and draw the graph of each equation.

64

65

66 Graph the solution of the following system. $\begin{cases} y > x^2 - 2 \\ y \le x + 1 \end{cases}$

MATHEMATICAL EXCURSION

EUCLID'S ALGORITHM
A shortcut to factoring large numbers

Factoring a polynomial by removing the greatest common factor is not a problem when the coefficients are quickly found:

$$14x + 21 = 7(2x + 3)$$

Suppose, however, that the coefficients are large and the greatest common factor is not quickly seen:

$$1219x + 437$$

By using a method called Euclid's algorithm, you can find the greatest common factor no matter how baffling the coefficients.

1. Write the larger number as the greatest possible multiple of the smaller, plus any remainder.

	Remainder
$1219 = 2(437) +$	345
$437 = 1(345) +$	92
$345 = 3(92) +$	69
$92 = 1(69) +$	23
$69 = 3(23) +$	0

2. Repeat step 1 for the number in parentheses and the remainder.
3. Continue this process until the remainder is 0.

The next-to-last remainder, in this problem 23, is the greatest common factor.

$$1219x + 437 = 23(53x + 19)$$

Factor.
1. $117x + 279$ 2. $663x - 286$
3. $867m + 1071$ 4. $3977h - 679$

$$1632x + 728$$

$$1632 = 2\ (728) + 176$$

$$728 = 4\ (176) + 24$$

$$176 = 7\ (24) + 8$$

$$24 = 3\ (8) + 0$$

GRAPHING OTHER PARABOLAS

Objectives

After studying this section, you will be able to
- Graph equations of the form $y = a(x - h)^2 + k$
- Find the x- and y-intercepts of a parabola
- Graph equations of the form $y = a|x - h| + k$

Part One: Introduction

Graphing $y = a(x - h)^2 + k$

Recall the graph of the function $f(x) = x^2$. What happens if a quadratic function has a coefficient in the x^2-term that is not 1?

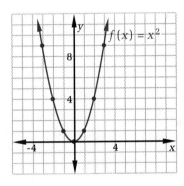

Example   *Graph the functions.*

a $g(x) = 2x^2$ **b** $h(x) = \frac{1}{3}x^2$ **c** $j(x) = -1x^2$

All of the functions resemble $f(x) = x^2$. Let's look at a table of values and the graph for each.

$g(x) = 2x^2$

x	-3	-2	-1	0	1	2
$g(x)$	18	8	2	0	2	8

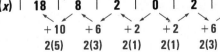

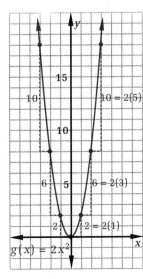

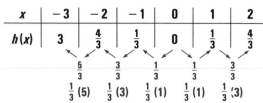

$h(x) = \frac{1}{3}x^2$

x	-3	-2	-1	0	1	2
$h(x)$	3	$\frac{4}{3}$	$\frac{1}{3}$	0	$\frac{1}{3}$	$\frac{4}{3}$

$\frac{5}{3}$ $\frac{3}{3}$ $\frac{1}{3}$ $\frac{1}{3}$ $\frac{3}{3}$

$\frac{1}{3}(5)$ $\frac{1}{3}(3)$ $\frac{1}{3}(1)$ $\frac{1}{3}(1)$ $\frac{1}{3}(3)$

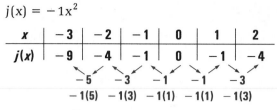

$j(x) = -1x^2$

x	-3	-2	-1	0	1	2
$j(x)$	-9	-4	-1	0	-1	-4

-5 -3 -1 -1 -3

$-1(5)$ $-1(3)$ $-1(1)$ $-1(1)$ $-1(3)$

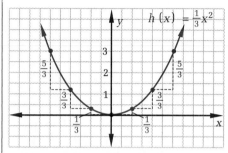

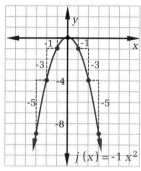

We can make a chart of what we have found.

Graphs of Functions

Function	Vertex	Axis of Symmetry	Pattern	Coefficient of x	Comparison with $f(x)=x^2$
$f(x)=x^2$	$(0,0)$	$x=0$	$1, 3, 5, 7,\dots$	1	
$g(x)=2x^2$	$(0,0)$	$x=0$	$2, 6, 10, 14,\dots$	2	narrower
$h(x)=\frac{1}{3}x^2$	$(0,0)$	$x=0$	$\frac{1}{3}, \frac{3}{3}, \frac{5}{3}, \frac{7}{3},\dots$	$\frac{1}{3}$	wider
$j(x)=-1x^2$	$(0,0)$	$x=0$	$-1, -3, -5, -7,\dots$	-1	upside down

Note: In the last example, the vertex is the highest, or maximum, point.

From the chart above, we can extend the ideas of Section 11.1.
For equations of the form $y = a(x - h)^2 + k$,
- The vertex is (h, k).
- The equation of the axis of symmetry is $x = h$.
- If $a > 0$, the graph opens upward and the vertex is the lowest, or minimum, point.
- If $a < 0$, the graph opens downward and the vertex is the highest, or maximum, point.
- As the x-values change by 1 from the vertex point, the pattern for the change in y-values is $1a, 3a, 5a, 7a, \dots$.

Finding the Intercepts of a Parabola

Recall that the intercepts of a graph are the points where the graph crosses the axes. The x-intercepts occur when $y = 0$, and the y-intercept occurs when $x = 0$.

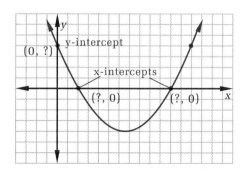

Example Find the x- and y-intercepts of the graph of $y = (x - 3)^2 - 4$.

The x- and y-intercepts can be found using either a graphing method or an algebraic method.

Method 1
Sketching a graph shows that the y-intercept is 5 or (0, 5) and the x-intercepts are 1 and 5 or (1, 0) and (5, 0). This technique works well if you can draw the graph quickly.

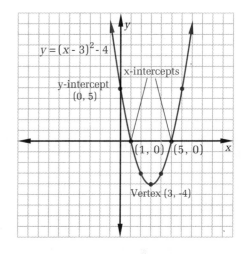

Method 2

To find the y-intercept algebraically, we can let x = 0	To find the x-intercept algebraically, we can let y = 0

To find the y-intercept algebraically, we can let x = 0
$$y = (x - 3)^2 - 4$$
$$y = (0 - 3)^2 - 4$$
$$y = 9 - 4$$
$$y = 5$$

To find the x-intercept algebraically, we can let y = 0
$$y = (x - 3)^2 - 4$$
$$0 = (x - 3)^2 - 4$$
$$4 = (x - 3)^2$$
$$\sqrt{4} = \sqrt{(x - 3)^2}$$
$$2 = |x - 3|$$
$$2 = x - 3 \text{ or } -2 = x - 3$$
$$5 = x \text{ or } 1 = x$$

With each method, we find that the y-intercept is 5 or (0, 5) and the x-intercepts are 1 and 5 or (5, 0) and (1, 0). Although the algebraic method is more precise, graphing is a good way to check.

Graphing $y = a|x - h| + k$

Consider the following example.

Example If $f(x) = 2|x - 3| + 4$, graph the function f.

Here is a table for this function.

x	−1	0	1	2	3	4	5	6
$f(x)$	12	10	8	6	4	6	8	10

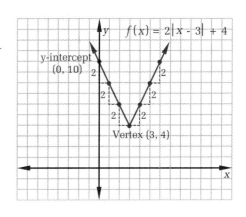

The vertex is (3, 4). The axis of symmetry is x = 3.

A coefficient a has the same effect on the graph of $y = a|x - h| + k$ as it has on the graph of the quadratic function $y = a(x - h)^2 + k$. For the equation and the graph of $y = a|x - h| + k$,
- The vertex is (h, k).
- The equation of the axis of symmetry is $x = h$.
- If $a > 0$, the graph opens upward.
- If $a < 0$, the graph opens downward.
- The pattern for the change in y-values per unit change in x-value from the vertex is always $1a$, $1a$, $1a$, ...

Part Two: Sample Problems

Problem 1   For each equation, answer the following.
  i Does the graph open upward or downward?
  ii Is the vertex the highest point or the lowest point?
  iii What are the coordinates of the vertex? Is the graph wider or narrower than the graph of $f(x) = x^2$?
  iv What is the pattern for the change in y-values as x-values change by 1 from the vertex point?

  a $y = -3(x + 2)^2 - 4$ **b** $y = \frac{1}{2}x^2$ **c** $y = x^2 - 4$

Solution   **a** Remember   **b** Remember   **c** Remember
  $f(x) = a(x - h)^2 + k$ $x^2 = (x - 0)^2$ $x^2 = (x - 0)^2$
  i Downward   **i** Upward   **i** Upward
  ii Highest   **ii** Lowest   **ii** Lowest
  iii $(-2, -4)$;   **iii** $(0, 0)$; wider   **iii** $(0, -4)$; the same
   narrower   **iv** $\frac{1}{2}, \frac{3}{2}, \frac{5}{2}, \ldots$ **iv** $1, 3, 5, \ldots$
  iv $-3, -9, -15, \ldots$

Problem 2   Make a quick sketch of the graph of each equation.
  a $y = \frac{1}{2}(x + 3)^2 - 2$ **b** $y = -2|x - 4| + 5$

Solution   **a** Vertex: $(-3, -2)$ **b** Vertex: $(4, 5)$
  Axis of symmetry: Axis of symmetry:
  $x = -3$ $x = 4$
  Opens upward   Opens downward
  Pattern: $\frac{1}{2}, \frac{3}{2}, \frac{5}{2}, \ldots$ Pattern:
   $-2, -2, -2, \ldots$

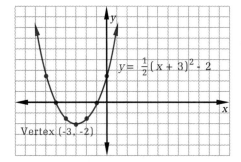
$y = \frac{1}{2}(x + 3)^2 - 2$
Vertex $(-3, -2)$

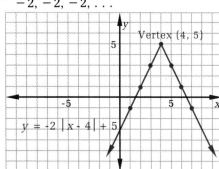
Vertex $(4, 5)$
$y = -2|x - 4| + 5$

Problem 3 Given the quadratic function $f(x) = 2x^2 + 16x + 32$, find the vertex and draw the graph of the parabola.

Solution First we change the equation to the form $y = a(x - h)^2 + k$.

$$2x^2 + 16x + 32 = 2(x^2 + 8x + 16)$$
$$= 2(x + 4)^2$$

Since $f(x) = 2(x + 4)^2$, the vertex is $(-4, 0)$.

The axis of symmetry is $x = -4$.

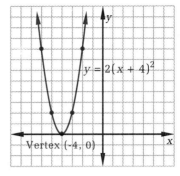

Problem 4 At Ocean World Park, Dolly the dolphin jumps out of the water on a parabolic path. If the x-axis coincides with the top of the water in Dolly's tank and the y-axis is in the center of the tank and perpendicular to the x-axis, then the path that Dolly travels is given by

$y = -\frac{5}{36}x^2 + 20$, where x and y are measured in feet.

a How far from the center of the tank does Dolly leave and reenter the water?

b What is Dolly's greatest height above the water?

Solution **a** Dolly leaves and reenters the water at the x-intercepts of the parabola. Therefore, we set $y = 0$ and solve for x.

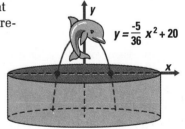

$$0 = -\frac{5}{36}x^2 + 20$$
$$\frac{5}{36}x^2 = 20$$
$$x^2 = 144$$
$$x = 12 \text{ or } x = -12$$

Dolly is 12 feet from the center of the tank both when she leaves the water and when she reenters the water.

b At the vertex of the parabola, Dolly will be at the greatest height. The vertex is $(0, 20)$, so Dolly jumps 20 feet out of the tank.

Part Three: Exercises and Problems

Warm-up Exercises

In problems 1–3, answer each question for each problem.

i Does the graph open upward or downward?

ii Is the vertex the highest point or the lowest point?

iii What are the coordinates of the vertex? Is the graph wider or narrower than the graph of $f(x) = x^2$?

iv What is the pattern for the change in y-values as x-values change by 1 from the vertex?

1 $y = -\frac{1}{3}x^2$ **2** $y = x^2 + 3$ **3** $y = 4(x - 1)^2 + 3$

In problems 4 and 5, find the x- and y-intercepts.

4 $y = \frac{1}{2}(x - 3)^2 - 8$ **5** $y = |x - 3| - 2$

In problems 6 and 7, write the equation for each graph pictured.

6

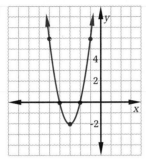

7

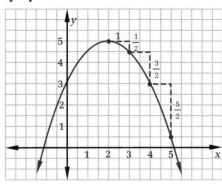

Problem Set

In problems 8–11, find the vertex and the axis of symmetry and determine whether the graph opens upward or downward.

8 $y = -2(x - 4)^2$ **9** $y = \frac{1}{2}(x + 2)^2 - 4$

10 $y = \frac{1}{3}x^2 + 6$ **11** $y = 4(x + 7)^2 - 3$

In problems 12–15, determine whether the graph opens upward or downward and give the pattern of change in y-values.

12 $y = 3(x - 2)^2$ **13** $y = -2(x + 1)^2 - 4$

14 $y = 3|x - 2| + 5$ **15** $y = -2|x + 1|$

In problems 16 and 17, find the x- and y-intercepts.

16 $y = (x - 2)^2 - 9$ **17** $y = |x + 3| - 6$

In problems 18 and 19, find x if y = 0.

18 $y = |x + 6| - 7$ **19** $y = |x + 6|$

In problems 20–25, make a quick graph of each equation.

20 $y = -\frac{1}{3}(x + 2)^2 - 5$ **21** $y = -\frac{1}{3}|x + 2| - 5$

22 $y = 2(x - 3)^2 - 4$ **23** $y = -\frac{1}{4}(x + 1)^2 + 6$

24 $y = -|x - 2| + 5$ **25** $y = \frac{1}{3}|x| + 1$

26 Johnny can pick 24 apples in 6 minutes. How many apples can Johnny pick in 1 minute? How many can he pick in 8 hours?

27 Graph $y = 3x$.

28 Write the equation of the parabola in the form $y = a(x - h)^2 + k$.

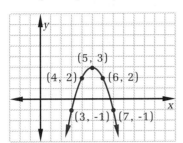

(5, 3)

(4, 2)   (6, 2)

(3, -1)   (7, -1)

29 Write the equation of the graph in the form $y = a|x - h| + k$.

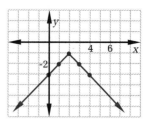

30 As a boat moves through water, waves are created. The distance between the waves is determined by the formula $d = \left(\frac{v}{1.2}\right)^2$ where d is in feet and v is in knots. How far apart are the waves formed by a boat traveling at 10 knots?

31 The height, in feet, of an object is described by the function $h(t) = -16t^2 + 10t + 15$. What is the initial upward velocity of the object? What is the initial height of the object?

In problems 32 and 33, find the vertex and the equation of the axis of symmetry of each graph.

32

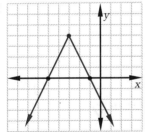

33

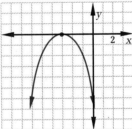

34 A suitcase fell out of an airplane at 10,000 feet. The initial velocity of the suitcase was 0 feet per second. Its height in feet h after t seconds is given by the function $h = -16t^2 + 10,000$. What was its height after 10 seconds? When will it hit the ground?

In problems 35 and 36, solve for y.

35 $(y - 3)^2 = 49$

36 $(3y + 4)(2y - 3)(y - 9) = 0$

In problems 37–39, multiply.

37 $(x + 7)^2$

38 $(2x - 3)^2$

39 $(5 + x)^2$

40 Dinah has 5 more dimes than Nicki has nickels. How much money does each have if the total number of coins they have is 21?

Problem Set, *continued*

41 Find x so that the areas are equal.

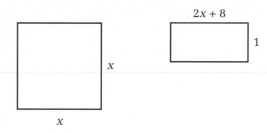

In problems 42–45, find the vertex and the x- and y-intercepts for each equation.

42 $y = x^2 - 4$ **43** $y = -x^2 + 9$

44 $y = |x| - 3$ **45** $y = -2|x| + 6$

46 Graph each equation on the same set of axes.

   a $y = -(x - 1)^2 + 2$ **b** $y = -2(x - 1)^2 + 2$ **c** $y = -\frac{1}{2}(x - 1)^2 + 2$

47 A ball is thrown into the air, and its height h at any time t in seconds is given by $h = -16(t - 1)^2 + 212$. When is the ball at its highest point above the ground? When is it on the ground?

48 The product of two consecutive integers added to twice the first integer equals 54. Find the integers.

49 Peter can pick 24 peppers in 4 minutes. Paul can pick 24 peppers in 3 minutes. How many peppers can each person pick in 1 minute? If they pick together, how many peppers can Peter and Paul pick in 1 minute? How long will it take them to pick 2590 peppers?

In problems 50 and 51, graph each equation.

50 $y = 2|x - 3| - 4$ **51** $y = -\frac{1}{3}(x + 2)^2 + 5$

52 If (1, 5) and (0, 3) are on $y = ax^2 + b$, find a and b.

53 Write a formula for the area A in terms of x. If the area is 16, find x. If the area is 3, find x.

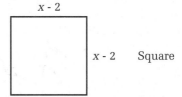

54 If A is the area of the shaded region, find a formula for A in terms of x. Find the sides of the original rectangle when the area of the shaded region is 27 square units.

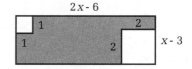

In problems 55 and 56, find the x- and y-intercepts.

55 $y = -2|x - 3| + 6$ **56** $y = \frac{1}{2}(x + 2)^2 - 16$

In problems 57 and 58, what is the equation of the graph?

57

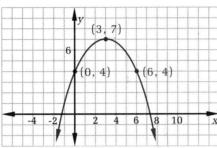

58

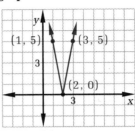

59 In preparation for a party, 4 liters of fruit juice are mixed with 2 liters of seltzer water. After 3 liters of the beverage are served, another liter each of fruit juice and seltzer is added to the mixture. How many liters of fruit juice are in the mixture now? What percentage of the mixture is seltzer?

60 Solve the system of inequalities by graphing.
$$\begin{cases} y \geq \frac{1}{2}(x - 3)^2 - 1 \\ y < -2(x - 1)^2 + 3 \end{cases}$$

61 Make a table of values and graph $y = x^3$. Use your answer to graph $y = (x - 2)^3$.

62 Ace motorcyclist Suzy Kee jumps her motorcycle off a 12-foot-high ramp. Her height above the ground at any horizontal distance x is given by

$$y = \frac{-3}{800}(x - 40)^2 + 18$$

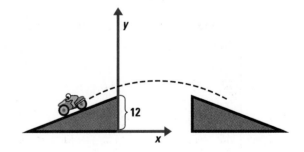

a What is the greatest height Suzy reaches?

b How far should the landing ramp be from the first ramp so that Suzy just reaches it on the way down?

c What horizontal distance has Suzy traveled when she is 16 feet above the ground?

63 Paul Vault and his brother Banks are Olympic vaulters. Paul can jump to a height of 17'6", and Banks can vault to 18'4". Each reaches the top of his vaults 1 second after leaving the ground. What initial upward velocity did each vaulter have?

11.3 COMPLETING THE SQUARE IN QUADRATIC FUNCTIONS

INPUT $x^2 - 10x - 3$ **X** OUTPUT $(x-5)^2 - 28$

Objectives

After studying this section, you will be able to
- Use the technique of completing the square to transform $y = ax^2 + bx + c$ into $y = a(x - h)^2 + k$

Part One: Introduction

Completing the Square

If an equation is not in the form $y = a(x - h)^2 + k$, it is difficult to find the coordinates of the vertex, to determine the equation of the axis of symmetry, or to graph the equation quickly. Now, we will look at how to change any equation in the form $y = x^2 + bx + c$ into the form $y = a(x - h)^2 + k$ by using the technique of *completing the square.* Let's try an example.

Example   Transform the equation $y = x^2 - 10x - 3$ by completing the square.

In section 10.4, we saw the following pattern.
$$(\square - \triangle)^2 = \square^2 - 2\triangle\square + \triangle^2$$
We can use this pattern to rewrite $y = x^2 - 10x - 3$ as a perfect square trinomial.

Step 1   We can rewrite the equation $y = x^2 - 10x - 3$
as $y = x^2 - 10x + \underline{\ ?\ } + \underline{\ ?\ } - 3$

Step 2   We find the third term
$y = x^2 - 2\underline{5}x + \underline{5}^2$
    $= x^2 - 10x + 25$
The missing term is 5^2 or 25.

In the rewritten equation of Step 1, we add the missing term and its opposite, with the net effect of adding zero.
$y = x^2 - 10x + \underline{\ 25\ } + \underline{\ -25\ } - 3$

Step 3 Now we can factor the perfect square trinomial and combine the like terms.

$$y = x^2 - 10x + 25 - 25 - 3$$

Factor   Combine

$$y = \quad (x - 5)^2 \qquad - 28$$

The equation is now in a form we can analyze and quickly graph.

What happens when the coefficient of the x^2 term is not 1? We can generalize our procedure and develop an algorithm.

Example

Transform $y = 3x^2 - 18x - 2$ into the form $y = a(x - h)^2 + k$. Then give the coordinates of the vertex and the equation of the axis of symmetry.

Step 1 We factor out the coefficient of x^2 from the first two terms of the trinomial. Do not change the third term.

$$y = 3x^2 - 18x - 2$$
$$y = 3(x^2 - 6x) - 2$$

Step 2 Next, we rewrite the equation with two blanks so that one value is added to the quantity inside the parentheses and one to the quantity outside.

$$y = 3(x^2 - 6x + \underline{\quad?\quad}) + \underline{\quad?\quad} - 2$$

Step 3 After finding the number that completes the square, we add the number and its opposite. *Be careful here.* It looks as if we should add 9 and -9, but we are completing the square of a quadratic that has the common factor 3. So we add 3(9), or 27, and -27.

$$+27$$

$$y = 3(x^2 - 6x + \underline{\quad9\quad}) + \underline{\quad-27\quad} - 2$$
$$y = 3(x - 3)^2 - 29$$

The vertex is $(3, -29)$. The axis of symmetry is $x = 3$.

Example

Use the function $f(x) = -2x^2 + 16x - 22$. Give the coordinates of the vertex and state whether it is a minimum or a maximum point. Give the equation of the axis of symmetry and then graph the function.

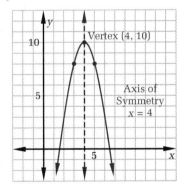

$$f(x) = -2x^2 + 16x - 22$$
$$= -2(x^2 - 8x) - 22$$
$$= -2(x^2 - 8x + \underline{\quad?\quad}) + \underline{\quad?\quad} - 22$$

$$-32$$

$$f(x) = -2(x^2 - 8x + \underline{\quad16\quad}) + \underline{\quad32\quad} - 22$$
$$f(x) = -2(x - 4)^2 + 10$$

The vertex $(4, 10)$ is a maximum point because the -2 causes the graph to open downward. The axis of symmetry equation is $x = 4$.

Part Two: Sample Problems

Problem 1

Refer to the figure.
a Write an equation for the area A of the shaded region.
b For what value of x will the area of the shaded region be equal to 20?

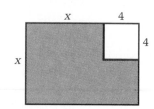

Solution

a The area of the shaded region is the area of the large rectangle minus the area of the small square.

$$A = x(x + 4) - 4(4)$$
$$= x^2 + 4x - 16$$

b Let $A = 20$ and solve for x.

$$20 = x^2 + 4x - 16$$
$$0 = x^2 + 4x - 36$$

Use the quadratic formula: $a = 1$, $b = 4$, $c = -36$.

$$x = \frac{-4 \pm \sqrt{4^2 - 4(1)(-36)}}{2(1)} = \frac{-4 \pm \sqrt{160}}{2}$$

$$x \approx 4.325 \text{ or } x \approx -8.325$$

Since x represents the side of a rectangle, the area of the shaded region is 20 if x is about 4.325.

Problem 2

Find the x- and y-intercepts of $y = x^2 - 12x + 40$ and graph the equation.

Solution

To find the x-intercepts, complete the square. Then let $y = 0$ and solve for x.

$$y = x^2 - 12x + 40$$
$$y = x^2 - 12x + \underline{36} + \underline{-36} + 40$$
$$y = (x - 6)^2 + 4$$
$$0 = (x - 6)^2 + 4$$
$$-4 = (x - 6)^2$$

To find the y-intercept, let $x = 0$ and solve for y.

$$y = x^2 - 12x + 40$$
$$y = 0^2 - 12(0) + 40$$
$$y = 40$$

The y-intercept is (0, 40).

There is no real value with a squared value equal to -4. Therefore, there are no x-intercepts. This can also be seen in the graph.

The vertex (6, 4) is a minimum point. The axis of symmetry equation is $x = 6$. The graph follows a 1, 3, 5, . . . pattern.

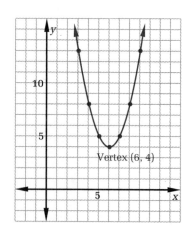

Problem 3   Write $y = -4x^2 - 36x - 65$ in the form $y = a(x - h)^2 + k$.

Solution   We use the following BASIC computer program.

```
10 REM     This program transforms y = ax^2 + bx + c into
20 REM     y = a(x - h)^2 + k by completing the square.
30 REM     It also gives the vertex and axis of symmetry.
40 PRINT "Enter a, b, and c, separated
      by commas: ";
50 INPUT a,b,c
60 IF a = 0 THEN GOTO 130
70 LET h = -b / (2*a)
80 LET k = -a * h^2 + c
90 PRINT "y = ";a;"(x - ";h;")^2 + ";k
100 PRINT "The vertex is: (";h;",";k;")"
110 PRINT "The axis of symmetry is: x = ";h
120 GOTO 140
130 PRINT "This is not a quadratic
      function!!"
140 END
```

Your computer screen will display the following:

```
Enter a, b, and c separated by commas: -4,
    -36, -65
y = -4(x - - 4.5)^2 + 16
The vertex is: (-4.5, 16)
The axis of symmetry is: x = -4.5
```

Part Three: Exercises and Problems

Warm-up Exercises

In problems 1 and 2, complete the square to form a perfect square trinomial.

1 $x^2 - 10x +$ __?__   **2** $x^2 + 7x +$ __?__

In problems 3–5, complete the square and factor the resulting trinomial.

3 $x^2 + 18x +$ __?__   **4** $x^2 - 4x +$ __?__   **5** $x^2 - 2x +$ __?__

In problems 6–9, transform each equation from the $y = ax^2 + bx + c$ form to the $y = a(x - h)^2 + k$ form.

6 $y = x^2 - 6x + 5$ **7** $y = 3x^2 + 18x + 10$

8 $y = -2x^2 + 8x - 4$ **9** $y = \frac{1}{3}x^2 - 2x + 9$

10 Find the x- and y-intercepts of $y = x^2 + 8x + 12$.

Problem Set

In problems 11–13, find the value of k that makes each trinomial a perfect square trinomial.

11 $x^2 + 8x + k$ **12** $x^2 - 10x + k$ **13** $x^2 + 5x + k$

In problems 14–17, complete the square and factor the resulting trinomial.

14 $x^2 - 12x +$ ___?___   **15** $x^2 + 6x +$ ___?___
16 $x^2 - 9x +$ ___?___   **17** $x^2 + 15x +$ ___?___

In problems 18 and 19, find the values of a, b, c, and d that complete the square and make the statement an identity.

18 $4x^2 - 16x = a(x^2 - bx + c) + d$ **19** $5x^2 - 30x = a(x^2 - bx + c) + d$

In problems 20–25, change each equation into the form $y = (x - h)^2 + k$ and graph it.

20 $y = x^2 + 10x$ **21** $y = x^2 - 4x - 5$ **22** $y = x^2 + 8x - 2$
23 $y = 2x^2 + 12x + 16$ **24** $y = x^2 + 9x + 12$ **25** $y = -x^2 - 4x + 1$

26 A ball is thrown upward from the top of a building. Its height in feet h above the ground is given by $h(t) = -16t^2 + 96t + 110$, where t is in seconds.

    a Write this equation in the form $h(t) = a(t - h)^2 + k$.
    b What is the greatest height of the ball?
    c When will the ball strike the ground?

27 Write an equation for the graph shown. Use the form $y = (x - h)^2 + k$.

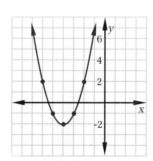

In problems 28–30, determine whether the parabolas open upward or downward.

28 $y = 2(x - 5)^2 + 3$ **29** $y = -\frac{1}{3}(x + 4)^2 - 7$ **30** $y = -3x^2 + 2$

In problems 31 and 32, simplify.

31 $\dfrac{9x^4 y^3}{3xy^5}$ **32** $\dfrac{(4x^5)^2 \, (3x^4)}{9x^8}$

In problems 33–35, factor completely.

33 $9x^2 - 12x$

34 $9x^2 - 25$

35 $4x^2 + 12x + 9$

In problems 36–39, graph.

36 $y = x^2 - 4$

37 $y = 2|x - 5| + 4$

38 $y = -2x^2 + 4x - 8$

39 $y = x^2 - 2x + 4$

In problems 40 and 41, solve each system.

40 $\begin{cases} 3x + 5y = 31 \\ x = 2y + 3 \end{cases}$

41 $\begin{cases} 4x - 3y = 38 \\ 2x + y = 14 \end{cases}$

42 Given $y = -x^2 + 6x + 7$, for what values of x is y = 0? For what values of x is y positive?

In problems 43 and 44, graph each equation and find the x-intercepts.

43 $y = \frac{2}{3}x - 4$

44 $y = -(x - 2)^2 + 5$

45 Refer to the figure.
  a Write a formula for the area A of the shaded region.
  b Write the formula for area A in the form $A = a(x - h)^2 + k$.

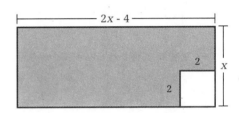

46 Find the vertex and the equation of the axis of symmetry.
  a $y = x^2 - 8x + 3$
  b $y = 2x^2 - 8x + 3$

In problems 47–50, complete the square and change each equation into the form $y = a(x - h)^2 + k$.

47 $y = 3x^2 + 6x$

48 $y = 3x^2 - 12x + 5$

49 $y = \frac{1}{2}x^2 + 10x$

50 $y = -2x^2 - 6x - 3$

In problems 51 and 52, change each equation into the form $y = a(x - h)^2 + k$. Then graph the equation.

51 $y = x^2 - 4.6x + 12.9$

52 $y = -x^2 + 7.6x - 14.2$

In problems 53–55, how many x-intercepts will each equation have?

53 $y = -2(x - 4)^2 + 5$

54 $y = -2(x - 4)^2 - 1$

55 $y = -2(x - 4)^2$

56 Refer to the equation $y = |x^2 + 6x + 5|$.
  a For which value(s) of x is y = 0?
  b Draw the graph of the equation.

Problem Set, *continued*

In problems 57–60, graph each equation.

57 $y = |2x - 10| + 3$

58 $y = -\left|\frac{2}{3}x + 6\right| - 1$

59 $y = \left|\frac{1}{2}x - 5\right| - 3$

60 $y = \left|\frac{3}{2}x - 6\right| + 1$

61 Make a table and sketch the graph of all pairs (x, y) that are solutions of $y = \frac{1}{x}$. Be sure to include some numbers between −1 and 1.

62 Solve for (x, y).
$$\begin{cases} y = \frac{1}{2}x + 6 \\ 2y = 3x - 4 \end{cases}$$

63 The diagram shows a rectangle that is transformed into a square. Find the missing area in order to complete the square of the original rectangle.

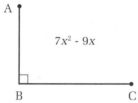

64 What values of x will make $\overline{AB}$ and $\overline{BC}$ perpendicular if angle B = $7x^2 - 9x$?

65 Make a table and sketch the graph of all ordered pairs (x, y) that are solutions of the equation $\frac{y}{4} = \frac{x}{2}$.

66 AB = CD. For what value of x does $\overline{AB}$ have the greatest length possible?

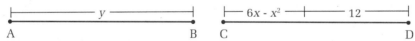

67 A parabola has an equation of the form $y = ax^2 + bx + c$. It passes through (0, 3), (1, 0), and (3, 0). Find the equation of this parabola in the form $y = a(x - h)^2 + k$.

68 The formula for projectile motion on the moon is $h(t) = -0.8t^2 + v_0t + h_0$.

a An astronaut on the moon hits a golf ball, giving it an initial upward velocity of 30 meters per second. When will the ball return to the surface of the moon?

b Find the greatest height above the moon's surface reached by the ball.

THE PARABOLA AND THE QUADRATIC EQUATION

Objectives

After studying this section, you will be able to

- Recognize the relationship between the x-intercepts of the graph of a quadratic function and the roots of a quadratic equation
- Use the discriminant to determine the number of x-intercepts of a graph of a quadratic function and the number of roots of a quadratic equation
- Prove the quadratic formula
- Use the discriminant to determine whether a quadratic equation can be solved by factoring

Part One: Introduction

The x-intercepts and Quadratic-Equation Solutions

A quadratic function is expressed as $f(x) = ax^2 + bx + c$ or $y = ax^2 + bx + c$. A quadratic equation is an equation in the form $0 = ax^2 + bx + c$. To see the relationship between the quadratic equation and the quadratic function, let's look at the next two examples.

Example   *Graph the quadratic function*
$f(x) = x^2 - 6x + 5$
and find the x-intercepts.

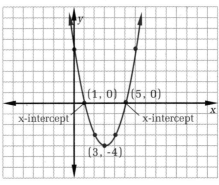

First we complete the square.
$f(x) = x^2 - 6x + \underline{} + \underline{} + 5$
$f(x) = x^2 - 6x + \underline{9} + \underline{-9} + 5$
$f(x) = (x - 3)^2 - 4$

We can read the x-intercepts from the graph. One x-intercept is 5. The other x-intercept is 1.

Example   *Find the roots of the quadratic equation $0 = x^2 - 6x + 5$.*

To find the roots means to solve the quadratic equation for x. We solve this quadratic equation by factoring.

$0 = x^2 - 6x + 5$
$0 = (x - 5)(x - 1)$
$x - 5 = 0$ or $x - 1 = 0$, so $x = 5$ or $x = 1$

The roots of the equation are 5 and 1.

The x-intercepts of the graph of the quadratic function $f(x) = x^2 - 6x + 5$ and the roots of the quadratic equation $0 = x^2 - 6x + 5$ are the same.

> ***Finding the roots of $0 = ax^2 + bx + c$ is the same as finding the x-intercepts of $f(x) = ax^2 + bx + c$.***

In order to find the x-intercepts of the graph of a quadratic function, we often use the quadratic formula.

Example *Find the x-intercepts of the graph of the quadratic function $g(x) = 2x^2 + 5x - 6$.*
Use the quadratic formula with $a = 2$, $b = 5$, $c = -6$.

$$x = \frac{-5 \pm \sqrt{25 - 4(2)(-6)}}{4}$$

$$= \frac{-5 \pm \sqrt{73}}{4}$$

$$\approx \frac{-5 \pm 8.544}{4}$$

The roots of the quadratic equation and the x-intercepts of the graph of the quadratic function are $x \approx 0.886$ and $x \approx -3.386$.

Example *The graph of $h(x) = x^2 - x - 20$ is shown. Use the graph to solve $0 = x^2 - x - 20$.*

The x-intercepts of the graph are the solutions of $0 = x^2 - x - 20$, so $x = 5$ and $x = -4$ are the solutions of $0 = x^2 - x - 20$.

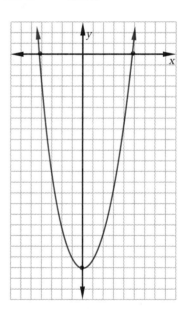

The Discriminant

Given the quadratic equation $0 = ax^2 + bx + c$, $b^2 - 4ac$, the quantity under the square root symbol in the quadratic formula, is the *discriminant.*

Let's look at the relationship between the discriminant and the number of x-intercepts.

Example   Sketch the graph of $f(x) = x^2 - 2x - 8$ and determine the number of x-intercepts.

We let $f(x) = 0$ and use the quadratic formula.

$$0 = x^2 - 2x - 8$$

$$x = \frac{2 \pm \sqrt{4 - 4(1)(-8)}}{2}$$

$$x = \frac{2 \pm \sqrt{36}}{2}$$

$$= \frac{2 \pm 6}{2}$$

$x = 4$ or $x = -2$

The graph has two real intercepts, 4 and -2.

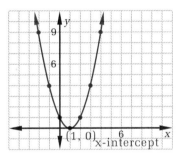

Example   Sketch the graph of $f(x) = x^2 - 2x + 1$ and determine the number of x-intercepts.

We let $f(x) = 0$ and use the quadratic formula.

$$0 = x^2 - 2x + 1$$

$$x = \frac{2 \pm \sqrt{4 - 4(1)(1)}}{2}$$

$$x = \frac{2 \pm \sqrt{0}}{2}$$

$x = 1$

The graph has one x-intercept, 1.

Example   Sketch the graph of $f(x) = x^2 - 2x + 6$ and determine the number of x-intercepts.

We let $f(x) = 0$ and use the quadratic formula.
$$0 = x^2 - 2x + 6$$

$$x = \frac{2 \pm \sqrt{4 - 4(1)(6)}}{2}$$

$$x = \frac{2 \pm \sqrt{-20}}{2}$$

Since $\sqrt{-20}$ is not a real number, this graph has no x-intercepts.

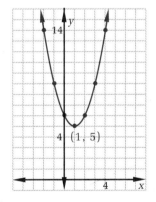

The values of the discriminant in these examples are 36, 0, and -20, respectively.

Discriminant	Number of x - intercepts	Number of Real Roots
Positive	2	2
Zero	1 (Vertex)	1
Negative	None	None

The value of the discriminant ($b^2 - 4ac$) indicates the number of x-intercepts for the parabola and the number of real roots to the quadratic equation.

Proof of the Quadratic Formula

The quadratic formula is one of the most useful formulas you will learn in algebra this year. When the quadratic formula was presented in Chapter 7, it was shown to work for a few examples, and you were asked to use it and to accept it on faith. You now have learned enough algebra to understand a proof of the quadratic formula based on completing the square for the general quadratic function $f(x) = ax^2 + bx + c$.

$$f(x) = ax^2 + bx + c$$

Factor out the common factor a
$$f(x) = a\left(x^2 + \frac{b}{a}x + \underline{\quad?\quad}\right) + \underline{\quad?\quad} + c$$

Complete the square
$$f(x) = a\left[x^2 + \frac{b}{a}x + \left(\frac{b}{2a}\right)^2\right] - a\left(\frac{b}{2a}\right)^2 + c$$

$$a\left(\frac{b^2}{4a^2}\right) = \frac{b^2}{4a}$$
$$f(x) = a\left(x + \frac{b}{2a}\right)^2 - \frac{b^2}{4a} + c$$

$$\left(\frac{4a}{4a}\right) = 1$$
$$f(x) = a\left(x + \frac{b}{2a}\right)^2 - \frac{b^2}{4a} + \left(\frac{4a}{4a}\right)c$$

$$f(x) = a\left(x + \frac{b}{2a}\right)^2 - \frac{(b^2 - 4ac)}{4a}$$

Now let's find the roots of the quadratic equation $0 = ax^2 + bx + c$.

$$0 = a\left(x + \frac{b}{2a}\right)^2 - \frac{(b^2 - 4ac)}{4a}$$

Add $\dfrac{(b^2 - 4ac)}{4a}$ to each side
$$\frac{(b^2 - 4ac)}{4a} = a\left(x + \frac{b}{2a}\right)^2$$

Multiply each side by $\dfrac{1}{a}$
$$\frac{(b^2 - 4ac)}{4a^2} = \left(x + \frac{b}{2a}\right)^2$$

Take the square root of both sides
$$\sqrt{\frac{b^2 - 4ac}{4a^2}} = \left|x + \frac{b}{2a}\right|$$

$$\pm\frac{\sqrt{b^2 - 4ac}}{2a} = x + \frac{b}{2a}$$

Add $-\dfrac{b}{2a}$ to each side
$$-\frac{b}{2a} \pm \frac{\sqrt{b^2 - 4ac}}{2a} = x$$

Add the fractions
$$x = \frac{-b \pm \sqrt{b^2 - 4ac}}{2a}$$

⟫ **The roots of the quadratic equation $ax^2 + bx + c = 0$ are**
$$x = \frac{-b \pm \sqrt{b^2 - 4ac}}{2a}.$$

When Will the Factoring Method Work?

When should we use the quadratic formula to solve an equation, and when can we use factoring? The discriminant can help us decide.

Let's calculate the discriminant of some quadratic equations that can be factored.

Equation	Discriminant
$x^2 - 11x + 18 = 0$	$(-11)^2 - 4(1)(18) = 49,$ or 7^2
$x^2 - 6x + 9 = 0$	$(-6)^2 - 4(1)(9) = 0$

Now let's calculate the discriminant of quadratic equations that can't be factored.

$x^2 - 5x - 7 = 0$	$(-5)^2 - 4(1)(-7) = 53$
$x^2 + 2x + 9 = 0$	$(2)^2 - 4(1)(9) = -32$

The value of the discriminant is a perfect square when the equation is factorable. Using the discriminant is a quick way to determine whether to factor or to use the quadratic formula as well as how many x-intercepts and real roots we will find.

Part Two: Sample Problems

Problem 1

How many real roots does each of the following quadratic equations have?

a $y = 3x^2 + 2x + 5$ **b** $y = x^2 - 6x - 10$ **c** $y = x^2 - 16x + 64$

Solution

In each case, use the discriminant.

a $a = 3, b = 2,$
$\quad c = 5$

$\quad b^2 - 4ac$
$\quad (2)^2 - 4(3)(5)$
$\quad = 4 - 60$
$\quad = -56$
$\quad -56 < 0$ None

b $a = 1, b = -6,$
$\quad c = -10$

$\quad b^2 - 4ac$
$\quad (-6)^2 - 4(1)(-10)$
$\quad = 36 + 40$
$\quad = 76$
$\quad 76 > 0$ Two

c $a = 1, b = -16,$
$\quad c = 64$

$\quad b^2 - 4ac$
$\quad (-16)^2 - 4(1)(64)$
$\quad = 256 - 256$
$\quad = 0$ One

Problem 2

Dolly the dolphin is hungry. When Dolly leaps, her height in feet h above the water is given by $h = -16t^2 + 35.2t$, where t is time in seconds.

Dolly's trainer, on a platform 10 feet above the water, holds a fish. Dolly jumps from the water at $t = 0$ seconds. How long is it before Dolly gets the fish?

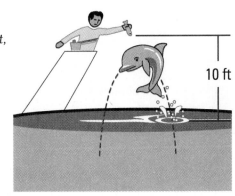

10 ft

Solution We must find the time when Dolly is 10 feet above the water. Using the equation for projectile motion, we let $h = 10$ and then solve for t.

$$h = -16t^2 + 35.2t$$
$$10 = -16t^2 + 35.2t$$
$$0 = -16t^2 + 35.2t - 10$$
$$t = \frac{-35.2 \pm \sqrt{(35.2)^2 - 4(-16)(-10)}}{2(-16)}$$
$$t \approx 0.335 \text{ or } t \approx 1.9 \text{ seconds}$$

Since Dolly would want to eat as soon as possible, she gets the fish in approximately 0.335 seconds.

Problem 3 *The area of the square is numerically equal to the perimeter of the rectangle. Give the dimensions of the figures.*

Solution Area of square $= x^2$
Perimeter of rectangle $= 2(3x) + 2(x + 4)$
$$= 6x + 2x + 8$$
$$= 8x + 8$$
$$x^2 = 8x + 8 \text{ or } x^2 - 8x - 8 = 0$$

$$x = \frac{-(-8) \pm \sqrt{(-8)^2 - 4(1)(-8)}}{2(1)}$$
$$= \frac{8 \pm \sqrt{96}}{2}$$
$$= \frac{8 \pm 4\sqrt{6}}{2}$$
$$\approx 4 \pm 4.9$$

Therefore, $x \approx 8.9$ or $x \approx -0.9$. Since x is a side of a square, x must be approximately 8.9. The sides of the square are about 8.9, and the sides of the rectangle are about 26.7 and 12.9.

Part Three: Exercises and Problems

Warm-up Exercises

In problems 1–4, how many real roots does each quadratic equation have?

1 $3x^2 + 2x + 5 = 0$
2 $x^2 - 6x - 10 = 0$
3 $x^2 - 16x + 64 = 0$
4 $x^2 + 2x + 0.5 = 0$

5 The x-intercepts of $f(x) = x^2 + bx + c$ are 3 and -4. Find the values of b and c.

6 The graph of $f(x) = ax^2 + bx + c$ is shown in the diagram. Is the discriminant of $0 = ax^2 + bx + c$ positive, negative, or zero?

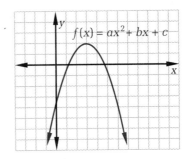

In problems 7–10, how many x-intercepts does the graph of each quadratic function have?

7 $f(x) = x^2 + 2x + 1$ **8** $f(x) = x^2 + 2x + 2$

9 $f(x) = x^2 + 2x - 3$ **10** $f(x) = x^2 + 2x - 0.1$

11 The graph of $f(x) = x^2 + 4x + 9$ is shown at the right. Find the solution(s) of $0 = x^2 + 4x + 9$.

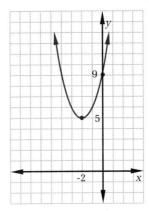

Problem Set

In problems 12–17, find the value of the discriminant.

12 $6x^2 - 3x - 3 = 0$ **13** $x^2 - 8x - 9 = 0$ **14** $x^2 + x + 2 = 0$

15 $4x^2 + 4x + 1 = 0$ **16** $25x^2 - 10x + 1 = 0$ **17** $x^2 - \frac{5}{6}x + \frac{1}{6} = 0$

In problems 18–20, use the discriminant to determine the number of real solutions for each quadratic function.

18 $f(x) = x^2 - 6x + 9$ **19** $g(x) = x^2 + 5x - 4$ **20** $h(x) = -2x^2 - 6x$

In problems 21–24, use the discriminant to determine the number of x-intercepts for each equation.

21 $y = 3x^2 + 2x + 9$ **22** $y = 3x^2 + 18x + 27$

23 $y = 3x^2 + 4x - 6$ **24** $y = -3x^2 + 5x + 4$

In problems 25–28, solve by factoring.

25 $x^2 - 4x - 21 = 0$ **26** $x^2 - 2x - 48 = 0$

27 $x^2 + 7x - 18 = 0$ **28** $x^2 - 4x - 5 = 0$

29 Given $f(x) = x^2 + 5x - 24$, find each of the following.

   a $f(0)$ **b** x if $f(x) = 12$

Problem Set, *continued*

30 It costs $350 to charter a bus for 8 hours. The bus company charges an additional $5 per person until the capacity of 54 is reached. If a group is more than 54 passengers, a second bus is needed. Find the cost of chartering a bus for each group below.

　a 18 passengers　　**b** 47 passengers　　**c** 65 passengers

In problems 31 and 32, the graph of the function is shown. Solve for x if f(x) = 0.

31 $f(x) = (x - 4)^2 - 9$

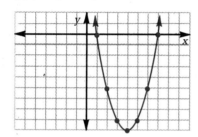

32 $f(x) = -(x - 4)^2 - 1$

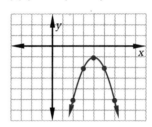

In problems 33–36, find the x- and y-intercepts of each quadratic function.

33 $f(x) = x^2 - x - 6$　　　**34** $g(x) = 2x^2 + 7x - 30$

35 $h(x) = x^2 + 8x + 16$　　**36** $k(x) = -x^2 + 6x - 11$

In problems 37–39, solve, using the quadratic formula. Leave your answers in the form $x = \dfrac{? + \sqrt{?}}{?}$ **or** $x = \dfrac{? - \sqrt{?}}{?}$.

37 $x^2 - 5x - 8 = 0$　　**38** $2x^2 - 3x - 4 = 0$　　**39** $x^2 + 3x - 2 = 0$

In problems 40–43, sketch the graph of each equation.

40 $y = |x - 4| + 3$　　　**41** $y = 2(x - 3)^2 - 5$

42 $y = |x - 5| - 6$　　　**43** $y = -2(x + 1)^2 + 4$

44 Write the equation of a line in slope-intercept form if the slope is -4 and the y-intercept is -12.

45 Marie is 11 years younger than her friend Juanita. The product of their ages is 60. How old is each friend?

In problems 46–48, factor.

46 $9x^3 + 12x^2y$　　　**47** $2x^2 - 15x - 27$　　　**48** $3x^2 + 30x + 75$

49 Write a table of values for $\dfrac{y}{3} = \dfrac{x}{4}$ and graph.

In problems 50 and 51, solve for y.

50 $\frac{9}{11} = \frac{y}{33}$

51 $\frac{y}{8} = \frac{11}{16}$

52 Does the horizontal line $y = -3$ intersect the parabola $y = x^2 + 4x + 2$?

53 In the triangle, find x in standard radical form and to the nearest thousandth.

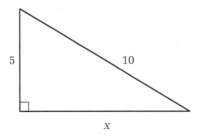

In problems 54 and 55, transform each equation into the form $y = a(x - h)^2 + k$ **by completing the square.**

54 $y = x^2 + 10x - 3$

55 $y = x^2 + 9x + 4$

In problems 56 and 57, write each expression in simplified radical form.

56 $\dfrac{8 + \sqrt{48}}{2}$

57 $\dfrac{-2 - \sqrt{72}}{2}$

58 Each diagram shows the graph of $f(x) = ax^2 + bx + c$. Will the discriminant of $0 = ax^2 + bx + c$ be positive, negative, or zero?

a
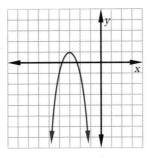

b
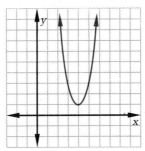

c
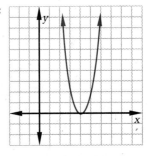

d
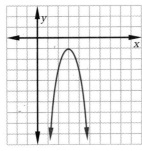

e
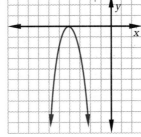

f
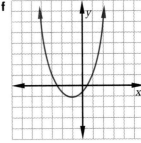

Problem Set, *continued*

59 In a basketball game, free throws score 1 point and baskets score 2 points. Wing scored 4 times as many baskets as free throws and scored 45 points. How many baskets did Wing make in the game?

In problems 60–62, solve each quadratic equation.

60 $x^2 - 6x + 8 = 0$ **61** $8x^2 - 6x + 1 = 0$ 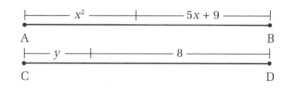 **62** $x^2 - 6x - 9 = 0$

63 A roast beef sandwich costs $0.90 more than a large soda. Elmo ate 4 roast beef sandwiches and had 3 large sodas. His bill was $8.50. How much does a roast beef sandwich cost?

64 Find the value of k so that the equation $x^2 + 6x + k = 0$ has one real root.

65 A ball is thrown into the air. Its height h in feet above the ground at any time t in seconds is given by the formula $h = -16t^2 + 146t$. When is the ball 20 feet above the ground? When does the ball hit the ground?

66 Find the point of intersection of the line $y = 7$ and the parabola $y = 2(x - 3)^2 + 7$.

67 Refer to the line segments.
  a If AB = CD, write an equation involving x and y to express the equality.
  b If $y = 25$, find x.

68 Find x if $\sqrt{x^2 - 3x} = 3\sqrt{6}$.

69 Find the area of the shaded region if $x = 5$.

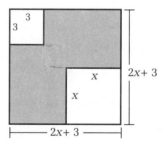

70 If $x \neq 0$, which of the following expressions is *not* equal to $x^2 - 6x + 9$?

  a $(x - 3)^2$ **b** $\dfrac{9x - 6x^2 + x^3}{x}$

  c $(3 - x)^2$ **d** $(2x + 3)^2 - 3x(x + 6)$

71 Write an equation to represent the graph.

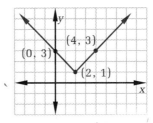

72 Find the distance between the origin and the vertex of the parabola $y = -2(x - 3)^2 + 6$.

73 Find x if the volume of the box is 500 cubic centimeters.

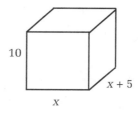

74 Twice the area of rectangle I equals the area of rectangle II. Find the area of each rectangle.

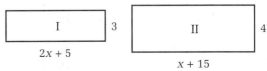

75 The perimeter of the rectangle is 26 meters. The area is 36 square meters. Find the length of each side.

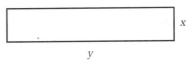

In problems 76–78, find the vertex of the graph of each function.

76 $f(x) = 3x^2 - 12x + 17$

77 $g(x) = -0.5x^2 - 4x - 13$

78 $h(x) = |12x - 41| + 7$

79 Find the values of k so that $x^2 - kx + 16 = 0$ will have two real roots.

80 Find the distance between the vertices of the graphs of $y = (x - 3)^2 + 2$ and $y = |x + 3| - 2$.

81 Find the area of the region enclosed by the graphs of $y = |x|$ and $y = 10 - |x|$.

82 Given the triangle, find x to two decimal places.

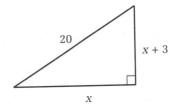

83 A parabola has an equation of the form $y = a(x - h)^2 + k$. The vertex is at $(4, -3)$, and the graph passes through the point $(6, 9)$. Find the equation of the parabola.

84 If $f(x) = x^2 - 5x - 14$, find all values of k so that $f(k - 3) = 0$.

85 Use each of the digits 2, 3, 4, 5, 6, and 7 exactly once to make two 3-digit numbers that have the largest possible product.

86 If $AB = \frac{1}{2}BC$, what is the longest possible length of $\overline{AB}$?

$$\overset{\displaystyle A}{\vdash}\; y \;\overset{\displaystyle B}{\dashv}\;\; -x^2 - 4x + 10 \;\overset{\displaystyle C}{\dashv}$$

87 Three polynomials are determined by the matrix product. Find the sum of the three polynomials.

$$\begin{bmatrix} 3 & -2 & 4 \\ -1 & 5 & 6 \\ 1 & 3 & -2 \end{bmatrix} \begin{bmatrix} x^2 \\ x \\ 1 \end{bmatrix}$$

CAREER PROFILE

EXPLORING SPACE WITHOUT LEAVING EARTH
Astrophysicist Lee Anne Willson tells how

What led Lee Anne Willson to choose astrophysics for a career? "When I was young, I read a lot of science fiction," she answers. "I was fascinated with the idea of exploring space." She first thought of becoming an astronaut and then turned to astronomy. At the age of thirteen, she joined an amateur astronomy group near her home in Nevada. She majored in physics as an undergraduate and earned her Ph.D. in astronomy at the University of Michigan. Dr. Willson is now a professor of astrophysics at Iowa State University.

"My major interest is in finding out how stars develop. I'm particularly interested in variable stars—stars that pulsate and change in brightness. Math is the basic tool in my work, and more and more we're using computer models. These, in a sense, allow us to bring stars here for analysis, and to speed up the time scale at which astronomical events occur."

Dr. Willson often uses a spectrograph in her work. When starlight passes through a prism in the instrument, it produces a spectrum crossed by chemical spectrum lines. The wavelengths of lines produced by a stationary object are known. By comparing them with the wavelengths of lines produced by a moving star, Dr. Willson is able to calculate the star's motion and whether the star is approaching or receding.

Wavelengths are measured in nanometers (1 nanometer $= 1 \times 10^{-9}$ meter). A star's motion (v) is found with the following formula, where $w =$ standard wavelength, $s =$ shift in wavelength, and $c =$ speed of light: 3×10^5 kilometers per second.

$$v = \frac{s}{w}c$$

For example, in the spectrum of the bright star Sirius, the standard line of wavelength of magnesium, 516.56 nanometers, is shifted 0.0137 nanometers. By using the formula, we find that Sirius is moving toward us with a speed of 8 km/sec.

PROJECTILE MOTION

Objectives

After studying this section, you will be able to
- Recognize projectile motion as a quadratic function
- Solve problems involving projectile motion

Part One: Introduction

Projectile Motion—A Quadratic Function

Projectile motion, such as the motion of a thrown ball or of a skier skiing off a jump, is one of the many physical situations that can be described by quadratic functions. Let's look at what happens when a basketball player tries to make a basket. The height h of the ball above the ground is a function of the time t that the ball is in motion and is given by the formula

$$h(t) = -\tfrac{1}{2}gt^2 + v_0t + h_0$$

where g = acceleration due to gravity (a constant)
v_0 = initial upward velocity of the object (if $t = 0$)
h_0 = initial height of the object (if $t = 0$)

In the case of the basketball, the formula becomes

$$h(t) = -\tfrac{1}{2}(32)t^2 + 30t + 7$$

where 32 is the force of gravity,
30 is the upward velocity of the released ball, and
7 is the ball's initial height above ground.

Gravity is a constant force that causes all objects on Earth to accelerate at the same rate, g. If a problem uses meters for distance, g is approximately 9.8 meters per second per second. If the problem uses feet, g is approximately 32 feet per second per second.

Part Two: Sample Problems

Problem 1   M.T. Climber, standing at the edge of a canyon 2500 feet above the canyon floor, throws a rock into the air with an initial upward velocity of 96 feet per second.
   a When will the rock return to the same height as M.T.?
   b When will the rock strike the floor of the canyon?

Solution   Height $h_0 = 0$ when time $t = 0$. Since our units are feet and seconds, $g \approx 32$ feet per second per second. The quadratic function is

$$h(t) = -16t^2 + 96t + 0$$

   a The rock will return to the same height when $h(t) = 0$ again.

$$0 = -16t^2 + 96t$$
$$0 = -16t(t - 6)$$
$$t = 0 \text{ or } t - 6 = 0$$
$$t = 0 \text{ or } t = 6$$

   The rock will return to the same height as M.T. in 6 seconds.
   b The floor of the canyon is 2500 feet below M.T. The rock will hit the canyon floor when $h(t) = -2500$.

$$-2500 = -16t^2 + 96t$$
$$0 = -16t^2 + 96t + 2500$$

   We use the quadratic formula and find $t \approx 15.85$ or $t \approx -9.85$. Therefore, at $t \approx 15.85$ seconds, the rock strikes the floor of the canyon. Why don't we use $t = -9.85$?

Problem 2   A ball is kicked from the ground with an initial upward velocity of 14.7 meters per second.
   a Write an equation to describe the height h of the ball at any time t.
   b What is the ball's greatest height above the ground?
   c When will the ball strike the ground?

Solution   **a** This is a projectile problem, so we use $h(t) = -\frac{1}{2}gt + v_0t + h$. The units are meters and seconds, so $g \approx 9.8$ meters/second and $v_0 = 14.7$ meters/second. The ball is kicked from the ground, so $h_0 = 0$.

$$h(t) = -\tfrac{1}{2}gt^2 + v_0t + h$$
$$= -\tfrac{1}{2}(9.8)t^2 + 14.7t + 0$$
$$= -4.9t^2 + 14.7t$$

   b To find the greatest height, we find the vertex of the parabola described by the quadratic function by completing the square.

$$h(t) = -4.9t^2 + 14.7t$$
$$= -4.9(t^2 - 3t + \underline{\quad?\quad}) + \underline{\quad?\quad}$$
$$= -4.9(t^2 - 3t + 2.25) + 11.025$$
$$= -4.9(t - 1.5)^2 + 11.025$$

   The vertex of the parabola is at (1.5, 11.025). The greatest height of the ball is 11.025 meters above the ground 1.5 seconds after the ball is kicked.

c The ball will strike the ground when the height above the ground is zero meters (when $h(t) = 0$).

$$h(t) = -4.9t^2 + 14.7t$$
$$0 = -4.9t^2 + 14.7t$$
$$0 = -4.9\,t(t - 3)$$
$$t = 0 \text{ or } t - 3 = 0$$
$$t = 0 \text{ or } t = 3$$

The height of the ball is zero at $t = 0$ seconds (when the ball is kicked) and $t = 3$ seconds (when the ball strikes the ground).
The vertex of the parabola occurs at $t = 1.5$ seconds. This makes sense—the ball takes just as long to fall back to the ground from the vertex as it takes to reach the vertex.

Part Three: Exercises and Problems

Warm-up Exercises

1 Jan, a water-skier, jumps off a 5-meter-high ski jump with an initial upward velocity of 7 meters per second. When is Jan back at the height of the ski jump? When is Jan at the highest point above the water? When does Jan hit the water?

Problem Set

2 For each of the following equations describing projectile motion, give the initial upward velocity v_0 and the height h_0 above the ground at $t = 0$ seconds, and determine whether the units are meters and seconds or feet and seconds.

a $h(t) = -\frac{1}{2}(9.8)t^2 + 56t$

b $h(t) = -\frac{1}{2}(32)t^2 + 32t$

c $h(t) = -16t^2 + 48t + 7$

d $h(t) = -4.9t^2 + 96t + 50$

3 At $t = 0$ seconds, a projectile has an initial velocity v_0 and an initial height h_0. Write an equation for the motion of the projectile using the values for v_0 and h_0 given below. Assume gravity is the only force acting on the projectile.

$gt^2 + vt + h$

a $v_0 = 128$ feet per second, $h_0 = 0$ feet
b $v_0 = 96$ feet per second, $h_0 = 124$ feet
c $v_0 = 35$ meters per second, $h_0 = 16$ meters
d $v_0 = 48$ meters per second, $h_0 = 0$ meters

4 For each set of data given in problem **3**, write an equation for the height of the particle and find the height when $t = 2$ seconds. Assume gravity is the only force acting on the particle.

5 Find the value of k so that $x^2 - 24x + k$ is a perfect square trinomial.

Problem Set, *continued*

6 Miguel correctly completed the square in this problem.

$f(x) = x^2 + 10x + 11$

$f(x) = (x^2 + 10x + \underline{\ a\ }) + 11 + \underline{\ b\ }$

$f(x) = (\underline{\ c\ })^2 + \underline{\ d\ }$

What values did Miguel use for a, b, c, and d?

7 If AB = BC, find x. Do the calculations mentally.

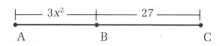

8 Find x. Write your answer in standard radical form. Then give an approximation to the nearest thousandth.

9 K. Icker kicks a football off the field for a field goal. The ball's initial upward velocity is 30 meters per second.

  a Write the equation for height h in meters after time t in seconds.

  b What will be the height of the ball after 3 seconds?

  c What will be the height after 6 seconds?

10 Find the x-intercepts of the quadratic function $3x^2 - 2x - 1$.

11 Point C is what percentage of the distance from point A to point B?

12 Four cold drinks and seven sandwiches cost $8.10. Elmo had two cold drinks and three sandwiches. Sandwiches cost twice as much as cold drinks. How much was Elmo's bill?

In problems 13–16, determine the number of real roots for each quadratic equation.

13 $4x^2 + 3x - 2 = 0$ **14** $3x^2 - 9x + 11 = 0$

15 $36x^2 + 12x + 1 = 0$ **16** $9x^2 + 2x - 1 = 0$

In problems 17 and 18, find the vertex and the axis of symmetry of each function.

17 $y = (x + 5)^2 - 9$ **18** $y = |x - 3| + 8$

19 A ball is thrown upward vertically from the ground at 64 feet per second.

  a Write the equation for the height of the ball.

  b After how many seconds will the ball hit the ground?

20 A trinomial is selected at random from the list below. Find the probability that the trinomial cannot be factored over the integers.

$x^2 - 6x - 7$ $6x^2 + 5x + 1$
$x^2 - 7x + 6$ $x^2 + 2x + 3$
$6x^2 + 7x + 1$

21 Multiply the matrices.

$$\begin{bmatrix} \frac{1}{3} & 6 \\ \frac{1}{2} & \frac{1}{4} \end{bmatrix} \begin{bmatrix} 12 \\ 8 \end{bmatrix}$$

22 Find the x^2-term in the product $(x^2 + 3x + 4)(2x^2 - x + 3)$.

In problems 23–25, solve each equation.

23 $\frac{9}{4} = \frac{x_1}{12}$

24 $y^2 + 13y + 36 = 0$

25 $8(2t + 5) - (3 - 4t) = 9(2t + 4)$

26 S. Piker served a volleyball from 1 meter off the ground with an upward velocity of 8 meters per second.

a Write an equation for the height of the ball h in meters after t seconds.
b What will be the height of the ball after 0.5 seconds?
c When will the ball again be at its initial height?
d If no one touches the ball, when will it hit the ground?

27 Find the x-intercepts of the quadratic function $f(x) = 2x^2 + 3x - 4$.

In problems 28 and 29, solve each system.

28 $\begin{cases} 3x + 2y = -7 \\ y = -4x - 1 \end{cases}$ **29** $\begin{cases} 3x - y = 12 \\ 2x + 3y = -14 \end{cases}$

In problems 30 and 31, draw a graph for each function.

30 $y = (x - 1)^2 + 3$ **31** $y = |x + 4| + 1$

32 Mr. Pike jumps off the 10-meter diving platform with an initial velocity of 3.8 meters per second.

a Write an equation to describe Mr. Pike's motion.
b When does he hit the water?
c How high above the water does he get?

Problem Set, *continued*

33 Find the area of the rectangle. Then find the perimeter and the semi-perimeter (one-half the perimeter).

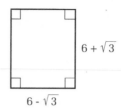

$6 + \sqrt{3}$

$6 - \sqrt{3}$

In problems 34–36, refer to the diagram.

34 Find the slope of ℓ.

35 Find an equation of ℓ.

36 Does the point $(-3, 12)$ lie on ℓ?

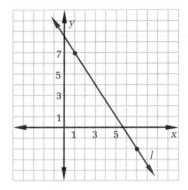

37 Find the vertex and the axis of symmetry of $f(x) = x^2 - 8x + 5$.

In problems 38 and 39, solve.

38 $2x^2 - 4x + 2 = 0$ **39** $x^2 + 6x - 7 = 0$

40 Find the area of $\triangle ABC$ if the equation of the parabola is $y = -(x - 3)^2 + 9$.

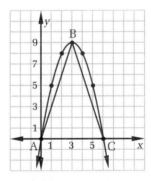

41 Pierre has 5 nickels and 15 dimes. He spends 10 of the coins with a total value of $0.85. Find the ratio of nickels spent to dimes spent.

42 Write an inequality to describe the shaded region.

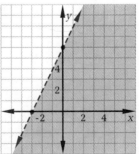

43 Dex Terity can juggle 3 balls in the air at once. He gives each ball an initial velocity of 16 feet per second. He releases each ball $\frac{1}{4}$ second after the previous one.

a Write the relation describing the motion of each ball.
b How high does each ball rise above the release point?
c What is the position of each ball at $t = \frac{7}{8}$ seconds?

44 At a party, Luanne served 4 liters of punch that was 40% seltzer water and 60% juice. Some additional guests arrived, so Luanne added 1 liter of seltzer to the punch. What percent seltzer was the new mixture?

45 On the same coordinate plane, carefully sketch the graph of each equation.

a $y = x^2$ 　　　　　　　　 **b** $y = 0$
c $y - 1 = 2(x - 1)$ 　　　 **d** $y - 4 = 4(x - 2)$
e $y - 9 = 6(x - 3)$ 　　　 **f** $y - 1 = -2(x + 1)$
g $y - 4 = -4(x + 2)$ 　　 **h** $y - 9 = -6(x + 3)$

46 Snoopy is in his Sopwith Camel, 4000 feet above the ground. He fires a missile at the Red Baron with an initial upward velocity of 320 feet per second. The Red Baron is 4700 feet above the ground.

a Write an equation describing the motion of the missile.
b When on the way up might the missile hit the Red Baron?
c If the missile misses the Red Baron on the way up, when might the missile hit the Red Baron on the way down?

47 Find the ratio of the x-intercept to the y-intercept for the line $3x - 2y = 12$.

48 If $9x^2 = 16y^2$, find the value of $\frac{x}{y}$.

49 Sky Diver jumps from an airplane at 8000 feet with no upward velocity. He falls freely for 6000 feet before opening his chute.

a Write an equation describing Sky Diver's motion.
b How soon after he leaves the airplane does he open his chute?
c Why is the answer to part **b** not realistic?

50 Find the values of k so that $x^2 + kx + 36 = 0$ will have one real root.

MEASURES OF DISPERSION

Objectives

After studying this section, you will be able to
- Find the range of a set of data
- Find the deviation scores of a set of data
- Find the mean deviation of a set of data

Range

In Section 7.7, you learned about measures of central tendency: the mean, median, and mode. Now you will learn about three *measures of dispersion,* or indicators of the variation from the mean of a set of data. Knowing about the dispersion in a set of data allows you to interpret that data more accurately than with a knowledge of only the mean or median. Let's look at some examples.

During his last six lessons at Star Driving School, Lefty Turner drove 23, 14, 45, 36, 31, and 9 miles. The low and high numbers of miles are 9 and 45. Therefore, his driving ranged from 9 to 45 miles during his lessons. The *range* of a set of data is the difference between the greatest and smallest numbers.

> *range = greatest number − smallest number*

The range of the data above is $45 - 9 = 36$ miles.

Problem 1   *Determine the range for each set of data.*

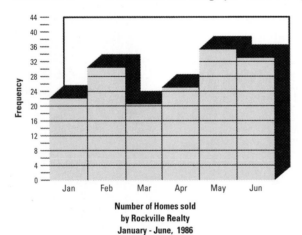

**Number of Homes sold
by Rockville Realty
January - June, 1986**

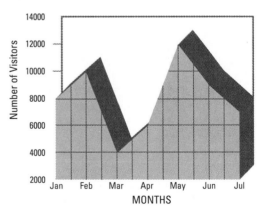

MONTHS

Number of Visitors to the
Mathern City Museum of History
January - July, 1987

| Solution | The high number is 42. The low number is 24. Range = 42 − 24 = 18. | The high number is 12,000. The low number is 4000. Range = 12,000 − 4000 = 8000. |

Deviation Scores

In a home-run hitting contest, 8 batters hit the following numbers of home runs: 4, 2, 7, 1, 2, 3, 6, and 5. Slugger Sam hit 7 home runs, while Line Drive Larry hit 1. We want to compare their numbers of home runs with the mean number of home runs hit.

The mean number of home runs hit was

$$\frac{4 + 2 + 7 + 1 + 2 + 3 + 6 + 5}{8} = 3.75.$$

To compare a number with the mean, we use the *deviation score,* or the difference between the score and the mean.

 deviation score = score − mean

We can find the deviation score of each hitter in order to make comparisons with the mean for each batter.

Slugger Sam's deviation score was 7 − 3.75 = 3.25.
Line Drive Larry's deviation score was 1 − 3.75 = −2.75.

We can represent the mean and deviation scores by the following diagram.

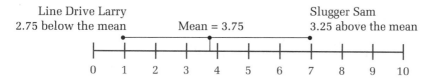

Slugger Sam's performance was 3.25 homers above the mean, while Line Drive Larry's performance was 2.75 homers below the mean.

| Problem 2 | Workers A, B, C, D, E, F, G, and H picked strawberries at rates of 16, 20, 13, 11, 9, 15, 22, and 14 quarts per hour. Determine the deviation score for each worker. |

| Solution | We begin by determining the mean and then construct the table. |

$$\text{Mean} = \frac{\text{number of quarts picked per hour}}{\text{number of workers}} = \frac{120}{8} = 15 \text{ quarts per hour}$$

Worker	Number of Quarts per Hour	Deviation Score
A	16	16 − 15 = 1
B	20	20 − 15 = 5
C	13	13 − 15 = −2
D	11	11 − 15 = −4
E	9	9 − 15 = −6
F	15	15 − 15 = 0
G	22	22 − 15 = 7
H	14	14 − 15 = −1

Mean Deviation

After six 9-hole rounds of golf, Paula Putter and Sam DeSlicer are tied for first place in the Tusine Mathematics Open Tournament. Both golfers have scores of 240. Their scores per round are shown.

| **Paula Putter** | 38, 41, 49, 32, 41, 39 |
| **Sam DeSlicer** | 37, 45, 43, 41, 39, 35 |

We want to know which golfer has been more consistent. To determine consistency, we use the **mean deviation score** for each golfer.

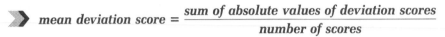

$$\text{mean deviation score} = \frac{\textit{sum of absolute values of deviation scores}}{\textit{number of scores}}$$

We use a chart to determine each golfer's mean deviation score.

Paula's mean score: $\frac{240}{6} = 40$. Sam's mean score: $\frac{240}{6} = 40$.

Score		Deviation Score (Score-Mean)		Absolute Value of Deviation Score	
Paula	Sam	Paula	Sam	Paula	Sam
38	37	-2	-3	2	3
41	45	1	5	1	5
49	43	9	3	9	3
32	41	-8	1	8	1
41	39	1	-1	1	1
39	35	-1	-5	1	5
240	240	0	0	22	18

$$\text{mean deviation score} = \frac{\text{sum of absolute values of deviation scores}}{\text{number of scores}}$$

Paula's mean deviation score: $\frac{22}{6} = 3\frac{2}{3} \approx 3.7$

Sam's mean deviation score: $\frac{18}{6} = 3$

Since Sam's mean deviation (3) is less than Paula's mean deviation (3.7), his scores tend to be closer to the mean than Paula's scores. Therefore, Sam appears to be more consistent than Paula.

Note Because Sam and Paula were tied, they had the same mean score. If they had had different mean scores, we would have used each mean score in determining each mean deviation.

Problem Set

1 Walter Payton's rushing touchdown statistics are given below.

Year	'75	'76	'77	'78	'79	'80	'81	'82	'83	'84	'85	'86	'87	Total
TD's	7	13	14	11	14	6	6	1	6	11	9	8	4	110

a Find the mean number of rushing touchdowns that Payton scored per year.

b Find the deviation score for his 1982 total.

c Why might he have scored so few touchdowns in 1982?

d Find the range of touchdowns he scored per year.

2 T. Nager is planning his spring vacation for April. He is considering a trip to Sunville or Palm Island. He has gathered this data.

April Average High Temperatures in °F

Year	'80	'81	'82	'83	'84	'85	'86	'87	'88	'89
Sunville	78	71	82	80	71	73	70	70	74	76
Palm Island	82	79	86	89	61	73	82	68	85	83

a Determine the mean of the April average high temperature for each vacation location.

b Determine the mean deviation score for each vacation location.

c If T. wants a consistent temperature, where should he vacation?

3 Dr. A.C. Ula was listing systolic blood pressure data for a group of his patients. The numbers were 135, 120, 111, 140, 124, 116, 108, 120, 132, 144, and 92.

a List the data from smallest to largest.

b What is the range of the data?

c Find the mean of the data.

d Hy Presher is the person with a blood pressure of 144. What is Hy's deviation score?

e Find the mean deviation.

4 Mr. Mobius graded his students' math tests. The scores were 82, 78, 81, 83, 75, 88, 90, 65, and 69.

a Find the median of the data.　　　**b** Find the mean.

c Find the range.　　　**d** Find the mean deviation.

Then Mr. Mobius found that each student had actually scored 6 more points than he thought. The new scores are 88, 84, 87, 89, 81, 94, 96, 71, and 75.

e Recompute the median, mean, range, and mean deviation for the new data.

5 Machine A and Machine B turn out batches of 1000 bolts. The data below represent the percentage of defective parts per batch.

Batch

	1	2	3	4	5
Machine A	1.1%	1.5%	0.7%	1.3%	0.5%
Machine B	1.4%	1.6%	1.5%	1.5%	1.7%

a Find the mean percentage of defective parts per batch for each machine.

b Find the mean deviation percentage for each machine.

c Which of the two machines has a more consistent quality?

6 The data x, $x + 10$, $x + 20$, $x + 25$, and $x + 50$ has a mean of 40.

a Find the value of x.

b Find the numerical value of each piece of data.

c Find the deviation score of each piece of data.

Chapter Summary

Concepts and Procedures

After studying this chapter, you should be able to

- Graph equations of the form $y = x^2$ (11.1)
- Graph equations of the form $y = (x - h)^2 + k$ (11.1)
- Compare the absolute value graph and the parabola (11.1)
- Graph equations of the form $y = a(x - h)^2 + k$ (11.2)
- Find the x- and y-intercepts of a parabola (11.2)
- Graph equations of the form $y = a|x - h| + k$ (11.2)
- Use the technique of completing the square to transform
  $y = ax^2 + bx + c$ into $y = a(x - h)^2 + k$ (11.3)
- Find the relationship between the roots of a quadratic equation
  and the x-intercepts of a quadratic function (11.4)
- Use the discriminant to determine the number of x-intercepts of
  the graph of a quadratic function and the number of roots of a
  quadratic equation (11.4)
- Prove the quadratic formula (11.4)
- Use the discriminant to determine whether a quadratic equation
  can be solved by factoring (11.4)
- Solve projectile motion problems (11.5)
- Recognize projectile motion as a quadratic function (11.5)
- Find the range of a set of data (11.6)
- Find the deviation scores of a set of data (11.6)
- Find the mean deviation of a set of data (11.6)

Vocabulary

axis of symmetry (11.1)
completing the square (11.3)
deviation score (11.6)
discriminant (11.4)
mean deviation (11.6)
measures of dispersion (11.6)
range (11.6)

1 Refer to the equation $y = x^2 - 8x + 12$.
  a Find x when $y = 0$.
  b Complete the table.

x	1	2	3	4	5	6	7
y							

  c Graph the equation using the data from part **b.**

2 Make a table of values and graph $f(x) = (x + 1)^2 - 9$. What is the lowest point on the graph?

In problems 3 and 4, find the vertex and the equation of the axis of symmetry for each equation.

3 $y = (x - 4)^2 + 7$ **4** $y = |x + 3| - 4$

5 The area A of a rectangle is given by $A = (x + 4)^2 + 13$. What is the smallest possible value for the area?

6 Graph the equation $y = -(x - 1)^2 + 3$.

In problems 7 and 8, give the vertex and the axis of symmetry and determine if each parabola opens upward or downward.

7 $y = -2(x - 3)^2 + 5$ **8** $y = \frac{1}{3}(x + 2)^2 + 6$

9 Graph the equation $y = \frac{2}{3}|x - 1|$.

10 If $f(x) = (x - 4)^2 - 10$, find the x- and y-intercepts of the graph.

11 As a cannonball travels through the air, its height h in meters above the ground at t seconds is $h(t) = -9.8(t - 10)^2 + 980$. For what time t does this equation have physical meaning? What is the highest point reached by the cannonball?

In problems 12 and 13, find the value of k that will make each polynomial a perfect square trinomial.

12 $x^2 - 18x + k$ **13** $x^2 + kx + 36$

Review Problems, *continued*

In problems 14 and 15, transform each equation into the form
$y = a(x - h)^2 + k$.

14 $y = x^2 + 6x + 5$ **15** $y = 2x^2 + 16x + 40$

16 Complete the square of $y = \frac{1}{2}x^2 + 5x + 2.5$. Then graph the equation.

In problems 17–19, find the discriminant and determine the number of real roots for each equation.

17 $x^2 + x + 1 = 0$ **18** $x^2 + 2x + 1 = 0$ **19** $x^2 + 3x + 1 = 0$

In problems 20 and 21, find the x- and y-intercepts.

20 $y = (x - 3)^2 - 16$ **21** $y = -(x - 7)^2 + 9$

In problems 22 and 23, use the given information and write the equation of a parabola in the form $y = (x - h)^2 + k$.

22 vertex (3, 5), axis of symmetry $x = 3$
23 vertex $(-2, 0)$, axis of symmetry $x = -2$

24 A soccer ball is kicked upward with an initial velocity of 48 feet per second. Write an equation for height h after t seconds. When will the ball hit the ground?

In problems 25–27, solve each equation.

25 $x^2 - 9x = 22$ **26** $10x^2 - 7x + 1 = 0$ **27** $x^2 = -12x$

28 Rachel Racquet hit a tennis ball. The height of the ball is described by $h(t) = -16t^2 + 80t$. When will the ball hit the ground?

In problems 29 and 30, determine whether it is possible to factor each equation.

29 $x^2 - 5x + 6 = 0$ **30** $3x^2 + 4x - 2 = 0$

31 Find the value of x so that the area of the square is $4x^2 + 9$.

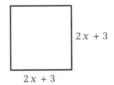

$2x + 3$

$2x + 3$

32 Two points are selected at random from the set $\{(0, 5), (-3, -4),$ $(2, 21), (-2, -3), (-4, -3)\}$.
   a Find the probability that both points are on the graph of $y = (x + 3)^2 - 4$.
   b Find the probability that one point is the vertex of the parabola.

In problems 33 and 34, solve each equation. Write the solution in standard radical form.

33 $x^2 - 10x - 3 = 0$ **34** $x^2 - 3x + 1 = 0$

35 Quickly graph each equation on the same coordinate plane.

    a $y - 2 = 3(x - 4)$ **b** $y = 3|x - 4| + 2$

    c $y = 3(x - 4)^2 + 2$

In problems 36 and 37, graph each quadratic inequality.

36 $y \geq (x - 2)^2 + 1$ **37** $y < (x + 3)^2$

38 If $h(t) = -3(x - 2)^2 + 7$, find the maximum value of $h(t)$.

39 A ball is thrown upward from the top of a building at $t = 0$ seconds. The height above the ground in meters h at any time $t \geq 0$ is given by $h(t) = -4.9t^2 + 117.6t + 42$.

    a Complete the square to transform the equation into the form $h(t) = a(t - h)^2 + k$.

    b How high is the building?

    c How high above the ground does the ball go?

    d When does the ball strike the ground?

40 If $h(t) = t^2 - 8t + 3$, find the minimum value of $h(t)$.

41 Refer to the quadratic equation $y = (x - 2)^2 - 5$.

    a Graph the parabola for the values of $0 \leq x \leq 6$.

    b What is the smallest y-value on the graph? What is the largest y-value?

42 If $y = x^2 + bx + c$ and two points on the graph are $(2, 7)$ and $(-1, -8)$, find b and c.

43 The graph of the quadratic equation $ax^2 + bx + c$ has a vertex at $(3, 10)$ and a y-intercept of -26. Find a, b, and c.

44 Write the equation of the parabola in the form $y = a(x - h)^2 + k$.

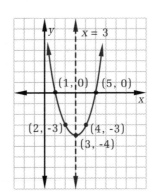

45 If $ab = 6$ and $a + b = 5$, evaluate each expression.

    a $a^2 + b^2$ **b** $(a - b)^2$

1 Refer to the equation $y = (x - 4.6)^2 + 2.7$.

    a Find the vertex of its graph.

    b Find the axis of symmetry of its graph.

    c Find the y-intercept of its graph.

    d Describe the shape of its graph.

In problems 2–5, graph each equation.

  2 $y = (x + 5)^2 - 4$ **3** $y = |x - 2| + 5$

  4 $y = \frac{-1}{4}(x + 3)^2 + 2$ **5** $y = 3|x - 2| + 1$

6 The product of two consecutive odd integers added to three times the first integer is 84. Find the integers.

In problems 7 and 8, change each equation into $y = a(x - h)^2 + k$ form.

  7 $y = 2x^2 - 12x + 14$ **8** $y = -x^2 + 4x - 1$

9 If an equation is chosen at random from the ones below, what is the probability that its graph has two x-intercepts? What is the probability that its graph has no x-intercepts?

    $y = \frac{-1}{2}(x - 3)^2 + 4$ $y = |x + 5|$ $y = x^2 - 8x + 16$

    $y = 5x^2 + 1$ $y + 3 = 2(x - 1)^2$

10 If $f(x) = 3x^2 - 14x - 5$, find the x-intercepts of the graph.

11 Lily hurtles off the 1-meter springboard with an initial upward velocity of 4.9 meters per second.

    a Write an equation to describe Lily's motion.

    b When does Lily hit the water?

    c How high above the water does Lily get?

12 Frank bowled nine times in March and scored games of 110, 155, 140, 142, 137, 161, 115, 140, and 137.

    a Find the mean, range, and mean deviation of Frank's bowling scores.

    b If two of the nine scores are chosen at random, what is the probability that at least one of them is within the mean deviation of the mean?

PUZZLES AND CHALLENGES

1 Find all real numbers x such that $x^{x^5 - 13x^3 + 36x} = 1$.

2 Ruke and Duke can complete a set of math problems in 24 minutes. If Ruke works alone he can do only $\frac{2}{3}$ as much of a set of math problems as Duke. How long would it take each person working alone to do a set of math problems?

3 A square hole is 12 inches on a side. Tom Sawyer has a rectangular piece of wood 9 inches by 16 inches. How can he cut the rectangle into two pieces and have it fit the square hole exactly?

4 What is wrong with the following BASIC computer program?

```
10 REM This program prints the squares
       of numbers 1 to 10
20 FOR y = 1 TO 10
30 READ x
40 LET y = x * x
50 PRINT x, y
60 NEXT y
70 DATA 1,2,3,4,5,6,7,8,9,10
80 END
```

5 Al Chemist had a 10-liter container of snake oil. Al used a small pitcher to remove a quantity of snake oil from the original container. He then refilled the container with castor oil and so mixed the two oils together. Al repeated the entire process once. The 10-liter container then contained equal amounts of snake and castor oil. What was the capacity of Al's pitcher?

6 Take a stick with a hole through it as shown. Pass a loop of string through the hole and tie it as shown in the diagram. Make sure the string is a bit too short to pass around the other end of the stick. Pass the loop through the top buttonhole of someone's shirt. The challenge is to have the person get the stick and loop free from the shirt without untying the loop or taking off the shirt.

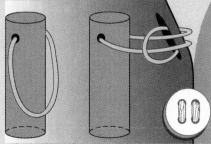

7 Pinocchio has two wooden cubes, one of which is just slightly larger than the other. A square hole is cut through the larger one so that the portion of the cube remaining is still in one piece. The other cube just barely passes through the hole. After the hole has been cut out, the larger cube is still heavier than the smaller cube. How is this possible?

12 PROPORTION AND RATIONAL EQUATIONS

I n a mathematical sense, the human brain, like a hurricane, a dripping faucet, and the odd wobble in the orbit of the planet Pluto, is chaotic. There is a hidden order in the apparently random way the brain's neurons fire, and this order is currently being studied using a relatively new mathematical theory, chaos theory.

Until recently most applications of chaos theory had been in the physical sciences, but a few scientists have now begun to apply this new theory to various aspects of physiology such as brain function.

Chaos theory is part of a larger field of mathematics called nonlinear dynamics, a field that has been attracting more and more attention. Nonlinear equations yield highly accurate descriptions of natural processes that cannot be described by more traditional means.

RATIO AND PROPORTION

Babe Ruth

Hank Aaron

Objectives

After studying this section, you will be able to
- Solve problems involving ratios
- Understand proportions and their properties

Part One: Introduction

Ratio Problems

The two major-league baseball players with the most lifetime home runs are Babe Ruth and Hank Aaron. Aaron hit 755 home runs, and Ruth hit 714. Which was the better home-run hitter?

One answer is that Aaron was better because he hit 41 more home runs than Ruth. Another approach is to compare the number of home runs each man hit with the number of times he came to bat. The *ratio* of times at bat to home runs hit tells us something about how often each man hit home runs. Aaron batted 12,364 times in his career, and Ruth batted 8399 times.

$$\text{Aaron} \quad \frac{\text{Times at bat}}{\text{Home runs}} = \frac{12{,}364}{755} \approx 16.4$$

$$\text{Ruth} \quad \frac{\text{Times at bat}}{\text{Home runs}} = \frac{8399}{714} \approx 11.8$$

Aaron hit a home run about every 16.4 times at bat. Ruth hit a home run about every 11.8 times at bat. So, it would seem that Ruth was the better home-run hitter.

A *ratio* is a fraction. By showing the relationship between two numbers, ratios help us express numerical information in meaningful ways.

Example   Which is the better buy?

Let's compare the cost per can.

$$\frac{100¢}{6 \text{ cans}} = 16\frac{2}{3}¢ \text{ per can}$$

$$\frac{85¢}{5 \text{ cans}} = 17¢ \text{ per can}$$

REGULAR PRICE
6 for
$1.00

TODAY ONLY
5 for
85¢

The better buy is 6 cans for $1.

In order to compare ratios, the units must be the same. That is the reason we changed $1 to 100¢.

Proportions and Their Properties

Many problems are solved by setting two ratios equal to each other and calculating the unknown value. A **proportion** is an equation stating that two ratios are equal. Suppose Ruth had had the same number of times at bat as Aaron and had continued to hit home runs at the same rate. You can use a proportion to predict how many career home runs Ruth would have hit.

<table>
<tr><td align="center">**Ruth's Actual
Statistics**</td><td></td><td align="center">**Ruth's Projected
Statistics**</td></tr>
</table>

$$\frac{\text{Actual number of home runs}}{\text{Actual times at bat}} = \frac{\text{projected number of home runs}}{\text{projected times at bat}}$$

$$\frac{714}{8399} = \frac{x}{12{,}364}$$

$$12{,}364 \cdot \frac{714}{8399} = \frac{x}{12{,}364} \cdot 12{,}364$$

$$1051 \approx x$$

If Babe Ruth had batted 12,364 times, he would have hit about 1051 home runs.

Example   Solve $\frac{x}{5} = \frac{4}{3}$ for x.

Multiply both sides of the equation by 5

$$\frac{x}{5} = \frac{4}{3}$$

$$5 \cdot \frac{x}{5} = 5 \cdot \frac{4}{3}$$

$$x = \frac{20}{3} \text{ or } \approx 6.67$$

By looking at some familiar proportions, you can see that if two ratios are equal, the reciprocals of the ratios are also equal.

If $\frac{4}{3} = \frac{8}{6}$, then $\frac{3}{4} = \frac{6}{8}$.   If $\frac{1}{3} = \frac{2}{6}$, then $\frac{3}{1} = \frac{6}{2}$.

Example   Solve $\dfrac{5}{x} = \dfrac{3}{4}$ for x.

The proportion $\dfrac{5}{x} = \dfrac{3}{4}$ is equivalent to $\dfrac{x}{5} = \dfrac{4}{3}$. We solved this proportion in the preceding example. Therefore, $x = \dfrac{20}{3}$, or $x \approx 6.67$.

 If $\dfrac{a}{b} = \dfrac{c}{d}$, then $\dfrac{b}{a} = \dfrac{d}{c}$, where a, b, c, and $d \neq 0$.
If two ratios are equal, then the reciprocals of the ratios are also equal.

Another notation for the proportion $\dfrac{a}{b} = \dfrac{c}{d}$ is $a:b = c:d$. This is read "a is to b as c is to d." Since a and d are at the ends of this notation, they are known as the *extremes*. The middle two terms, b and c, are known as the *means*.

Proportion	Proportion	Means	Extremes	Product of Means	Product of Extremes
$\dfrac{3}{4} = \dfrac{6}{8}$	3:4 as 6:8	4 and 6	3 and 8	24	24
$\dfrac{3}{2} = \dfrac{6}{4}$	3:2 as 6:4	2 and 6	3 and 4	12	12

If $\dfrac{a}{b} = \dfrac{c}{d}$, then $ad = bc$.
In a proportion, the product of the means equals the product of the extremes.

Example   Solve $\dfrac{4}{15} = \dfrac{12}{x}$ for x.

The product of the means equals the product of the extremes.

$$\dfrac{4}{15} = \dfrac{12}{x}$$
$$4x = 12 \cdot 15$$
$$4x = 180$$
$$x = 45$$

Part Two: Sample Problems

Problem 1   Solve $\dfrac{y}{4} = \dfrac{y-1}{y}$ for y.

Solution   The product of the means equals the product of the extremes.

$$\dfrac{y}{4} = \dfrac{y-1}{y}$$
$$y \cdot y = 4(y-1)$$
$$y^2 = 4y - 4$$
$$y^2 - 4y + 4 = 0$$
$$(y-2)^2 = 0$$
$$y - 2 = 0$$
$$y = 2$$

Problem 2   The sum of the measures of two angles is 90. The measures of the angles are in a ratio of 2:3. Find the measure of each angle.

Solution Fractions of the form $\dfrac{2 \cdot n}{3 \cdot n}$ are in a 2:3 ratio. Let 2n represent the measure of one angle and 3n the measure of the other.

$$2n + 3n = 90$$
$$5n = 90$$
$$n = 18$$

The measure of one angle is 2(18), or 36. The measure of the other angle is 3(18), or 54.

Problem 3 *Mark R. made a mistake of 0.1 inch when measuring a foot-long marker. Mia Sure made a mistake of 1 foot when measuring a mile-long bridge. Who had the smaller error ratio?*

Solution Error ratio $= \dfrac{\text{error}}{\text{distance}}$ (Units must be the same.)

Mark's error ratio $\dfrac{0.1 \text{ inch}}{12 \text{ inches}} \approx 0.0083$

Mia's error ratio $\dfrac{1 \text{ foot}}{5280 \text{ feet}} \approx 0.00019$

Mia had the smaller error ratio.

Part Three: Exercises and Problems

Warm-up Exercises

In problems 1 and 2, determine the better buy in each pair of choices.

1 Three sweaters for $72 or two sweaters for $55

2 Two loaves of bread for $0.59 or five loaves of bread for $1.42

In problems 3–5, solve each proportion.

3 $\dfrac{3}{2} = \dfrac{x}{3}$ **4** $\dfrac{6}{x} = \dfrac{2}{7}$ **5** $\dfrac{x-2}{x} = \dfrac{x}{4}$

6 The sum of the measures of ∠PQR and ∠PQS is 180. The ratio of the measure of ∠PQR to ∠PQS is 1 to 5. Find the measure of each angle.

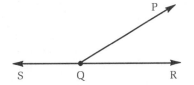

In problems 7–9, solve each proportion.

7 $\dfrac{y}{2} = \dfrac{3}{12}$ **8** $\dfrac{9}{4} = \dfrac{x}{7}$ **9** $\dfrac{16}{15} = \dfrac{12}{p}$

10 Find the ratio of vowels to consonants in the word *Mississippi*.

Problem Set

11 Consider the proportion $\frac{15}{20} = \frac{x}{12}$. What are the means? What are the extremes? What is the product of the means? Write the proportion in $a{:}b = c{:}d$ form.

12 Find two numbers whose ratio is 3 to 5 and whose sum is 88.

13 Refer to $\overline{AD}$.
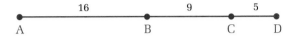

    a Find the ratio of AB to BC.

    b Find the ratio of BC to CD.

    c Which ratio is larger: $\dfrac{AB}{BC}$ or $\dfrac{BC}{CD}$?

In problems 14–17, solve for y.

14 $\dfrac{y}{12} = \dfrac{2}{3}$ **15** $\dfrac{y}{4} = \dfrac{7}{20}$ **16** $\dfrac{7}{8} = \dfrac{y}{2}$ **17** $\dfrac{24}{36} = \dfrac{6}{y}$

18 A carton of eight 16-ounce bottles of juice costs $6.50. A carton of six 12-ounce bottles costs $4.20. Which is the better buy?

19 Refer to $\overline{AD}$.
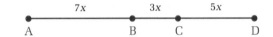

    a Find the ratio of AB to BC.

    b Find the ratio of BC to CD.

20 Simplify $\dfrac{8-3}{3-8} + \dfrac{8+3}{3+8}$.

In problems 21–23, find the vertex and the axis of symmetry of each parabola, and quickly sketch each graph.

21 $y = (x - 3)^2 + 1$ **22** $y = x^2 + 2$ **23** $y = (x + 4)^2$

24 Consider $\left\{\frac{4}{7}, \frac{5}{9}, \frac{6}{11}, \frac{7}{13}, \frac{8}{15}\right\}$. Which ratio is the largest?

25 Write the expression $18x^3 + 24x^6$ in factored form.

26 Graph $\dfrac{y}{x} = \dfrac{3}{2}$.

27 A bag initially contains 16 red chips and 4 white chips. What percentage of the chips in the bag are white? If 5 white chips are added to those in the bag, what percentage of the chips in the bag are now red?

28 Two supplementary angles are in the ratio of 3 to 2. Find the measure of the larger angle.

29 Consider the set of positive integers that are less than 20. Find the ratio of prime numbers to composite numbers.

30 During his playing career in the National Football League, Jim Brown gained 12,312 yards. He carried the ball 2359 times. Walter Payton gained 16,726 yards during his playing career. He carried the ball 3838 times. If Brown had carried the ball as many times as Payton, how many yards would he have gained?

31 Refer to the table of values. Find the ratio of the change in y to the change in x.

x	−6	−3	0	3
y	−6	−2	2	6

32 Find two numbers whose ratio is 1 to 4 and whose product is 64.

33 Consider $\left\{\frac{1}{3}, \frac{2}{5}, \frac{3}{5}, \frac{5}{7}, \frac{4}{9}\right\}$. If a ratio is selected at random from the set, what is the probability that the ratio selected is less than $\frac{1}{2}$?

34 Solve the proportion $\frac{a - 2}{4} = \frac{12}{a}$ for a.

35 The table below represents the data for the Redville girls' basketball team. The field-goal or free throw percentage is determined by dividing the number of field goals or free throws scored by the number of attempts.

	Field Goals			**Free Throws**		
	Attempted	**Scored**	**Percentage**	**Attempted**	**Scored**	**Percentage**
Jane Smith	167	59		62	41	
Rita Morales	147	43		53	31	
Jenny Kim	227	100		88	71	
Susan Jones	183	99		69	53	
Carol Willis	104	34		41	23	

a Calculate the field-goal percentages to the nearest thousandth.
b Calculate the free-throw percentages to the nearest thousandth.
c Which girl scored the most field goals?
d Which girl had the best field-goal percentage?

36 Find the ratio of the area of the smaller square to the area of the larger square.

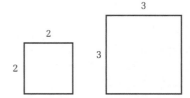

37 In 1986 Roger Clemens pitched 254 innings and gave up 77 runs. A baseball game is usually 9 innings long. Find the ratio of runs given up to games pitched. (This ratio is called an earned run average.)

38 Refer to the rectangle and triangle in the diagram.

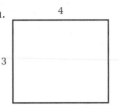

   a Find the ratio of the perimeter of the
rectangle to the perimeter of the
triangle.

   b Find the ratio of the area of the rectangle to the area of the triangle.

39 What is the ratio of the circumference of a circle to its diameter?

40 The roots of a quadratic equation are in the ratio of 2 to 3. The
sum of the roots is 15. Find the equation.

41 Find the ratio of the volume of cube A to
the volume of cube B.

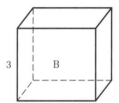

In problems 42–44, solve each equation.

42 $\dfrac{z}{2z} = \dfrac{5}{10}$ **43** $\dfrac{b}{b+1} = \dfrac{3}{2}$ **44** $\dfrac{w}{w+2} = \dfrac{w+1}{w+5}$

45 Select any point on the graph of $y = \frac{2}{3}x$. Find the ratio of y to x.

46 In the diagram, $\overline{AB}$ is perpendicular to
$\overline{BD}$. Find the ratio of the measure of
$\angle ABC$ to the measure of $\angle CBD$.

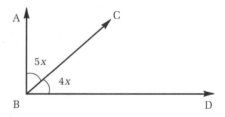

47 A special $1000 savings certificate pays 10% interest at the end of
1 year. What is the ratio of the amount of money in the bank
after 1 year to the amount originally invested? After 2 years?
After 3 years?

48 L-MART discounted the price of an item by 10%. A week later
the new price was increased by 10%. Find the ratio of the final
price to the original price.

49 In April the game warden tagged 3000 trout. In July she caught
4500 trout in new nets and discovered that 400 of them were
tagged. What conclusion might the game warden draw?

50 Given $\dfrac{x}{y} = \dfrac{5}{3} \cdot \dfrac{a}{b}, \dfrac{a}{b} = \dfrac{4}{11} \cdot \dfrac{c}{d}$, and $\dfrac{c}{d} = \dfrac{2}{7} \cdot \dfrac{e}{f}$, find the ratio of $\dfrac{x}{y}$ to $\dfrac{e}{f}$.

APPLICATIONS OF PROPORTION

Objectives

After studying this section, you will be able to

- Use proportions to interpret scale factors
- Use proportions to convert units
- Use proportions to solve similar triangle problems

Part One: Introduction

Scale Factors

Maps are drawn to scale, and the scale is given in the legend of the map. The scale of the map of Florida is given as 1 inch equals 120 miles. The ratio that represents the scale on the map is $\frac{1 \text{ inch}}{120 \text{ miles}}$.

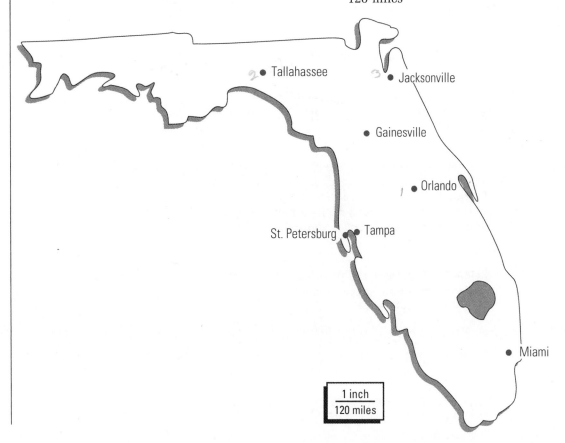

Example   The distance from Tampa to Jacksonville is about $1\frac{5}{8}$ inches on our map. What is the approximate distance in miles between these two cities?

Let's set up the given proportion and solve the equation.

$$\frac{1.625 \text{ inches}}{x \text{ miles}} = \frac{1 \text{ inch}}{120 \text{ miles}}$$

$$1x = (1.625)(120)$$

$$x = 195$$

The distance between the two cities is 195 miles.

Conversions

You can write conversion factors as equations or as ratios.

Metric Conversions		English Conversions	
Equations	**Ratios**	**Equations**	**Ratios**
1 meter = 100 centimeters	$\frac{1 \text{ m}}{100 \text{ cm}}$	1 gallon = 4 quarts	$\frac{1 \text{ gal}}{4 \text{ qt}}$
1 kilometer = 1000 meters	$\frac{1 \text{ km}}{1000 \text{ m}}$	1 mile = 5280 feet	$\frac{1 \text{ mi}}{5280 \text{ ft}}$
1 meter = 1000 millimeters	$\frac{1 \text{ m}}{1000 \text{ mm}}$	1 foot = 12 inches	$\frac{1 \text{ ft}}{12 \text{ in.}}$

To convert between the metric system and the English system, we need a conversion table that relates the two systems. Although most conversion tables use equal signs, the conversions between systems are approximations.

Length

2.54 centimeters = 1 inch, or 1 centimeter = 0.394 inch

1 meter = 3.28 feet, or 1 meter = 39.37 inches

1 kilometer = 0.6214 mile, or 1.609 kilometers = 1 mile

Volume

0.946 liter = 1 quart, or 1 liter = 1.06 quarts

250 milliliters = 1 cup

You can convert from one unit to another by writing a proportion for which both sides of the equation are numerically equal to 1.

Example   Use the tables of conversion factors to convert each of the following.

a   54 in. = __?__ cm

$$\frac{1 \text{ in.}}{2.54 \text{ cm}} = \frac{54 \text{ in.}}{x \text{ cm}}$$

$$x = (54)(2.54) = 137.16$$
54 in. = 137.16 cm

b   800 ml = __?__ cups

$$\frac{1 \text{ cup}}{250 \text{ ml}} = \frac{x \text{ cups}}{800 \text{ ml}}$$

$$x = \frac{800}{250} = 3.2$$

800ml = 3.2 cups

Example   *Romeo and Juliet are in Canada, driving 385 kilometers from Detroit to Niagara Falls. They have a full tank of gasoline. If the gasoline tank holds 15 gallons of gasoline and the car averages 18 miles per gallon, can they make it to Niagara Falls without having to stop for gasoline?*

The car can go 18 · 15, or 270, miles on one tank of gasoline. However, Romeo and Juliet are in Canada, where distances are given in kilometers. We need to convert 270 miles to kilometers. Using the conversion table, we set up a proportion.

$$\frac{x \text{ km}}{270 \text{ miles}} = \frac{1 \text{ km}}{0.6214 \text{ mile}}$$

$$x = \frac{(270)(1)}{0.6214} \approx 435$$

270 miles ≈ 435 km

Romeo and Juliet should have no difficulty reaching Niagara Falls on one tank of gasoline.

Similar Triangles

Triangles that have the same shape but not necessarily the same size are called *similar triangles.*

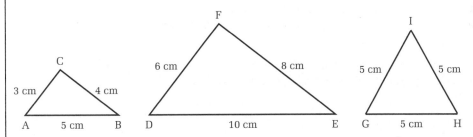

△ABC and △DEF are similar; this is written as △ABC ~ △DEF.
△ABC and △GHI are not similar.

> **The lengths of corresponding sides of similar triangles are proportional.**

In △ABC and △DEF, side AB corresponds to side DE, side BC corresponds to side EF, and side AC corresponds to side DF. Since the lengths of corresponding sides of similar triangles are proportional, the following statements are true.

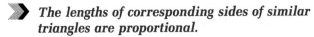

$$\frac{AB}{DE} = \frac{BC}{EF} = \frac{AC}{DF} \text{ or, using numbers, } \frac{5}{10} = \frac{4}{8} = \frac{3}{6}$$

Example   △RST ~ △MNO. *Find the length of side MN.*

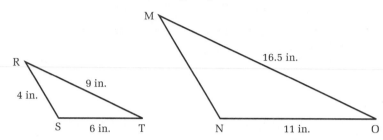

Since the triangles are similar, we know that corresponding sides are proportional.

$$\frac{MN}{RS} = \frac{NO}{ST}$$

$$\frac{MN}{4} = \frac{11}{6}$$

$$MN = \frac{44}{6}, \text{ or } \frac{22}{3}, \text{ or } 7.\overline{3}$$

The length of side MN is approximately 7.3 inches.

Part Two: Sample Problems

Problem 1   *Donald wants to find the distance between Disneyland, in Anaheim, California, and Disney World, in Orlando, Florida. On a map in his atlas, the distance between the cities measures 22 centimeters. The map's scale indicates that 6 centimeters is equal to 600 miles and 3.7 centimeters is equal to 600 kilometers. What is the distance between the two parks in miles and kilometers?*

Solution   Since 6 cm = 600 mi, 1 cm = 100 mi. Therefore, 22 centimeters on the map represents 22 · 100, or 2200, miles as the actual distance between Disneyland and Disney World.

To find the distance in kilometers, Donald needs a proportion.

$$\frac{\text{cm on map}}{\text{km actual distance}} = \frac{3.7}{600}$$

$$\frac{22}{x} = \frac{3.7}{600}$$

$$13{,}200 = 3.7x$$

$$3568 \approx x$$

The distance between Disneyland and Disney World is about 3568 kilometers.

Donald checked his answers using the conversion 1 kilometer equals 0.6214 miles. He found that 3568 kilometers equals 3568(0.6214), or about 2217.2, miles. This is very close to the earlier calculation of 2200 miles.

Problem 2 A snapshot is 3 inches wide and 5 inches high. It is enlarged to make a poster that is 40 inches high. What is the poster's width?

Solution We will let the new width equal w.

$$\frac{\text{Old width}}{\text{Old height}} = \frac{\text{new width}}{\text{new height}}$$

$$\frac{3}{5} = \frac{w}{40}$$

$$\left(\frac{3}{5}\right)(40) = w$$

$$24 = w$$

The new width is 24 inches.

Problem 3 Are the two triangles similar?

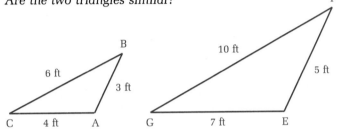

Solution Two triangles are similar if all of their corresponding sides are proportional in length.

$$\frac{AB}{EF} = \frac{3}{5}; \frac{BC}{FG} = \frac{6}{10}; \frac{AC}{EG} = \frac{4}{7}$$

$$\frac{AB}{EF} = \frac{BC}{FG} \text{ because } \frac{3}{5} = \frac{6}{10}.$$

$$\frac{BC}{FG} \ne \frac{AC}{EG} \text{ because } \frac{6}{10} \ne \frac{4}{7}.$$

Since not all the corresponding sides of these two triangles are proportional, these triangles are not similar.

Part Three: Exercises and Problems

Warm-up Exercises

In problems 1 and 2, use the map of Florida at the beginning of Section 12.2 to find the distance between the given cities.

1 Miami to Gainesville

2 Orlando to St. Petersburg

3 How many kilometers are there in one mile?

4 How many inches are there in one centimeter?

5 Let $\triangle ABC \sim \triangle XYZ$, and let $AB = 2$, $BC = 4$, $AC = 5$, and $XY = 3$. Find YZ and XZ.

In problems 6–8, complete each conversion.

6 3 in. = __?__ cm 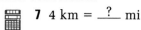 **7** 4 km = __?__ mi **8** 4.24 qt = __?__ l

9 Arch E. Techt needs to draw plans for a shopping center that will be built on a city block. (Hint: A city block is approximately 450 feet by 450 feet.) Arch is using paper that is 3 feet square. What is the largest scale he can choose?

Problem Set

In problems 10–13, solve for S_1.

10 $\dfrac{S_1}{82} = \dfrac{11}{82}$ **11** $\dfrac{18}{12} = \dfrac{3}{S_1}$ **12** $\dfrac{S_1}{12} = 6$ **13** $10 = \dfrac{40}{S_1}$

14 A football field is 100 yards long. How long is the football field in feet? How long is the football field in meters?

15 A 24-minute phone call to Punxsutawney cost Phil $1.80. The next month he called again and talked for 35 minutes. How much was he charged for the second call? (Hint: Assume that the per-minute charge is the same for each minute of the call.)

16 Given △ABC ~ △PQR. If AB = 12, BC = 24, AC = 20, and PQ = 8, what are QR and PR?

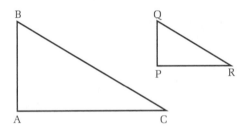

17 Chef Patti Fours needs 5 eggs for every 3 dozen cream puffs she makes. How many eggs are needed for 18 dozen cream puffs?

18 Let x represent the number of inches and $f(x)$ represent the corresponding number of centimeters.

a Complete the table.

Inches (x)	0	1	2	3	4	x
Centimeters f(x)	0	2.54	5.08			

b Write a formula in function notation.
c What is the domain of the function?
d Draw a graph of the function.

19 Complete the proportion if △ACB ~ △DFE.

$\dfrac{BC}{EF} = \dfrac{?}{DE} = \dfrac{AC}{?}$

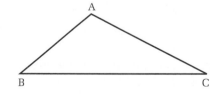

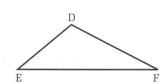

20 Given △GHI ~ △KPQ.

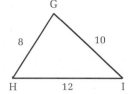

a Complete the proportion. $\dfrac{GH}{?} = \dfrac{?}{PQ} = \dfrac{?}{KQ}$

b Find x and y.

In problems 21 and 22, evaluate $\dfrac{x - 3y}{3y - x}$ **for the given values.**

21 x = 1 and y = −5   **22** x = −4 and y = 2

23 Factor $x^2 + 8x + 12$ over the integers.

24 If △GIH ~ △QPT, complete the proportion. $\dfrac{GH}{QT} = \dfrac{?}{?} = \dfrac{?}{?}$

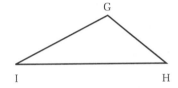

25 Refer to the map on page 607. Willie travels from Orlando to Tallahassee to Jacksonville and back to Orlando every week on his sales tour. His company pays $0.23 per mile for travel. How much should Willie be paid to cover his travel expenses each week?

26 In this scale drawing of a living room, 1 inch represents 6 feet. What are the dimensions of the living room? How many square yards of carpeting are needed to carpet this room? Find the cost of carpeting the living room if carpet costs $20 per square yard and the installation cost is $90.

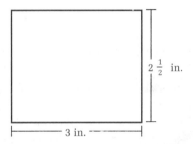

27 Three and one-half tablespoons of coffee make a pot of coffee that fills 5 cups. Melissa expects the parents at the school's open house to drink 30 cups of coffee. How many tablespoons of coffee will she need?

28 Solve the system for (x_1, y_1). $\begin{cases} 3x_1 + 8y_1 = 14 \\ 2x_1 - 4y_1 = 28 \end{cases}$

29 Jerry Bilt receives a kit for building a model airplane. The kit uses a scale of $\frac{1}{4}$ inch to 3 feet.

a One inch of the model's length corresponds to how many feet on the actual airplane?

b If the completed model is $6\frac{1}{2}$ inches in length, what is the length of the actual airplane?

Problem Set, *continued*

30 If $\dfrac{x}{2x + 5} = \dfrac{1}{2}$, what is x?

31 For a school concert the ratio of tickets sold to parents, children, and faculty is 25:20:3. If 240 tickets are sold, how many tickets are sold to each group?

32 Express in simplest terms the ratio of the volume of the large box to the volume of the small box.

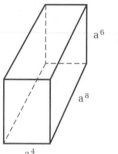

33 If 1000 Greek drachmas is equivalent to $7.92, how much is 3250 drachmas worth in U.S. currency?

34 If two triangles are similar, the corresponding angles are equal in measure. Given $\triangle ABC \sim \triangle DEF$, find x, y, and z.

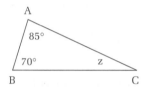

35 A 10-foot-long section of a beam weighs 2520 pounds. What is the weight of an 8-foot-long section of the beam?

36 Refer to the two circles. Express each ratio in simplest form.
  a The ratio of the circumferences
  b The ratio of the areas

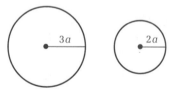

37 If a machinist needs 3.5 hours to produce 12 bearings, how long must he work to produce 20 bearings?

38 Find the ratio of the volume of the cone to the volume of the cylinder.

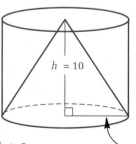

In problems 39 and 40, solve for *K*.

39 $\dfrac{K}{K + 3} = \dfrac{2K}{K + 8}$

40 $\dfrac{K + 3}{K} = \dfrac{K + 8}{2K}$

41 Consider the sequence of numbers $a_1, a_2, a_3, \ldots, a_n$, where $a_1 = 1$ and $a_{n+1} = a_n + 2$. Find the first 8 numbers in the sequence.

42 "Quality on the rise!" the ad proclaims, with a perspective, truncated graph to prove it.

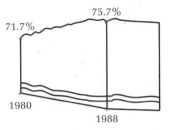

a Use a ruler to measure the height of the graph for 1980 and 1988. What is the percentage increase in height from 1980 to 1988?

b Based on the numbers given, what is the actual percentage increase?

43 Consider the sequence of numbers $a_1, a_2, a_3, \ldots, a_n$, where $a_1 = 1$ and $a_{n+1} = 2 \cdot a_n$. Express the first 8 numbers of the sequence as powers of 2.

44 The area of the shaded region is $40x + 4$.

a Find x.

b The area of a small square is what percentage of the area of the large square?

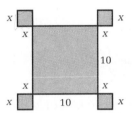

45 Find the ratio of a to b if $2a = 3c$ and $12c = 7b$.

46 Before leaving London for Paris, Darnell decided to convert 42 pounds to francs. He read that 1 pound was equivalent to $1.8941 and that 1 franc was equivalent to $0.1877. To the nearest franc, how many francs should Darnell get in the exchange?

47 Given $\triangle ABC \sim \triangle DEF$.

a Find x and y.

b Find the ratio of BC to AC.

c Find the ratio of EF to DF.

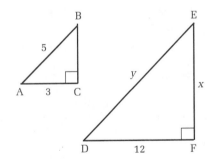

48 The starship Interprize has enough fuel to travel 6000 miles in 8 hours at normal speed or 2000 miles in 1 hour at hyperspeed. Its destination is 800 Sretems away. A distance of 250 Sretems equals 1250 miles.

a How far away is the ship's destination in miles?

b If refueling takes 30 minutes, will the ship get there faster by using normal speed or by using hyperspeed?

c How much sooner will the ship get to its destination by using the quicker method?

DIRECT AND INVERSE VARIATION

Objectives

After studying this section, you will be able to
- Solve direct-variation problems
- Solve inverse-variation problems

Part One: Introduction

Direct Variation

In some proportion problems, as one variable increases, the other variable also increases. In other proportion problems, one variable increases as the other variable decreases. In this section, you will learn about these two patterns of variation.

Proportion problems of the first type arise when several proportions have a common ratio. Consider a baker who makes cream-puff pastries. The number of eggs he uses daily depends on the number of cream puffs he makes each day, which depends on how many are ordered for that day. The recipe requires 5 eggs for every 3 dozen cream puffs. At the beginning of the week the baker has the following orders.

Day	Order
Monday	12 dozen
Tuesday	16 dozen
Wednesday	83 dozen

The baker can find a formula for the number of eggs he needs each day by setting up and solving a proportion. Then he can evaluate the formula to find the number of eggs needed.

Proportion $\dfrac{\text{Eggs}}{\text{Dozen puffs}} = \dfrac{e}{p} = \dfrac{5}{3}$

Formula $e = \dfrac{5}{3}p$

Now all he has to do each day is evaluate the formula $e = \dfrac{5}{3}p$.

Day	Order	Number of Eggs
Monday	12 dozen	$e = \frac{5}{3}(12) = 20$
Tuesday	16 dozen	$e = \frac{5}{3}(16) \approx 27$
Wednesday	83 dozen	$e = \frac{5}{3}(83) \approx 138$

The ratio $\frac{e}{p}$ is always $\frac{5}{3}$.

Any situation where two variables are always in the same ratio is called a **direct variation.** Two variables are in direct variation if their ratio is a constant.

Notice that when you solve $\frac{e}{p} = \frac{5}{3}$, you obtain the formula $e = \frac{5}{3}p$. This formula is of the form $y = kx$, where k is a known number. You can say that y *varies directly as* x. In the baker problem, the number of eggs used varied directly as the number of pastries ordered. The known number k is known as the **constant of variation.** The constant of variation in the baker's formula is $\frac{5}{3}$.

The graph of a formula of the form $y = kx$, where k is a known number, is a line through the origin with slope k. Its x-intercept and y-intercept are both 0.

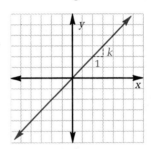

Here are some other examples of direct variation.

- An automobile is traveling at the constant rate of 50 miles per hour. The distance traveled is $d = 50t$. In this case, distance varies directly as time.
- A person is paid $5.50 an hour. The wages earned are $w = 5.50h$. Wages vary directly as hours worked.
- A computer printer prints 80 characters per second. The number of characters printed is $c = 80s$. The number of characters printed varies directly as the number of seconds.

In each illustration, as one variable increases, the other increases proportionally. For example, as one variable is doubled, the other is doubled, or as one variable is halved, so is the other.

Inverse Variation

Tina wanted to read 36 short stories during her summer vacation. She made a table to help her plan a schedule.

Number of Stories Read Per Day	Number of Days Needed to Finish
1	36
2	18
3	12
4	9

According to her table, as the number of short stories read per day increases, the number of days needed to complete the task decreases. This is an example of *inverse variation.*

A formula to represent Tina's information is $R \cdot t = 36$, where R is the number of stories read per day and t is the number of days needed to finish reading all the stories. In inverse variation, the product of the variables is a constant. Two variables are in *inverse variation* if their product is a constant.

A formula of the form $xy = k$, where k is a known number, describes an inverse variation. We say that x *varies inversely as* y. The number of days needed for Tina to read all the stories varies inversely with the number of stories she reads per day. Again, the constant k is called the constant of variation. The constant of variation in Tina's formula is 36.

Here is another example of inverse variation. If the area of a rectangle is 50 square feet, then $lw = 50$. The length varies inversely as the width. If you double the width, you must halve the length to keep the same area of 50 square feet.

Part Two: Sample Problems

Problem 1   *The value of p varies directly as q, and p is 12 when q is 8. Complete the table.*

q	−0.5	8	16.2	20.1
p				

Solution   Since $\frac{p}{q}$ is a constant, $\frac{p}{q} = \frac{12}{8} = 1.5$ is the constant of variation. We can express the direct variation as $\frac{p}{q} = 1.5$ or $p = 1.5q$.

We can substitute the values of q from the table to compute the values of p.

q	−0.5	8	16.2	20.1
p	−0.75	12	24.3	30.15

Problem 2   *The value of p varies inversely as q, and p is 12 when q is 8. Find p when q is 14.*

Solution   The product of pq is a constant equal to 12 · 8, or 96.
The inverse variation is

$$pq = 96$$
$$p(14) = 96$$
$$p = \frac{96}{14}, \text{ or } \approx 6.86$$

Problem 3   In business, the time it takes to complete a job is measured in worker hours. This means that the number of hours required to complete the job is inversely proportional to the number of workers required. If a job is estimated to take 4000 worker hours for completion and the job needs to be completed in 130 hours, how many people should work on the job?

Solution   The number of worker hours is the product of the number of people working and the amount of time each works.

people · time = worker hours
people · 130 = 4000
people ≈ 31

It will take 31 people to complete the job in 130 hours.

Problem 4   Korn's Discount Bookstore discounts all paperback books by 14%. Gordy's job is to mark all paperbacks with the discounted price. Devise an efficient method for calculating the discounted prices.

Solution   We will write a computer program to generate a table of values. To use the program to generate other tables, we let the input be starting and ending values as well as the constant of variation. This will help Gordy if the manager decides to change the amount of discount.

```
10  REM    This program prints out a table of values
20  REM    that vary directly.
30  REM    -------------- Data Entry --------------
40  PRINT "Enter the minimum and maximum values for
45  PRINT your table separated by a comma";
50  INPUT MN,MX
60  PRINT "Enter the increment for the values in your
65  PRINT table";
70  INPUT S
80  PRINT "Enter the constant of variation";
90  INPUT CV
100 REM    --------------- Output ---------------
110 PRINT "REG PRICE","DISC PRICE"
120 FOR   X = MN TO MX STEP S
130 LET   Y = CV*X
140 PRINT X,Y
150 NEXT  X
160 END
```

The cheapest book is $0.50, the most expensive book is $9.75, and all book prices end in either a 5 or a 0. Gordy can run the program, enter a minimum value of 0.50, a maximum value of 9.75, and an increment of 0.05. For the constant of variation, Gordy enters 0.86 because a 14% discount means the selling price will be 86% of its original price.

Part Three: Exercises and Problems

Warm-up Exercises

In problems 1–4, classify each equation as direct variation, inverse variation, or neither.

1 $y = 2x$ **2** $y = 2x + 5$ **3** $25 = xy$ **4** $x = \dfrac{3}{y}$

5 If p varies directly as q, and if p is 8 when q is 2, what is q when p is 1?

6 If p varies inversely as q, and if p is 9 when q is 3, what is p when q is 27?

7 Find the value of x on the map.

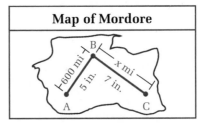

8 Evaluate the expression $\dfrac{a - b}{b - a}$ for $a = 5$ and $b = -2$.

Problem Set

In problems 9–11, determine whether the given relationship is a direct variation, an inverse variation, or neither.

9 The distance d traveled by an airplane after t hours if the plane's speed is 370 miles per hour

10 The volume v in each of n bottles used to package 300 gallons of perfume

11 The number of hours h, at w dollars per hour, necessary to work in order to earn $20,000

12 If P is 12 when Q is 6, and if P varies inversely as Q, what is the value for Q when P is 8?

13 If P is 12 when Q is 18, and if P varies directly as Q, what is Q when P is 30?

14 Sari drove 240 miles in 5 hours. How fast did she drive? If the speed limit is raised and she makes the same trip in 1 hour less time, how fast does she drive?

15 The speed of a plane is inversely proportional to the time it takes to make a trip. If a trip takes 4.7 hours at 325 miles per hour, how long will the trip take at 425 miles per hour?

16 Simplify $\dfrac{24x^3}{32x^8}$.

In problems 17 and 18, factor each polynomial.

17 $x^2 - 11x - 26$ **18** $4x^2 - 5x + 1$

19 A job is estimated to take 19,000 worker hours to complete. If the job must be finished in 30 days, how many people should work on the job? If 18 people work on the job, how long will it take?

20 In a school hockey game, the number of goals n is directly proportional to the number of shots s attempted. Write a formula to represent this relationship using a constant of variation c. Find c to the nearest hundredth if $n = 2$ when $s = 17$.

21 Solve $y_1{}^2 + 5y_1 = 6$ for y_1.

22 Hooke's Law for an elastic spring states that the distance a spring will stretch varies directly as the force applied. If a force of 20 pounds will stretch a spring 9 inches, how far will a force of 30 pounds stretch the spring?

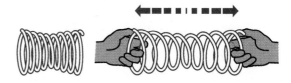

23 The number of British thermal units (BTU's) of heat necessary to heat a building varies inversely as the outside temperature. If 500 BTU's are required when the outside temperature is 20°F, how many BTU's will be required to heat the building for a day if the outside temperature is 4°F?

24 If 5 people take 3 hours to paint an office, how long will 7 people take to paint 4 offices the same size?

In problems 25 and 26, graph each equation.

25 $\frac{x}{y} = 2$ **26** $y = \frac{1}{2}x$

27 Let $y = 3x + 4$.

   a Complete the table.
   b Is the ratio of y to x a constant value?
   c Does the graph of $y = 3x + 4$ pass through the origin?

x	y	$y{:}x$ or $\frac{y}{x}$
-4		
-2		
-1		
1		
5		

28 Sven needs to draw a 28-inch-by-36-inch map on an 8-inch-by-12-inch piece of paper. What is the largest scale he can use?

29 The cost of a pizza varies directly as the area of the pizza. If a 12-inch-diameter pizza costs $7.20, how much is a 16-inch-diameter pizza?

Problem Set, *continued*

30 The amount of homework math students do is inversely proportional to the temperature outside. If math students do 45 minutes of homework when the temperature is 50°, how many minutes of homework do they do when the temperature reaches 90°?

31 Modify Gordy's computer program in Sample Problem **4** so that it will print a sales-tax table. Assume the sales tax is 7%.

In problems 32 and 33, graph each equation.

32 $y = 3x$ **33** $\dfrac{y}{x} = 3$

34 Complete the table so the lever is in balance for each value of *d*.

d	50	20	10	5	2	1
w						

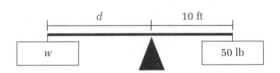

35 A painter made 28 gallons of paint using white pigment, linseed oil, dryer, and turpentine in the ratio of $3:2:1:1$. How many gallons of each material did she use?

36 A rectangle has an area of 24 square feet. Its sides are integers. Find the probability that its perimeter is greater than 20 feet.

37 The pressure on a point in a liquid varies directly with the distance from the surface to the point. The pressure at a depth of 8 meters is 75 kilograms per square meter for a certain liquid. Find the pressure at a depth of 10 meters.

38 Given $\triangle ABC \sim \triangle EDC$.

   a Complete the proportion.
$$\frac{AB}{ED} = \frac{AC}{?} = \frac{BC}{?}$$
   b Find x and y.

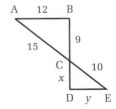

39 Imagine a rectangle whose area is always 80 square centimeters but whose width and length can vary. Are its width and length directly or inversely proportional to each other? If its length is 3.47×10^5 centimeters, what is its width?

40 The cost of installing carpet varies directly as the number of square yards of carpet installed. If it costs $75 to install a 12-foot-by-18-foot carpet, how much will it cost to install a 20-foot-by-24-foot carpet?

41 Refer to the diagram.

  a 1 square yard = ___?___ square feet

  b Complete the table below.

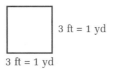

3 ft = 1 yd

3 ft = 1 yd

Number of Square Yards x	1	2	3	4	5	6	x
Number of Square Feet $f(x)$							

  c Write a formula or function to convert square yards to square feet.

  d Graph the function from part **c**.

42 The speeds (S_1 and S_2, in revolutions per minute) of the pulleys vary inversely as their diameters (d_1 and d_2).

  a Write a formula for the relationship.

  b Find the speed of the fan if the speed of the first pulley is 900 revolutions per minute.

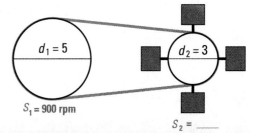

$d_1 = 5$

$d_2 = 3$

$S_1 = 900$ rpm

$S_2 =$ _____

HISTORICAL SNAPSHOT

FRACTIONS WITHIN FRACTIONS
How to simplify continued fractions

A *continued fraction* is a rational expression that looks complex. All but the last fraction have a denominator that consists of a whole number plus a fraction. Continued fractions have fascinated some of the world's greatest mathematicians, from Archimedes (287?–212 B.C.) to Ramanujan (see page 507).

$$\cfrac{1}{3 + \cfrac{1}{3 + \cfrac{1}{3 + \frac{1}{3}}}}$$

To simplify continued fractions, start at the lower right and work upward one step at a time:

$$\cfrac{1}{3 + \cfrac{1}{3 + \cfrac{1}{3 + \frac{1}{3}}}} = \cfrac{1}{3 + \cfrac{1}{3 + \cfrac{1}{\frac{10}{3}}}} = \cfrac{1}{3 + \cfrac{1}{3 + \frac{3}{10}}} =$$

$$\cfrac{1}{3 + \cfrac{1}{\frac{33}{10}}} = \cfrac{1}{3 + \frac{10}{33}} = \cfrac{1}{\frac{109}{33}} = \frac{33}{109}$$

To convert a fraction, such as $\dfrac{329}{1051}$, to a continued fraction, use the following method, patterned after Euclid's Algorithm (see page 552).

$$1051 = 3(329) + 64$$
$$329 = 5(64) + 9$$
$$64 = 7(9) + 1$$
$$9 = 9(1) + 0$$

Write the coefficients on the right in order (3, 5, 7, and 9) as the whole-number parts of a continued fraction:

$$\frac{329}{1051} = \cfrac{1}{3 + \cfrac{1}{5 + \cfrac{1}{7 + \frac{1}{9}}}}$$

Convert each fraction to a continued fraction.

1. $\dfrac{4}{5}$ 2. $\dfrac{13}{30}$ 3. $\dfrac{15}{82}$ 4. $\dfrac{294}{3893}$

SIMPLIFYING RATIONAL EXPRESSIONS

Objectives

After studying this section, you will be able to
- Simplify rational expressions
- Determine the restrictions on a rational expression

Part One: Introduction

Simplifying Rational Expressions

In this section, we begin to work with fractional expressions that have polynomials in the numerator and denominator. These fractions are called **rational expressions.**

In arithmetic, you learned to simplify fractions.

$$\frac{28}{16} = \frac{4 \cdot 7}{4 \cdot 4} = 1 \cdot \frac{7}{4} = \frac{7}{4}$$

In Chapter 9 you learned how to simplify algebraic expressions.

$$\frac{8x^6}{18x^4} = \frac{2x^4 \cdot 4x^2}{2x^4 \cdot 9} = \frac{2x^4}{2x^4} \cdot \frac{4x^2}{9} = 1 \cdot \frac{4x^2}{9} = \frac{4x^2}{9}$$

In both cases you found the largest factors common to the numerator and denominator. The ratio of these common factors is equal to 1.

Consider the rational expression $\dfrac{5(x + 3)}{3(x + 3)}$. The expression can

also be written as $\dfrac{x + 3}{x + 3} \cdot \dfrac{5}{3}$. Since $\dfrac{x + 3}{x + 3} = 1$, this expression

simplifies to $\dfrac{5}{3}$.

Example *Simplify* $\dfrac{3y - 12}{5y - 20}$.

We factor the numerator and denominator, then find common factors.

$$\frac{3y - 12}{5y - 20} = \frac{3(y - 4)}{5(y - 4)}$$

$$= \frac{3}{5} \cdot \frac{(y - 4)}{(y - 4)}$$

$$= \frac{3}{5} \cdot 1 = \frac{3}{5}$$

Example   Simplify $\dfrac{y - 2}{2 - y}$.

We factor -1 from the numerator to try to get common factors.

$$\dfrac{y - 2}{2 - y} = \dfrac{-1(-y + 2)}{2 - y}$$

$$= \dfrac{-1(2 - y)}{2 - y} = -1$$

Note   Whenever the numerator and the denominator are opposites, as in $\dfrac{d}{-d}$, $\dfrac{y - 2}{2 - y}$, or $\dfrac{a - b}{b - a}$, the simplified fraction is -1.

Restrictions on Rational Expressions

Consider the following two examples.

Example   For what value of x is $\dfrac{x^2 + 5x + 4}{x + 1}$ undefined?

A fraction is undefined when the denominator is zero. If $x = -1$, the denominator would be zero and the fraction would be undefined. Such a value is called a **restriction.**

Example   Simplify $\dfrac{x^2 + 5x + 4}{x + 1}$ and state any restrictions.

$$\dfrac{x^2 + 5x + 4}{x + 1} = \dfrac{(x + 4)(x + 1)}{(x + 1)}$$

$$= x + 4$$

The simplified version is defined when $x = -1$, but the original fraction is undefined when $x = -1$. When working with rational expressions it is important to refer to the original denominator to note where the expression is undefined. The simplified answer is $x + 4$, with the restriction $x \neq -1$.

In computer programming, division by zero will cause a program to crash. Computer programmers must be aware of such restrictions.

Part Two: Sample Problems

Problem 1   For what values of x is $f(x) = \dfrac{x^2 + 3x}{x^3 - 9x}$ undefined?

Solution   Restrictions make the denominator zero.

$$x^3 - 9x = 0$$
$$x(x^2 - 9) = 0$$
$$x(x - 3)(x + 3) = 0$$

The function is undefined at $x = 0$, $x = 3$, or $x = -3$.

Problem 2 Simplify $\dfrac{12z^3 + 27z^2}{36z^2 + 12z}$ and give any restrictions.

Solution

$$\dfrac{12z^3 + 27z^2}{36z^2 + 12z}$$

$$= \dfrac{3z^2(4z + 9)}{12z(3z + 1)}$$

$$= \dfrac{3z}{3z} \cdot \dfrac{z(4z + 9)}{4(3z + 1)}$$

$$= \dfrac{z(4z + 9)}{4(3z + 1)}$$

The restrictions occur when the original denominator is zero.

$$36z^2 + 12z = 0$$
$$12z(3z + 1) = 0$$
$$z = 0 \text{ or } z = -\tfrac{1}{3}$$

The restrictions are $z \neq 0$ and $z \neq -\tfrac{1}{3}$.

Problem 3 Simplify $\dfrac{x^2 + 6x - 16}{2x^2 - 8}$ and give any restrictions.

Solution

$$\dfrac{x^2 + 6x - 16}{2x^2 - 8}$$

$$= \dfrac{(x + 8)(x - 2)}{2(x - 2)(x + 2)}$$

$$= \dfrac{x + 8}{2(x + 2)}$$

The restrictions are $x \neq 2$ and $x \neq -2$. These are the values for which the original denominator, $2x^2 - 8$, equals zero.

Problem 4 Solve $\dfrac{x^2 - 6x + 9}{4x - 12} = \dfrac{x^2 - 25}{5 - x}$ for x.

Solution First let's simplify each side of the equation.

$$\dfrac{x^2 - 6x + 9}{4x - 12} = \dfrac{x^2 - 25}{5 - x}$$

$$\dfrac{(x - 3)(x - 3)}{4(x - 3)} = \dfrac{(x + 5)(x - 5)}{-1(x - 5)}$$

$$\dfrac{(x - 3)}{4} = \dfrac{x + 5}{-1}$$

$$-1(x - 3) = 4(x + 5)$$
$$-x + 3 = 4x + 20$$
$$-17 = 5x$$
$$\dfrac{-17}{5} = x$$
$$-3.4 = x$$

Using a calculator is the best way to check this problem.

Part Three: Exercises and Problems

Warm-up Exercises

In problems 1–3, simplify.

1 $\dfrac{14x^5y}{21x^4y^2}$

2 $\dfrac{4y(y-3)}{8(y-3)}$

3 $\dfrac{8x-24}{3x-9}$

In problems 4–6, for what values of x is each expression undefined?

4 $\dfrac{7}{2x-8}$

5 $\dfrac{x}{(x-5)(x+5)}$

6 $\dfrac{x^2+9x}{x^2-9x}$

7 What is the ratio of minutes in an hour to seconds in an hour?

Problem Set

In problems 8–10, simplify each expression and indicate restrictions.

8 $\dfrac{x^2-x-2}{x^2+x-6}$

9 $\dfrac{3x^2-6x-9}{6x-3}$

10 $\dfrac{4x^2-12x-16}{2x^2-6x-8}$

In problems 11–13, give any restrictions.

11 $\dfrac{2}{3x-12}$

12 $\dfrac{x}{2x^2+5x-3}$

13 $\dfrac{3x^2+x-2}{x^2+3x+2}$

In problems 14–16, simplify and give any restrictions.

14 $\dfrac{4x^3-4x}{6x^2-6}$

15 $\dfrac{4x^2+20x}{x^2+6x+5}$

16 $\dfrac{x-1}{1-x}$

In problems 17 and 18, evaluate each expression for $x = 3$ and $y = 7$.

17 $\dfrac{x-y}{y-x}$

18 $\dfrac{3y-2x}{2x-3y}$

19 The value of w varies inversely as m. If $w = 8$ when $m = 25$, what is m when $w = 20$?

20 Find the ratio of the area of Region I to the area of Region II.

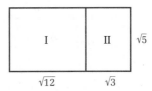

21 The cost of beveling a circular mirror varies directly as the radius. If it costs \$1.60 to bevel a mirror with a 10-inch radius, how much will it cost to bevel a mirror with a 24-inch radius?

Problem Set, *continued*

In problems 22 and 23, simplify and give any restrictions.

22 $\dfrac{2x^2 + 7x - 15}{x^2 + x - 20}$

23 $\dfrac{4x^2(x^2 - 7x + 6)}{12x^3(x^2 + 2x - 3)}$

24 The resistance of a length of wire varies inversely with the wire's cross-sectional area. A certain copper wire has a resistance of 32 ohms and a cross-sectional area of 40 square millimeters. Find the resistance of a copper wire of the same length whose cross-sectional area is 60 square millimeters.

25 The number of representatives a state is allowed in Congress is proportional to the state's population. In 1980, California's population was 23,667,565, and Connecticut's was 3,107,576. Connecticut had 6 representatives. How many representatives should California have had? Ohio had 21 representatives. Estimate its population.

In problems 26 and 27, simplify and give any restrictions.

26 $\dfrac{36x - 4x^3}{2x^2 + 6x - 36}$

27 $\dfrac{25 - x^2}{x^3 - 25x}$

28 If Hawkeye can hit a target 90% of the time, how many times will he hit the target if he makes 450 attempts?

29 Make a table of values for $f(x) = \dfrac{x^2 - 2x - 24}{x - 6}$ using integers from -3 to 3 for values of x.

In problems 30–32, simplify and give any restrictions.

30 $\dfrac{x^2 + x - 42}{2x^2 + 9x - 35}$

31 $\dfrac{16x^2(x - 3)}{4x(3 - x)}$

32 $\dfrac{x^2 + 8x - 20}{x^2 - 100}$

33 E varies directly as F. If E is 24 when F is 6, what is E when F is 24?

34 The graph shows that b varies directly as a.

  a Find the constant of variation.
  b Write an equation to express this variation graph for b in terms of a.

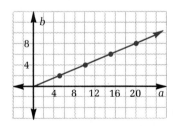

35 An alloy of tin and silver weighs 175.5 pounds. If the ratio of tin to silver is 12:1, how many pounds of silver are in the alloy?

In problems 36 and 37, solve for x.

36 $\dfrac{x^2 - 7x + 10}{x - 2} = \dfrac{2x^2 + x - 3}{x - 1}$

37 $\dfrac{x^3 - 3x^2}{x} = \dfrac{7x - 14}{x - 2}$

38 In a storage battery, the ratio of acid to water is $1:7$. If there are 14 ounces of water in a cell, how many ounces of acid are there per cell?

39 Solve $\dfrac{z + 1}{4} = \dfrac{3}{z + 12}$ for z.

40 Find all values of x that satisfy the equation $\dfrac{x^3 - 3x^2}{x - 3} = 9$.

41 Ignoring restrictions on x, if one of the following expressions is chosen at random, what is the probability that it is equal to $x + 5$?

$\dfrac{x^2 + 25}{x + 5}$ $\qquad$ $\dfrac{x^2 - 25}{x - 5}$ $\qquad$ $\dfrac{x^2 + 5x}{x}$ $\qquad$ $\dfrac{x^2 + 10x + 25}{x + 5}$

In problems 42–44, simplify and give any restrictions.

42 $\dfrac{3x^2 - 10x - 8}{6x^2 - 19x - 20}$ $\qquad$ **43** $\dfrac{x^2 - 9}{x^2 + 9}$ $\qquad$ **44** $\dfrac{20x^2 + 15x^3}{25x + 20x^2}$

45 Solve for (x, y).

$$\begin{bmatrix} 1 & 0 \\ -2 & 3 \end{bmatrix} \begin{bmatrix} y \\ x \end{bmatrix} = \begin{bmatrix} 2x \\ 6 \end{bmatrix}$$

In problems 46 and 47, solve for x.

46 $\dfrac{x^2 - 4x}{2x} = \dfrac{x^2 - 9}{x + 3}$ $\qquad$ **47** $\dfrac{x - 4}{x} = \dfrac{5}{x + 2}$

48 The graph shows that a varies inversely as b.

   a Find the constant of variation.
   b Write an equation of the variation.

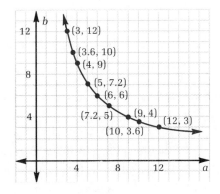

49 Two numbers are in the ratio of 3 to 4. If the smaller number is increased by 10 and the larger number is decreased by 10, the results are equal. Find the two numbers.

Problem Set, *continued*

50 Consider a sequence of numbers, $a_1, a_2, a_3, \ldots, a_n$, where
$a_1 = 1$, $a_2 = 2$, and $a_{n+2} = a_{n+1} \cdot a_n$. Find the first 8 numbers
in the sequence. What are these 8 numbers expressed as powers of 2?

51 The voltage across the coils of a transformer varies directly as the number of
turns on the coils.

  a Write a proportion to describe the
relationship shown in the diagram.

  b Solve for V_2.

  c A step-down transformer is wound
with 550 turns on the input and 45
turns on the output. Find the output
voltage if the input voltage is 110
volts.

  d Find the voltage at the spark plugs if a 6-volt alternator is
connected to a coil with an input winding of 50 turns and an
output winding of 50,000 turns.

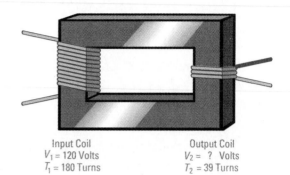

Input Coil
$V_1 = 120$ Volts
$T_1 = 180$ Turns

Output Coil
$V_2 = $? Volts
$T_2 = 39$ Turns

52 Consider two squares where the first square has side s_1 and the
second has side s_2. For each pair of squares below, find the ratio
of the area of the first square to the area of the second. Find the
ratio of the perimeter of the first to the perimeter of the second.

  a $s_1 = 3$, $s_2 = 4$ **b** $s_1 = 2$, $s_2 = 5$ **c** $s_1 = x$, $s_2 = y$

53 The path shown travels through squares
in a spirallike manner. Continuing in the
same pattern, find the area of the eighth
square.

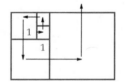

54 The area of a rectangle is 36. The lengths of its sides, a and b, are
integers. Find the probability that its perimeter is greater than 28.

55 If $\dfrac{AB}{EF} = \dfrac{BC}{FG} = \dfrac{AC}{EG}$, what are y and z if
$x = 5$?

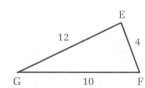

56 Refer to the system of three gears.

  a Find S_1 and S_2.

  b Which way do gears 1 and 2 turn?

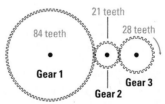

21 teeth

84 teeth

28 teeth

Gear 1

Gear 3

Gear 2

$S_1 = \underline{\ ?\ }$ rpm $S_2 = \underline{\ ?\ }$ rpm $S_3 = 450$ rpm

MULTIPLICATION AND DIVISION OF RATIONAL EXPRESSIONS

Objectives

After studying this section, you will be able to
- Multiply rational expressions
- Divide rational expressions

Part One: Introduction

Multiplying Rational Expressions

In multiplying rational expressions, such as $\dfrac{15x^4}{9x} \cdot \dfrac{12x^5}{35x^3}$, our goal is to find the simplest possible expression for the product. To do this, we look for common factors in the numerator and denominator of the product. Remember that to multiply fractions, multiply their numerators and multiply their denominators.

$$\frac{15x^4}{9x} \cdot \frac{12x^5}{35x^3}$$

$$= \frac{15 \cdot 12 \cdot x^4 \cdot x^5}{9 \cdot 35 \cdot x \cdot x^3}$$

$$= \frac{3 \cdot 5 \cdot 3 \cdot 4 \cdot x^4 \cdot x^5}{3 \cdot 3 \cdot 5 \cdot 7 \cdot x^4}$$

$$= \left(\frac{3 \cdot 3 \cdot 5 \cdot x^4}{3 \cdot 3 \cdot 5 \cdot x^4}\right) \cdot \left(\frac{4 \cdot x^5}{7}\right)$$

$$= 1 \cdot \frac{4x^5}{7}$$

$$= \frac{4x^5}{7}$$

Note   By not actually carrying out the multiplications, we can more easily recognize common factors.

Example   *Multiply* $\dfrac{x^2 + 5x - 14}{8x^2} \cdot \dfrac{4x^2 - 12x}{3x + 21}$ *and give all restrictions.*

Our strategy will be to factor the numerator and denominator of each fraction and then look for common factors.

$$\frac{x^2 + 5x - 14}{8x^2} \cdot \frac{4x^2 - 12x}{3x + 21}$$

$$= \frac{(x + 7)(x - 2)}{4x \cdot 2x} \cdot \frac{4x(x - 3)}{3(x + 7)}$$

$$= \frac{(x + 7) \cdot 4x}{(x + 7) \cdot 4x} \cdot \frac{(x - 2)(x - 3)}{2x \cdot 3}$$

$$= 1 \cdot \frac{(x - 2)(x - 3)}{6x}$$

$$= \frac{(x - 2)(x - 3)}{6x}$$

Restrictions are $x \neq 0$ and $x \neq -7$.

Dividing Rational Expressions

Recall that to divide a fraction by a fraction, multiply the first fraction by the reciprocal of the second fraction. For example, $\frac{3}{5} \div \frac{4}{7} = \frac{3}{5} \cdot \frac{7}{4} = \frac{21}{20}$. This same method is used when dividing two rational expressions.

Example   *Divide* $\dfrac{15x^4}{9x} \div \dfrac{12x^5}{35x^3}$.

$$\frac{15x^4}{9x} \div \frac{12x^5}{35x^3}$$

$$= \frac{15x^4}{9x} \cdot \frac{35x^3}{12x^5}$$

$$= \frac{3 \cdot 5 \cdot 35 \cdot x^7}{3 \cdot 3 \cdot 12 \cdot x^6}$$

$$= \frac{175x}{36}$$

Example   *Divide* $\dfrac{x^2 - 3x - 10}{x^2 - 4x} \div \dfrac{x^2 + 4x + 4}{x^2 - 16}$ *and give all restrictions.*

$$\frac{x^2 - 3x - 10}{x^2 - 4x} \div \frac{x^2 + 4x + 4}{x^2 - 16}$$

$$= \frac{x^2 - 3x - 10}{x^2 - 4x} \cdot \frac{x^2 - 16}{x^2 + 4x + 4}$$

$$= \frac{(x - 5)(x + 2)(x + 4)(x - 4)}{x(x - 4)(x + 2)(x + 2)}$$

$$= \frac{(x + 2)(x - 4)}{(x + 2)(x - 4)} \cdot \frac{(x - 5)(x + 4)}{x(x + 2)}$$

$$= \frac{(x - 5)(x + 4)}{x(x + 2)}$$

To find restrictions, we must consider all quantities that were denominators or are now denominators. We must find restrictions for $x^2 - 4x$, $x^2 - 16$, and $x^2 + 4x + 4$. The restrictions are $x \neq 0$, $x \neq 4$, $x \neq -4$, and $x \neq -2$.

One of the powerful uses of algebra involves showing why rules and relationships work. The following explains why we can multiply by the reciprocal when dividing fractions.

The expression $\frac{a}{b} \div \frac{c}{d}$ can be written as $\dfrac{\frac{a}{b}}{\frac{c}{d}}$. Since $\dfrac{\frac{d}{c}}{\frac{d}{c}} = 1$,

$$\frac{\frac{a}{b}}{\frac{c}{d}}$$

$$= \frac{\frac{a}{b} \cdot \frac{d}{c}}{\frac{c}{d} \cdot \frac{d}{c}}$$

$$= \frac{\frac{a}{b} \cdot \frac{d}{c}}{1}$$

$$= \frac{a}{b} \cdot \frac{d}{c}.$$

As you can see, $\dfrac{a}{b} \div \dfrac{c}{d} = \dfrac{a}{b} \cdot \dfrac{d}{c}.$

Part Two: Sample Problems

Problem 1 Divide $\dfrac{4x^2}{3}$ into $2x$ and give any restrictions.

Solution Rewrite $2x$ as $\dfrac{2x}{1}$.

$$\frac{2x}{1} \div \frac{4x^2}{3}$$

$$= \frac{2x}{1} \cdot \frac{3}{4x^2}$$

$$= \frac{2x \cdot 3}{2x \cdot 2x}$$

$$= \frac{2 \cdot x}{2 \cdot x} \cdot \frac{3}{2x}$$

$$= \frac{3}{2x}, \; x \neq 0$$

Problem 2 Divide $\dfrac{90x^6 - 10x^8}{x} \div \dfrac{x^2 - 9}{5x^3}$ and give any restrictions.

Solution

$$\frac{90x^6 - 10x^8}{x} \div \frac{x^2 - 9}{5x^3}$$

$$= \frac{90x^6 - 10x^8}{x} \cdot \frac{5x^3}{x^2 - 9}$$

$$= \frac{10x^6(9 - x^2)}{x} \cdot \frac{5x^3}{x^2 - 9}$$

$$= \frac{10x^6 \cdot 5x^3}{x} \cdot \frac{9 - x^2}{x^2 - 9}$$

$$= 50x^8 \cdot (-1)$$

$$= -50x^8, \; x \neq 0, \; x \neq 3, \; x \neq -3$$

Part Three: Exercises and Problems

Warm-up Exercises

In problems 1–5, multiply and simplify.

1 $\dfrac{5x^2}{10y^3} \cdot \dfrac{4xy}{x^3y^2}$

2 $\dfrac{18y^2z}{4y^3w} \cdot \dfrac{6yzw}{27}$

3 $\dfrac{2(x-6)}{6-x} \cdot \dfrac{1}{3}$

4 $\dfrac{5-y}{y^2} \cdot \dfrac{y^2}{y-5}$

5 $\dfrac{4(x-3)}{x^2} \cdot \dfrac{x(x+4)}{(x-3)(x+4)}$

In problems 6–9, simplify and give any restrictions.

6 $\dfrac{x^2-y^2}{x+y} \div \dfrac{x-y}{a}$

7 $\dfrac{(2x)^3y}{xy^2} \cdot \dfrac{y}{4x}$

8 $\dfrac{x-2}{x+5} \cdot \dfrac{x^2+7x+10}{x+2}$

9 $\dfrac{x^3-x}{x^2+x-2} \div \dfrac{4x^2+4x}{x^2-2x-8}$

Problem Set

In problems 10 and 11, multiply and give any restrictions.

10 $\dfrac{x^2+4x-5}{6x^2} \cdot \dfrac{9x^2-18x}{3x+15}$

11 $\dfrac{x^2+2x-3}{x^2+x-12} \cdot \dfrac{x^2-x-6}{x^2+x-6}$

In problems 12 and 13, divide and give any restrictions.

12 $\dfrac{24x^3}{5x} \div \dfrac{12x^2}{15}$

13 $\dfrac{2x^2+5x-3}{x^2-5x+6} \div \dfrac{x^2+5x+6}{x^2-4}$

14 The number of characters a computer printer will print varies directly with the time the printer operates. How long, in minutes, will it take to produce a document of 120,000 characters if the printer prints 15 characters per second?

In problems 15–18, find the missing rational expressions.

15 $\dfrac{3y}{y-3} \cdot \dfrac{?}{?} = \dfrac{6y^2-3y}{5y-15}$

16 $\dfrac{6y^2-3y}{5y-15} \div \dfrac{3y}{y-3} = \dfrac{?}{?}$

17 $\dfrac{5y^2}{y-5} \cdot \dfrac{?}{?} = \dfrac{y}{2}$

18 $\dfrac{x+4}{x-3} \cdot \dfrac{?}{?} = \dfrac{x^2-16}{5x-15}$

19 The following BASIC program was written to generate a table of values for $y = \frac{1}{x}$ from $x = -5$ to $x = 5$. What's wrong with the program?

```
10 FOR x = -5 TO 5
20 LET y = 1/x
30 PRINT x, y
40 NEXT x
50 END
```

20 A typewriter prints in either elite or pica type. There are 102 letters per line of elite type and 85 letters per line of pica type. For both elite and pica, there are 55 lines per page. If a paper typed in pica is 12 pages long, how long would the paper be if it were typed in elite type?

21 Simplify $\dfrac{9 - 12y}{12 - 16y}$.

In problems 22–24, divide and simplify.

22 $\dfrac{5x^4}{3z^5} \div \dfrac{4w^6}{7y}$

23 $\dfrac{3x^2}{5x^4} \div \dfrac{12x^5}{25x^{12}}$

24 $\dfrac{18y^5}{8y^2} \div \dfrac{9x^2}{16x^5}$

25 Solve $\dfrac{y + 3}{4} = \dfrac{2}{8}$ for y.

26 Jim, Jock, and Jack created a table to compare shoe size to foot length.

    a Write a linear equation that relates shoe size to foot length.

    b Does this equation represent a direct variation?

Name	Shoe Size	Foot Length (in inches)
Jack	9	$10\frac{1}{2}$
Jim	10	$10\frac{3}{4}$
Jock	12	$11\frac{1}{4}$

In problems 27 and 28, simplify and give any restrictions.

27 $\dfrac{4x^3}{x^2 - 9} \cdot \dfrac{x^2 - 4x - 21}{2x^3 - 14x^2}$

28 $\dfrac{x^2 - 2x}{x^2 + x - 6} \div \dfrac{x^3 - 64x}{x^2 + 11x + 24}$

29 A boy is born when his father is 30 years old.

Father's Age	30									
Son's Age	0	1	2	3	5	6	10	15	30	x
Ratio of Father's Age to Son's Age										

    a Copy and complete the chart.

    b For what value of x will the ratio of the father's age to the son's age be $\frac{3}{2}$?

    c For what value of x will the ratio of the father's age to the son's age be $\frac{11}{10}$?

In problems 30 and 31, find the missing rational expression.

30 $\dfrac{x}{x + 1} \div \dfrac{?}{?} = \dfrac{x(x + 2)}{(x + 1)(x - 1)}$

31 $\dfrac{x + 4}{x + 2} \cdot \dfrac{?}{?} = \dfrac{5x + 20}{x^2 + 2x}$

Problem Set, *continued*

In problems 32–34, solve for *x*.

32 $\frac{1}{2}x + \frac{3}{4} = \frac{5}{8}$

33 $\frac{1}{2}x = \frac{3}{5}$

34 $\frac{1}{2}x^2 + x + \frac{1}{2} = 0$

35 Number 10 gauge steel weighs 5.47 pounds per square foot. Find the weight of a 10-gauge steel plate measuring 6 feet by 4 feet 6 inches.

In problems 36 and 37, simplify and give any restrictions.

36 $\dfrac{x^2 + 4}{x + 2} \div \dfrac{x^2 - 4}{x - 4}$

37 $\dfrac{9 - x^2}{x^2 + 5x - 6} \cdot \dfrac{x^2 - 36}{4x^2 - 12x}$

38 Given that $\triangle FAN \sim \triangle SIT$, find FN if FA = 8, FN = SI, and ST = 18.

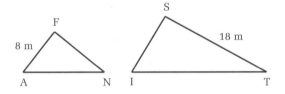

In problems 39 and 40, find the missing rational expression.

39 $\dfrac{x^2}{4x - 8} \div \dfrac{?}{?} = \dfrac{1}{4}$

40 $\dfrac{x}{x + 2} \cdot \dfrac{?}{?} = \dfrac{x + 2}{x}$

41 For a certain engine, 8 ounces of oil are mixed with $1\frac{1}{2}$ gallons of gasoline. How many ounces of oil are needed for 20 gallons of gasoline? $1 : 24$

In problems 42 and 43, divide, simplify, and give any restrictions.

42 $\dfrac{x + 3}{x - 1} \div \dfrac{1 - x}{3 + x}$

43 $\dfrac{x^2 + 3x}{5x + 5} \div \dfrac{10x + 30}{15x^2 + 15x}$

44 Express the ratio of the area of the shaded region to the area of the large circle in simplest form.

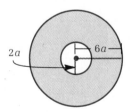

45 What are the restrictions on x?

$$\dfrac{3x(x - 1)}{(x + 7)(x - 2)} \div \dfrac{(x - 3)(x + 4)(x - 8)}{(x - 5)(x + 6)}$$

46 Find the missing rational expression.

$$\dfrac{x}{x - 1} \div \dfrac{?}{?} = \dfrac{x - 1}{x}$$

47 Gear 1 has 45 teeth. The inside circle of gear 2 has 30 teeth, and the outside wheel of gear 2 has 72 teeth. Gear 3 has 54 teeth. The speed of gear 1, S_1, is 100 revolutions per minute.

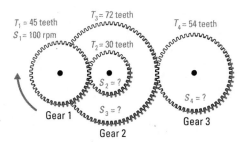

a Find S_2, S_3, and S_4.
b Which way is gear 3 turning if gear 1 is turning clockwise?

48 Simplify.
$$\frac{x^2 + 2x + 1}{x^2 - 1} \cdot \frac{x^2 + 3x + 2}{x^2 + 1} \cdot \frac{x^2 + 4x + 3}{x^2 + 5x + 6}$$

49 Fill in the missing polynomials.
$$\frac{15(x - 2)}{5x(x + 6)} \cdot \frac{x(x + 6)}{?} = \frac{?}{6(x + 3)}$$

50 What simplified rational expression must be multiplied by $\dfrac{x^2 + 4x + 3}{x^2 + 5x + 4}$ to give an answer of $\dfrac{x + 3}{x + 2}$?

51 In the figure, $\dfrac{E}{R} = \dfrac{R_d}{E_d}$. To pull out a nail, a carpenter must exert a force (E) of 8 pounds at a distance from the fulcrum (E_d) of 12 inches. Find the resisting force (R) of the nail if the distance of the nail from the fulcrum (R_d) is 2 inches.

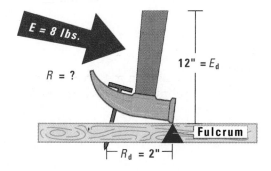

In problems 52 and 53, simplify and give any restrictions.

52 $\dfrac{x^2 - 25}{25 + 5x} \div \dfrac{25 - 10x + x^2}{5x - 25x^2}$

53 $\dfrac{x^2 + 4x}{x^2 - 4} \div \dfrac{x^2 + 8x + 16}{x^2 - 16} \cdot \dfrac{x^2 + 4x + 4}{x^2 + 2x}$

In problems 54–56, find all values of x.

54 $\sqrt{x} + 12 = 21$ **55** $3\sqrt{x} = 75$ **56** $\sqrt{x + 2} = 4$

57 The wavelength w in meters of a radio wave varies inversely as the frequency f in kilocycles per second. This relation is described by $wf = 300,000$.

a Find the wavelength of radio station WINK, which broadcasts at a frequency of 760 kilocycles per second.
b Find the wavelength of station WONK, which broadcasts at a frequency of 1140 kilocycles per second.

SOLVING RATIONAL EQUATIONS

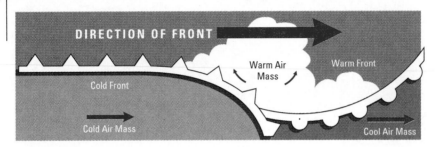

DIRECTION OF FRONT

Warm Air Mass

Warm Front

Cold Front

Cold Air Mass

Cool Air Mass

Objectives

After studying this section, you will be able to
- Solve rational equations
- Solve rate problems
- Solve work problems

Part One: Introduction

Rational Equations

A proportion is a special type of rational equation. Now you will see how we solve other types of rational equations.

 A general strategy for solving equations involving fractions is to multiply both sides of the equation by an expression that eliminates the fractions and reduces the equation to one you already know how to solve.

Example   Solve $\dfrac{5}{y} + \dfrac{2}{3} = \dfrac{5}{6}$ for y.

We can eliminate the fractions by multiplying both sides of the equation by $2 \cdot 3 \cdot y$, a common multiple of the denominators.

$$\frac{5}{y} + \frac{2}{3} = \frac{5}{6}$$

Multiply both sides by $2 \cdot 3 \cdot y$

$$2 \cdot 3 \cdot y\left(\frac{5}{y} + \frac{2}{3}\right) = 2 \cdot 3 \cdot y\left(\frac{5}{6}\right)$$

$$\frac{2 \cdot 3 \cdot y \cdot 5}{y} + \frac{2 \cdot 3 \cdot y \cdot 2}{3} = \frac{2 \cdot 3 \cdot y \cdot 5}{6}$$

Solve the linear equation

$$30 + 4y = 5y$$
$$30 = y$$

Check the solution in the original equation.

Example   Solve $\dfrac{w}{8} + \dfrac{w+3}{12} = \dfrac{5}{6}$ for w.

The least common multiple of the denominators is 24.

$$\frac{w}{8} + \frac{w+3}{12} = \frac{5}{6}$$

$$24\left(\frac{w}{8} + \frac{w+3}{12}\right) = 24\left(\frac{5}{6}\right)$$

$$24\left(\frac{w}{8}\right) + 24\left(\frac{w+3}{12}\right) = 24\left(\frac{5}{6}\right)$$

$$3w + 2(w+3) = 4 \cdot 5$$

$$5w + 6 = 20$$

$$5w = 14$$

$$w = \frac{14}{5}, \text{ or } 2.8$$

Check
We can use a calculator to check the solution.

Left Side

$$\frac{w}{8} + \frac{w+3}{12}$$

Enter 2.8 $\boxed{\div}$ 8 $\boxed{=}$ $\boxed{\text{STO}}$ 2.8 $\boxed{+}$ 3 $\boxed{=}$ $\boxed{\div}$ 12 $\boxed{=}$ $\boxed{+}$ $\boxed{\text{RCL}}$ $\boxed{=}$

The display shows $\boxed{0.8333333}$.

Right side

$$\frac{5}{6}$$

Enter 5 $\boxed{\div}$ 6 $\boxed{=}$

The display shows $\boxed{0.8333333}$.

If $w = 2.8$, the sides are equal, so the answer checks.

More Rate Problems

We can use the formula $d = r \cdot t$, in the form $\dfrac{d}{r} = t$, to solve another type of rate problem.

Example   *Jim Shue jogs 9 miles from home, then walks back. The entire trip takes 6 hours. If he jogs twice as fast as he walks, how fast does he jog?*

Let $r =$ the walking rate. Then $2r =$ the jogging rate. Since $\dfrac{d}{r} = t$, Jim's jogging time is his distance divided by his rate, or $\dfrac{9}{2r}$. Similarly, his walking time is $\dfrac{9}{r}$. The total time is 6 hours.

$$\frac{9}{2r} + \frac{9}{r} = 6$$

Multiply both sides by $2r$ $$2r\left(\frac{9}{2r} + \frac{9}{r}\right) = 2r \cdot 6$$

$$9 + 18 = 12r$$

$$2.25 = r$$

Since his jogging rate is $2r$, Jim jogs at 4.5 miles per hour.

Work Problems

Another type of problem involving rational equations occurs when we need to know how much time it takes to do a job.

Example

When only the cold-water faucet runs, a sink fills in 80 seconds. When only the hot-water faucet runs, the sink fills in 90 seconds. If both faucets run, how long will it take to fill the sink?

Let t represent the number of seconds it takes both faucets to fill the sink. The cold-water faucet fills $\frac{1}{80}$ of the sink in 1 second, so it fills $\frac{t}{80}$ of the sink in t seconds. The hot-water faucet fills $\frac{1}{90}$ of the sink in 1 second, so it fills $\frac{t}{90}$ of the sink in t seconds.

The part the cold-water faucet fills	+	The part the hot-water faucet fills	=	One filled sink
$\dfrac{t}{80}$	+	$\dfrac{t}{90}$	=	1
$720\left(\dfrac{t}{80}\right.$	+	$\left.\dfrac{t}{90}\right)$	=	720(1)
9t	+	8t	=	720
		17t	=	720
		t	≈	42.4

If both faucets run, the sink fills in about 42.4 seconds.

Part Two: Sample Problems

Problem 1

Chip and Biff formed a lawn-mowing company for the summer. Working alone, Chip can mow 1 acre in 150 minutes. Biff can mow 1 acre in 120 minutes by himself. How long will it take Biff and Chip to mow 3 acres if they work together?

Solution

Let x represent the number of minutes it takes Chip and Biff to mow 3 acres if they work together.

Chip mows $\frac{1}{150}$ acre in 1 minute, so in x minutes he mows $\frac{x}{150}$ acre.

Biff mows $\frac{1}{120}$ acre in 1 minute, so in x minutes he mows $\frac{x}{120}$ acre.

After x minutes, 3 acres are mowed.

$$\frac{x}{150} + \frac{x}{120} = 3$$
$$600\left(\frac{x}{150} + \frac{x}{120}\right) = 600 \cdot 3$$
$$4x + 5x = 1800$$
$$9x = 1800$$
$$x = 200$$

Working together, Chip and Biff can mow 3 acres in 3 hours and 20 minutes.

Problem 2 Solve $\dfrac{18}{x^2 + 3x} - \dfrac{6}{x} = \dfrac{x}{x + 3}$ for x.

Solution

Factor the denominators to determine common factors

Multiply both sides of the equation by $x(x + 3)$

$$\frac{18}{x^2 + 3x} - \frac{6}{x} = \frac{x}{x + 3}$$

$$\frac{18}{x(x + 3)} - \frac{6}{x} = \frac{x}{x + 3}$$

$$x(x + 3)\left(\frac{18}{x(x + 3)} - \frac{6}{x}\right) = x(x + 3)\left(\frac{x}{x + 3}\right)$$

$$\frac{x(x + 3)18}{x(x + 3)} - \frac{x(x + 3)6}{x} = \frac{x(x + 3)x}{x + 3}$$

$$18 - 6(x + 3) = x^2$$

$$18 - 6x - 18 = x^2$$

$$0 = x^2 + 6x$$

$$0 = x(x + 6)$$

$$x = 0 \text{ or } x = -6$$

There are two restrictions on x: $x \neq 0$ and $x \neq -3$. So $x = -6$ is the only solution.

Problem 3 Solve $\dfrac{x}{2} + \dfrac{4}{x} = 6$ for x.

Solution The least common multiple of the denominators is 2x.

$$\frac{x}{2} + \frac{4}{x} = 6$$

$$2x\left(\frac{x}{2} + \frac{4}{x}\right) = 2x \cdot 6$$

$$2x\left(\frac{x}{2}\right) + 2x\left(\frac{4}{x}\right) = 2x \cdot 6$$

$$x^2 + 8 = 12x$$

$$x^2 - 12x + 8 = 0$$

$$x = \frac{12 \pm \sqrt{144 - 32}}{2}$$

$$x \approx 11.29 \text{ or } x \approx 0.71$$

Part Three: Exercises and Problems

Warm-up Exercises

In problems 1–3, solve each equation.

1 $\dfrac{a}{5} + \dfrac{a - 2}{2} = \dfrac{2}{3}$ **2** $\dfrac{b}{2} + \dfrac{3}{b} = 8$ **3** $\dfrac{x}{x - 1} - \dfrac{3}{x^2 + x - 2} = \dfrac{x}{x + 2}$

4 Sharon can shovel 40 feet of sidewalk in 20 minutes if the snow is 4 inches deep. Shirley needs 30 minutes to do the same job. How long will it take them together to shovel 40 feet of sidewalk with snow 4 inches deep?

5 Molly can walk from her house to a movie theater in 20 minutes. It takes her sister Alice 30 minutes. How long does it take them to walk to the theater together?

6 Martha walked to the park, which is 12 blocks from her home, and jogged back. The entire trip took 1.5 hours. If Martha jogged three times faster than she walked, how fast did she walk?

Problem Set

In problems 7–9, solve for w.

7 $\dfrac{w}{4} - \dfrac{2}{3} = \dfrac{1}{2}$

8 $\dfrac{4}{w} - \dfrac{3}{2} = 2$

9 $\dfrac{2}{w} + \dfrac{3}{5} = \dfrac{5}{6}$

10 Pedro can bike twice as fast as he can run. One day he biked 10 miles to his grandmother's house, and he ran back. The entire trip took 2.5 hours. How fast did Pedro run?

11 Divide and simplify $\dfrac{x}{3 + x} \div \dfrac{2x}{x + 3}$.

In problems 12 and 13, solve for x.

12 $\dfrac{x}{x + 2} - \dfrac{4}{x^2 + 2x} = \dfrac{2}{x}$

13 $\dfrac{4}{x + 3} - \dfrac{7}{x - 3} = \dfrac{8x}{x^2 - 9}$

14 Tom can whitewash a fence alone in 4 hours, and Huck can whitewash the same fence in 5 hours working by himself. Tom whitewashes with Huck for 1 hour and then leaves. How long will it take Huck to finish whitewashing the fence?

In problems 15–17, solve for x.

15 $\dfrac{2x}{x^2 - 4x} - \dfrac{6}{x - 4} = \dfrac{4}{x}$

16 $\dfrac{9}{7x} - \dfrac{3}{2x} = \dfrac{7}{2x^2}$

17 $\dfrac{x}{3} + \dfrac{9}{x} = 4$

18 Timmy can fill his wading pool with water from the garden hose in 45 minutes. Timmy's big brother can pump water from the well and fill the pool in 30 minutes. How long would it take to fill the pool using both the garden hose and the pump?

19 In the diagram, $\dfrac{1}{x} + \dfrac{1}{y} = \dfrac{1}{z}$. Find z if x = 10 and y = 8. Find x if z = 10 and y = 15.

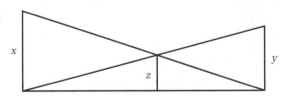

In problems 20–22, solve each equation.

20 $\dfrac{w + 3}{5} = \dfrac{w}{3}$

21 $\dfrac{x}{5} + \dfrac{3}{2} = \dfrac{x}{2}$

22 $\dfrac{t + 2}{6} + \dfrac{t}{9} = \dfrac{5}{18}$

23 Ole M. Picks ran the 100-meter dash in 9.8 seconds with a head wind. He then turned around and ran the same distance in 9.4 seconds with a tail wind. How fast would Ole have run the 100-meter dash if there had been no wind?

24 Find the slope of the line that passes through the points $(-3, 7)$ and $(-1, -4)$. Write an equation for this line.

25 Ms. C. T. Dweller walks 2 miles to work in the same time it takes Mr. Sub Urbin to drive 10 miles to work. Mr. Urbin drives 15 miles per hour faster than Ms. Dweller walks. What is each worker's speed?

26 Find the missing rational expression.

$$\frac{3x - 2}{2(x + 7)} \cdot \left(\frac{?}{?}\right) = \frac{x + 5}{2(x - 3)}$$

27 If it takes one man 14 minutes to replace the crystal of a watch, how long does it take 14 men to replace the crystal on a watch?

In problems 28 and 29, multiply.

28 $\dfrac{10x^2 - 5x}{5xy^3} \cdot \dfrac{3y^3}{6x - 3}$

29 $\dfrac{x^2 - 49}{2x + 14} \cdot \dfrac{6x^2}{x^2 - 7x}$

30 A river has a current of 2 miles per hour. Kay can paddle a canoe downstream 10 miles in the same time it takes her to paddle upstream 6 miles. How fast can Kay paddle in still water?

31 Leo Lightning runs 4 kilometers per hour faster than Slo Poke. Leo runs 10 kilometers, and then Slo runs 14 kilometers. The total elapsed time is 6 hours. How fast does each person run?

32 Solve $\dfrac{1}{x^2 + 3x + 2} + \dfrac{1}{x^2 - 4} + \dfrac{3}{x^2 - x - 2} = 0$ for x.

33 Ethel Lete runs 12 miles and then walks 16 more miles. She can run twice as fast as she can walk. The total elapsed time is 5 hours. How fast does Ethel walk?

34 Evaluate the expression $\dfrac{x^2 + 6x - 27}{x^2 - 81} \cdot \dfrac{x + 3}{x - 3}$ for $x = -3$.

35 Three pipes are connected to a water tank. One of the pipes can fill the tank in 30 minutes. The second pipe can fill it in 20 minutes. The third pipe can fill the tank in 40 minutes. How long will it take to fill the tank if all three pipes are opened together? If the slowest pipe is shut off after 3 minutes and the fastest pipe is shut off 3 minutes later, how long will it take the remaining open pipe to finish filling the tank?

36 Copy machine #7347 can make 48 copies per minute, while copy machine #7734 can make 64 copies per minute. How long will it take the two machines running together to make 3024 copies?

37 The height of the image of a man on film is inversely proportional to the distance of the camera from the man. At a distance of 15 feet from the camera, a 6-foot-tall man creates a 12-millimeter image on the film. What would the distance have to be to obtain a 4-millimeter image on the film?

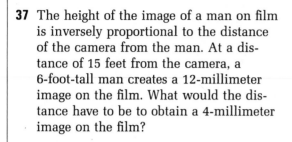 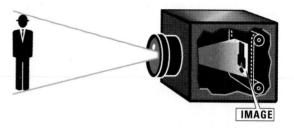

IMAGE

38 Sun D. Driver drove in the country 20 miles per hour faster than in the city. She traveled 15 miles in the city and 40 miles in the country. If the trip took 1.5 hours, at what speed did she travel in the city?

39 Solve $\dfrac{5}{x} + \dfrac{x}{x+3} = \dfrac{14}{x^2 + 3x}$ for x.

40 The sum of a number and its reciprocal is equal to the opposite of the product of the number and its reciprocal. Find the number.

41 Thirty cows can eat 10 bales of hay in 8 hours. How long would it take 12 cows to eat 3 bales of hay?

42 A faucet can fill a sink in 8 minutes. The drain can empty the sink in 6 minutes. If the sink is full, the faucet is running, and the drain is open, how long does it take for the sink to drain?

43 At 10:00 A.M. a snowstorm is 250 miles west of St. Louis. The storm travels 150 miles eastward at a constant rate, and then its speed decreases by 5 miles per hour. If the storm reaches St. Louis at 8:00 P.M., what was the storm's original speed?

44 Simplify $\dfrac{x-2}{(x-1)x-2}$.

45 In 1955, Jim Treadway was driving from Wausau, Wisconsin, to Moorhead, Minnesota. The speed limit in Wisconsin was 10 miles per hour faster than the speed limit in Minnesota, and Jim always drove the speed limit. The distance from Wausau to the state line is 140 miles, and the distance from the state line to Moorhead is 240 miles. If Jim made the trip in 6 hours, what were the speed limits in these states?

46 Find all ordered pairs of positive integers (a, b) so that
$$\frac{1}{a} + \frac{1}{b} = \frac{1}{2}.$$

47 The starship Interprize has only two speeds, normal and hyper. It has enough fuel to travel 6000 miles in 8 hours at normal speed or 2000 miles in 1 hour at hyperspeed. The ship must make a 4000-mile trip. How far should it travel at each speed to arrive at its destination in the least time possible, using all of the fuel it has?

48 Simplify $\dfrac{(3x + 8)x + 4}{(5x + 12)x + 4}$.

49 If a chicken and a half can lay an egg and a half in a day and a half, how long does it take one chicken to lay one egg?

A HABITAT STUDY OF ALASKAN BIRDS
Biologist Rebecca Field explains how and why

The North Slope of Alaska is vast and the winters are long. How can a research scientist conduct a meaningful study of the area's great numbers of wildlife during the short summer season available each year? The answer is simple: sample!

Rebecca Field, a wildlife research biologist, led the North Slope Bird and Habitat Study for the U.S. Fish and Wildlife Service. She explained how the team sampled the region, choosing areas typical of various habitats. They laid numbered grids over large areas. "Then, using random numbers, we chose our study sites," she said.

The sites were staked so they could be identified year after year. Dr Field's teams studied how migratory birds used habitats during and after the breeding season. Biologists at each site counted the number of birds of each spe-

cies and recorded habitat types. Analysis of the results after several seasons allow Dr. Field to predict how birds use habitats. Those predictions are being tested. Meanwhile, the results of her study will be used by the Fish and Wildlife Service to advise agencies and managers on how proposed activities—oil and gas development, for example—will affect the area's wildlife.

It was a love of the outdoors fostered during family camping trips and birding expeditions that led Dr. Field to her profession. She earned her Ph.D. at Johns Hopkins University. Now she is the leader of the Massachusetts Cooperative Wildlife Research Unit with the U.S. Fish and Wildlife Service in Amherst, Massachusetts.

ADDITION AND SUBTRACTION OF RATIONAL EXPRESSIONS

Objectives

After studying this section, you will be able to
- Add and subtract rational expressions with like denominators
- Add and subtract rational expressions with unlike denominators

Part One: Introduction

Rational Expressions with Like Denominators

You've learned that to add or subtract fractions with the same denominator you add or subtract their numerators.

$$\frac{3}{13} + \frac{5}{13} = \frac{3+5}{13} = \frac{8}{13} \text{ and } \frac{3}{13} - \frac{5}{13} = -\frac{2}{13}$$

The same method is used for rational expressions.

Example   *Simplify* $\dfrac{3+x}{x+1} - \dfrac{5+2x}{x+1}$.

Since the fractions have the same denominator, we subtract the numerators.

$$\frac{3+x}{x+1} - \frac{5+2x}{x+1}$$
$$= \frac{3+x-(5+2x)}{x-1}$$
$$= \frac{3+x-5-2x}{x+1}$$
$$= \frac{-x-2}{x+1} \text{ or } -\frac{x+2}{x+1}$$

Example   *Simplify* $\dfrac{x+5}{2} + \dfrac{3x+1}{2}$.

$$\frac{x+5}{2} + \frac{3x+1}{2}$$
$$= \frac{x+5+3x+1}{2}$$
$$= \frac{4x+6}{2}$$
$$= \frac{2(2x+3)}{2}, \text{ or } 2x+3$$

Rational Expressions with Unlike Denominators

Recall that to add or subtract two fractions with unlike denominators we rewrite the fractions with common denominators and then add or subtract.

$$\frac{3}{5} + \frac{2}{7} = \frac{3}{5} \cdot \frac{7}{7} + \frac{2}{7} \cdot \frac{5}{5} = \frac{21}{35} + \frac{10}{35} = \frac{31}{35}$$

We use the same method for rational expressions when the denominators are unlike.

Example Simplify $\dfrac{2x}{3} + \dfrac{4x}{5}$.

The least common denominator is $3 \cdot 5$, or 15.

$$\frac{2x}{3} + \frac{4x}{5}$$

$$= \frac{5}{5} \cdot \frac{2x}{3} + \frac{3}{3} \cdot \frac{4x}{5}$$

$$= \frac{10x}{15} + \frac{12x}{15}$$

$$= \frac{22x}{15}$$

Example Simplify $\dfrac{4x + 5}{4} - \dfrac{1.25x + 3}{x}$.

The least common denominator is $4 \cdot x$, or $4x$.

$$\frac{4x + 5}{4} - \frac{1.25x + 3}{x}$$

$$= \frac{x}{x} \cdot \frac{4x + 5}{4} - \frac{4}{4} \cdot \frac{1.25x + 3}{x}$$

$$= \frac{x(4x + 5) - 4(1.25x + 3)}{4x}$$

$$= \frac{4x^2 + 5x - 5x - 12}{4x}$$

$$= \frac{4x^2 - 12}{4x}$$

$$= \frac{4(x^2 - 3)}{4x}, \text{ or } \frac{x^2 - 3}{x}$$

Example Add $\dfrac{a}{b} + \dfrac{c}{d}$.

The least common denominator is bd.

$$\frac{a}{b} + \frac{c}{d}$$

$$= \frac{a}{b} \cdot \frac{d}{d} + \frac{c}{d} \cdot \frac{b}{b}$$

$$= \frac{ad}{bd} + \frac{bc}{bd}$$

$$= \frac{ad + bc}{bd}$$

Part Two: Sample Problems

Problem 1   Given $f(x) = \dfrac{x}{x^2 + 2x} + \dfrac{2}{x^2 + 2x}$. *Copy and complete the table.*

x	-4	-3	-2	-1	0	1	2	3	4
$f(x)$									

Solution   Let's simplify the expression before we evaluate.

$$f(x) = \frac{x}{x^2 + 2x} + \frac{2}{x^2 + 2x}$$

$$= \frac{x + 2}{x^2 + 2x}$$

$$= \frac{x + 2}{x(x + 2)}$$

$$= \frac{1}{x}, \; x \neq 0, \; x \neq -2$$

Now we can complete the table for $f(x) = \frac{1}{x}$. Remember that $f(x)$ is undefined for $x = 0$ and $x = -2$.

x	-4	-3	-2	-1	0	1	2	3	4
$f(x)$	$-\frac{1}{4}$	$-\frac{1}{3}$	und.	-1	und.	1	$\frac{1}{2}$	$\frac{1}{3}$	$\frac{1}{4}$

Problem 2   *Simplify* $\dfrac{4}{x^2 - 6x} - \dfrac{2}{x^2 - 3x}$.

Solution   Let's begin by factoring the denominators.

$$\frac{4}{x^2 - 6x} - \frac{2}{x^2 - 3x}$$

$$= \frac{4}{x(x - 6)} - \frac{2}{x(x - 3)}$$

$$= \frac{(x - 3)}{(x - 3)} \cdot \frac{4}{x(x - 6)} - \frac{(x - 6)}{(x - 6)} \cdot \frac{2}{x(x - 3)}$$

The least common denominator is $x(x - 3)(x - 6)$

$$= \frac{(x - 3)4}{(x - 3)x(x - 6)} - \frac{(x - 6)2}{(x - 6)x(x - 3)},$$

$$= \frac{4x - 12 - (2x - 12)}{x(x - 3)(x - 6)}$$

$$= \frac{4x - 12 - 2x + 12}{x(x - 3)(x - 6)}$$

$$= \frac{2x}{x(x - 3)(x - 6)}$$

$$= \frac{2}{(x - 3)(x - 6)}, \; x \neq 0, \; x \neq 3, \; x \neq 6$$

Part Three: Exercises and Problems

Warm-up Exercises

In problems 1–3, add or subtract.

1 $\dfrac{5x - 3}{x} + \dfrac{2x - 1}{x}$

2 $\dfrac{3}{x} + \dfrac{x}{4}$

3 $\dfrac{5}{2x} - \dfrac{3x}{x + 10}$

4 Add $\dfrac{x}{m} + \dfrac{y}{n}$.

5 Simplify $\dfrac{3x + 2}{x + 2} + \dfrac{x + 6}{x + 2}$.

6 Simplify $\dfrac{2x}{x - 1} - \dfrac{x}{x - 1}$ and give any restrictions.

7 Solve $\dfrac{x}{8} = \dfrac{x + 5}{10}$ for x.

In problems 8 and 9, simplify.

8 $\dfrac{x + 2}{3} + \dfrac{x - 1}{6}$

9 $\dfrac{3x}{x + 2} \cdot \dfrac{2x}{x + 2}$

10 Louis can sort 1000 index cards in 20 minutes. Bob needs 30 minutes to sort 1000 cards. How long will it take them to sort 1000 cards if they work together?

Problem Set

11 Solve $\dfrac{f}{3} + \dfrac{f}{4} = \dfrac{1}{12}$ for f.

In problems 12–17, simplify each expression and solve each equation.

12 $\dfrac{5}{x + 2} - \dfrac{7}{x + 2}$

13 $\dfrac{3}{5} + \dfrac{x}{5} = 5x$

14 $\dfrac{x}{4} + \dfrac{x}{3}$

15 $\dfrac{9}{x - 7} + 1 = \dfrac{3}{x - 7}$

16 $\dfrac{x}{2y} + \dfrac{3x}{2y}$

17 $\dfrac{a}{b} - \dfrac{b}{a}$

18 Maranda makes $3 per hour more than Belinda. As a result, Belinda must work 51 hours to earn as much as Maranda earns in 26 hours. How much does Maranda earn in 1 hour?

In problems 19–22, simplify and give any restrictions.

19 $\dfrac{4}{x^2 + x} - \dfrac{9}{x^2 - x}$

20 $\dfrac{x + 2}{4} - \dfrac{x - 7}{9}$

21 $\dfrac{3}{2x + 4} - \dfrac{3}{2x}$

22 $\dfrac{x}{x + 5} + \dfrac{3}{x - 5}$

Problem Set, *continued*

23 Solve $\dfrac{3}{m} = \dfrac{m}{27}$ for m.

24 Bart can fix 6 flat tires in 1 hour. Art can fix 16 flat tires in 3 hours. Today, they have to fix 68 flat tires. How long will it take them if they work together?

25 Simplify $\dfrac{2x + 4}{x^2 + 4x + 4} - \dfrac{x}{x + 2}$ and give any restrictions.

26 If 4x = 9y, what is the ratio of x to y?

In problems 27–29, make a quick graph of each equation.

27 $y = x^2 - 4$ **28** $y = \frac{1}{2}x^2 - 4$ **29** $y = 2x^2 - 4$

In problems 30 and 31, simplify.

30 $\dfrac{x}{x - 3} - \dfrac{x - 1}{3 - x}$ **31** $\dfrac{5}{y - 2} + \dfrac{3}{y^2 - 4y + 4}$

32 A boat near the shore is traveling 20 miles per hour slower than a car traveling along the shore road. The boat travels 15 miles in the same time that the car travels 75 miles. What is the rate of each vehicle?

In problems 33–35, simplify each expression and solve each equation.

33 $\dfrac{x}{5} + \dfrac{3x}{10} + \dfrac{1}{2}$ **34** $\dfrac{2x}{3} + \dfrac{x}{4} = \dfrac{5}{6}$ **35** $\dfrac{3}{x} = \dfrac{5}{7x} + \dfrac{1}{4}$

36 The sum of a number and its reciprocal equals twice the product of the number and its reciprocal. Find the number.

37 Simplify $\dfrac{2x}{x + 1} - \dfrac{x}{x - 1}$.

38 If 7b + 10 = 2(B + 5), what is the ratio of B to b?

In problems 39 and 40, simplify and give any restrictions.

39 $\dfrac{x}{2x - 18} - \dfrac{11x}{2x^2 - 14x - 36}$ **40** $\dfrac{6}{x - 3} - \dfrac{1}{x + 3} + \dfrac{2x}{x^2 - 9}$

41 Find the value of x if the area of the rectangle is 72.

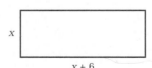

x

x + 6

42 Subtract $\dfrac{11y}{x - 3y}$ from $\dfrac{2x + 5y}{x - 3y}$ and simplify.

43 If $\dfrac{2}{x} = \dfrac{3}{y}$ and $\dfrac{x}{4} = \dfrac{6}{y}$, what is (x, y)?

In problems 44–47, simplify each expression and solve each equation.

44 $\dfrac{x}{x + 1} + \dfrac{2}{x + 2}$

45 $\dfrac{x}{x + 1} = \dfrac{2}{x + 2}$

46 $\dfrac{3}{x^2 + x} - \dfrac{2}{x^2 - x}$

47 $\dfrac{2}{x^2 + x} \div \dfrac{4}{x^2 - x}$

48 When a number is added to the numerator and denominator of $\dfrac{4}{7}$, the resulting fraction equals 0.8. Find the number.

49 Hy Topps jogged 10 miles farther than he walked. He walked at 4 miles per hour and jogged at 6 miles per hour. The total trip took 3 hours. How far did he jog and how far did he walk?

50 Solve $xy = \dfrac{PQZ}{RW}$ for W and give any restrictions.

51 Refer to the graph of mean baseball batting averages.

  a In what year did the mean batting average hit its lowest point? Approximately what was the mean average that year?
  b What is the range of the batting averages?

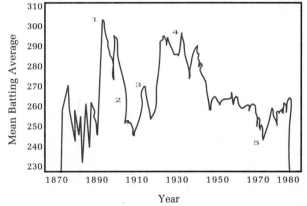

52 If $(-2)^3 = -8$, then what is $(-3)^2$?

53 Copy machine #7347 makes 48 copies per minute. Copy machine #7734 makes 64 copies per minute. The boss needs 50,000 copies of an announcement about Glory Days celebration. For three hours, both machines work together. Then machine #7347 breaks down. It is repaired in 2 hours, but then machine #7734 breaks down and cannot be repaired. If the machines started at 8:00 A.M., when will the job be completed? Calculate your answer to the nearest minute.

54 Max has 80 marbles. Half of them are red. The store sells packs of 3 marbles, each pack containing 1 red marble, 1 blue marble, and 1 green marble. How many packs must Max buy if he wants $\dfrac{2}{5}$ of his marbles to be red and does not want to throw out any marbles?

STEM-AND-LEAF PLOTS AND BOX-AND-WHISKER PLOTS

Objectives

After studying this section, you will be able to
- Draw and interpret stem-and-leaf plots
- Draw and interpret box-and-whisker plots

Stem-and-Leaf Plots

The following data represent the temperatures (in °F) recorded at 1:00 P.M., January 20, 1988, in 25 major U.S. cities.

38, 5, 21, 16, 44, 49, 62, 13, 29, 52, 57, 68, 70, 11, 56, 44, 39, 78, 9, 30, 39, 62, 15, 28, 50

A *stem-and-leaf plot* is a way of displaying such data.

To draw a stem-and-leaf plot, we must first identify the low temperature, 5°, and the high temperature, 78°. We use the tens digits as the *stems* of the plot. We list the stems vertically with a line drawn to their right.

```
        0 |
        1 |
        2 |
        3 |
 Stems  4 |
        5 |
        6 |
        7 |
```

Next we read each piece of data. The first number, 38, has a stem of 3. The units digit, 8, is called its *leaf*. We put the leaf 8 to the right of the stem 3. The second number, 5, has a stem of 0 and a leaf of 5. We put the leaf 5 to the right of the stem 0. If we continue through all the data, we have the plot shown.

```
        0 | 5 9
        1 | 6 3 1 5
        2 | 1 9 8
        3 | 8 9 0 9
 Stems  4 | 4 9 4
        5 | 2 7 6 0
        6 | 2 8 2
        7 | 0 8
            Leaves
```

We rearrange each row of leaves in order from smallest to largest.

```
        0 | 5 9
        1 | 1 3 5 6
        2 | 1 8 9
        3 | 0 8 9 9
 Stems  4 | 4 4 9
        5 | 0 2 6 7
        6 | 2 2 8
        7 | 0 8
            Leaves
```

Below each plot we provide a legend to explain what the numbers mean.

4 | 9 represents a temperature of 49°F on January 20, 1988, at 1:00 P.M. for a major U.S. city.

The stem-and-leaf plot can be converted into a bar graph by rotating the stem-and-leaf plot as shown.

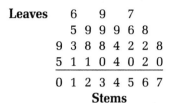

Leaves   6   9   7
            5 9 9 9 6 8
          9 3 8 8 4 2 2 8
          5 1 1 0 4 0 2 0

          0 1 2 3 4 5 6 7
                Stems

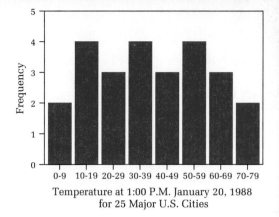

Temperature at 1:00 P.M. January 20, 1988
for 25 Major U.S. Cities

Box-and-Whisker Plots

The data represent the bowling scores of 19 students.

> 81, 85, 91, 96, 105, 110, 113, 127, 136, 143, 148, 149, 151, 160, 162, 168, 180, 184, 219

The low score is 81, and the high score is 219. These scores are called the ***outlier scores*** of the data. The number 143 is the median of the data. Consider the nine scores below 143. Their median is 105. Of the nine scores above 143, the median score is 162.

We will use the two outliers, 81 and 219, the median of the entire data, 143, and the medians of the two halves, 105 and 162, to draw a ***box-and-whisker plot*** for the 19 bowling scores.

First we draw to scale a line that contains the numbers 81, 105, 143, 162, and 219. Then we use the numbers 105, 143, and 162 to draw a *box*. The line segments to the left and right of the box are called the *whiskers* of the plot.

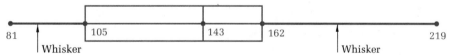

Notice that the box-and-whisker plot is divided into four sections (2 whiskers and 2 boxes). Included within each section is $\frac{1}{4}$, or 25%, of the data.

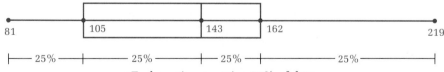

Each section contains 25% of data

The three numbers 105, 143, and 162 divide the data into four sections. Each number is called a ***quartile.*** The lowest number is denoted by Q_1, the second of the three (the median) is denoted by Q_2, and the highest number is denoted by Q_3.

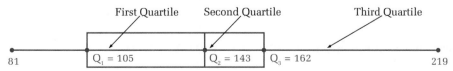

First Quartile   Second Quartile   Third Quartile

$Q_1 = 105$ $Q_2 = 143$ $Q_3 = 162$

Problem   *Draw a box-and-whisker plot for the following data.*
2, 2, 5, 7, 8, 10, 11, 17, 18, 23

Solution   The outlier values are 2 and 23, since they are the smallest and largest values of the data.

We find the median, Q_2, by taking the mean of the two middle scores, 8 and 10. The median is 9. Next, we take the median of all the data below Q_2 to find Q_1. The median of 2, 2, 5, 7, and 8 is 5, so Q_1 is 5.

The five scores above the median Q_2 are 10, 11, 17, 18, 23. The median of this data, Q_3, is 17.

We can use the outliers and Q_1, Q_2, and Q_3 to draw the box-and-whisker plot.

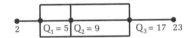

Problem Set

1 As Mr. Al G. Berra graded his class's tests, he wrote down the scores. There were 120 points possible.

85, 49, 92, 113, 102, 88, 99, 118, 66, 75, 111, 108, 75,
68, 88, 105, 90, 115, 107, 90, 75, 99, 102, 78, 56

a Draw a stem-and-leaf plot for the data.
b Mr. Berra believes that the top 6 students should get A's. What should he set as a cutoff score for an A?

2 A consumer group compared prices on several popular electronic items. They collected data on television sets, video recorders, and portable radios. Their box-and-whisker plots are shown.

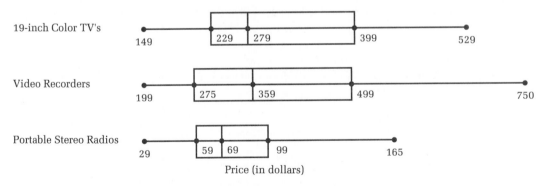

a What range describes the middle 50% of the prices of video recorders?
b What is the range of prices of the cheapest 25% of portable radios?
c What are the quartiles (Q_1, Q_2, and Q_3) for the color TV's?
d Do more radios cost more than $69 or less than $69?

3 The data in the chart represent the number of videotapes rented from Vic's Video Rental during a two-week period.

Week	Sunday	Monday	Tuesday	Wednesday	Thursday	Friday	Saturday
1	89	36	52	55	62	88	97
2	85	30	68	72	61	80	89

a Draw a stem-and-leaf plot for the data.
b Draw a bar graph for the data.
c Why do certain days seem to have a large or small number of rentals?

4 Refer to the box-and-whisker plot.

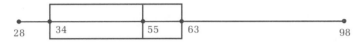

a Determine Q_1, Q_2, and Q_3.
b Determine the range for the data represented.
c Determine the mean, median, and mode for the data.
d Which range contains more data, the range from 28 through 34 or the range from 63 through 98?

5 The following data represent the winning run totals for Apollo High School's baseball games during the 1987 season.

$$6, 3, 9, 2, 11, 7, 5, 7, 9, 3, 4, 8, 10, 7, 1, 4, 6, 8, 5,$$
$$10, 4, 3, 7, 9, 8, 4$$

a Find the outliers of the data.
b Find Q_1, Q_2, and Q_3.
c Draw a box-and-whisker plot of the data.

6 The data represent the test scores for two algebra classes.

4th-Period Algebra Class	Stems	8th-Period Algebra Class
8 7 0	9	3 4 6
9 7 7 6	8	0 1 1 1 2 7
9 8 8 7 5 5 5 3 2	7	0 2 3 3 4 6 9
7 4 2 2 2 0	6	4 7 8
7 1	5	
	4	3
	3	
	2	
	1	
	0	

a Find the mean, median, and mode for each class.
b Draw a box-and-whisker plot for each class.
c Combine the data in a single stem-and-leaf plot.
d Find the mean, median, and mode for the stem-and-leaf plot.
e Draw a box-and-whisker plot for this stem-and-leaf plot.

CHAPTER SUMMARY

CONCEPTS AND PROCEDURES

After studying this chapter, you should be able to
- Solve problems involving ratios (12.1)
- Understand proportions and their properties (12.1)
- Understand scale factors (12.2)
- Convert units (12.2)
- Use proportions to solve similar triangle problems (12.2)
- Solve direct-variation and inverse-variation problems (12.3)
- Simplify rational expressions (12.4)
- Determine the restrictions on rational expressions (12.4)
- Multiply and divide rational expressions (12.5)
- Solve rate problems (12.6)
- Solve work problems (12.6)
- Solve rational equations (12.6)
- Add and subtract rational expressions (12.7)
- Draw and interpret stem-and-leaf plots (12.8)
- Draw and interpret box-and-whisker plots (12.8)

VOCABULARY

box-and-whisker plot (12.8)
constant of variation (12.3)
direct variation (12.3)
extremes (12.1)
inverse variation (12.3)
means (12.1)
outlier scores (12.8)

proportion (12.1)
quartile (12.8)
ratio (12.1)
rational expression (12.4)
restriction (12.4)
similar triangles (12.2)
stem-and-leaf plot (12.8)

REVIEW PROBLEMS

In problems 1–3, solve each proportion.

1 $\dfrac{x}{3} = \dfrac{8}{9}$

2 $\dfrac{12}{w} = \dfrac{7}{3}$

3 $\dfrac{12}{t} = \dfrac{16}{t+1}$

4 Multiply $\dfrac{x}{4x^2 + 2x} \cdot \dfrac{3x+6}{9}$ and simplify.

5 The altitude of a hot-air balloon varies inversely as the number of passengers. If a balloon carrying 5 people floats at a height of 350 feet, how high could the balloon float with 2 fewer passengers?

6 Solve $\dfrac{3}{x+1} + \dfrac{3x}{4} = 3$ for x.

7 Chip can mow a lawn in 45 minutes, and Biff can mow the same lawn in 1 hour. How long will it take to mow the lawn if they work together?

8 Write an equation to indicate that x and y vary inversely.

9 If 3 zorks cost 5 rallods, how many rallods are needed to buy 17 zorks?

In problems 10 and 11, give the restrictions on each equation.

10 $\dfrac{5}{x+1} = \dfrac{9}{x^2 - 2x}$

11 $\dfrac{a}{b} \div \dfrac{c}{d} = \dfrac{a}{b} \cdot \dfrac{d}{c}$

In problems 12–14, simplify each expression and give any restrictions.

12 $\dfrac{1}{a} - \dfrac{3}{a} + \dfrac{7}{a}$

13 $\dfrac{b}{3} + \dfrac{4}{b}$

14 $\dfrac{c+3}{2c^2 + 6c} - \dfrac{4c+5}{c}$

15 Given $\triangle ABC \sim \triangle ADE$. If BC = 4, DE = 3, and AD = 5, what is AB?

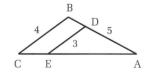

16 Divide $\dfrac{9}{x + 3} \div \dfrac{27}{x^2 + 6x + 9}$.

In problems 17–19, simplify and give any restrictions.

17 $\dfrac{2x^2 - 13x - 24}{6x^2 + 7x - 6}$

18 $\dfrac{4x^3 - 16x}{9x^2(x - 2)}$

19 $\dfrac{3y^4(5y - 5)}{15y^3(1 - y)}$

In problems 20 and 21, convert.

20 4500 milliliters to liters

21 1 gallon to liters

22 Shelli walks 3 miles per hour faster than Randie. Shelli can walk as far in 2 hours as Randie walks in 4.4 hours. How far can Shelli walk in 2 hours?

23 Hob E. Ist wants to make a model of the United States Coast Guard's tall ship *Eagle*, which is 267 feet long. His display case has shelves 24 inches long. What scale should he use so that the model will be as large as possible and still fit in the display case?

24 What is the constant of variation if $m = 14$ when $w = 9$ and if m and w vary directly? If m and w vary inversely?

In problems 25 and 26, solve for x**.**

25 $\dfrac{2x - 6}{7} = \dfrac{2}{x + 3}$

26 $\dfrac{x^2 - 4x + 4}{x - 2} = \dfrac{9x + 9}{3(x + 1)}$

27 If $\frac{3}{4}$ pound of peanuts costs $2.75, how much should 2 pounds of peanuts cost?

In problems 28–31, simplify and give any restrictions.

28 $\dfrac{6xy^2}{(2y)^3} \cdot \dfrac{y}{8x}$

29 $\dfrac{y(2x - 5)}{4y^4} \cdot \dfrac{y^3}{5 - 2x}$

30 $\dfrac{(x - 3)^2}{4} \div \dfrac{x^2 - 6x + 9}{2(x - 3)}$

31 $\dfrac{x^2 - 8x}{x^2 - 6x + 16} \div \dfrac{3x}{9(x - 2)}$

32 Ernest Miler can run directly from point A to point C in 45 minutes. If he runs at the same rate, how long will it take him to run from point A to point B and then to point C?

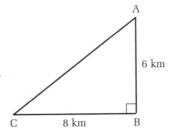

33 Fill in the missing rational expression.

$$\dfrac{x}{x + 1} \div \dfrac{?}{?} = \dfrac{x + 2}{x + 3}$$

34 Hussain drove 10 miles per hour faster than Ashvin. Consequently, Hussain drove 330 miles in the same amount of time it took Ashvin to drive 270 miles. Find the speeds of Hussain and Ashvin.

35 Tippie K. New was paddling her canoe in a 2-mile-per-hour current. She paddled 3 miles upstream, then turned around and returned to her starting point. The total trip took $1\frac{1}{8}$ hours. How fast was she paddling?

36 Multiply $\dfrac{x^2 + x - 6}{x^2 - 9} \cdot \dfrac{x^2 - 5x + 6}{x^2 - 4x + 4}$ and simplify.

In problems 37 and 38, solve for x.

37 $\dfrac{9}{x} + \dfrac{22}{x^2 - 4x} = \dfrac{x}{x - 4}$

38 $\dfrac{3}{5x} - \dfrac{1}{3x} = \dfrac{4}{3x^2}$

39 Felix can ride his bike 20 miles in 1.5 hours. Oscar can ride 25 miles in 1.5 hours. If Felix and Oscar ride together, how far can they go in 1.5 hours?

40 Solve $\dfrac{x + 1}{\sqrt{3}} = \dfrac{\sqrt{3}}{x}$ for x. Express the answer in standard radical form.

41 If $\dfrac{3}{x} = \dfrac{5}{y}$ and $xy = 1$, what is (x, y)?

In problems 42 and 43, simplify.

42 $\dfrac{x + 2}{(x + 3)x + 2}$

43 $\dfrac{x + 1}{(3x + 4)x + 1}$

44 Alex can wash 20 dishes in 8 minutes. Jason washes 30 dishes in 9 minutes. Working at separate sinks, how long would it take them to wash 300 dishes? Working at separate sinks, how many could they wash in an hour?

In problems 45 and 46, simplify and give any restrictions. Write your answer in simplest form.

45 $\dfrac{9x}{3x - 6} - \dfrac{9x^2}{x^2 - 4}$

46 $\dfrac{6}{x - 5} + \dfrac{25}{x^2 - 25}$

47 Pamela and Frances want to paint the kitchen ceiling. They have only one ladder. Pamela can do the job by herself in 2 hours, while it takes Frances 2.5 hours. They want to make certain that each works the same amount of time, but they cannot work together. How long should Pamela work before she stops to let Frances finish?

1 A mechanic and an apprentice install an alternator for $75. Their wages are in the ratio of 11:4. How much does each earn?

2 Select two points (x_1, y_1) and (x_2, y_2) on the graph of $y = \frac{3}{4}x + 9$. Find the ratio of $y_2 - y_1$ to $x_2 - x_1$.

3 One hundred Lucky Cluck split fryer chickens were weighed, and the results were displayed as a box-and-whisker plot.

42   54   64   69   73

Weights of Split Fryers (in ounces)

a Find the median weight.
b Based on the plot, if you chose a fryer at random, what is the probability that it would weigh 3 pounds 6 ounces or less? (Remember: 1 pound = 16 ounces.)

4 Roger's car can go 10 miles per hour faster than Leo's car. In the same time that Leo drives 180 miles, Roger drives 210 miles. Find the speed of each car.

In problems 5–7, simplify and give any restrictions.

5 $\dfrac{x}{x + 5} \div \dfrac{x + 6}{x + 7}$

6 $\dfrac{x^2 - x}{x^2 - 1} \cdot \dfrac{x + 1}{x^2}$

7 $x - \dfrac{2x}{x^2 - 1} + \dfrac{3}{x + 1}$

8 Each inch of a scale model automobile represents 16 inches on the actual automobile. Find the length of the automobile in feet if the length of the model is $9\frac{1}{4}$ inches.

9 The cost of a pizza varies directly as the area of the pizza. If a pizza that is 12 inches in diameter costs $8.10, how much is a pizza that is 16 inches in diameter?

10 The speeds (revolutions per minute) of two pulleys are inversely proportional to their diameters.

a Write a formula to describe this relationship.
b Find S_2.

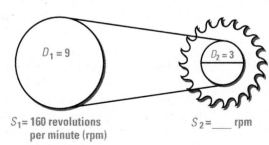

$S_1 = 160$ revolutions per minute (rpm)

$S_2 = \_\_\_$ rpm

Multiplication and Division Properties of Inequality (5.1)

If both sides of an inequality are multiplied or divided by the same positive number, then the result is an inequality having the same order. If both sides of an inequality are multiplied or divided by the same negative number, then the result is an inequality having reversed order.

Positives

If $a > b$ and $c > 0$, then $ac > bc$ and $\frac{a}{c} > \frac{b}{c}$.

If $a < b$ and $c > 0$, then $ac < bc$ and $\frac{a}{c} < \frac{b}{c}$.

Negatives

If $a > b$ and $c < 0$, then $ac < bc$ and $\frac{a}{c} < \frac{b}{c}$.

If $a < b$ and $c < 0$, then $ac > bc$ and $\frac{a}{c} > \frac{b}{c}$.

Multiplication Property of Equality (2.3, 2.6)

If $a = b$, then $ac = bc$. If $a = b$ and $c = d$, then $ac = bd$.

Multiplication Property of Exponents (9.2)

When we multiply two numbers with the same base, we add the exponents. The base remains the same. $a^m \cdot a^n = a^{m+n}$

Multiplication Property of -1 (3.7)

$a(-1) = -a$ and $-1(a) = -a$

Multiplication Property of Zero (2.6, 3.7)

$0(a) = a(0) = 0$; $a \cdot 0 = 0$ and $0 \cdot a = 0$

Multiplicative Identity Property (2.6, 3.7)

There is a number 1, called the multiplicative identity, such that $1 \cdot a = a \cdot 1 = a$, and $a \cdot 1 = a$ and $1 \cdot a = a$.

Multiplicative Inverse Property (2.6, 3.7)

For every number a, $a \neq 0$, there is a number $\frac{1}{a}$, called the multiplicative inverse (or reciprocal) of a, such that $a \cdot \frac{1}{a} = 1$ and $\frac{1}{a} \cdot a = 1$.

Power to a Power Property (9.2)

When we raise a power to a power, we multiply the exponents. The base remains the same. $\left(a^m\right)^n = a^{mn}$

Property of the Opposite of a Quantity (3.7)

$$-(a + b) = -1(a + b)$$
$$= (-a) + (-b)$$
$$-(a - b) = -1(a - b)$$
$$= -a + b$$

Property of Squares of Real Numbers (5.5)

For all real numbers a, $a^2 \geq 0$.

Quotient Property (2.6)

$a \cdot \frac{1}{b} = \frac{a}{b}$

Reflexive Property of Equality (2.6)

$a = a$

Substitution Property (2.6)

If $a = b$, then either one can be substituted for the other.

Subtraction Property of Equality (2.3, 2.6)

If $a = b$, then $a - c = b - c$; if $a = b$ and $c = d$, then $a - c = b - d$.

Symmetric Property of Equality (2.6)

If $a = b$, then $b = a$.

Transitive Properties of Inequality (3.7, 5.5)

If $a < b$ and $b < c$, then $a < c$. If $a > b$ and $b > c$, then $a > c$.

Transitive Property of Equality (2.6)

If $a = b$ and $b = c$, then $a = c$.

Trichotomy Property (3.7, 5.4)

Given any two numbers a and b, one of the following must be true: $a > b$ or $a < b$ or $a = b$.

Zero Product Property (2.3, 2.6)

If $ab = 0$, then $a = 0$ or $\mathbf{b} = 0$.

TABLE OF FORMULAS

A rectangle has length _l_ and width _w_.

1 Area $= lw$

2 Perimeter $= 2l + 2w$

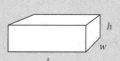

3 Volume of a rectangular prism $= lwh$

A circle has radius _r_ and diameter _d_.

4 Area $= \pi r^2$

5 Circumference $= 2\pi r = \pi d$

A square has four equal sides, _s_.

6 Area $= s^2$

7 Perimeter $= 4s$

A triangle has sides _a_, _b_, _c_ and height _h_ and angles A, B, C.

8 Area $= \dfrac{bh}{2}$

9 Perimeter $= a + b + c$

10 $\angle A + \angle B + \angle C = 180°$

A right triangle has legs l_1 and l_2 and hypotenuse _h_.

11 Pythagorean Theorem: 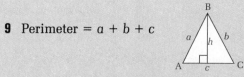 $l_1{}^2 + l_2{}^2 = h^2$

12 Distance $=$ rate $\cdot$ time $(d = rt)$

13 Average of a set of numbers $= \dfrac{\text{sum of all numbers}}{\text{number of numbers}}$

14 Probability $= \dfrac{\text{number of winners}}{\text{number of possibilities}}$

SELECTED ANSWERS

1.1 Getting Started

Warm-up Exercises

1 21 **2** 15 **3** 32.4 **4** 54 **5** $\frac{1}{2}$ or 1 to 2 or 1:2 **6** CD
7 True, $\frac{3}{5} + \frac{5}{8} = \frac{49}{40}$ **8** 8.68

Exercises and Problems

9 $\frac{1}{24}$ **11** 125 **13** 2.118 **15** 135.201 cm²; 51.86 cm
16 a $4.13 **b** $63.08 **c** $9.46 **17 a** $7\frac{1}{2}$ in. **b** $20\frac{1}{2}$ in.
19 37 **21** ≈0.1818182 **23** 4.5 **24** 4.5 in.³
25 Displays error (E) **27** Alternates 6 and 2 in the display **29 a** $1.7 million

b

Profit in Millions

c 2
30 a $94.34 **b** $5.66

1.2 Expressing Numbers

Warm-up Exercises

1 6^5 **2** x^5 **3** 6^9 **4** $(A = \frac{1}{2}bh)$ 402.5 mm² **5 a** 25.8 sq
cm **b** 82.35 sq mm **c** 28.47 sq in. **6** $0.78, $12.71
7 a ≈58 sec **b** ≈57.89 sec **8** Answers will vary.
a These are usually timed on a measured course.
b The pace is slow. If it were computed to tenths or more, the answer would be 0. **c** By exact timing and by estimation **d** Cannot be answered by information given **e** No **f** Man and perhaps quarterhorse and greyhound

Exercises and Problems

9 a 13 is prime **b** 2^5 **c** $2 \cdot 3^2 \cdot 11$ **10 a** 15 **b** 125
c 15 **11** 253 **13** 10 **15** 1, 17 **17** z = 10 **18** $140
19 a 32 **b** 32

20

x	1	2	3	4	5
3x = 2	5	8	11	14	17

21 7.19 **22** d = 5 **23** 31 **24** ≈14%

1.3 Beginning to Work With Algebraic Expressions

Warm-up Exercises

1 17 **2** 28 **3** −625 **4** 8 **5** 17 **6** 1440 **7** 38 **8** 4.8
9 a 11 **b** $5 + 6\sqrt{11}$ or 24.9 **10** 10

Exercises and Problems

11 n + 4 **13** $\frac{n+5}{6}$ **14** 48 **15** The sum of 5 and x
17 2 cubed times 7 **19** The sum of x and 2 divided by y **21** 23 **22** 31.5 cm **23 a** 40% to 100% **b** 72.2%
c 73% **24 a** 13 in. **b** 5 in.
25 32 **27** 32 **28** 32 **29** 4 **31** 19 **32 a** 2h **b** 5h
c 8h **33** 47.3 **35** 9

36

x	1	2	3	4	5
3x + 2	1	4	7	10	13

37 25

38 (5, 14) **39** No, the measure of angle P is 89.57°.

1.4 Understanding Equations and Inequalities

Warm-up Exercises

1 = **2** > **3** < **4** = **5** k = 19 **6** x = 25 **7** x = 2
8 x = 2 **9** x = 8 **10** x = 13

Exercises and Problems

11 Yes **13** True **14** No **15** A ≈ 132.73
16 a 6x + 10 = 60 **b** $2x^2 + 10x = 100$ **17** 3, 5, 7
19 7 **21** 4n + 6 **22** a = 8.0826 **23** x ≈ 3.21
24 y = 23 **25** 48° **26** y = 43 **27** $S_{10} = 1440$

28

.70473	0.705	0.70	0.7
.73	0.737	0.74	0.7
$\frac{7}{16}$	0.438	0.44	0.4
$\frac{5}{7}$	0.714	0.71	0.7
$\sqrt{7}$	2.646	2.65	2.6

29

Cereal	Calories	Grams Protein	Grams Fat	Mg. Sodium
Oat Way	160	8	4	210
Wheaties	150	7	3	170
Rice Crunchies	170	6	2	340

30 2 and 5 **31** 153.9 ft² **32** A ≈ 498.8 cm² **33** 3
35 x ≈ 22.90 **36** $x_1 = 6.5$ or $\frac{13}{2}$ **37** No **38** 162.63
39 No **40** 3x = 22.5, x = 7.5 **41 a** m = 2
b m = −4 **42** Answers may vary. 3 < x < 3.8
43 Sometimes

1.5 Ways to Represent Data

Warm-up Exercises

1 {6} **2** {2, 4} **3** {4} **4** {4} **5** w = 16, x = 8, y = 6,
z = 42 **6** 40 **7** Yes; x = 2 **8** Yes **9** (Tuesday, 40°)
(Wednesday, 55°) (Thursday, 35°) (Friday, 45°)

Exercises and Problems

11 Matrix **13** x = 111 **15** x = 3 **17** True **19** False
20 b = 9 **21** {20} **23** {3, 5, 6} **24 a** The number of

minnows Al, Bob, and Carl each bought **b** The number of worms Bob bought **c** 21 **25 a** 5 **b** 47 or 48 **c** The store would give away 90 discs **d** $0.18 **27** x = 3 **29** x_2 = 4 **31** y = 14 **32** $\frac{1}{20}$ of the wall **33** Yes **34** No **35** x = 3, y = 1, z = 2 **37** x = 4 or x = 0

1.6 Graphing

Warm-up Exercises

1 a (1, 2), I **b** (2, 6), I **c** (−3, 4), II **d** (−2, −2), III **e** (0, 5) **f** (1, −3), IV **g** (−3, 0) **h** (3, 0) **2 a** E **b** Origin **c** F **3 a** −3 **b** 4 **4** (3, 3)

Exercises and Problems

5

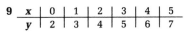

x	1	2	3	4
y	1	4	7	10

6 64 **7 a** Juan **b** $310 **c** $205 **d** Juan **8** y = $\frac{14}{3}$ or $3\frac{5}{3}$

9

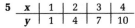

x	0	1	2	3	4	5
y	2	3	4	5	6	7

10 $\frac{1}{30}$ **11** x + 10 = 16 **12 a** (3, 2) **b** 7 units **13** 2880 **14** x = 14 **15** $\sqrt{5}$ **16** No; $2\frac{3}{4} \neq \frac{1}{2}(3\frac{1}{4}) + 1$

17

x	0	1	2	3
y	3	3.5	4	4.5

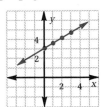

19 (3, −2), (−3, 2) **20** x = 5, y = 15, z = 20
21 The point (2, 9) does not lie on a line that fits the remaining points.

22 (3, 5)

23

x	4	6	8	10	12
y	0	1.414	2	2.449	2.828

1.7 Translating Between Words and Symbols

Warm-up Exercises

1 5x **2** n + 4 **3** n − 6 **4** $\frac{n+6}{4}$ **5** $(\frac{n}{3})^2$ **6** Answers

---

may vary. Half of the sum of two numbers. **7** Fifteen less than a number. **8** Three times a number plus six.

Exercises and Problems

9 a 7 − x **b** $(x + 4)^2$ **10** m = $\frac{2}{3}$ **11** x + x + 17 **13** x = 4 **15** 25q cents **16** $\frac{1}{y}$ **17** 3.7 **19**

20 a {2} **b** {0, 1, 2} **21 a** x(x − 8) **b** $\frac{1}{2}$x + $\sqrt{17}$ **22** $\frac{p}{b}$ **23 a** x + 8 + 14 = 38 **b** x = 16 **24** (−2, −8) **25** 33

26 D | 7 | 11 | 11 |

27 x = 4, y = $\frac{1}{2}$ **28 a** (2, 1), (6, 1), (6, 4), (2, 4) **b** 4; 3 **29** $\frac{1}{12}$ or .08$\overline{33}$ **30** c **31** (4, 3) **32** 30

1.8 Probability

Warm-up Exercises

1 $\frac{3}{5}$ **2** $\frac{4}{10}$ or $\frac{2}{5}$ **3** 0 **4** $\frac{5}{8}$ **5** $\frac{3}{6}$ or $\frac{1}{2}$ **6 a** $\frac{3}{5}$ **b** 0

Exercises and Problems

7 $\frac{5}{6}$ or .8$\overline{3}$ **9** $\frac{2}{3}$ or .6$\overline{6}$ **11** $\frac{7}{10}$ or .7 **13** 1 **14** b **15** 6
16 a Yes **b** (5, −1) **c** $\frac{1}{2}$ **17** 3$\frac{1}{2}$ **18** −2.6 **19** $\frac{3}{10}$
20 a 2.3 cm² **b** $\frac{1}{4}$ or .25 **21 a** $\frac{2}{9}$ or .2$\overline{2}$ **b** $\frac{2}{3}$ or .6$\overline{6}$
22 Sometimes. If x < 0 or x > 1, then x² > x. But if x is between 0 and 1, then x > x².

Review Problems

1 11 **2** {5, 7} **3** y = 2 **5** x_1 = 12 **6** 14 **7 a** 77.5% **b** 95% **8** ≈3.32 **9** Quadrant II **10** y = 39 **11** 4 **12** Yes **13** 475.3 m² **14** 2³ · 5

15

x	−2	−1	0	1	2
y	1	2	3	4	5

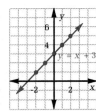

16 2x + 4 **17** x − 4 **18** (5, 9) **19** q = 16, r = 8.5, s = 1, t = 12 **21** r = 4 **22** 24 **23** 10d cents **24** 3280 mi **25** 2x + 3 = 39 **26** 44.3 **27** $\frac{2}{5}$ **29** {2, 3} **30** 25 yards **31** d ≈ 34.21 **32** m ≈ −6.56 **33** y ≈ 1016.34 **35** 12 **36** $\frac{1}{2}$ **37 a** The number of shingles needed to build the contemporary doghouse **b** The number of boards, shingles, and nails needed to build the split-level doghouse **c** 200 **39** 47 **41** 12 **42** $16.80 **43** (5, 2) **44** $\frac{1}{31}, \frac{30}{31}$ **45** $\frac{1}{6}$

2.1 Algebraic Basics

Warm-up Exercises

1 Equation **2** Inequality **3** Expression **4** Inequality **5** Expression **6** Equation **7** Expression **8** Inequality **9** Equation **10** $15x_3$ **11** $8x^2 - 7x$ **12** 37 **13** $4y^2 + y - 36$ **14** Yes **15** Yes **16** No

Exercises and Problems

17 $2x^3 + 3x$ **19** No **20** $x - 7 = 12$ **21 a** $x + 11 = 27$ **b** $3x = 12$ **22** No **23** {0, 3} **24** 3 and 10 **25** $20.905x + 3.8y$ **26** No solution **27** $104\frac{17}{18}$ or ≈ 104.94 **29** $5n$ **31** $122 + 5n$ **32** Yes **33** 3 **35** $4x + 8x^3 + 10y^3 - 2x^2$ **37** Any real number **39** $2x + 3y = 83$ **40** $x^2 + 3 = 28$ **41** $\frac{1}{4}$ **42** No **43** {(2, 8), (0, 2) (1, 5)} **44** $2x + 3y = 83$ **45 a** $P = 35x$ **b** 119

46 Answers may vary in table.

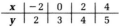

x	-2	0	2	4
y	2	3	4	5

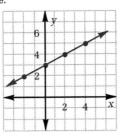

47 No **49** 18 **50** {1, 2, 3} **51** 6 and 13 **53** $x = 2$ **54** $\frac{1}{14}$ or ≈ 0.071

55 $\begin{bmatrix} 4 & 64 \\ 16 & 4 \end{bmatrix}$ **56** 4:3 or $\frac{4}{3}$ **57** 988 **58** {(0, any real number), (any real number, 0)} **59** {2, 3}

2.2 Solving Equations

Warm-up Exercises

1 Subtracting 47.1 **2** Adding 76 **3** Dividing by $\frac{2}{5}$ or multiplying by $\frac{5}{2}$ **4** Multiplying by $\frac{3}{2}$ or dividing by $\frac{2}{3}$ **5** $m = 104$ **6** $y = 47$ **7** $z = 22$ **8** $m = 44$ **9** $s = 603$ **10** $x = 16$ **11** $t = 17$ **12** 11 **13** $x = 52$

Exercises and Problems

15 $4x^2 + 10x$ **17** $4x_1 + 11y$ **19** $6.2 + 2x$ **20** $30.\overline{3}$ or $\frac{91}{3}$ **21** 15 people **22 a** $x + 2 + 2x + 3 + 3y - 4$, $3x + 3y + 1$ **b** 31 **23** $x = 0$ **25** $y = 2.38$ **27** $y = 61$ **29** 14 **30** 13 **31** $x = 2.45$ **33** $x = 16$ **35** $y = 24$

37 $x = 0$ **39** $m = 3124.85$ **41** $x = 9$ **42** $\frac{1}{3}$ **43** Width = 29 in.; length = 58 in. **44** 1014 mi. **45** 48 mph **46** 2659 trips each **47** $x = b - a$ **48** $x = \frac{c - b}{a}$ **49** $x = 45$ **50 a** 6 **b** 18 **51** $\frac{26}{25}$ **52** 45 **53** $x = 0$ or $x = 3$

2.3 Properties of Equality

Warm-up Exercises

1 Subtraction Property of Equality **2** Multiplication Property of Equality **3** Zero Product Property **4** Addition Property of Equality **5** Division Property of Equality **6** Multiplication or Division Property of Equality **7** $x = 0$ **8** $x = 0$ or $x = 2$ **9** $x = 4$ or $x = 2$ **10** $x = 0$ or $x = $ any real numbers provided $y = 0$

Exercises and Problems

11 Subtract. Prop. of Equal.; $x = 288$ **13** Add. Prop. of Equal.; $x = 53.1$ **15** Mult. or Div. Prop. of Equal.; $x = 27$ **17** Add. Prop. of Equal., Div. Prop. of Equal.; $x = 27$ **19** Add like terms, Div. Prop. of Equal.; $x = 101$ **20** $\frac{2}{3}$ **21** $x = 9$ **23** $21x + 12$ **25** $\frac{3}{4}x$ **27** $x = 0$ **29** 18 **30** $w = 14$ cm **31 a** $500x$ **b** 6500 **c** 85 **33** $y = 0$ or $y = 13.2$ **35** $x = 0$ **37** $x = 4$ or $x = 7$ **38** 1 **39** $x = 2042$ **41** $z = 6$; Add. Prop. of Equal.; Div. Prop. of Equal. **43** $x = 274$; Mult. or Div. Prop. of Equal. **45** $x = 0$ or $x = 7$; Zero Product Property **47** $m = 1.1$; Combine like terms, Div. Prop. of Equal. **48** $x + .30 (400) = 700$ or $x + 120 = 700$; 580 **49** $\approx .36$ **50 a** $\frac{1}{10}$ or .1 **b** $\frac{19}{100}$ or .19 **c** $\frac{271}{1000}$ or .271 **51** $\frac{2}{3}$ **52** 15 **53** $x \approx 3.65$

2.4 The Substitution and Distributive Properties

Warm-up Exercises

1 $5 + y = 15$ **2** $8 + 3y = 11$ **3** $2y + 3 = 9$ **4** $5y - 4 = 6$ **5** $2x - 2y$ **6** $2y$ **7** $y^2 - 2y$ **8** $y(2y + 5)$ **9** $10x$ **10** $4x + 12$ **11** $x(x + 9)$ **12** $3y^2 + 4y$ **13** $y = 8.25$ **14** $y = 8.25$

Exercises and Problems

15 $x = 5$ **17** $y = \frac{29}{4}$ **19** a; c; h **20** 6 **21** $6y + 24$ **23** $(8 + 6)n$ or $14n$ **25** 220 seconds **26** $x = 3.8$ **27** $x = 13$ **29** $x = 17$ **31** 144 **33** 1 **35** $\frac{1}{4}$ or .25 **37** $x = 3$ **39** $p = 0$ **41** $x = 20.\overline{6}$ **43** $x = 3.25$ **45** $8x + 32$ **47** $x = 9$ **49** $w = 0$ **51** $x = 18$ **53** $11y + 15$ **55** 0 **56** $y = x*(3*x + 7)$ **57** $x = 9$ **59** $15x + 9$ **60** $x = 10$ **61** $x = \frac{4}{3}$ or $x = -\frac{5}{2}$ **63** $x = 0$ or $x = 3$ **65** Yes **66** $1.75 **67 a** $\approx 68\%$ **b** 4 **c** No

2.5 Applications of Equation Solving

Warm-up Exercises

1 a $50t$ mi **b** $385 - 50t$ mi **c** $385 - 50t = 35$ **d** 7 hr
2 $55h + 3.5m$

Exercises and Problems

3 a \$68; \$114; \$183 **b** $23y + 45$ **c** $160 = 23y + 45$
d 5 yd **4 a** \$57 **b** $24 + 16.5h$ **c** $65.25 = 24 + 16.5h$
d 2 hr 30 min or 2.5 hr **5 a** \$685; \$1320; \$3225
b $635x + 50$ **c** $c = 635x + 50$ **d** \$4495 **e** \$2069
6 a 36 mi; 60 mi **b** $12h$ **c** $90 = 12h$ **d** 7 hr 30 min
or 7.5 hr **7 a** \$172.25 **b** \$257.25 **c** $42.5b + 2.25$
d $1149.75 = 42.5b + 2.25$ **e** 27 **8 a** 140 ft; 168 ft; 189
ft **b** $7r + 70$ **c** $280 = 7r + 70$ **d** 30 rows/side or 60
rows total **e** 3600 **9** Barb was charged \$7.86 per
package instead of \$7.68 (numbers transposed)
10 a 21,439 ft **b** $10,000 + 123x$ **c** ≈ 203.25 sec
11 30 **12 a** \$204 **b** $(s - 45)12$ **c** 64 mph
13 a $3.50 + 0.75x$ **b** \$9.50 **c** 15 toppings
14 a ≈ 172.4 mph **b** ≈ 161.2 mph **c** 200 mph
15 a 23 **b** $0.65y$ **c** 60 **16 a** 17 or 18 **b** 54
c $4x + 0.35x$ or $4.35x$ **17 a** 8.5 mi **b** 7 mi
c $\frac{r}{6} + \frac{w}{15} = 10$

2.6 Formal Properties

Warm-up Exercises

1 Commutative Property of Addition **2** Multiplicative
Inverse Property **3** Commutative Property of
Multiplication **4** Commutative Property of Addition
5 Associative Property of Addition **6** Multiplication
Property of Equality **7** Addition Property of Equality
8 Substitution Property of Equality

Exercises and Problems

9 $x + (p + q)$ **11** Dist. Prop. of Mult. over Add.
13 $8x$ **15** $(4y) \cdot 3$ **17** Distrib. Prop. of Mult. over Add.
19 Zero Product Property **20 a** Comm. Prop. of Add.
b Dist. Prop. of Mult. over Add. **c** Addition; Mult.
Iden. Prop. **21** Comm. Prop. of Add. **23** Comm. Prop.
of Mult. **25** Trans. Prop. of Equal. **27** Assoc. Prop. of
Add. **29 a** Dist. Prop. of Mult. over Add. **b** Addition
c Mult. Prop. of Eq. **d** Assoc. Prop. of Mult. **e** Mult.
Iden. Prop. **31** $x = 0$ or $x = \frac{9}{2}$ **32** $y = 78$; Sub. Prop.,
Div. Prop. **33** $x = 4$ **34 a** $19.95d + 0.12m$ **b** \$142.59
c 725 mi **35** $6 - 1 \neq 1 - 6$ **37** $10 \div 5 \neq 5 \div 10$
38 Dist. Prop. of Mult. over Add. **39** a and e
40 a 90; 63.52; 16,916 **b** Yes; No **c** Yes, 0 **d** $0, \frac{1}{2}$
e No; $(4 \cdot a) * (4 \cdot x) = 16 \cdot (a * x)$

Review Problems

1 {7} **3 a** $3x = 12$ **b** $x = 4$ **c** $33.\overline{3}\%$ **5** $q = 37.57$
7 $9 + \frac{28}{15}c$ **9** $3w + 15$ **11** $x = 120$ **12 a** $6x + 6 = 84$
b $x = 13$ **c** 29 **13** $y = 0$ or $y = 15$ **15** $y = 6$
17 $2.2n + 16.1$ **19** $9u^2 - 6u_2 + 7^2$ **21** $x = 33$ **23** 45

---

24 a \$167.50 **b** $35h + 45$ **c** $141.25 = 35h + 45$
d 2.75 hr or 2 hr 45 min **25** $s = 1$ **27** $y = 5$
29 $f = 2$; $v = 8$ **30** 23 **31** Distrib. Prop. of Mult. over
Add. **33** Comm. Prop. of Add. **35** Div. Prop. of Equal.
37 $\frac{2}{17}$ or ≈ 0.12 **38 a** $3x + 3y = 42$ **b** $x = \frac{13}{2}$ or 6.5
39 $11m + 9n$ **41** $17r + 11q$ **43** $30x + 14x^2$
44 a $n + 5$ **b** $n + 15$ **c** $n + 15$ **d** $n + 5$
e $0.05n + 0.10(n + 15) + 0.25(n + 5)$
f $5.95 = 0.05n + 0.10(n + 15) + 0.25(n + 5)$ **45** 861
46 a Beemer, 14 min **b** $8\frac{1}{3}$ mi **c** 57 min **47** \$130.23
48 a $\frac{5}{6}$ **b** Yes; because $\frac{1}{a} + \frac{1}{b} = \frac{1}{b} + \frac{1}{a}$ **c** No; $\frac{1}{a}$
cannot $= 0$ **d** $\frac{1}{2}$ **e** $\sqrt{2}$

3.1 The Number Line

Warm-up Exercises

1 E **2** D **3** B **4** A **5** F **6** C **7** True **8** False **9** True
10 True **11** False **12** True

Exercises and Problems

13 Integer, Real, Rational **15** Rational, Real
17 Integer, Real, Rational **19** Rational, Real
21 Irrational, Real **23** Rational, Real **25** 4 degrees
lower

27

29

30 14 to the left **31** 246 ft **32 a** 18 **b** -36 **c** 24
d -18 **33** 0 **35** $3\frac{1}{3}$ **37** Answers will vary.
38 a $\{-3, -2, -1, 0, 1, 2, 3\}$ **b** $\frac{5}{12}$ **c** $\frac{5}{66}$ **39** $5d + 10$
41 $16f + 36$ **43** $16d^2 + 24d^3$ **45** $9.2h + 17.53k$
47 \$42.50; $15.5 + 0.75r = 42.50$; $r = 36$ games
49 $x = 0$ or $x = -5$ **51** Comm. Prop. of Add.
52-56

57 2.6 **59** $-\pi$ **61** $\frac{-1}{200}$ **63** $\frac{1}{4}$ **64** \$11 **65 a** 7°F
b -10°F **67** $x = 170$ **69** $x = 75$ **71** $x = 87$ **72** A:
$-2\frac{7}{8}$; B: -1.6; C: $-\frac{1}{3}$; D: $\frac{3}{4}$; E: 2.2; F: 3.75 **73** -8 **75** 9
77 26 **78** The Irons will win with a force of 3
pounds to the right. **79 a** (4, 5) **b** $(-3, -1)$
c (4, -1)
80 a

b $x + x + (x + 5) + (x + 5) = 40$ or $4x + 10 = 40$;
$x = \frac{15}{2}$ mm or 7.5 mm **81** $x = 3$; $y = 7$ **82 a** 26

minutes **b** Mileage markers from a certain location.
c 60 mph **83** Answers will vary. **84** $\frac{1}{12}$

3.2 Comparing Numbers on the Number Line

Warm-up Exercises

1 True **2** False **3** False **4** True **5** True **6** True
7 False **8** True **9** True **10** True **11 a** iv **b** iii **c** i
d ii

Exercises and Problems

13 $-\sqrt{7}$ **15** 8.8 **16** 19 **17** 0 **19** 5x **21** 112 **23** x
25 0 **26** 7 **27** 27 **29** 0

31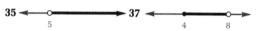
10

33 ◀━━━━━●━━━━▶
7

35 ◀━━○━━━━━▶
5

37 ◀━━━━●━━━○━▶
4   8

39 $x \le -2$ **41** $x \le \sqrt{5}$ **43** 27 **45 a** 9 **b** 6 **c** 7
46 27 **47 a** \$5.45 **b** \$8.25 **c** \$252.00 **48** 50
49 217.44 **51** $x = -12$ **53** $x = 12$

55

x	-3	-2	-1	0	1	2	3
y	3	2	1	0	1	2	3

57 $y = \frac{5}{2}$ or $y = -\frac{5}{2}$ **59** 22

61 $\begin{bmatrix} 3.3 & 29 \\ 2 & 3 \end{bmatrix}$ **62 a** \$2310 **b** \$2300 **c** No **63** A

number greater than negative three and less than or
equal to three **64** 7 cartons **65** That of the figure on
the right. **67** Sometimes **69** Sometimes **70** \$96; 20%
of \$120 is greater than 20% of \$100

3.3 Addition of Real Numbers

Warm-up Exercises

1 6 **2** 2 **3** -15 **4** -17 **5** -y **6** $-19x^2$
7 $-7\sqrt{7} + (-3\sqrt{5})$

Exercises and Problems

9 -0.225 **11** -13 **13** -102 **15** 0.01 **16** ≈1.414
17 (-5, 8) **19** $y = -7$ **21** $x = 4.5$ **23** $6a - 8b$

24

x	-3	-2	-1	0	1	2	3
y	-5	-4	-3	-2	-1	0	1

25 5 floors down **27** 0

29 $\begin{bmatrix} -3.9 & -1.05 \\ -\frac{1}{6} & -2.15 \end{bmatrix}$ **31** ◀━━━━━○━━▶
-10

33 ◀━━━━━●━━▶
3

35 25π or ≈78.5 **37**

39 -41.6 **41** -14.35 **43** 12.6
45 Dist. Prop. of Mult. over Add.

47

x	-5	-4	-3	-2	-1	0	1	2	3
y	3	2	1	0	-1	-2	-3	-4	-5

48 ≈345.605 **49** $-10.\overline{6}$ **50** 98
51 a   **b** 6, 16

c (-8, 19) and (-2, 3) **53** $-3x^2 + (-7x)$ **55** $x = 0$ or
$x = -4$ **57** $x = 0$ or $x = -5$ **58** 2008
59 $5(x + 2y + 7)$ **60** (-14, -16) **61** $x = \frac{b}{a}$

3.4 Subtraction of Real Numbers

Warm-up Exercises

1 $\begin{bmatrix} -9 & 4 \\ -6 & -6 \\ -8 & -2 \\ 8 & -8 \end{bmatrix}$

2 -5x **3** 5x **4** 5x **5** 78 □ − □ 105 □+/−□ □ = □
6 6.92 □+/−□ □ − □ 2.37 □ = □
7 2 □√□ □+/−□ □ + □ 3 □ = □

Exercises and Problems

9 0 **11** 3 **13** -47 **15** -9 **17** 140 **19** 17 **21** 44
23 -28 **25** -1 **27** 18 **29** 0 **31** $-6y - 16$
33 $x = -28$ **35** 19x **37** $x = 0$ or $x = 4$

38 $\begin{bmatrix} 9 & -21 & -40 \\ -30 & 9 & -3.1 \\ -.2 & -2 & 0 \end{bmatrix}$

39 $x \ge -10$ **41** $x < 0$ **43** -49.5 **45** 109 **47** 60
49 -3.38 **51** 5.2 **53** -81.66 **54** \$101; approximately

2.25 hr **55** -38.3667 **57** 66.2 **58** $\begin{bmatrix} 2 & 0 \\ 2 & -6 \end{bmatrix}$

59 (-17, -9) **60** $\frac{-13}{8}$ **61** -11.46 **63** -5
65 Property of the Opposite of a Quantity
67 Multiplication Property of Equality **69** $x = 23$
71 60; (3, 5) **73** $-9 < x < 9$ **74 a** Quadrant IV **b** $\frac{5}{32}$

3.5 Multiplication and Division of Real Numbers

Warm-up Exercises

1 -6 **2** -2 **3** -2 **4** -8 **5** -1 **6** -4 **7** -8 **8** -1
9 -13 **10** -3

Exercises and Problems

11 45 **13** -12 **15** -48 **17** $-\frac{3}{4}$ or -0.75

5.1 Solving Equalities

Warm-up Exercises

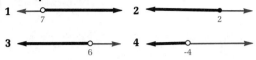

$7\ x \geq 3$ $8\ x < \frac{10}{3}$ $9\ x \leq 1$ $10\ x > -1$

Exercises and Problems

11 4 is greater than y. **13** -2 is less than or equal to n. **15** $y < -9$

17 $-9 \geq m$

19 $m > -19$

20 $0 < x < 6$ **21** $\{x: x > 3\}$ **23** $\{x: x > 32\frac{4}{5}\}$ **25** $\{x: x > 25\}$ **27** $x \geq 3$ **29** $x < 4.5$ **31** True **33** True

35 $x \geq 6$ **36** $\frac{3}{7}$ **37** $\begin{bmatrix} 18 \\ -52 \end{bmatrix}$ **38** $3(x + 3) + 5 < 71$ or $3x + 14 < 71$, $x < 19$ **39** 144

41 $x < -3$

43 $x \geq 5$

44

x	−4	−3	−2	−1	0	1	2	3	4
y	−19	−16	−13	−10	−7	−4	−1	2	5

45 20 **46** $x \geq \frac{9}{2}$ **47** $x > 5$ **49** $y = 0$ or $y = 3$
51 $y = 0$ or $y = 1$ **53** -1.78 **54** $x = 13$ **55** $x = 5$ or $x = -5$ **57** $x = 7$ or $x = -13$ **59** 1, 2, and 3 **60** 29, 30, and 31 **61 a** 2 **b** $n + 2$ **c** $n - 2$ **d** $n + 5$
63 $-6 \leq x \leq 6$ or $|x| \leq 6$ **65** $x < \frac{11}{2}$ **67** $x \geq -6$
69 $y = 0$ or $y = 12$ **70** 62
71 $3x + 13 < 50$, $x < \frac{37}{3}$ **72** 73 and 75 **73** $x < 68$; $x < 29.6$ **74 a** Monday through Thursday **b** Friday through Sunday **c** Amount of time available in one's schedule to watch movies **d** Reduce prices
75 a $0.59x + 10.08$ **b** $0.59x + 10.08 < 12.5$ **c** 4
76 $(6, \frac{15}{2})$ **77** $x = 3$ or $x = -1$ **79** 3, 4, 6, 8; 9, 12; 12, 16 **80** 4:00 A.M. the next day **81** $x = 9$ or $x = -3$
82 Let y be the number of elements in set Y. Then $0 \leq y \leq 30$. **83** 169 **84** $\frac{1}{3}$ and $\frac{3}{4}$

5.2 Using Inequalities

Warm-up Exercises

1 Obtuse **2** Acute **3** Right **4** Straight **5** Acute
6 Right **7** Acute **8** Obtuse **9** $10(2x - 50) < 300$ and

$2x - 50 > 0$ **10** $\frac{87}{2} < y < \frac{177}{2}$ **11** $0 < x < 30$

Exercises and Problems

12 a 126°; obtuse **b** 4°; acute **c** 180°; straight **d** 184°; unclassified **13** $x > -10$

15 $x < 115$ **16** $0 < x < 60$

17 14 **19** ≈ 43 min **20 a** $1500 + 755t > 10{,}000$; $t > \approx 11.3$ weeks **b** ≈ 119.2 more weeks **21** $x < \frac{7}{2}$

23 $x = 4$ or $x = -4$ **25** $x = -\frac{1}{6}$ **27** $\begin{bmatrix} -13 & 14 \\ 14 & -28 \end{bmatrix}$

28 $14\frac{1}{4}$ hr or 14 hr, 15 min **29** $y = 27\frac{1}{3}$ **31** $x = 20$

32 15 **33** $-40 < x < 75$ **34 a** $\frac{2}{3}$ **b** $\frac{1}{6}$ **c** $\frac{1}{6}$ **d** 0

35 $\{x:x > -5\}$ **37** $\{x:x < -15\}$ **38** 10 yr

39

x	0	5	10	15	20	25
y	6	3	0	−3	−6	−9

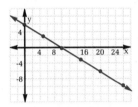

40 a 1976 **b** 1970 **c** 1974, 1976-1979 **41** $x > \frac{7}{12}$
43 $x = 76$ **45** $x^2 + x$ **47** True **49** True
50 $\angle 1$: $\approx 41.54°$, acute; $\angle 2$: $\approx 138.46°$, obtuse
51 a $500{,}000 - 15t$ **b** $15t > 50{,}000$; $t > 3333\frac{1}{3}$ hr or $t > 3333$ hrs, 20 min **52** $\frac{2}{5}$ **53** 27; 63 **54** 12

5.3 Compound Inequalities

Warm-up Exercises

1 d **2** c **3** a **4** b **5** $-3 \leq x < 4$ **6** $x < -3$ or $x > -1$ **7** {a, b, g, h} **8** {a, b, c, i, k} **9** $x \leq 6$ and $x > -1$; All numbers less than or equal to 6 and greater than -1

10 $x < -1$

or $x \geq 6$ **11** $x < 1$ or $x > 6$;

All numbers less than 1 or greater than 6

12 $x \geq -4$ and

$x \leq -1$ **13 a** $18t \leq 45$;

$t \leq 2.5$ **b** $100 - 18t$ **c** $100 - 18t \leq 28$; $t \geq 4$ **d** There is no time when S.H. is in listening range of both WARP and WUFF.

Exercises and Problems

15 [number line: 0 to 3.5]

17 $x < 5$ [number line at 5]

19 [number line: −3.5 to 9.5]

21 [number line: −3, 0, 5]

23 $x < -3$ or $x \geq 5$; The empty set **25** $-2, -1, 0, 1, 2, 3, 4, 5, 6, 7$ **26** From ≈ 4.64 hr to ≈ 8.21 hr

27 a **b**

29 [number line: −2, −1, 0]

30 34 **31** Between ≈ 248.6 miles and ≈ 350.3 miles
32 a $10 < x < 23.\overline{3}$ **b** $33.\overline{3} < x < 53.\overline{3}$.
33 \$63.75 to \$106.25 **34** 7.5 min to 22.5 min
35 $x = 2$; $y = -4$ **36** $25 < x < 43$ **37 a** {8, 16, 24, 32, 40, 48} **b** {6, 12, 18, 24, 30, 36, 42, 48} **c** {24, 48}
d {6, 8, 12, 16, 18, 24, 30, 32, 36, 40, 42, 48} **39** $x \leq 3$ and $-14 \leq x$ or $-14 \leq x \leq 3$; {x: $-14 \leq x \leq 3$}

[number line: $-14 \leq x \leq 3$, −14, 3] **41** $x < \frac{7}{4}$ or $x > \frac{7}{4}$ or $x \neq \frac{7}{4}$;

{x:x = $\frac{7}{4}$} [number line: $x < \frac{7}{4}$ or $x > \frac{7}{4}$, $\frac{7}{4}$]

42 [number line: −5, 0, 5]

43 35x; between 2142.86 ft² and 3142.86 ft²

5.4 Absolute Value and Other Inequalities

Warm-up Exercises
1 $x < 9$ and $x > -9$ **2** $x = 2$ or $x = -8$ **3** $x < 2$ and $x > -8$ **4** $x > 2$ or $x < -8$ **5** $x \geq -3$ and $x \leq \frac{19}{3}$
6 $x \leq \mid$ and $x \geq \frac{-17}{3}$ **7** 4, −32 **8** 2, −8 **9** {x:x > 2 or x < −9} **10** {x: $-4 \leq x \leq 5$} **11** $x > 3$ **12** 30; 40

Exercises and Problems
13 $x > 2$ or $x < -2$ **15** $-2 \leq x \leq 4$ **17** $x \geq 3$ or $x \leq -\frac{1}{3}$ **19** 10; 30 **20** $y = 22$ **21** 19; 47
23 $-4 < x < 8$ **25 a** 18,750 mi **b** 8000 mi **c** 1000 mi **27** [number line: −2, 0]

29 [number line: 0, 7]

31 [number line: −2, −1, 0] **32** $x > -1$ or $x < -10$

33 Between 182 and 252 mi **34** 4; 11
35 $-3 < x < -1$ **37** $|x| < 3$ **39** $\frac{2}{5}$ **41** ≈ 2.63
43 $|x| \leq 8$ **45** $x > 3$ or $x < -2$ **47 a** False **b** True
c False **d** True **48 a** 0 **b** $\frac{1}{5}$ **c** $\frac{4}{5}$
49 $x > 6$ or $x < -2$ [number line: x < −2 or x > 6, −2, 0, 6]

51 [number line] x can be any number.

53 $x > \frac{5}{2}$ or $x < -\frac{3}{2}$ [number line: $x < -\frac{3}{2}$ or $x > \frac{5}{2}$, −1.5, 2.5]

54 Between \$664 and \$913
55 a $11 < x < 21$ **b** $13 < x < 43$ **c** $13 < x < 21$
56 $\frac{1}{5}$ **57 a** $3{,}000{,}000 - 160x$
b $3{,}000{,}000 - 160x \geq 80{,}000$; $18{,}250 \geq x$
59 $-2 \leq x \leq 0$ or $x \geq 4$ **61** $\frac{-17}{2} \leq x \leq \frac{3}{2}$
63 $-3 \leq x \leq 0$ or $x = 2$ **64** $x = \frac{9}{4}$; $y = 4$
65 $\frac{12}{35}$

5.5 Properties of Inequality

Warm-up Exercises
1 Mult. Prop. **2** Trichotomy Prop. **3** Trans. Prop.
4 Mult. Prop. **5** Prop. of Opposites **6** Ineq. Prop. of Reciprocals **7 a** Given **b** Sub. Prop. of Ineq. **c** Def. of Sub. **d** Comm. Prop. of Add. **e** Assoc. Prop. of Add. **f** Add. Inv. Prop. **g** Add. Iden. Prop. **h** Div. Prop. of Ineq. **i** Division **j** Mult. Iden. Prop.

Exercises and Problems
8 B; Div. Prop. of Ineq **9 a** $> $ **b** $< $ **c** $= $ **d** $< $ **e** $> $ **f** $>$ **10 a** True **b** False **c** True **d** True **e** True
f True **11 a** $\frac{1}{3}$ **b** $\frac{1}{2}$ **c** B **d** Ineq. Prop. of Recips.
12 a Torry, Charles, Lin **b** Trans. Prop. of Ineq.
13 $\begin{bmatrix} 55 \\ -35 \end{bmatrix}$ **14** x can be any real number
15 $x \leq -2$
16 $\frac{3}{4}, \frac{5}{6} = \frac{15}{18}, \frac{7}{9}, \frac{8}{9}, \frac{11}{12}$ **17 a** $x = 36$ **b** $x = 21$
c $21 < x < 36$ **d** $6 < x < 21$ **19** $A \cup B = \{1, 2, 3, 4, 5, 6, 7, 8, 9,\}$; $A \cap B = \{\ \}$ **21** $x > \frac{9}{2}$ or $x < -\frac{7}{2}$
23 $y \geq -13$ and $y < -2$ **25 a** A, C, G, and H **b** Between 317.6 and 397 mi² **c** A, B, D, E, and F **d** Yes
26 a False **b** True **c** False **d** False **27 a** All values **b** Some values **c** All values **d** All values **e** All values **f** Some values **g** Some values **h** Some values **i** All values **28** $10 \leq 7 - 6x$, Given;
$10 - 7 \leq 7 - 6x - 7$, Subtraction Property of Equality;
$10 - 7 \leq 7 + (-6x + -7)$, Definition of Subtraction;

10 − 7 ≤ 7 + (−7 + −6x) Commutative Property of Addition; 10 − 7 ≤ (7 + −7) + −6x, Associative Property of Addition; 3 ≤ 0 + −6x, Addition;

3 ≤ −6x, Identity Element of Addition; $-\frac{3}{6} \geq \frac{-6x}{-6}$,

Division Property of Inequality; $-\frac{1}{2} \geq 1x$, Division;

$-\frac{1}{2} \geq x$, Identity Element of Multiplication

29 a 14 < x < 29 **b** 24 < x < 54
30 a |d − 0.035| ≤ 0.002 **d** Between 0.033 and 0.037 inches **31** 13x < 8x − 12, Given; 13x − 8x < 8x − 12 − 8x, Subtraction Property of Inequality; 13x + −8x < 8x + −12 + −8x, Definition of Subtraction; 13x + −8x < 8x + −8x + −12, Commutative Property of Addition; 13x + −8x < (8x + −8x) + −12, Associative Property of Addition; 5x < (8x + −8x) + −12, Addition; 5x < 0 + (−12), Additive Inverse Property; 5x < −12, Additive Identity Property; $\frac{5x}{5} < -\frac{12}{5}$, Division

Property of Inequality; $|x < -\frac{12}{5}$, Division; $x < \frac{-12}{5}$,

Multiplicative Identity Element **32 a** 2000 + 65t
b 2000 + 65t > 7500 **c** Between 84.6 and 123.1 minutes **d** 5000 < 2000 + 65t < 7500; between about 46.2 min and about 84.6 min **33 a** True **b** False
c True **d** False **e** True **f** False **34** 40 min

35 a 35t > 65; $t > \frac{13}{7}$

b 170 − 35t > 45; $t < \frac{25}{7}$

c Between about 1.9 and about 3.6 hours after leaving Mudville

36 a False **b** False **37** $X > \frac{17}{4}$ or $X < -\frac{7}{4}$

5.6 Circle Graphs, Pictographs, and Artistic Graphs

Problem Set

1 a Cray **b** Cray, $58\frac{1}{3}$%; Fujitsu, $4\frac{2}{3}$%; CDC, ETA

Systems, 14%; Hitachi, 19%; NEC, 4% **c** CDC

2

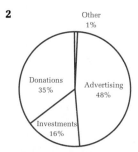

3 a 25% basketball, 25% football, $12\frac{1}{2}$% hockey, $37\frac{1}{2}$%

swimming **b** basketball: 300; hockey: 150; swimming: 450
4 a 1985 **b** March **c** January **d** No

5 a

Flavor	Pounds Sold	Percent of Sales
Mixed	432	39.3%
Orange	265	24.1%
Lemon-lime	113	10.3%
Coconut	93	8.5%
Tropical	195	17.8%

b

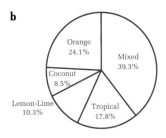

6 a

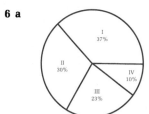

b

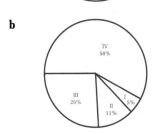

7 a 2:1 **b** 2:1 **c** 8 **d** 64 **e** 8:1 **f** 8:1 **g** No. The February TV is 8 times as large as the January TV, but the number of viewers is only twice as large. It is likewise from February to March. The pictograph is very misleading.

Review Problems

1 ◄────────────►
    -3.25

3 ◄──●────|────●──►
      -2.5   0   2.5

5 A ∪ B = {1, 2, 4, 6, 7, 8, 10, 13}; A ∩ B = {4, 10}
7 a y = 21 **b** y = 17 **c** y > 17 **d** 17 < y < 21

9 −5 ≤ z   ◄──────●──|──►
              -5   0   -5 ≤ z

10 z ≥ −11   ◄──●────|──►
               -11   0   z ≥ -11

13 ◄────○────────○────►
         -5   7

14 $(22, -34)$ **15** Between 727,600 and 761,600 people
16 a True; $169 = 169$ **b** True; $-27 < 0$ **c** False;
$7 \neq 17$ **17 a** $x < 4$ **b** $x > -5$ **c** $-5 < x < 4$
18 a 37% **b** Netherlands, W. Germany
c

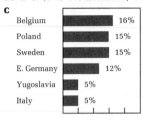

Belgium	16%
Poland	15%
Sweden	15%
E. Germany	12%
Yugoslavia	5%
Italy	5%

d Hungary; the percentage is greater.
19 $x = \frac{19}{7}$
21 $-30x + 62$ **23** Mae, Jenny, Beth; Trans. Prop. of Ineq. **25** $x \geq 6$ or $x \leq 0$ **27** $x < -7$ or $x > 0$ **28** $\frac{1}{3}$; 0;
$\frac{1}{6}$; $\frac{1}{2}$ **29** $3 \geq x$ or $x \geq 13$

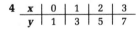

31 $x > 4$ or $x < -4$

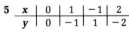

33 The necessary score is 101, but it is not possible for Joan to earn that score. **34** No such integers
35 a $0 < x < 90$ **b** $0 < y < 70$ **c** $x = 40$
37 $-2 < x < 12$ **39** $x < 6$ or $x > 24$ **41** No solution
42 $1587 **43 a** $x = 46$ **b** $-5 < x < 42$ **45** $x > \frac{6}{5}$ or $x < 1$ **47 a** $\frac{1}{3}$ **b** $\frac{1}{2}$ **c** II **d** Recip. Prop. of Ineq.

6.1 Tables, Graphs, and Equations

Warm-up Exercises

1 Right 1 unit and up 2 units **2** Right 3 units and up 2 units **3** Right 4 units and down 1 unit

4

x	0	1	2	3
y	1	3	5	7

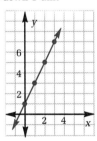

5

x	0	1	−1	2
y	0	−1	1	−2

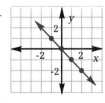

6

x	0	3	−3
y	−4	−6	−2

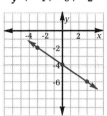

7 $y = 6x + 14$ **8** $y = \frac{-2}{5}x + 2$

9

x	−3	−2	−1	0	1	3	9
y	−7	−3	1	5	9	17	41

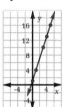

10

x	0	1	3	−2
y	5	6	8	3

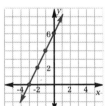

Exercises and Problems

11

x	−5	−4	−3	−2	−1	0	1	2	3	4	5
y	−4	−2	0	2	4	6	8	10	12	14	16

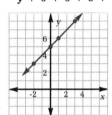

13

x	−5	−4	−3	−2	−1	0	1	2	3	4	5
y	27	22	17	12	7	2	−3	−8	−13	−18	−23

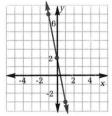

15 $\frac{5}{6}$ or 0.83 **17** $y = -8x + 25$ **19** $y = 3x - 5$

20 $\frac{3}{8}$ or 0.375 **21** $p > 3$ **22 a** AB = 3; BC = 2 **b** $\frac{2}{3}$

c CD = 6; DE = 4 **d** $\frac{2}{3}$ **e** $\frac{2}{3}$ **23** $\frac{-3}{2} > x$ **25 a** (6, 2)

b ≈ 9.4 **26** $y = -5x + 12$

27

x	0	1	2	3	4	5	6
y	14	12	10	8	6	4	2

28 a (9, 6)

x	4	9	14	19	24	29
y	12	6	0	−6	−12	−18

b $y = -\frac{6}{5}x + \frac{84}{5}$ **29** $y = \frac{3}{2}x + 3$ **31 a** (3, 2), (6, 4),
(9, 6), (12, 8) **b** (−3, −2), (−6, −4), (−9, −6) **c** (3, 6),
(6, 8), (9, 10), (12, 12)

33

35

x	−1	0	1	2	3	4	5	6	7	8	9
y	−8	−5	−2	1	4	7	10	13	16	19	22

36

x	−5	−4	−3	−2	−1	0	1	2	3	4	5
y	26	17	10	5	2	1	2	5	10	17	26

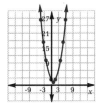

37 $x = 4$; $y = -14$ **38** $y = \frac{5}{2}x - \frac{23}{2}$ **39** $x > \frac{7}{3}$ or
$x < -\frac{17}{3}$ **41 a i** 10 **ii** 5 **iii** 15 **b** Yes **c i** $\frac{3}{4}$ **ii** $\frac{3}{4}$
iii $\frac{3}{4}$ **42 a** $h = -25x + 30,000$

b

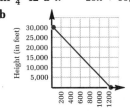

c $x = 1000$ sec **d** 27,000 ft **43 a** (19, 11); (25, 13)
b $y = \frac{1}{3}x + \frac{14}{3}$

44 a

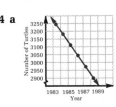

b $N = -70(y - 1983) + 3260$ **c** 2840 **d** 2001
45 a $C = 3.5L + 3W$

b

Width	Length				
	20	**25**	**30**	**35**	**40**
10	100	117.5	135	152.5	170
15	115	132.5	150	167.5	185
20	130	147.5	165	182.5	200
25	145	162.5	180	197.5	215
30	160	177.5	195	212.5	230

c He can use any dimensions except 30 by 40.
46 $b = 12$

47

x	−8	−6	−4	−2	0	2	4	6	8
y	68	40	20	8	4	8	20	40	68

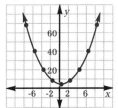

49

x	−8	−6	−4	−2	0	2	4	6	8
y	12	10	8	6	4	2	0	2	4

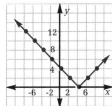

50 a $x = \pm 23$ **b** $y = 1994$ **c** $y = |x|$
51 a $y = 1024$ **b** $x = 8$ **c** $y = 2^x$

52 a

Ounces	3	6	12	18	24	32
Cost in Cents	$44\frac{1}{2}$	89	178	267	356	$474\frac{2}{3}$

b $\frac{89}{6}$ cents or ≈ 14.83 cents **c** $y = \frac{89}{6}x$ or $14.83x$
53 a Add two previous of same variable **b** No **c** No
answer

6.2 Slope-Intercept Form of an Equation

Warm-up Exercises

1 1; 4; $x + 4$ **2** $-\frac{2}{3}$, −1; $y = -\frac{2}{3}x - 1$ **3** $\frac{9}{5}$; 1

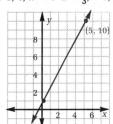

4 $-1; 0$

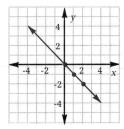

5 $\frac{2}{3}$ **6** $-\frac{2}{5}$ **7** $y = 3x - 1$ **8** 1

9

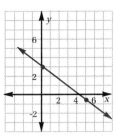

10

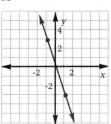

c

x	15	20	25	30	35	40	45	50	55	60
y	211	208	205	202	199	196	193	190	187	184

x represents age in years; y represents pulse rate (after aerobics) in beats per minute.

30 $0.5; -3; -\frac{3}{.5}$ or -6 **31** $2; -3$ **33** $\frac{2}{3}; 6$ **35** 8
36 $(-3.0, 2.9)$ **37 a** $(0, 5)$ and $(2, 2)$ **b** y decreases by 3 **c** y decreases by $\frac{3}{2}$ or 1.5 **d** $-\frac{3}{2}$ **e** $(0, 5)$
f $y = -\frac{3}{2}x + 5, -2 \le x \le 4$ **38** $x = \frac{20}{3}; y = \frac{1}{3}$

39 $(x, y) = (\frac{30}{7}, \frac{2}{7})$ **40** FD5, RT90, FD10
41 a, b

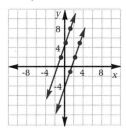

c $y = 3x - 4$
42 a

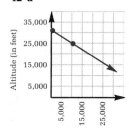

b ≈ 1.33 ft **c** $31{,}125$ ft **d** $\approx 15{,}840$ ft
43 $y = \frac{18 - 3x}{2}$ or $9 - \frac{3}{2}x$ **44** $x = \frac{18 - 2y}{3}$ or $6 - \frac{2}{3}y$
45 a, d, e **46** $20; 32; 30$ **47** $\frac{1}{5}$

Exercises and Problems

11 $3; 8$ **13** $-4; 0$ **15** $1; 5.4$ **17** $-2; 5; y = -2x + 5$
19 5 **20** $-\frac{3}{4}$ **21** $x > \frac{87}{2}$ **23** $x \ge \frac{4}{7}$ **25** No solution
26 a $\frac{5}{8}$ **b** $(3, 1)$ **c** $(-5, 6)$ **d** $-\frac{5}{8}$ **27** $(-936, 872),$
$(-935, 945), (-934, 1018)$
29 a

x	1	2	3	4	5	6	7	8	9	10
y	0.25	0.45	0.65	0.85	1.05	1.25	1.45	1.65	1.85	2.05

x represents the weight in ounces; y represents the postage in dollars.

b

x	32	41	50	59	68	77	86	95	104	113
y	0	5	10	15	20	25	30	35	40	45

x represents the Fahrenheit temperature; y represents the Celsius temperature.

6.3 The Geometry of Slope

Warm-up Exercises

1 a **2** $\frac{8}{5}$ or 1.6 **3** $\frac{-2}{3}$ **4** Yes **5** They are noncollinear.
6 $(\frac{3}{2}, 0)$

Exercises and Problems

7 -1 **9** 0 **11** a and c **12** $(-1, -2)$ **13** Down 2, right 3 **14 a** $\frac{1}{4}$ **b** 1 (Any two points are collinear.)
15 Yes **17 a** x increases by 2 **b** y increases by 4 **c** $\frac{4}{2}$
or 2 **18** $-\frac{2}{3}$ **19** $p = 6$ **20** $n = -\frac{20}{7}$ **21** $(1, 8)$

22 $+36°$; $-54°$; $25°$ **23** $(8, 0)$, $(8, 4)$, $(5, 4)$;

0, undefined, $\frac{1}{2}$, $\frac{4}{5}$ **24** -4 **25** $-\frac{1}{4}$

26
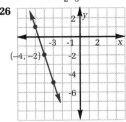

27 $-\frac{4}{7}$

28 a $k = 3$ **b** $k = -3$

29 Graph shows \$35,000 in sales spread over 3 months. Previous monthly averages were higher. **30** $p = 35$

31 ≈ 8201 ft **32** $\overline{BD}$: $\frac{5}{3}$; $\overline{AC}$: -6 **33** $y = x - 4$

35 $y = -\frac{1}{3}x + 2$ **37** $y = 2x$ **38** $q = 23$ or $q = -23$

39 a $\frac{3}{8}$; $-\frac{8}{3}$ **b** The slopes are negative reciprocals of each other. The product of their slopes is -1. **c** Right angle **41** $y = x + 3$

6.4 Other Forms of Linear Equations

Warm-up Exercises

1
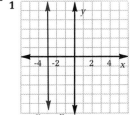

2
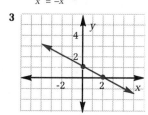

3

4 $(-2, 0)$; no y-intercept **5** No x-intercept; $(0, 3)$
6 $(6, 0)$; $(0, 4)$ **7** $(-1, -3)$, $(0, -3)$, $(1, -3)$; $y = -3$
(Other points are possible.) **8** $(4, 9)$

Exercises and Problems

9
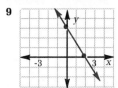

11
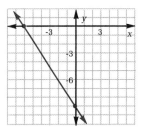

13
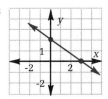

15 $-\frac{1}{3}$ **17** L_1: $y = x + 6$; L_2: $y = x + 3$; L_3: $y = x$;

L_4: $y = x - 3$ **19** $-\frac{17}{2}$ **21** -3

22 a, b, c
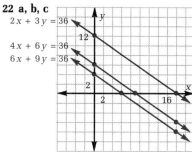
$2x + 3y = 36$
$4x + 6y = 36$
$6x + 9y = 36$

23 $a = \frac{2}{5}$; $b = \frac{5}{8}$ **25**
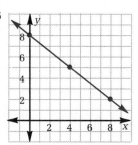

27 a $(2, 2)$ **b** 13 **c** Undefined **d** 0 **e** $-\frac{5}{12}$ **28** No

29 Yes **31** $y = \frac{5}{3}x - 10$

33
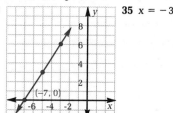
35 $x = -3$

37 $2x - 3y = -18$ **39 a** $(-1, -7)$ **b** $(\frac{2}{5}, 7)$
40 7:03 A.M. **41** 6 **42** 81 mi; 26.4 ft/sec

43 $\frac{1}{3}$ **45** 56 **47** Yes **49** $y = -\frac{3}{2}x + \frac{5}{2}$ **51** 1350 ft;

720 ft; 1530 ft, $\frac{15}{8}$ **52 a**

t	x	y
−2	−3	−7
−1	−1	−4
0	1	−1
1	3	2
2	5	5
3	7	8

b $\frac{3}{2}$ **c**

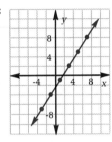

d $y = \frac{3}{2}x - \frac{5}{2}$ **e** $\frac{5}{3}$ **f** $-\frac{5}{2}$ **53** $\frac{10.1}{-3.8}$ or ≈ -2.66

55 $x = -2$ and $y = 8$ **56** $\frac{3}{10}$

57 $y = 2$ or $y = -2$

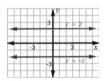

59 $x - 3y = 6$ or $x - 3y = -6$

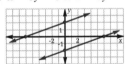

60 $27 < x < 57$

6.5 One More Form of a Linear Equation

Warm-up Exercises

1 $y - 593 = \frac{-77}{93}(x + 187)$ **2** Slope $= \frac{6}{5}$;
y-intercept $= -21$ **3**

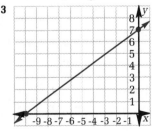

4 $y - 7 = \frac{2}{3}(x - 8)$ **5** $y - 4 = -\frac{4}{5}(x - 3)$
6 $y - 2 = \frac{2}{7}(x - 6)$ **7** $y = 0$ **8** $(0, -4)$ and others
9 $\approx (6.4, 0)$ and others **10** $(4, -1)$ and others

Exercises and Problems

11 4 **12** $y + 6 = -\frac{2}{3}(x - 4)$ **13** $3x - y = 4$
15 $-4x + y = 22$ **17** $y - 2 = -\frac{4}{5}(x - 4)$ **18** $(5, 3)$,
$(8, 5)$, $(11, 7)$, and $(14, 9)$ **19** $y - 3 = \frac{2}{3}(x + 2)$

21 $y = 7$ **23** $y = 4x + 8$ **24** $\frac{28}{3}$ **25** $y = -\frac{8}{3}x - 4$

26 a $y = 1$ **b** $x = 7$ **c** $y - 1 = \frac{3}{2}(x - 3)$ **d** $(7, 7)$

27 $y - 18.5 = 0.71(x - 1974)$ **28 a** $y - 6 = \frac{1}{6}(x + 8)$

b $y - 8 = \frac{1}{6}(x - 4)$ **c** $y = \frac{1}{6}x + \frac{22}{3}$ and $y = \frac{1}{6}x + \frac{22}{3}$

29 704 ft; ≈ 762 ft **30** $y + 1 = \frac{3}{4}(x + 4)$

31 $-\frac{17}{3} \le x \le \frac{7}{3}$ **32** $y = 2x + 10$; $y = -2x + 10$;
$y = 4$ **33**

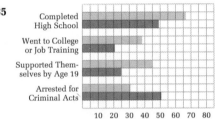

35

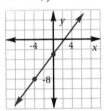

Percent

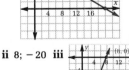

□ Preschool ■ No Preschool

37 $y = \frac{7}{5}x - 7$ **39 a** $y - 3 = -\frac{3}{2}(x + 4)$

b $y = -\frac{3}{2} - 3$ **40** $y = -9$ **41 a** $25\pi \approx 78.54$ cm²
b $9\pi \approx 28.27$ cm² **c** $16\pi \approx 50.27$ cm²

42 $(2, 4)$ and $(2, -4)$ **43 a ii** $\frac{x}{20} + \frac{y}{12} = 1$ **ii** 20; 12

iii

iv $-\frac{3}{5}$ **b i** $\frac{x}{8} - \frac{y}{20} = 1$

ii 8; −20 **iii**

iv $\frac{5}{2}$

44 a $2x + 3y = 10$ and $5x + y = 12$
b  **c** $(2, 2)$

6.6 Nonlinear Graphing

Warm-up Exercises

1 Solid **2** Dashed **3** Solid **4** No
5 **6** $(-5, -2)$ **7** $(3, 2)$

Exercises and Problems

9 **11 a**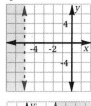

12 a, b, and c make the inequality true; d makes it false **13** The boundary line of $y \le 2x - 3$ is solid; that of $y < 2x - 3$ is dashed. **14** Possible answers: $(0, -7), (-1, -8)$

15 $x = \frac{11}{3}$; $y = \frac{7}{6}$ **17**

x	−5	−1	7	11	15
y	29	21	5	13	21

18 d **19** x-intercepts 1, 5; y-intercept 5 **20** $x = 6$ or $x = -6$ **21** 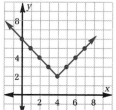 **23**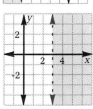

24 a 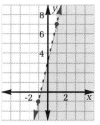 **b**

c **25**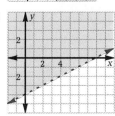

28 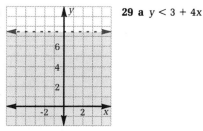 **29 a** $y < 3 + 4x$

b 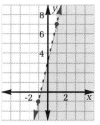 **c** $y > 3$

30

x	0	1	2	3	4	5
y	3	2	1	2	3	4

31 a $y = \frac{7}{4}x$ **b** $y \le \frac{7}{4}x$ **32** $x \ge -5$ **33 a** $\frac{1}{4}$ **b** $\frac{1}{4}$ **c** $\frac{7}{16}$

34 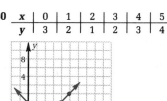 **35** L_1: $y = \frac{2}{3}x + 4$; L_2: $y = \frac{2}{3}x + 2$; L_3: $y = \frac{2}{3}x - 2$ **36 a** Possible answer: $k = 2$

b Possible answer: $k = 1$ **c** Possible answer: $k = 0.9$
37 Possible answers: $a = -1$, $k = -1.25$
38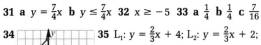

39

x	0	1	2	3	4	5	6
y	9	4	1	0	1	4	9

40 a $350 **b** Between $150 and $350 **c** No **d** $\approx$$251

41

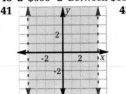

43

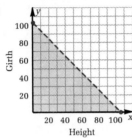

44 100 **45 a** $\frac{x}{-4} + \frac{y}{10} = 1$ **b** $y = 5\frac{x}{2} + 10$ **c** Lines with intercepts at the origin, $(0, 0)$. The denominator of a fraction cannot be 0. **d** $y = -\frac{b}{a}x + b$

3 $\frac{x}{\frac{8}{3}} + \frac{y}{-2} = 1$ **46**

47 a The x-values do not have constant change.
b $y = \sqrt{x}$ **c** No

Review Problems

1

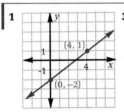

3

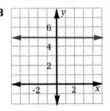

5

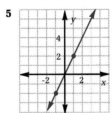

7

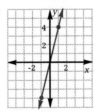

9

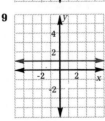

10 a Increases by 5 **b** 5; 11

c $y = 5x + 11$ **11** $p = 6$; $q = -\frac{23}{6}$ **13** $x_1 = 9$ or $x_1 = -5$ **15** Length = 22; width = 9.6

16 a-e

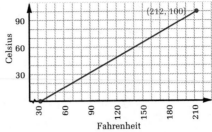

f 37°C **g** 122°F **h** $\frac{5}{9}$ **17 a** $(6, 4)$ **b** 20, 24 **c** $-\frac{2}{3}, \frac{2}{3}$ **d** $\approx$7.21 **18 a** 250 **b**

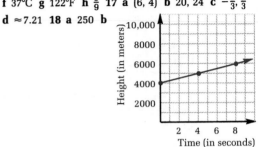

c 11,500 m **d** 12 sec **19** $-\frac{3}{5}$ **21** $y + 5 = -\frac{3}{8}(x - 7)$

23 $y - 3 = 7(x - 6)$ **25** $y = 11$ **26 a** $\frac{4}{5}$ **b** $\frac{1}{5}$
27 6, -4; I, III, and IV **28** $k = -49$ **29** $(20, 15)$

31

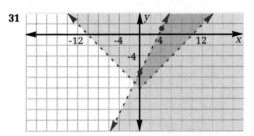

32 $k = 2$ **33** a, b, c **34** 1 **35 a** $h = \frac{4}{100}d + 900$
b 1028 ft **c** 17,500 ft **37**

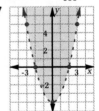

39 $V = \frac{14,125}{4t} + 12,000$; $79,093.75; 1974; $170,906.25

41 $y = -\frac{4}{5}x + 8$

7.1 Working with Formulas

Warm-up Exercises

1 $A = 81$ **2** $m = 0$ and $m = -2$ **3** $31.50 **4** $P = 3a$; $P = 3f + g$; $P = 12 + h$ **5** $\frac{b - d}{a - c}$ or $\frac{d - b}{c - a}$ **6** $d = rt$

7 $v = 5n + 10d$ **8** $v = 0.05n + 0.10d$ **9** 32° **10** 0°
11 98.6° **12** 40.5° **13** $P = 45$

Exercises and Problems

15 2 or 1 **17** 2 or 1 **18** $c = 540h$
19 a $c = 2.35 + 0.42m$ **b a** $3.19
21

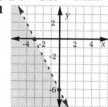

22 a $a = 9.99r + 13.79c + 11.49t$ **b** $171.75
c $148.87 **d** 13 discs **23** $\begin{bmatrix} 0 & -30 \\ -35 & 20 \end{bmatrix}$ **24** $\frac{13}{20}$ or .65

25 ≈ 1087.18 ft/sec **27** 0 ft/sec; Waves do not
propagate when it's that cold **28** $x = -1$ or $x = -1.5$
29 $y = \frac{-1}{4}x + \frac{27}{4}$ **31** $y = \frac{8}{3}x + 8$ or $3y - 8x = 24$
32 $x + y = 180$; $y = 180 - x$
33 $\begin{bmatrix} 20 & 30 \\ 12 & 5 \\ 6 & 20 \\ 15 & 8 \end{bmatrix} \cdot \begin{bmatrix} 5 \\ 5.25 \end{bmatrix} = \begin{bmatrix} 152.50 \\ 86.25 \\ 135.00 \\ 117.00 \end{bmatrix}$

35 24 cm **36 a** $t = 0$ **b** $t = -30$ **c** $t = \pm 4$ **d** $x = 2$
and $x = 3$ **37** ≈ 10.3 gal **39** None; it would cost $1.17
41 $56.62 **43** ≈ 74.58 mph **44** Yes; 50 mph ≈ 80
km/hr **45** $\frac{5}{6}$ **46 a** $450; $1200 **b** $1950 **c** More
d March 6 **e** $125 per day **f** $P = 125d + 75$
47 ≈ 471.24 ft³
48 a $x \le 5$ **b** 3

c

x	5	4	3	2	1	0	-1	-2	-4
y	3	4	≈ 4.4	≈ 4.7	5	≈ 5.2	≈ 5.4	≈ 5.6	6

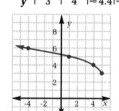

49 a Yes

b

t	0	1	2	3	4	5
h	0	128	192	192	128	0

c $t = 0$ and $t = 5$ **d**

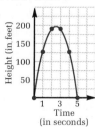

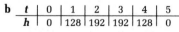

51 $\approx $21,000

7.2 Special Formulas of Geometry

Warm-up Exercises

1 a $(-4, 0)$ **b** ≈ 8.06 **c** $(-\frac{1}{2}, 0)$ **d** ≈ 8.06 **2 a** ≈ 141.4
cm³ **b** ≈ 0.16 **3** ≈ 64.3 ft² **4** 179.25 **5** 875 cal
6 ≈ 37.6 cal **7** ≈ 526.9 cal **8** 90 cm² **9** 196π in.³ or
≈ 615.8 in.³ **10** $-\frac{4}{3}$ **11** 5 **12** 2 or $-\frac{1}{2}$

Exercises and Problems

13 4 **15** 25 **17** $x = \pm 8$ **19** $(1, 1)$ **20 a** 11 hours
b $27.50 **c** $\approx $3.93 **21** $-\frac{1}{3}$ **23** 20π m or ≈ 62.8 m
25 480 ft³ **27** 34 and 56 **28** $x = -3$ or $x = -2$
29 10 **31** ≈ 12.08 **32** 68 **33 a, b**

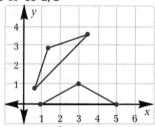

34 $p = -4$; $q = 2$ **35** $k > 4$ **36** $\frac{3}{5}$ or .6 **37** 110.25π m²
or ≈ 346.36 m² **38** ≈ 64.3 mph
39 a

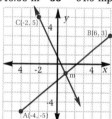

b $(1, -1)$ **c** -2

d $y + 1 = -2(x - 1)$ or equivalent **40** $24 + 6x + 4y$
41 128 ft² **42 a** Bill $= 25p$ **b** $400 **43 a** $\frac{5}{12}$ **b** $8\frac{1}{3}$ ft
c $21\frac{2}{3}$ ft **44 a** Parallelogram **b** $(5, 7\frac{1}{2})$ **c** $(5, 7\frac{1}{2})$
45 a $(3, 3)$ **b** $(\frac{1}{2}, -1)$ **c** $(5\frac{1}{2}, 7)$ **46** $166.\overline{6}\pi$ m³ or
≈ 523.6 m³ **47** $A = 6$ **49 a** $\frac{1}{8}$ mi; $\frac{5}{8}$ mi; $\frac{1}{4}$ mi
b ≈ 0.159 mi **c** ≈ 10.7 sec **d** ≈ 43.7 sec
51 $(16 - 4\pi)$ in.² or ≈ 3.43 in.² **53** ≈ 1.91 mi²

7.3 Using the Quadratic Formula

Warm-up Exercises

1 $a = 2$, $b = 0$, $c = -7$ **2** $a = 0$, $b = 5$, $c = -3$
3 $a = 1$, $b = 2$, $c = -3$ **4** No **5** $n = \pm 6$ **6** $x = 0$ or
$x = 2$ **7** $x = 1$ or $x = -3$

Exercises and Problems

8 b and c **9** $a = 2$, $b = 5$, $c = -9$ **11** $a = -2$,
$b = -5$, $c = 4$ **13** $a = 1$, $b = 0$, $c = 12$ **15** 8 and 9 or

-9 and -8 **17** $\{-\frac{1}{8}\}$ **19** $\{\frac{1}{2}, -3\}$ **20 a** $x = 36$ **b** $54°$
c $36°$ **d** $3{:}2$ **21** $x = \pm 4$ **23** $x = 0$ or $x = -5$
24 $c = 4(2y + x) + 6x$ or $c = 8y + 10x$ **b** \$1480
25 4 by 9 **26** No real solutions **27 a** $x^2 - 3x + 4 = 0$,
$a = 1$, $b = -3$, $c = 4$ **b** $2x^2 + 14x = 0$, $a = 2$, $b = 14$,
$c = 0$ **c** $5x^2 - 45 = 0$, $a = 5$, $b = 0$, $c = -45$
d $3x^2 + 17x - 15 = 0$, $a = 3$, $b = 17$, $c = 15$ **28** 42
and 43 or -43 and -42 **29** ≈ 18.97 **31** $(8, 3)$
33 $t = 2$ sec and $t = 4$ sec **34 a** $\approx 35.7\%$ **b** Shelby's
actually has about 75.65% as many defectives as Brand
X. **35** $\{-3, -2\}$ **37** $\{0, 9\}$ **39 a i** $\{\approx 1.54, \approx -0.87\}$
ii $\{0, -5\}$ **iii** $\{-3\}$ **iv** No real-number solutions
b Because $b^2 - 4ac = 0$ **c** Because the computer tried
to take the square root of a negative number
41 $x \approx 0.449$ or $x = -4.45$ **43** 26
44 a 75 ft **b** 360 ft **c** ≈ 292 ft

7.4 Literal Equations

Warm-up Exercises

1 $y = \frac{9 - ax - c}{2}$ **2** $\frac{x_1 y_1}{y_2}$ **3** $y = 5g$ **4** $x \approx \pm 4.12$

5 $x = \pm 3$ **6** $x = 0$ or $x = -5$ **7** $A = \frac{W}{V}$ **8** $V = \frac{W}{A}$

9 ≈ 220.6 volts **10** $P = \frac{nRT}{V}$ **11** $R = \frac{PV}{nT}$ **12** $n = \frac{PV}{RT}$

Exercises and Problems

13 $w = \frac{A - 2lh}{2l + 2h}$ **14** $x = 166.\overline{6}g$ **15** $r = \frac{d}{t}$

16 $h = \frac{2A}{b_1 + b_2}$ **17** $t = \frac{d}{r}$ **19** $t = \frac{i}{pr}$ **20** $C = \frac{5}{9}(F - 32)$;
$-5°C$ **21** $h = \frac{3V}{\pi r^2}$; ≈ 6 cm **22** $b_1 = \frac{2A}{h} - b_2$; $b_1 = 1$ in.
23 a $x + y = 90$ **b** $y = 90 - x$ **c** The angles are
complementary. **25** $x = 3A - x_1 - x_2$ **27** $\frac{Fr^2}{mG}$
28 $x = 11$ or $x = -6$ **29** $x_4 = 4A_v - x_1 - x_2 - x_3$; 95
31 18 **33** 0 **34 a** 1/9/88; 170 points **b** 12/31/87;
1/5/88; 1/6/88; 1/8/88 **c** 1/7/88 **d** 1 **e** 1/5/88

35 $r = 0.7$ **37** Slope $= \frac{6}{5}$, y-intercept $= \frac{11}{5}$

39 Slope $= \frac{5}{2}$, y-intercept $= 5$ **40 a** $C = \frac{N}{(1.10)^T}$
b 10 INPUT N,T
20 LET C = N/(1.10)↑T
30 PRINT C
40 END
c \$2135.05 **d** \$950.42 **e** \$13,348.60
41 $k = 4$ **43** $2 - \sqrt{7} \approx -0.65$ **44 a** $t = 6$ sec
b $t \approx 4.66$ sec or $t \approx 1.34$ sec **c** $t = 3$ sec **d** No; You
can't take the square of a negative number.

7.5 Functions and Relations

Warm-up Exercises

1 $\{x{:}x \le 1\}$ **2** $\{x{:}x \ne \pm 3\}$ **3** $\{x{:}x \in \mathcal{R}\}$ **4** x is a
function of y **5** y is a function of x **6** y is a function
of x **7 a** Nonzero real numbers **b** Yes **8** A relation
is any set of ordered pairs. A function is also a set of
ordered pairs but to be a function, the ordered pairs

must pair each input with exactly one output. This
restriction does not apply to a relation.

Exercises and Problems

9 $\{0, 2, -2, 4, -4\}$ **10** $\{5, 5, 12\}$ **11** a and c
12 a Nonnegative real numbers **b** Yes **13** No

15 $\ell = \frac{V}{wh}$ **17** $\ell = t^2$ **18 a** Yes **b** Yes **19** No; Five is
paired with 2 and 7. **21** Yes; Each input has one
output. **22 a** $C = 1.80i + 2.49p$ **b** \$21.03

23 $p \approx 2.58$ or $p \approx -0.58$ **25** $x \ge 4$ **27** $x = 3$ or
$x = 1$ **29** $\frac{6}{36}$ or $\frac{1}{6}$ **31 a** $y = 5$ or $y = -5$ **b** Yes

32 Yes **33** $x = \frac{d - b}{a - c}$ **34** $Q = 4G$; nonegative numbers

35 $x \ge 3$ **37** $x = 8$ **39** $y = -\frac{2}{3}x - \frac{2}{3}$ **40** $x = 7$
41 a Yes **b** No **42 a** $-3 \le x \le 3$ **b** $0 \le y \le 9$
c Yes **43** 60

44 a

	x	7
x	x^2	7x
3	3x	21

b $(x + 7)(x + 3) = A$
$x^2 + 10x + 21 = A$
$x(x + 7) + 3(x + 7) = A$
$x(x + 3) + 7(x + 3) = A$
45 No, each input for q yields two outputs for p.

47 93.75 lb **48 a** $\frac{3}{5}$ **b** $\frac{3}{5}$ **49 a** $E(-2, 5)$; $F(-1, -1)$;

$G(5, 0)$; $H(4, 6)$ **b** $(\frac{3}{2}, \frac{5}{2})$ **c** $(\frac{3}{2}, \frac{5}{2})$

51 $-3.56 < x < 3.56$ **53** 4.47 by 22.36
55 Input: month
Output: interest rate
Domain: June, July
              August, September

Range: 7%, 8% $9\frac{1}{4}\%$, $7\frac{1}{2}\%$

7.6 Function Notation and Graphing

Warm-up Exercises

1 $2\sqrt{3} + 1$ **2** 3 **3** 3 **4** 3 **5** $\{x{:}x \ge 1\}$ **6** $\{x{:}x \ne 4\}$
7

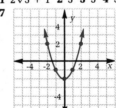

Exercises and Problems

9 -1 **11**

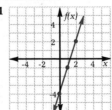

37

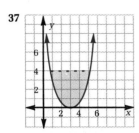

9.1 Large Numbers

Warm-up Exercises

1 602,000,000,000,000,000,000,000 **2** 3.24×10^4
3 6.25×10^1 **4** 1.7643×10^0 **5** 2^{10} or 1024 **6** 2^6 or 64
7 2^{10} or 1024 **8** 3^{18}; 3^{20} **9** 1; a; 4 **10** 3; x; 1 **11** 3.25;
10; 12 **12** -7; 5; 12

Exercises and Problems

13 3.4598×10^2 **15** 1.89×10^1 **17** 89,754.23
19 $n = 3$ **21** $n = 6$ **23** 19,683 **25** 1,048,576 **27** 25
29 24,583 **31** True **33** False

34

x	-1	0	1	2	3
y	$\frac{1}{3}$	1	3	9	27

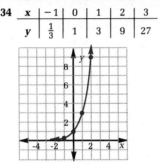

35 1:8 **37** $y \approx 8.3$ **39** $p \approx 0.153$ **40** $9.\overline{6} \times 10^{14}$,
9.7×10^{14}, 10^{15}, 7.3×10^{15}, $7.\overline{3} \times 10^{15}$, 83.7×10^{14},
3.2×10^{16}, 3.23×10^{16} **41** $\approx 3.45 \times 10^{12}$
43 $\approx 2.24 \times 10^{11}$ **44** Hopps; $9685.75 **45** ≈ 6433.9
47 $\approx 1.3 \times 10^{10}$ **49** 9 **51** 9 **52** $-3.5x_1{}^4$
53 $\approx 1.12 \times 10^6$ or $\approx 1,120,000$
54 a, b, c

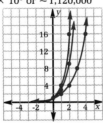

55 $x = 1$ or $x = 3$ **56** $\approx 5.87 \times 10^{12}$ mi
57 $\approx 2.47 \times 10^5$ **59** 3^{11} **60** The 49th day **61** The area
decreased by 4%. **63** $\approx 8.0 \times 10^{16}$ **64** $2265 **65** 60
67 30 **69** $-\frac{2}{7}$ **71** $\frac{3}{5}$ **73** 9 **75** 16 **77** 48 **78** 1:8
79 $\approx \$12,987.01$ **81** -3.166×10^{16} **82** $\approx 8.36 \times 10^{24}$
83 (50, 70) **84** $y = -3$ or $y = -0.5$ **85 a** 32, 64, 128,
256 **b** $\frac{1}{32}, \frac{1}{64}, \frac{1}{128}, \frac{1}{256}$ **c** 6.25, 3.125, 1.5625, 0.78125
d 81, -243, 729, -2187

9.2 Multiplication Properties of Exponents

Warm-up Exercises

1 y^{16} **2** a^9 **3** $25x^6y^2$ **4** $x_1{}^3x_2{}^4$ **5** 10^7 or 10,000,000
6 $6x^6 - 18x^5 + 15x^4 - 6x^2$ **7** False **8** False **9** False
10 True **11** False **12** False **13** $12a^3 + 18a^2 + 30a$

Exercises and Problems

15 $-x^4y^{12}$ **17** $x = 9$ **19** 4 **21** 4 **22 a** Yes **b** Yes
c Yes **d** Yes **e** No; $\frac{2}{x}$ is not a monomial. **f** No; 2^x is
not a monomial. **23** $2^{54} \approx 1.801 \times 10^{16}$
25 $6^{20} \approx 3.656 \times 10^{15}$ **26** 12 m^2 **27** y^{15} **29** $-x^7y^{11}z^3$
30 a $\approx 2.4 \times 10^{13}$ mi **b** $\approx 2.4 \times 10^7$ hr or $\approx 2.74 \times 10^3$
yr **31** $6x^8 + 196x^6 - 28x^5 - 84x^3$ **33** 2.4×10^{10}
35 (4, 17) **36 a** $2.28 **b** $184.10 **37** 1875 **39** -1875
41 $81x^8y^4$ **43** $n = 20$ **45** Maria is 15; Pedro is 30.
46 a 7203 **b** 194,481 **c** In part **b**, both 3 and x are
raised to the fourth power. **47** 32 **49** 2187
51

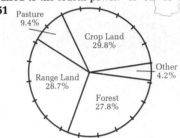

52 a 81 **b** -81 **c** -243 **d** -243 **e** A negative
number raised to an odd power, as in Part **c**, will
always be negative. A negative number raised to an
even power, as in Part **a**, will always be positive. The
opposite of an even number, as in Parts **b** and **d**, is
always negative. **53** $-3x^9$ **55** $-64x^3$ **57** $13x^3$
59 $20x^2$ **61** $-128x^7y$ **63** Approximately -5.07×10^{16}
65 $16x^8y^6z^{12}$

66 $\frac{4}{6.35 \times 10^{11}} \approx 6.3 \times 10^{-12}$ **67** 160 **68 a** False
b False **c** False **69 a** ≈ 990.46 **71** 11.9
73 $\approx 4,571,632.4$ **75** 6×10^{10} drops **76** 0 **77** $12x^5$,
$-30x^8$, $-10x^9$, $8x^{12}$ **79** True **80** $\approx 6.63 \times 10^7$ mi^2;
$\approx 3.88 \times 10^{22}$ ft^3 **81** $-14x^3 + 60x^2 + 22x$
83 $20x^3 + 25x^2 + 30x$ **84** $x_1 = 3$ **85** 429,981,696
87 1,073,741,824 or 1.0737×10^9 **89** $-50.653x^6y^9$
91 $\frac{3}{5}$ **92 a** Yes **b** No **c** Yes **d** No **e** Yes **f** No **93** 1
94 $\approx 2.97 \times 10^{14}$ drops **95 a** 40,320 **b** 40,320
c $\approx 1.72 \times 10^{12}$ **d** $n = 69$ (The number may vary
depending on calculator model.) **96** $\frac{3}{5}$
97 $\approx 4.07 \times 10^{-3}$

9.3 Division Properties of Exponents

Warm-up Exercises

1 $\frac{1}{4}$ **2** $\frac{2a^2}{b^2}$ **3** $1 + \frac{3}{b}$ **4** $\frac{1}{4}$ **5 a** -16 **b** -16 **c** The
expressions are equivalent expressions.

Exercises and Problems

7 $\frac{x^3}{2y^4m}$ **9** 25 **11** 100 **13** 1 **15** $\frac{9x^3}{y^2}$ **17** $\frac{y}{2x^2}$ **19 a** 64
b 4096 **c** $\frac{512}{w^3}$ **21** $\frac{1}{9}$ **23** 36 **24** $\approx 1.84 \times 10^{19}$
25 a Yes **b** Yes **c** No **d** No **27** -0.4 **29** 0.5; 0.25;
0.04; 0.001 **30 a** \$540 **b** \$734.66 **c** \$1,099,880.63
31 $10x^4 - 3x^2 + 4x + 5$ **33** ≈ 3.88 sec **35** $\frac{8}{5}$ **37** 16
39 a $\approx 9.821 \times 10^8$ ft/sec **b** 31,536,000 sec
c $\approx 3.097 \times 10^{16}$ ft
41 $\frac{-3x}{8192y^7}$ **43** $(3.2 \times 10^5)^2$, $(3.2 \times 10^2)^5$, $(3.2 \times 10^6)^2$,
$(3.2 \times 10^3)^4$ **44** $9x + \frac{8}{x}$ **45** $\{(5, 17), (-6.5, \approx 18.64)\}$
46 10^{30} **47** 200,000 plants **48 a** 25 **b** 13 **c** 25
d $(x + y)^2 = x^2 + 2xy + y^2$ **49** About \$311.11 **50** a^9
51 $2(x_2 + 3x_1) + 6(x_2 + 3x_1)$ **53 a** $\approx 5.067 \times 10^{21}$ ergs
b $\approx 3.737 \times 10^{19}$ foot-pounds **54** 1, 3, 5, 15, -1, -3,
-5, -15 **55** 9^4, 9^{12}, $6 \cdot 9^8$ **56** 1990 **57** $x = 3$

9.4 Negative and Zero Exponents

Warm-up Exercises

1 4^{-2} or $\frac{1}{16}$ **2** 1 **3** 4.65×10^{-3} or 0.00465 **4** $\frac{1}{9}$ **5** $\frac{1}{2x^5}$
or $\frac{x^{-5}}{2}$ **6** $\frac{2y^3z^3}{3x^5}$ **7** $\frac{x^{14}y^6}{4}$ **8** $a + b$ **9** 3.59×10^{-3}
10 0.0000243 **11** 3.15×10^{-5}

Exercises and Problems

12 -4.3×10^4, 2.1×10^{-3}, 10^{-2}, 7.31×10^2 **13** 5^3 or
125 **15** 5^3 or 125 **17** 1 **19** 1 **20** 2.16×10^8 **21** x^8
23 a^6b^{-11} **25** 3.2109×10^{-1} **27 a** Yes **b** No **c** No
d Yes **29** 0.403 **31** 1,200,000; $\approx 1.46 \times 10^6$ **33** $768x^6$
35 $8192x^6$ **37** $162x^5y^6$ **39** $144x^3y^4$ **41** 0 **43** 1
44 a 96 **b** 1536 **c** $\frac{384}{w^2}$ **d** $\frac{55,296}{w^2}$ **45** 8×10^{10} **47** 3^{16}
49 3 **51** $\frac{y^2}{9x^5}$ **53** $\{x:x < 0 \text{ or } x > 0\}$ **55** $\{x:x \in \mathcal{R}\}$
56 $(5 \times 10^8, 7 \times 10^6)$ **57** $n = 7$ **59** $n = -8$ **60 a** 6
b 3 **c** 2 **d** 6 **61 a** 1080 ft/min **b** $\frac{2}{3}$ mi/min
63 $\frac{4}{9}$ **65** $\approx \$28,972.60$ **67** $x = 1$ **69** No solution
70 a S.A. $= 52a^2$ **b** $\approx 5.13 \times 10^{10}$ mm^2 **c** 10,000 mm
or 1×10^4 mm **71** $\frac{y^3}{64x^6}$ **73** $\frac{4}{3}(x + y)$ **75** $x = \frac{a}{2} + 3$
76

x	10^4	10^3	10^2	10^1	10^0	10^{-1}	10^{-2}	10^{-3}	10^{-4}
y	10^{-4}	10^{-3}	10^{-2}	10^{-1}	10^0	10^1	10^2	10^3	10^4

77 $x = 2^{10}$ **79** 54 m^2 **80** 1
81 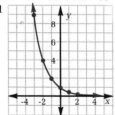 **83** $x = -3$ **84** $(0, 0)$

85 a $V = 5\pi a^3$ **b** 40π or ≈ 125.66 **c** 135π or ≈ 424.12

d $\frac{8}{27}$ **86 a i** 5 **ii** 4 **iii** 3 **iv** 2 **v** -2 **vi** -3 **b i** 6
ii -6 **iii** -1 **iv** 0 **c** ≈ 1.5; $10^{1.5} \approx 32$

9.5 Simplifying Radicals

Warm-up Exercises

1 5 **2** 7 **3** 13 **4** 17 **5** $2 + 2\sqrt{3}$ **6** $13\sqrt{3} - 3\sqrt{5}$
7 $2\sqrt{5} + 5\sqrt{3}$ **8** $4\sqrt{3}$ **9** $2\sqrt{5}$ **10** $3\sqrt{10}$ **11** 14
12 $20\sqrt{2}$ **13** $x = 2\sqrt{13}$ or ≈ 7.21

Exercises and Problems

15 $2\sqrt{7}$ **17** 14 **19** $4 + \sqrt{6}$ **21** 90 **23 a** $3\sqrt{6}$ **b** $\sqrt{30}$
25 0.2214 **27** 0.02214 **29** 0.007 **31 a** $10\sqrt{3}$ cm
b 18 cm^2 **33 a** About 0.026 mi/sec **b** About 0.43 sec
35 $x = -4$ **37** $x = -2$ **39** 36π or ≈ 113.1 **41** 25
43 0.38 **45** 0.45 **47** 1.21×10^2 **48** $2\sqrt{30}$ in.
49 a $\frac{-3}{7}$ **b** $y - 5\sqrt{2} = \frac{-3}{7}(x - 3\sqrt{2})$
51 $\sqrt{\sqrt{9} + \sqrt{16}} < \sqrt{9} + \sqrt{16}$ **52** $(-6\sqrt{2}, -3)$ **53** $\frac{1}{3}$
55 $\frac{2\sqrt{15}}{3}$
57 $15\sqrt{3}$ **58** $(3\sqrt{2}, -2\sqrt{2})$
59

x	1	2	3	4	5	6	7
y	—	0	1	≈ 1.4	≈ 1.7	2	≈ 2.2

61 $-14\sqrt{2}$ **63 a** $6\sqrt{35}$ or ≈ 35.5 **b** $24\sqrt{35}$ or ≈ 141.99
c $6\sqrt{5}$ or ≈ 13.42 **64** $x = -3 + \sqrt{15}$ or $x = -3 - \sqrt{15}$
65 $(\sqrt{2}, \sqrt{3}, 2, \sqrt{5})$
66 $(\frac{7\sqrt{5}}{5}, \frac{-2\sqrt{3}}{5})$ **67** $x = 0$ or $x = 1$ **69** $x = \frac{-19}{4}$ or
$x = \frac{-21}{4}$

9.6 Rationalizing

Warm-up Exercises

1 $\frac{4}{7}$ **2** 20 **3** $7\sqrt{3}$ **4** 2 **5** $\sqrt{15}$ **6** $\frac{2}{3\sqrt{2}}$ **7** $\frac{5}{2\sqrt{3}}$ **8** $\frac{1}{5}$
9 $\frac{\sqrt{5}}{3}$ **10** $3\sqrt{2}$ **11** $x = \frac{\sqrt{161}}{20}$; $y = 1$

Exercises and Problems

13 $\frac{3}{2\sqrt{3}}$ **15** $\frac{2}{3\sqrt{3}}$ **16** 6.4×10^{-2}, $(0.5)^2$, $\sqrt{0.49}$, 0.8 or
$\sqrt{\frac{16}{25}}$ **17** $5\sqrt{2}$ **19** $4\sqrt{2}$ **21** $x = \frac{11\sqrt{2}}{2}$ **23** 3 **25** $a^4\sqrt{6}$
27 $2x^4 + x^3 + 3x^2 - \frac{9}{2}x$ **29** $x = 0$ or $x = \sqrt{2}$
30 $5\sqrt{2}$ cm **31** 2 **33** $\sqrt{10}$, $\sqrt{6}$ **35** $8\sqrt{3}$ cm
37 $8\sqrt{3} - \sqrt{2}$ **38** 4 **39** $\frac{1}{\sqrt{2}}$ **41** $\frac{3x}{\sqrt{15}}$ **43** ≈ 2.214
45 ≈ 22.14 **46** $x = 2\sqrt{10}$ **47** $x = \frac{\sqrt{6}}{2} \approx 1.22$
49 $x = 7$ **51** $x = 3\sqrt{3}$ **52** Yes **53** $[\frac{5\sqrt{2}}{2}, \frac{\sqrt{3}}{3}]$ **54** 42
square units **55** $-6\sqrt{3} < x < 4\sqrt{3}$ **57** $\sqrt{2}$ **59** $3\sqrt{2}$
61 $5\sqrt{2}$ **63** $90\sqrt{2}$ **64** 25 **65** $12\sqrt{3}$ **66** $\frac{4\sqrt{3}}{3}$
67 Choose negative values for a and b.
68 $x = 3\sqrt{2} \approx 4.24$ m **69** $x = \sqrt{2}$

9.7 Radical Equations

Warm-up Exercises

1 Add -4 to both sides. **2** Square both sides. **3** Add the radicals. **4** Divide both sides by 10. **5** No real solution **6** $x = 3$ **7** $x = \frac{17}{4}$ **8** $x = 49$

Exercises and Problems

9 $x_1 = 225$ **11** $x_1 = 223$ **13** $a = 144$ **15** $y = 64$
16 a Yes **b** No **c** No **d** Yes **e** No **f** No
17 $x_1 = -11$ **19** $x_1 = 121$ **20** $x = 3$ or $x = -3$
21 $a = 9$ **23** $y = 143$ **25** $x = 321$ **26** $x = 6$ or $x = -1$ **27 a** About 14 **b** About 154 **29** True **31** 10
33 $x = 62$ **35** $x\sqrt{57}$ or $x = -\sqrt{57}$ **37** No real solution **39** $4x^2$ **41** $y = 169$ **42** $x = 5$ **43** $x = 4\sqrt{2}$
45 $x = 1$ or $x = 5$ **47** $x \geq -3$ **48** 3:2 **49** 9:4
50 $A = 3.008 \times 10^9$; $P = 2.22 \times 10^5$ **51** $10\sqrt{3}$
52 Some possible answers are: **a** Simplify $\sqrt{12}$ **b** Simplify $\sqrt{50}$ **c** Simplify $\sqrt{80}$ **d** Simplify $\sqrt{28} - \sqrt{112}$ **53** $6\sqrt{3} - 6 - 3\sqrt{2a}$ **54 a** ≈ 2.01 sec **b** ≈ 2.23 m
55 $x = 4$ **56** $x = 103$ **57** $x = 4$ **58 a** $V = \frac{a^8\pi}{3}$
b $V \approx 2.37 \times 10^{29}$ **59** $2\sqrt{26}$ **60** 1:16
61 $x = 49$ **63** $N = 16$ **64** W_2 **65** $x = \pm\sqrt{7}$
67 $x = 0$ **69** 16

9.8 Other Roots and Fractional Exponents

Warm-up Exercises

1 4 **2** 81 **3** 3 **4** -3 **5** No real equivalent **6** 1.1
7 a ≈ 1.86 **b** ≈ 4.22 **8** 2

Exercises and Problems

9 $\sqrt{32} = 4\sqrt{2}$ **11** ≈ 1.741 **13** 2.000 **15** $-8\sqrt{7}$ **16** $5\frac{1}{2}$
hr **17** $2\sqrt{2}$ **19** $2\sqrt[3]{2}$ **21** $4\sqrt{5}$, $4\sqrt{6}$, 10, $6\sqrt{3}$, $8\sqrt{2}$
23 $2x^2\sqrt[3]{5}$ **24 a** $8\sqrt{2}$, $4\sqrt{6}$, $4\sqrt{14}$ **b** $32\sqrt{3}$ **25** $x = 81$
27 $y = -4$

28

x	2	3	4	5	6	7	8
$64^{\frac{1}{x}}$	8	4	2.83	2.30	2	1.81	1.68

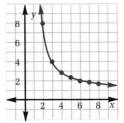

29 $x = 64$ **31** $x = -2$

33 $2\sqrt[3]{10}$ m or ≈ 4.31 m **35** $2y$ in.
37

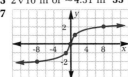

39 1, 0
40 1, 0, -1 **41** $n = 3$ **43** $n = 16$ **45** $x = 4$

47 ≈ 1.59 **49** 2 **50 a** $4\sqrt{2}$ or ≈ 5.66 **b** $128\sqrt{2}$ or ≈ 181.02 **51** $\sqrt[3]{15}$, $2\sqrt[3]{2}$, $2\sqrt[3]{3}$, $3\sqrt[3]{2}$

52

x	0	1	2	3	4	5	6
$f(x)$	1	2.1	4.41	9.26	19.45	40.84	85.77

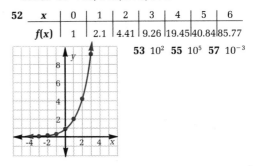

53 10^2 **55** 10^5 **57** 10^{-3}

59 10^{-6} **61** 2; 10; 5; 15; -3; -11; -6; -18 **62** $6\sqrt[3]{2}$ cm or ≈ 7.56 cm **63** 2 **65** $\frac{\sqrt[3]{12}}{2}$ **66** All positive odd integers **67 a** $36\sqrt{3}$ or ≈ 62.35 **b** $12\sqrt{3}$ or ≈ 20.78 **c** $\left[\frac{\sqrt{3}}{2}\right]$ or ≈ 0.87 **68 a** The cube with $2\sqrt[3]{2}$ as its edge **b** The cube with $2\sqrt[3]{2}$ as its edge
69 a $e = 3$ **b** $e = 2\sqrt[3]{225}$ or ≈ 12.16 **c** $e = \frac{2\sqrt[3]{450}}{\sqrt{2}}$ or ≈ 13.65

9.9 Scattergrams

Problem Set

1 a $y = 11x + 239$ **b** \$316, \$327 **c** $y = 10x + 240$ **d** \$310, \$320 **2 a**

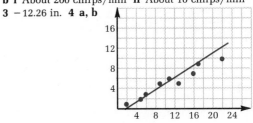

b i About 200 chirps/min **ii** About 10 chirps/min
3 -12.26 in. **4 a, b**

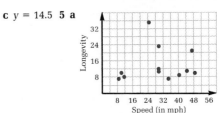

c $y = 14.5$ **5 a**

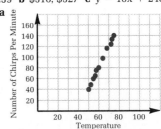

b The data do not follow a linear pattern; longevity and speed are not correlated.

6 a

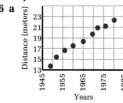

b $y = 0.2656x - 503.34$ **c** 23.61 m **d** The prediction is only an educated guess at the actual outcome.

7 Answers will vary.

a, b

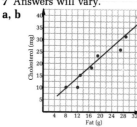

c $y = \frac{5}{2}x - 7$ **d** Answers may vary; about 41 g

Review Problems

1 $x = 6\sqrt{2} - 2$ **2** $-10^{12}, 10^{28}$ **3** $16x^4$ **5** $16x^4$
7 $r = 2\sqrt[3]{\frac{25}{\pi}}$ or ≈ 6.708 **9** ≈ 6.708 **11** $\frac{1}{6}$ **13** False
15 $g = 6$ or $g = -6$ **17** $g = -1$
19 $6x^4 - 10x^3 - 24x^2$ **21** $3x - 6 - \frac{2}{x}$ **23** 15,625
25 1024 **27** 1024 **29** -512 **31** $\frac{2}{3}$ **32** 6 cm **33** $(8, -1)$
35 $x = 2$ **37** $\approx 5.29 \times 10^7$ **38** Answers will vary

a, b

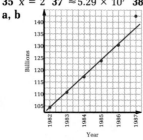

c 160; since it is a prediction, it will be possible to verify in 1990-1991. **39** $x = 16$ **41** No real solution
42 a $\frac{16\sqrt{2}}{3}, \approx 7.54$ **b** $\frac{15.625\sqrt{2}}{12}, \approx 1.84$ **c** $\frac{\sqrt{2}}{2}, \approx 0.71$
43 $n = 20$ **45** $n = 3y^4$ **46** $x = -2 + \sqrt{105} \approx 8.25$ or $x = -2 - \sqrt{105} \approx 12.25$ **47** $x = 3$ **49** $x = 5$ or $x = -5$ **50** $x = 2\sqrt{2}$; radicals **51** 40,960,000 bytes; about 9309 pages

52

x	0	1	2	3	4	5	6
f(x)	1	10	100	1,000	10,000	100,000	1,000,000

x	10^0	10^1	10^2	10^3	10^4	10^5	10^6
g(x)	0	1	2	3	4	5	6

53 $4\sqrt{170}$ or ≈ 52.15

10.1 Anatomy of a Polynomial

Warm-up Exercises

1 h **2** d **3** a, b **4** b, e **5** a, d, f **6** g, i **7** a, g **8** b, c

Exercises and Problems

9 Yes **11** Yes **13** $-12x - 48x^2 + 12x^3 + 12x^4$
15 Degree: 9; Coefficient: ≈ 0.67 or $\frac{2}{3}$ **17** Degree: 1;
Coefficient: 0.50 or $\frac{1}{2}$ **18** $8x^2 - x + 3$ **19 a** 4 **b** 7, 4,
5, 6 **c** 7 **20** 0.5 or $\frac{1}{2}$ **21** $2x^3 + 6x^2 + 8x$
23 $-79.8x^3y^5 - 35.7x^2y^3$ **24** $\triangle = 1$; $\square = 1$
25 $x = 4\sqrt{5}$ or ≈ 8.94 **27** $x = 0$ or $x = -8.50$
29 $g(1) = 11$; $g(-2) = 17$; $g(\sqrt{5}) = 15$ **30** $P(0) = 1$;
$P(5) = 32$; $P(-3) = \frac{1}{8}$ or ≈ 0.13 **31** $x \approx 12.88$ or
$x \approx -3.88$ **33** -233.60 **35** $18x^5 - 12x^4 + 42x^3$
37 a G **b** The vertex is the extreme point of the graph. **38** $x^3 - 3x^2 + 5x - 7$; 2.375 **39** 143 **41** 144
43 32

45

x	-3	-2	-1	0	1	2	3
y	9	4	1	0	1	4	9

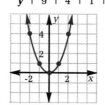

47 Total area: $5x^4 + 15x^3 + 10x^2 + 20x$
48 $(5x + 6)x + 8$; 64 **49 a** $8x - 12$ **b** It is impossible to write length AE as a monomial.
51 $4w^3z^4 - 11w^2z^3 - 3wz^2$ **52** $(2x)(x^2 - 10x)(3x)$ or $6x^4 - 60x^3$

53

x	-3	-2	-1	0	1	2	3	4	5
y	36	25	16	9	4	1	0	1	4

55 $4x^4 + 12x^3 + 23x + 31x + 15$ **56 a** $7(3 - 2x)$
b $11(5x + 3)$ **c** $x(x + 3)$
57 a

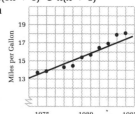

b Approximately 20 miles per gallon **58** 5, x, y, y^2, 5x, 5y, $5y^2$, xy, xy^2, 1, $5xy^2$
59 $x = 0$ or $x = 5$ **61** $x = -12$

10.2 Addition and Subtraction of Polynomials

1 $-2x^5 - 3x^4 - 2x^2 - 4$ **2** $8x^3 + 4x^2 + 4x - 7$ **3** No
4 No **5** Yes

Exercises and Problems

7 $13x - 6y - 5z$ **9** $8x^2 + 11x - 6$ **11** $24x^2$

13 $35x^5y^2 - 21x^4y^3 + 42x^3y^4$ **14** $\frac{2}{4}$ or .50

15 $\begin{bmatrix} 2x^2 & 5x + 7 \\ 15x - 9 & 15 \end{bmatrix}$

16 a $\frac{1}{2}(6x)(x^2 + 2x + x + 5)$ or $3x^3 + 9x^2 + 15x$

b $\frac{1}{2}(6x)(x^2 + 2x)$ or $3x^3 + 6x^2$

c $3x^3 + 9x^2 + 15x - (3x^3 + 6x^2)$ or $3x^2 + 15x$
17 $a = 5; b = -1; c = 1; d = 0; e = -8$
18 $2x^2 + 2x - 5$ **19** $24x^2 + 15x + 36$

21

x	-2	-1	0	1	2
y	2	1	0	1	2

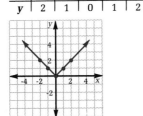

23 $p = 4; q = -\frac{1}{2}$ **24** $5x^2 + x + 3$ **25** Coefficient:
-6; degree: 3 **27** $-81x^4$ **29 a** $A = 20x^2; B = 10x;$
$C = 12x; D = 6$ **b** $20x^2 + 22x + 6$ **31** $x = 3$
33 $x \le 4.8$ **34** $-7x^3 + 6x^2 + 5x + 1$ **35** $x = 2$ or
$x = -2$ **37** x^6 **39** $16x^2 - 14x - 21$

40

	$3x$	$5x$	1
$6x^3$	$18x^4$	$30x^4$	$6x^3$

41 4501 **43** $-18x^3 + 4x^2 - 14x - 10$ **44** $x = -5$
45 a $3x^3 + 12x^2 + 15x$ **b** $10x^2 + 15x + 20$
c $3x^3 + 22x^2 + 30x + 20$ **46** ≈ 1547.9 **47 a** $20x$

b $16x^2$ **c** $x = \frac{5}{4}$ or $1\frac{1}{4}$ **48** 41 or 42 **49** $3x + 12y$

50 a $(3x + 4)(x + 5)$ **b** $x = -5$ or $x = -\frac{4}{3}$ or ≈ -1.33
51 $x = 8; y = -2$ **52** 8π or ≈ 25.13 **53** $15x^9$

55 a

	40% red	60% white
30% tall	12%	18%
70% short	28%	42%

b 18 red tall, 27 white tall, 42 red short, 63 white short
57 $x = \frac{1}{2}$ **58** $a = 3; b = 8; c = 6$

10.3 Multiplication of Polynomials

1 $x^3 + 5x^2 + 14x + 40$ **2** $8a^2 + 5ab - 3b^2$
3 $\sqrt{15} + \sqrt{5} + \sqrt{3} + 1$ **4** $-12x^4 + 16x^3 - 4x^2$
5 $16p^2 - q^2$ **6** $x = 1 \pm 2\sqrt{2}$ **7** No real solution

Exercises and Problems

8 $20x^2 + 43x + 14$ **9** $x^2 + 2x - 15$ **11** $x^2 - 13x + 36$
13 $x^2 - 10x + 24$ **15** $x^2 - 5x - 36$
17 $x_1 - 2x_1x_2 + x_2^2$ **18 a** $(3z + 1)(z^2 + 3z + 5)$
b $3z^3 + 10z^2 + 18z + 5$ **19** $1, -5; -1, 5$ **21** $1, 12;$
$-1, -12; 2, 6; -2, -6; 3, 4, -3, -4$
23 a $p = 2(x - 3)^2 + 8$ **b** $x = 7$ or $x = -1$
24 $4x^2 + 13$ **25** 2 **26** $x\sqrt{11} - 1 \approx 2.32$ or
$x = -\sqrt{11} - 1 \approx -4.32$ **27** $x = 4$ or $x = -1.50$
29 $4 + 2\sqrt{3}$ or ≈ 7.46 **30** $x = 0$ or $x = -8$ **31** -4

33

x	-3	-2	-1	0	1	2	3
y	18	8	2	0	2	8	18

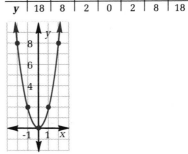

35 $x^2 - 9$ **37** $x^2 + 16x + 64$

39

	$5x$	7
$3x$	$15x^2$	$21x$
4	$20x$	28

41 $3(2x + 5y^2 - 10)$ **43** The x^2-term is $65x^2$. **44** 7, 8,
13, $-7, -8, -13$
45 a $x^2, (x + 10)(x - 6)$ **b** $x^2 = x^2 + 4x - 60$ **c** 225
46 Any three consecutive integers.

10.4 Special Multiplications

1 $25x^2 + 90xy + 81y^2$ **2** $49y^{10} - 1$ **3** $21x^2 + 40x - 21$
4 9 **5** $\pm 30x$ **6** $-\frac{13}{3\sqrt{3} + 12}$ **7** $x^2 + \frac{1}{2}x - \frac{15}{2}$

Exercises and Problems

9 $y^2 - 49$ **11 a** $5y + 2a$ **b** $5y - 2a$ **c** $25y^2 - 4a^2$
13 $x^2 + 20x + 100$

15 a

	x	$+$	4
x	x^2		$4x$
$+$ 4	$4x$		16

b I and IV **c** II and III **d** $x^2 + 8x + 16$ **17** $x^2 - 169$
19 $25 - x^2$ **21** $R^2 - r^2$ **23** $\pm 24x$ **25** $x^2 + x - 42 = 0$
27 $x = 9$ or $x = -2$ **28** $2x + 7y$
29 a, b, and **c** **30** $-2a^2 - 4a + 8$ **31** $(y - 7)(y + 7)$
32 $15\sqrt{2}$ and $-5\sqrt{2}$ **33 a** $x > 4$ **b** $x = 3.75$
c $4 < x \le 17.5$ **35** $x^2 + 10x + 25$ **37** $x^3 + 125$
39 $20x^2 + 41w + 20$ **41** $(3.2)^8 \approx 10,995.12$ **43** 100 in.²

45

x	-3	-2	-1	0	1	2	3
y	6	1	-2	-3	-2	1	6

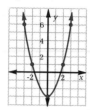

47 $\frac{5 + \sqrt{3}}{2}$ **49**

	$2x$	9
$3x$	$6x^2$	$27x$
8	$16x$	72

51 -7 and -5, or 5 and 7
53 $5\sqrt{7} + 10$ **55** ≈ 9.84

10.5 Factoring

Warm-up Exercises

1 $-6a^2b(3a^2b - 2ab^2 + 4)$ **2** $3xy(2x^2 - 3xy^2 + 4)$

3 $x = 0$ or $x = -\frac{3}{2}$ **4** $x = 0$ or $x = -\frac{2}{5}$

5 $((2x + 1)x - 3)x - 1$

Exercises and Problems

7 x^3 **9** 11 **11** $8y$ or $-8y$ **12** $50a^2 + 10ab$
13 $4x(4x + 3)$ **15** $25x(x^2 + 3x + 1)$ **17** No
18 $24x^3 - 16x^2 + 8x$ **19** $8x(3x^2 - 2x + 1)$
20 $x^2 + 8x + 15$ **21** $(x + 5)(x + 3)$
23 $-7x(x^2 + 3x - 2)$ **25** $x^2(x^3 - x^2 + 3x + 2)$
27 $2y(x^2 + 4x + 1)$ **28** No; a common factor of 2
remains in the binomial factor. **29** $4(2x^2 + 5x + 4)$
30 $3x$, $5x^3y$, -2 **31** $8c^4 + 10c^3$ **33** $x = 7$ or $x = -7$
34 $(-1, -1)$ **35** $x^2 + 5x - 24 = 0$ **36 a** $-9, -8, -8$
b $x = 2$ or $x = 8$ **c** $x = 5$ **37** $4x + 3$ **39** ≈ 734.69
40 $x = 8$ **41 a** $x = \pm 3$ **b** $x = \pm 3$ **42 a** 0 ft **b** 0 ft
c 6 sec **43** $a^2 + 12a + 36$ **45** $c^2 - 4d^2$
47 $(b - 8)(b + 8)$ **49** $x = 6$
51 $x = 0$ or $x = 4$ **53** $x = 0$ or $x = -3$ **55** ≈ 34.08
57 $(2x^2 + 3)x + 15$; ≈ 15.23 **59** $((x + 5)x + 3)x + 4$;
≈ 4.26 **60** $x = 32$ **61** $x^2 + 2x - 35 = 0$
63 $x^2 - 12x + 36 = 0$ **64 a** -10 **b** -6 **c** 10
65 $(7, 5)$ **66** $4x^3 - 3x^2 - 36x + 27 = 0$

10.6 Factoring Trinomials

Warm-up Exercises

1 $(x - 4)(x + 3)$ **2** $2(x + 6)(x + 1)$ **3** $3(x^2 - 7x + 8)$
4 $x = -4$ **5** No real solution **6** $x \approx 1.24$ or
$x \approx -3.24$

Exercises and Problems

7 $13x$ **9** $-5x$ **11** $(x + 1)(x + 11)$ **12** 25, 14, 11, or 10
13 $3(x^2 + 7)$ **15** $x = \frac{5}{2}$ or $x = \frac{-8}{3}$ **17** $(x + 1)(x + 7)$
19 $(x + 1)(x - 7)$ **21** $3x^2 - 5x - 100$
22 $(3x - 20)(x + 5)$ **23** 6 and -6 **24** $(1, 3)$

25 $(x - 18)(x - 1)$ **27** $(x - 6)(x - 3)$
29 $(x + 9)(x + 2)$ **31** $-1(x^2 + 5x - 9)$
33 $-1(2x^2 - 3x + 7)$ **34** $x = 18$ or $x = -5$

35 $-1(x + 5)(x - 1)$ **37** $-1(x + 4)(x + 2)$ **39** $x < -\frac{1}{2}$
40 $x + 3$ by $x + 5$; $x^2 + 8x + 15$ **41** $3x^3 - 15x^2 - 33x$
43 $2x^3 - 28x^2 + 98x$ **45** $5x(x + 4)(x + 2)$ **47** $(15, -1)$
49 $x = 6$ or $x = 7$ **51** ≈ -2838.56
53 $((x + 3)x + 7)x + 11$ **54** $x = 1$
55 $x^2 - 2x - 63 = 0$ **57 a** $(x + 4)(x - 4)$
b $(x - 8)(x + 2)$ **c** $(x - 1)(x + 16)$ **d** Cannot be
factored **59** $2x^4$ **61** $x = 9$ or $x = 6$
63 a $(x + 2)(x + 1)$ **b** $(x + 4)(x - 1)$ **c** $(x + 5)(x - 2)$
d $(x + 6)(x - 3)$
64 $x = 8$ **65** $(x - 5)(x - 8)$ **67** $(x + 10)(x + 4)$
69 $(x + 40)(x - 1)$ **71** $(90, 45)$ **73** $5y(2x - 1)(x - 1)$

75 $\frac{8}{15}$ **76** $x = 8$ **77** $-1(x - 4)(x - 1)$

79 $2(x - 1)(x - 3)$ **80** 12 **81** $x \approx 5.035$ m
82 $x = -1$ or $x = -14$; $y = 2$ or $y = -7$
83 $x = -2$, $x = -4$, or $x = 1$ **84** No real solutions

85 $x = \frac{-8c}{a}$ or $x = \frac{d}{3a}$ **86** $\angle BCF = 94°$ **87** $a = 2\sqrt{2}$;
$b = -16$ **88** $(x - 6)(x + 2)(x - 2)$ **89** $x = 6$, $x = -2$,
or $x = 2$

10.7 More About Factoring Trinomials

Warm-up Exercises

1 $(3x + 4)(2x + 1)$ **2** $(4x - 1)(2x + 3)$

3 $4(x - 1)(3x + 2)$ **4** $x^2 + \frac{7}{2}x - 2 = 0$ **5** $r = 2$ or
$r = \frac{2}{3}$

Exercises and Problems

7 $(2x + 1)(x + 3)$ **9** $(2x + 1)(x - 3)$ **10** 13, 8, 7, -7,
$-8, -13$ **11** $(7x - 3)(x - 2)$ **12** $\frac{1}{9}$ m **13** $x = -\frac{10}{3}$ or
$x = -1$ **15** $n = 8$ or $n = -5$ **17** $(x - 2)(2x - 5)$
19 $(2x - 3)(x - 4)$ **21** $y^2 - 169$ **23** $y^2 - 16$
24 $(5z + 3)(2z - 1)$ **25** $x = 3$ **27** $x(x - 6)(x + 1)$
29 $4v^2 + 36v + 81$ **30** 5 m by 20 m **31** $x = -5$;
$y = -8$ **33** $6(3x + 1)(x - 7)$ **35** $5(3x + 4)(2x + 5)$
37 -8 **39** $x(x + 1)^2$ or $x(x + 1)(x + 1)$
41 $\pi Rh(R + 2)$ **42** $a = -36$ **43** $(3m - 7)(4m + 3)$
45 $(2p - 3)(35p + 12)$ **47 a** $x = 0$ or $x = 15$
b $x = 16$ or $x = -1$ **49** $x^2 + 20x + 100 = 0$

50 a

	$2x$	7
x	$2x^2$	$7x$
4	$8x$	28

b $2x^2 + 15x + 28$ **c** $x = 2.5$ **51** $4(3m + 7)(m - 1)$

53 $x = 1.5$ or $x = 3$ **55** $x = \frac{1}{4}$ or $x = -2$ **57** Cannot
be factored **59** $x = -0.5$; perimeter is 16 m
61 $3(5y + 12)(y + 2)$ **63** $(4, 16)$ or $(-2, 4)$ **64** 0, 9, 16,
21, 24, 25 **65** 4 m by 5 m **66 a** $x = 0$ or $x = 9.\overline{3}$
b $x = 0.\overline{3}$ or $x = 9$ **67** $(3v + 1)^2$ **69** 8 in.
70 a 288 ft **b** $t = 3$ or $t = 8$ seconds because the
rocket could be at 384 feet going up or coming down

c 11 sec **71** $(3z - 1)(4z + 35)$ **73** $(6z + 7)(2z - 5)$
74 $x = 1$, $x = -1$, $x = \frac{\sqrt{30}}{6} \approx 0.91$, or
$x = \frac{-\sqrt{30}}{6} \approx -0.91$ **75** 2 cm by 6 cm by 9 cm
76 $x = 1.1\overline{6}$ and $x = -1$ **77** $(19y + 31)(19y - 31)$
79 $-(12x + 25)(x - 2)$

10.8 Factoring Special Polynomials

Warm-up Exercises

1 $(y + 11)(y - 11)$ **2** $(y - 1)(y - 1)$ **3** $3(x^2 + 4)$
4 $(x + 8)(x + 2)$ **5** $4(y + 2)(y - 2)$ **6** $(2x + 1)^2$ **7** 9
8 $\pm 30x$

Exercises and Problems

9 $10y$ **11** $12x$ **13** 49 **15** 144 **17** $(m + 9)(m - 9)$
19 $(p - 9)^2$ **21** $(x - 6y)(x + 6y)$ **22** $x = 2$ **23** $14d$ or
$-14d$ **25** $6z$ or $-6z$ **27** $x \geq 5$ or $x \leq -9$

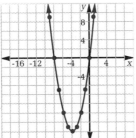

$x \leq -9$ or $x \geq 5$

29 No **31** Yes **33** No
35 $(11 - 5z)(11 + 5z)$ **37** $x = 7$; $y = 2$ **39** 1.1×10^8
41 $4(x + 4)(x - 4)$ **43** $(4x + 7)^2$ **44** 64 **45** $(x + y)^2$
47 $(y + 4)^2$ **49** $r = -0.\overline{27}$ or $\frac{-3}{11}$ **51** $(x - 1)^2$, $x \neq 0$
53 20, 5 **54** 9 **55 a** $y + 16 = x^2 + 8x + 16$
b $(x + 4)^2$ **c** $y = (x + 4)^2 - 16$

55 d

x	-9	-8	-7	-6	-5	-4	-3	-2	-1	0	1
y	9	0	-7	-12	-15	-16	-15	-12	-7	0	9

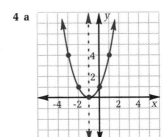

57 $(w + 4)(w + 9)$ **59** $x = -6$ or $x = \frac{7}{2}$
60 $x^2 - 49 = 0$ **61** No **63** Yes **64** $\pm 40y$
65 a $f(x) + 25 = x^2 - 10x + 25$ **b** $(x - 5)^2$
c $f(x) = (x - 5)^2 - 25$ **67** $x = \frac{63}{16}$ or ≈ 3.94 **69** $y = 8$
71 $x = -3$ **73** $x = 6$cm **75** $(z - 8)^2$
77 $2x(x + 3)(x - 3)$ **79** $(4x - 5)(2x + 3)$ **80** $a > \frac{35}{3}$ or
$a > 11.6$ **81** $(x - 3)^2$ **82** $x = 9$ or $x = -3$ **83** $x = 9$
or $x = -3$ **84** $a = 8$ m **85** $((x - 6)x + 7)x + 9$
87 $b = 6$ or $b = -6$ **89** $w = -\frac{5}{4}$ or -1.25
91

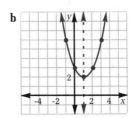

93 $(x + 2)^2(x - 2)^2$ **94** $z = 5$ or $z = -5$ **95** $s = 3$ cm
97 $(\sqrt{6}x - \sqrt{7}y)(\sqrt{6}x + \sqrt{7}y)$ **98 a** 56 ft **b** $t = 3$ sec
c 200 ft **d** $t = 6.54$ sec

Review Problems

1 $10x^2 + 5$ **3** Monomial **5** Binomial **7** $45x^3 + 30x^2$
8 $\frac{7}{11}$ **9 a** $A = 3x^2$; $B = 2x$; $C = 12x$; $D = 8$
b $3x^2 + 14x + 8$ **11** $2x^2 + 2x - 12$ **13** $2(x^2 - 9)$
15 $3xy(3x + 2y)$ **17** $(3 - 2k)(3 + 2k)$ **19** $4x(x - 5)^2$
21 $x = 8$ or $x = -4$ **22** $(x + 5)(x - 11) = 0$ or
$x^2 - 6x - 55 = 0$ **23** $(2x - 3)(x + 1)$ **25** -59 and
-57, or 57 and 59 **27** $6x$ or $-6x$
29 $2x^3 + 4x^2 - 6x$ **31** $(2x - 3)(x - 1)$
33 $(2x + 5)(2x - 5)$ **34** $3x + 12$ **35 a** -4 **b** 8
36 $x = \frac{1}{3}$ or $x = -\frac{1}{2}$ **37** $2x^3 - 2x^2 + 28x$
38 $8x^2 - 4x + 1$ **39** $(x - 8)(x - 5)$
41 $(x - 10)(x + 4)$ **43** $35y(y - 4)$ **45** $x = 9$ cm
47 $3x + 7$ **49** $x = -1$ or $x = -9$ **51** $x = \frac{4}{3}$ or
$x = -\frac{4}{3}$ **53** $x = 1$ or $x = 3$ **54** $x \leq \frac{1}{3}$ or $x \geq \frac{1}{2}$
55 ≈ 54.37 **56** $x = 5$ **57** $(x - 7)x + 11$ **59** 1
61 $8 + 4\sqrt{3}$ **62** $x = 4$ cm
63 $9, -9, 15$, and -15 **64** $x = 16$ or $x = -6$ **65** $8x^2$
67 $(x + 3)(x - 3)(x + 2)(x - 2)$ **69** $(x - 1)^2(x + 1)^2$
71 $x \geq 7$ or $-1 \leq x \leq 0$ **72** $(2x + 1)(4x - 3) = 0$ or
$8x^2 - 2x - 3 = 0$ **73** $x = 3$ or $x = -1$ **74** $\frac{81}{4}$ or 20.25

11.1 Graphing the Parabola

Warm-up Exercises

1 a $(2, 4)$ **b** $x = 2$ **c** parabola, "∪" **2 a** $(2, -3)$
b $x = 2$ **c** absolute value, "V" **3 a** $(3, 4)$ **b** $x = 3$
c parabola, "∪"

4 a

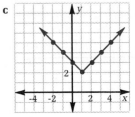

b

c

5 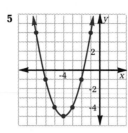 **6**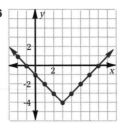

b $t = 5$ sec **c** 45 m **d**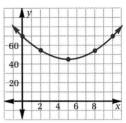

7 $y = (x - 3)^2 - 1$ **8** $y = |x + 2|$

Exercises and Problems

9 a $y = 5$ **b** $y = 14$ **c** $y = 14$ **11** $(-5.4, -3.2)$;
$x = -5.4$ **13** $(0, 0)$; $x = 0$ **14 a** $x = 5$ or $x = -1$
b $x = 2$ **c** $x = 4$ or $x = 0$

52 a $y = (x - 2)^2 + 5$

15 a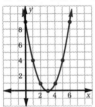

b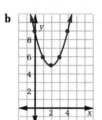

c The sides of the square are zero at $(2, 5)$. **53** $k = 1$
or $k = -1$ **54** $4x^2 - 2x + 3$

55 $\begin{bmatrix} 6x^2 - x - 6 \\ 2x^2 + 3x - 18 \end{bmatrix}$

b 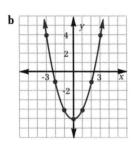 **c**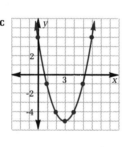

57 $(y - 4x)(y + 4x)$
59 $y = (x - 1)^2 + 5$ **60 a** $(x - 4)^2 = y - 2$

17 $(2, 0)$; $x = 2$ **19** $(-5, -4)$; $x = -5$ **21** $(-3, 2)$;
$x = -3$

b 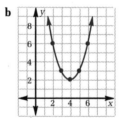 **c** $(2, 6)$ or $(6, 6)$

23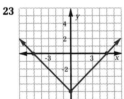

61

25 $-\frac{12}{13}$ or -0.92 **27** $5\sqrt{2}$ **28** $y = (x + 3)^2 + 5$; 230
29 $y = |x + 2| + 5$ **30** $y = (x - 6)^2 + 4$ **31** $x = 4$
33 $19x - 3$ **35** $y = (x - 4)^2 + 1$ **36** $(x, y) = (7, -2)$
37 87 min or 1 hr 27 min
38 $y = |x - 4| + 7$ **39** x^{15}
41 $\frac{1}{4}$ **43** $2x(3x + 4y + 5z)$

45

r	0	1	2	3	4	5
A	0	π	4π	9π	16π	25π

46 $y = (x + 2)^2 - 4$ **47** $(0, 0)$, $(1, 1)$ $(-1, 1)$
48 $y = (x - 4)^2$
49 $y = 8$ **50** $x = 5$ or $x = -1$ **51 a** 145 m

63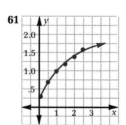

65 $|x - 3| + 4 = y$

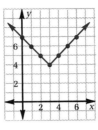

66 No real values.

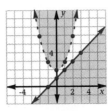

11.2 Graphing Other Parabolas

Warm-up Exercises

1 i Downward **ii** Highest **iii** $(0, 0)$, wider **iv** $-\frac{1}{3}$, $-1, \frac{-5}{3}, \ldots$ **2 i** Upward **ii** Lowest **iii** $(0, 3)$, the same **iv** $1, 3, 5, \ldots$ **3 i** Upward **ii** Lowest **iii** $(1, 3)$, narrower **iv** $4, 12, 20, \ldots$ **4** $-1, 7; -3\frac{1}{2}$ **5** $1, 5; 1$

6 $y = 2(x + 3)^2 - 2$ **7** $y = -\frac{1}{2}(x - 2)^2 + 5$

Exercises and Problems

9 $(-2, -4)$; $x = -2$; upward **11** $(-7, -3)$; $x = -7$; upward **13** Downward; $-2, -6, -10, \ldots$ **15** Downward; $-2, -2, -2, \ldots$ **17** $(3, 0)$, $(-9, 0)$; $(0, -3)$ **19** $x = -6$ **21**

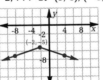

23

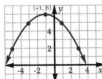

25

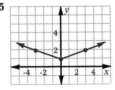

26 4; 1920 **27**

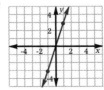

29 $y = -|x - 2| - 1$ **30** ≈ 69.4 ft **31** 10 ft/sec; 15 ft **33** $(-3, 0)$; $x = -3$ **34** 8400 ft; $t = 25$ sec **35** $y = 10$ or $y = -4$ **37** $x^2 + 14x + 49$ **39** $25 + 10x + x^2$ **40** Dinah, \$1.30; Nicki, \$0.40 **41** $x = 4$ **43** $(0, 9)$;

$(3, 0)$ and $(-3, 0)$; $(0,9)$ **45** $(0, 6)$; $(3, 0)$, $(-3, 0)$; $(0, 6)$
46 a, b, c

47 $t = 1$ sec; $t \approx 4.64$ sec **48** 6 and 7 or -9 and -8
49 Peter: 6, Paul: 8; 14; 185 min or 3 hr 5 min
51

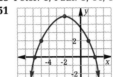

52 $a = 2$; $b = 3$ **53** $A = (x - 2)^2$; $x = 6$; $x \approx 3.73$
54 $A = 2(x - 3)^2 - 5$; 8 by 4 **55** $(6, 0)$, $(0, 0)$; $(0, 0)$
57 $y = \frac{-1}{3}(x - 3)^2 + 7$ **59** 3; 40%

60

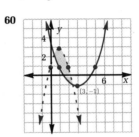

61 a

x	0	1	-1	2	-2
y	0	1	1	8	-8

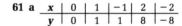

b

62 a 18 ft **b** 80 ft **c** ≈ 16.9 ft and ≈ 63.1 ft **63** Paul: $V_0 = 33.5$ ft/sec; Banks: $V_0 = 34.3$ ft/sec

11.3 Completing the Square in Quadratic Functions

Warm-up Exercises

1 25 **2** $\frac{49}{4}$ or 12.5 **3** 81; $(x + 9)^2$ **4** 4; $(x - 2)^2$ **5** 1; $(x - 1)^2$ **6** $y = (x - 3)^2 - 4$ **7** $y = 3(x + 3)^2 - 17$
8 $y = -2(x - 2)^2 + 4$ **9** $y = \frac{1}{3}(x - 3)^2 + 6$ **10** $(-6, 0)$; $(-2, 0)$; $(0, 12)$

Exercises and Problems

11 $k = 16$ **13** $k = \frac{25}{4}$ or 6.25 **15** 9; $(x + 3)^2$ **17** 56.25;
$(x + 7.5)^2$ **19** $a = 5$; $b = 6$; $c = 9$; $d = -45$
21 $y = (x - 2)^2 - 9$

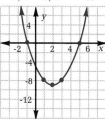

23 $y = 2(x + 3)^2 - 2$

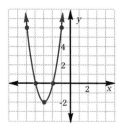

25 $y = -(x + 2)^2 + 5$

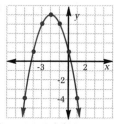

26 a $h(t) = -16(t - 3)^2 + 254$ **b** 254 ft **c** $t \approx 6.98$
sec **27** $y = (x + 4)^2 - 2$ **29** Downward **31** $3x^3y^{-2}$ or
$\frac{3x^3}{y^2}$ **33** $3x(3x - 4)$ **35** $(2x + 3)^2$ **37**

39

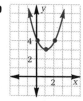

41 $(x, y) = (8, -2)$ **42** $x = 7$ or $x = -1$; $-1 < x < 7$
43 $x = 6$

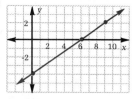

45 a $A = 2x^2 = 4x - 4$ **b** $A = 2(x - 1)^2 - 6$
46 a $(4, -13)$; $x = 4$ **b** $(2, -5)$; $x = 2$
47 $y = 3(x + 1)^2 - 3$ **49** $y = \frac{1}{2}(x + 10)^2 - 50$
51 $y = (x - 2.3)^2 + 7.61$

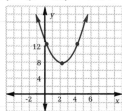

53 2 **55** 1 **56 a** $x = -5$ and $x = -1$
b

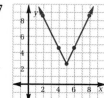

57

59

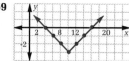

61

x	-4	-2	-1	$-\frac{1}{2}$	$-\frac{1}{4}$	$\frac{1}{4}$	$\frac{1}{2}$	1	2	4
y	$-\frac{1}{4}$	$-\frac{1}{2}$	-1	-2	-4	4	2	1	$\frac{1}{2}$	$\frac{1}{4}$

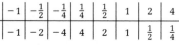

62 $(x, y) = (8, 10)$ **63** 9 **64** $x = \frac{30}{7}$ and $x = -3$

65

x	-3	-2	-1	0	1	2	3
y	-6	-4	-2	0	2	4	6

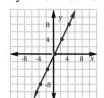

66 $x = 3$ **67** $y = (x - 2)^2 - 1$ **68 a** $t = 37.5$ sec
b 281.25 m

11.4 The Parabola and the Quadratic Equation

Warm-up Exercises

1 None **2** Two **3** One **4** Two **5** $b = 1; c = -12$
6 Positive **7** One **8** None **9** Two **10** Two **11** No
real solutions

Exercises and Problems

13 100 **15** 0 **17** $\frac{1}{36}$ **19** Two **21** None **23** Two
25 $x = 7$ or $x = -3$ **27** $x = 2$ or $x = -9$
29 a $f(0) = -24$ **b** $x = -9$ or $x = 4$ **30 a** $440
b $585 **c** $1025 **31** $x = 1$ or $x = 7$ **33** x-intercepts:
(3, 0) and $(-2, 0)$; y-intercept: $(0, -6)$ **35** x-intercept:
$(-4, 0)$; y-intercept: (0, 16) **37** $x = \frac{5 + \sqrt{57}}{2}$ or
$x = \frac{5 - \sqrt{57}}{2}$ **39** $x = \frac{-3 + \sqrt{17}}{2}$ or $x = \frac{-3 - \sqrt{17}}{2}$
41 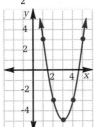 **43**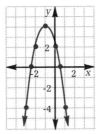

44 $y = -4x - 12$ **45** Marie is 4; Juanita is 15
47 $(2x + 3)(x - 9)$

49

x	-8	-4	0	4	8
y	-6	-3	0	3	6

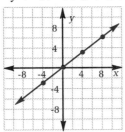

51 $y = 5.5$ **52** No **53** $x = 5\sqrt{3}$; ≈ 8.660
55 $y = (x + 4.5)^2 - 16.25$ **57** $-1 - 3\sqrt{2}$
58 a Positive **b** Negative **c** Zero **d** Negative **e** Zero
f Positive **59** 20 **61** $x = \frac{1}{2}$ or $x = \frac{1}{4}$ **63** $1.60
64 $k = 9$ **65** $t \approx 0.139$ sec and $t \approx 8.986$ sec;
$t = 9.125$ sec **66** (3, 7) **67 a** $x^2 + 5x + 9 = y + 8$
b $x = 3$ **68** $x = 9$ or $x = -6$ **69** 135 square units
70 All are equal. **71** $y = |x - 2| + 1$ **72** $3\sqrt{5}$ or
≈ 6.71 **73** $x = 5$ **74** 37.5 square units; 75 square
units **75** 9 m, 4 m **77** $(-4, -5)$
79 $k < 8$ or $k > 8$ **80** $2\sqrt{13} \approx 7.21$ **81** 50 square
units **82** $x \approx 12.56$ **83** $y = 3(x - 4)^2 - 3$ **84** $k = 10$
or $k = 1$ **85** $742 \times 653 = 484,526$ **86** 7 units
87 $3x^2 + 6x + 8$

11.5 Projectile Motion

Warm-up Exercises

1 $t \approx 1.43$ sec; $t \approx 0.714$ sec; $t \approx 1.95$ sec

Exercises and Problems

2 a 56 m/sec; 0 m **b** 32 ft/sec; 0 ft **c** 48 ft/sec; 7 ft
d 96 m/sec; 50 m **3 a** $h(t) = -16t^2 + 128t$
b $h(t) = -16t^2 + 96t + 124$
c $h(t) = -4.9t^2 + 35t + 16$ **d** $h(t) = -4.9t^2 + 48t$
4 a $h(2) = 192$ ft **b** $h(2) = 252$ ft **c** $h(2) = 66.4$ m
d $h(2) = 76.4$ m **5** $k = 144$ **6** 25; -25; $x + 5$; -14
7 $x = 3$ or $x = -3$ **8** $x = 5\sqrt{2}$ or ≈ 7.07
9 a $h(t) = -4.9t^2 + 30t$ **b** 45.9 m **c** 3.6 m **10** x
$= 1$ or $x = \frac{-1}{3}$ **11** 25% **12** $3.60 **13** 2 **15** 1
17 $(-5, -9)$; $x = -5$ **19 a** $h = -16t^2 + 64t$ **b** 4

20 $\frac{1}{5}$ **21** $\begin{bmatrix} 52 \\ 8 \end{bmatrix}$ **22** $8x^2$ **23** $x_1 = 27$ **24** $y = -9$ or

$y = -4$
25 $t = \frac{-1}{2}$ or -0.5 **26 a** $h = -4.9t^2 + 8t + 1$ **b** 3.775
m **c** After about 1.63 sec **d** After about 1.75 sec
27 $x = \frac{-3 + \sqrt{41}}{4}$ or $x = \frac{-3 - \sqrt{41}}{4}$ **29** $x = 2$; $y = -6$
31

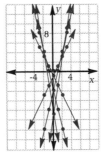

32 a $h(t) = -4.9t^2 + 3.8t + 10$ **b** $t \approx 1.87$ sec
c ≈ 10.74 m **33** 33; 24; 12 **35** $y + 2 = \frac{-3}{2}(x - 7)$
37 $(4, -11)$; $x = 4$ **39** $x = -7$ or $x = 1$ **40** 27 **41** $\frac{3}{7}$
or 3:7 **42** $y < 2x + 6$ **43 a** 1st ball: $h(t) = -16t^2 + 16t$;
2nd ball: $h(t) = -16(t - \frac{1}{4})^2 + 16(t - \frac{1}{4})$; 3rd ball:
$h(t) = -16(t - \frac{1}{2})^2 + 16(t - \frac{1}{2})$ **b** 4 ft **c** 1st ball:
1.75 ft; 2nd ball: 3.75 ft; 3rd ball: 3.75 ft **44** 52%
45 a-h

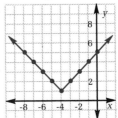

46 a $h(t) = -16t^2 + 320t + 4000$ **b** $t = 2.5$ sec
c $t = 17.5$ sec **47** $\frac{-2}{3}$ **48** $\pm\frac{4}{3}$

49 a $h(t) = -16t^2 + 8000$ **b** ≈ 19.36 sec **c** If he opened his chute any sooner, he would drift.
50 $k = 12$ or $k = -12$

11.6 Measures of Dispersion

Problem Set

1 a About 8.5 **b** -7.5 **c** In 1982, the NFL players were on strike, and very few games were played. **d** 13
2 a Sunville: 74.5; Palm Island: 78.8 **b** Sunville: 3.60; Palm Island: 6.88 **c** Sunville **3 a** 92, 108, 111, 116, 120, 124, 132, 135, 140, 144 **b** 52 **c** 122 **d** 22
e About 11.8 **5 a** Machine A: 1.02%; Machine B: 1.54% **b** Machine A: .34%; Machine B: .09%
c Machine B **6 a** $x = 19$ **b** 19, 29, 39, 44, 69 **c** -21, -11, -1, 4, 29

Review Problems

1 a $x = 6$ or $x = 2$
b

x	1	2	3	4	5	6	7
y	5	0	-3	-4	-3	0	5

c
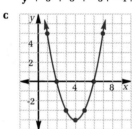

2 $(-1, -9)$ **3** $(4, 7)$; $x = 4$ **5** 13
6
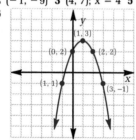

7 $(3, 5)$; $x = 3$; downward
9
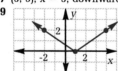

10 ≈ 0.84, ≈ 7.16; 6 **11** $0 \le t \le 20$; 980 m
13 $k = \pm 12$ **15** $y = 2(x + 4)^2 + 8$
16 $y = \frac{1}{2}(x + 5)^2 - 10$ **17** -3; none **19** 5; 2
21 x-intercepts: (10, 0) and (4, 0); y-intercept: (0, -40)
23 $y = (x + 2)^2$ **24** $h = -16t^2 + 48t$; 3 sec **25** $x = 11$ or $x = -2$ **27** $x = 0$ or $x = -12$ **28** 5 sec after it was hit **29** Yes **31** $x = 0$ **32 a** 1 **b** $\frac{2}{5}$ **33** $5 + 2\sqrt{7}$, $5 - 2\sqrt{7}$

35 a, b, c
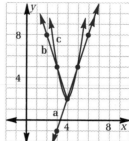

37
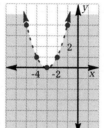

41a
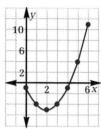

38 7 **39 a** $h(t) = -9.8(t - 6)^2 + 394.8$ **b** 42 m
c 394.8 m **d** $t \approx 12.3$ sec **40** -13 **41 b** -5; 11
42 $b = 4$; $c = -5$ **43** $a = -4$; $b = 24$; $c = -26$
44 $y = (x - 3)^2 - 4$ **45 a** 13 **b** 1

12.1 Ratio and Proportion

Warm-up Exercises

1 Three sweaters for $72 **2** Five loaves for $1.42 **3** $\frac{9}{2}$ or 4.5 **4** 21 **5** No real solution **6** $\angle PQR = 30°$; $\angle PQS = 150°$ **7** $y = \frac{1}{2}$ **8** $x = \frac{63}{4}$ **9** $p = \frac{45}{4}$ **10** $\frac{4}{7}$

Exercises and Problems

11 x and 20; 15 and 12; 20x; 15:20 = x:12 **12** 33 and 55 **13 a** $\frac{16}{9}$ **b** $\frac{9}{5}$ **c** $\frac{BC}{CD}$ **15** $y = \frac{7}{5}$ **17** $y = 9$ **18** The carton of 16-oz bottles **19 a** $\frac{7}{3}$ **b** $\frac{3}{5}$ **20** 0 **21** (3, 1); $x = 3$ **23** $(-4, 0)$; $x = -4$ **24** $\frac{4}{7}$ **25** $6x^3(3 + 4x^3)$

26
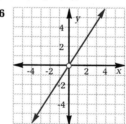

27 20%; 64% **28** 108 **29** $\frac{8}{10}$ **30** Approximately 20,031 yd, assuming he had continued to perform at the same level **31** $\frac{4}{3}$ **32** 4 and 16 or -4 and -16
33 $\frac{3}{5}$

704 Selected Answers

34 $a = 8$ or $a = -6$ **35 a** ≈ 0.353; ≈ 0.293; ≈ 0.441; ≈ 0.541; ≈ 0.327 **b** ≈ 0.661; ≈ 0.585; ≈ 0.807; ≈ 0.768; ≈ 0.561 **c** Jenny Kim **d** Susan Jones **36** 4:9

37 ≈ 2.73 **38 a** $\frac{7}{6}$ **b** $\frac{2}{1}$ **39** π **40** $x^2 - 15x + 54 = 0$

41 $\frac{8}{27}$ **43** $b = -3$ **45** $\frac{2}{3}$ **46** $\frac{5}{4}$ **47** $\frac{11}{10}$; $\frac{121}{100}$; $\frac{1331}{1000}$ **48** $\frac{99}{100}$

49 That there were about 33,750 trout in the stream

50 $\frac{40}{231}$

12.2 Applications of Proportion

Warm-up Exercises

1 330 mi **2** 105 mi **3** 1.609 **4** 0.394 **5** 6, $7\frac{1}{2}$ **6** 7.62

7 2.4856 **8** ≈ 4.01 **9** 1 in. = 12.5 ft

Exercises and Problems

11 $S_1 = 2$ **13** $S_1 = 4$ **14** 300; ≈ 91.44 **15** $2.63

16 16; $\frac{40}{3}$ or $13\frac{1}{3}$ **17** 30

18 a

Inches (x)	0	1	2	3	4	x
Centimeters f(x)	0	2.54	5.08	7.62	10.16	2.54x

b $f(x) = 2.54x$ **c** $x \geq 0$ **d**

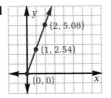

19 AB; DF **20 a** KP, HI, GI **b** $x = 5$; $y = 6$ **21** -1

23 $(x + 6)(x + 2)$ **24** $\frac{GI}{QP} = \frac{IH}{PT}$ **25** About $127.65

26 18 ft × 15 ft; 30 yd²; $690 **27** 21 **28** $(10, -2)$

29 a 12 ft **b** 78 ft

30 No real solutions **31** Parents: 125; children: 100; faculty: 15 **32** a^9:1 **33** $25.74 **34** $x = 80°$; $y = 40°$; $z = 25°$ **35** 2016 lb **36 a** $\frac{3}{2}$ **b** $\frac{9}{4}$ **37** 5 hr 50 min

38 $\frac{1}{3}$ **39** $K = 0$ or $K = 2$

41 1, 3, 5, 7, 9, 11, 13, 15 **42 a** 50% **b** 4% **43** 2^0, 2^1, 2^2, 2^3, 2^4, 2^5, 2^6, 2^7 **44 a** $x = 4$ or $x = 6$ **b** If $x = 4$, 16%; if $x = 6$, 36% **45** $\frac{7}{8}$ **46** 424 **47 a** $x = 16$; $y = 20$ **b** $\frac{4}{3}$ **c** $\frac{4}{3}$ **48 a** 4000 mi **b** By using hyperspeed **c** 2 hr 50 min

12.3 Direct and Inverse Variation

Warm-up Exercises

1 Direct **2** Neither **3** Inverse **4** Inverse **5** $\frac{1}{4}$ **6** 1 **7** $x = 840$ mi **8** -1

Exercises and Problems

9 Direct **11** Inverse **12** $Q = 9$ **13** $Q = 45$

14 48 mph; 60 mph **15** ≈ 3.6 hr **16** $\frac{3}{4x^5}$ or $\frac{3}{4}x^{-5}$

17 $(x - 13)(x + 2)$ **19** 80; 132 days **20** $n = cs$ or $\frac{n}{s} = c$; $c \approx 0.12$ **21** $y_1 = -6$ or $y_1 = 1$ **22** 13.5 in.

23 2500 **24** $8\frac{4}{7}$ hr **25**

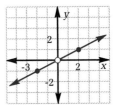

27 a

x	y	y:x or $\frac{y}{x}$
-4	-8	2
-2	-2	1
-1	1	-1
1	7	7
5	19	$\frac{19}{5}$

b No **c** No **28** 1 to $3\frac{1}{2}$ **29** $12.80 **30** 25 min

31 Change line 130 to: Let Y = INT(100∗CV∗X + .5) This will give the tax table in cents, rounded to the nearest cent. If a tax table in dollars is desired, change line 130 to: Let Y = INT(100∗CV∗ + .5)/100 Also change line 110 to: Print "AMOUNT," "TAX"

33

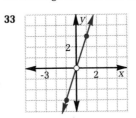

34

d	50	20	10	5	2	1
w	10	25	50	100	250	500

35 12 gal white pigment, 8 gal linseed oil, 4 gal dryer, 4 gal turpentine **36** $\frac{3}{4}$ **37** 93.75 k per m² **38 a** EC, DC **b** $x = 6$; $y = 8$ **39** Inversely; 2.3×10^{-4} cm **40** $166.67 **41 a** 9

b

Number of Square Yards x	1	2	3	4	5	6	x
Number of Square Feet f(x)	9	18	27	36	45	54	9x

c $f(x) = 9x$ **d**

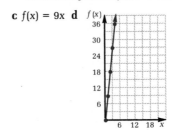

42 a $S_1 d_1 = S_2 d_2$ **b** 1500 rpm

12.4 Simplifying Rational Expressions

Warm-up Exercises

1 $\frac{2x}{3y}$ **2** $\frac{y}{2}$ **3** $\frac{8}{3}$ **4** $x = 4$ **5** $x = 5$, $x = -5$ **6** $x = 0$, $x = 9$ **7** $\frac{1}{60}$

9 $\frac{(x-3)(x+1)}{2x-1}$, $x \neq \frac{1}{2}$ **11** $x \neq 4$ **13** $x \neq -2, x \neq -1$

15 $\frac{4x}{x+1}$, $x \neq -5, x \neq -1$ **17** -1 **19** $m = 10$

20 2:1 **21** $3.84 **23** $\frac{x-6}{3x(x+3)}$, $x \neq -3, x \neq 0, x \neq 1$

24 $21\frac{1}{3}$ ohms **25** 46; approximately 10,876,516 **27** $-\frac{1}{x}$, $x \neq 0, x \neq 5, x \neq -5$ **28** 405

29

x	-3	-2	-1	0	1	2	3
y	1	2	3	4	5	6	7

31 $-4x$, $x \neq 0, x \neq 3$

33 96 **34 a** $\frac{2}{5}$ **b** $b = \frac{2}{5}a$ **35** 13.5 lb **37** $x = \frac{3 \pm \sqrt{37}}{2}$

38 1.75 oz **39** $z = 0$ or $z = -13$ **40** $x = -3$ **41** $\frac{3}{4}$

43 $\frac{x^2-9}{x^2+9}$, no restrictions **45** $(-6, -12)$ **47** $x = 8$ or $x = -1$

48 a 36 **b** $ab = 36$ or $a = 36 \cdot \frac{1}{b}$ or $b = 36 \cdot \frac{1}{a}$ **49** 60 and 80 **50** 1, 2, 2, 4, 8, 32, 256, 8192; $2^0, 2^1, 2^1, 2^2, 2^3,$ $2^5, 2^8, 2^{13}$ **51 a** $\frac{120}{180} = \frac{V_2}{39}$ **b** 26 volts **c** 9 volts **d** 6000 volts **52 a** $\frac{9}{16}; \frac{3}{4}$ **b** $\frac{4}{25}, \frac{2}{5}$ **c** $\frac{x^2}{y^2}; \frac{x}{y}$ **53** 441 **54** $\frac{3}{5}$

55 $y = 12; z = 14$ **56 a** 150, 600 **b** Clockwise; counterclockwise

12.5 Multiplication and Division of Rational Expressions

Warm-up Exercises

1 $\frac{2}{y^4}$ **2** z^2 **3** $-\frac{2}{3}$ **4** -1 **5** $\frac{4}{x}$ **6** $a, x \neq \pm y, a \neq 0$

7 2x, $x \neq 0, y \neq 0$ **8** $x - 2, x \neq -2, x \neq -5$ **9** $\frac{x-4}{4}$, $x \neq 0, x \neq \pm 1, x \neq -2, x \neq 4$

Exercises and Problems

11 $\frac{x^2+x-2}{x^2+2x-8}$, $x \neq 2, x \neq 3, x \neq -3, x \neq -4$

13 $\frac{2x-1}{x-3}$, $x \neq \pm 3, x \neq \pm 2$ **14** $133\frac{1}{3}$ min **15** $\frac{2y-1}{5}$, or an equivalent expression **17** $\frac{y-5}{10y}$, or an equivalent expression **19** When $x = 0$, the program will crash because the expression $\frac{1}{x}$ will be undefined.

20 10 pages **21** $\frac{3}{4}$ or 0.75 **23** $\frac{5}{4}x^5$ **25** $y = -2$

26 a $\frac{1}{4}x + \frac{33}{4} = y$, where x represents shoe size and y represents foot length **b** No **27** $\frac{2x}{x-3}$, $x \neq 0, x \neq 7, x \neq \pm 3$

29 a

Father's Age	30	31	32	33
Son's Age	0	1	2	3
Ratio of Father's Age to Son's Age	undefined	31	16	11

35	36	40	45	60	30 + x
5	6	10	15	30	x
7	6	4	3	2	$\frac{30+x}{x}$

b 60 **c** 300, but it is doubtful they will live to see it

31 $\frac{5}{x}$ or an equivalent expression **33** $x = \frac{6}{5}$ **35** 147.69 lb **37** $-\frac{(3+x)(x-6)}{4x(x-1)}$, $x \neq 0, x \neq 1, x \neq 3, x \neq -6$

38 12 m **39** $\frac{x^2}{x-2}$ or an equivalent expression

41 $106\frac{2}{3}$ oz **43** $\frac{3}{10}x^2$, $x \neq 0, x \neq -1, x \neq -3$ **44** $\frac{8}{9}$

45 $x \neq 2, x \neq -7, x \neq 3, x \neq -4, x \neq 8, x \neq 5, x \neq -6$ **46** $\frac{x^2}{(x-1)^2}$ or an equivalent expression

47 a 150 rpm, 150 rpm, 200 rpm **b** Clockwise

48 $\frac{(x+1)^3}{(x-1)(x^2+1)}$ **49** $18(x+3), x - 2$ **50** $\frac{x+4}{x+2}$

51 48 lb **53** $\frac{x-4}{x-2}$, $x \neq 0, x \neq \pm 2, x \neq \pm 4$

55 $x = 625$ **57 a** 394.74 m **b** ≈ 263.16 m

12.6 Solving Rational Equations

Warm-up Exercises

1 $a = \frac{50}{21} = 2\frac{8}{21} \approx 2.38$ **2** $b \approx 15.6$ or $b \approx 0.38$ **3** No solution **4** 12 min **5** 30 min **6** 10.7 blocks per hour

Exercises and Problems

7 $w = \frac{14}{3}$ or ≈ 4.67 **9** $w = \frac{60}{7}$ or ≈ 8.57 **10** 6 mph

11 $\frac{1}{2}$ **13** No real solution **14** 2.75 hr or 2 hr 45 min

15 $x = 2$ **17** $x = 3$ or $x = 9$ **18** 18 min **19** $z = \frac{40}{9}$; $x = 30$ **21** $x = 5$ **23** 9.6 sec **24** $-\frac{11}{2}$;

$y - 7 = -\frac{11}{2}(x + 3)$ or $y + 4 = -\frac{11}{2}(x + 1)$ **25** Ms. Dweller: 3.75 mph; Mr. Urbin: 18.75 mph

26 $\frac{(x+7)(x+5)}{(x-3)(3x-2)}$ **27** 14 min (Only one man at a time can fix a watch.) **29** 3x **30** 8 mph **31** Leo: ≈ 7.06 km per hr; Slo: ≈ 3.06 km per hr

32 No real solution **33** 4.4 mph **34** 0 **35** $9\frac{3}{13}$ min or ≈ 9.23 min; $12\frac{3}{4}$ min **36** 27 min **37** 45 ft **38** ≈ 24.75 mph **39** $x = \frac{-5 + \sqrt{21}}{2} \approx -0.21$ or $x = \frac{-5 - \sqrt{21}}{2} \approx -4.79$ **40** No real solution **41** 6 hr

42 24 min **43** ≈ 27.25 mph **44** $\frac{1}{x+1}$

45 Wisconsin: 70 mph; Minnesota: 60 mph

46 (4, 4),(3, 6), (6, 3) **47** 3000 mi at normal speed; 1000 mi at hyperspeed **48** $\frac{3x+2}{5x+2}$ **49** A day and a half

12.7 Addition and Subtraction of Rational Expressions

Warm-up Exercises

1 $\frac{7x-4}{x}$ **2** $\frac{12+x^2}{4x}$ **3** $\frac{-6x^2+5x+50}{2x(x+10)}$ **4** $\frac{xn+ym}{mn}$ **5** 4

6 $\frac{x}{x-1}$, $x \neq 1$ **7** $x = 20$ **8** $\frac{x+1}{2}$ **9** $\frac{6x^2}{(x+2)^2}$

10 12 min

11 $f = \frac{1}{7}$ 13 $x = \frac{1}{8}$ 15 $x = 1$ 17 $\frac{a^2 - b^2}{ab}$ 18 $6.12

19 $\frac{-5x - 13}{x(x^2 - 1)}$, $x \neq 0$, $x \neq \pm 1$ 21 $\frac{-3}{x(x + 2)}$, $x \neq 0$,

$x \neq -2$ 23 $m = 9$ or $m = -9$ 24 6 hr 25 $-\frac{x - 2}{x + 2}$, $x \neq -2$ 26 9:4

27 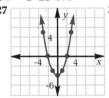 29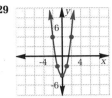

31 $\frac{5y - 7}{(y - 2)^2}$ 32 Boat: 5 mph; car: 25 mph 33 $\frac{x + 1}{2}$

35 $x = \frac{64}{7}$ 36 1 37 $\frac{x^2 - 3x}{x^2 - 1}$ 38 7:2 39 $\frac{x}{2(x + 2)}$, $x \neq -2$, $x \neq 9$ 41 $x = 6$ 42 2 43 $(4, 6)$ or $(-4, -6)$ 45 $x = \sqrt{2}$ or approximately 1.41, or $x = -\sqrt{2}$ or approximately -1.41 47 $\frac{x - 1}{2(x + 1)}$ 48 8 49 Jogged 13.2 mi; walked 3.2 mi 50 $W = \frac{PQZ}{Rxy}$, $R \neq 0$, $W \neq 0$, $x \neq 0$, $y \neq 0$ 51 a 1884; about .233 b About 0.075 52 9 53 8:42 P.M. 54 40

12.8 Stem-and-Leaf Plots and Box-and-Whisker Plots

Problem Set

1 a
```
 4 | 9
 5 | 6
 6 | 6 8
 7 | 5 5 5 8
 8 | 5 8 8
 9 | 0 0 2 9 9
10 | 2 2 5 7 8
11 | 1 3 5 8
```

b 106 or 107 2 a $275 to $499 b $29 to $59 c 229, 279, 399 d The same number cost more than $69 as cost less.

3 a
```
9 | 7
8 | 0 5 8 9 9
7 | 2
6 | 1 2 8
5 | 2 5
4 |
3 | 0 6
```

b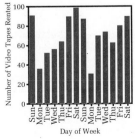

c Weekends are usually busiest 4 a 34, 55, 63 b 70 c Median: 55; mean and mode cannot be determined d They have the same amount 5 a 1 and 11 b 4, 6.5, 8 c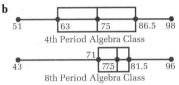

6 a 4th period: mean, 75.04; median, 75; modes, 75 and 62. 8th period: mean, 76.7; median, 77.5; mode 81.

b

4th Period Algebra Class: 51, 63, 75, 86.5, 98

8th Period Algebra Class: 43, 71, 77.5, 81.5, 96

c
```
9 | 0 3 4 6 7 8
8 | 0 1 1 1 2 6 7 7 7 9
7 | 0 2 2 3 3 3 4 5 5 5
  | 6 7 8 8 9 9
6 | 0 2 2 2 4 4 7 7 8
5 | 1 7
4 | 3
```

d Mean: approximately 75.80; median: 75.5; modes: 62, 73, 75, 81, 87

e

43, 67.5, 75.5, 84, 98

Review Problems

1 $x = \frac{8}{3}$ or ≈ 2.67 3 $t = 3$ 4 $\frac{x + 2}{12x + 6}$ 5 ≈ 583.3 ft

6 $x = 0$ or $x = 3$ 7 ≈ 26 min 8 $y = \frac{k}{x}$, $xy = k$, or $x = \frac{k}{y}$ 9 $28\frac{1}{3}$ or ≈ 28.33 11 $b \neq 0$, $c \neq 0$, $d \neq 0$

13 $\frac{b^2 + 12}{3b}$, $b \neq 0$ 15 $\frac{20}{3}$ or ≈ 6.67 16 $\frac{x + 3}{3}$

17 $\frac{(2x + 3)(x - 8)}{6x^2 + 7x - 6}$, $x \neq \frac{-7 \pm \sqrt{193}}{12}$ 19 $-y$, $y \neq 0$, $y \neq 1$

21 ≈ 3.78 22 11 mi 23 1 in. on the model represents 11 ft 1.5 in. on the ship 24 $\frac{14}{9}$ or ≈ 1.56; 126

25 $x = \pm 4$ 27 $7.33 29 $-\frac{1}{4}$, $y \neq 0$, $x \neq \frac{5}{2}$

31 $\frac{3(x - 8)(x - 2)}{x^2 - 6x + 16}$, $x \neq 0$, $x \neq 2$ 32 1 hr 3 min

33 $\frac{x(x + 3)}{(x + 1)(x + 2)}$ or an equivalent expression

34 Hussain: 55 mph; Ashvin: 45 mph 35 6 mph

36 1 37 $x = 7$ or $x = 2$ 39 20 mi 40 $x = \frac{-1 + \sqrt{13}}{2}$ or $x = \frac{-1 - \sqrt{13}}{2}$

41 $\left(\frac{\sqrt{15}}{5}, \frac{\sqrt{15}}{3}\right)$ and $\left(\frac{-\sqrt{15}}{5}, \frac{-\sqrt{15}}{3}\right)$ or ($\approx .77$, ≈ 1.29) and ($\approx -.77$, ≈ -1.29) 43 $\frac{1}{3x + 1}$ 44 ≈ 51.4 min; ≈ 350 dishes 45 $\frac{6x(1 - x)}{x^2 - 4}$, $x \neq \pm 2$ 47 $1\frac{1}{9}$ hr

GLOSSARY

absolute value (3.2) The distance of a real number from zero on the number line. The symbol for the absolute value of a number n is $|n|$.

acute angle (5.2) An angle whose measure is less than 90°.

additive identity (2.6) The number 0 such that $a + 0 = 0 + a = a$.

additive inverse of a (3.2) The number $-a$ such that $a + (-a) = 0$. See also *opposites*.

algorithm (5.4) A step-by-step procedure for doing a specific task in a finite number of steps.

axis of symmetry (11.1) A line that divides a graph into halves that are mirror images of each other.

base (9.1) The quantity that is raised to a power. In the expression $5x^7$, x is the base.

binomial (10.1) A polynomial with two terms.

box-and-whisker plot (12.8) A statistical graph that shows the outliers, the median, and the quartiles.

boundary algorithm (5.4) A four-step method for solving absolute value inequalities.

circumference (7.2) The perimeter of a circle, $c = 2\pi r$ or $c = \pi d$.

coefficient (3.3, 9.1) A number multiplying the variable. In the term $5x$, 5 is the coefficient.

collinear (6.3) Lying on the same line.

complete the square (11.3) To rewrite a trinomial as the sum of a perfect square trinomial and a constant.

completing the square (10.8) To fill in a term so that each resulting trinomial will be a perfect square trinomial.

composite number (1.2) A whole number with more than one prime factor. For example, 8, 9, 27, and 51 are composite numbers.

compound inequality (5.3) The combination of two inequalities joined by *and* or *or*.

conjugates (10.4) Two binomials whose only difference is the sign of one term.

consistent equations (8.2) Equations in a system that have at least one common solution.

constant function (7.5) A relation in which each input, or domain element, is paired with the same output, or range element.

constant of variation (12.3) The value of the ratio of two variables in direct variation.

counting number (3.1) See *natural number*.

cube root of d (9.8) The number c such that $c^3 = d$.

degree of a monomial (10.1) The sum of the exponents of the variables.

degree of a polynomial (10.1) The largest of the degrees of the individual terms.

dependent equations (8.2) Equations in a system that have identical solution sets.

dependent variable (7.6) In a function, the variable whose value is determined by the independent variable. Also called *output variable*.

deviation score (11.6) The difference between a score and the mean in a set of data.

difference of squares (10.4) The product of two binomials that are the sum and difference of the same two terms.

direct variation (12.3) When the ratio of two variables is constant.

discriminant (11.4) In the quadratic formula, the quantity under the square root symbol.

distance formula (7.2) The distance between points (x_1, y_1) and (x_2, y_2) is given by $d = \sqrt{(x_2 - x_1)^2 + (y_2 - y_1)^2}$.

domain (7.5) The set of all inputs of a function or relation.

empty set (4.5) The set that has no members, written as $\{\ \}$.

equal matrices (4.2) Two matrices that have the same number of rows and columns, and of which corresponding elements are equal.

equal sets (1.5) Sets containing exactly the same elements.

equation (1.4) A mathematical statement that two quantities are equal.

equilateral (7.2) Having all sides of equal length.

equivalent equations (2.2) Two or more equations with exactly the same solutions.

evaluate (1.3) To find a numerical value of an expression.

exponent (9.1) In the expression 10^{36}, 36 is called the exponent.

extraneous solution (4.6, 9.7) An apparent solution of an equation that does not check.

extremes (12.1) In the proportion $a:b = c:d$, a and d are the extremes.

factor (1.2) A number that evenly divides another number is a factor of that number.

factor (10.5) To write an expression as a product of two or more expressions.

fitted line (9.9) A line approximating a set of data.

formula (7.1) An equation that states a general rule or principle in mathematical language or symbols.

function (7.5) A relation in which each input is paired with exactly one output.

general linear form (6.4) An equation of a line written as $Ax + By = C$.

graph (6.1) A picture of the solutions of an equation or inequality.

Horner's form (10.5) See *nested form*.

identity (4.2) An equation that is always true.

inconsistent equations (8.2) Equations in a system that have no common solutions.

independent equations (8.2) Equations in a system that have different solution sets.

independent variable (7.6) In a function, the variable whose value is subject to choice. The independent variable affects the value of the dependent variable. Also called *input variable*.

index (9.8) The number that indicates the root to be found. In the expression $\sqrt[3]{125}$, 3 is the index.

inequality (1.4) A mathematical statement that two quantities are not equal.

input axis (7.6) The horizontal axis of the graph of a function. Also called *domain axis*.

input variable (7.6) See *independent variable*.

integer (3.1) A number in the set $\{\ldots, -3, -2, -1, 0, 1, 2, 3, \ldots\}$.

intersection (5.3) For all sets A and B, the set of all elements that are common to both sets.

inverse operations (2.2) Two operations that reverse the effects of each other.

inverse variation (12.3) When the product of two variables is constant.

irrational number (3.1) A decimal that is nonterminating and nonrepeating.

lattice point (8.5) A point having integral coordinates.

leading coefficient (10.1) The coefficient of the first term of a polynomial written in descending order.

like radical terms (9.5) Radicals with the same radicands.

like terms (2.1) Terms that have exactly the same variables raised to the same exponents.

linear system (8.1) A system of two or more linear equations.

literal equation (7.4) An equation with two or more different variables.

mean (7.7) The average obtained by dividing the sum of a set of terms by the number of terms.

mean deviation score (11.6)

$$\frac{\text{sum of absolute values of deviation scores}}{\text{number of scores}}$$

means (12.1) In the proportion $a:b = c:d$, b and c are the means.

measures of dispersion (11.6) In a set of data, indicators of the variation from the mean.

median (7.7) The middle number of a given set of data.

midpoint formula (7.2) The coordinates (x_m, y_m) of the midpoint of the segment joining (x_1, y_1) and (x_2, y_2) are given by

$$(x_m, y_m) = \frac{x_1 + x_2}{2}, \frac{y_1 + y_2}{2}.$$

mode (7.7) The number that occurs the greatest number of times in a given set of data.

monomial (9.2) A real number, a variable, or the product of a real number and variables.

Multiplication-Addition Algorithm (8.4) A five-step process for solving systems of equations.

multiplicative identity (2.6) The number 1 such that $1 \cdot a = a \cdot 1 = a$.

multiplicative inverse of a (2.6) The number $\frac{1}{a}$ for every a not equal to 0 such that $a \cdot \frac{1}{a} = 1$. Also called the *reciprocal of a*.

natural domain (7.5) The largest possible set of inputs for which a relation or function has meaning.

natural number (3.1) A number in the set $\{1, 2, 3, \ldots\}$. Also called a *counting number*.

negative number (3.1) A number corresponding to a point to the left of zero on the number line.

nested form (10.1) A form of polynomial expression used to simplify calculator and computer calculations. Also known as *Horner's form*.

nonlinear system (8.1) A system in which at least one of the equations has a graph that is not a straight line.

obtuse angle (5.2) An angle whose measure is greater than 90°.

opposites (3.2) Numbers that have the same absolute value but are on opposite sides of zero on the number line. Also called *additive inverses*.

order of operations (1.3) The order in which the operations within an expression are done. (1) Simplify expressions within grouping symbols, such as parentheses, brackets, and fraction lines. (2) Simplify exponents and roots. (3) Do multiplication and division in order from left to right. (4) Do addition and subtraction in order from left to right.

outlier scores (12.8) The high and the low items in a set of data.

output axis (7.6) The vertical axis of a graph of a function. Also called *range axis*.

output variable (7.6) See *dependent variable*.

parabola (6.6) A U-shaped graph of an equation that contains a squared variable term.

perfect square trinomial (10.4) The square of a binomial.

pictograph (5.6) A graph in which a picture represents a specified piece or amount of data.

point-slope form (6.5) An equation of a line written as $y - y_1 = m(x - x_1)$, where (x_1, y_1) is a point on the line that has slope m.

polynomial (9.2) A monomial, a sum of monomials, or a difference of monomials.

positive number (3.1) A number corresponding to a point to the right of zero on the number line.

prime number (1.2) A whole number greater than or equal to 2 whose only factors are 1 and itself.

proportion (12.1) An equation stating that two ratios are equal.

Pythagorean Theorem (4.5) In any right triangle, the square of the length of the hypotenuse equals the sum of the squares of the lengths of the legs.

(one leg)^2 + (the other leg)^2 = (hypotenuse)^2

quadratic equation (7.3) An equation in one variable that can be written in the form $ax^2 + bx + c = 0$, where a, b, and c are numbers and a is not zero.

quadratic formula (7.3) The formula

$$x = \frac{-b \pm \sqrt{b^2 - 4ac}}{2a},$$ which gives the

solutions of the quadratic equation $ax^2 + bx + c = 0$.

quartiles (12.8) Three numbers that divide a set of data into four equal-sized parts.

radical (9.5) An expression with the form $\sqrt{a}$. The radical sign is also called the square root symbol.

radicand (9.5) In the expression $\sqrt{5}$, 5 is the radicand.

range (7.5) The set of all outputs of a function or relation.

range (11.6) The difference between the greatest and the smallest numbers in a set of data.

range axis (7.6) See *output axis*.

ratio (12.1) A fraction.

rational expression (12.4) A fraction that has polynomials in the numerator and denominator.

rationalize (9.6) To change a radical denominator to an integer.

rational number (3.1) A number that can be written in the form $\dfrac{an\ integer}{a\ natural\ number}$ or as a repeating or terminating decimal.

real number (3.1) A number in the set of rational and irrational numbers.

reciprocal (3.6) For any nonzero number $\frac{p}{q}$, the reciprocal is the number $\frac{q}{p}$. See also *multiplicative inverse*.

relation (7.5) A set of ordered pairs.

right angle (5.2) An angle whose measure is exactly 90°.

Row Reduction Algorithm (8.4) A process commonly used on computers to solve a system.

scalar multiplication (3.5) To multiply each element of a matrix by the same number.

scattergram (9.9) Data points plotted on a coordinate plane.

scientific notation (9.1) A method of writing very large and very small numbers as the product of a number with one nonzero digit to the left of the decimal point and the number 10 raised to a power.

set (1.5) A collection of objects.

similar triangles (12.2) Triangles that have the same shape but not necessarily the same size.

simplified form (2.1) Said of an expression whose like terms have been combined.

simultaneous equations (8.1) See *system of equations*.

slope (6.2) (1) The value of m in the equation $y = mx + b$. (2) The ratio $\dfrac{change\ in\ y}{change\ in\ x}$ when moving from one point to another on the graph of a line. (3) The rate of change in y along a line when the change in x is 1.

slope-intercept form (6.2) An equation of a line written in the form $y = mx + b$.

solution (2.1) Value or values of a variable that make an equation or inequality true.

solve (2.1) To find all values of a variable or variables that will make an equation or inequality true.

square root of d (4.5) The nonnegative number c such that $c^2 = d$.

standard radical form (9.5) A radical term written as the product of a number and a radical with a radicand that contains no perfect square factors.

statement (2.1)   An equation or inequality that is either true or false.

stem-and-leaf plot (12.8)   A way of organizing data in a shape resembling a horizontal bar graph.

straight angle (5.2)   An angle whose measure is 180°.

subscripts (1.3)   In the term x_3, the 3 is a subscript.

substitution (2.4)   To replace a variable with a number or an expression.

substitution method (8.3)   An algebraic method to solve systems of equations. (1) Solve one equation for one of the variables in terms of the other. (2) Substitute the expression for the variable in the other equation. (3) Solve the new equation. (4) Substitute the value of the variable into one equation and solve for the other variable. (5) Check the solution in both equations.

system of equations (8.1)   Two or more equations with the same variables. Also called *simultaneous equations*.

system of inequalities (8.5)   A system involving two or more inequalities instead of equations.

term (2.1)   The product of a number and a variable. For example, the expression $3x + 2x$ has two terms: $3x$ and $2x$.

trinomial (10.1)   A polynomial with three terms.

union (5.3)   For all sets A and B, the set of all elements that are either in set A or in set B or in both sets.

variable (1.3)   A symbol used to represent a number.

Venn diagram (5.3) A diagram that shows the relationship between two or more sets.

vertex (5.2)   The point where two lines meet to form an angle.

whole number (3.1)   A number in the set $\{0, 1, 2, 3, \ldots\}$.

x-intercept (6.2)   The point at which the graph of an equation crosses the x-axis.

y-intercept (6.2)   The point at which the graph of an equation crosses the y-axis.

INDEX

A

Abscissa, 29
Absolute value, 101, 227
  roots of squared quantities
    and, 179, 185
Absolute value equations, 178,
  185
  graphing, 290, 545-46, 555-56
Absolute value inequalities,
  220-21
Acute angle, 208-209
Addition
  Associative Property of, 82
  Commutative Property of, 82
  Distributive Property of
    Multiplication over, 69,
    83,164, 425, 496
  as inverse operation, 58
  of like terms, 53, 110
  of matrices, 110
  in order of operations, 15
  of polynomials, 490
  of radicals, 447
  of rational expressions,
    646-47
  of real numbers, 108-110
Addition Properties of
  Inequality, 200, 227
Addition Property of Equality,
  64, 81
Additive Identity Property, 82,
  133
Additive inverse, 102
Additive Inverse Property, 133
Algebra, defined, 4
Algorithm, 221
  boundary
    four-step, 221
    three-step, 289-90
  Euclid's, 552
  Multiplication-Addition,
    391-95
  Row Reduction, 394-95
Analytic geometry, 316-17
Angles, classifying, 208-209
Approximating, 8-9, 17
  calculators and, 60
  money and, 8
Area formulas, 314

Artistic graph, 235
Associative Property of
  Addition, 82
Associative Property of
  Multiplication, 82
Axes, 29, 347
Axis of symmetry, 544-46, 554,
  556
  computer program for
    finding, 565

B

Bar graph, 139
Base (in exponential
  expression), 9, 417
Best fit, line of, 472
Binomials, 485
  multiplication of, 497,
    501-503
Boolean algebra, 219
Boundary algorithm
  four-step, 221
  three-step, 289-90
Box-and-whisker plot, 653-54
Broken line graph, 140

C

Calculator, 5
  and approximating, 60
  for checking solutions, 152,
    639
  exponents and roots and, 10,
    467
  graphing, 289, 365, 382
  negative numbers and, 110,
    116
  nested form and, 486, 510
  quadratic formula and, 327
  scientific notation and,
    416-18, 441
Career Profiles, 38, 80, 114,
  163, 233, 288, 323, 373, 458,
  521, 580, 645
Cartesian coordinate system,
  29-30
Central tendency, measures of,
  353-54
Circle graph, 234

Circumference, 313
Closed set, 132
Closure properties, 132
Coefficient, 110, 417
Collinear points, 268
Common factor, 508-509
Commutative Property of
  Addition, 82
Commutative Property of
  Multiplication, 82
Completing the square, 531,
  562-63
Composite number, 9
Compound inequality, 214-15
Computers, 5
  BASIC programs, 131, 262,
    280, 329, 332, 336, 394-95,
    524, 565, 619
  exponents in computer
    language, 10
  graphing software, 289
Conjugates, 503
Consistent system, 365, 377
Constant function, 339
Continued fractions, 623
Conversions, 608-609
Coordinates, 29
Coordinate system, 29-30
Counting numbers, 94

D

Data analysis
  box-and-whisker plots,
    653-54
  graphs, 138-40, 234-35,
    472-74
  measures of central
    tendency, 353-54
  measures of dispersion,
    588-90
  stem-and-leaf plots, 652-53
  survey projects, 191
Degree (of monomial or
  polynomial), 484, 485
Denominators
  like, 646
  rationalizing, 453
  unlike, 647
Density Property, 95

line, 138
pictograph, 235
scattergram, 472-74

H

Historical Snapshots, 43, 57, 184, 297, 330, 471, 507, 623
Horner's form. *See* Nested form.
Hypotenuse, 180

I

Identity, 156
Inconsistent system, 375, 377
Independent system, 375, 377
Independent variable, 346
Index, root, 466
Inequalities, 20-21, 52-53, 102
  absolute value, 220-21
  boundary algorithms for, 221, 289-90
  classifying angles and, 208-209
  compound, 214-15
  distance method of solving, 220
  graphing, 102, 201, 220-21, 289-90
  solving, 200-202, 220-21
  symbols for, 21
  systems of, 401-402
Inequality, properties of, 133, 200, 202, 227-28
Inequality Properties of Opposites, 228
Inequality Properties of Reciprocals, 228
Input, 306-307, 337-340
Input axis, 347
Input-output diagram, 306-307, 337
Integers, 94-95, 96
Intercepts, 257, 275, 554-55, 569-72
Intersection of sets, 214, 402
Inverse operations, 58-59, 179
Inverse variation, 617-18
Irrational numbers, 95-96

L

Lattice point, 401
Leading coefficient, 485
  of 1, 514-15
  other than 1, 522-23
Leg (of right triangle), 180
"Less than," definition of, 227
Like denominators, 646
Like terms, 53
  addition of, 110
  radical, 447

Linear equations, 249
  general linear form, 274, 282
  graphing, 30, 246-48, 257-59, 273-75
  point-slope form, 281-82
  slope-intercept form, 257-58, 282
  solving, 58-59, 150-51, 164-65
  systems of, 364-66, 374-76, 382-83, 391-95
Line graph, 138
Line of best fit, 472
Literal equation, 331-32

M

Mapping, to represent relations, 338-39
Mathematical Excursions, 7, 125, 219, 272, 352, 390, 495, 552
Matrices, 25-26
  addition of, 110
  computer program for multiplying, 131
  equal, 26, 157
  multiplication of, 126-27
  multiplication of, by scalar, 122
  subtraction of, 116-17
Matrix equations, 165
Mean, 353, 473, 589
Mean deviation, 590
Means (of proportion), 602
Measures of central tendency, 353-54
Measures of dispersion, 588-90
Median, 353, 653
Member (of set), 25
Metric conversion, 608-609
Midpoint formula, 316-17
Mode, 353
Money, approximating and, 8
Monomials, 425
  degrees of, 484
  division by, 434
  multiplication by, 425
Multiplication, 9, 14
  Associative Property of, 82
  of binomials, 497, 501-503
  Commutative Property of, 82
  Distributive Property of, over Addition or Subtraction, 69, 83, 164, 425, 496
  Distributive Property of Exponentiation over, 424
  Distributive Property of Square Root over, 446
  as inverse operation, 58
  of matrices, 126-27
  by −1, 126
  in order of operations, 15

of polynomials, 496-97, 501-503
of polynomials by monomials, 425
of rational expressions, 631-32
of real numbers, 120-22
scalar, 122
short method, 496-97
Multiplication-Addition Algorithm, 391-95
Multiplication Property of Equality, 64, 81
Multiplication Property of Exponents, 423
Multiplication Property of Inequality, 201-202, 228
Multiplication Property of −1, 133
Multiplication Property of Zero, 82
Multiplicative Identity Property, 82, 133
Multiplicative Inverse Property, 82, 133

N

Natural domain, 340
Natural numbers, 94, 96
Negative exponents, 439-40
Negative numbers, 30, 94, 108, 110, 116. *See also* Real numbers.
Negative 1, multiplication by, 126
Negative slope, 265
Nested form, 486, 510
Nonlinear systems, 364, 383-84
Number line, 94-96, 101-102, 108-109
Numbers, sets of, 94-96. *See also* Real numbers.
Numerators, rationalizing, 453

O

Obtuse angle, 208-209
Opposite, 101-102, 126
  of a Quantity, Property of, 116, 133
  subtraction as addition of, 115
Opposites, Inequality Properties of, 228
Ordered pairs, 25
  graphing and, 30
  to represent relations, 337-38
  as solutions of systems, 364-65
Order of operations, 15-16
Ordinate, 29
Origin, 29
Outlier scores, 653

Cover

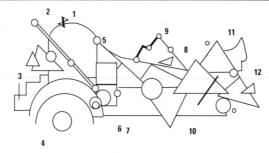

1: © 1988 Peter L. Vidor, all rights reserved; 2,4,8,12: National Space Science Data Center, operated by NASA under the direction of Dr. Bradford A. Smith; 3,6,7: JPL, NASA's Regional Planetary Image Facilities; 5: Courtesy Murphy/Jahn; 9: Courtesy John F. Hughes; 10: Gary Brettnacher/TSW/Click Chicago; 11: © Ronald Sheridan/TSW/Click Chicago.

Credits

South Latitudes of Mars at the Time of the Spring Equinox, 1977, NASA's Regional Planetary Image Facilities, Mars Mosaic ID # 211-5340: *v,* 3; © 1988 Peter L. Vidor, all rights reserved: *vi,* 43; Doug Armand/TSW/Click Chicago: *vii,* 265 (right); *Mistress and Maid* (detail), mid-5th century, The Achilles Painter, Lekythos, The Museum of Fine Arts, Boston: *viii,* 184; Cambridge University Press, England: *ix,* 507; H. Armstrong Roberts, Chicago: *x* (top), 483, 587; Don Jones, Fort Worth: 2, 38; NASA: 4, 312, 362, 373; Chart excerpted from "Running and Jumping" by David Willoughby, *Natural History* 83, no. 3 (March 1974), copyright the American Museum of Natural History, 1974: 12; © 1989 Comstock, New York: 20, 148, 150, 198; Tom Grill/© 1985 Comstock, New York: 32; AP/Wide World Photos, New York: 39 (left), 199, 324, 331; Ken Lax/The Stock Shop, New York: 39 (right); Yasuhiro Tanaka: 50, 80; Palomar Observatory, Mt. Palomar, California, courtesy Timothy Ferris: 51; *The Banquet,* 1951, David Smith, private collection, New York: 52; The Bettmann Archive, New York: 57 (both), 219, 495; *Yellow Whale,* 1958, Alexander Calder, painted sheet metal, wire, 45", courtesy Jean and Howard Lipman, from *Calder's Universe* by Jean Lipman (New York: Viking Press), in cooperation with the Whitney Museum of Art: 64; Nigel Snowden/© TSW/Click Chicago: 79; Michael Stuckey/© 1989 Comstock, New York: 81; The Weather Channel R: 92; Joe Golden, NOAA, Rockville, Maryland: 93; L.L.T. Rhodes/TSW/Click Chicago: 94; Alexandria King: 114; Jan Kopec/TSW/Click Chicago: 115; © Custom Medical Stock Photo, Chicago: 130; © Reed Kaestner/Zephyr Pictures, Del Mar, California: 149; "Top Sellers by Category: Word Processors" chart reprinted from *PC Magazine,* 2nd November 1988, © 1988 Ziff Communication Company: 162; Cristin's Candid Photography, Oil City, Pennsylvania: 163(above); © John Montsarratt/Root Resources, Evanston, Illinois: 163 (below); © 1980 Lee Marshall/FPG International, New York: 208; Geri Meyers: 233; Jeff Rotman, Somerville, Massachusetts: 244; Paul Berger/© TSW/Click Chicago: 245; © TSW/Click Chicago: 264, 437; Hugh Sitton/© TSW/Click Chicago: 265 (left); Algimantas Kezys: 289; Stanford University News Service; Stanford, California: 297; Camerique/H. Armstrong Roberts, Chicago: 304; © Georg Gerster/Comstock, New York: 305; Neal J. Edwards, National Geographic Society: 323; Historical Pictures Service, Chicago: 330; Bruce Peterson/H. Armstrong Roberts, Chicago: 362; © Manfred Kage/Peter Arnold, Inc., New York: 363; © Jeff Kaufman/FPG International, New York: 394; Ron Behrman, Albuquerque, New Mexico: 414, 458; Kay Elemetrics Corp., Pine Brook, New Jersey: 415; © 1986 Patricia Peticolis/Fundamental Photographs, New York: 417; Dennis Di Cicco/Peter Arnold, Inc., New York: 428; Paul Silverman/Fundamental Photographs, New York: 436; The Granger Collection, New York: 471; Stained-glass leaded windows with wooden frames, 1911–12, Frank Lloyd Wright, The Metropolitan Museum of Art, New York, purchase, 1967 Edward C. Moore, Jr. gift and Edgar J. Chalatele Foundation gift (67.231-3): 501; © 1989 Mike and Carol Werner/Comstock, New York: 482; UPI/Bettmann, New York: 508,600 (both); Sue Conner: 521; ISU Photos, Ames, Iowa: 542; Don Smetzer/© TSW/Click Chicago: 543; George Bowen: 580; © 1987 Globus Brothers/The Stock Market, New York: 581; James Gipe: 598; Ralph Clavenger/

West Light, Los Angeles: 599; "Mean Batting Average by Year" chart adapted from Philip Simòne/© 1986 *Discover*: 651.

McDougal, Littell and Company has made every effort to locate the copyright holders for the images used in this book and to make full acknowledgment for their use.

Illustrations

Robert Voigts: 8, 75, 78, 107, 113, 120, 137, 147, 167, 174, 185, 217, 232, 233, 235, 236, 240, 246, 279, 285, 303, 336, 353, 364, 382, 390, 396, 400, 401, 413, 484, 490, 522, 525, 535, 542, 552, 557, 561, 562, 573, 588, 597, 601, 607, 616, 621, 623, 630, 637, 638, 644, 660, 661.